Enterprise and Small Business

Principles, Practice and Policy

Second Edition

Edited by

Sara Carter and Dylan Jones-Evans

Prentice Hall

FINANCIAL TIMES

An imprint of **Pearson Education**

Harlow, England • London • New York • Boston • San Francisco • Toronto • Sydney • Singapore • Hong Kong
Tokyo • Seoul • Taipei • New Delhi • Cape Town • Madrid • Mexico City • Amsterdam • Munich • Paris • Milan

Pearson Education Limited
Edinburgh Gate
Harlow
Essex CM20 2JE
England

and Associated Companies throughout the world

Visit us on the World Wide Web at:
www.pearsoned.co.uk

First published 2000
Second edition published 2006

ISBN-13: 978-0-273-70267-2

British Library Cataloguing-in-Publication Data
A catalogue record for this book is available from the British Library

Library of Congress Cataloging-in-Publication Data
A catalog record for this book is available from the Library of Congress

10 9 8 7 6 5 4 3 2
10 09 08 07

Typeset in 10/12pt Sabon by 35
Printed and bound in Great Britain by Henry Ling Limited, at the Dorset Press, Dorchester, DT1 1HD.

The publisher's policy is to use paper manufactured from sustainable forests.

Enterprise and Small Business

Principles, Practice and Policy

We work with leading authors to develop the
strongest educational materials in business, bringing
cutting-edge thinking and best learning practice
to a global market.

Under a range of well-known imprints, including
Financial Times Prentice Hall, we craft high quality
print and electronic publications which help
readers to understand and apply their content,
whether studying or at work.

To find out more about the complete range of our
publishing, please visit us on the World Wide Web at:
www.pearsoned.co.uk

Contents

11 Family and entrepreneurship

Denise Fletcher

12 Social entrepreneurship

Alex Nicholls

13 Technical entrepreneurship

Sarah Cooper

List of figures

List of tables

List of contributors

Zoltan Acs is University Professor at the School of Public Policy, George Mason University, Fairfax, VA, US.

Giles Barrett is a Lecturer in Human Geography at Liverpool John Moores University, UK.

Dinah Bennett is Project Director of 'Women into the Network' and Senior Tutor at Durham Business School, UK.

Robert Bennett is Leverhulme Research Professor in the Department of Geography at the University of Cambridge, UK.

David Brooksbank is Professor of Enterprise and Small Business and Head of the Department of Enterprise and Economic Development at the University of Glamorgan, UK.

David Brown is Professor of Strategy and Information Systems at Department of Management Science at the University of Lancaster, UK.

Sara Carter is Professor of Entrepreneurship in the Department of Management and Organization, University of Stirling, UK.

Steve Conway is Senior Lecturer in Innovation at the University of Leicester Management Centre, UK.

Sarah Cooper is Senior Lecturer in Entrepreneurship in the Hunter Centre for Entrepreneurship at the University of Strathclyde in Glasgow, UK.

Per Davidsson is Professor of Entrepreneurship in the Brisbane Graduate School of Business at Queensland University of Technology, Australia, and at the Jönköping International Business School, Sweden.

Frédéric Delmar is Professor of Entrepreneurship in the Department of Strategy and Organization at EM Lyon, France.

Denise Fletcher is Director of Entrepreneurship Research, Nottingham Business School, Nottingham Trent University, UK.

Francis Greene is Lecturer in Entrepreneurship at the Centre for Small and Medium Sized Enterprises, Warwick Business School, University of Warwick, UK.

Kevin Ibeh is Senior Lecturer in International Marketing in the Department of Marketing, University of Strathclyde in Glasgow, UK.

Robin Jarvis is Head of Small Business at the ACCA and Professor of Accounting and Finance at Kingston University, UK.

Dylan Jones-Evans is Adjunct Professor of Entrepreneurship at the Turku School of Economics and Business Administration in Finland, and Director of the National Entrepreneurship Observatory at Cardiff University, UK.

Oswald Jones is Professor of Innovation and Entrepreneurship, Centre for Enterprise, Manchester Metropolitan University Business School in Manchester, UK.

Trevor Jones is at the Centre for Research in Ethnic Minority Entrepreneurship at De Montfort University, UK.

David Kirby is Professor of Entrepreneurship and Deputy Head of School at the University of Surrey Management School, UK.

Nigel Lockett is Relationship Manager for InfoLab and E-Business in the Department of Management Science at the University of Lancaster, UK.

Susan Marlow is Professor of Small Business and Entrepreneurship in the Department of Human Resource Management at De Montfort University, Leicester, UK.

Colin Mason is Professor of Entrepreneurship, Head of Department and Academic Director of the Hunter Centre for Entrepreneurship, Strathclyde Business School, University of Strathclyde in Glasgow, UK.

Kevin Mole is Lecturer in Enterprise in Warwick Business School at the University of Warwick, UK.

Alex Nicholls is Lecturer in Social Entrepreneurship at the Skoll Centre for Social Entrepreneurship, Said Business School, University of Oxford, and Fellow of Harris Manchester College, Oxford, UK.

Colm O'Gorman is Senior Lecturer in Entrepreneurship at UCD Business School, University College Dublin, Ireland.

David Purdy is Research Fellow at Westminster Business School, University of Westminster in London, UK.

Monder Ram is Professor of Small Business and Director of the Centre for Research in Ethnic Minority Entrepreneurship at De Montfort University, UK.

David Smallbone is Professor of Small Business and Entrepreneurship and Associate Director of the Small Business Centre at Kingston University, UK.

John Stanworth is Professor of Enterprise Studies at Westminster Business School, University of Westminster, UK.

David Stokes is Research Fellow in Small Business Studies and Director of Innovation at the Enterprise Exchange, Kingston University, UK.

Peter Wyer is Reader in Entrepreneurship at CEEDR, Middlesex University, UK.

Publisher's acknowledgements

We are grateful to the following for permission to reproduce copyright material:

Crown copyright: Table 2.1 from the Bolton Committee (1971) Report of the Committee of enquiry on Small Firms, Cmnd 4811; Table 2.3 from Small Business Service (2004), *SME Statistics*, www.sbs.gov.uk/smes; Figure 2.2 from Office for National Statistics (2005) *UK Workforce Jobs (seasonally adjusted), 1959–2004*; Table 3.1 from Labour Market Trends (2005), Office for National Statistics; Table 3.2 from M. Daly, 'The 1980s: a decade of growth in enterprise', *Employment Gazette*, March 1991, Office for National Statistics; Tables 3.3, 3.5 and 3.7 from 2001 Census, www.statistics.gov.uk; Table 3.4 from 2005 Census, www.statistics.gov.uk; Table 3.6 from Labour Force Survey (2005), Office for National Statistics, www.statistics.gov.uk; Figure 4.2 from figure 2, 'Cross cutting review of services to small businesses', HM Treasury 2002. Crown copyright material is reproduced with the permission of the Controller of Her Majesty's Stationery Office and the Queen's Printer for Scotland.

Other copyright: Figure 2.4 from D. Pilat, *The Major Growth Regions in Comparison: Some Findings from Recent OECD Work on Growth Productivity and Productivity*, OECD Breakfast Series in partnership with NABE, 18 Feb., © OECD, 2004; Figure 6.1 adapted from figure 5.1 in *Understanding the Small Business Sector* Routledge (Storey, D. 1994); Figure 7.1 from 'The individual-opportunity nexus' (Shane, S. and Eckhardt, J.) in *Handbook of Entrepreneurship Research* (eds. Z.J. Acs and D.B. Audretsch 2003), Kluwer Academic Publishers © 2003, with kind permission of Springer Science and Business Media; Figure 15.1 from Yukl, Gary A., *Leadership in Organizations*, 5th Edition, © 2002. Adapted by permission of Pearson Education, Inc., Upper Saddle River, NJ; Table 19.1 from Angel Investing: Matching Start-Up Funds with Start-Up Companies, Jossey Bass Wiley, (Van Osnabrugge, M. and Robinson, R.J. 2000); Figure 22.5 adapted from Brown, D. and Lockett, N., 'The Potential of Critical Applications for Engaging SMEs in E-Business', 2004, *European Journal of Information Systems*, Vol. 13 No. 1, Palgrave Macmillan, reproduced with permission of Palgrave Macmillan; Table 24.1 from Globalisation and Small and Medium Enterprises (SMEs), © OECD, 1997; Figure 22.6 adapted from 'Engaging SMEs in E-Business: The Role of Intermediaries within E-Clusters' in *Electronic Markets*, Vol. 11 No. 1, Taylor and Francis Ltd., http://www.tandf.co.uk/journals (Brown, D. and Lockett, N. 2001); Figure 23.4 from *The Corporate Paradox – Power and Control in the Business Franchise*, Routledge (Felstead, A. 1993); Mansueto Ventures LLC via the Copyright Clearance Centre for an extract from the article 'Two men and a bottle' by Tom Scott, published in *Inc: The Magazine for Growing Companies* 15th May 1998 © 1998 Mansueto Ventures LLC.

In some instances we have been unable to trace the owners of copyright material, and we would appreciate any information that would enable us to do so.

CHAPTER 1

Introduction

Sara Carter and Dylan Jones-Evans

1.1 Background

Attitudes towards entrepreneurship have changed considerably in the past 30 years. Gone are the days when the entrepreneur would be viewed as a 'deviant' individual on the margins of society. Today, individuals such as Richard Branson and Bill Gates are world renowned for their entrepreneurial prowess and are revered as role models that many would wish to emulate. In the same way that entrepreneurs have become an accepted part of everyday life, the influence of the small firm has also grown considerably. While this has been driven by various factors, such as the decline of large businesses, the development of an 'enterprise culture', market fragmentation and technological development, the increasing regard for small firms has been fuelled by a widespread recognition of their crucial economic and social role.

Small firms are, perhaps, most valued for their contribution to employment creation. While the abilities of an individual small firm to create a large number of jobs are restricted to a very few high growth 'gazelles', the sheer number of smaller enterprises ensures that their collective contribution to employment generation is substantial. For example, in the European Union, large firms have experienced employment losses in nearly every member state, whilst employment by small firms has grown considerably. In addition to creating employment, small firms also play a variety of other roles. For example, while the economies of scale in production and distribution enable large firms to make a significant contribution to the economy, many of them could not survive without the existence of small companies, who sell most of the products made by large manufacturers direct as well as providing them with many of the services and supplies they require to run a competitive business. Small firms have also introduced many products and services to the consumer, especially in specialised markets that are too small for larger companies to consider worthwhile. Finally, small businesses also provide an outlet for entrepreneurial individuals, many of whom would have found it almost impossible to work for a large organisation.

1.2 The purpose of this book

The increased importance of entrepreneurship and the small firm sector has led to considerable growth in interest in entrepreneurs and the companies they establish and grow. Although the study of entrepreneurship originated in the work of eighteenth-century economists, such as Richard Cantillon, the field has grown considerably during the past 40 years to encompass disciplines as varied as sociology, psychology, management studies and anthropology. Indeed, the chapters within this book draw on various approaches to explain broad issues relating to the enterprise environment, entrepreneurial processes and individuals, and small business management. The field of entrepreneurship and small business studies has always been diverse, and this book is intended both to reflect this diversity and to present an overview of each of the key themes relating to enterprise and small business.

Contemporary interest in the subject essentially dates from the early 1970s, when a number of critical events saw both a loss of confidence in large-scale industry and growing popular and governmental interest in small businesses. Even before this period, however, there had been research analysing the small firms sector from historical, geographical and socio-economic perspectives. What changed in the 1970s was both the volume of research undertaken and its direct role in influencing national economic policy. For the first time also, academics researching the field from within different disciplines formed associations, held international conferences to advance research in the area, and established a number of university-based centres focusing on the study of small business and entrepreneurship. These early initiatives have developed considerably. The modern field of entrepreneurship is recognised as a distinctive division within the Academy of Management, while the range of scholarly journals dedicated to the field has increased both in number and in specialisation. A further development has been seen in the growing number of university-based enterprise and small business research centres. Importantly, many of these centres have increasingly sought to disseminate their work within the mainstream university curricula by offering courses to undergraduate and postgraduate students. At the same time, there have been an increasing number of business schools around the world now offering small business and entrepreneurship as an integral element of business and management studies. While the US was an early leader in this area, Business Schools in Europe, the Middle East, Asia and Australasia have followed in developing courses in entrepreneurship and small business studies.

Despite these developments, entrepreneurship and small firms' research is often described as a new and emerging research field. Clearly, this is no longer the case. As each of the contributions in this volume demonstrates, research undertaken over the past 40 years has led to substantial theoretical and methodological advances. The field is far from exhausted, however. Each chapter within this volume demonstrates the extent, and also the incompleteness, of our understanding of many issues surrounding the small business sector. The development of the subject has not been confined to research; it has also been seen in the teaching of small business studies. The growing trend to include small business studies as part of the mainstream university curricula reflects both popular interest in small firms and their importance in economic development. Like many management subjects, small business studies draws from a range of disciplinary sources including, among others, economics, sociology, psychology, history and geography. We have tried to reflect the broad base of the subject in the breadth of the themes covered in this volume.

As the small business research field has grown and diversified over the past 30 years, so too has the number and content of small business courses taught in universities and colleges throughout the world. However, there is no single text book that encapsulates the range of small business themes in the depth required for undergraduate and post-graduate work. This book has been designed specifically to address the need for a single reference point for the growing number of students undertaking courses in small business and entrepreneurial studies. In determining the themes to be included in this book, guidance was taken from the syllabi of several university and college courses. Many of the initial small business courses taught in universities, such as the Graduate Enterprise Programme, were designed to encourage and enable students to actually start an enterprise. Increasingly, however, courses are designed to provide students with a more comprehensive insight into the small business sector. This reflects both the broad policy imperative to encourage students to start in business for themselves, and also the future careers of graduates who are increasingly likely to be employed within the small business sector or in occupations that directly or indirectly support the sector. Today, courses in small business studies are taught by a range of subject departments, including business and management, social sciences, arts and humanities. By including a broad range of themes in the required depth, we hope that this book will satisfy all students of the subject, irrespective of departmental affiliation.

This book contains 24 chapters from 31 contributors. Each contributing author was asked to present an overview of the specific body of work and explain how the field had developed over time. Even in such a large volume as this, not all issues can be explained in the depth which may be required, but we believe that each chapter amply fulfils the criteria of providing a strong starting point for students. One of the advantages of an edited collection of work is the ability to draw on acknowledged subject experts to provide specialised accounts of their specific research areas. We would like to thank each contributor not only for their chapter contributions, but also for giving their time and enthusiasm so freely. This book represents a substantial body of knowledge which we hope will provide an excellent reference point for students, researchers and teachers alike.

1.3 Structure of this book

The book is divided into three main parts that essentially reflect the three areas that concern the small firm today. These are first, the environment surrounding entrepreneurship and small business ownership; second, the various types of individuals who start and subsequently manage the venture; and thirdly, the various functions which have to be managed within the firm in order for it to succeed. As you will see when reading the various chapters, there are often no distinct boundaries between the issues discussed within the various chapters and, where possible, we have linked the relevant sections of chapters to those of others within the book.

The first part – The enterprise environment – focuses on the enterprise environment, and starts with two chapters that define the context of the book. Chapter 2 examines the definitions of small businesses and provides an analysis of the overall trends in the number of small businesses in various economies. Chapter 3 provides an overview of self-employment, profiling the main characteristics of individuals engaging in self-employment and business ownership. The three remaining chapters in this part extend beyond numbers and trends to explore first the role of government in supporting the small business sector (Chapter 4), the role of small businesses as contributors of innovation (Chapter 5), and issues of growth and development in the small business sector (Chapter 6).

The second part – The entrepreneur – focuses on entrepreneurship within the small firm. One of the defining characteristics of entrepreneurs is their ability to recognise and develop opportunities. This theme is examined in Chapter 7 on the entrepreneurial process. A great deal of research interest has focused on the distinctive personality characteristics of entrepreneurs and their relationship with business success. Chapter 8 explores the various approaches to the psychology of the entrepreneur. The next six chapters in this part each examine distinctive types of entrepreneurs: female, ethnic minority, family-based, social, technological and corporate – each group demonstrating specific characteristics which differentiate them from other types of owner manager. The final chapter in this part examines the relatively under-explored issue of leadership, entrepreneurship and small business management (Chapter 15).

The final part – The enterprise environment – focuses on the specific management functions within the small business. Mainstream management subjects such as strategy, HRM, finance and marketing are discussed from the specific viewpoint of the small firm and its stakeholders. Entrepreneurship and small business research has emphasised certain managerial functions as both central and specific to the small business. Thus, a chapter on marketing and the small business (Chapter 17) is preceded by a chapter focusing on the importance of networks in the small business sector. Similarly, a chapter on finance and the small business (Chapter 18) is extended by an accompanying chapter exploring venture capital and business angel investment (Chapter 19). The growing importance of e-commerce is discussed in Chapter 22, while Chapter 23 explores franchising, now seen as a long-established route into business ownership for many individuals. The final chapter in this part concludes the book by examining the internationalisation strategies of SMEs.

PART 1

The enterprise environment

CHAPTER 2

Defining and measuring the small business

Francis Greene and Kevin Mole

2.1 Introduction

This chapter begins by considering a sample of the definitions used by researchers and governments to describe smaller enterprises and shows that there is no single or uniform definition of smaller enterprises. It also examines the number of enterprises in the United Kingdom (UK), the European Union (EU) and internationally, and although there are measurement problems in calculating the number of smaller enterprises, this chapter demonstrates that smaller enterprises represent the overwhelming number of enterprises in any economy.

Empirical evidence suggests that in the UK, and internationally, there has been a general increase in the numbers of smaller enterprises since the 1980s and whilst most OECD (Organisation for Economic Cooperation and Development) countries follow this pattern, there are notable exceptions such as France, Japan and the US. In this context, the various reasons why smaller enterprises have 're-emerged' since the 1980s are considered, including changes in the cost structure of industry, rapid technological development, innovation, an increase in the service economy, changes in the labour market and shifts in government policy, although none of these explanations provide in themselves the single explanation for the growth of smaller enterprises. Section 2.7 looks at the US and explores the dynamic contribution of entry and exit and the importance of fast-growth enterprises.

2.2 Learning objectives

There are four learning objectives in this chapter:

1 To outline the various international definitions of smaller enterprises.

2 To describe the methodological issues faced in measuring smaller enterprises.

3 To show that smaller enterprises constitute the vast majority of enterprises in any economy.

4 To account for the reasons why the number of smaller enterprises have increased over the last 30 years.

Key concepts

■ definition of the small firm ■ role of small firm in the economy
■ small business trends

2.3 Definitions of smaller enterprises

This section begins by looking at two early attempts to provide a definition of smaller enterprises and then considers how authorities in the UK, the EU and elsewhere have defined smaller enterprises.

There is no simple or single definition of what constitutes a small enterprise. One of the earliest attempts to provide a definition was provided by the Bolton Report (1971). Bolton suggested two definitions for the small enterprise. First, he suggested a qualitative or economic approach that tried to capture the range and diversity of the smaller enterprise relative to the larger enterprise. This definition suggested that a small enterprise was so if it met three criteria:

■ independent (not part of a larger enterprise);

■ managed in a personalised manner (simple management structure);

■ relatively small share of the market (the enterprise is a price 'taker' rather than price 'maker').

Such criteria are useful because they reflect central features of smaller enterprises. Other than size itself, one factor that distinguishes smaller enterprises from their larger counterparts is the nature of the uncertainty they face. As smaller enterprises are often reliant upon a limited number of customers and have a limited product portfolio (Cosh and Hughes, 2000), they tend to be exposed to greater levels of uncertainty in their markets. In contrast, larger enterprises are able to limit the uncertainty in their markets simply because they have diversified product portfolios. The independence and personalised nature of the smaller enterprise further promotes uncertainty. Keasey and Watson (1993) have argued that small enterprise owner-managers often run sole proprietorships or partnerships. This means that their fortunes are often tied up directly with the success or otherwise of the enterprise: without the protection of limited liability, owner-managers may end up personally liable for their debts if their enterprise fails. Owner-managers of smaller enterprises also face, relative to larger firms, higher fixed management costs. This, again, may make their situation precarious as they may not have the necessary 'skill-set' to attend to the various areas of the business (e.g. financial or human resource management) equally well.

Bolton's attempt to reflect the uncertainty situation faced by small enterprises does present problems. Storey (1994) has criticised Bolton as it is often unclear when exactly the locus of management control shifts from the owner-manager to a functional or hierarchical management structure in a growing business. Enterprises that run into the thousands of employees may be run in a highly personalised manner. Storey and Johnson (1987) have also argued that 'independence' is a relative concept: some enterprises, whilst legally independent, may be entirely reliant upon one large enterprise for their economic activity. On the other hand, some enterprises with two or more

Table 2.1 **The Bolton Report's (1971) quantitative definitions of smaller enterprises**

Sector	Definition
Manufacturing	200 employees or less
Construction	25 employees or less
Mining and quarrying	25 employees or less
Retailing	Turnover of £50,000 or less
Miscellaneous Services	Turnover of £50,000 or less
Motor trades	Turnover of £100,000 or less
Wholesale trades	Turnover of £200,000 or less
Road transport	Five vehicles or less
Catering	All excluding multiples and brewery-managed houses

Source: Bolton Committee (1971)

establishments may expect each of these establishments to function independently. Finally, one or two employee enterprises may have a high degree of market power because they work in a highly specialised market niche.

Bolton also proposed a more quantitative definition of the smaller enterprise. Again, the concern was to capture the heterogeneity of smaller enterprises. This is because no single measure such as assets, turnover, profitability or employment is likely to fully account for the size of an enterprise. For example, an automotive manufacturer may consider itself small if it employs 300 workers. An enterprise of the same size, however, may be considered to be large if it is in motor repairs. Bolton, therefore (Table 2.1), suggested a variety of measures to reflect sectoral heterogeneity. Hence, employment was used for sectors such as manufacturing, turnover for motor trades, assets for transportation and ownership for catering.

There are obvious problems with such a definition. For a start, although it appears 'grounded' in the differences between sectors, many small enterprise owner-managers may not agree with such definitions either then or now (Woods *et al.*, 1993). Perhaps a more pertinent problem is that measures such as turnover and employment are eroded over time by the influence of inflation and productivity, respectively. Equally, the absence of a uniform definition makes it extremely difficult to chart differences or similarities between countries.

A more uniform definition has been adopted by the EU. This was first introduced in 1996 but was updated in 2004 to account for the impact of inflation and productivity changes. Table 2.2 shows that the EU considers there are three types of smaller enterprise: micro, small and medium-sized. Each of these have differing employee, turnover

Table 2.2 **EU definition of SMEs**

Enterprise category	Head count	Turnover or	Balance sheet
Micro	<10	€2m	€2m
Small	<50	€10m	€10m
Medium-sized	<250	€50m	€43m

Source: European Union (2005)

and asset thresholds. These three size groups of non-subsidiary independent businesses make up what are termed small and medium-sized enterprises (SMEs).

Although recommended by the EU, this definition is only binding for institutions or businesses that seek EU funding. Individual countries may adopt their own interpretation of what constitutes an SME. The UK government, for instance, tends to define an SME as:

- micro firm: 0–9 employees
- small firm: 0–49 employees (includes micro)
- medium firm: 50–249 employees.

Internationally, there is a wide variety of definitions. Countries such as the US or Canada define an SME as one that employs fewer than 500 employees. Hong Kong has an alternative definition: SMEs are manufacturing enterprises with fewer than 100 employees or non-manufacturing with fewer than 50 employees. This obviously makes it difficult to compare SMEs across various countries, particularly with regard to turnover or assets. Transnational studies, therefore, have tended to concentrate upon simple employment thresholds when measuring SMEs.

This section has shown that there is no easy, simple or optimal definition of smaller enterprises. In essence, whatever definition is used involves some form of a trade-off. What definitions such as Bolton's offer are insights into the managerial and behaviourial characteristics of smaller enterprises. Such definitions, though, cannot be easily generalised across industries and regions or countries.

2.4 Numbers of firms

If there are difficulties about defining the small enterprise, there are also methodological issues in measuring the number of smaller enterprises. This section looks at these issues but also shows that SMEs constitute nearly all of the enterprises and make a large contribution to overall employment in a given economy.

One reason for the lack of precision in terms of the actual number of enterprises in an economy is that there is no census of economic activity. Even if there were, there would still be the issue of informal economic activity. For instance, levels of illegal economic activity such as drug dealing are difficult to estimate (Fairlie, 2002). Equally, more legal forms of part-time or *ad hoc* activity such as homeworking or network marketing (individuals who are self-employed distributors selling to their family and friends (Pratt, 2000)) are also very difficult to pin down. Individuals who may be thought to be employees often find themselves 'falsely' self-employed because it allows for them or their 'employer' to reduce their tax liabilities (OECD, 2000).

In the absence, then, of a census of legal economic activities, much of what is known about SMEs is largely derived from two sources. First, governments throughout the developed world rely upon Labour Force Surveys (LFS) to estimate the number of self-employed individuals and unincorporated businesses. Second, governments often make use of particular registers such as value added tax (VAT) or credit referencing companies (e.g. Experian, Dun and Bradstreet) to estimate the number of incorporated enterprises. There are a number of problems with both these data sources.

In terms of LFS data, individuals may choose, for whatever reason, to misrepresent their economic status. It is also likely that the LFS underestimates younger people because they are likely to be more geographically mobile than older individuals. The biggest problem, though, with LFS data is that it is a survey. As such, it is an incomplete appraisal of unincorporated business activity: for example, the enterprise population for the UK was revised upwards in 2003 because it was found that the UK LFS had underestimated the number of enterprises by more than 70,000 enterprises.

Registers of enterprises also have well known biases. Credit referencing data is likely to offer better coverage of larger enterprises, companies, enterprises in particular sectors (manufacturing and construction), and enterprises that seek external finance (Storey and Johnson, 1986, 1987). VAT registration data is just as problematic. Governments seeking to reduce regulatory burdens on smaller businesses may elect to substantially increase the VAT threshold. This occurred in the UK in 1991 when the government increased the VAT threshold from an annual turnover level of £25,400 to £35,000. Alternatively, if they are seeking to raise taxes they may decrease the threshold level. In either case, this has an impact on the robustness of VAT time-series data.

There are other problems with VAT data. Certain enterprises such as children's clothes manufacturers are excluded from VAT registration because they are not liable to VAT. VAT registration is also not synonymous with firm 'birth'. An enterprise may take a number of years to reach the point where their sales justify being registered for VAT. Similarly, VAT deregistration does not necessarily mean that the enterprise has 'failed'. Enterprises may simply deregister because they have fallen below the turnover threshold.

The best estimate, therefore, of the enterprise population is often derived from a mix of survey information and registration information. In the UK, the enterprise population, as Table 2.3 shows, numbered just over 4 million in 2003. The vast bulk of these, some 2.9 million (70.1%) of enterprises, were made of enterprises that had no employees (the figures for employees (337,000 or 1.4%) represent partners of the business).

In terms of those enterprises with employees, the table shows that there were 1.23 million such enterprises. Again, the vast bulk of these were small enterprises either employing 1–4 employees (0.8 million) or 5–9 employees (0.22 million). Cumulatively, micro enterprises (0–9 employees) represent 95% of all enterprises, one-quarter of total employment and 22.3% of turnover. Table 2.3 also shows that the numbers of enterprises decline with employment size: 170,000 enterprises have between 10 and 49 employees whilst there are just 29,000 enterprises with between 50 and 249 employees. Nonetheless, the overall picture is that SMEs (<250 employees) represent 99.8% of enterprises. Based upon this it is tempting to suggest that SMEs represent business activity. This neglects the fact that although large firms represent only 0.2% of enterprises, they contributed 52.4% of employment and 49.8% of sales in 2003.

2.4.1 International comparisons

Table 2.4 shows an estimate of the number of enterprises in the EU (EU-15). Italy, Germany, Spain, France and the UK (in that order) clearly have the largest number of enterprises in the EU. In all EU countries, SMEs account for more than 99% of the total number of enterprises.

Table 2.3 Number of enterprises, employment and turnover in the whole economy by number of employees, UK start 2003

	Number of enterprises	Employment (000s)	Employees (000s)	Turnover[1] (£ million)	Enterprises (%)	Employment (%)	Employees (%)	Turnover[1] (%)
Whole economy								
All enterprises	4,097,095	27,959	24,337	2,400,741	100.0	100.0	100.0	100.0
With no employees[2]	2,870,180	3,159	337	177,506	70.1	11.3	1.4	7.4
All employers	1,226,915	24,800	24,000	2,223,235	29.9	88.7	98.6	92.6
1–4	802,860	2,311	1,733	213,411	19.6	8.3	7.1	8.9
5–9	215,260	1,517	1,403	143,977	5.3	5.4	5.8	6.0
10–19	112,780	1,575	1,515	157,881	2.8	5.6	6.2	6.6
20–49	59,015	1,822	1,790	184,540	1.4	6.5	7.4	7.7
50–99	17,740	1,241	1,234	137,197	0.4	4.4	5.1	5.7
100–199	9,155	1,274	1,270	144,712	0.2	4.6	5.2	6.0
200–249	1,855	414	413	45,267	0.0	1.5	1.7	1.9
250–499	3,770	1,317	1,315	175,268	0.1	4.7	5.4	7.3
500 or more	4,485	13,330	13,326	1,020,983	0.1	47.7	54.8	42.5

1. All turnover figures exclude Section J (financial intermediation) where turnover is not available on a comparable basis.
2. 'With no employees' comprises sole proprietorships and partnerships comprising only the self-employed owner-manager(s), and companies comprising only an employee director.

Source: Small Business Service (2004); (www.sbs.gov.uk/smes)

Table 2.4 SMEs in EU-15

	Total number of enterprises (000s)	SMEs as % of enterprises	Average employment size	SME as % of employment
Austria	268	99.63	11	71.85
Belgium	438	99.77	7	69.45
Denmark	206	99.51	10	72.62
Finland	222	99.55	7	64.54
France	2,501	99.76	8	66.63
Germany	3,019	99.64	10	64.76
Greece	771	100.00	2	86.55
Ireland	97	100.00	10	69.75
Italy	4,489	99.93	4	83.55
Luxembourg	24	100.00	9	73.33
Netherlands	572	99.65	12	65.21
Portugal	694	99.86	5	78.91
Spain	2,677	99.89	6	81.66
Sweden	486	99.79	7	67.97
United Kingdom	2,234	99.64	11	59.20
EU-15	18,698	99.79	7	69.74

Source: ENSR (2004); adapted from Tables IV.2, IV.3 and IV.4

There are differences, though, between the employment profile of European countries. Table 2.4 shows that there is a distribution in terms of the average employment size of a business. Countries below the EU average (seven employees) include Mediterranean countries such as Greece with two employees per enterprise, Italy with four, Portugal with five and Spain with six per enterprise. By comparison, countries such as the Netherlands, the UK and Austria have enterprises that are, on average, more likely to employ greater numbers of individuals. A similar distribution is also evident when we consider the employment shares of individual countries in relation to SMEs and larger enterprises.

Countries such as Greece, Italy, Spain and Portugal are more reliant on SMEs than economies such as the UK, Finland and Germany. For instance, SMEs contribute around 80% of employment in the four Mediterranean countries whilst in the UK, Finland and Germany they contribute less than 65% of total employment. These differences have led to the assertion that economies dominated by smaller-sized enterprises are less prosperous: 'there is a strong correlation between average enterprise size and economic prosperity, as measured by per capita GDP' (ENSR, 2004: 28).

Comparisons between the EU, Japan and the US further demonstrate the importance of SMEs. Table 2.5 indicates again that more than 99% of enterprises in these three economic area are SMEs. Equally, the EU and the US have similar distributions in terms of the percentage share of micro, small and medium-sized enterprises. This is also true for EU and US SMEs in terms of average employment size and employment share. Where, however, the EU and Japan differ from the US is in terms of the employment share of micro enterprises and large-scale enterprises (LSEs). Here, the average

Table 2.5 SMEs in the EU, Japan and US

	SME				LSE	Total
	Micro	Small	Medium	Total		
Enterprises US, 2000						
Number of enterprises (000s)	19,988	1,009	167	21,164	59	21,223
Percentage of enterprises	94.18	4.75	0.79	99.72	0.28	
Average employment size	1	20	94	3	1,119	6
Employment share (%)	22	15	12	49	51	
Enterprises Japan, 2001						
Number of enterprises (000s)	n/a	n/a	n/a	4,690	13	4,703
Percentage of enterprises				99.72	0.28	
Average employment size	n/a	n/a	n/a	5	975	8
Employment share (%)	n/a	n/a	n/a	67	33	
Enterprises Europe – **19 countries, 2003**						
Number of enterprises (000s)	17,820	1,260	180	1,927	40	19,310
Percentage of enterprises	92.28	6.53	0.93	9.98	0.21	
Average employment size	3	19	98	5	1,052	7
Employment share (%)	39	17	13	70	30	

Source: Table 3.5, ENSR (2004)

US micro enterprise is likely to be a sole proprietor whereas in the EU the average number of employees in a micro-sized enterprise is three. A bigger contrast, though, is the employment share of LSEs. In the US, LSEs contribute more than half of all employment; in Japan and the EU, LSEs contribute one-third of employment.

This section has demonstrated – despite their being problems in estimating the number of smaller enterprises in any given economy – that SMEs in the UK and internationally constitute around 99% of all enterprises and make a significant contribution to employment. It has also shown that the average size of an enterprise tends to be that of a micro business (0–9 employees). Nonetheless, larger enterprises remain critical to very many economies, particularly in the US.

2.5 Trends in SME statistics

The economic importance of SMEs in terms of employment and output has not always been evident. In this section, consideration is given to empirical evidence from the UK and internationally which suggests that SMEs prior to the 1980s were declining both numerically and in economic importance. Since the 1980s, the numbers of SMEs have grown dramatically. This section goes on to show that this general or 'U'-shaped increase is not common to all OECD countries. Notably, some countries such as France and Japan have seen their numbers of business owners decrease whilst the US has an 'n'-shaped distribution to its rates of business ownership.

Looking first at the situation prior to the 1980s, early empirical evidence from UK manufacturing employment data shows that the employment share of small manufacturing enterprises (<200 employees) declined from around 45% in the 1920s and 1930s until it reached around 30% in the 1960s and the 1970s (Figure 2.1).

Figure 2.1 Percentage of UK total manufacturing employment in small establishments (<200 employees), 1924–88

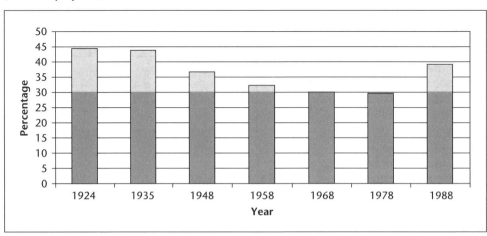

Source: Figure 2.2, Storey (1994)

Figure 2.2 **UK self-employment, 1959–2004** (seasonally adjusted)

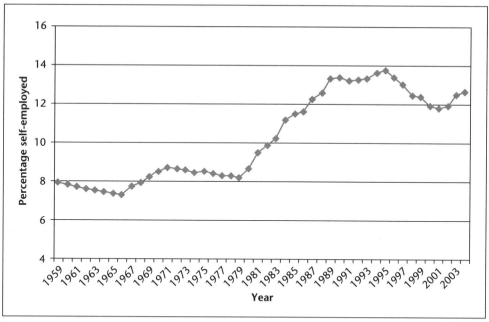

Source: Figure 1.2, Office for National Statistics (2005). www.statistics.gov.uk

Further evidence of the shift away from small-scale enterprises is shown in Figure 2.2. This shows the self-employment rate (as a percentage of workforce jobs) from 1959–2004. It indicates that after 1959 the self-employment rate fell to below 8% but showed a modest recovery in the 1970s. Subsequent to 1979, the self-employment rate shot up in the 1980s and the 1990s: by 1995 the self-employment rate had reached nearly 14% which represents a slightly more than 50% increase in self-employment rates in 15 years.

These changes in the self-employment rate are also mirrored in the changes in the total UK enterprise population and are discussed in more detail in Chapter 3. Figure 2.3 shows that the number of enterprises in the UK increased from 2.4 million in 1980 to a level of 4 million in 2003. This represents more than a 50% increase in the UK enterprise population. Much of this increase took place in the 1980s when the number of enterprises increased to around 3.8 million. Figure 2.3 further demonstrates, except for the recessionary period in the early 1990s, that the enterprise population has remained fairly constant since the 1980s. It would appear, at least for the UK, that SMEs who make up the vast bulk of all enterprises 're-emerged' after the 1980s.

These dramatic increases in small-scale enterprise activity in the 1980s and early 1990s, and the subsequent stabilisation of the enterprise population, might be a peculiarly UK phenomenon. Early evidence from Loveman and Sengenberger's (1991) study of six OECD countries in the 1980s (Japan, France, Germany, Italy, the UK and the US), however, showed that the employment share of SMEs in these countries broadly followed a 'U'-shaped pattern. In the US, for example, small businesses' share of

Figure 2.3 **UK enterprise population, 1980–2003**

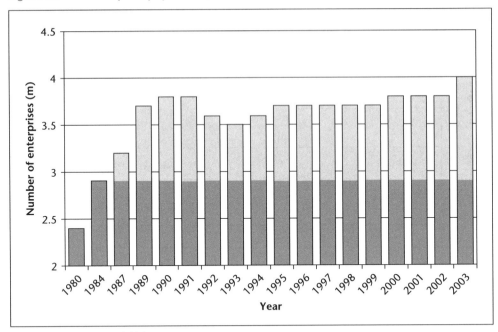

Source: Small Business Service (2005)

employment was 41,300,000 in 1958. This fell to 39,900,000 in 1967 before rising to 45,700,000 in 1982.

Blanchflower (2004) has nonetheless indicated that, in terms of self-employment (percentage of non-agricultural employment), the picture has not been consistent (Table 2.6). Blanchflower indicates that only certain economies (UK, Australia, New Zealand, Mexico and Ireland) have seen a steady increase in their self-employment rates over the last 50 years.

Other countries do not display this pattern. For example, the US has, with the exception of the recovery of the 1970s, seen a steady decrease in its rate of self-employment. This is also common to the economies of Austria, Denmark, France, Japan and Norway. Other economies, perhaps more in keeping with the UK statistics, show a 'U'-shaped self-employment pattern. Hence, Canada, Italy, the Netherlands and Portugal show rates falling in the 1970s and 1980s before returning to higher levels of self-employment more recently. Other countries (Belgium, Greece and Germany), could be further characterised as constants since the self-employment rates in these countries have remained relatively stable over the last 50 years.

Self-employment is only one measure of enterprise activity. A perhaps more complete measure is the evidence supplied by the COMPENDIA database, which contains business ownership rates (defined as the number of unincorporated and incorporated non-agricultural self-employed as a share of the labour force) for 23 OECD countries over the period 1972–2002 (only the even years). In Table 2.7 we can see that the average business ownership rate for these 23 countries was 10% in 1972. This rate fell

Table 2.6 Self-employment (% of all non-agricultural employment) in selected OECD countries, 1956–2002

	1956	1966	1976	1986	1996	2002
Australia		10.2	11.1	12.8	11.9	12.1
Austria		13.6[a]	9.5	6.3	7.0	7.8[b]
Belgium	13.0	14.4	11.4	13.1	14.5	14.1[c]
Canada	9.6	7.7	6.1	7.2	9.2	8.7
Denmark	15.5[d]	14.3[f]	9.6	7.1	7.2	7.2
France	19.5	14.2	10.9	9.8	7.7	6.7
Germany	10.1[e]	8.7	8.8	8.7	9.0	9.5
Greece	30.9[d]		30.9[i]	29.0	29.1	26.4
Ireland		9.8	10.6	11.1	12.9	12.7
Italy	27.6[k]	26.1	22.5	22.6	24.3	23.2
Japan	22.8	15.6	14.7	13.6	10.1	9.1
Mexico		19.0[h]	21.6[l]	20.7[m]	27.4	27.2
Netherlands	16.6	14.7[j]	8.9	8.2	9.9	9.9
New Zealand	9.3[j]	8.3	9.5	13.5	16.6	15.8
Norway	10.9	9.5	7.1	6.6	5.5	4.9
Portugal	16.7	15.0	11.8	16.9	19.9	17.7
UK	6.4	5.6	7.0	10.8	12.0	11.0
USA	10.3	8.7	6.8	7.4	7.3	6.4

Notes: a=1968; b=2001; c=1999; d=1960; e=1957; f=1965; g=1959; h=1970; i=1977; j=1961; k=1958; l=1980; m=1990; n=1988

Source: Blanchflower (2004); OECD Labour Force Statistics

throughout the rest of the 1970s and the early 1980s before returning to its 1972 level in 1986. Thereafter, the average rate of business ownership increased, reaching a peak in the mid to late 1990s. Overall, the average rate across all the 23 countries is 'U'-shaped for the period 1972–2002.

Four groups are discernable from Table 2.7. The first of these groups are countries that saw gradual increases in their rate of business ownership over the period (see Table 2.8). These 'increasers' include three Mediterranean countries (Greece, Italy and Portugal) as well as countries as seemingly divergent as Finland, the UK, Canada and Switzerland.

Within this group, it is also clear that the countries with the highest rates of business ownership in 1972 tend to have the highest rates in 2002. Over the period, therefore, there is little sign of convergence within this group: the three Mediterranean countries have rates (ranging from 11.2% to 16.1% in 1972 and 13.7% to 19.3% in 2002) that are persistently above that of Finland and Switzerland (6.6% in 1972 and 7.6–7.9% in 2002). The only country to change its relative position in 1972 was Ireland. In 1972 it had a business ownership rate of 7.7% which was just below the UK rate. By 2002, Ireland had a rate that was 0.5% above that of the UK.

It is further evident from Table 2.8 and the data in Table 2.7 that there are a group of countries (France, Luxemburg, Japan and Norway) that have seen an overall decline in their rates of business ownership. For example, both France (11.3%) and Japan (12.5%) in 1972 had rates of business ownership that were well above the average rate

Table 2.7 Percentage business ownership rate (number of business owners/total labour force)

	1972	1974	1976	1978	1980	1982	1984	1986	1988	1990	1992	1994	1996	1998	2000	2002
Australia	12.6	13.7	14.7	16.0	16.8	16.1	16.0	16.5	16.4	16.3	16.9	17.1	15.5	15.6	15.8	16.4
Austria	9.3	8.1	7.7	7.7	7.3	6.5	6.5	6.6	6.9	7.2	6.9	7.2	7.4	8.0	8.3	8.3
Belgium	10.5	10.0	9.8	9.9	9.8	9.9	10.2	10.6	10.9	11.2	11.4	11.6	11.9	11.8	11.7	11.3
Canada	7.9	7.5	7.8	8.5	8.7	9.0	10.0	10.0	10.6	10.8	10.9	12.1	12.8	14.0	13.1	12.2
Denmark	8.2	8.1	8.1	7.9	7.4	7.0	6.6	6.3	5.6	6.3	5.8	5.9	6.4	6.4	6.1	6.7
Finland	6.6	6.2	5.9	5.9	6.4	6.2	6.6	6.6	7.6	8.1	7.5	7.7	8.0	8.2	8.1	7.9
France	11.3	10.9	10.5	10.3	10.1	10.0	9.8	9.8	9.9	9.8	9.6	9.0	8.8	8.4	8.3	8.1
Germany	7.6	7.3	7.0	6.7	6.6	6.6	6.8	6.9	7.0	7.2	7.3	7.8	8.2	8.5	8.7	8.6
Greece	16.1	17.3	17.9	18.5	18.2	18.6	17.7	18.2	18.6	19.4	20.2	20.1	19.7	19.3	19.1	19.3
Iceland	11.1	10.2	9.9	10.0	8.8	8.6	9.1	9.9	10.1	10.9	11.7	12.5	13.0	13.2	13.3	12.3
Ireland	7.7	8.2	8.2	8.2	8.6	8.3	8.9	8.7	10.1	10.9	11.1	11.3	11.2	11.3	11.3	11.2
Italy	14.3	14.4	14.2	14.6	14.8	15.8	16.5	16.7	16.9	17.5	17.9	17.7	18.3	18.2	18.5	18.3
Japan	12.5	12.7	12.6	13.0	13.1	12.9	12.6	12.5	12.3	11.6	11.0	10.5	10.1	10.0	9.7	9.2
Luxembourg	10.7	10.0	9.3	9.2	8.7	8.2	8.3	7.8	7.5	6.9	6.4	6.7	6.7	6.3	5.9	5.4
New Zealand	10.6	10.2	10.2	9.5	9.0	10.1	11.4	11.5	11.4	11.5	12.3	12.9	13.9	13.8	14.2	13.5
Norway	9.7	9.2	8.9	8.7	8.4	8.6	8.7	8.4	8.4	7.7	7.8	7.8	7.1	6.9	6.4	6.5
Portugal	11.3	11.0	11.0	11.7	11.9	11.8	10.6	10.8	11.6	12.9	15.0	15.3	15.6	14.4	13.5	13.7
Spain	11.8	11.6	10.9	10.7	11.0	10.8	11.2	11.4	12.3	12.3	12.9	12.6	13.0	13.0	12.6	12.9
Sweden	7.4	7.1	6.8	6.8	7.0	7.4	7.2	6.6	6.4	6.9	7.2	8.0	8.1	8.2	8.3	8.1
Switzerland	6.6	6.5	6.9	6.8	6.5	6.6	6.8	7.0	7.1	7.3	7.0	7.4	8.5	9.1	8.7	7.6
Netherlands	10.0	9.7	9.2	8.7	8.5	8.1	8.1	8.2	8.2	8.5	8.9	9.7	10.2	10.4	10.9	10.8
UK	7.8	7.7	7.4	7.1	7.4	8.2	8.6	8.9	10.1	11.2	10.5	11.1	11.1	11.0	10.5	10.7
USA	8.0	8.2	8.1	8.8	9.5	9.9	10.4	10.3	10.7	10.6	10.3	10.5	10.4	10.3	9.8	9.5
Average	10.0	9.8	9.7	9.8	9.8	9.8	9.9	10.0	10.3	10.6	10.7	11.0	11.1	11.1	11.0	10.8

Source: EIM COMParative ENtrepreneurship Data for International Analysis (COMPENDIA, 2002.1)

Table 2.8 Patterns of business ownership in 23 OECD countries

Increasers	Decreasers	'U'-shaped	'Outliers'
Greece	France	Spain	Denmark
Italy	Luxemburg	Iceland	Australia
Portugal	Japan	Belgium	US
New Zealand	Norway	The Netherlands	
Canada		Germany	
Ireland		Austria	
UK		Sweden	
Finland			
Switzerland			

of 10%. These rates declined in the 1970s and the 1980s in line with the OECD average but in the 1990s rates in the four 'decliner' countries did not improve. Each of the four countries by 2002 had rates of business ownership that were below the average rate of 10.8%.

A third group are countries also have a 'U'-shaped pattern to their rates of business ownership. The Netherlands, for instance, began the 1970s with a rate of just over 10%, sank down to 8.1% in 1984 and then recovered to 10.8% in 2002. Other countries in this group display similar patterns although it is interesting to note some differences. First, Spain, unlike the other three Mediterranean countries, saw a marked fall in its business ownership rate in the late 1970s to the early 1980s.

Hence, from having a business ownership rate (11.9%) which was above Portugal (11.3%) in 1972, by 2002 the situation had reversed: Spain had a rate (12.9%) compared with Portugal's rate of 13.7%. A similar situation is evident with Austrian rates. Data from Table 2.7 also show that Sweden had, in fact, two separate 'U'-shaped periods. The first period was between 1972 and 1982. Rates here fell and then recovered to their 1972 levels. After 1982 rates again fell before returning to higher business ownership rates.

Table 2.8 suggests that there were three countries (Denmark, Australia and the US) that may be described as outliers in that they do not fit any of the patterns evident in the three other groups. Denmark is unusual in the sense that, although like very many other countries, business ownership rates decline in the 1970s and in the 1980s, they stabilised from 1988 at around 6%. Australia is also different from other countries because its rate of business ownership jumps from 12.6% in 1972 to 16% in 1978. Since then, Table 2.7 shows that business ownership rates in Australia have been, except for the mid-1990s, around 16%. The third outlier is the US. The pattern here may be described as 'n'-shaped in that business ownership rates increased from 8% in 1972 to 10.7% in 1988 before falling to 9.5% in 2002.

This section has shown that smaller enterprises 're-emerged' in the UK. In fact, from 1980 both self-employment and the more general business ownership data suggest that the UK enterprise population increased by 50% in the 1980s. Since then, with the exception of the recessionary period of the early 1990s, business ownership rates have gently increased since 1995. This evidence is in line with international data which suggests that the UK has seen its business ownership rates increase.

This section has also shown that the majority of other economies either follow this pattern or have a 'U'-shaped pattern to business ownership rates. The section, however, has pointed to some notable exceptions such as 'decreasers' (e.g. France and Japan) or those with unusual patterns (e.g. the US's 'n'-shaped pattern).

2.6 Explanations for the changes in business ownership

Given the heterogeneity of changes in business ownership rates over the last 30 or so years, it is unlikely that there is a unique explanation for such changes. The evidence from the previous section clearly showed that being above or below the average rate for all 23 countries does not necessarily indicate the likely direction of change in the rate of business ownership. Countries such as Japan and France were above the average but subsequently saw their rates decline. Australia, too, was above the average rate in 1972 but went on to have rates of business ownership well above the average. Similarly, countries like Canada or Ireland began below the average and were above the average by 2002.

In this penultimate section, therefore, a number of factors that seek to explain these changes are presented. These factors – changes in the cost structure of industry, rapid technological development, innovation, an increase in the service economy, changes in the labour market and shifts in government policy – should not be seen in isolation. Indeed, such factors are very likely to interact with each other. Furthermore, these factors tend to explain why ownership rates in the majority of OECD countries have either increased gradually over time or recovered from a dip in the 1970s to 1980s.

2.6.1 Cost disadvantages

Looking first at why business ownership rates declined prior to the 1980s, one reason may have been that smaller enterprises were at a cost disadvantage. In an era of mass production, larger enterprises were able to produce goods much more cheaply (economies of scale). Mass production also meant that the optimal size of plants (minimum efficient scale (MES)) needed to be larger. Smaller enterprises, therefore, found it more difficult to compete against rising volumes, falling costs and cheaper prices. The rising optimal plant size had two other effects: it tended to deter new entrants and it promoted concentration of ownership in an industry. Another impact of consolidating ownership is that it reduces uncertainty in the market place. As Coase (1937) had shown, enterprises who wish to sell their products or services in the market place face two principal transactional costs. First, both sellers (enterprises) and buyers (consumers) have costs: sellers have to market/advertise their goods/services whilst buyers have to search for these goods/services. Second, there is no guarantee that enterprises will gain payment for their goods/services. Hence, they need contractual terms that ensure that buyers of goods/services will not default on their payment.

Such uncertainties have led Galbraith (1967) to argue that it made sense for enterprises to limit such transaction costs. He argued that this was best done by larger enterprises working together to manipulate the behaviour of buyers through advertising and marketing. Bigger enterprises were also able to reduce uncertainty by vertically integrating their business with others in the supply chain. In essence, therefore, larger enterprises sought to economise on the market: 'the visible hand of managerial direction has replaced the invisible hand of market mechanisms, however, in coordinating flows and allocating resources in major modern industries' (Chandler, 1990: 95). Prior to the 1980s then, business ownership rates seemed to have declined as MES rose and economies of scale became more important. Little wonder, therefore, that Boswell (1973) lamented 'because many small firms appear to be inefficient, traditionalist and family-ridden, the small firm-sector as a whole is seen as inimical to progress and professionalism' (p. 19).

2.6.2 Technological changes

The empirical evidence (Table 2.7) shows that business ownership rates generally began to increase in the 1980s. One reason for this is that technological change reduced the importance of economies of scale in production. Instead of the optimal form of technology being mass production techniques similar to that first employed by Henry Ford, the introduction of new technologies (e.g. computer aided design, robots), organisation processes (e.g. 'just in time') and management techniques (e.g. total quality management) have had a profound impact on the cost structure of manufacturing. It has become increasingly possible for enterprises to operate at lower optimal sizes (Acs *et al.*, 1990). Along with this 'de-scaling' (smaller-sized optimal plants), new technologies allowed for greater flexibility (Kaplinsky, 1990). This meant is that it was possible to produce much more efficiently smaller batches of manufactured goods (Carlsson, 1989).

Another impact of technological change is that 'de-scaling' and increased flexibility allowed smaller enterprises to enter sectors previously closed to them. It also meant that smaller enterprises had the potential to compete much more effectively against larger enterprises as there was little efficiency differences (Dosi, 1988). For example, Acs *et al.* (1991) found that: 'in industries in which numerically controlled machines are extensively used, small firms have accounted for an increased share of subsequent sales in the market' (p. 317). Piore and Sabel (1984) also argued that the new technology offered distinct advantages to smaller enterprises. Based on a study of North Eastern and Central Italy (the 'Third Italy'), they suggested that new technology allowed groups of autonomous smaller enterprises to network together for their mutual benefit. Because the industries in this area (e.g. textiles, clothing, shoes) required skilled craft labour, individual workers were able to quickly adapt to new product runs. Equally, the enterprises themselves were able to share and coordinate management functions such as purchasing and marketing. New technology, therefore, allowed smaller enterprises to gain a competitive advantage because they were able to 'flexibly specialise'.

A consequence of the introduction of new technologies is that it created new industries. These new industries (e.g. microelectronics, biotechnologies and information communication technologies) have led to the notion that we have entered a fifth Kondratieff wave. These waves, lasting around 50 years, are said to bring with them profound economic change (Freeman, 1991). Hence, in the past, each of the previous four waves (iron, steam and cotton (1780s to 1840s); steel, coal, and the railways (1850s to 1890s); electricity, chemicals, the internal combustion machine and synthetic materials (1890s to 1930s); and electrical and light engineering, petrochemicals, and automotive manufacture

(1940s to 1980s)), has markedly altered economic activity. Hence, one reason why business ownership rates may have increased is that, in the early years of a Kondratieff wave, newer and smaller enterprises are responsible for creating and diffusing new technologies.

2.6.3 Innovation

In parallel with technological change arguments, some researchers have also argued that the re-emergence of smaller enterprises has much to do with the innovatory capacity of smaller enterprises. In part, smaller enterprises are said to have a competitive advantage because they are less bureaucratic and, therefore, more flexible to changing market conditions (Rothwell, 1989; Scherer, 1991). Imitation lags are also said to have fallen so that new products are brought much sooner to market (Jovanovic, 2001). Given this, Acs and Audretsch (1989) in the US and Pavitt *et al.* (1987) in the UK have argued that SMEs have a rate of innovation (innovations per employee) that is higher than larger enterprises in particular industries.

Too much emphasis can perhaps be given to the impact of technological change. Acs and Audretsch (1990) point to the fact that the most innovative firms in the US are larger enterprises. Moreover, technological change is not new: Klepper's (2002) study of earlier, mass production, industries (automotives, televisions, tyres and penicillin) showed that in the early years of these industries there were particularly high rates of entry and exit. Similarly, new technology, in itself, does not necessarily confer competitive advantages to smaller enterprises. New technology may allow larger enterprises to reduce set-up times and produce a wider variety of goods (economies of scope). The MES of an industry may also rise. Although the semiconductor industry is relatively new, Ernst and O'Connor showed that even back in 1992 it cost around US$1bn for a production facility that met the MES. Equally, Amin (1989) has questioned the notion that flexible specialisation helped liberate craft production. Instead, the suggestion was that many of the labour conditions were those of a sweatshop (low wages, poor working conditions and limited job security).

2.6.4 Large firm fragmentation

Another possible reason for the development in business ownership rates since the 1980s is that there has been a radical shift in the business practices of larger enterprises. Shutt and Whittington (1987), for instance, have argued that 'the sector's [small enterprise] rise does not represent an independent source of new employment but merely a transfer of employment from large units to small' (p. 21). This claim is derived from three suggested economic changes to the large firm's environment: producing innovative products became riskier; consumers and the macro-economy became more uncertain (e.g. increases in commodity prices, more fickle consumers); and it was increasingly difficult to control workers (e.g. increased wage demands, strikes). In response to these challenges, Shutt and Whittington (1987) contend that larger enterprises sought to vertically disintegrate by hiving off enterprise activities into subsidiaries or franchised operations. This idea is supported by Harrison (1994) who has argued that the seeming growth of small businesses is the result of a determined and concerted effort by multi-national firms to increase their flexibility. Hence, Harrison cites a determination of many such firms to concentrate upon their 'core competencies' and, thereby, seek to transfer risk to smaller enterprises. Empirically, Rainnie (1991) provides support for such a view. He showed that large enterprises responded to change not by vertically disintegrating but drawing in smaller enterprises into sub-contracting relationships. Similar changes in employment contracts are evident in other industries: milk delivery (Boyle, 1994), hairdressing (Drucker *et al.*, 1997) and book publishing (Stanworth and Stanworth, 1995).

2.6.5 Development of the service sector

The adoption of fragmentation strategies by larger enterprises is not supported by Hakim (1988a). She showed that comparatively few enterprises sought to exchange employees for the supposed flexibility of self-employed workers. Nonetheless, there would seem to be strong evidence to suggest that the nature of consumer demand has changed. Instead of being content with standardised mass produced goods, consumers have increasingly sought tailor-made goods and, in particular, individual services. For example, the number of financial service businesses in the UK doubled from 80,000 in 1980 to 160,000 by 1993. Similarly, between 1994 and 2003 business services, in general, increased by 314,000 to 500,000. This represents a 63% increase. Researchers such as Keeble *et al.* (1992) and Bryson *et al.* (1997) have also argued that the reason why businesses such as management consultancies and medical, health, and IT providers have grown is due to systemic changes in demand among business to business (B2B) services and consumer services for households and personal consumers.

Such businesses, particularly smaller-sized businesses, may have been able to exploit these sectors because there exist few opportunities for the development of economies of scale given that consumption is often at the point of purchase. Moreover, for Keeble *et al.* (1992) and Bryson *et al.* (1997) small service businesses have other, perhaps more intangible, competitive advantages: 'for small business service firms the most important competitive advantages are "personal attention to client needs", "specialised expertise or products" and "established reputation"' (Bryson *et al.*, 1997: 352).

2.6.6 Changes in the labour market

Alongside the development of particular niches to meet more sophisticated forms of demand, researchers have pointed to changes in the labour market to explain the growth of business ownership rates. For instance, researchers have pointed to the population change, increased wealth (Reynolds *et al.*, 1994), immigration (21.8% of UK individuals whose ethnic origin was Pakistani were self-employed in 2001–02 (Social Trends, 2002)), and, above all, unemployment as being explanations for the growth in business owner-ship rates. In the UK context, Greene (2002) has shown that unemployment reached over three million in the 1980s. Concomitant with this, the 1980s also saw dramatic increases in the enterprise population. The implication, therefore, is that unemployed individuals were 'pushed' into self-employment due to the lack of alternative employment.

2.6.7 Public policy

Another explanation for changes in business ownership rates is the role played by public policy since the 1980s. Greene (2002) has argued that faced with unprecedented levels of unemployment in the 1980s, the UK government of the time sought to shift the risk preferences of individuals towards setting up their own businesses. Hence, they supported a range of publicly or quasi-publicly supported schemes (e.g. the Enterprise Allowance Scheme, Small Business Loan Guarantee Scheme, Enterprise Zones, and the Prince's Trust) that sought to improve the conditions for setting up a business.

Similarly, following on from the UK's deregulation and privatisation of many of its public utilities in the 1980s, other OECD governments have sought to implement policies in the belief that over-regulated economies inhibit the entrepreneurial abilities of individuals. For instance, France which has seen a long-term decline in its business ownership rates has sought to reduce the administrative burdens faced by individuals seeking to set up a business (Henriquez *et al.*, 2002).

This section has provided some explanations that attempt to account for the dramatic increase in the business ownership rates in very many OECD countries. Hence, prior to the 1980s, the business environment may be judged to be inimical to smaller enterprises given that consumer demand was relatively stable and, as such, there were cost advantages in developing economies of scale. Since the 1980s, though, consumer demand has become more uncertain and consumers more demanding. This has led to the development of particular niches. Equally, labour market changes and government policies may also have fostered changes in people's propensities towards setting up a business. Finally, the section has shown that larger enterprises have sought to substitute capital for labour to compensate for uncertain demand and the rapid rate of technological change.

2.7 The 'n'-shaped puzzle of the US

The previous section provided some accounts for why for many OECD countries have seen business ownership rates increase. Such interpretations can also be stretched to include 'decreasers' such as France and Japan if it is believed that these countries are dominated by larger enterprises and a burdensome regulatory environment. What is not clear is why the US has followed an 'n'-shaped business ownership pattern or why self-employment rates have declined in the US. These questions are important because the US is often seen as a model of technological change, rapid innovation and a country that has been responsible for driving much of the global economic growth in the 1990s. The US is also seen as a country that strongly promotes entrepreneurship and has very few administrative burdens to inhibit individuals setting up or growing a business (Global Entrepreneurship Monitor (GEM), 2004).

One obvious explanation for the 'n'-shaped distribution of business ownership in the US is that the COMPENDIA dataset is a partial measure of business ownership in the US. Because COMPENDIA is designed to measure international business ownership rates, the particular measure it has chosen (the number of unincorporated and incorporated non-agricultural self-employed as a share of the labour force) may be thought to poorly reflect the actual nature of entrepreneurship in the US. Earlier on, Table 2.5 showed, for example, that the US has significantly more larger enterprises than either Europe or Japan. The COMPENDIA data may then underestimate the contribution of larger enterprises to entrepreneurship in the US as they measure the rate of business ownership rather than the contribution of particular businesses. Indeed, given that the US is a large, well-integrated market with a flexible labour force, ENSR (2004) have suggested that larger enterprises predominate in the US because it allows for the development of economies of scale and scope. The implication, therefore, is that the economic growth of the US is due to the economic activities of larger enterprises.

Another potential explanation for the US is that the 'n'-shaped pattern is appropriate for the US economy. Carree *et al.* (2002) argue that there is an equilibrium rate between economic development and business ownership. Using the same COMPENDIA data, they find that countries that deviate from an equilibrium rate suffer: 'by and large, a five percent point deviation implies a growth loss of three percent over a period of four years' (p. 285). Given that Carree *et al.* (2002) find that the US tends to follow the equilibrium rate, this then may give some insights into the economic performance of the US.

These arguments are essentially static arguments: they point to what is happening rather than why it is happening. For example, the US economy may be dominated by large multinational businesses such as Microsoft or Dell, but this ignores the fact that these very enterprises are relatively new. Jovanovic (2001) has shown, for the period 1926–96, that smaller enterprises significantly outperformed larger, more established, enterprises.

A more dynamic explanation for the US is that what matters is not the rate of business ownership but the degree of 'churn' (rate of entry and exit) in the economy. Because the US places relatively fewer regulatory burdens on business start-up, entry barriers are lower and this may, in turn, encourage greater numbers of new enterprises. These new entrants stimulate competition in the sector so as to ensure that enterprises that are inefficient exit the sector. The overall effect, therefore, is to drive up efficiency and innovation in the sector.

There is some evidence to support the idea of the dynamic role of new enterprises. GEM (2004), for example, looks at the numbers of individuals in a given economy that are seeking to set up a new venture or who have a new venture. GEM (2004) calls this rate total entrepreneurial activity (TEA). The US, like Australia and New Zealand, had TEA rates that were among the highest in the OECD in 2004. It goes on to argue that there is a correlation between TEA and GDP growth. Similarly, for the UK, Disney *et al.* (2003) have argued that the dynamic nature of enterprise birth and death can have a large impact on productivity: 'Between 1980 and 1982, single establishment firms (25% of manufacturing employment) experienced no productivity growth among survivors; all productivity gains for this group came from entry and exit' (p. 691). Moreover, it may be more than coincidental that the VAT registration and deregistration rates for the UK mirror regional inequalities. Prosperous regions such as London and the South East (e.g. Sussex and Buckinghamshire) had VAT registration rates of 36,600 and 30,300, respectively, in 2003. Their deregistration rates were also high: 34,600 (London) and 27,800 (South East). This compares with registration/deregistration rates of 4,600/4,000 for less prosperous regions such as the North East of England (e.g.

Tyne and Wear) or 3,800/4,000 for Northern Ireland. Armington and Acs (2002) have also shown that there are similar regional disparities in the US. In 1994, the average annual firm birth rate in the US was 3.85 per 1,000 of the labour force. Well above this average were the South and West of the US whilst the Northeast and Midwest of the US were well below this average.

This evidence points to the view that the 'n'-shaped pattern of business ownership in the US is the outcome of the dynamic nature of entry and exit. If so, it may be anticipated that the US would have higher rates of entry and exit compared with other economies. Evidence from 10 OECD economies suggests (Figure 2.4) that this is not the case.

Figure 2.4 shows that the US tends to have higher rates of manufacturing and service entry and exit than most of the nine other economies but that these differences tend to be relatively small. Moreover, simply encouraging yet larger numbers of new entrants into particular sectors does not necessarily improve efficiency or innovation. Many of these individuals may have skills that are unsuited to running an enterprise. If they enter, they may not have any discernable impact upon efficiency or innovation because they do not have the skills to compete effectively with existing enterprises in the sector (Greene et al., 2004).

An alternative but equally dynamic explanation for business ownership rates in the US is the role played by fast-growth enterprises. Again, as with enterprise churn, what matters here is not the rate of business ownership but the patterns of enterprise activity. Fast-growth enterprises have long been seen as important. Storey (1985) showed that over a ten-year period (with an enterprise exit rate of 60%), 4% of enterprises will

Figure 2.4 **EU–US entry and exit rates**

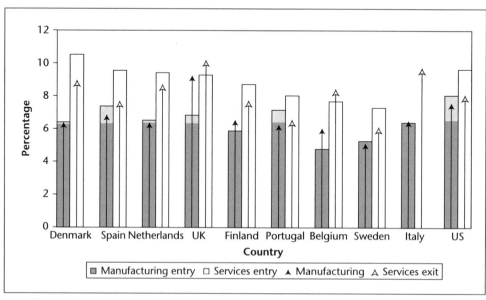

Source: Pilat (2004)

Figure 2.5 Employment gains of surviving firms after two years

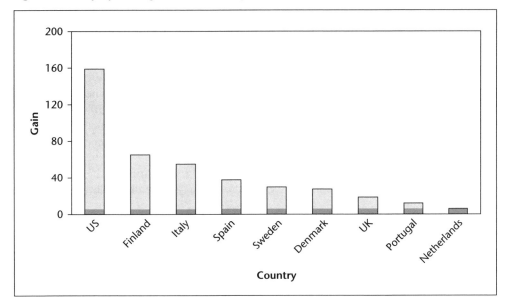

contribute 50% of employment. Such a result is fairly typical: Birch *et al.* (1997), for example, showed that 'gazelles' – around 3% of all US enterprises – were responsible for about 70% of gross job growth.

Therefore, the argument is that the US should have higher rates of growth among its enterprise population. This is a view supported by Scarpetta *et al.* (2002) who suggest that the US, unlike the EU, has lower regulation and stricter employment legislation. This allows individual entrepreneurs to enter a market at a small scale so that they can test their ideas out. Subsequently, those that find that their ideas are novel or efficient are able to expand. The impact of this is shown in Figure 2.5 which shows the employment gains of surviving firms over a two-year period (as a percentage of initial employment). Figure 2.5 clearly shows that US enterprises have rates of employment growth that are more than double the nearest EU country (Finland) and more than four times that of economies such as the UK or Denmark.

This evidence suggests that what matters is fast-growth enterprises. However, it should not be assumed that entry and exit rates are unimportant. Scarpetta *et al.* (2002) also indicate that entry and exit accounts for from 20–40% of total productivity growth.

This section has shown that there are a variety of explanations for the 'n'-shaped pattern to business ownership rates in the US. Some of it may be due to measurement issues, the relative size and integration of the US economy or because the US is better able to balance its business ownership rates with economic development. This section has also shown that a more dynamic explanation is the influence of enterprise churn and fast-growth enterprises. These factors, rather than more static interpretations, are likely to drive economic growth in the US and in other OECD countries.

2.8 Chapter summary

This chapter has sought to provide various international definitions of smaller enterprises. It has shown that these vary internationally. Despite this, and the methodological problems of using a mix of survey (Labour Force Survey) and registration data (e.g. VAT registration), this chapter has clearly shown that SMEs account for the vast majority of enterprises in any given economy. The chapter has also demonstrated that the number of smaller enterprises has tended to increase over the last 30 years in most OECD countries. A variety of explanations – changes in the cost structure of industry, rapid technological development, innovation, an increase in the service economy, changes in the labour market and shifts in government policy – have been offered to explain why it is that the general pattern of business ownership has been increasing or 'U'-shaped. These explanations, however, should not be seen in isolation with each other.

The chapter has also looked at economies that do not follow this pattern. Hence, it has looked at 'decreasers' such as France or Japan. The main concentration in the final section of the chapter has been on the US. It has shown that there are various static reasons for the US's 'n'-shaped pattern: measurement issues, the importance of larger enterprises or equilibrium rates. Two more dynamic interpretations were also offered: entry and exit; and the importance of fast-growth enterprises. Whilst the actual contribution of these two interpretations is still debatable, it is evident that what matters is not the actual static rate of business ownership in an economy but the dynamic nature of that economy.

Questions

1 What are the advantages and disadvantages of describing a small business (a) quantitatively and (b) qualitatively?

2 Why do you think there are differences in small firm formation rates between countries?

3 What are the main reasons for the growth in the number of small firms?

4 What are the main reasons for the recent decline in business ownership in the US and does this make a difference to the impact of the small firm sector?

Web links

www.europa.eu.int/comm/enterprise/enterprise_policy/sme_definition/index_en.htm
This site presents the background to the new EU definition of the small business.

www.sbrt.co.uk/
The Small Business Research Trust undertakes a quarterly survey of small firms that provides statistical analyses of the progress of smaller businesses in the light of economic and political change.

www.sbs.gov.uk
This is the website of the Small Business Service in the UK. The section 'research and statistics' contains up-to-date information on the small firm sector in the UK.

www.europa.eu.int/comm/enterprise/enterprise_policy/analysis/observatory_en.htm
The Observatory of European SMEs was established by the European Commission in 1992 to improve the monitoring of the economic performance of SMEs in Europe. This website provides a list of reports produced by the Observatory.

CHAPTER 3

Self-employment and the small business

David J. Brooksbank

3.1 Introduction

This chapter provides a general introduction to the core statistical data on the self-employed in the UK. The chapter starts by providing an overview of the self-employed, who they are, why they entered self-employment, their personal characteristics, their jobs and the industrial sectors they enter. A key feature discussed in this chapter is the growth in self-employment over the past 20 years and, although this chapter concentrates on the UK situation, this trend has been apparent in many other countries.

3.2 Learning objectives

There are three learning objectives in this chapter:

1 To appreciate the numbers of individuals involved in self-employment in the UK and their importance to the economy.
2 To be aware of the major trends and changes to the stock of self-employed over the past two decades.
3 To link the important themes, covered elsewhere in the text, to the baseline data.

Key concepts
■ self-employment ■ personal characteristics ■ self-employment treads

3.3 The self-employed

Detailed and comprehensive analysis of the self-employed received very little attention from the economics profession prior to the 1980s. Set against a background of declining numbers stemming from the days of the industrial revolution this is hardly surprising. However, during that decade something new happened to self-employment in the UK: the numbers of self-employed rose by approximately 60% to 3.4 million, forming almost 13% of the workforce. This dramatic rise has caused a well-deserved resurgence of interest. The increases in self-employment in the 1980s and the subsequent fall during the recession at the start of the 1990s have given rise to a lively debate about the types of people tempted to give self-employment a try.

The first part of this chapter presents the data on these people and will allow you to link themes and trends to the rest of the text. Research undertaken by Meager *et al.* (1996) studied the income distribution of the self-employed – both male and female. (Other authors have also added interesting material to this debate including Jenkins (1994) and Parker (1997, 2004).) On average, over all the self-employed, they earn as much as wage earners but there is a significant dispersion with one group of very high earners at one end of the spectrum (usually male) while at the other end there exists a large and growing group of poor self-employed. To elaborate, a self-employed person has more than three times the chance of falling into the bottom 10% of the income distribution than a comparable type of employee (i.e. earning approximately £40–£50 per week).

Meager *et al.* also comment that self-employment, even if it forms only part of a working career, can put peoples' future financial security at risk. If a person has a 'punctuated' work history with periods of employment, unemployment and self-employment, then they are more likely to be pushed into the poorer group of self-employed workers in later life because they are less likely to have a stable occupational pension and less likely to have a significant volume of savings. This in turn implies a greater dependency upon the state pension in later life. The increased heterogeneity of the self-employed population means that those at the bottom end of the earnings spectrum cannot expect things to improve dramatically over the next few years.

There is no automatic link between self-employment and poverty, although equally there is no such link between self-employment and success. Storey (1994) believes that it is important for the self-employed to have a realistic understanding of what they are undertaking. He has discovered instances where people have entered self-employment and then run up considerable personal debt. They survive in business only by working very long hours at low rates of pay (although in some cases this provides them not only with employment, but a certain status within society).

If self-employment risks leading to debt and poverty, then why are so many people choosing it? Anecdotal evidence suggests that some of the new self-employed have been actively forced into it by their companies. Citizens' Advice Bureaux across the country have noticed that for the last five or six years an increasing number of people are coming to them with problems associated with self-employment. One major problem is that self-employment status has been imposed upon them. Employers see the advantages, in a short-term sense, of having a self-employed workforce. The rights of these people are then adversely affected by this when the company is no longer liable for pension contributions and employer's National Insurance Contributions (NICs). It is hard to determine how many of these types of people there are among the total self-employed, but such reluctant entrepreneurs should be kept in mind.

A larger group who have entered self-employment are those who were previously unemployed. The encouragement of the unemployed to become their own bosses has been a constant of government policy since the early 1980s. There has been a succession of initiatives: the Enterprise Allowance Scheme (EAS), the Business Start-Up scheme and the Enterprise Support Programme. These schemes all require a moderate amount of capital to be injected prior to registration and often banks are reluctant to lend to people who have previously been unemployed. Lack of capital or assets to act as collateral is a major problem which has been well studied. Research by Black, De Meza and Jeffreys (1996), for example, has shown that house price inflation and financial liberalisation in the 1980s permitted people to borrow and start up on their own far more easily than was previously and is now the case. The illiquid wealth stored in houses could be freed as a result of this financial liberalisation. A deliberate focus of government policy was, therefore, to allow people the chance of entrepreneurship after years of being stuck with few liquid funds. Robson (1996a) has thrown some doubt on the role played by housing collateral in his informative study of business start-ups, although his later paper did indicate a positive relationship between regional house prices and regional rates of self-employment activity (Robson, 1998). The different results make this an interesting area for future work.

Meager *et al.* (1996) have also undertaken research that has convinced the authors that the necessary attributes for success in self-employment cannot easily be inculcated by training. They believe that entrepreneurs are more likely to be born with these attributes and one of the best predictors of someone becoming self-employed and succeeding is whether either or both of their parents have been self-employed.

The sorts of people who come from a family tradition of self-employment (a small business culture where the things that are necessary to succeed like knowledge of contracts and the need to save in the form of a pension for old age) are more likely to stay in business. However, a picture is also emerging of many people entering from other backgrounds. Many have been employees all their lives, as have their parents, and after redundancy they set up on their own but are less likely to have the skills and attributes which are a good predictor of success. This is likely to be one of the explanations of why these people fall disproportionately into the low-income sector of the self-employed.

Storey (1994) takes the analysis further by emphasising that self-employment for the unemployed (including those made redundant) is no guarantee of an entrepreneurial society. There is a notion that if somehow the unemployed can be transformed into self-employed this has a number of advantages. The first is that the people are no longer registered as unemployed and, second, some additional output must be created. In reality, however, the unemployed enter the easy to enter industries (e.g. window cleaning, hairdressing or vehicle repairing) and displace people already there. These people enter unemployment with possible adverse social consequences for themselves. There is a circularity of moving from self-employment into unemployment and back again, not having an impact upon aggregate employment or on wealth creation.

The numbers of those becoming self-employed is rising again after levelling off at the depths of the recession in the early 1990s. However, the new evidence suggests that a significant number of these people will be reluctant entrepreneurs. Without prospects of a secure job people are forced to give self-employment a try.

3.4 Who are the self-employed and what do they do?

This section begins by finding out what the aggregate data say about the self-employed: How many are there? Which jobs do they do? Where do they live? How have these factors changed over time? The major source of data is the Labour Force Survey (LFS) for Great

Britain and updates of the analysis of self-employment figures in it by Campbell and Daly (1992) for the Employment Department provide the basis for the review that follows.

3.4.1 Aggregate data

In Great Britain the total number of self-employed persons (calculated using the grossing-up procedures adopted for the Labour Force Survey) was some 3,633,000 in 2005. This represents an increase of 1,855,000 (104%) since 1979. The figure rose steadily throughout the 1980s and only declined as the recession of 1990 took effect. Since 1991 the rate has climbed and then remained relatively stable. The remarkable rise and then plateau is illustrated in Figure 3.1 below.

Figure 3.1 Self-employment in the UK, 1979–2005 (thousands)

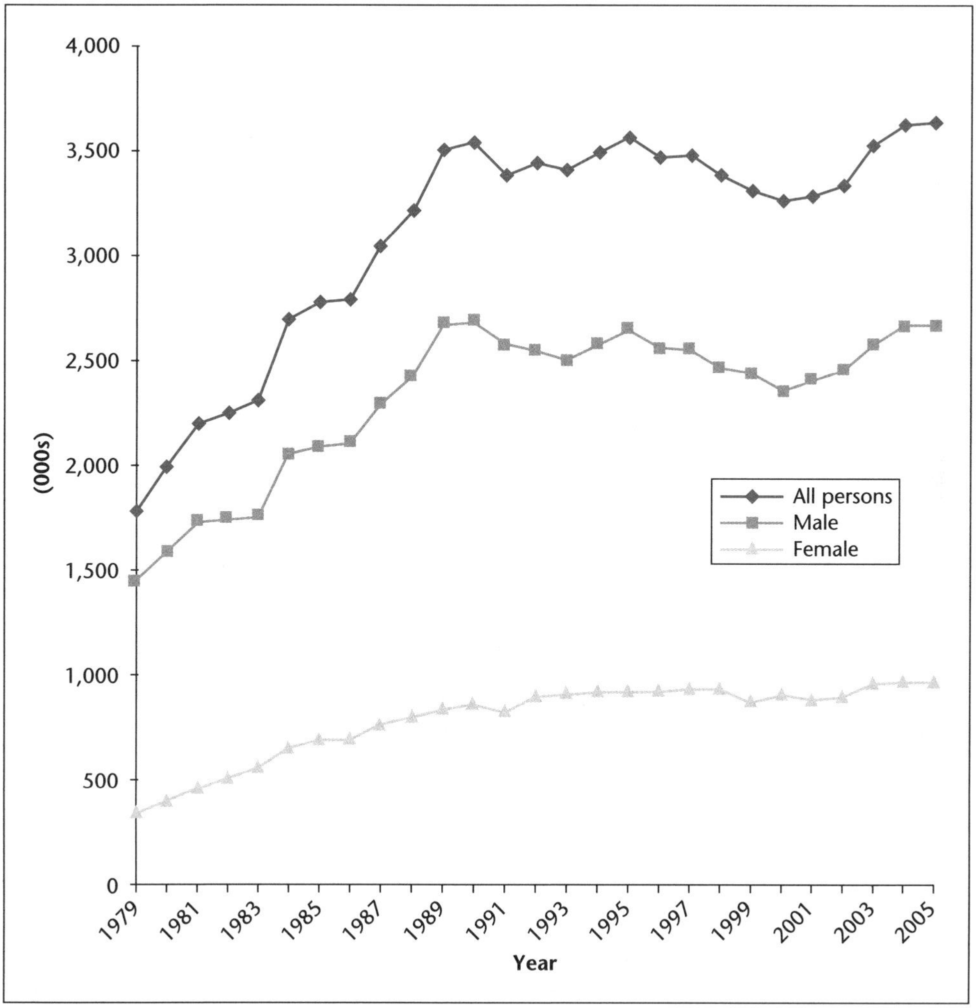

Source: Labour Force Surveys

Table 3.1 **Numbers self-employed by gender (thousands), 1979–2005**

	All persons	Male	Female
1979	1,778	1,442	337
1981	2,201	1,745	455
1983	2,301	1,751	550
1984	2,695	2,050	646
1985	2,778	2,086	691
1986	2,789	2,105	685
1987	3,044	2,287	756
1988	3,216	2,425	791
1989	3,504	2,672	832
1990	3,542	2,686	855
1991	3,384	2,568	816
1992	3,447	2,550	897
1993	3,409	2,501	908
1994	3,494	2,576	918
1995	3,562	2,647	914
1996	3,475	2,560	915
1997	3,479	2,551	928
1998	3,386	2,464	922
1999	3,311	2,438	873
2000	3,260	2,354	906
2001	3,281	2,406	875
2002	3,339	2,454	885
2003	3,530	2,577	953
2004	3,628	2,665	963
2005	3,633	2,675	858
% changes			
1981–1991	54	47	79
1991–2001	−3	−6	7
2001–2005	11	11	−2

Source: Labour Market Trends (2005), seasonally adjusted

A more detailed analysis of the rise during the last decade is shown in Table 3.1, which also provides a breakdown by gender. The figures are for Great Britain.

The share of the self-employed in total employment increased from under 9% in 1981 to over 12% in 1991, where it remained at the Census date in 2001. However, whilst the increase in absolute numbers of self-employed continued in the second half of the 1980s, during this period they increased their share of the total labour force at a slightly lower rate than at the start of the decade. This was matched by a corresponding increase in the rate of growth in the number of employees.

A prominent concern recently has been the growth in part-time employment (self-employment). In 1987, 2,464,000 (83%) were full-time self-employed and 503,000 (17%) were part-time self-employed. In 2005, 2,820,000 (78%) were full-time and 813,000 (22%) were part-time. There is no discernible pattern or split between the proportions of male or female self-employed moving to part-time work over the period.

This is not the case for employees in employment where there has been a noticeable shift towards female part-time as the main job.

Hakim (1988b) noted that the statistics generally do not support the popular view that unemployment pushes people into self-employment. Only around 20% of the inflow to self-employment each year comes from the ranks of the unemployed. Some government schemes, such as the Enterprise Allowance Scheme (EAS), have clearly accounted for some of the new entrepreneurial activity, but by no means all of it. However, the flow of unemployed into self-employment is proportionately higher than the representation of the unemployed within the workforce as a whole would suggest.

Research that has tried to measure the impact of the EAS has shown that many participants were not unemployed for over a year. They may not, therefore, have been included within the unemployment totals for the year prior to the survey dates and so the LFS, from which Meager (1991) takes his data, could be a poor indicator of the impact of this particular policy.

Daly (1991a) also considered the aggregate flows into and out of self-employment. He noted that changes in self-employment rates are likely to follow changes in total employment. Between 1981 and 1987 the rise in self-employment was primarily caused by increases in the proportion of people who were self-employed. After that date, total employment increases rapidly, which accounted for most of the increases in self-employment rates. Additional research by Abell, Khalif and Smeaton (1995) using LFS data for 1975–91 studies flows into and out of self-employment from other states of the labour market. The LFS devoted part of its questionnaire to employment state one year prior to the interview and from this it is possible to analyse transitions between alternative states. The conclusion reached is that much of the apparent increase in self-employment between 1979 and 1989 (with entries greater than exits during this time) can be explained by wage employees becoming self-employed.

3.4.2 Patterns of self-employment

The rest of this review concentrates upon the empirical patterns of self-employment in a number of key areas. These are:

- the role of personal characteristics in the determination of employment status;
- important characteristics of the jobs that the self-employed choose to do; and
- the flows into and out of self-employment.

A distinctive feature of self-employment is that it involves taking risks which entail the possibility of failure. Once a self-employed person establishes a business, some risks decline, but they never disappear. The penalties of failure vary with the degree of personal commitment, the availability of alternative wage or self-employment, and the extent of a social safety net, but they usually involve high personal cost. An employee may be made redundant but there is often some financial compensation, perhaps guaranteed by the State, and there is a social concern that offers at least nominal encouragement. However, the bankrupt self-employed person (who may not be able to take advantage of any bankruptcy protection) has less of a safety net, and he (and even his family) may be deprived of all financial assets. While the risks are inherent, self-employment would be more attractive if fewer of those who entered were likely to fail. If the standard of entrants were higher the survival rate would be higher. If that is achieved by more rigorous screening rather than an upgrading of human resources, less labour would enter the sector and the government's programmes for encouraging the sector would be less effective.

The self-employed are concentrated mainly in industries and trades where there are many producers, where entry is relatively easy and competition vigorous. The resulting crowding can lead to market saturation, and the self-employed often operate close to the margin. When times are difficult (in general, or in their particular trade), they drive themselves and their families harder; when circumstances are easier they reap the benefits. Hakim (1988b) notes that the self-employed exhibit a tendency to increase their hours and effort during tough times rather than cut staff. In better times they then cut hours and effort rather than strive only for financial reward. It is largely a private question as to how badly or how well they treat themselves in terms of hours and conditions of work. For those with employees the danger is that they will expect the employees to accept the same treatment that they themselves tolerate, or worse. As a consequence, the self-employed are sometimes seen as bad employers. They are concentrated in service trades where many employees are paid low wages; these wages may be further reduced when the employer's earnings fall. Employers may also be tempted to extend hours of work and neglect safety conditions and there is little guarantee that in good times the gains of self-employment will be shared with the employees.

In many trades where self-employment is extensive the enterprises are too small for there to be any real likelihood that trade unions can organise the employees. Moreover, where trade unions endeavour to do so, small employers and often their employees as well may resist these efforts. Trade unions tend, therefore, to be suspicious of self-employment. Laws and regulations may not apply or may be difficult to enforce. Employment terms accepted by employees of very small-scale employers may be seen as a threat to the terms which trade unions negotiate in larger firms. Employees in trades where the self-employed are a significant element may find their terms and conditions of work constrained. Their employers may argue that they have to face competition from very small firms and thus cannot afford 'excessive' labour costs. Poor employment conditions of employees in some very small firms, although at the margin of an industry, may have a wider depressing effect on wages and working conditions. Trade unions may believe that it is the owners of micro enterprises with whom they cannot negotiate who weaken their bargaining power in other enterprises where they are organised.

3.5 Personal characteristics of the self-employed

3.5.1 Gender

Table 3.1 showed that males make up a significantly greater proportion of the self-employed than do females. They have continued to do so throughout the period covered by the table and there appears to be no reason to suspect that this will change dramatically over the next few years. However, it is also clear that female self-employment has grown over the total period by twice as much as has male self-employment. This phenomenon has been debated recently in the literature. Some commentators have argued that the role of 'the female entrepreneur' has become steadily greater as the preconceptions of society about the role of women in the workplace have changed (see, for example, Carter and Cannon (1988) and Hakim (1988a)). Other writers have argued that the figures obtained from the LFS exaggerate the true picture. Curran and Burrows (1989) use the General Household Survey (GHS) to show that the ratio of male to female self-employment has remained relatively constant over the years.

The two distinct arguments are resolved when one decomposes the relative changes into two segments. In the first half of the 1980s there was a very rapid increase in female self-employment relative to male. In later years the increases have been similar in proportionate terms. The absolute rise in female self-employment is partly caused by the overall increase in the number of women in the labour market as a whole. Over the period 1979–2005 the female self-employment rate has changed very little, from approximately 5% in 1979 to just over 7.4% in 2005. Daly (1991a) reports that almost all of the increase for females, in the late 1980s, was due to the increasing numbers in total employment, not as a result of an increase in the self-employment rate.

Analysis of the flows into and out of self-employment by gender reveals that the inflow of females was relatively higher than the outflow and higher than the inflow for males over the early part of the 1980s. After 1987 this trend, whilst still applicable to the inflow data, does not hold for the outflow. There was a definite increase in the numbers of women leaving self-employment in the late 1980s. This could be due to differing success rates between sexes or, as Meager (1991) suggests, simply a 'statistical phenomenon' caused by the rapid rise in female self-employment in the earlier period. This issue is discussed further in Chapter 9.

3.5.2 Age

Table 3.2 shows the numbers of self-employed by age and also splits the data by gender.

Examining the information contained in Table 3.2 it is clear that self-employment becomes an increasingly inviting option as one nears middle age. This may be due to a potential entrepreneur reaching a capital threshold and being able to afford the start-up costs of a new venture. Alternatively, the former employee may have accumulated sufficient knowledge or experience of a certain trade to try going into business alone. One factor explaining the increased prevalence of middle-aged self-employed could be that this is the vulnerable age for redundancies in times of recession. Experienced and motivated managers and workers made redundant may well be tempted to try their hand in their own enterprise.

Another feature of the table is the increase in the participation of the over-65s. This reflects a number of key points. First, if the business was the creation of the entrepreneur, there may be considerable reluctance to retire. The self-employed can adjust their hours and effort to cope with the effects of old age and can, therefore, stay on much longer. Second, the self-employed may well not be covered as adequately as much of the employed sector by pension arrangements. They may have to rely on only a state pension and it could very well be that, to some extent, the self-employed cannot afford to retire. Third, many occupations require that their workforce retire at some statutory age and in recent years many firms have actively used an early retirement policy to rationalise the workforce. A good example of this is the local government sector; as

Table 3.2 **Age profile of the self-employed, 2001**

	1981		1991		2001	
	Thousand	Percent of total employment	Thousand	Percent of total employment	Thousand	Percent of total employment
Male						
16–24	108	4.2	198	7.9	70	3.6
25–44	884	13.8	1,291	17.9	1,013	14.9
45–54	387	14.4	591	21.6	634	21.5
55–59	149	11.7	201	19.5	275	25.1
60–64	107	13.1	130	19.9	176	27.4
65+	90	28.0	100	32.3	107	45.5
All	1,726	12.2	2,511	17.4	2,274	16.7
Female						
16–24	26	1.2	48	2.2	22	1.3
25–44	236	5.9	441	8.0	399	7.0
45–54	103	5.2	195	8.8	246	9.6
55–59	38	4.7	59	8.0	93	10.9
60–64	24	7.0	30	9.2	46	13.9
65+	24	13.8	31	20.1	33	22.6
All	451	4.7	805	7.2	839	7.4
All persons						
16–24	134	2.8	246	5.2	92	2.5
25–44	1,120	10.7	1,733	13.6	1,412	11.3
45–54	491	10.5	786	15.8	880	15.9
55–59	187	8.9	260	14.7	368	18.9
60–64	131	11.3	160	16.3	222	22.8
65+	141	23.0	131	30.4	140	36.8
All	2,177	9.2	3,316	13.0	3,114	12.4

Source: Census (2005); Daly (1991a)

councils are merged with districts it has been important to shed employees. Compulsory dismissals would be unpopular in what is a highly unionised sector.

The comparatively low level of self-employment among the younger age groups reflects the difficulty of establishing any enterprise without sufficient funds or experience. Meager (1991) poses the question of how great is the effect on economic activity rates from the distinct growth in the 65+ group, as growing numbers of people reach normal retirement age? If people are being pushed into self-employment because of redundancy or other factors (and the growth is not coming from the traditional *petit bourgeoisie*) then are the financial structures which society has designed to deal with 'ordinary retired employees' adequate for this new class of older entrepreneur?

The age distribution for the self-employed is roughly similar for both sexes. Meager (1991), however, illustrates that the propensity for males to enter self-employment at an early age is almost four times that of similarly aged females. The ratio falls to about two to one in middle age and then rises again among the oldest age groups. Family commitments and other social factors can explain the mid-range figures. However, it is not at all clear why young women should be so small a proportion of those entering self-employment. The pattern of overall self-employment rates is similar across the range of ages, with some tendency for the increases to be concentrated among the very young and the much older age groups. This does not imply, however, that the average age of the self-employed has become older over the period. The explanation for the growing self-employment rates in the older age range lies in the changes which took place over the same period in the number of employees. Overall, the number of employees grew slightly until 1991, but this growth was particularly rapid among the 20–44 year old age groups, more than offsetting the significant decline in the 45+ age ranges. Given this latter decline, therefore, the self-employed accounted for a growing proportion of all those in work in these older age ranges.

The age profile of the self-employed did change over the 1980s. In particular the average age of the sector fell over the period, although analysis of the flows shows that this was not primarily due to new entrants being younger. Instead, the phenomenon appears to have been caused by the rapid increase in new entrants, who are, by definition, younger than those who comprise the existing stock. Splitting the decade in half, it appears also that the increase in numbers of young entrants in the first half is offset by an increase in outflow of these people in the second.

3.5.3 Marital status

Daly (1991a) analyses the marital status of the self-employed in some detail. The self-employment rate is much lower for single people than it is for people in other categories (such as married, widowed, divorced or separated). This reflects, in part, the fact that people below the age of 25 are less likely to be married than those in the older age categories. However, it also appears that single people of whatever age are less likely to be self-employed. Marriage seems to provide support in establishing a successful enterprise and spouses are often partners in such schemes. Meager (1991) notes that it is often assumed that the female partner plays the role of 'housewife' while her husband goes out to run his own business. Women should therefore be seen to have less of an impact on the self-employment data if they are married because of this minor role. In fact, the financial support of a spouse may actually be equally (or more) important. If the spouse is already employed, and providing a steady and stable income, there is every reason to expect that this will be of benefit to the potential entrepreneur. This factor can work equally well for women as well as for men.

There are a few differences to note between the sexes. Divorced men have higher self-employment rates than divorced women. This is probably caused by the fact that in many of the family partnerships the man plays a fairly dominant role and he is likely to continue running the business after a divorce or separation. Widowed women have a higher self-employment rate than all other categories. This may be because they inherit such businesses from their deceased husbands. Some will have been partners of the firm before the death, but a large number may well have been ordinary employees elsewhere.

Daly (1991a) stresses the importance of dependent children in determining self-employment rates. Over all age groups there is little difference between men with and those without dependent children. Disaggregating by age group shows that self-employment rates are far higher among men with dependent children in the age brackets 25–34 and 45–54. Men aged 35–44 showed no difference, whilst there was a large difference in the opposite direction for those aged 16–24. Further effects of children are also identified. Women with dependent children are more likely to be self-employed, but they are then less likely to employ others. For men, the opposite is true. LFS data also points to the fact that a large proportion of married people who are both self-employed are partners in the same firm, although responses to the LFS questionnaire do not show this directly. It is possible to show, however, that most respondents placed themselves in the same industrial category and it seems reasonable to conclude that this implies some sort of partnership. Further evidence for this is that almost one third of self-employed couples are in the hotel and catering industries where partnership is the norm.

3.5.4 Ethnic group

The ethnic minority population in the UK tends to be concentrated in fairly distinct geographical regions. Communities appear to stick together, where cultural traditions can be observed and family businesses established. Curran and Burrows (1989) used the GHS to examine 'ethnicity' and found that self-employment was high among the Asian population, whilst it was much lower (relative to Whites) among those of West Indian origin. They qualify their arguments by stating that 86% of Asians still work for someone else. Those people who are of Mediterranean background (Cyprus, Malta and Gibraltar) were found to be over twice as likely to be self-employed as those of Asian background and over four times as likely as Whites. However, according to the GHS, ethnic minority groups comprised only 7% of the whole self-employed sample and so the arguments about higher propensities among these groups must be kept in perspective. It is true to say that this proportion is higher than their proportion in the working population as a whole, which in 1992 was about 4.5%.

The only group of workers to experience a consistent upward trend over much of the last two decades has been the 'White' sector. The West Indian group did not share in the overall increases, whilst the rest did grow in absolute terms (although this growth was not a consistent trend). Table 3.3 shows the proportions of self-employed by ethnic group from the 2001 Census. People in employment from Pakistani and Chinese groups are more likely to be self-employed than those in other ethnic groups in Great Britain. According to the LFS, in 2002/03, around one quarter (23%) of Pakistanis in employment were self-employed, as were around one fifth (18%) of Chinese people. This compared with around one in ten (12%) White British people and fewer than one in ten Black people. It appears that whilst certain ethnic groups have experienced an increase in self-employment participation rates, care should be taken when analysing the significance of these sectors. Traditional beliefs about the 'corner shop' family businesses associated with certain ethnic groups are not disproved by the research. However, the relative size of these minorities must be stressed before conclusions about their role in influencing economy-wide self-employment rates are reached.

Clark and Drinkwater (1998) use GHS and Census of Population data to examine how both 'push' and 'pull' factors may lead members of the non-White, ethnic minority

Table 3.3 **Ethnicity and self-employment: England and Wales, 2001**

	All self-employed	Percentage of self-employed	Percentage of economically active within ethnic group
ALL PEOPLE	3,114,490	100	12.4
White – British	2,743,066	88.1	12.4
White – Irish	46,105	1.5	14.3
White – Other White	102,175	3.3	14.2
Mixed – White and Black Caribbean	4,447	0.1	6.9
Mixed – White and Black African	2,296	0.1	8.6
Mixed – White and Asian	6,500	0.2	10.6
Mixed – Other Mixed	5,448	0.2	10.2
Asian or Asian British – Indian	75,481	2.4	14.8
Asian or Asian British – Pakistani	37,194	1.2	17.2
Asian or Asian British – Bangladeshi	8,523	0.3	11.1
Asian or Asian British – Other Asian	15,342	0.5	13.9
Black or Black British – Black Caribbean	18,762	0.6	6.5
Black or Black British – Black African	14,466	0.5	6.8
Black or Black British – Other Black	2,037	0.1	5.3
Chinese or Other Ethnic Group – Chinese	22,570	0.7	21.6
Chinese or Other Ethnic Group – Other Ethnic Group	10,078	0.3	10.2

Source: Census (2001). www.statistics.gov.uk

groups to enter self-employment. They motivate their work by quoting the evidence of Metcalfe *et al.* (1996), who found that the desire to avoid labour market discrimination in the form of low-paid jobs was a principal explanation for the entry of minorities into self-employment. Clark and Drinkwater (1998) find that there is substantial variation between ethnic minority groups in self-employment, but in general they earn less than Whites, even Whites with similar characteristics. They conclude that any analysis of ethnic self-employment must take into account differences in ethnicity within the minority groups and must avoid amalgamating a particularly heterogeneous sector. The issue of ethnicity and enterprise is discussed further in Chapter 10.

3.5.5 Levels of education

The level of education achieved by the potential entrepreneur has long been seen as a crucial factor in determining both the actual entry into self-employment and, thereafter, the longer-term success of the venture. There have been a number of attempts to analyse these factors over the past few years. The results of the studies have thrown up an interesting inconsistency. Curran and Burrows (1989) used GHS data to show that self-employed men are less qualified than men in wage employment. Men in self-employment with employees are more likely to have formal qualifications than those in self-employment without employees. For women, however, those in self-employment with employees are less well qualified than their male counterparts, whilst those without employees are better qualified than their male counterparts and women wage employees

Table 3.4 **Qualifications of employees and the self-employed: England and Wales, 2001**

	All employees	All self-employed	Male employees	Male self-employed	Female employees	Female self-employed
Higher level qualifications	25.1	22.3	24.8	20.3	25.5	27.7
Lower level qualifications	50.2	43.8	48.5	42.4	52.1	47.7
No qualifications or level unknown	24.7	33.9	26.7	37.3	22.5	24.7

Note: The term 'no qualifications' describes people without any academic, vocational or professional qualifications. The term 'lower level' qualifications is used to describe qualifications equivalent to levels 1 to 3 of the National Key Learning targets (i.e. GCSEs, 'O' levels, 'A' levels, NVQ levels 1–3). The term 'higher level' refers to qualifications of levels 4 and above (i.e. first degrees, higher degrees, NVQ levels 4 and 5, HND, HNC and certain professional qualifications).

Source: Census (2005). www.statistics.gov.uk

generally. They are, however, less well qualified than male wage employees. The paper concludes that the self-employed appear to have a lower level of educational attainment than wage earners, although there is some overlap between the two groups.

Daly (1991a) and Meager (1991) used the LFS to analyse the issue. They both found that, generally, the self-employed appear to have a higher level of educational achievement than employees. Table 3.4 shows the 2001 Census data on qualifications. Whilst earlier findings by authors such as Meager (1991) tend to show the highest rates of self-employment are among those with their highest qualification being 'A' Levels or equivalent, Table 3.4 shows that the self-employed (in aggregate) are slightly less well qualified than employees. The lowest rates are among those with higher education below degree level. These qualifications are typically courses associated with a vocational career and include banking exams and nursing diplomas.

There is clearly a complex relationship between educational qualifications and participation rates for the self-employed. That relationship depends critically upon the definitions used in defining the data sets and, indeed, upon which survey is used to compile that data.

Turning to the flows into and out of self-employment, there appears to be an overall increase in the qualifications of the sector over time. This is particularly shown at the extremes of the qualification ladder. The number of people with a degree or equivalent shows a larger inflow than outflow and the proportion within this inflow is higher than that in the stock of self-employed. A similar pattern is seen for those entering the sector with GCSE or equivalent. There are a number of reasons why one might expect a swing towards more highly qualified entrants. First, the data suggests that women in self-employment are, in general, more qualified than men. Since the data also shows a higher entrance rate for women, a higher general level of education should result. Second, as time passes and more young people enter the sector the average level of qualifications will rise because the educational standards of the younger, newly available, workforce are higher than those already self-employed. The final factor may be linked to the increase in the number of schemes that have promoted self-employment over the past few years. The ability of young entrepreneurs to start their own businesses, either by an easing of credit conditions or by direct policy intervention, has meant a larger number of graduates and other highly qualified people being attracted into self-employment.

3.6 The jobs of the self-employed

3.6.1 Industrial division

The responses that make up the LFS allow the applied researcher to place the self-employed into various standard industrial categories. Intuitively, one would expect most respondents to fall into sectors that are traditionally associated with entrepreneurial or family enterprise. There are high rates of participation in sectors such as agriculture, construction and private sector services whilst there are low participation rates in areas such as manufacturing and those sectors that are dominated by the public sector. Table 3.5 shows the way in which the self-employed make up the major industrial sectors. The main feature is that the self-employed are very highly specialised and concentrated in a few sectors.

The sectors in which self-employment has a foothold are those (with the exception of agriculture) which have experienced higher than average employment growth during the 1980s. The sectors which have been in decline are those in which it appears difficult for the option of self-employment to be feasible. Approximately 50% of those working in agriculture are self-employed, yet agriculture only accounts for about 0.1% of total employment.

The recent patterns of self-employment propensities exhibited by an analysis of the changes over the last two decades prompt an important question. Is the recent, and unusual, growth in self-employment caused by structural change in the economy, with a growth in the service sector and a decline in manufacturing? Or is it also heavily influenced by an increase within individual sectors? Research has been performed using 'shift-share' analysis. This decomposes the changes over time into that change which would have occurred had the self-employment rates within each industry remained

Table 3.5 **Self-employment by industrial sector: England and Wales, 2001**

	Male (%)	Female (%)	All (%)
All People	17.9	7.8	13.3
A. Agriculture, Hunting, Forestry	54.1	45.9	5.9
B. Fishing	66.9	31.6	0.1
C. Mining & Quarrying	7.2	3.5	0.1
D. Manufacture	8.5	6.4	8.9
E. Electricity, Gas and Water Supply	6.2	1.8	0.3
F. Construction	40.3	12.5	19.1
G. Wholesale and Retail trade, Repair of Motor Vehicles	17.3	7.1	15.7
H. Hotels and Restaurants	19.8	11.1	5.3
I. Transport Storage and Communication	14.6	5.9	6.4
J. Financial Intermediation	9.4	2.8	2.1
K. Real Estate, Renting and Business Activities	22.4	11.2	17.2
L. Public Administration & Defence, Social Security	2.2	1.5	0.8
M. Education	8.1	3.6	2.9
N. Health and Social Work	14.1	6.4	6.5
O, P, Q. Other	23.8	20.4	8.6

Source: Census (2001). www.statistics.gov.uk

unchanged over the period and a residual growth element comprising the growth within sectors over time. Both Meager (1991) and Daly (1991a) illustrate that the sectoral component of growth over the 1980s was much smaller than that associated with the within sector growth. This does not follow the pattern established by the Organisation for Economic Cooperation and Development (OECD) (1986).

In six OECD countries (excluding Great Britain) most of the increase in self-employment over the first half of the 1980s was attributed to a sectoral shift. Meager (1991) notes that it is this feature, of rapid within sector growth, that distinguishes the changes in self-employment in Great Britain from those changes that occurred elsewhere. Hakim (1989a) draws these points out in some detail. There appears to have been a change in the attitudes of employers to using sub-contracted labour both in the construction industry and elsewhere. This 'demand-side' effect is not easy to distinguish from supply-side influences because in most cases it has not been possible to work at a sufficiently disaggregated level. Such details would probably show a larger industry shift component, but at the moment it remains unlikely that such effects could account for more than a small proportion of the total change.

The analysis of flow data for industries is interesting. The pattern of inflow and outflow is broadly similar to the raw data for stocks. However, certain industrial categories do show greater growth rates than others. In particular the construction industry has a much larger inflow in the early years than outflow, which is consistent with a higher degree of sub-contractor use in the sector. Also, the banking sector shows rapid growth commensurate with the establishment of a great many financial services companies. The recession at the end of the decade is highlighted by a very large outflow from many of these sectors which experienced such growth earlier on. Indeed a large part of the fall in the recession of the early 1990s appears to be accounted for by a substantial fall in the numbers employed in the construction industry in the South East.

3.6.2 Regional differences

Table 3.6 illustrates the self-employment rate by government office region in 2001. The highest rate of 14.7% in Great Britain is the South West (an area hit particularly hard during the recession at the end of the 1980s and beginning of the 1990s) and the lowest rate is the North East at 8.3%.

The regional variations in self-employment rates are not as pronounced as those for the sectoral differences. However, the strong influence of industry type on these propensities suggests that regions where, for example, there is a majority of manufacturing firms may well have a lower than average self-employment rate. This can be seen in the cases of the North, where there is a concentration of manufacturing, and the South East, which relies heavily on construction and services. This industrial effect can explain some of the variation across regions, but not all of it. To help to decompose the effects of industrial concentration a shift-share analysis is used.

Another important area that is covered by an analysis of the regional factors associated with self-employment is that concerned with the correlation between regional unemployment and self-employment. Creigh et al. (1986) failed to find any positive relationship between the variables. They argued that the conventional wisdom that states that unemployment pushes people into self-employment does not appear to hold.

Table 3.6 **Self-employment by GB government office region, 2005**

	Self-employment (thousands)	Self-employed as % of all in employment aged 16+
Eastern	364	13.3
East Midlands	250	12.3
London	519	15.1
North East	91	8.3
North West	356	11.4
Scotland	235	9.7
South East	591	14.5
South West	360	14.7
Wales	155	11.9
West Midlands	286	11.6
Yorkshire & The Humber	256	11.0
GB	3,463	12.6

Source: Labour Force Survey (2005), not seasonally adjusted

Furthermore, the depressed conditions that are associated with regional unemployment mean that conditions are not suitable for positive entrepreneurial activity and therefore any 'push' effect will be cancelled out by these depressed circumstances. Meager (1991), however, does find a positive correlation between unemployment and self-employment for certain regions (the exceptions being Northern Ireland, which had the highest unemployment rate, and the East Midlands, which had a rate slightly below the national average). Blanchflower and Oswald (1991) also found a positive relationship at the regional level, but their model did not include an industrial structure variable.

There is then some debate as to what are the major factors that determine differences in self-employment rates across regions. There is an industrial factor and there is a labour market factor. However, it is not clear what else influences the propensities. Creigh *et al.* (1986) put the explanation down to an unspecified bundle of 'other factors', whilst Blanchflower and Oswald (1991) offer no further guidance. Curran and Burrows (1989) do identify long-standing historical factors as one major influence. They claim that the industrial structure among former generations has a significant impact today. This might suggest that policies aimed at promoting self-employment should be targeted at regions that have a history of such entrepreneurial activity, rather than, perhaps, giving block assistance to every region.

It also suggests that differences across regions may well persist even if the other factors, such as industrial mix and the labour market, change over time. Analysis of flow data also shows that regional differences appear to be maintained over time. There are similar proportional representations in the flows as there are in the figures available for the stocks.

3.6.3 Occupations of the self-employed

The section above analysed the self-employed in terms of industrial sectors. It is also possible to examine more carefully the occupational categories that these people fall into. A common problem is the urge for most self-employed persons to classify themselves as managers. There is, therefore, a need to compare these responses carefully with those that make up the industrial category decomposition. Such a review is carried out in Meager (1991). The article concludes that female self-employment is much higher than male self-employment in the 'managerial' categories. This result is consistent with the results described above, which showed that better qualified women had a relatively higher self-employment rate. One possible explanation for this, put forward by Meager (1991), is that labour market rigidities (perhaps even in the form of positive sex discrimination) prevents these well-qualified women achieving in the employee sector. They are then pushed into self-employment in order to fulfil their ambitions.

The flows data given by the LFS reinforces these ideas. Large net inflows are apparent in those sectors that, primarily, cover the service industries. One notable feature is that the construction occupation does appear to have a relatively larger outflow than inflow towards the end of the decade. This is consistent with the idea that construction work may be very sensitive to the business cycle.

3.6.4 Other factors associated with self-employment

There are a number of supplementary factors. These include hours of work, employees and the temporary nature of some self-employment jobs. The self-employed report themselves as working longer hours, in general, than ordinary employees. Self-employment is typically characterised as a very demanding role and, whilst there may be some degree of over-reporting, over 60% of respondents to the LFS throughout the 1980s said that they worked more than 40 hours per week. This compares with less than 40% for employees. The differential is even greater for those claiming to work more than 60 hours per week. The self-employed with employees tend to work longer hours than those without. This finding is supported by Creigh *et al.* (1986) and by Curran and Burrows (1989). It is also interesting to note that religious background appears to be related to self-employment. As Table 3.7 illustrates, those people of the Jewish faith have the highest percentage involved in self-employment according to the 2001 Census.

Table 3.7 **Self-employment and religion: England and Wales, 2001**

	Self-employed	Percentage of self-employed	Percentage of self-employed within religious group
All people	3,114,490	100.0	12.4
Christian	2,169,828	69.7	12.2
Buddhist	14,637	0.5	18.6
Hindu	43,626	1.4	15.3
Jewish	33,873	1.1	28.0
Muslim	74,254	2.4	15.2
Sikh	23,695	0.8	14.8
Any other religion	15,340	0.5	17.2
No religion	527,544	16.9	12.2
Religion not stated	211,693	6.8	12.5

Source: Census (2001). www.statistics.gov.uk

Meager (1991) reports that two-thirds of the self-employed have no employees of their own. Most of the rest have fewer than 25 employees. Hakim (1988b) stresses that the self-classification of individuals responding for the LFS may lead some small business owners to label themselves as employees rather than as self-employed. This could mean that the figures for those self-employed with employees is underestimated. Turning finally to the classification of employment as full- or part-time, it appears that there is a lower rate of part-time working among the self-employed. This is probably explained by the under-representation of women in the self-employed group.

3.7 Chapter summary

This chapter has reviewed some of the data on the incidence of self-employment in the UK. Central to the first part was the rise in self-employment from 1979 to 1990. In particular, male self-employment rose from 1,642,000 to 2,689,000 over that period in the UK – a rise of 63%. The predominant flow into self-employment was from wage employment and the flow was concentrated in industries that favoured the sector (e.g. construction, distribution and services). The decade was also characterised by extensive financial liberalisation, when access to loans became easier, and by explicit government policies aimed at promoting new enterprise.

The major question, of course, is how one interprets all of this evidence to put together a story about the rise in self-employment. There is now clear evidence that it was caused by the coincidence of a number of factors which had not previously been combined in such a setting. The economic recession caused a large number of manufacturing workers to become unemployed, many of whom had redundancy funds to act as collateral in starting new businesses. This inflow was boosted further by government schemes such as the Enterprise Allowance Scheme and Small Firms' Loan Guarantee Scheme, and later in the decade by unprecedented financial liberalisation. Loans from banks and institutions became simple to obtain and, coupled with a government drive to create an 'Enterprise Culture', business start-ups accelerated.

Outflows from the sector still took place, many of which were new small businesses set up by the inexperienced. However, the inflow exceeded the outflow and the numbers continued to rise. Further stimulus was also provided as existing (and surviving) large employers started to sub-contract much of their non-core work. This was done for reasons of taxation and (presumably) to allow for ease of lay-off. Employment (or 'self-employment') of this type became the norm in construction, as well as other manufacturing processes.

When the recession hit at the end of the decade the position was rapidly reversed. Loans became very hard to obtain and repossessions and calling in of debt became commonplace. Business confidence started to fail, followed immediately by a greater outflow than inflow in the small self-employed business sector. Whilst the 1979–80 recession hit manufacturing (in particular in the North and the West Midlands) and thus provided a pool of willing potential entrepreneurs, the early 1990s recession hit those industries favouring self-employment and for the first time had a big effect on the South East and London. The demand for the services provided by the self-employed fell and this caused unemployment of these workers in the construction, distribution and services sectors. Only as the economy has started to pull out of the recession has the position started to improve. The continued problems in the housing market have meant that recovery via construction industry recruitment has been extremely slow.

Prospects for the self-employed were alluded to briefly in the introduction. Many commentators believe that entry to self-employment in the future will be at the margins: entry as a wealthy entrepreneur (the 'pull' hypothesis) mixed with entry as reluctant entrepreneurs at the other end of the income spectrum (the 'push' hypothesis).

Questions

1 Describe the different factors that may influence an individual's decision to become self-employed or to start a new business.

2 Using the empirical data provided in this chapter, describe some of the typical characteristics of the self-employed population.

3 Given the recent trends regarding the self-employed and small business ownership, what are the future prospects for the numbers of self-employed people and small business ownership.

Web links

www.statistics.gov.uk/cci/nscl.asp?ID=7850
This site contains various papers from the UK Office for National Statistics on self-employment trends.

www.ncge.org.uk
Website of the UK's National Council for Graduate Entrepreneurship. Under the policy section, there is a paper that examines graduates in self-employment and their characteristics.

www.pfrc.bris.ac.uk/publications
The Personal Finance Research Centre at Bristol University has published a number of papers on self-employment in deprived communities.

CHAPTER 4

Government and small business

Robert J. Bennett

4.1 Introduction

This chapter seeks to introduce how government and small businesses inter-relate with each other. How can government act most effectively to help small firms, in particular, and the economy as a whole? Where can government best focus its attention? What are its limitations, and how has recent small business policy developed in Britain.

4.2 Learning objectives

There are four learning objectives in this chapter:

1 To introduce the case for government action to help small businesses.
2 To understand the limitations on government actions to help small businesses.
3 To appreciate the different aims, methods and forms that government actions may take.
4 To become acquainted with the main examples of government help to small businesses in Britain, and their strengths and weaknesses.

Key concepts
■ market failure ■ business climate ■ regulation ■ bureaucratic failure
■ targeting ■ advice and consultancy

4.3 The role of government

The first point on which it is important to be clear is that entrepreneurs and managers, not governments, develop small businesses. But government can have a profound effect on how all firms, particularly small firms, operate and their opportunities to grow. Indeed, government policy and its influence on the 'institutional environment' of a country, region or locality has become a key focus of efforts to help improve how small firms develop and economies compete. As a result, almost all countries now have an active policy for improving competitiveness within which is a strong element focused on what, in policy terms, are usually referred to as small and medium-sized enterprises (SMEs). There are three main dimensions to the government role:

4.3.1 Government as regulator

Government and legal rules determine how trade rules operate (nationally and internationally) and the legal form of companies, the extent of legal limits on company liabilities and the strength of anti-trust, restrictive practices and anti-monopoly regulations. Government also influences regulation on conditions at work, consumer protection, food, health, safety, environmental and planning regulation and licensing.

4.3.2 Government as economic agent

Government taxes, charges fees, raises debts and spends. The way in which this operates has a profound effect on business finance and risk taking:

■ Taxation and fee levels affect entrepreneurial incentives and market entry; government debt levels severely affect the economic climate.

■ Spending influences the competitive environment and procurement rules for government contracts influence markets; the growth of government services (particularly education, health and transport services) influences the factor inputs for SMEs.

■ As a significant employer, government wage rates and employment conditions impact on local and national pay bargaining, the role of trade unions and employment conditions.

■ Government redistribution policies and social engineering influence work incentives and the labour market.

4.3.3 Government as strategic planner and promoter

Government finance can be used to offer grants, subsidies, loans, or information and advisory support to SMEs; and can seek to improve the infrastructure of business factor inputs. Notable examples are:

■ education and skills

■ research and development

■ marketing and productivity initiatives

■ international trade protection or barriers.

Over time, the consensus on the extent and form of government policy in each of these areas has changed radically. Up to the early nineteenth century, government sanctioned large monopolistic companies (charter companies such as the East India Company). Few other limited liability companies could exist and hence most businesses were very small traders who had limited scope to grow because they could not compete with the few large monopolies. The industrial revolution and the creation of laws to allow the establishment of limited liability companies (in Britain in 1844 and 1856) at first allowed a large number of small companies to be established, but as time progressed there was consolidation of economic power into a small number of large concerns. By 1910, 16% of British manufacturing output was generated by the 100 largest companies; by 1970 the 100 largest companies accounted for 47% of output and covered 36% of employment (Hannah, 1976; Prais, 1976).

The large firm dominance of the economy was encouraged by government in several ways. First, planning of supply during both World Wars led to considerable consolidations. Second, until the 1960s, government policy encouraged price cartels and collusion between firms, which frequently led to amalgamations and takeovers. The scope for SMEs was limited by these growing behemoths. Third, and at the same time, the growth of socialism and the Labour Party led to an ideological decision to nationalise many strategic industries, to provide them with large subsidies and to control politically the means of production through extensive economic committees. By 1960, 13% of GDP was produced by nationalised industries and they employed 10% of the workforce excluding dockyards and munitions factories (Pryke, 1981). Inevitably the scope for SMEs was limited by both these large firms and nationalised industries in terms of market entry and scope to compete.

The result was a significant long-term decline in the number of business, particularly small firms, up to the 1960s, with major waves of merger occurring in the 1920s and 1930s, and in the 1950s and 1960s, (Hannah 1976, Table A.1). This evolution is shown in Figure 4.1, which also shows the relatively limited development of self-employment (single person businesses).

The apogee of this period was the establishment in 1962 of the National Economic Development Council (NEDC) which was to be a means 'to seek agreement on ways of improving economic performance, competitive power and efficiency' (Selwyn Lloyd, Chancellor of the Exchequer, 1962; quoted in Middlemas, 1983, p. ix). This led to a network of tripartite committees between trade unions, government and businesses (generally represented by the Confederation of British Industries (CBI)) to inform negotiations on wages and economic policy, which were modelled on the French Commissariat du Plan and the Japanese MITI. These committees covered 60% of all manufacturing industry. The collapse of the committee-driven approach was inevitable as one industry after another suffered increased international competition, its management was unable to respond, its sales collapsed and, as its profits fell, subsidies increasingly became necessary. In Middlemas' words (1983, p. 66), this national process of economic planning was 'too close to government, too dependent on what government did or did not do, too subject to the (political) pendulum'. Most importantly it could not cope with rapid change, increased global competition, and it ignored small firms.

From the late 1960s a significant and rapid change began to occur. The Restrictive Practices Act prevented cartels and price fixing; joining the European Community in 1976 restricted state aids to industry; privatisation of former nationalised industries after 1979 reduced government control radically; and new technologies increased the scope for innovative management by small and innovative businesses and their ability to compete with large businesses. A rapid growth in small firms has been the result, so that in Britain SMEs are now 150% of their number in the 1960s and self-employment has nearly doubled.

Figure 4.1 Number of self-employed and number of establishments (1930–2004)

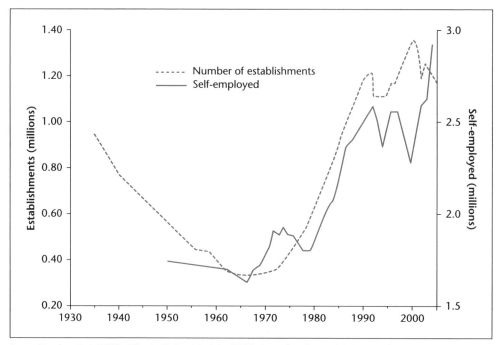

Source: Data from Prais (1976); Office for National Statistics (2003); Bannock and Peacock (1989); Small Business Service (various years)

4.4 The case for government action for SMEs

In general, government action for SMEs has been justified by three main arguments: that market failures exist which inhibit small firm development; that there is a special public interest in SMEs because of their capacity to create jobs; and that government can develop and act on a strategic vision for the economy which individual SMEs cannot.

The market failure argument suggests that small firms will not invest or develop some fields and, therefore, government should assist. The main basis of this argument is that, because SMEs are small, they lack control of the markets in which they operate and will, therefore, underinvest. An example might be training, where SMEs may be discouraged from training their personnel because they are concerned about other firms 'poaching' them at higher salaries – particularly larger firms. This is a so-called 'free rider' problem where the non-training firm gains cost advantage over the firm that trains. Similar examples may apply to implementation of environmental controls or research and development, where those firms that do invest may not be able to gain full benefits because of undercutting or poaching by others. These arguments suggest a role for government as a regulator (to impose an obligation on *all* firms e.g. to train, to conform to regulations, etc.) or as a supplier (to provide government-financed training or a subsidy to private provision).

A further component of the market failure argument has been that small firms are less aware of advice, information or other business services that are available, are more sceptical about their value and can be more unwilling to seek external support (see Gibb and Dyson 1984; Storey, 1994). This argument is frequently used to justify government advice and information initiatives. But whilst there may have been reluctance by small firms in the 1970s, there is little evidence to suggest that it is true today. Extensive surveys of the small firm take-up of external advice, consultancy, training and other services suggests that they are usually just as likely to use these supports as any other firm, with the possible exception of the start-up and very early stages of growth (Bennett and Robson, 1999a; Ramsden and Bennett, 2005).

The most important aspect of possible market failures for small firms is that they suffer specific barriers or unequal treatment which, on grounds of equity, government should help to remove. This was a fundamental plank of the argument by the Bolton Report (1971) which suggested that a level of government action was justified to help SMEs because they were disadvantaged compared with larger firms. In the market, larger firms will gain advantage of economies of scale in a number of ways, for example the purchase of inputs at lower unit costs because of bulk purchasing discounts or economics of administration arising from having specialist skills available in personnel, financial, managerial and other fields. Ironically, however, one of the strongest arguments that is usually used to justify government action is that government itself creates disadvantages for small firms because the costs of compliance with its regulatory and administrative requirements tend to have severe diseconomies of scale. For example, studies of the costs of compliance with government procedures suggest that they are two to ten times higher for small firms as costs per employee, on cost per £ of turnover, than they are for large firms (Bannock and Peacock, 1989; Sandford, 1989, 1995; Cressy, 2000; Poutziouris *et al.*, 1999, 2001, 2003).

This disadvantage is particularly strong for the smallest businesses (of under ten employees) and tends to diminish with size; diseconomies are of little consequence for firms with over 200 employees. There is also variation between different regulatory streams: compliance costs with labour market directives tend to be more costly than taxation requirements, which are in turn more costly than licensing processes. For some businesses, health and safety requirements, in terms of both the costs and the form of regulatory monitoring and inspection, can be so costly as to close the business.

A summary of some of the main market gaps is as follows (see e.g. Bolton Committee, 1971; Bannock, 1981, 1990; Storey, 1994; Curran and Blackburn, 1994; Curran and Storey, 2002; DE, 1990; DTI, 1998a, 2003a; SBS 2002, 2004; SBC, 2004a):

■ *Taxation* distorts incentives and the capital market and places proportionately higher burdens of compliance costs on small firms.

■ *Regulation and bureaucracy* is highly regressive with firm size (proportionately much higher on small firms).

■ *Purchasing* – large firms and public sector purchasing is heavily biased towards other large firms and public sector suppliers.

■ *Competition policy* is a largely discretionary aspect of government activity in the UK and generally has to reach high levels of abuse before government acts: it thus tends to strongly weaken the possibilities of entry by small firms.

■ *Education and research* has tended to have little focus on business and enterprise, particularly in the small firms sector: it has been biased towards either management or employee status rather than entrepreneurship and pure research rather than technological innovation and development.

■ *Social legislation* – as with other regulatory impacts, the effects on incentives to individuals, costs to businesses (especially labour costs), and forms of employment (part-time, full-time) all have regressive effects on small firms.

These arguments have been used as a basis for a range of special policies to help small business, ranging from subsidies to reducing regulatory requirements, and to specialised provision of advice and information. The range of initiatives is considerable and the size and complexity of these initiatives is large in almost all countries. A survey for EU countries is contained in the European SMEs Observatory reports (1994, 1995, 1996). A survey of the main market gaps in policies to meet them is shown in Table 4.1.

Table 4.1 Market imperfections: causes and areas of policy action required

Market gap	Cause of market gap	Policy action needed
Supply of entrepreneurs	Social and economic bias in favour of employment and unemployment rather than self-employment	Welfare system, education and tax system
Supply of innovations	Inadequate R&D	Education and research policy Misallocated R&D expenditure Tax system
Lack of capital	Distortions in capital markets	Tax system Subsidised lending Monopoly policy Labour relations policy
Lack of premises	Imperfections in property markets	Urban redevelopment Planning regulations Infrastructure investment Tax system
Bureaucracy and compliance costs	Growth of government	Simplification, exemption, changes to taxation Reorganisation of central and local government
Purchasing	Imperfections in supplier markets	Monopoly policy Tax system Government 'crowding out' business and small firms
Marketing	Imperfections in seller markets	Promotional activities

Source: Developed from Bolton (1971); Bannock (1981, 1990)

The second argument for government action for small businesses is that they have become major parts of the economy. Hence, specific policies for small business are a way to encourage the growth of the economy as a whole. This has been viewed as particularly important since small businesses can create a major growth in jobs. This argument gained considerable popularity in the 1970s and 1980s, which was a period in which large firms, mainly in the manufacturing sector, were shedding jobs at an enormous rate. An influential study was that by Birch (1979) that suggested that two thirds of the increase in employment in the US between 1969 and 1976 was in firms employing less than 20 workers. Although these findings are disputed, there is no doubt that all governments in western economies see job creation as one of the major motives for SME policies.

The third argument, that government can develop and act on a strategic vision for the economy that small firms cannot, overlaps with the objective of job generation. With a shift from the scope for government to act as protectionist sources of support to their economies, governments instead have sought to take on a role in trying to boost economic growth. This is often framed in terms of increasing a nation's competitiveness. This strategy has been summarised in a range of competitiveness white papers (e.g. DTI, 1998, 2001, 2003a; HM Government, 1994, 1995; Cabinet Office, 1996b) and has found its way into specific small business policy (e.g. SBS, 2002, 2004). An individual firm is unlikely to be able to see the whole economic picture, even if it is a large firm, so government has a role in taking the larger strategic view and seeking to plug gaps or stimulate what would not otherwise occur. This has led to a burgeoning of reports on how countries should fill their skills gap, infrastructure gap, research gap, financing gap, etc. For example, the British government has argued that 'it is government's role to offer support to business to increase productivity and invest in innovation. Government investment in training should particularly address areas of market failure, by supporting employers in training their low-skilled workers' (DfES, 2003a, pp. 22–3).

A good statement of the objectives of small business policy is that by the European Commission (2003a, 2004) which in a green paper has sought to identify a perceived problem of EU business development and possible policy solutions. The perceived European problem is that people prefer employee over self-employed status with a resulting lower business birth rate in the EU than many other countries, a less dynamic business sector as a whole and hence higher unemployment levels. The chief policies advocated are reduction of entry barriers to starting a business, trying to reduce risk and increase reward levels, fostering capacity and skills and broadening the accountability of businesses across society. Specific policy actions are in the fields of education, better regulation, reducing financial gaps and improving cultural supports.

The argument for government action for small firms is, however, much more difficult to implement as specific and effective actions than they are to dream up as a policy designer. Even in the words of one of the economists who is most widely drawn on to justify government intervention, effective actions are very constrained: 'The important thing for government is not to do things which individuals are doing already' (Keynes, 1926, p. 47). Keynes felt that actions should be restricted to the aggregate level – the economy as a whole. Analysed below are the difficulties of government action for SMEs.

4.5 Finding a niche for government action

It is difficult to find evidence that there is a *general* phenomenon of market failure or need for major government actions for small firms. Taking the normal definitions, SMEs are 90–99% of all businesses, account for nearly 60% of GNP and over 60% of employees and have grown from 2.3 million in 1979 to 4 million in Britain by 2004. SMEs are, therefore, a successful sector of the economy. It is not obvious that they need government help. Of course, it is possible that they could be even more success-ful. However, if we take evidence of the features that hold back SME development from previous research and from surveys of SMEs themselves, there is little evidence of a generalised market failure. Most survey responses focus on the need for govern-ment to stabilise the economic environment or improve its own regulatory regime (e.g. Storey, 1994; Curran and Blackburn, 1994; SBRC, 1992; Cosh and Hughes, 2003). The NatWest SERT quarterly surveys of small business consistently show economic climate and regulation as the first and second main concerns of small firms since 1999, although in the earlier 1990s cash flow and payments were also important concerns. The con-cern with regulation is reinforced in the large-scale surveys such as Your Business Matters (IOD, 1996; Better Regulation Task Force, 2002b), which show the concerns of small firms to be chiefly with the interface with government itself (legal requirements, VAT, availability of grants, etc.); only in training is government seen as a major source of support and then preferably as an enabler rather than a provider. These conclusions are further reinforced by the Bank of England's well-balanced assessment (e.g. Bank of England, 1996), which emphasises the role of market agents in overcoming small firm deficiencies and questions the effectiveness of most policy areas.

The implications of these results are as follows:

- The main needs that businesses have are maintaining and developing their products, markets and internal processes.

- Businesses chiefly want government to maintain a strong and stable economic envir-onment and a *transparent* and *stable* regulatory environment in which compliance costs are low, risks can be assessed reliably and long-term strategies developed.

- There is no overwhelming demand for government to do things for specific firms or sectors.

- There is no *general* evidence of a market failure where business needs are not being met by the private sector business services that are available. Where so-called needs have been identified they relate to areas where well-developed markets already exist: for example venture capital; marketing; advice and consultancy; information; skills and training; prompt payment, credit and bad debt collection. Although there may be gaps and deficiencies in some of these markets, there are existing agents that should be able to tackle them, i.e. the market should be able to respond itself, or perhaps by partnership of public and private sectors, rather than by direct government activity.

- Where needs are identified that are generic to many firms, or to all or most sectors, they chiefly concern the quality of factor inputs, such as education and skills or transport infrastructure. This suggests that government action needs to be focused primarily not on provision of specific supports or contacts to individual firms, but instead on: the form of regulatory framework that influences market provision; and the quality of public sector services that influence factor inputs.

■ In cases where individual firms can benefit from specific support, this is usually related to specific business needs which government is unlikely to be able itself to meet (e.g. product development, design and marketing). This suggests that any support from government has to be channelled through standard business-to-business (B2B) interfaces of business services, rather than through government offices.

■ In some cases, specific needs relate to local problems such as the absence of suitable sites, premises or scope for expansion; gaps in transport and infrastructure; skills shortages; and the influence of the local 'business climate'. Many of these firm-specific needs relate to the roles played by other private sector providers of business services but in some cases the role of local and central government through planning and local services is a target for concern. But even in these cases it is the *general* nature of governmental approaches to the SME's specific problems that is important (e.g. speed of planning decisions, willingness to develop new infrastructure, pro-business climate, etc).

These findings do not suggest that large-scale or focused SME policies should ever be a key feature of government policies. Nor do they suggest, in most cases, that government policy regarding SMEs should be very different from that for other larger businesses.

4.6 Limitations on government action

The difficulties of finding a niche for government actions are increased by the difficulties of acting effectively once a cause for intervention is found. The existence of a market failure or 'need' in itself does not justify government action. Not only are there other non-market approaches as alternatives to government, but also, and most importantly, attempts to overcome market failure may result in actions which do more harm than good, because there is also possible government or bureaucratic failure. The result of such failures is that government can harm small firms and can reduce the welfare of society though diverting resources, deflecting or impeding businesses. As a result, the costs may exceed the benefits of intervention and far exceed the costs of accepting the market failure that existed in the first place. Market failure problems and 'needs', therefore, do not necessarily always have effective government policy solutions.

In general, the difficulties of government action cover each stage, from problem identification to policy execution. At the design stage, how is it that government and its officers, who are not themselves running a business, are likely to be better than a small business at identifying a development problem and designing a solution for business? The constraints on government action are:

■ lack of appropriate and up-to-date information

■ lack of technical business skills

■ adoption of targets for public policy rather than business policy

■ difficulty of policy termination (admitting that mistakes have been made and exiting)

- difficulty providing help that adds to total net output, rather than helping one firm and thus displacing another (achieving additionality of policy)
- difficulty of aligning and coordinating policies so that they do not conflict with each other
- embeddedness of policy with multiple layers of complex decision making with many and conflicting targets that are slow to change.

As noted by Peacock (in Bannock and Peacock, 1989, p. 6) 'Too often it is assumed that a case for public production . . . is the sole answer to so-called "market failure" . . . (but) when consumers have only an indirect control over what is produced and how it is produced, the checks operating on bureaucratic efficiency are weak.' Peacock goes on to identify four specific weaknesses. First, consensus views are usually necessary in policy implementation; this means that the aims are deliberately obfuscated to keep everyone happy and this suits bureaucrats and politicians since it is then less easy to identify when the policy fails. Second, there are no real costs or risks to policy makers when things go wrong, especially if the aims are unclear in the first place. Hence, the quality of design is not incentivised and correction of error is slow; policy termination in the face of failure is rare. Third, proliferation of specific schemes fosters clients who defend pet schemes. Instead of the small firms focusing on business development, they put extra resources into bargaining and lobbying with government; this is distortionary, undermines firm efficiency and creates dependency and clientelism. Fourth, the costs and benefits of alternatives are rarely assessed and there is no civil service career to be made from not spending allocated public finance and, therefore, reducing tax burdens and improving general economic conditions; as a result, improvement in government policies is usually, at best, slow. Indeed a recent Treasury Review (2002, p. 153) admitted that: 'A variant of Gresham's Law might operate, in that bad services drive out good.'

4.7 Possibilities for targeting

This discussion has shown that there are usually rather narrow possibilities for policies that target small business. Despite this, there has been a strong tendency that seeks to target. For example, a number of initiatives target growth businesses, distinguishing them from those which cannot or are unwilling to grow (which are usually termed 'lifestyle' businesses). The focus on growth companies is, for example, strongly built into most DTI objectives. The usual means of targeting policy is to target those businesses which either:

- will benefit to the greatest extent from assistance (a 'need' measure), or
- will yield the greatest policy benefit ('leverage' or 'value for money' measures), and
- avoid as far as possible displacement and non-additionality effects ('additionality' measures).

The potential benefits of targeting of policy are obvious: it can reduce the range of expenditure, it may focus resources where they are 'needed' and it is easier to market.

A focus on growth businesses, for example, yields a target market of approximately 200,000 businesses (taking the definitions of growth businesses of 10–200 employees used by the DTI (1992)). A focus on exporting business yields a target market of about 100,000 businesses (Institute of Export, 1995; quoted in Bank of England, 1996). A focus on innovation or high-technology businesses is a more fuzzy concept but yields a target of perhaps 100,000 businesses. If it is possible to distinguish *SMEs* within these groups, the proportion will be even smaller (Smallbone, 1997). Targeting is thus very attractive as a public policy approach, whether viewed from a perspective of 'need', 'leverage' or avoidance of non-additionality.

But there are great dangers in attempting to target the market in this way which derive from the variety within the target market, however far it is narrowed. First, the starting point for any change in business activity, as we have argued, must be the entrepreneur's own marginal appraisal of costs and benefits of the change, judged by the characteristics of its supply, customer and trading environment, and its internal capacities and structures. Any decisions have to be market-driven in the two senses: that only the business itself can make the decisions and it must judge its decisions on the criteria of its own capacity to continue to meet its customer's needs. Any policy targeting can, therefore, be only of the crudest kind in the sense of identifying a target for possible take-up rather than identifying a specific group where all will need to respond. In addition the target group is not stable. Those businesses that are growth, export or innovation businesses in one period may not have the same characteristics in another period. Although we know that there is a strong correlation of each of these business characteristics over time (i.e. growth businesses tends to continue to be growth businesses and are also often the innovators and exporters), there is no prior set of conditions that strongly allows identification of the upward performers. Hence it is not possible to define a stable or exclusive group as potential targets for government action.

There is also a rather strange conflict in-built into a government policy that seeks to give greater support to these businesses that are already growing and hence are successful. There are also particular dangers in trying to distinguish between growth and lifestyle businesses. Any good business is good business! Maintaining a business is a competitive world in itself and major success and the lifestyle business of today may well be the growth business of tomorrow. The managerial gateway to access policy benefits must, therefore, be a flexible one, both for entry and exit. This in turn has implications for management and design of policy contact networks, databases and marketing. But the safest policy of all is not to target, and leave open the choice of policy supports used to those best able to assess them – the small business itself.

4.8 Forms of government action for small business

There is a variety of ways in which government can seek to help small business. It is possible to distinguish these between the underlying policy aims, the policy method and the targeting.

The underlying *aims* of government support can be distinguished between three broad approaches:

- *Cost reduction* – The use of grants, subsidies or reduced-rate loans to reduce the cost of inputs into the business. These can be targeted (e.g. a grant to a specific business) or general (e.g. to reduce energy costs, to reduce general taxation or to reduce labour costs by government finance to improve the general level of education and training).

- *Risk reduction* – The use of macro-economic policies (such as taxation, interest rates and other instruments) to stabilise the economy and reduce oscillations and uncertainties. Government's regulatory environment itself is a key contribution to the level of risk small businesses experience.

- *Increase the flow of information* – To make information more readily available on international trends in markets, national and local issues, and on government policies that affect small businesses. This can be via targeted supports (and information services) or general publicity.

The *methods* of government support cover four broad fields namely:

- finance (grants and subsidies; cost effects of taxation and compliance)
- providing information
- providing specialist advice
- helping with training and personnel development.

Targeting can focus on:

- stages of business development including idea formation/entrepreneurship, start-up, early growth, development and expansion;
- types of business, by firm size, exporters/non-exporters, by sector, by location (e.g. rural, inner city, community-based, ethnic minority);
- factor inputs and resources, including capital, land and premises, personnel and skills and innovation/technology transfer;
- general business climate such as culture of entrepreneurialism and workplace ethics, regulatory environment and the macro-economic environment.

These are only examples of a large, complex and overlapping field of possible instruments that government can implement in its desire to help small business. To help understand how these instruments have developed in practice, the next section summarises the main initiatives in the UK at three levels: national, sector and local.

4.9 National policy

4.9.1 Better regulation

UK governments have attempted to respond to criticisms of the regulatory burdens that undermine small firms development through better regulation initiatives. An important step was the establishment in 1994 of first a Deregulation Task Force and, since 1997, a Better Regulation Task Force. Demonstrating the breadth and difficulty of the problem of controlling government regulation, both of these Task Forces have operated outside the main government departments. They have been administered within the Cabinet Office, but are independent with an independent chair, reporting to a Cabinet Committee chaired by the Deputy or the Prime Minister. This Task Force approach has been prominent in attempting to seek to change the way in which government departments work so as to encourage greater sensitivity to the problems of business compliance and costs, particularly for smaller firms. Its principles of good practice are: proportionality, accountability, consistency, transparency and targeting. The chief efforts have been as follows:

- All departmental proposals with an impact on businesses must carry a compliance cost assessment and a risk assessment, personally approved by the minister responsible.

- A quarterly report from all departments must be produced on what secondary legislation has been introduced and its compliance costs to business.

- A streamlined procedure for primary legislation to be amended or repealed for deregulation purposes, as well as improving fairness, transparency and consistency of enforcement procedures.

- Simplification and improved information on relevant business licences and regulatory requirements with an alignment of registration and notification for start-up businesses (with a single point of contact for all tax, social security and VAT matters being developed).

- Reduction of burdens of completing government surveys to businesses with less than ten employees, plus reduced compliance costs for other surveys.

- Simplification of many official forms, including Intrastat (recording imports and exports between EU countries).

- Reducing or amending existing regulation and abolishing some licences.

- Attempts at improved and more business-friendly enforcement procedures with clearer appeals mechanisms.

- Attempts to reduce compliance burdens for *all* businesses with respect to health and safety, building regulations etc., to ensure regulations apply only to relevant businesses.

- Repeal of all local government acts in England and Wales that duplicate or contradict national requirements, plus setting up pilots of 'one-stop-shops' by local government to provide a single point of contact on planning, building and fire safety.

It is also sought to enforce change through a Regulatory Impact Unit, also situated within the Cabinet Office (see Deregulation Task Force, 1995, 1996; Steering Group, 1996; Cabinet Office, 1995; Better Regulation Task Force, 2000, 2002a 2003, 2004; www.cabinetoffice.gov.uk/regulations; www.brtf.gov.uk).

Some specific examples of changes are proposals to change the Consumer Credit Act, following the recommendations by the Office of Fair Trading, that businesses should be excluded from the scope of the Act, but progress has been shown. The statutory audit requirement for small firms with a turnover of less than £90,000 was abolished from 1996 and extended to all companies with less than £350,000 turnover from April 1997. Various attempts have been made to modify the rules for corporate insolvency for small businesses and late payment legislation. Progress on these has also been slow.

Despite some developments the chairs of these Task Forces have been critical (e.g. Deregulation Task Force, 1996): 'the culture of Whitehall needs to change more. Regulation is a form of government spending. The Government forces businesses and people to spend their own money to meet public interest objectives. But whereas there are stringent controls that inhibit the growth of conventional public spending, no comparable constraints exist for new regulation'. There has thus been doubt whether the government's 'impact and risk assessment' procedures carry enough weight to inhibit growth of regulatory burden. Indeed one Task Force member threatened to resign in 1997 because there 'was not enough support from ministers who are too willing to accept new regulations from Brussels' (ibid.). For the case of new European fire regulations, for example, there was 'an absolutely clear-cut example where there are no benefits and absolutely enormous costs' (see Fisher, 1996). Similar conclusions are drawn for the effect of employment regulations (SBC, 2004b). The Better Regulation Task Force (2004) comes to a similar conclusion: 'It is time we did something more to reduce the burden, to achieve deregulation as well as better regulation – a spring clean of existing stock . . . I think we need to target a better balance' (Graham, 2004). The Bank of England (1996) has also commented that too much attention has been given to reducing the number of regulations rather than ameliorating the negative impacts of new legislation.

A Small Business Council was established in 2000 to act as the voice of small business across government. Although slow to develop real teeth, it has also become a prominent critic of the growth of regulation. Its 2004 report states that: 'it is time that the cost of being governed should start to reduce year on year. The regulatory burden needs measuring, particularly as it has a disproportionate effect on small firms. The cost of regulation should be reduced. The appraisal process by civil servants should be changed . . . to provide incentives for officials not to introduce new regulations' (SBC, 2004a, pp. 3–4). Despite these comments, progress is slow.

The constraints on all these better regulation initiatives is that they work outside the main departmental decision making that creates the regulations in the first place. What is clearly required is for the designers of regulations to be far more sensitive to the needs of those who have to comply with them in business. The criticism has been that, rather than simplifying, civil servants over-design or 'gold-plate' regulations with needless detail and complexity (Better Regulation Task Force, 2004). Overcoming this requires a culture change in Whitehall with major re-training of staff and politicians.

4.9.2 Financial assistance to SMEs

The major national governmental financial package available to small businesses from government is the Small Firm Loan Guarantee. This provides a government guarantee for loans by approved lenders (chiefly the major banks). Loans are intended to be for businesses or individuals who cannot obtain commercial finance because of lack of security or a proven track record. The guarantees generally cover 75% of the loan and are available to businesses that are over two years old. Most loans are less than £70,000 for periods of two to seven years. The minimum is £5,000 and maximum £250,000. The scheme has run since the early 1980s, but has become more significant in number of loans and total value since 1994 (see Table 4.2). Since 1995 simplification of SMART

Table 4.2 **The Loan Guarantee Scheme**

Financial year	1989–90	1991–92	1994–95	1996–97	1998–99	2000–01	2002–03
Number	3,124	2,917	6,207	5,081	4,482	4,312	3,916
Total, value (£m)	94.0	68.7	245.9	201.3	188.8	240.5	269.5
Average loan size (£)	30,103	23,579	39,630	39,626	42,124	55,765	68,870

Source: Small Business Service, quoted in Bank of England, *Quarterly Report on Small Business Statistics,* various years

and SPUR schemes has focused about £2.3m per year on technological development feasibility studies. EU funding elements are important in these programmes, but complexity and inflexibility are criticised. There is also a Phoenix Fund and other special initiatives for deprived areas.

Following a review of start-up assistance in 1994, central government grants to small firms, which had been initiated in 1982, were terminated in 1995, with the resources now available through neighbourhood or urban regeneration schemes or Business Link (see Section 4.12). The former Enterprise Allowance Scheme and Business Start-up Scheme had a major impact on stimulating self-employment through the 1980s and these have evolved to new forms of grant assistance for the unemployed since 2000. Other sources of small grants and loans are via Scottish and Welsh development bodies, English Regional Development Agencies and Business Link. Larger grants of £10,000–100,000 may be available in Assisted Areas (relating to EU Structural Funds regions) through Regional Selective Assistance (re-named Selective Finance for Investment in 2004), provided that they create new jobs or safeguard old ones. Since 2004 this scheme is also evaluated by the increase in gross value added per full-time employee. These are discretionary grants related to relocations or expansions. In addition there are smaller grants for Innovation Projects in eligible locations.

Important tax incentives have also been introduced since 1995, which have subsequently been extended, for Enterprise Investment Schemes, Venture Capital Trusts and Business Angels to encourage equity participation in small firms, as well as participation in management development by Angels. In addition the Alternative Investment Market (AIM) aspect of the Stock Exchange has had significant success in improving equity flows into larger SMEs; the European market EASDAQ will further enhance this development. It should be noted that, as well as government initiatives, Britain has one of the best developed venture capital markets in Europe, the largest agent being 3i, although it does not rival that in the US.

For small firm management training, there have been Small Firms Training Loans available from government through major banks. There have also been Career Development Loans to individuals from government through major banks for education or training (Marshall *et al.*, 1993). For the unemployed a number of other special assistance schemes exist. The main framework since 2003 is Learn Direct, a directory of training providers and financial supports. This directs small firms, their employees, or the unemployed, to Work Based Learning provision for adults, or New Deal to get people into employment through training. There are also the Prince's Youth Business Trust and Livewire for those aged 16–25, which are sponsored initiatives by major companies.

In addition, since 1994, the government, with the Bank of England, has sought to stimulate, debate and improve the relations between SMEs and banks and other financial institutions. Banks are the largest source of funds for SMEs, lending £40bn in 2004. Significant changes have been:

- a lower and more transparent pattern of bank charges for small businesses – a previously much-criticised area;
- a shift of resources by the banks towards the mid-corporate sector (approximately in excess of £500,000 turnover) to which they devote more time and advice, conversely turning services to micro firms into a more basic service at lower cost;
- most significantly, a shift away from overdraft to term loans, accounting for about 75% of bank lending to SMEs in 2003, increased from 50% in 1992, which now comes close to many European countries – for example in Germany it is over 80% (Bank of England, 2004) – and has important implications: namely, to encourage longer-term thinking by small firms and closer working with their bankers.

4.9.3 Exporting and importing

Exporters are only about 1% of all SMEs and it has been a major concern of policy to try to expand the export outlook, particularly since most SMEs that do export are chiefly concerned with European and not wider world markets.

The chief aspects of UK export support are the Export Credit Guarantee Scheme (which insures against non-payment for exports) and a range of DTI/Foreign and Commonwealth Office services (marketed through Trade Partners UK). These services were enhanced in the late 1990s by the reorganisation of foreign staff positions in embassies, to give a higher priority to trade issues, and the establishment of a more focused DTI approach regarding its staff in this area. The main activities are trade fairs, outward missions, overseas seminars, overseas promotions, and inward missions and funds to facilitate development in specific overseas markets. Trade fairs and outward missions have been given a particularly strong emphasis.

4.9.4 Research and innovation

The emphasis on support for small firm R&D and technological innovation in the UK has historically been low, with a preference for development of pure research in universities and institutes and an implicit bias towards larger firms. Some attempt to change this is occurring through Innovation and Technology Counsellors in Business Links, through greater pressure on research councils, universities and research institutes to be more involved with applied R&D, particularly in SMEs, and through various innovation and research tax credits introduced by the Chancellor since 2000. Much of this development is slow or uncertain as yet. The applied R&D spend is still low in the UK and connections are weaker between research and business than in many other countries, particularly in the US, Korea or Germany. At present, therefore, most initiatives are small and localised rather than diffusing to the whole network of SMEs or research bodies. European programmes are often disproportionately significant as a result, although their economic output is often unclear. Important research funding initiatives are EUREKA, Regional Technology Centres, Teaching Company Scheme, Shell Technology Enterprise Programme, and Innovation Research and Development Grants. Some local university initiatives such as science parks have been particularly successful (e.g. Cambridge, Heriot Watt, Warwick), though the success elsewhere is patchy. Shifts in university funding regimes since about 2000 have sought to emphasise technology transfer and innovative research spin-offs through so-called 'third stream funding' (which is additional to teaching and general research income).

4.9.5 Education and training

It has long been recognised that one of Britain's chief competitive weaknesses has been a poor general level of education and training. This has been reflected, not so much at the most senior levels of management, but chiefly in the employee semi-skilled and un-skilled categories, and has been argued to have led Britain into a so-called 'low-skill equilibrium' (Finegold and Soskice, 1988). As recently as 1981 Britain had only 50% of workers with recognised qualifications and only 13% of the population going into higher education. By 1989, 45% of children left school at 16 with no qualification or only one pass at GCSE level. The pattern has improved significantly but there is still a long way to go, particularly at the level of basic and vocational skills. For example, in 2003, 40% of the adult population aged 16–65 was classed as functionally innumer-ate; 14.9 million adults had numeracy skills below that expected of 11-year olds, and 5.2 million adults had literacy below that level (DfES, 2003b). The deficiency of basic school achievements confirms that, whilst Britain is continuing to produce a very good level of output of highly qualified people, at the basic and vocational levels there is still a major deficiency and this has severe impacts on small firms. This is thrusting atten-tion to the earlier years of basic schooling (age 5–14) as well as to the more vocational area (age 14–19). For example, in the first ever national test statistics for 11-year-olds in England published in March 1997, 25% of pupils failed to achieve level 4 or above (the required standard) in English, Maths and Science. These deficiencies have pro-found implications for SME workforces and for policy on school management and teacher training which are only beginning to be tackled.

Poor education and training skills are arguably one of the most crucial constraints on small firm growth in Britain. SMEs rely to a greater extent on the general quality of the labour market, especially on government-financed basic education and skills, because they more than all other companies can usually least afford training. In addition, they are more subject to labour poaching because they have a less dominant market position and frequently can be outbid in wages. A more formalised training system, such as that in Germany, has many advantages for SMEs in overcoming these problems. Deficient education also undermines the more general scope for entrepreneurism, the culture of enterprise and spirit of risk taking.

There have been various attempts to improve SMEs' workforce training. For example: in the 1990s a Small Business Initiative gave a 1% reduction in overdraft interest rate, or £150 reduction in bank charges per year, for three years, in exchange for a pattern of management training agreed with a bank; and Skills for Small Business involved firms of fewer than 50 employees identifying a key worker who was given subsidised training and assessment skills to develop a company's training programme. Since 2000 much of this effort has devolved to training providers, industry-led bodies and Sector Skills Councils, including the Small Firms Lead Body, to develop specific qualifications and standards for small firms. In addition, apprenticeships targeted on higher vocational skills, and Investors in People (IiP) have been used to improve training standards assessment and badging of companies to accredited training levels. Other subsidised training to encourage start-ups, business development and business skilling in specific areas such as finance, marketing and management are run through Business Link (see Section 4.12).

Whilst there has been a lot of activity to develop the education and training system in Britain since the late 1980s, it is still far from clear that the right mix of programmes and incentives exists to encourage smaller firms. Indeed it is increasingly being recognised, as noted above, that the most important investments needed for business developments as a whole, but small firms in particular, are in the most basic skill areas of literacy and numeracy.

4.9.6 Information and advice

Failures in the supply of information are a recognised problem for small firms, which inter-relates with their relatively low level of market power. In Britain until the mid-1980s the main government-supported information service was focused through the Small Firms Service, which was set up at a regional level largely in response to the 1971 Bolton Report. The Department of Trade and Industry also acted as a direct supplier of information, as did other departments in relation to the specific industrial sectors with which they were concerned.

From about 1990 this system began to change with a greater emphasis being placed on local delivery and access points. From 1993 a system of Business Links has been used as the main delivery mechanism (see Section 4.12).

As well as direct government-supported providers of information and advice, there are also many other providers, nationally, sectorally and locally. Major policy efforts have been made to bring some degree of integration to these systems by signposting, referrals and one-stop shops, across the public and private sectors, and between central and local government. The form of this exchange is now becoming highly focused either on sectoral or local approaches, although it is far from clear that these two approaches are themselves integrated with each other (see below).

4.10 Sector policy

Up to the 1960s, sector policy was a key part of government national economic planning, as discussed earlier, but this was abolished in 1979. However, following an initiative launched to the CBI in 1993, a number of government attempts have been made to focus on the development of business sectors. An early change was the re-organisation of the DTI itself into a 'Sponsoring Division' from 1994. The aim was for the government to help each sector develop competitiveness. Inevitably some of this development has focused on SMEs, but probably there has still been a bias towards larger companies.

Potentially more important for SMEs have been attempts to encourage the role of trade associations and training organisations. These are voluntary bodies in Britain but they receive recognition by government and some funding to support training and businesses to develop initiatives. They suffer from a variable business membership but many trade associations are an important source of service to SMEs. Indeed most surveys of businesses show trade associations to be the first and main point of call for services after banks, accountants, lawyers and other professionals, ahead of local chambers of commerce and well ahead of any government-backed agencies (Bennett and Robson, 1999a). The main services provided by trade associations are government lobbying, information and advice, conferences and benchmarking for businesses. Standard setting, legal and arbitration services are more common in professional associations and bodies serving the smallest firms of the self-employed and owner-managers (Bennett, 1997a, 1999). As it is a voluntary system, membership is variable, but density of membership is generally much higher for sector bodies than any other UK business associations (Bennett, 1997a): on average market penetration is 62% for trade associations and 50% for professional associations. Hence, sector associations are important interfaces and suppliers of services to SMEs and have been sought by government as partners in policy initiatives.

In the mid-1990s, attempts were made by government to improve trade associations so that they could provide a better basis to inform and work with government. In 1993 a Benchmarking Challenge initiative provided modest DTI funds to help trade associations set up 'clubs' to help their members to benchmark against each other in terms of competitiveness, in 1995 an Export Challenge invited trade associations to propose methods to help their members promote exporting. In 1996 a Network Challenge sought innovative proposals from trade associations in the use of IT (see Cabinet Office, 1996a; Berry, 1997). Most significant, however, has been the promotion since 1996 of a 'model' trade association with criteria and targets of best practice (DTI, 1996b; Bennett, 1997b; Berry, 1997). This aimed to encourage benchmarking of trade associations against each other, and to guide government departments towards those associations which met 'model' criteria. This was thus a source of 'recognition' of trade associations by government. Generally, the 'model' trade association was well received and was very widely disseminated. Since 1997 this initiative has been taken over and managed by the CBI, through a Trade Association Forum, but with continued modest government support. Since 2001 a key role of these sector associations has been to work with government through Sector Skills Councils. These seek to help government develop and promote vocational training standards, apprenticeships and the diffusion of take-up of training between companies.

4.11 Local policy

For most small firms the local context is far more important than it is for larger firms. Small firms depend to a greater extent on the local labour market, local financial services and any sources of information and advice available locally. Because of lower absolute resources, thresholds for entry and lower market power, small firms usually have much less time for search and evaluation, so that the local context can be crucial to them. This also makes the general skill level, general role of banks, general level of information and general availability of advice more important to small firms. As a result, the role of national policy is in fact often the most crucial for SMEs, even if its effects are consumed by businesses chiefly through the local level.

At a local level, national and sectoral issues come together and are reinforced by the specific local conditions that determine how fertile the local environment is, both for new firm formation and for the development. Some geographical areas have a more positive supporting environment to market development than others. A good deal of analysis has gone into assessing policies that can improve local environments. In general, it has been found that the extent of existing entrepreneurialism and growth of small firms in an area is a strong stimulus to enterprise, along with occupational structures related to commerce, services (rather than manufacturing) and to management and the professions. High rates of job loss can be strong 'push' factors, whilst long-term unemployment and high levels of employment in branch plants are usually impediments. More general factors such as high levels of educational attainment, availability of skills, premises, local capital and the general business climate are also important in encouraging small firms to develop (Moyes and Westhead, 1990). Indeed, one of the strongest forces that can promote or impede small firms is the general institutional structure and capacity of an area (e.g. see Stohr, 1990; Bennett and McCoshan, 1993; Bennett and Krebs, 1994). This has led to the general conclusion, phrased particularly strongly by Sweeney (1987), that small firm development is as much a social as a technological or financial phenomenon.

Various initiatives in Britain have sought to improve the local environment for small firms. Mainly these have been seen as supply-side approaches to overcome the market gaps outlined earlier. An early approach was the financial support by government grants and projects for a network of local Enterprise Agencies. From about 1980, these grew to a network of 400 agencies in 1994 across Britain, chiefly concerned with small business start-ups and immediate aftercare. Since 1995 these have been subsumed within Business Link and subsequently Regional Development Agencies (RDAs) (see below; and Bennett and Payne, 2000).

Local government throughout the 1980s was also a major agent in SME support, chiefly as a provider of information, sites and physical regeneration initiatives. Central government limits on local government running of companies restricted activities, but new local government initiatives continue to be announced and this has been given added support since 2001 by the role of the local government's new local development powers. Many of local government SME actions are made in partnership with other agents such as local chambers of commerce. As a voluntary system, unlike the compulsory systems in France, Germany, Italy or Spain, membership of chambers of commerce in Britain varies. Membership is about 8% of the total UK business population, but much higher among established SMEs, and about 23% for firms of 20–200 employees. The chambers offer representation and lobbying, and also provide information and basic advice; export/import documentation, information and advice; foreign trade fairs and missions (for which they are an agent of the DTI); management training;

and employee training (via government contracts, for which they are now the main UK supplier in some areas).

In Scotland and Wales, development agencies were established in the 1970s and 1980s and continue to play a major role. Urban development bodies have sought to stimulate focused development in inner city areas since the 1980s. The Rural Development Commission was important in rural areas. These bodies have been the main agents administering the grants and other financial supports discussed earlier. They may also be important in land preparation and provision of premises, environment improvements and SME advice (particularly for minorities, ethnic and women's groups, etc.).

The scene changed after 1990 with the establishment of local Training and Enterprise Councils in England and Wales and Local Enterprise Companies in Scotland. These were general-purpose bodies that took over the administration of many government SMEs grants and advice schemes. They were also the chief local agent of central government to finance vocational training for the unemployed. There were 85 of these bodies in England and Wales and 22 in Scotland.

In the period between their launch in 1990 until their abolition in 2001, the Training and Enterprise Councils developed a wide range of small business activities. The most prominent were counselling and training, with a major emphasis on consultancy support and specific advice to start-ups. Much of this was delivered through other agents under contract (Bennett and Krebs, 1994). Surveys showed the full range of activities to be very extensive, but often too broad and ill focused to make any major local impact. Partly as a result of these criticisms, the government launched a new initiative in 1993 of what became Business Link (see Section 4.12).

The scene changed radically again in 2001 with the launch of RDAs in England and greater powers devolved to the Scottish Parliament and Welsh Assembly. Business Link and most business development initiatives were then devolved to RDAs, with the result that different 'business support' strategies now operate in each English region, Scotland and Wales. The result is usually viewed as a rather fragmented structure. Various assessments of it have referred to a 'patchwork quilt', 'chaos', 'labyrinth of initiatives', a 'muddle' (Audit Commission, 1989, 1999; PIU, 2000; Treasury, 2002). The Better Regulation Task Force (2002b, p. 43) 'struggled with the justification for so many bodies active on the ground . . . Our stakeholders struggled too . . . it will take more than protocols or pieces of paper to ensure close working'. Figure 4.2 summarises the range of government departments and agents, and their relative expenditure, seeking to help businesses, mostly smaller businesses.

A survey of the different organisational and funding structures is shown in Figure 4.3. This shows the different central and regional government departmental roles (across the top of the figure), separated for England, Scotland and Wales. From these flow different funding programmes, which are supposed to be coordinated at regional level (RDAs, Scottish Enterprise, Highlands and Islands Enterprise, and Welsh Assembly/ Welsh Development Agency); in turn at local level specific delivery agents such as Business Link are again supposed to coordinate the different funding programmes, working with local partners (chiefly local government) and other agents (such as trade associations, chambers of commerce, etc.).

Figure 4.2 **Expenditure on small firms by Government Bodies 2001/2 (total £2.5bn)**

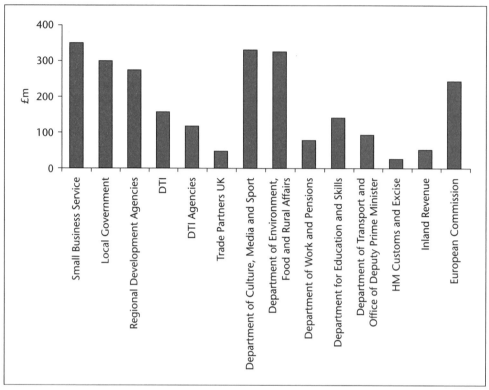

Source: HM Treasury (2002: fig. 2)

4.12 A case study of advice and support schemes – Business Link

In most countries, government initiatives for small business in recent years have focused on providing advice and support to firms at various stages, from start-up, through early growth, to later innovation and strategic change processes. This is seen as one of the best ways of overcoming areas of market failure (e.g. unequal access to information) with least distortion to markets. This has been the main approach of the US Small Business Administration and is also now followed by most EU countries (EU SMEs Observatory, 1996). Within Britain, the provision of advice has been focused on a range of local agencies, called Business Link in England, Business Gateway in Scotland, and Business Connect in Wales. The case of Business Link is instructive since it provides a good example of the potential for government support to small business and also its limitations.

Before the 1970s there was no government advisory service for small firms in Britain; the focus, as we have seen, was on national policies, larger firms and nationalised industries. The Bolton Report in 1971, however, suggested the establishment of a single information and advice helpline. This became the Small Firms Service, which operated

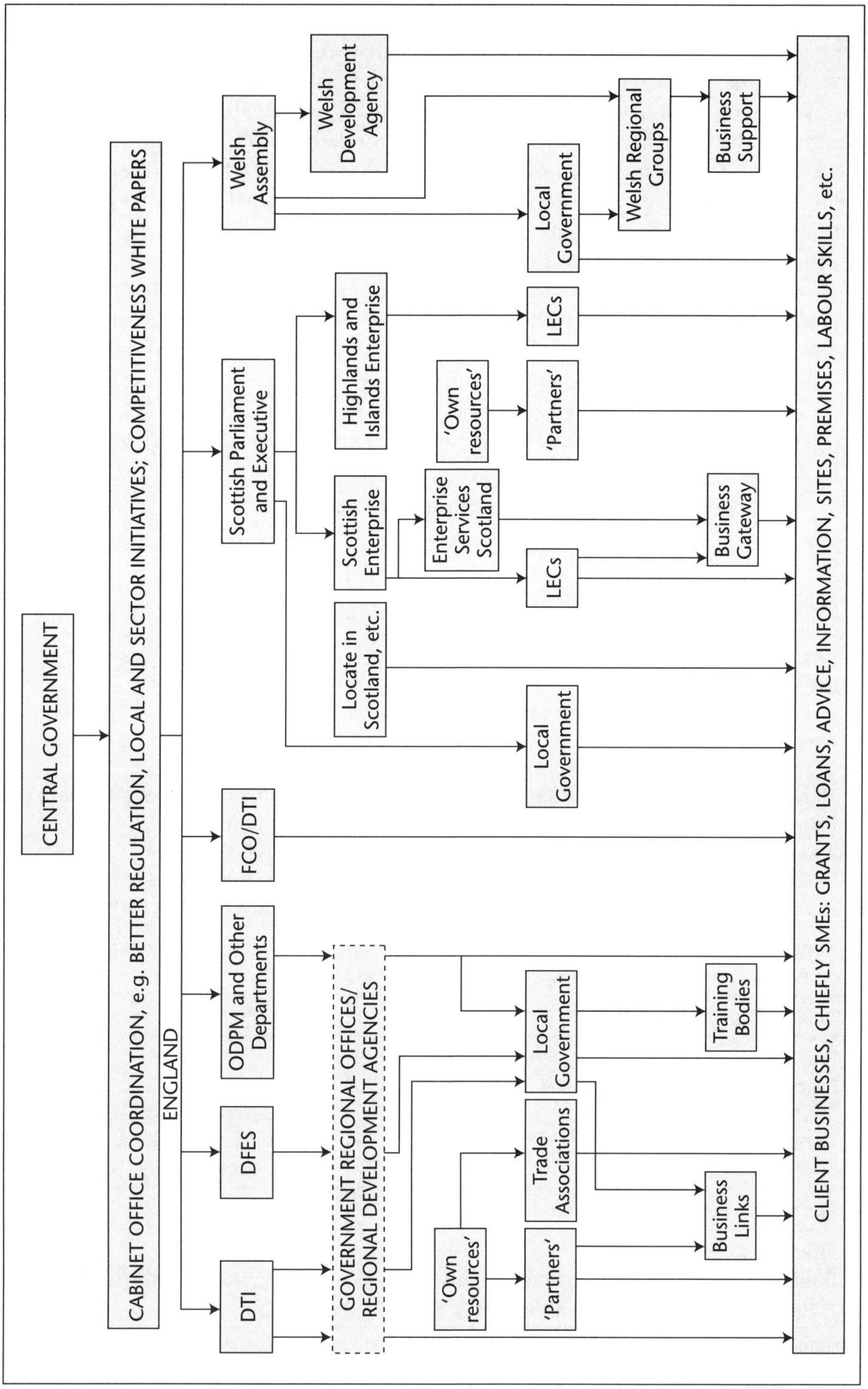

Figure 4.3 Organisation of finance and department responsibility between central government, its agents, local government and small businesses

between 1973 and 1993. It was a centralised, telephone-based helpline, with civil service staff who referred callers to other specialist suppliers in the private and public sector. All small firms were eligible. High volumes of enquiries were dealt with (250,000 per year) and high satisfaction was achieved (95% of customers). In addition, a more specialist Business Development Service responded to 20,000 requests a year for low-cost counselling, which was often provided by secondees from larger businesses on a semi-voluntary basis. The service was supplemented from 1988 to 93 by the Enterprise Initiative that provided higher levels of government grant support for consultancy and staffing. Again high take-up and satisfaction levels were achieved.

From 1993 this limited, but successful, approach was abolished and replaced by Business Link. This decentralised the management to local partnerships in 85 areas, with 200 even more local satellites. The aim was to use these local delivery points as a means to integrate a wide range of central government small business services: to integrate delivery. The full range of services is summarised in Table 4.3. The service was targeted on 10–200 employee firms 'with growth potential' and there were incentives

Table 4.3 **Services to be provided in Business Links**

Information and advice	
Provide high-quality information and advice on: Grants and support schemes Finance Late payment VAT, tax and uniform business rates Licensing requirements Legislation (health and safety, planning, etc.) Standards (including BS5750/BS7850 and TQM) BSI services Information (including new legislation)	Business start-up Technology and innovation Training Marketing Design Product sourcing Environmental issues (including BS7750) Application of IT* Property* Patents, trademarks and copyright* Education/Business Partnerships*
Personal Business Advisors who maintain regular contact with a portfolio of companies and construct an integrated package of services to meet their ends.	
Counselling/consultancy	
Provide *access* to: Diagnostic health check services Start-up counselling General business counselling Survival counselling	Investors in People Other subsidised consultancy schemes Commercial consultancy Business consultancy
Business skills and awareness	
Provides *access* to Business skills seminars (including business planning, quality, marketing, purchasing, etc.)	Business start-up schemes

*Indicates that a service is desirable, but not essential.

Source: Derived from Department of Trade and Industry (1992: Prospectus, Annex 2) and Bennett *et al.* (1994: Table 9.15)

to provide intensive consultancy and advice services through a new group of employees called 'personal business advisors' (PBAs). There were financial targets for fee income (initially of 25% of the total budget for Business Link) with the intention that the Business Link would have an ongoing relationship with the small firm being advised and be partially self-financing. The result was a take-up of advice and more intensive counselling similar to the earlier Small Firms Services, but with much lower satisfaction levels (60% on average), and with high variability between areas (satisfaction varying from 20% to 90%).

From 2001 this system was reformed though a reduction in the number of geographical areas covered to 45, removal of fee incentives and changed management structures. In the period 2001–03 take-up reduced as Business Link managers restructured and refocused, but satisfaction was raised to about 85%, although variability between areas remained.

From 2005 direct control of Business Link passed from the central government DTI to the English RDAs. Each has followed different paths. In the South East, which has had limited government resources since it has fewer economic problems, the service is highly focused on signposting and referral to private sector advisors, with a limited group of businesses with growth potential selected for high levels of advisor and financial support.

At the other extreme, in the North East and North West Regions, there are large public funds available, which derive from multiple British and EU initiatives. In these regions an attempt is being made to integrate small business support with urban regeneration, neighbourhood renewal and industrial restructuring initiatives. Less referral and signposting is attempted and more small firms, in targeted areas, are able to gain grants or subsidies.

The evolution of Business Link provides a major internationally relevant case study of lessons in how government should, and should not, seek to support small businesses. It has been extensively monitored and assessed. You can read these assessments in Bennett and Robson (1999c, 2000, 2003, 2004, 2005; Bennett *et al.*, 2001) and Priest (1999), HoC (1996a, 1996b). The role of the advisor (PBA) has been given detailed assessment by Sear and Agar (1996), Tann and Laforet (1998), Mole (2002a, 2002b) (see also www.businesslink.gov.uk). The following summarises the main lessons learnt.

1 Integration of government central and local services, which was a major aim of decentralisation to local agencies, has only partially occurred. Government departments, local government and other 'partners' have remained jealous of their own areas, and 'turf wars' have occurred. There has been little real rationalisation of the number of government-financed agencies operating locally: policy termination remains rare.

2 Inter-related with 'turf wars', referral to non-public agents has been very limited. Referral was perhaps 5% of Business Link actions up to 2001, whilst under the Small Firms Service in the 1980s it was about 90%.

3 The model of intensive support through PBA consultancy has proved elusive to achieve. Most demand from government sources is in fact for simple information and advice, not for intensive specialisms. The hope to create long-term relationships with small firms ignored the market for advice, which is generally for one-offs (Riddle, 1986; Hill and Nealey, 1991; Clark, 1995). Encouraging small firms to come into

long-term relationships furthermore risked 'moral hazard' problems, that they would take unwarranted risks and become dependent on public support. This is proving to be a continuing problem with regional approaches, where they are heavily funded, such as those in the North West and North East England.

4 The target of raising fee income proved both unrealistic ('who wants to pay for government services?') and severely distorting of manager and advisor behaviour. This more than any other factor made referral less likely as advisors held on to small business enquirers in order to sell them a service and charge a fee. This in turn increased dissatisfaction levels.

Finally, the decentralisation to a wide range of local areas has proved difficult to quality assure. Whilst the aim of bringing advisors and administrators closer to the small firm was laudable, in practice it has proved difficult to recruit sufficient advisors of high enough quality to make the system effective. Typical comments on advisors are: 'poor quality', 'unprofessional', 'too bureaucratic', 'poor skill levels' (Ramsden and Bennett, 2005). In effect, the policy was over-designed, producing a model for support that few businesses wanted and which was difficult to implement. High variability between areas resulted, which was the inevitable outcome of differences in management capacity of different local Business Links and differences in advisor competence within each area.

4.13 Chapter summary

This chapter has explored how governments have sought to help small businesses, in the last sections focusing on the example of British government schemes and the particular case of Business Link. A key conclusion is that, whilst there is some scope for government to help small businesses, much of this effort has to be focused on general rather than specific schemes. This is because government is not going to have the technical capacity to be able to segment its strategies in an effective way, nor is it clear that there are good arguments why some types of business should be helped more than others.

This means that government action can be most effective where it improves the generic environment for entrepreneurship and business growth (through education policy, skills training, infrastructure) rather than specific and targeted initiatives. Moreover, the actions of government in its own activities, as regulator, economic agent and planner/promoter, are the key areas where its policy should focus. Too often government initiatives disadvantage small businesses because of the diseconomies of scale that they experience in being able to cope with compliance with government procedures. Hence, better regulation and improvement of government services is usually the main action that government can take to help small firms.

This conclusion is not surprising, since each small business is trading in a unique business environment of suppliers and customers with its own specific internal staff, product and management characteristics. Whilst there are many generic features to SMEs, and these are often focused on policy targeting, the practical demand from small firms is investments and actions that are specific to individual market niches and opportunities. These aspects of the market for SMEs' products and services are *highly segmented*. Thus an appropriate policy intervention or support for small firms needs to be general to all (allowing them to adapt what is on offer to their different trading environments). It should not be surprising, therefore, that there are no simple or generic solutions for SME policy. Even when looking at a single field of activity, such as training, advice, exporting or better regulation, it is difficult for government to design programmes that are likely to fit a firm's specific needs. As noted by the Bank of England (1996): 'There is no single solution which will bring about sudden or dramatic improvement'. As a result there have been many different policy initiatives with a 'patchwork quilt' of programmes. This outcome seems to be inevitable as a result of efforts to target and segment supports and is as true in Europe as it is in Britain. The discussion here suggests that government policy support should normally focus on generic and supply-side issues and remove itself from attempts at specialised targeting.

Questions

1 Which main form of government action is most likely to help small business?

2 Assess the arguments for segmenting policy to target parts of the small business market.

3 Does the pattern of small business support in Britain provide a coherent and effective package for small firms?

4 Using the case of Business Link to illustrate your argument, what are the most effective strategies that should be followed by a government advice service for small firms?

Web links

www.businesslink.gov.uk
This is the website of the main government support agency for small business in the UK.

www.sba.gov
The Small Business Administration was established to maintain and strengthen the US economy by aiding, counselling, assisting and protecting the interests of small businesses.

www.europa.eu.int/comm/enterprise/enterprise_policy
The European Commission's DG Enterprise website which contains policy documents on a range of issues related to entrepreneurship and small business at a European level.

CHAPTER 5

Innovation and the small business

Zoltan J. Acs

5.1 Introduction

Just as the economy has been besieged by a wave of technological change that has left virtually no sector of the economy untouched, scientific understanding of the innovative process – that is, the manner by which firms innovate, and the impact such technological change has in turn on enterprises and markets – has also undergone a revolution, which, if somewhat quieter, has been no less fundamental. Well into the 1970s, conventional wisdom about the nature of technological change was shaped largely by Schumpeter (1942). This conventional wisdom confirmed to a generation of scholars and policy makers that innovation and technological change lie in the domain of large corporations and that small business would fade away as the victim of its own inefficiencies.

While this conventional wisdom about the singular role played by large enterprises with market power prevailed during the first three decades subsequent to the close of World War II, more recently a wave of new studies has challenged this wisdom. Most importantly, these studies have identified a much wider spectrum of enterprises contributing to innovative activity, and that in particular small entrepreneurial firms as well as large established incumbents play an important role in the innovation and process of technological change.

In the global economy, the continued entry of new technology-based firms (NTBFs) into the economy is a crucial public policy issue. Government plays an important role in small firm innovation by increasing small business access to the R&D infrastructure, diffusing risk and providing capital.

5.2 Learning objectives

There are six learning objectives in this chapter:
1 To understand how entrepreneurship, firm size and innovative activity are interrelated.
2 To gain basic understanding of the knowledge production function.
3 To illustrate how conventional empirical measures of innovative activity may be misleading.

76

4 To recognise how the external industry environment, knowledge spill-overs, geographic location, and scale economies influence the innovative process.

5 To observe that entrepreneurship and small firms play a key role with respect to technological change and innovation.

6 To understand how public policy promotes small firm innovation.

Key concepts

■ **entrepreneurship**   ■ **innovative activity**   ■ **firm size**   ■ **technological change**
■ **knowledge production function**

5.3 The knowledge production function

With regard to theories of innovation, firms are considered exogenous and their performance in generating technological change endogenous. For example, in the most prevalent model found in the literature of technological change, the model of the *knowledge production function*, formalised by Griliches (1979), firms exist exogenously and then engage in the pursuit of new economic knowledge as an input to the process of generating innovative activity. The most decisive input in the knowledge production function is new economic knowledge. The greatest source generating new economic knowledge is generally considered to be R&D.

When it came to empirical estimation of the knowledge production function, it became clear that measurement issues played a major role. The state of knowledge regarding innovation and technological change has generally been shaped by the nature of the data that were available to scholars for analyses. Such data have always been incomplete and, at best, represented only a proxy measure reflecting some aspect of the process of technological change. The greatest obstacle to understanding the economic role of technological change was a clear inability of scholars to measure it. More recently, Cohen and Levin (1989) warned: 'A fundamental problem in the study of innovation and technical change in industry is the absence of satisfactory measures of new knowledge and its contribution to technological progress. There exists no measure of innovation that permits readily interpretable cross-industry comparisons.'

Measures of technological change have typically involved one of the three major aspects of the innovative process:

1 a measure of the inputs into the innovative process, such as R&D expenditures, or else the share of the labour force accounted for by employees involved in R&D activities;

2 an intermediate output, such as the number of inventions which have been patented; or

3 a direct measure of innovative output.

These three levels of measuring technological change have not been developed and analysed simultaneously, but have evolved over time, roughly in the order of their presentation. That is, the first attempts to quantify technological change at all generally involved measuring some aspects of inputs into the innovative process. Measures of R&D inputs – first in terms of employment and later in terms of expenditures – were only introduced on a meaningful basis enabling inter-industry and inter-firm comparisons in the late 1950s and early 1960s.

A clear limitation in using R&D activity as a proxy measure for technological change is that R&D reflects only the resources devoted to producing innovative output, but not the amount of innovative activity actually realised. That is, R&D is an input and not an output in the innovation process. In addition, R&D measures incorporate only efforts made to generate innovative activity that are undertaken within formal R&D budgets and within formal R&D laboratories. The extent of informal R&D is considerable, particularly in smaller enterprises, and not all efforts within a formal R&D laboratory are directed towards generating innovative output in any case. Other types of output, such as imitation and technology transfer, are also common goals in R&D laboratories.

As systematic data measuring the number of inventions patented were made publicly available in the mid-1960s, many scholars interpreted this new measure not only as being superior to R&D but also as reflecting innovative output. In fact, the use of patented inventions is not a measure of innovative output, but is rather a type of intermediate output measure. A patent reflects new technical knowledge, but it does not indicate whether this knowledge has a positive economic value. Only those inventions that have been successfully introduced in the market can claim that they are innovations as well. While innovations and inventions are related, they are not identical. The distinction is that an innovation is 'a process that begins with an invention, proceeds with the development of the invention, and results in the introduction of a new product, process or service to the marketplace' (Edwards and Gordon, 1984, p. 1).

Mansfield (1984, p. 462) has explained why the propensity to patent may vary so much across markets: 'The value and cost of individual patents vary enormously within and across industries . . . Many inventions are not patented. And in some industries, like electronics, there is considerable speculation that the patent system is being bypassed to a greater extent than in the past. Some types of technologies are more likely to be patented than others.' The implications are that comparisons between enterprises and across industries may be misleading. According to Cohen and Levin (1989): 'There are significant problems with patent counts as a measure of innovation, some of which affect both within-industry and between-industry comparisons.'

Thus, even as the US Patent Office has introduced new and superior sources of patent data, such as the new measure of patented inventions from computerisation, the reliability of these data as measures of innovative activity has been severely challenged. For example, Pakes and Griliches (1980, p. 378) warn that 'patents are a flawed measure (of innovative output); particularly since not all new innovations are patented and since patents differ greatly in their economic impact.' And in addressing the question, 'Patents as indicators of what?', Griliches (1990, p. 1669) concludes that: 'Ideally, we might hope that patent statistics would provide a measure of the (innovative) output . . . The reality, however, is very far from it. The dream of getting hold of an output indicator of inventive activity is one of the strong motivating forces for economic research in this area.'

Besides the fact that many, if not most, patented inventions do not result in an innovation, a second important limitation of patent measures as an indicator of innovative activity is that they do not capture all of the innovations actually made. In fact, many inventions that result in innovations are not patented. The tendency of patented inventions to result in innovations and of innovations to be the result of inventions which were patented combine into what Scherer (1983a) has termed as the propensity to patent. It is the uncertainty about the stability of the propensity to patent across enterprises and across industries that casts doubt upon the reliability of patent measures. According to Scherer (1983): 'The quantity and quality of industry patenting may depend upon chance, how readily a technology lends itself to patent protection, and business decision-makers' varying perceptions of how much advantage they will derive from patent rights. Not much of a systematic nature is known about these phenomena, which can be characterised as differences in the propensity to patent.'

Just as for the more traditional measures of technological change, there are also certain limitations associated with the direct measure of innovative activity. In fact, one of the main qualifications is common among all three measures – the implicit assumption of homogeneity of units. That is, just as it is implicitly assumed that each dollar of R&D makes the same contribution to technological change, and that each invention which is patented is equally valuable, the output measure implicitly assumes that innovations are of equal importance. As Cohen and Levin (1989) observe: 'In most studies, process innovation is not distinguished from product innovation; basic and applied research are not distinguished from development.' Thus, the increase in the firm's market value resulting from each innovation, dollar expended on R&D, and patent, is implicitly assumed to be homogeneous – an assumption which clearly violates real-world observation.

The knowledge production function has been found to hold most strongly at broader levels of aggregation. The most innovative countries are those with the greatest investments to R&D. Little innovative output is associated with less-developed countries, which are characterised by a paucity of production of new economic knowledge. Similarly, the most innovative industries also tend to be characterised by considerable investments in R&D and new economic knowledge. Not only are industries such as computers, pharmaceuticals and instruments high in R&D inputs that generate new economic knowledge, but also in terms of innovative outputs (Audretsch, 1995). By contrast, industries with little R&D, such as wood products, textiles and paper, also tend to produce only a negligible amount of innovative output. Thus, the knowledge production model linking knowledge-generating inputs to outputs certainly holds at the more aggregated levels of economic activity.

Where the relationship becomes less compelling is at the disaggregated microeconomic level of the enterprise, establishment or even line of business. For example, while Acs and Audretsch (1990) found that the simple correlation between R&D inputs and innovative output was 0.84 for four-digit standard industrial classification (SIC) manufacturing industries in the US, it was only about half, 0.40, among the largest US corporations. The model of the knowledge production function becomes even less compelling in view of the recent wave of studies revealing that small enterprises serve as the engine of innovative activity in certain industries. These results are startling, because, as Scherer (1991) observes, the bulk of industrial R&D is undertaken in the largest corporations; small enterprises account only for a minor share of R&D inputs.

As an example of the R&D carried out in different countries, the following comparison (UNICE Benchmarking Report, 1999) of business expenditures on R&D per capita (in $, based on 1997 data), suggests that the US is a global leader of knowledge production (see Figure 5.1). Figure 5.2 compares knowledge outputs. The number of

Figure 5.1 International comparisons of business research and development

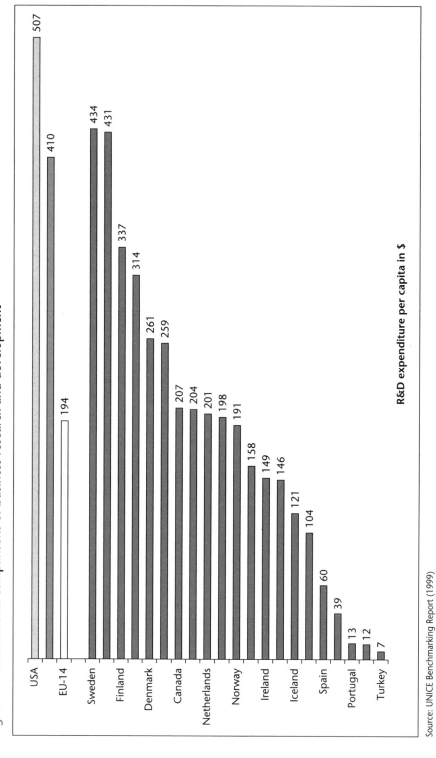

R&D expenditure per capita in $

Source: UNICE Benchmarking Report (1999)

Figure 5.2 International comparisons of patent numbers

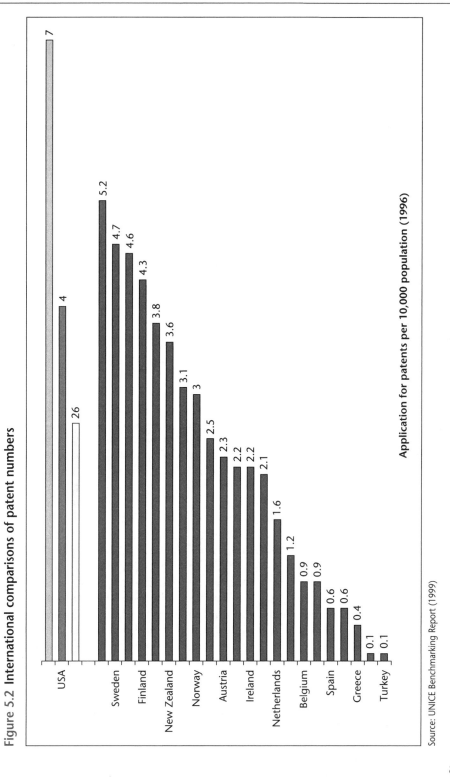

USA 7
4
26

Sweden 5.2
4.7
Finland 4.6
4.3
New Zealand 3.8
3.6
Norway 3.1
3
Austria 2.5
2.3
Ireland 2.2
2.2
Netherlands 2.1
1.6
Belgium 1.2
0.9
Spain 0.9
0.6
Greece 0.6
0.4
Turkey 0.1
0.1

Application for patents per 10,000 population (1996)

Source: UNICE Benchmarking Report (1999)

yearly patent applications is a potential indicator of newly created knowledge that is intended for commercialisation. While the US is historically the largest investor in R&D on the global market, when entrepreneurial activity measurements are based on the number of patent applications submitted (1996 data, per 10,000 population), the US ranks only second after Japan.

5.4 The role of firm size

At the heart of the conventional wisdom has been the belief that large enterprises able to exploit at least some market power are the engine of technological change. This view dates back at least to Schumpeter, who in *Capitalism, Socialism and Democracy* (1942, p. 101) argued that: 'The monopolist firm will generate a larger supply of innovations because there are advantages which, though not strictly unattainable on the competitive level of enterprise, are as a matter of fact secured only on the monopoly level.' The Schumpeterian thesis, then, is that large enterprises are uniquely endowed to exploit innovative opportunities. That is, market dominance is a prerequisite to undertaking the risks and uncertainties associated with innovation. It is the possibility of acquiring quasi-rents that serves as the catalyst for large-firm innovation.

Five factors favoring the innovative advantage of large enterprises have been identified in the literature. First is the argument that innovative activity requires a high fixed cost. Second, only firms that are large enough to attain at least temporary market power will choose innovation as a means for maximisation. This is because the ability of firms to appropriate the economic returns accruing from R&D and other knowledge-generating investments is directly related to the extent of that enterprise's market power. Third, R&D is a risky investment; small firms engaging in R&D make themselves vulnerable by investing a large proportion of their resources in a single project. However, their larger counterparts can reduce the risk accompanying innovation through diversification into simultaneous research projects. The larger firm is also more likely to find an economic application of the uncertain outcomes resulting from innovative activity. Fourth, scale economies in production may also provide scope economies for R&D. Economies of scale in promotion and in distribution facilitate the penetration of new products, thus enabling larger firms to enjoy a greater profit potential from innovation. Finally, an innovation yielding cost reductions of a given percentage results in higher profit margins for larger firms than for smaller firms.

A number of explanations have emerged why smaller enterprises may, in fact, tend to have an innovative advantage, at least in certain industries. The factors yielding small firms with the innovative advantage generally emanate from the difference in management structures between large and small firms. For example, the bureaucratic organisation of large firms is not conducive to undertaking risky R&D. The decision to innovate must survive layers of bureaucratic resistance, where an inertia regarding risk results in a bias against undertaking new projects. However, in the small firm the decision to innovate is made by relatively few people. Second, innovative activity may flourish most in environments free of bureaucratic constraints (Link and Bozeman, 1991). That is, a number of small-firm ventures have benefited from the exodus of researchers who felt thwarted by the managerial restraints in a larger firm. Finally, it has been argued that while the larger firms reward the best researchers by promoting them out of research to management positions, the smaller firms place innovative activity at the centre of their competitive strategy.

Scherer (1988, pp. 4–5) has summarised the advantages small firms may have in innovative activity: 'Smaller enterprises make their impressive contributions to innovation because of several advantages they possess compared to large-size corporations. One important strength is that they are less bureaucratic, without layers of "abominable no-men" who block daring ventures in a more highly structured organisation. Second, and something that is often overlooked, many advances in technology accumulate upon a myriad of detailed inventions involving individual components, materials, and fabrication techniques. The sales possibilities for making such narrow, detailed advances are often too modest to interest giant corporations. An individual entrepreneur's juices will flow over a new product or process with sales prospects in the millions of dollars per year, whereas few large corporations can work up much excitement over such small fish, nor can they accommodate small ventures easily into their organizational structures. Third, it is easier to sustain a fever pitch of excitement in small organizations, where the links between challenges, staff, and potential rewards are tight. "All-nighters" through which tough technical problems are solved expeditiously are common.'

Two other ways that small enterprises can compensate for their lack of R&D is through spill-overs and spin-offs. Typically an employee from an established large corporation, often a scientist or engineer working in a research laboratory, will have an idea for an invention and ultimately for an innovation. Accompanying this potential innovation is an expected net return from the new product. The inventor would expect to be compensated for their potential innovation accordingly. If the company has a different, presumably lower, valuation of the potential innovation, it may decide either not to pursue its development, or that it merits a lower level of compensation than that expected by the employee.

In either case, the employee will weigh the alternative of starting their own firm. If the gap in the expected return accruing from the potential innovation between the inventor and the corporate decision maker is sufficiently large, and if the cost of starting a new firm is sufficiently low, the employee may decide to leave the large corporation and establish a new enterprise. Since the knowledge was generated in the established corporation, the new start-up is considered to be a spin-off from the existing firm. Such start-ups typically do not have direct access to a large R&D laboratory. Rather, these small firms succeed in exploiting the knowledge and experience accrued from the R&D laboratories with their previous employers.

The research laboratories of universities provide a source of innovation-generating knowledge that is available to private enterprises for commercial exploitation. Jaffe (1989) found that the knowledge created in university laboratories 'spills over' to contribute to the generation of commercial innovations by private enterprises. Feldman (1994) found persuasive evidence that spill-overs from university research contribute more to the innovative activity of small firms than to the innovative activity of large corporations. Large firms are more active in university-based research. However, small and medium-sized enterprises apparently are better able to exploit their university-based associations and generate innovations. Link and Rees (1990) conclude that, contrary to the conventional wisdom, diseconomies of scale in producing innovations exist in large firms. They attribute these diseconomies of scale to the 'inherent bureau-cratisation process which inhibits both innovative activity and the speed with which new inventions move through the corporate system towards the market' (Link and Rees, 1990, p. 25).

Thus, just as there are persuasive theories defending the original Schumpeterian hypothesis that large corporations are a prerequisite for technological change, there are also substantial theories predicting that small enterprises should have the innovative advantage, at least in certain industries. As described above, the empirical evidence based on the input measure of technological change, R&D, tilts decidedly in favour of the Schumpeterian hypothesis. However, as also described above, the empirical results are somewhat more ambiguous for the measure of intermediate output – the number of patented inventions. It was not until direct measures of innovative output became available that the full picture of the process of technological change could be obtained.

Using this new measure of innovative output from the US Small Business Adminis-tration's Innovation Data Base, Acs and Audretsch (1990) show that, in fact, the most innovative US firms are large corporations. Further, the most innovative American cor-porations also tended to have large R&D laboratories and be R&D intensive. At first glance, these findings based on direct measures of innovative activity seem to con-firm the conventional wisdom. However, in the most innovative four-digit standard industrial classification (SIC) industries, large firms, defined as enterprises with at least 500 employees, contributed more innovations in some instances, while in other indus-tries small firms produced more innovations. For example, in computers and process control instruments small firms contributed the bulk of the innovations. By contrast in the pharmaceutical preparation and aircraft industries the large firms were much more innovative.

Probably their best measure of innovative activity is the total innovation rate, which is defined as the total number of innovations per one thousand employees in each industry. The large-firm innovation rate is defined as the number of innovations made by firms with at least 500 employees, divided by the number of employees (thousands) in large firms. The small-firm innovation rate is analogously defined as the number of innovations contributed by firms with fewer than 500 employees, divided by the num-ber of employees (thousands) in small firms.

The innovation rates, or the number of innovations per thousand employees, have the advantage in that they measure large- and small-firm innovative activity relative to the presence of large and small firms in any given industry. That is, in making a direct comparison between large- and small-firm innovative activity, the absolute number of innovations contributed by large firms and small enterprises is somewhat misleading, since these measures are not standardised by the relative presence of large and small firms in each industry. When a direct comparison is made between the innovative activity of large and small firms, the innovation rates are presumably a more reliable measure of innovative intensity because they are weighted by the relative presence of small and large enterprises in any given industry. Thus, while large firms in manufac-turing introduced 2,445 innovations in 1982, and small firms contributed slightly fewer, 1,954, small-firm employment was only half as great as large-firm employment, yielding an average small-firm innovation rate in manufacturing of 0.309, compared with a large-firm innovation rate of 0.202.

The most important and careful study to date documenting the role of German SMEs (enterprises with fewer than 500 employees) in innovative activity was undertaken by a team of researchers at the Zentrum für Europaeische Wirtschaftsforschung (ZEW) led by Harhoff and Licht (1996). Harhoff and Licht show that the likelihood of a firm not innovating decreases with firm size. For example, 52% of firms with fewer than 50 employees were not innovative. By contrast, only 15% of the firms with at least 1,000 employees were not innovative. More striking is that the smallest firms that do innovate have a greater propensity to be innovative without undertaking formal research and development. While only 3% of the largest corporations in Germany are innovative without undertaking formal R&D, one-quarter of the innovative firms with fewer than 50 employees are innovative without formal R&D.

Systematic empirical evidence also suggests that too long a high gestation period required to innovate was a very important barrier to innovative activity. Other major barriers to innovative activity include legal restrictions and restrictive government policies, an excessive time required to obtain government approval for a new product, a shortage of finance capital, a lack of competent employees, and too high a risk.

Thus, there is considerable evidence suggesting that, in contrast to the findings for R&D inputs and patented inventions, small enterprises apparently play an important generating innovative activity, at least in certain industries. By relating the innovative output of each firm to its size, it is also possible to shed new light on the Schumpeterian hypothesis. In their 1991 study, Acs and Audretsch find that there is no evidence that increasing returns to R&D expenditures exist in producing innovative output. In fact, with just several exceptions, diminishing returns to R&D are the rule. This study made it possible to resolve the apparent paradox in the literature that R&D inputs increase at more than a proportional rate along with firm size, while the generation of patented inventions does not. That is, while larger firms are observed to undertake a greater effort towards R&D, each additional dollar of R&D is found to yield less in terms of innovative output.

The contribution of small firms to technical change is uneven across technologies. Table 5.1 examines the presence of small firms in each technology using two measures. First, the table reports the small firm share of patents in each technology area, and the total number of patents. The second measure, the share of firms that are small by technology area, is more complicated because each firm had to be classified into a technology area based on where most of its patents are found. Firms with presence in two areas were counted into both technology areas. Therefore, the sum of the number of firms across technology areas exceeds the number of firms in the study.

Overall, one-third of the top 1,000 most patenting US firms are small, and small firms have a 6% share of patenting. In biotechnology however, small firms produce one-quarter of the patents and account for 71% of the patenting firms. They are also over represented in the other health-related areas – pharmaceuticals, medical equipment and medical electronics. Patenting in chemicals and agriculture is related to the health areas and so the pattern is similar though weaker there.

The unclassified patents are another area of small firm strength. Unclassified patents encompass, among other things, patents on gaming – golf, snowboarding, toys, casino gaming, etc. – and 21% of them belong to small firms. In information technology (IT) the pattern is different. In health-related technologies small firms produce a higher

Table 5.1 **Small firm share of patenting by technology in the US**

Technology area	Percentage of patents from small firms	Number of patents	Percentage of firms that are small	Number of firms
Biotechnology	25	3,886	71	45
Pharmaceuticals	19	6,453	68	59
Medical Equipment	11	8,437	45	88
Unclassified	11	2,511	31	26
Medical Electronics	11	2,974	64	14
Chemicals	9	15,760	29	91
Agriculture	8	2,561	28	18
Glass, Clay and Cement	7	1,003	50	2
Wood and Paper	7	1,961	29	21
Food and Tobacco	6	1,453	19	16
Textiles and Apparel	6	1,837	19	16
Power Generation and Distribution	6	2,045	80	5
Fabricated Metals	5	2,313	36	11
Industrial Process Equipment	5	5,480	28	39
Primary Metals	5	586	22	9
Electrical Appliances and Computers	5	10,436	28	64
Other Transport	5	1,136	10	10
Miscellaneous Manufacturing	5	9,313	16	73
Heating and Ventilation	5	1,026	43	7
Telecommunications	5	19,099	33	91
Semiconductors and Electronics	5	13,893	44	43
Miscellaneous Machinery	4	6,181	17	54
Office Equipment and Cameras	4	9,268	43	37
Measuring and Control Equipment	4	8,201	26	39
Plastics, Polymers and Rubber	4	7,187	21	28
Industrial Machinery and Tools	3	8,050	20	54
Motor Vehicles and Parts	3	5,774	22	37
Computers and Peripherals	3	31,645	36	101
Aerospace and Parts	2	1,147	0	1
Oil and Gas	1	2,660	6	17
All technology areas	6	193,976	33	1,116

Source: CHI Research (2003): 17

share of patents, and account for a higher share of firms whose patents focus on health technologies. Small firms account for one-third of patent share, which is in line with their presence overall. However, in information technologies – areas such as semiconductors and office equipment – the small firm share of patents is lower than 6%, but the share of firms that are small is higher than one-third. In other IT areas, telecommunications and computers, the share of patents is low while the share of firms is about one-third. This suggests that although small firms are relatively more active in these areas, large firms have a higher propensity to patent than in other areas and so overshadow the small firm effort when simple patent counts are examined.

Areas where small firms are weakest include: oil and gas, aerospace, motor vehicles and industrial machinery. In all these areas, small firms have less than half the share of patenting we would expect given their overall presence in the study, and small firms account for less than one-third of firms. Health and information technologies were the fastest growing areas of patenting for US innovators over the past decade (Hicks *et al.*, 2001). The strength of small firm innovators in these burgeoning areas of technology is not an accident. The small firms no doubt made innovation in these technologies more dynamic, and small firms were no doubt attracted into these areas because they offered great technical opportunity. The greater small firm presence in these newer industries is in line with previous research that has established that small firms play an important role in innovation early in the evolution of industries (Audretsch, 1995; Freeman and Soete, 1997).

5.5 The industry context

In comparison with the number of studies investigating the relationship between firm size and technological change, those examining the relationship between innovation and the external industry structure or environment are what Baldwin and Scott (1987, p. 89) term 'minuscule' in number. While it has been hypothesised that firms in concentrated industries are better able to capture the rents accruing from an innovation, and therefore have a greater incentive to undertake innovative activity, there are other market structure variables that also influence the ease with which economic rents can be appropriated. For example, Comanor (1967) argued and found that, based on a measure of minimum efficient scale, there is less R&D effort (average number of research personnel divided by total employment) in industries with very low-scale economies. However, he also found that in industries with a high minimum efficient scale R&D effort was also relatively low. Comanor interpreted his results to suggest that, where entry barriers are relatively low, there is little incentive to innovate, since the entry subsequent to innovation would quickly erode any economic rents. At the same time, in industries with high entry barriers, the absence of potential entry may reduce the incentives to innovate.

Because many studies have generally found positive relationships between market concentration and R&D, and between the extent of barriers to entry and R&D, it would seem that the conventional wisdom built around the Schumpeterian hypothesis has been confirmed. However, when the direct measure of innovative output is related to market concentration, there appears to be unequivocal evidence that concentration exerts a negative influence on the number of innovations being made in an industry.

Not only does market structure influence the total amount of innovative activity but also the relative innovative advantage between large and small enterprises. The differences between the innovation rates of large and small firms examined in the previous section can generally be explained by: the degree of capital intensity; the extent to which an industry is concentrated; the total innovative intensity; and the extent to which an industry is comprised of small firms. In particular, the relative innovative advantage of large firms tends to be promoted in industries that are capital-intensive, advertising intensive, concentrated and highly unionised. By contrast, in industries that are highly innovative and composed predominantly of large firms, the relative innovative advantage is held by small enterprises.

5.6 The geographic context

How can small firms' innovative activity be explained? While many explanations have been offered for the innovative prowess of small firms, one that is consistent with both entrepreneurship and fundamental US American values is the role of property rights. Their relatively more generous property rights may explain small firms' greater innovative capacity. People must be able to keep a portion of the fruits of their labour or they will not innovate. An innovator in a large company often has very limited property rights protection: the new product generally belongs to the firm, not the employee who invented it. Creative employees have less incentive to work hard for the company. The less-than-perfect incentive structure in many large corporations can allow bureaucratic inertia to drive corporate decisions. Managers' and employees' interests lie in protecting their claims on the firm's cash flow. Small firms are better able to protect their property rights, which means that there is more incentive to work hard.

There are many incentives to work in addition to property rights. Corporate culture also affects motivation and incentives for hard work. For example, employees of Sun Microsystems (a large firm) have a commitment to succeed that is enhanced by the large number of people sharing it; that may be inspirational to the point of making people want to work harder. A small firm may not provide the commonly shared culture of a large organisation and may therefore require more self-motivation to get new ideas out. New technology-based firms (NTBFs) gain their comparative innovative advantage by exploring new technological spaces that may have been overlooked by larger firms. In many industries small firms receive funding for such efforts. Regional networking facilitates this process and permits small firms to obtain and use knowledge more efficiently in order to make radical innovations. Because their research is closely tied to that of other institutions and firms, it diffuses quickly.

Knowledge is localised for both start-ups and other firms, but start-ups are more closely tied into regional networks because they depend on networks for critical knowledge inputs. If knowledge flows are localised, then firms located in distant regions are excluded from knowledge networks. Where this occurs, large firms must get knowledge inputs internally. Both small and large firms play important roles in innovative activity. Small firms tend to have the innovative advantage in industries with high technological opportunity and where large firms dominate. This suggests a division of labour between large and small firms. Small firms are superior in commercialising new knowledge; large firms are superior in their ability to appropriate returns from these innovations, either by buying property rights or acquiring the small firms. Thus, the greatest synergy might be achieved through continual mergers of new small firms with innovative products into large firms with international market access. For example, highly innovative small pharmaceutical companies are continuously absorbed into larger multinational firms as the industry is forced to become more efficient.

The evidence revealing small enterprises to be the engine of innovative activity in certain industries, despite an obvious lack of formal R&D activities, raises the question about the source of knowledge inputs for small enterprises. The answer emerging from a series of studies is from other, third-party, firms or research institutions, such as universities. Economic knowledge may *spill over* from the firm or research institution creating it for application by other firms.

That knowledge spills over is rarely disputed. However, the geographic range of such knowledge spill-overs is greatly contested. In disputing the importance of knowledge externalities in explaining the geographic concentration of economic activity, Krugman (1991) and others do not question the existence or importance of such knowledge spill-overs. In fact, they argue that such knowledge externalities are so important and forceful that there is no compelling reason for a geographic boundary to limit the spatial extent of the spill-over. According to this line of thinking, the concern is not that knowledge does not spill over but that it should stop spilling over just because it hits a geographic border, such as a city limit, state line or national boundary.

A recent body of empirical evidence clearly suggests that R&D and other sources of knowledge not only generate externalities, but that such knowledge spill-overs tend to be geographically bounded within the region where the new economic knowledge was created. That is, new economic knowledge may spill over but the geographic extent of such knowledge spill-overs is limited (Jaffe, 1989). Krugman (1991, p. 53) has argued that economists should abandon any attempts at measuring knowledge spill-overs because 'knowledge flows are invisible, they leave no paper trail by which they may be measured and tracked.' But 'knowledge flows do sometimes leave a paper trail' – in particular in the form of patented inventions and new product introductions.

5.7 The knowledge production function reconsidered

The model of the knowledge production function becomes even less compelling in view of the evidence documented earlier that entrepreneurial small firms are the engine of innovative activity in some industries, which raises the question: Where do new and small firms get the innovation producing inputs, that is the knowledge?

The appropriability problem, or the ability to capture the revenues accruing from investments in new knowledge, confronting the individual may converge with that confronting the firm. Economic agents can and do work for firms, and even if they do not an incumbent firm can potentially employ them. In fact, in a model of perfect information with no agency costs, any positive economies of scale or scope will ensure that the appropriability problems of the firm and individual converge. If an agent has an idea for doing something different from what is currently being practised by the incumbent enterprises – both in terms of a new product or process and in terms of organisation – the idea, which can be termed as an innovation, will be presented to the incumbent enterprise. Because of the assumption of perfect knowledge, both the firm and the agent would agree upon the expected value of the innovation. But to the degree that any economies of scale or scope exist, the expected value of implementing the innovation within the incumbent enterprise will exceed that of taking the innovation outside the incumbent firm to start a new enterprise. Thus, the incumbent firm and the inventor of the idea would be expected to reach a bargain splitting the value added to the firm contributed by the innovation. The payment to the inventor – either in terms of a higher wage or some other means of remuneration – would be bounded between the expected value of the innovation if it was implemented by the incumbent enterprise on the upper end, and by the return that the agent could expect to earn if he used it to launch a new enterprise on the lower end.

A different model refocuses the unit of observation away from firms deciding whether to increase their output from a level of zero to some positive amount in a new industry, to individual agents in possession of new knowledge that, due to uncertainty, may or may not have some positive economic value. It is the uncertainty inherent in new economic knowledge, combined with asymmetries between the agent possessing that knowledge and the decision-making vertical hierarchy of the incumbent organisation with respect to its expected value, that potentially leads to a gap between the valuations of that knowledge.

Divergences in the expected value regarding new knowledge will, under certain conditions, lead an agent to exercise what Hirschman (1970) has termed as *exit* rather than *voice*, and depart from an incumbent enterprise to launch a new firm. But who is right, the departing agents or those agents remaining in the organisational decision-making hierarchy who, by assigning the new idea a relatively low value, have effectively driven the agent with the potential innovation away? *Ex post* the answer may not be too difficult. But given the uncertainty inherent in new knowledge, the answer is anything but trivial *a priori*.

This initial condition of not just uncertainty but greater degree of uncertainty *vis-à-vis* incumbent enterprises in the industry is captured in the theory of firm selection and industry evolution proposed by Jovanovic (1982). The theory of firm selection is particularly appealing in view of the rather startling size of most new firms. For example, the mean size of more than 11,000 new-firm start-ups in the manufacturing sector in the US was found to be fewer than eight workers per firm. While the minimum efficient scale (MES) varies substantially across industries, and even to some degree across various product classes within any given industry, the observed size of most new firms is sufficiently small to ensure that the bulk of new firms will be operating at a suboptimal scale of output. Why would an entrepreneur start a new firm that would immediately be confronted by scale disadvantages?

An implication of the theory of firm selection is that new firms may begin at a small, even suboptimal, scale of output, and then if merited by subsequent performance expand. Those new firms that are successful will grow, whereas those that are not successful will remain small and may ultimately be forced to exit from the industry if they are operating at a suboptimal scale of output.

An important finding of Audretsch (1995) is that although entry may still occur in industries characterised by a high degree of scale economies, the likelihood of survival is considerably less. People will start new firms in an attempt to appropriate the expected value of their new ideas, or potential innovations, particularly under the entrepreneurial regime. As entrepreneurs gain experience in the market they learn in at least two ways. First, they discover whether they possess *the right stuff*, in terms of producing goods and offering services for which sufficient demand exists, as well as whether they can produce that good more efficiently than their rivals. Second, they learn whether they can adapt to market conditions as well as to strategies engaged in by rival firms. In terms of the first type of learning, entrepreneurs who discover that they have a viable firm will tend to expand and ultimately survive. But what about those entrepreneurs who discover that they are either not efficient or not offering a product for which there is a viable demand? The answer is that *it depends on the extent of scale economies as well as on conditions of demand*. The consequences of not being able to grow will depend, to a large degree, on the extent of scale economies. Thus, in markets with only negligible scale economies, firms have a considerably greater likelihood of survival. However, where scale economies play an important role the consequences of not growing are substantially more severe, as evidenced by a lower likelihood of survival.

What emerges from the new evolutionary theories and empirical evidence on the role of small firms is that markets are in motion, with a lot of new firms entering the industry and a lot of firms exiting out of the industry. The evolutionary view of the process of industry evolution is that new firms typically start at a very small scale of output. They are motivated by the desire to appropriate the expected value of new economic knowledge. But, depending upon the extent of scale economies in the industry, the firm may not be able to remain viable indefinitely at its start-up size. Rather, if scale economies are anything other than negligible, the new firm is likely to have to grow to survive. The temporary survival of new firms is presumably supported through the deployment of a strategy of compensating factor differentials that enables the firm to discover whether or not it has a viable product.

The empirical evidence supports such an evolutionary view of the role of new firms in manufacturing, because the post-entry growth of firms that survive tends to be spurred by the extent to which there is a gap between the MES level of output and the size of the firm. However, the likelihood of any particular new firm surviving tends to decrease as this gap increases. Such new suboptimal scale firms are apparently engaged in the selection process. Only those firms offering a viable product that can be produced efficiently will grow and ultimately approach or attain the MES level of output. The remainder will stagnate and depending upon the severity of the other selection mechanism – the extent of scale economies – may ultimately be forced to exit out of the industry. Thus, the persistence of an asymmetric firm-size distribution biased towards small-scale enterprise reflects the continuing process of the entry of new firms into industries and not necessarily the permanence of such small and sub-optimal enterprises over the long run. Although the skewed size distribution of firms persists with remarkable stability over long periods of time, a constant set of small and suboptimal scale firms does not appear to be responsible for this skewed distribution. Rather, by serving as agents of change, entrepreneurial firms provide an essential source of new ideas and experimentation that otherwise would remain untapped in the economy.

5.8 Innovation and public policy in the US

The federal government has played an active role in financing new high-technology firms since the Soviet Union launched the Sputnik satellite in the late 1950s. In recent years, European and Asian nations, and many US states, have adopted similar incentives. While these programmes' precise structures have differed, the efforts have been predicated on two shared assumptions: that the private sector provides insufficient capital to NTBFs and that the government can identify firms where investments will ultimately yield high social and/or private returns.

Since 1980, the federal government has instituted active policies in support of these dynamic NTBFs. Building on experiences in the states, Congress and the executive branch created new programmes in which government and the private sector are partners in developing and deploying new technologies. These programmes include the Small Business Innovation Research (SBIR) programme, the Small Business Technology Transfer (STTR) programme, the Advanced Technology Program (ATP), the Manufacturing Extension Partnership (MEP) programme, and several financing programmes for high-technology companies administered by the US Small Business Administration.

These programmes stress commercialisation potential, non-financial assistance and better intellectual property rights protection. They represent only a small fraction of America's total investment in research and development (R&D), but in leveraging money to the public and private sectors they have an economic impact far greater than that suggested by the programme budget alone. Taken together, the programmes represent an important commitment to the process that allows small technology-based businesses to use their unique competencies to address federal research needs, create new products and processes, and bring them to commercial markets.

In addition to providing basic management, technical and research assistance to pre-venture entrepreneurs and existing small businesses, a number of SBDCs are emphasising assistance to technology companies. Specialised services include commercialisation help, assistance to inventors and manufacturers, SBIR application assistance and services to NTBFs. The SBA has also established an agreement with the US Department of Commerce to establish SBDC field offices at manufacturing extension centres to improve the competitiveness of small and medium-sized manufacturers by providing management and marketing consulting and guidance.

5.8.1 Financial support for NTBFs

The US Small Business Administration (SBA) has several loan programmes that assist small businesses whose primary activity is in the high-technology industry. Two programmes that currently assist some 2,000 high technology businesses annually are the Section 7(a) and 504 loan. The Section 7(a) loan programme authorises the SBA to guarantee loans made by lenders to small businesses that cannot obtain financing on reasonable terms through normal lending channels. The SBA can guarantee 75% of the loan amount up to $750,000. For loans of $100,000 or less, the guarantee rate is 80%. The interest rate is not to exceed 2.75% over the prime-lending rate.

Through certified development companies (CDCs), the 504-loan programme provides long-term, fixed-rate financing to small businesses to acquire or construct facilities for their operations or to purchase machinery and equipment with a useful life of ten or more years. Typically, project proceeds are provided as follows: 50% of the project cost is financed by an non-guaranteed bank loan, 40% by an SBA-guaranteed debenture that is sold to investors at a fixed rate, and 10% by the small business. The maximum SBA debenture is $750,000, except under certain circumstances when it can be up to $1m. Job creation and retention is the main purpose of the programme.

In addition to these established loan programmes, the two-year pilot capital access programme was conceived to help direct the SBA's limited loan resources to businesses that may have a greater impact on the nation's overall economic well-being. It is based in part on a proprietary computer-based market segmentation programme developed by Citibank that identifies and targets businesses involved in the development and utilisation of newer technologies, potential job creators and prospective exporters. Minority-, women- and veteran-owned firms are also targeted under this programme. The programme includes a mutually agreed set of credit standards and a streamlined loan application process. So far, nine loans for a total of $1,663,000 have been made to high-technology firms under the programme.

5.8.2 Angel Capital Electronic Network

A series of nine focus groups sponsored by the SBA's Office of Advocacy between September 1995 and March 1996 confirmed the existence of a significant gap in equity capital for rapidly growing firms needing between $500,000 and $1.5m. Entrepreneurs can often raise amounts under $500,000 from their personal resources (investments, second mortgages, credit cards, families, friends and colleagues). For amounts up to $1.5m, however, it is very difficult to raise the third-party equity capital so essential to the success of rapidly growing high-technology businesses.

Popular mythology has it that the organised venture capital industry has sufficient capital to meet the needs of high-potential small businesses, that the shortage is not of capital but of 'good deals'. The myth is both popular and false: the organised venture capital industry has always been a limited market. Fewer than 1,000 deals are consummated in a year and fewer than 100 are starting or seed deals. As the amount of funding flowing into the industry has increased, the number of deals has remained essentially static. The average size of a deal has increased dramatically: organised venture capitalists rarely fund deals under $3m.

Many of the NTBFs with promising technologies, products and markets need relatively small amounts of equity capital to commercialise and produce their products. These firms have traditionally turned to the informal private equity capital that goes under the name 'angel capital'. This market has been estimated at 30 times the size of the venture capital market. Because angel capital is both informal and private, knowledge about the nature and extent of the market is limited. The Office of Advocacy's nine focus groups examined the problems associated with angel capital and its potential to meet the needs of rapidly growing small businesses. The focus groups confirmed that despite the essential role angel financing plays, the market has inefficiencies associated with a lack of organisation and high transaction costs.

SBA's Office of Advocacy, in cooperation with the University of New Hampshire's Center for Venture Research, recently examined how the process could be improved. Clearly, the market would work better if the angel investors had access to more potential deals and the entrepreneurs had exposure to more potential investors. The trick was to design a system that would provide greater dissemination of information without notably increasing the potential for fraud and abuse. The new system, unveiled in October 1996, is ACE-Net, the Angel Capital Electronic Network. ACE-Net covers eight of the most successful regional angel capital networks with a password-controlled, secure Internet network. The network will serve as a locator for serious investors and entrepreneurs interested in finding each other. A series of carefully crafted security mechanisms will help protect the process from fraud and abuse.

ACE-Net addresses the problem of high transaction costs by introducing a set of standard terms to reduce the time and cost involved in each transaction. The primarily university-based regional networks are ideally positioned to provide education and information about the angel financing process to potential angels and entrepreneurs. As the network begins to operate, it should increase the number of angels, the potential amount of angel financing available, and the efficiency of the process.

5.8.3 Small Business Innovation Research programme

Federal research and development that strengthens the national defence, promotes health and safety, and improves the nation's highways and airports is vital to the long-term interests of the United States and its citizens. The SBA, through the Small Business Innovation Research (SBIR) programme and its smaller companion programme, the Small Business Technology Transfer (STTR) programme, helps ensure that innovative ideas developed by quality small businesses are a part of these efforts. These programmes ensure that some $1bn in federal R&D projects goes to small businesses each year. SBIR is an integral component of a national technology strategy and the primary access point for NTBFs to participate in federal R&D efforts.

In 1982 Congress passed the Small Business Innovation Development Act, authorising the SBIR programme. The nation had just undergone a long period of economic stagnation and policymakers were looking for new economic answers. International competition, particularly in producing and marketing technology, was growing more intense. The US had the largest R&D effort in the world – a scale of scientific enterprise unequalled in history – and America's international competitors were becoming more successful at producing and marketing innovations derived from that research.

The SBIR programme was designed to address these perceived problems in several ways. It increased the competition for federal R&D work by opening it to small businesses. The scope and funding of each project was designed to attract talented entrepreneurs. Projects were chosen to fulfill each government agency's requirements for innovative solutions to their technology-oriented problems. To improve the nation's economic competitiveness, the programme was designed to encourage entrepreneurs to bring innovations derived from federal R&D into the marketplace.

Today's SBIR programme is a competitive procurement activity designed to meet the R&D needs of the federal government. Each federal agency with an extramural R&D budget in excess of $100m must designate a certain percentage of this budget for small business. Ten federal agencies currently participate in the programme: the Departments of Defense, Agriculture, Commerce, Education, Health and Human Services, Transportation and Energy, the Environmental Protection Agency, the National Air and Space Administration and the National Science Foundation.

In the three-step SBIR process, small businesses can earn awards up to $100,000 for phase I and up to $750,000 for phase II. Phase III looks to the private sector for funding. Successful bidders can be awarded up to $100,000 to perform a feasibility study as phase I. If the small firm and the agency then agree, the firm can be awarded a phase II contract or grant for actual R&D resulting in a model or prototype. In the third phase – commercialisation – the small firm is encouraged to bring the innovation to market.

At the completion of the second phase the government has the rights to the innovation for its own use only; that is, the government will never pay the firm a royalty. But the small firm keeps all other rights to the innovation and is encouraged to patent, copyright or take other measures to protect its position. The firm can then bring the innovation to the marketplace, producing the product or service directly or working out co-venturing or licensing arrangements.

By some measures the SBIR programme has been highly successful. Since its inception in the 1983 financial year, small high-technology firms have submitted more than 220,000 proposals resulting in more than 33,000 awards. Although the programme's primary purpose is to meet the government's R&D requirements, the incidental benefit is substantial: more than 25% of SBIR projects have become products or services sold in the marketplace. The public reaps the benefits of the government research and the business participants improve their competitive positions and profitability. The SBIR programme is meeting not only the research goals of the funding agencies, but also a special need for high-risk seed and start-up capital. The current level of almost $1bn in SBIR funding each year is more than ten times the funding provided by the institutional venture capital organisations to these small technology firms.

5.8.4 Small Business Technology Transfer programme

The Small Business Technology Transfer (STTR) programme is a three-year pilot programme, funded in 1994 through a small allocation from five federal agencies' extramural R&D budgets. The purpose of STTR is to tap research institutions for the enormous reservoir of ideas that have not yet been deployed effectively for the nation's economic benefit. These research institutions employ one in four R&D scientists and engineers in the US and are involved in more than $40bn in R&D each year. They have helped position the US as undisputed world leader in basic research and many areas of applied research. The one-quarter million scientists and engineers in these institutions often recognise that their research has important commercial applications, but few have efficient mechanisms to pursue these applications.

STTR is an important step toward harnessing this research for America's economic advancement. By merging the innovative ideas of the researcher at the research institution with the entrepreneurial skills of a small technology company, STTR creates an efficient vehicle for moving the ideas to market. University collaboration with new technology-based firms has the potential to stimulate innovation more than R&D performed solely in a company lab. Route 128 in Massachusetts and Silicon Valley in California are centres of high-tech economic development precisely because of university interaction with small, innovative companies.

Both STTR and SBIR programmes serve the purpose of transforming innovative research into commercial reality. STTR uses the approach established in the SBIR programme, which has proven remarkably efficient in stimulating technological innovation. But whereas SBIR funds R&D projects at small firms and limits the participation of research institutions to a subcontracting or consulting role, STTR funds cooperative R&D projects between an NTBF and a research institution. STTR enables a researcher at a university to spin off a commercially promising idea by joining forces with a small technology company. Thus, STTR is a mechanism for small businesses to tap into the vast reservoir of ideas in the nation's research institutions.

5.8.5 Advanced Technology Program

Small firms are thriving in the rigorous, hard-fought competitions of the Advanced Technology Program (ATP), which is managed by the US Department of Commerce's National Institute of Standards and Technology (NIST). Of the 280 awards made by the ATP from 1990 to 1996, nearly half went to individual NTBFs or to joint ventures led by a small business. The awards are valued at $970m in ATP funds and more than $1bn in industry cost-share. Many more NTBFs are participating in or benefiting from the programme as members of ATP-funded joint ventures, and as subcontractors, suppliers and customers of ATP awardees. And small means small in the ATP. Many of the awardees have been start-ups or still in the early development stages. More than half of the 100 small, single-company awardees had fewer than 25 employees and more than 85 had fewer than 100 employees at the time they received the ATP award.

In partnership with the ATP, these NTBFs are developing high-risk, enabling technologies that they can translate into new business opportunities, new industrial processes to improve their productivity and the productivity of other US producers, and new products and services for the world's markets. Some of these technologies are path breaking in that they will revolutionise existing ways of doing things or create whole new industry sectors. Some provide the technical infrastructure critical to productivity advances within an industry sector. And some have many different uses across a variety of industry sectors.

Although most of the ATP-funded projects are still in their early stages, the participants, including the small companies, have begun to report promising results. The ATP awards are enabling these companies to pursue challenging research projects that otherwise would have been delayed, scaled down or not done at all. As a result, many of the companies now have important new technical capabilities that enable them to attract other sources of capital and pursue new commercial opportunities. Some are growing rapidly. New and improved processes, products and services are emerging that benefit not just the award-recipient companies but also other researchers, producers, consumers and, ultimately, the nation.

5.8.6 Manufacturing Extension Partnership

The Manufacturing Extension Partnership (MEP) is a growing nationwide system that gives smaller manufacturers unprecedented access to new technologies, resources and expertise. At the heart of the system is a network of affiliated, locally based manufacturing extension centres. Each centre is a partnership, typically involving federal, state and local governments; industry; educational institutions; and other sources of expertise, information and funding support.

Centres are private, non-profit organisations rather than offices of the federal government. The programme began with three extension centres in 1989. Today, nearly all states and Puerto Rico already have or are planning centres affiliated with MEP, linking firms with engineers and other specialists with manufacturing or business experience to address specific needs. Through this network, MEP is putting hard-to-find technical assistance and the newest business practices within the reach of the nation's 381,000 small and medium-sized manufacturing establishments.

5.9 Chapter summary

Within a generation, scholarship has produced theories, evidence and new insights that have dramatically changed the prevalent view about the role of entrepreneurship in innovation and technological change. The conventional wisdom held that small firms inherently have a deficit of knowledge assets, burdening them with a clear and distinct disadvantage in generating innovative output. This view was certainly consistent with the early interpretation of the knowledge production function that to compete globally you have to be big.

More recent scholarship has produced a revised view that identifies entrepreneurial small firms as making a crucial contribution to innovative activity and technological change. There are two hypotheses why scholarship about the role of small firms has evolved so drastically within such a short period. First is that, as explained in this chapter, the measurement of innovative output and technological change has greatly improved. As long as the main instruments to measuring innovative activity were restricted to inputs into the innovative process, such as expenditures on formal R&D, many or even most of the innovative activities by smaller enterprises simply remained hidden from the radar screen of researchers. With the development of measures focusing on measures of innovative output, the vital contribution of small firms became prominent, resulting in the emergence of not just the recognition that small firms provide an engine of innovative activity, at least in some industry contexts, but also of new theories to explain and understand how and why small firms access knowledge and new ideas. This first hypothesis would suggest that, in fact, small firms have always made these types of innovative contributions, but they remained hidden and mostly unobserved by scholars and policy makers.

The alternative hypothesis is that, in fact, the new view towards the innovative capacity of small firms emerged not because of measurement improvements, but because the economic and social environment actually changed in such a way as to shift the innovative advantage more towards smaller enterprises. This hypothesis would say that the conventional wisdom about the relative inability of small firms to innovate was essentially correct – at least for a historical period of time. Rather, the new view of small firms as engines of innovative activity reflects changes in technology, globalisation and other factors that have fundamentally altered the importance and process of innovation and technological change. As Jovanovic (2001, pp. 54–55) concludes: 'The new economy is one in which technologies and products become obsolete at a much faster rate than a few decades ago . . . It is clear that we are entering the era of the young firm. The small firm will thus resume a role that, in its importance, is greater than it has been at any time in the last 70 years or so.' Future research may sort out which of these two hypotheses carries more weight. However, one important conclusion will remain. Scholarship has clearly changed in its assessment of the role of small firms in the process of innovation and technological change from being mostly unimportant to carrying a central role.

Future economic growth is closely tied to the growth of small, new technology-based firms. The federal government has instituted a number of policies in support of these NTBFs, including the Small Business Innovation Research, Small Business Technology Transfer and Advanced Technology programmes, the Manufacturing Extension Partnership and several US Small Business Administration financing programmes for high-technology companies. While these programmes represent only a small fraction of America's total investment in research and development, they have a significant impact. They represent a national commitment to encourage small technology-based businesses to address federal research needs and to create and commercialise new products and processes.

Questions

1 What limitations in the measurement of the knowledge production function distort empirical information regarding innovative activities and technological change in small firms?

2 How is recent research challenging the conventional wisdom that monolithic enterprises exploiting market power are the driving engine of innovative activity?

3 What are some of the innovative advantages characteristic of small enterprises?

4 In what way do spill-overs and spin-offs affect the innovative activities of small enterprises?

5 How does the federal government support and promote small firm innovation?

Web links

www.mpiew-jena.mpg.de
The website of the Max Planck Institute for Economics. Under research, the Entrepreneurship, Growth and Public Policy body has published a range of papers on knowledge spill-overs and entrepreneurship.

www.cordis.lu/innovation-policy/studies
A list of studies commissioned by the European Commission's Enterprise and Innovation Directorate. Under published studies, there is a paper on 'Innovative SMEs and employment creation'.

www.cric.ac.uk
Results from the ESRC Centre for Research on Innovation and Competition (CRIC) project examining the innovation performance of small firms.

www.sba.gov/advo/research
Research and publications by the Small Business Administration in the US. A research report 'Small Firms and Technology: Acquisitions, Inventor Movement, and Technology Transfer' published in January 2004 should be of interest.

CHAPTER 6

Growth and development in the small business

David Smallbone and Peter Wyer

6.1 Introduction

There has probably been more written about small business growth in recent years than any other aspect of the development or management of small firms. One of the reasons for this is the contribution of growing firms to economic development and employment generation, which has attracted the attention of policy makers in many countries. In this regard, there is a growing body of research evidence that demonstrates a positive relationship between entrepreneurship and economic growth (e.g. Audretsch *et al.*, 2002; Carree *et al.*, 2002; Reynolds *et al.*, 2003; Wennekers and Thurik, 1999). At the same time, there is little understanding of how this occurs and what the nature of the causal relationships is. Nevertheless, the issue is very topical in the early years of the twenty-first century, which is evidenced by the widespread interest and support by policy makers for the Global Entrepreneurship Monitor (GEM) study.

For private sector business service providers such as banks, growing businesses are potentially attractive customers because business growth is likely to be associated with a demand for finance and other services. For some individual business owners, the high casualty rates among new firms, in particular, focuses attention on the elusive 'success factors', the identification of which has been the subject of a large number of studies (e.g. Smallbone *et al.*, 1995; Davidsson and Delmar, 1997; Warren and Hutchison, 2000). Whilst growth may be judged by some as an indicator of business success, it can also present managers with problems which often focus on the need to relate expansion to the resources available or those that can be realistically mobilised.

In this context, this chapter considers some of the main issues relating to growth that confront small business owners/managers, as well as those individuals and organisations concerned with assisting or doing business with them. After a brief discussion of what is meant by 'growth' in small firms, the question of how growth can be explained is considered, drawing on a number of major research studies. The second half of the chapter focuses on some of the management issues associated with growth in small firms, including the main barriers to growth and how these can be managed.

6.2 Learning objectives

There are four learning objectives in this chapter:

1 To consider what is meant by growth in small firms.

2 To consider some of the theories and concepts that have been used to help explain growth in small firms.

3 To assess the main barriers and constraints to growth in small firms.

4 To identify some of the main issues facing managers in growing small firms and discuss ways in which these may be successfully dealt with.

Key concepts

■ business growth ■ development ■ management constraints
■ external environment

6.3 Growth and development in the small firm

Much of the literature that has been written about small business growth defines growth in terms of employment (Storey, 1994; Keeble, 1993; Barkham *et al.*, 1996; Schutgens and Wever, 2000). Part of the reason for this is the interest of public policy makers in facilitating growth in employment opportunities. In this context, various studies have demonstrated the disproportionate contribution of a minority of fast growth firms to employment generation (see Chapter 2). For example, among new firms, it has been suggested that 'out of every 100 created, the fastest growing four firms will create half the jobs in the group over a decade' (Storey *et al.*, 1987). Another study which was concerned with the development of a group of 306 mature manufacturing SMEs over an 11-year period showed that 23% of the firms (i.e. those achieving high growth) contributed 71% of all new jobs created in the panel (Smallbone *et al.*, 1995).

Although employment generation may be an appropriate growth criterion for public policy, for most SME owners/managers it is a consequence of growth rather than a prime objective of business development. Where owners seek to expand their business, this is more likely to be in terms of profitability, sales turnover or net assets than employment per se, since few have set up their businesses primarily to create employment for others. At the same time, a number of studies have demonstrated the close correlation that typically exists between employment growth and sales growth in small firms over a long period of time (Storey *et al.*, 1987; Smallbone *et al.*, 1995), although increased employment is less clearly related to a growth in profitability.

Although the policy context is one of the reasons why many academic studies define small business growth in terms of increased employment, another reason is related to data availability and reliability. Financial data (such as sales turnover or profits) are notoriously less reliable in small firms than in large firms and also less commonly available, particularly in countries (such as the UK), where the smallest firms are exempt from annual financial reporting requirements. This means that researchers typically have to rely on self-reported financial data which presents both confidentiality and reliability issues, particularly with respect to sales and profitability.

One of the issues that needs be recognised in any discussion of small business growth is that not all owners see growth as an important business objective. One of the reasons is that there are a variety of factors that contribute to individuals starting and running businesses, which means that lifestyle and non-business objectives may result in a lack of growth orientation (Curran, 1986a). Moreover, the importance of business growth in relation to other goals that individual entrepreneurs may aspire to can change over time. The growth orientation of an individual small firm can also vary at different stages of business development, as well as in response to changes in external factors. For example, in a newly established business, some growth is likely to be a necessity for survival, although a period of rapid growth may need to be followed by a period of consolidation, if expansion is not to outstrip the ability of the firm's resource base to support it. For these reasons, the extent to which the owner of a small firm is seeking to grow (i.e. its growth orientation) can vary over time as well as between firms.

6.4 Explaining growth in small firms

Although a great deal has been written about the growth of small enterprises, there is no single theory which can adequately explain growth patterns in small businesses nor, as Gibb and Davies (1990; 1991) have suggested, is there much likelihood of such a theory being developed in the future. The main reason for the absence of such a growth model is the variety of different factors which can affect the growth of small firms, as well as the way in which these factors interact with one another. At the same time, there is broad agreement about what the main influences on small business growth are, summarised in the framework developed by Storey (1994). As a result, a slightly modified version of the Storey framework is used in this chapter to consider the factors influencing small firm growth. This will incorporate aspects of the four main theoretical approaches to small business growth identified by Gibb and Davies (1990; 1991) as well as selected empirical evidence where appropriate. The aim is to highlight those aspects which appear to be characteristic of growing and high-growth enterprises.

Our framework includes the three influences on growth identified by Storey – namely characteristics of the entrepreneur, characteristics of the firm and management strategies – but also the influence of the external environment, which Storey does not consider separately. The external environment is separately identified here in order to emphasise its influence, since one of the size-related differences between large and small firms is connected with their differing abilities to control or shape external environmental influences. Hence it is our intention to make explicit that a prime influence on the growth performance of small firms is the way in which their managers address the enabling and constraining forces emanating from their operating context (see Figure 6.1). Each of the four components identified in Figure 6.1 will be discussed in turn.

6.4.1 Characteristics of the entrepreneur

Since one of the distinguishing characteristics of small firms compared with large firms is the close correspondence between ownership and management, the characteristics of

Figure 6.1 Growth in small firms

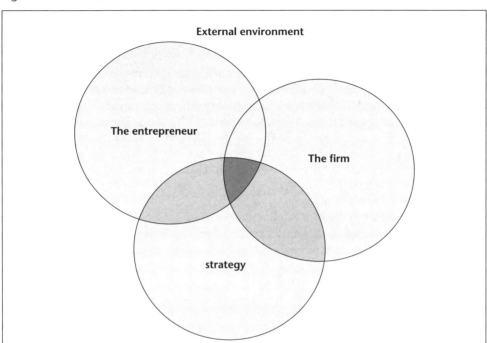

Source: Based on Fig. 5.1 in Storey (1994: 124)

individuals who start and run small firms can have a major impact on their growth orientation and performance, as well as on their organisational culture (see Chapter 8 for a more detailed discussion). In this context, one of the approaches to understanding small business growth identified by Gibb and Davies (1990; 1991), was the so-called 'personality-dominated approach', in which the entrepreneur is seen as the key to the development of the business. For example, the personal goals of an entrepreneur are likely to influence why a business was started in the first place, as well as the strength of the firm's growth orientation once it was established. *A priori*, one might expect that a business which was set up to exploit a clearly defined market opportunity for a product or service (and/or because the entrepreneur is strongly motivated to make money) would show a higher propensity to grow than a start-up where the main drivers are 'push' factors, such as unemployment (or the threat of it), dissatisfaction with present employment or personal lifestyle reasons. This distinction refers to what is described in the GEM study as 'opportunity driven' and 'necessity-driven' entrepreneurship.

In their seminal work on small business growth, Stanworth and Curran (1976) distinguished between three different identities of small business owners, thus emphasising the variety of goals that are apparent in relation to why individuals start and run businesses. The identities were defined as:

■ an *artisan identity*, where the owner's role centres on the intrinsic satisfaction associated with the personal autonomy that running one's own business can entail;

103

- the *classical entrepreneurial* identity, where the owner's role emphasises earnings and the generation of profits; and

- the *managerial identity*, where it is suggested that the owner's priorities are focused on looking for the recognition of others.

Empirical evidence suggests that whilst growth orientation, in the sense of growth being actively sought as a business objective, does not necessarily lead to actual growth performance, one of the characteristics which distinguishes high-growth firms from other firms is the commitment of the owner(s) to expand the business. For example, in a study of 306 established manufacturing SMEs (up to 100 employees) referred to earlier in the chapter, it was found that the propensity to achieve high growth from 1979–90 was significantly associated with the strength of their commitment to grow: 70% of high-growth firms referred to strong commitment to grow during this period compared with 32% of other firms (Smallbone *et al.*, 1995).

Some insight into the distinctive characteristics of entrepreneurs involved in high-growth performing small businesses can be obtained from research undertaken in relation to a recent government initiative in England, to provide targeted support for start-ups with high growth potential. When the programme was introduced in 1999, it was intended to be a highly selective intervention aimed at the top 0.5% of start-ups, in terms of their growth potential. The research involved surveying young businesses that had actually achieved high growth during the first years of trading, defined as reaching an annual sales of £150,000 by the end of the first year and/or £1m by the end of year three (Smallbone *et al.*, 2002). By surveying a sample of businesses drawn from Dun and Bradstreet, it was found that 75% of these businesses were started by people with previous management experience, which was typically gained in a medium or large enterprise. In fact, 29% had been developed out of a previous business, which typically reflected a situation where entrepreneurs had worked in a larger firm in a related activity, but had reached a stage where they felt they could start their own firm (sometimes with others) in a similar or related business activity, either in competition with their previous employer, or as a supplier, and/or by exploiting a new market niche which they had identified. The profile that emerges from this research appears distinctive in comparison with the small business population as a whole.

Researchers who have focused on the role of the entrepreneur's personality on the firm's growth performance (e.g. Chell *et al.*, 1991; Kets de Vries, 1977; Smith-Hunter, Kapp and Yonkers, 2003), have highlighted its influence on attitudes to risk (which can affect the willingness of a business owner to use external finance), the emphasis placed on personal autonomy (which can affect the willingness of the entrepreneur to collaborate with other firms, or even to use consultants), and managerial competencies, particularly in relation to strategic management skills. With regard to the role of the entrepreneur's personality, a Euro-wide study of fast-growing enterprises found the most successful firms to be characterised by 'strong leadership' and pursuing highly outward-looking, customer-focused strategies (EFER, 1996).

With regard to the role of the entrepreneur's personality in contributing to business growth, a recent longitudinal study by Moran (1999) found high-growth performance to be associated with personalities that showed a strong orientation towards being in charge of people, who were decisive and showing a preference for hands-on engagement with the world (i.e. learning by doing). At the same time, it should be noted that all of the firms featuring in Moran's study had been through some form of management development programme that may have contributed to building their personal capabilities and a more strategic outlook on their businesses.

Whilst such factors can undoubtedly affect the performance of the firm in a number of respects, some types of research in this paradigm are more controversial. These include attempts to use typologies based on profiling the personality traits of entrepreneurs to predict business success, which tend to ignore the capacity of people to learn and change over time, or indeed their motivation. For example, an owner's motivation for expanding a business may decline once they have achieved what they consider to be a satisfactory level of income from their enterprise and/or their personal/family circumstances change as they grow older. In this respect, Chell and Haworth (1992) have pointed to an association between the age and experience of the leader of the firm and the stage of development of the business reached.

Some of the manufacturing SMEs that achieved high growth in the longitudinal study referred to above (Smallbone *et al.*, 1995 op. cit.), were started by what Stanworth and Curran characterised as 'artisans' but who changed to a more entrepreneurial stance over time. This is an important point because it demonstrates how individuals can change their orientation to growth in response to changes in external circumstances, as well as their own learning experiences, and/or in their personal circumstances. An example includes a business started by a founder from a craft printing background but who ten years later was beginning to think like an entrepreneur seeking to manage the assets of the business to increase his returns, rather than simply to run a production plant. This had involved firms setting up a property management arm to the business which the owner ran himself, recruiting a production manager to run the core printing activity which the owner had become increasingly bored with.

Storey's emphasis on the role of the characteristics of entrepreneurs on business performance places less emphasis on personality *per se* and more on those personal characteristics which influence access to resources. These include educational background and qualifications, which can affect the management resource base of the business, as well as the entrepreneur's motivation for running it, because of the higher earnings expectations of more educated business owners. Whilst recognising that educational qualifications are no guarantee of business success, Storey suggests that their role is likely to vary between sectors and will be higher in technology and knowledge-based activities and lower in the more traditional and craft-based sectors (see Chapter 13). Other personal characteristics of entrepreneurs considered by Storey include:

- previous management and/or entrepreneurial experience (if any) prior to establishing the current enterprise
- family history
- functional skills and previous training
- previous knowledge and/or experience of the sector in which the business has been established.

However, whilst most of these factors can be shown to contribute to small business growth in one or more major empirical studies, none appears to make a dominant contribution. Indeed, the search for the identikit picture of the successful entrepreneur has not proved fruitful and, whilst undoubtedly relevant, the characteristics and previous experience of the founder appear to have only a modest effect on the success of the business in terms of its growth performance. Moreover, for many of us who have spent some years researching small business behaviour it is the unpredictability and variety of conditions associated with small business success that help to make the topic so fascinating.

One characteristic that has been attracting increasing attention in recent years has been portfolio ownership (Scott and Rosa, 1997) which refers to the fact that some entrepreneurs may be involved in a number of enterprises. Some studies have suggested that portfolio entrepreneurs are more likely to be associated with growth-orientated firms, since multiple ownership is itself a sign of a degree of entrepreneurial flair. It has also been pointed out that, whilst early studies of portfolio entrepreneurship tended to emphasise its role in reducing business risk, it has been increasingly recognised as an important growth strategy, particularly in sectors where economies of scale can be achieved at a low level (Carter, 1999).

6.4.2 Characteristics of the firm

Although organisational characteristics may reflect those of the entrepreneur, they are different in the sense that they are based on decisions made by the owner either at the time the business was started or at some time after. Storey's review of the relationship between organisational profile characteristics and the propensity of small firms to grow includes age and size as well as other variables. With respect to age, Storey reports that most UK and US research shows that younger firms grow more rapidly than older firms, reflected in the statement that 'most small firms grow only in the first few years and stabilise' (Burns, 1989). Whilst this may be statistically accurate as far as surviving businesses are concerned, it partly reflects the need for newly established firms to increase the scale of their operations if they are to accumulate sufficient resources to be able to withstand unforeseen external shocks. At the same time, other research has demonstrated that even some very mature firms can grow strongly, sometimes following a long period of stagnation (Smallbone and North, 1996). Indeed, growth in small firms (where it occurs) is rarely a continuous and sustained process, so that a firm's age will never be a completely reliable predictor of its growth prospects.

One of the approaches used to explain small business growth identified by Gibb and Davies (1990) was the so-called 'organisational' approach, which emphasises the development sequences of a firm as it passes through a series of stages at different points in its life-cycle. The original idea was that since every product or service faces a life-cycle, then so do businesses. There are a number of variants of the 'life-cycle' or 'stages of growth' models. Churchill and Lewis (1987) propounded a five-stage developmental model. This model considers each development stage of a firm in terms of enterprise factors and management factors, the nature, form and significance of which change over time as the firm develops.

Application of such a model (see the example in Figure 6.2) might, for instance, highlight the pivotal management roles and activities of the owner-manager at the start-up

Figure 6.2 An indicative 'stages' of growth/life-cycle model

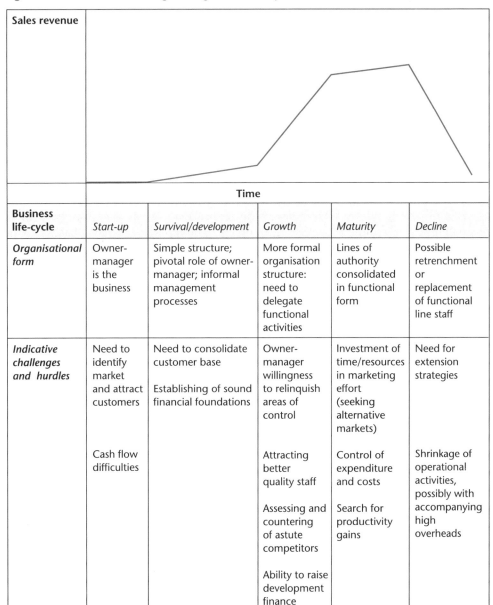

Business life-cycle	Start-up	Survival/development	Growth	Maturity	Decline
Organisational form	Owner-manager is the business	Simple structure; pivotal role of owner-manager; informal management processes	More formal organisation structure: need to delegate functional activities	Lines of authority consolidated in functional form	Possible retrenchment or replacement of functional line staff
Indicative challenges and hurdles	Need to identify market and attract customers	Need to consolidate customer base Establishing of sound financial foundations	Owner-manager willingness to relinquish areas of control	Investment of time/resources in marketing effort (seeking alternative markets)	Need for extension strategies
	Cash flow difficulties		Attracting better quality staff Assessing and countering of astute competitors Ability to raise development finance	Control of expenditure and costs Search for productivity gains	Shrinkage of operational activities, possibly with accompanying high overheads

and survival stages of the business, when simple organisation structure and informal management processes predominate. Significantly, the model focuses attention on the ways in which these enterprise and management factors will need to be adapted through the various development stages of the firm. Corresponding development hurdles that the small firm may face at identified development stages and the likely changing nature of impacting problems are also mapped onto some models.

Typical of such models is the highlighting of the inadequacy of informal management approaches as a small business strives to grow, with a subsequent need for the owner-manager to relinquish all-embracing control of management tasks and begin to formalise the organisation structure. As the business progresses toward a sustainable growth path, recruitment of quality staff may become a priority and formalisation of organisation structure necessary, including the increasing delegation of management responsibilities. Tighter control over day-to-day operations and finances may be required, as may the ability to identify and act upon development opportunities, together with a more formalised approach to planning and monitoring activities and assessment of competitor actions.

Although critical thresholds separating distinctive phases of the development of a small firm often exist, the formalised 'stages' models, such as those of Churchill and Lewis (1987) or Steinmetz (1969), have little application as tools to explain the growth of small firms for a number of reasons. In practice, boundaries between phases may be fuzzy rather than distinct and some small businesses commonly develop more rapidly in relation to certain functions or dimensions than others. As a result, it is often difficult to position firms empirically and thus apply the model in practice.

More fundamentally, such an approach implies that a firm's development path is determined, whereas in practice the number of stages that can be identified is variable. Moreover, in practice, the order of stages is not fixed, which means that some firms that may ultimately grow further may move back then forward rather than continuously forward in the sequence of stages. Overall, the value of such models is more to help diagnose organisational problems and bottlenecks that need to be addressed by the owner-manager if a firm is to grow further, rather than as an explanation of what actually occurs. Nevertheless, such models are only concerned with internal constraints and thresholds, divorcing the firm's development path from any inter-relationship with the firm's external environment (for an excellent critique of stage models of growth, see O'Farrell and Hitchens, 1988).

Empirical studies have shown that one of the most critical thresholds with respect to growth as far as organisational development is concerned relates to the willingness of the owner to delegate decisions (Storey, 1994; Lybaert, 1998). This can be illustrated with reference to an analysis of the distinctive characteristics and strategies of a group of high-growth SMEs over an 11-year period, referred to earlier in the chapter (Smallbone *et al.*, 1995). One of the most significant differences between high-growth firms and their low-growth or non-growth counterparts was their propensity to have made changes that were designed to create more time for the leaders to manage the firm strategically. Previous writers had suggested that 'creating time to manage is one of the key internal factors influencing the process of change in small firms' (Gibb and Dyson, 1982). The results from the long-term longitudinal research showed it to be a key discriminating feature between firms which were able to achieve high growth over 11 years and those that were simply able to survive. Whether this is a cause or effect of growth is less important in practical terms than recognising that the issue needs to be prioritised by entrepreneurs if sustained growth over a long period of time is to be achieved.

6.4.3 Management strategy

In considering the role of strategy as a factor influencing small firm growth, we refer to management actions taken by the owner once the business has started to trade that affect the development path of the firms. These actions may be planned and explicit but more typically are implicit and emergent in smaller companies (see Chapter 21). Storey's review of areas where management strategy may influence the growth of a small firm includes product development and innovation, market strategy, business planning, production technology, the financial base and external equity, management training and recruitment, workforce training and the use of external advice and assistance (Storey, 1994). As a result, strategies for mobilising resources are included and, by implication, management competence, since this underpins management actions and is central to the way in which finance, labour and other resources are mobilised.

Several key strategy factors which are evident in growing firms were identified by Storey, from his review of key empirical studies. First, a willingness to share equity with external individuals or organisations was frequently identified in small firms that actually achieved high rates of growth. A second factor relates to the ability of rapidly growing firms to identify market segments or niches where they can build customer bases founded on their distinct advantages and selling points (see Chapter 17). Moreover, exploitation of this type of non-price competitive advantage will often relate to the utilisation of relevant technologies and a willingness to introduce new products. Finally, an owner-manager's willingness to delegate and devolve decision making was found to be a crucial facilitator of growth in a number of studies which would also require an ability to attract, retain and enthuse managerial personnel who are capable of accepting this delegated authority.

One of the main approaches to understanding the growth process identified within the literature is characterised by Gibb and Davies (1990; 1991) as the 'business management' approach, which focuses on the importance of business skills and the role of functional management, planning, control and formal strategic orientations. This body of literature offers valuable guiding insights into how a growing business might achieve sustainable development, by making internal adjustments that are commensurate with identified opportunities in its external change environment. Thus, informative works on business strategy such as that of Johnson and Scholes (2004) emphasise the growing need for managers to sensitise themselves to what is an increasingly turbulent operating environment, offering management approaches and techniques to aid the manager in this respect. Certainly, the work of Johnson and Scholes offers support for Storey's propositions with respect to key strategy factors. However, much work within the 'business and management' field continues to be based upon assumptions that organisations utilise rational decision-making approaches to identifying, and acting upon, development opportunities within their external change environment. This rationality manifests itself in recommendations and prescriptions with regard to the essential roles of long-term planning and financial control for underpinning organisational growth. However, such prescription seems to overlook the ability of management tools of this nature to accommodate the nature, form and variety of change situations which impact on contemporary businesses. This particularly applies in the case of smaller firms, which have limited ability to shape or control external environmental influences (see Chapter 21).

Whilst management activities such as 'strategic planning' and 'control' may have a part to play in sustaining the growth of some small businesses, the use of formal planning is rare in small firms, being more characteristic of larger businesses. This is partly because of the higher propensity of large firms to employ managers that are professionally trained, although it also reflects a greater ability to reduce some of the uncertainties in the external environment that is typical in the case of small firms. It appears, therefore, that whilst management approaches contained in the wider business literature have some potential for aiding our understanding of organisational growth, there is a need to be selective in applying this knowledge to the small business context, where owners and managers typically face an uncertain external environment with a limited resource base.

6.4.4 External environmental influences

Arguably, it is the impact of external influences and the unpredictable manner in which they emerge, or change, which provide the greatest impact on the nature and pace of small business growth (Wyer, Mason and Theodorakopoulos, 2000). Small businesses can face major problems in identifying and dealing with environmental change because of a lack of understanding, management expertise and time. In this context, Cohn and Lindberg (1974) emphasise that 'because small firms generally engage in a narrower range of activities, use a narrower range of materials, employ fewer skills and serve single markets, it is probably even more important for them to anticipate changes in the factors impinging on their welfare than it is for large firms. A great change in one factor is likely to have more effect on a small company [than a large one]'. For example, in relation to finance, Welsh and White (1984) underline how 'external forces tend to have more impact on small businesses than on large businesses. Changes in government regulations, tax laws and labour and interest rates usually affect a greater percentage of expenses than they do for large organisations'.

Certainly, two of the broad categories of approaches to explaining growth in small firms, identified by Gibb and Davies (1990; 1991), address the importance of the impact of the external environment upon organisations: first, the so-called 'business management' approaches discussed above; and second, the so-called 'sectoral and broader market led approaches'. For Gibb and Davies (1991), these sectoral studies concentrate on the identification of external constraints and opportunities facing small firms. For example, within the context of small high-tech businesses, the need to keep abreast of technological change and 'the importance of building marketing into quality, design and development from the early stages' are key sectoral conditions affecting potential business success. In other sectors, the position and role of large firms in the external operating environment can exert considerable influence over the ability of small firms to grow, because of supply chain based relationships, which in some cases can result in highly dependent relationships between small firms and their dominant large-firm customers. For example, the strategies of large firms with regard to sub-contracting, 'make or buy' decisions and strategic partnerships can be key influences on the growth potential of individual small firms. Integral to the concept of partnership is the potential for the small firm to access know-how and resources from large firms, in relation to R&D, technology and management skills. While Gibb and Davies emphasise that the existing literature does not provide clear guidelines in the form of predictive theory, the existing knowledge base provides some insight that may be used as a guiding frame of reference with regards to small firm growth processes.

In relation to external environmental influences, sectoral variations on the growth rates of small firms are to be expected because of differences in market trends and competitive conditions between different activities, which may themselves vary over time. However, since market conditions vary between individual product markets, the amount of sectoral variation in growth performance, which is identified in practice, tends to vary according to the level of sectoral disaggregation. This is because the narrower the sectoral definition that is used, the less variety that exists within sectoral categories, which means there is less of a tendency for buoyant conditions in one product market to be offset by weak trends in another, or vice versa.

A firm's location is another characteristic that can affect its growth prospects, since it reflects spatial variations in local environmental conditions. On the demand side, variations in the size, scope and buoyancy in local markets might be expected to affect a firm's opportunities to grow. On the supply side, variations in the cost and availability of some factors of production (such as labour and premises) and resources (such as access to information and business services) may also be an influence. At the same time, the adaptability of SMEs to local external conditions should not be underestimated (Smallbone et al., 1999a). Whilst the employment growth of small firms may vary considerably between different types of location (Keeble et al., 1992; Hoogstra and Van Dijk, 2004) because of differences in labour market conditions, the growth performance of small firms measured in terms of sales growth tends to show much less variation (Smallbone et al., 1993). This is because of differences in the types of strategy used by SME owners or managers to develop their businesses in different locations, which is an indication of the adaptability of successful SMEs to local conditions (North and Smallbone, 1996).

6.5 Barriers and growth constraints – the external operating context

In this section, we consider the main external barriers that may constrain small business development and which have to be circumvented, or managed, if effective growth is to be sustained.

6.5.1 A rapidly changing environment

If contemporary business organisations are to survive and prosper, their managers must learn to cope with unprecedented levels of change. The origins of such change are multi-sourced, deriving from factors such as increasing globalisation associated with the emergence of new sources of production; developments in information and communications technology; and the emergence of the better educated and more discerning consumers in mature market economies. In combination, such factors have contributed to a more competitive and rapidly changing environment facing business managers.

111

For the small business, its weakness in being able to control and relate to the environment is a key distinguishing characteristic. Moreover, when one conceptualises 'change' at a more specific level, the complexity of the management task in small firms becomes highly apparent. Change situations may be conceptualised in terms of closed-, contained- and open-ended change (Stacey, 1990). Faced with closed change, a firm can predict events and actions with regard to timing and consequences, such as if a major customer increases their order. In such circumstances, the form and timing of its consequences are knowable and allow for prediction in terms of the required resources and cash flows. Contained change relates to events occurring that involve repetition of past events, such as where a seasonal pattern of sales allows for a degree of predictability. In the case of both closed- and contained-change situations, the small business manager can undertake rational short-interval planning activity in order to underpin organisational control.

However, as Stacey and others have emphasised, much of the change that faces contemporary business organisations is unknowable and unpredictable in terms of its timing and its consequences. In other words, such change is open-ended, and it is often unclear what is changing or why it is changing, making it virtually impossible to predict the consequences for the operating environment of individual businesses. For example, the unanticipated emergence of cost reductions and quality improving technology from overseas competitors can have an indeterminate impact on a small business. Under such operating conditions, sustainable business development can only be effected by small business management processes that can facilitate the identification and understanding of open-ended change situations as a basis for determining appropriate internal adjustment activity within the small firm.

6.5.2 Industry structure, competition and market limitations

Porter (1980) emphasises that the key aspect of a firm's environment is the industry or industries in which it competes. For Porter, the competitive rules of the game and strategies potentially available to a firm are substantially influenced by industry structure (see Chapter 21). He sees the intensity of competition in an industry transcending the behaviour of current competitors, with its roots in the industry's underlying economic structure. For him, it is the collective strength of five basic competitive forces which determine the profit potential in an industry. These forces, which drive industry competition, are: the threat of new entrants; bargaining power of suppliers; bargaining power of buyers; the threat of substitute products or services; and the intensity of rivalry among existing firms.

In order to effect sustainable development within a given industry, a small firm would need to build up an understanding of the underlying structural features that underpin the basic competitive forces described above. This is because it is knowledge of the underlying sources of these competitive forces that allows a firm to determine its critical strengths and areas of weakness. For example, the threat of new entrants to an industry (or, put another way, the difficulty of gaining access to an industry) can be understood with reference to the underlying sources of barriers to entry. These might include the existence of economies of scale within the industry; established firms having achieved product differentiation; high-level capital requirements; the presence of switching costs; the need for new entrants to secure access to distribution channels; and the possession by established firms of cost advantages independent of scale (such as product know-how or design characteristics retained through patents or secrecy; access to raw materials; or favourable locations).

For the smaller business, one keystone to growth may be a recognition that 'markets tend to become more heterogeneous over time, evolving into progressively finer segments as buyer tastes and technological opportunities change'. Such 'heterogeneity of the market permits market segmentation and the use of product differentiation to create "specialist" or "niche" strategies by firms' (McGee, 1989). At the same time, significant potential barriers often exist, which may prevent the small firm from effecting such development. These barriers include the need to identify and respond to such market segments or niches, requiring both the determination of the form of the 'distinctiveness', which will provide the differentiation of product to match the customer needs; and the ability to produce and sustain that distinctiveness. In this context, it has been suggested that those firms achieving growth are those that can identify the key criteria upon which to compete in certain segments (including design, price, quality, delivery) and are then able to develop a competitive advantage around these criteria (O'Farrell and Hitchens (1988)). The barriers also include the difficulty of coping with direct competitors who may ultimately be attracted by the returns associated with the emerging segment or niche, and the broader forces of competition, as discussed above.

Moreover, even where a small business has appropriately identified underlying industry and market structure characteristics in a manner which continues to facilitate ongoing sustainable development, the unfolding of unknowable open-ended change situations can confound that development without warning. For example, the effect of 9/11 on the willingness of many US citizens to travel abroad had sudden and significant effects on firms engaged in tourism in London and other major tourist centres.

6.6 Barriers and growth constraints – the internal operating context

This section reviews some of the major internal constraints which affect growth in the small firm. These relate to the influence of the owner-manager and the relative small scale of the enterprise.

6.6.1 Owner-manager and size-related constraints

For many small-medium size enterprises, 'size-related factors affect their ability to identify and respond to developmental opportunities in their external environment' (Wyer and Smallbone, 1999). This emphasises how owner-manager and size-related characteristics help to shape the enabling and constraining forces that affect the ability of smaller firms to identify, cope with and positively respond to external environmental changes. Size-related characteristics thus contribute substantially to shaping strategic activity and underlying management actions. Relevant owner-manager and size-related characteristics include the following.

Organisational culture

In an owner-managed business, the 'organisational culture' typically reflects the personality traits and aspirations of the owner-manager which, in turn, shapes the enabling and constraining forces affecting the firm. The pervading sets of norms and values, ways of doing things and the freedoms afforded to different individuals are often reflected in informal and idiosyncratic structures, systems and processes, which themselves often reflect the personality traits of the main owner (see Chapter 8). Whilst over time a firm's historical development path and its markets and its technologies will all affect this culture, the owner-manager is likely to have a predominant influence, particularly in the early stages of a business. In this context, a key potential constraint on future development can be the extent to which the small business culture/structure remains embedded in the owner-manager. This is a key management issue which is addressed later.

Finance

A well-documented constraint on small business growth is that of an inadequate financial resource base (see Chapter 18), which can be a particular constraint on growing firms, where an ongoing need for development funds creates a strong demand for finance. On the one hand, financial constraints can result from a lack of the required levels of collateral – perhaps because the firm's assets are already being used to secure existing debt – combined with the absence of a proven track record in the case of new and young firms, which can affect their ability to raise external finance. It also reflects the firm's financial management skills, which can affect its ability to generate investment funds internally. Whilst Storey (1994 op. cit.) has identified a willingness to share equity as a factor influencing the growth potential of a small firm, the operation of the formal venture capital markets makes it difficult for firms to raise sums of less than approximately £250,000 from this source. The potential importance of equity financing to high-growth small firms is emphasised by the fact that for risky projects and those requiring long-term funding, equity capital is often the only possible source (Ruda, 1999). Whilst informal risk capitalists (or business angels) are a possible source of such finance, as well as publicly funded venture capital funds that, in some cases, may be specifically targeting seed and early stage financing, entrepreneurs must have the knowledge and ability to identify a feasible development project and produce a supporting business plan to realise finance from these sources. As it is, an ignorance of formal and informal sources of risk capital may itself be a constraint on the growth of many potentially successful small businesses.

Attracting and retaining quality people

Many small businesses face a marginal labour market whereby they cannot offer the same wage and salary levels or career path opportunities as large companies. This can affect their ability to attract the most able, committed and/or experienced workers, which can in turn impact on the consistency of product or service quality. The latter is essential in building image and a satisfied customer base, and can be difficult to realise if there are staffing problems (see Chapter 20). The solution must be to encourage more owners to adopt a greater staff-focused approach to human resource management, recognising that potentially the workforce can be one of the firm's most important assets.

Marketing problems

Developing effective marketing and distribution systems can represent a particular challenge for small businesses, especially for those firms attempting to grow through market development activities into overseas markets (see Chapter 24). For example, Smallbone *et al.* (1999) found that, within a recent seven-country study of internationalisation and SME development, in all countries SMEs faced difficulties in obtaining information about foreign markets, which was, in part at least, due to their tendency to rely on informal marketing methods. It was felt that whilst reliance upon informal methods is often adequate in some domestic markets, such methods may be inadequate abroad. Carson (1991) suggests that our understanding of small business marketing will derive from greater consideration of factors such as the character and personality of the owner-manager and the inherent flexibilities and informalities of small business management. Implicit in this view is the possibility that (any small business attempt to draw upon the essentially large-company-oriented formal marketing management literature for guidance, with its emphasis on more formalised marketing methods, could, in some instances, act as a constraint on the firm's development rather than a facilitator.)

We conclude this sub-section by emphasising that the distinctive characteristics of small businesses, described previously, may threaten their potential flexibility and responsiveness, which small firms can potentially exploit in competing with larger firms. If such problems are not circumvented or effectively managed, they are likely to prove a major constraint on the ability of the small business to grow.

6.6.2 Inadequacy of existing assets for underpinning growth

Many of the above size-related constraints can exert pressure on management to attempt to 'squeeze more' out of existing assets in order to facilitate the growth path to which they are committing themselves. For example, 'rapidly growing companies are especially vulnerable to cash difficulties, because the need for working capital increases in a fairly constant ratio to turnover. As a result, there is likely to be an increasing demand for finding working capital as turnover increases' (Winckles, 1986). This can lead to a phenomenon known as over-trading, which can result from failure to plan carefully the underlying financial requirements of a development project, or from an attempt to expand too rapidly. For instance, taking on additional customer orders on the assumption that existing resources can cope (when in practice they are insufficient) can lead to cash flow problems. This in turn may contribute to relations with the firm's workforce and suppliers being soured, as the firm finds itself unable to pay staff wages and/or suppliers.

Growth can also lead to pressure on the firm's human resource base, which is exacerbated if management is either unwilling or unable to recruit externally. Such firms must focus on existing human resources within the firm, placing an emphasis on getting the best out of those workers. Within this context, small businesses have been found to be constrained in several areas. For example, in order to motivate and enthuse management and supervisory level staff, and to fully utilise their expertise and capabilities, it may be necessary to give staff more responsibility, involving them more substantially in management decision-making processes. However, the management style of many owner-managers has tended to be autocratic and underpinned by a reluctance to delegate decision making (Kets de Vries, 1977). A further issue concerns confidence and capability levels of staff (including the owner-manager) to undertake new tasks, which they will inevitably be asked to complete as the firm proceeds along its growth path. This in turn raises the issue of the need for upgrading management skills, although a number of constraining forces have been found to restrict the uptake of management training within the small firm. These include an owner-manager reluctance to utilise outside advice; time constraints; willingness to pay the market price; and the inappropriateness of much of the training provided to the needs of a heterogeneous small business sector. One of the biggest challenges for those providing training is the proposition that the most effective learning mode for small firms may be through experience rather than formal external training (Gibb, 1997).

The pace of growth can also exert pressure on physical resources. For example, a reluctance to invest in additional or new machinery may be the result of a lack of confidence; a lack of ability to assess new available technologies; or it may reflect concern with regard to the integration of new systems and processes into existing activities. In this regard, Ekanem and Smallbone (2004) have demonstrated the key role of experiential learning in relation to investment decision making in small manufacturing firms rather than using appraisal methods based on formalised learning. A further developmental difficulty revolves around premises. Since the pace of growth may result in a small business outgrowing its existing facilities, both availability and cost of alternative premises can result in a firm attempting to utilise existing premises to the limit, which may have severe repercussions in terms of efficiency of operation and ability to meet customer demands with regard to quality and delivery. Moreover, a fear that increased overheads associated with any expansion may not be adequately covered because of the firm's inability to achieve requisite rates of growth in sales can also result in a reluctance to take up new premises (Wyer and Smallbone, 1999).

6.6.3 Difficulties associated with team building and team management

In order to establish a newly developing firm as an effective organisation capable of sustaining itself in the market-place, the owner manager has to ensure that all tasks are appropriately allocated on an individual and/or small group basis. At an early stage in a firm's development, those 'sub-units' of individuals organised to work together may appear to be working as a 'team', although in practice may be no more than a 'group', lacking a collective rationale, in which it is clearly understood that individual performance contributes directly to the overall good (Godfrey, 1990; Ensley and Pearce, 2001; Ucbasaran et al., 2003). Arguably, though, for a small organisation to sustain ongoing development, there is a need for its management to recognise that the concept of a 'team' is preferable to simply that of a 'group', However, whilst recognising that the transition from 'group' to 'team' working is a pre-condition for effecting sustainable small business development, the problems associated with team building and team management can prove a major constraint on organisational development in practice (see Chapter 20).

6.7 Managing growth

Since one of the major challenges facing the contemporary small business is that of coping with unknowable, unpredictable open-ended change, a key issue relates to how small firms attempt to strategically control their operations. This section first considers the potential and limitations of formal, rational long-term planning modes of management to underpin small-firm development. Empirical insight is then utilised to suggest the potential utility of an organisational learning perspective to effecting small-business growth.

6.7.1 The uses and limitations of rational long-term planning modes of management

Considerable support continues to be afforded to the view that a rational, systematic step approach to managing the dynamic, volatile and fast-changing operating environment in which the modern-day small business finds itself is the most effective way to underpin sustainable long-term development. Brown and McDonald (1994) emphasise how it is critical 'to recognise that a series of systematic steps can be useful in formulating strategies when the stakes are high and the resource commitment is significant to the firm. It reduces the risk of leaving out key issues, and it highlights the assumptions on which strategies are based and resources are committed'. McDonald (1980) underlines that business problems are in fact less amenable to highly structured analytical methods to be found in the sciences, but that it is the very complexity of business problems which lends itself to some kind of structured procedure to help identify problems.

A structured approach to problem solving underpins the rational analytical planning models of management, which typically involves the following:

■ awareness of the problem

■ exploration of the problem

■ deciding what to do

■ taking action to implement the decision

■ examination and feedback of results (Luffman *et al.*, 1991).

Within a strategic planning context, the approach assumes that a small business can approach the strategic control of its fast-changing operating environment through undertaking a series of rational, systematic steps. This process is depicted in Figure 6.3.

The propounded strength of this model lies in its processual form. Strategic planning encourages a careful and systematic reading of shifts in technology, competitor position and customer tastes, leading to the formulation of actions in response. Moreover, it has been suggested that strategic planning helps the small business concentrate on its competitive nature by encouraging an external focus on key environmental factors to determine where the firm fits, as well as internally focusing on the firm's strengths and weaknesses. The overall analytical and evaluatory process should then lead to the setting of a formal direction for the business, helping to determine where the business is going (Fry and Stoner, 1995).

117

Figure 6.3 **Indicative steps in strategic analysis**

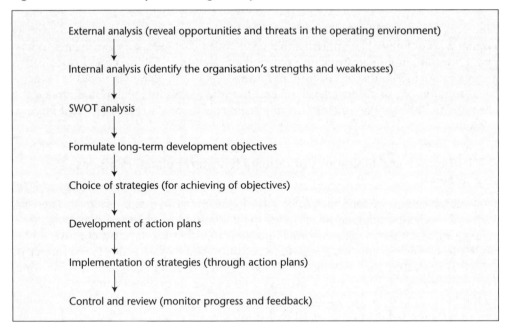

External analysis (reveal opportunities and threats in the operating environment)

↓

Internal analysis (identify the organisation's strengths and weaknesses)

↓

SWOT analysis

↓

Formulate long-term development objectives

↓

Choice of strategies (for achieving of objectives)

↓

Development of action plans

↓

Implementation of strategies (through action plans)

↓

Control and review (monitor progress and feedback)

However, the real utility of rational planning models in small organisations is debatable (Wyer *et al.*, 2000). First, the utility of rational analytical planning should be considered within the context of the assumptions upon which the approach is based, which include the quality of information and an ability to extrapolate future events from past experiences. Its value is also affected by the fact that resource constraints limit the ability of most small firms to formally scan their external environment. Much of the change that contemporary small businesses must be able to cope with is open-ended change, which is unknowable and unpredictable rather than closed or contained change. In addition, coping must be undertaken in the context of more limited internal resources than are available to larger firms. As a consequence, it is questionable whether formal, rational long-term planning methods of management are compatible with the challenges facing small business managers, and the idiosyncrasies and informalities of small-firm management processes, or whether such modes of management are adequate for dealing with open-ended change situations (Stacey, 1990).

Whilst some studies do suggest positive correlation between formal planning activity and growth (Schwenk and Shrader, 1993) and some association is suggested between strategic planning intensity and success in achieving primary business objectives (Peel and Bridge, 1998), there is still little evidence of causal relationship between planning and long-term business performance. Moreover, as Shane (2003) points out, similar correlation has been found in studies that have examined the founder's tendency to plan, rather than the creation of business plans per se (Miner *et al.*, 1989; 1994), thereby emphasising the role of planning as a process.

6.7.2 An organisational learning perspective

Drawing upon Personal Construct Theory (Kelly, 1955) and contemporary learning theory (Hawkins, 1994), Wyer and Boocock (1996) have offered insight into the ways in which small business owner-managers learn and have provided foundations for considering how small firms cope with open-ended change. The thrust of their work is founded on Kelly's proposition that all individuals utilise a personal construct system (derived from inherent personal characteristics and accumulated experience) which is used as a frame of reference to interpret the world. In brief, we all have personal constructs that act as frames of reference to help us view the world which confronts us and deal with new situations which arise.

If change situations impact on small firm owner-managers they will use their existing personal constructs to cope with the change. On many occasions, minor adjustments to the construct may allow the owner-manager to deal with the change, simply because a *similar situation* has been dealt with in the past. This can be characterised as *simple* learning (Stacey, 1996) which takes place when the owner-manager her confirmed the validity of their current constructs by using them to make sense of a new situation. However, sometimes change situations arise for which existing constructs are inadequate. This requires them to be extended through a process that entails the questioning of the underlying assumptions upon which the existing constructs are based. This is a more *complex* learning process which is why simple learning is more common (Stacey, 1996).

Such a conceptualisation of how individuals cope with change has far-reaching implications for the growth-oriented small business. If owners are confronted by unknowable, unfolding change forces, success in coping with such a challenge in a manner that can lead to sustainable business development will depend to a considerable extent on their ability and willingness to 'extend' personal construct systems; that is, to change their mindset or frames of reference and to engage in complex learning. This may include an ability and willingness to anchor the understanding and learning of other key members of the organisation to enhance collective organisational understanding (Wyer and Mason, 1998). This means that the role of dialogue, both between internal organisational members and with key external informants on the boundaries of the small firm's operating environment, is a crucial learning activity.

Foundation studies that have drawn on an organisational learning perspective to investigate strategic development processes in small firms based on in-depth case studies have revealed a number of insights into strategic management processes (Wyer, Mason and Theodorakopoulos, 2000; Wyer and Mason, 1998a). They confirm that whilst few small firms have written short- or long-term plans, many owner-managers demonstrate strategic awareness (Gibb and Scott, 1985) in the sense of having a mental target of the preferred development path for the business. The study also demonstrated the role of informal networking with key external actors and informants in contributing to emergent strategy, which was typically developed in a trial and error way (see Chapter 16). Significantly, however, some of the most successful firms in the study were able to loop back the results of what they had learned to make adjustments to their strategic or operational activities. In other words, successful SMEs in the study were led by owner-managers who appeared to have learned how to learn.

6.7.3 Managing finance to facilitate expansion

In order to facilitate sustainable growth it is necessary for the small firm's management to progressively enhance its financial management capabilities (see Chapter 18). In the early stages of development, when activity and sales levels are relatively low, control can be maintained through the use of relatively informal systems. However, as the business grows, it is necessary to enhance finance skills and formalise the approach to financial management, but also to recognise the interdependencies between finance and other areas of functional activity within the firm. For example, the projection of financial requirements to underpin a period of expansion must derive to a considerable extent from the forecasting of future sales and the determination of income and costs associated with that sales expansion. This requires a marketing capability to provide an understanding of the target customer base and of change forces to which that customer base is, or may become, sensitive, in order to provide such estimates. In other words, effective financial management depends to some extent on other functional management capabilities.

With regard to the financing of growth, two crucial areas are the management of fixed and working capital. Expansion will require close attention to fixed capital needs in terms of the firm's ability to acquire requisite premises, plant and/or equipment. In this context, the firm's management needs to acquaint itself with the various methods of raising long-, medium- and short-term finance and to develop understanding of what would be an appropriate mix of these categories of finance to effectively underpin development. Integral to this is consideration of the wider variety of sources of such finance, including the ability to recognise innovative sources of finance (such as 'business angels' discussed above and, in more depth, in Chapter 19) and how innovative 'finance packages' can be used to leverage further funds from elsewhere (Krantz, 1999). A crucial ability in this regard relates to the need to consider the appropriate balance of external and internal funds. For example, the balance of debt (long- and medium-term external funding) to equity (the owner's own internal funding) is a crucial issue. The ratio of this funding (known as the gearing ratio) can be critical in terms of facilitating or constraining small firm growth. With a high gearing ratio (where the firm is relying on external interest-bearing borrowings), in times of slow sales and high interest rates a firm may find its potential for future growth severely constrained because of the financial drain imposed upon it by having to meet high interest costs on borrowings.

The small business will also have to make sufficient provision for working capital in order to facilitate growth. Working capital relates to the ongoing provision of stocks of appropriate levels of raw materials and component parts, the financing of debtors and the access to cash to meet day-to-day expenditures and running costs. It thus incorporates the firm's current assets and current liabilities. The complexity of the management tasks underpinning the determination of the forms and levels of working capital to facilitate growth include: the need to forecast sales, from which estimates of the costs likely to be incurred and anticipated income can be made; plans for future growth, including time scales for each step and estimation of all inherent costs; consideration of possible developmental problems which may result in delay (hold-ups and inefficiencies); and examination of the current and likely costs of borrowing and consideration of repayment periods (Bennett, 1989).

Inevitably, over time, growth will require additional fixed and working capital and the ability to ensure that adequate and appropriate funding underpins that growth clearly points to the need for an ongoing enhancement of financial capabilities. For example, the management of working capital will require close control of debtors to ensure a balance between, for example, credit being used as a 'promotional' and competitive tool, while controlling debtor periods to avoid undue financial pressures on the business. Stock levels must be managed to ensure a free-flowing production activity and an ability to serve customers in a timely manner, though not at a level that results in stocks of raw materials or component parts idling on the shelves and thus tying up cash. With regard to creditors, there is a need to negotiate credit periods which contribute effectively to a positive cash flow, while at the same time recognising that creditors should not be exploited in a manner that can sour the relationship and lead to a deterioration in the quality or timing of supplies, or which precludes the uptake of discounts for early settlement.

However, a crucial issue is that the nature of financial management skills developed by the growing small business must reflect and accommodate the nature and form of the growth and change patterns of the business. For example, Bennett's proposition that decisions on working capital needs should be based on a consideration of anticipated activity levels, requiring the forecasting of sales and costs, will be a more straightforward task if the small business is operating in a relatively stable external environment, in which it has been able to track a pre-determined development path. However, if a small firm is facing open-ended unknowable change, in which it may have to seek development opportunities through trial and error, the relationship between financial management skills, marketing capabilities and strategic awareness are closely inter-related.

6.7.4 Developing the marketing function

Analysis of a small business in its early stages of development is unlikely to reveal a marketing approach or activity which even vaguely reflects formal marketing management as represented by the mainstream marketing literature (see Chapter 17). Instead, it is an understanding and application of the concept of marketing that is important, namely 'a matching between a company's capabilities and the wants of customers in order to achieve the goals of the firm' (McDonald, 1984). Whilst this may appear to be an obvious and fundamental concept, which must underpin the sustained development of any successful small business, there is much evidence of small firms going out of business because of a failure to fully understand the needs of its targeted customers and of firms founded on the mistaken premise that they have the 'company capability' to serve the needs of an identified group of customers (Smallbone, 1990). In the early stages of small business development the nature and form of marketing are often embedded in the owner-manager. In many instances it is the owner-manager's close interface and relationship with his customers that allows for the 'matching process' between the small firm capability and the wants of customers to be effectively achieved.

Whilst an informal 'market orientation' may be a keystone for sustainable growth and development of the small firm, the effective facilitation of sustainable growth may require an increasing formalisation of the firm's marketing activity. For McDonald, it is not essential for a firm 'to have a formalised marketing department for the analysis, planning and control of the matching process'. However, with growth in a firm's product range and customer types, the management of marketing may need to be brought under one central control function. Growth brings with it the need to coordinate all of those functional activities within the firm, which participate in the matching process. The crucial issue is not whether a department, an individual or group of individuals is responsible for a firm's marketing, but the extent to which marketing is embedded within the organisation. This means that key individuals within the firm have a clear understanding that the profit which the company strives to earn is a return founded on depth of understanding of the needs of the firm's target customer groups and their ability to organise the firm's resources in their totality so as to satisfy those needs. Within the context of the growing small business, a key management art appears to relate to the ability to extend the marketing concept in the business as it develops.

6.7.5 Broadening the customer base while coping with existing customers

A major challenge facing the growth-oriented small business is to sustain the level of service provision to an existing clientele, which may itself be increasing demands on the firm, both quantitatively and qualitatively, while at the same time seeking to broaden its customer base. However, as we have already seen, the actual process of identifying opportunities which can facilitate a widening of customer base is itself a difficult one. It is likely to exert considerable strain upon the small firm's ability to continue to serve the increasing demands of its existing customer base. The process of effecting internal adjustments to exploit new opportunities can place such stress on the operations of the small firm that its ability to service the needs of existing customers is adversely affected. The broadening of the firm's product-market definition will require an expansion of physical, financial and human resources at a time when the existing customer base may be demanding ongoing management attention and additional resource allocations. Within a highly competitive environment, the small firm will find itself having to continuously seek efficiency improvements, both within the business and in its interface with service providers such as suppliers and distributors, in order to maintain a competitive edge in its existing markets. This, together with the need to improve existing products, will be a prerequisite to protecting existing customer bases and market shares, so as to cement current foundations, both to maintain current levels of activity and to facilitate any future expansion. Clearly, any move to broaden the existing product-market definition within the small business must be accompanied by a careful evaluation of the adequacy of existing resources and abilities, as a basis for sustainable development of the firm in its totality (that is, an ability to expand into new areas of activity while effectively maintaining and enhancing those existing areas with ongoing developmental potential). Such evaluation should also incorporate the potential for complementing existing resources and abilities in a manner that can facilitate the identified expansion opportunities.

6.7.6 Deciding when to introduce new managers and modify organisational structure

A key developmental issue is to what extent a small business, which is striving for growth, can continue to rely upon an organisational framework in which the owner-manager is the pivotal centre of all activity, based on an informal structure for the direction and fulfilment of operational activities. The answer is likely to be contingent upon the individual business and its personnel, the nature of the firm's development path and of the environment and markets it is operating in.

Handy (1976) explains how 'each organisation, each part of an organisation has a culture, and a structure and systems appropriate to that culture'. Thus, in a large company we may find several sub-cultures and different forms of structure throughout the organisation. However, in small businesses it is common to find culture in a form which Handy terms a *power* culture. Its structure is depicted by a *web*: that is, 'the culture depends on a central power source, with rays of power and influence spreading from that central figure. They are connected by functional or specialist strings but the power rings are the centre of activity'. The organisation with its few rules and procedures tends to work on precedent with staff often anticipating the wishes and decisions of the owner-manager, the central power source. The owner-manager often exercises control by selection of key individuals for particular activities, or through 'occasional summonses to the centre'.

As the small business grows this culture/structure is likely to prove inadequate to facilitate a rapid pace of development. Indeed, as reported earlier in the chapter, firms that are successful in achieving high growth over an extended period are characterised by an ability to modify the structure to accommodate an evolving role for the leader of the firm. A typical evolving response by the owner-manager might be to gradually formalise structure in terms of the allocation of formal responsibilities and the development of linking mechanisms between the newly emerging roles. The result is a formal *hierarchy* type of structure and an underpinning *role* type culture (see the pioneering work in this area by Taylor (1947) and Fayol (1949)). However, for a small business to evolve into a formal hierarchical structure in its pure form would be to overlook the inherent weaknesses of such a structure. The classical organisational model views a business in terms of a network of inter-linking job descriptions rather than a network of human relationships, treating the organisation as a closed system (the inputs of the business are viewed as easily controlled), when in reality any business is faced with the complexities of a dynamic external environment, that is, it is an open system (Lawrence and Lee, 1989). Thus, the timing and form of adjustment to organisational structure in a small firm context is a complex issue, with a danger that adjustment towards a formal hierarchy, with its rigidity and inward focusing tendency, may reduce the ability of the firm to relate and adapt to its fast-changing environment.

6.8 Chapter summary

Growth-oriented small businesses make a major contribution to economic development and employment generation within local communities and are a crucial engine for the development of national economies. For this reason they attract a great deal of attention, not least from policy makers and support providers hoping to encourage and influence their ongoing growth. However, the existing knowledge base, about how successful growth businesses effectively sustain development, is limited, although there have been a growing number of empirical studies. Commencing from the premise that there is no single theory which can adequately explain small-firm growth, this chapter first sought to draw upon major research studies to highlight aspects which appear to be characteristic of high-growth enterprises. Crucial in many small firms is the central and pivotal role of the owner-manager, though many research studies have had limited success in their attempts to identify key personality traits and characteristics which can be said to typify owner-managers of growth-oriented firms. Nevertheless, the combination of ownership and management, sometimes in a single individual, is a recurrent feature distinguishing small firms from large companies. As a result, the characteristics and capabilities of individuals operating small firms impact substantially on the form of organisation culture of particular small firms and their orientation towards, and success in achieving, sustained growth.

Many studies have focused on the characteristics and development issues of the small firm itself. One such approach is the life-cycle or stages model approach which, whilst a useful vehicle for aiding the diagnosis of organisational problems and difficulties that an owner-manager may have to circumvent if growth is to be achieved, is of less value when seeking to explain growth. Similarly, the body of 'business management' literature provides guiding insight to enhance understanding of ways in which organisations may sustain growth through adoption of development choices regarding potential adjustment to their market, product and/or process activities. But much of such insight appears overly rational and systematic when compared with the reality of small business management. In addition, it may be inappropriate for coping with the unpredictable contemporary change environment with which the modern-day small-business manager must struggle. Indeed, an emphasis throughout this chapter is that a prime determinant of growth is the way in which the growth-oriented small business must successfully address the enabling and constraining nature of its external operating context.

It appears, therefore, that the literature provides foundation insight and guiding frames of reference for enhancing understanding of key issues underpinning small-firm growth, without providing an integrated theory of growth. Moreover, much of those areas of literature that are 'business management' based seem to be substantially large-company-oriented, failing to fully address the idiosyncracies and problems impacting on smaller firms. As a result, this chapter has made a selective utilisation of relevant literature, which has facilitated a consideration of major barriers that may constrain small-business development, and which must be circumvented or managed if effective growth is to be sustained. Commencing with the external operating context, emphasis is placed on the predominance of totally unpredictable open-ended change and how this must be identified and understood if the small firm is to grow effectively. With regard to the competitive environment, the small business needs to be sensitive to underlying industry and market structure characteristics if it is to understand the broad sources of competition.

In terms of the internal operating context of the small firm, it is suggested that small businesses can be viewed as a 'potential unique problem-type' facing problems and barriers to growth, which are owner-manager and/or size-related. Particular attention has been afforded to internal barriers impacting on growth in the form of the potential inadequacy of existing assets, as well as the ability of management to team build and team manage, in order to effectively facilitate the nature and pace of development. Having focused on key barriers that can potentially impede growth, the final section of the chapter considered first the limited utility of rational long-term planning in a small business context and, second, an alternative organisational learning perspective to effecting sustainable strategic development in small businesses. In total, the chapter provides an overall context for considering key management issues facing growing small firms.

Questions

1 To what extent do life-cycle and stages models of business development help in enhancing understanding of the small firm growth process?

2 In what ways may rational long-term planning modes of management be inadequate for aiding the small business to effect sustained growth?

3 What are likely to be the key constraints impacting upon a small business in its attempts to effect growth through the broadening of its customer base?

Web links

www.inc.com/inc500
Inc Magazine's list of the fastest growing firms in the US.

www.europes500.com/
A list of the 500 fastest job creators in Europe.

www.fasttrack.co.uk/
A list of the fastest growing companies in the UK.

www.fsb.org.uk/barriers2006
Presents the 'Lifting the Barriers to Growth 2006' produced by the Federation of Small Businesses (2006), which examines issues relating to the growth of small businesses such as employment, finance, business advisory services and legislation. It also examines a range of current business issues and their effects on the small business sector, including issues relating to the National Minimum Wage uprate, new employment directives, environmental compliance and business-related crime.

www.ihh.hj.se/eng/research
Website of the Jonkoping International Business School, which contains a range of working papers on small firm growth, including 'Theoretical and Methodological issues in the study of firm growth' by Davidsson and Wiklund (1999), which gives a detailed background to the research undertaken on growth firms.

PART 2

The entrepreneur

CHAPTER 7

The entrepreneurial process

Per Davidsson

7.1 Introduction

This chapter will focus on research-based insights into the entrepreneurial process. By that is meant the process of setting up a new business activity resulting in a new market offer. This new offer may be made by a new or an existing firm, although the main focus here is on the start-up of new, independent firms. Further, the new offer may be innovative, bringing to the market something that was not offered before, or imitative, i.e. a new competitor enters the market with products or services very similar to those other firms are already offering. While the latter type of process may be less complex and also have less market impact it entails most of the steps that typically have to be taken in order to get a business up and running. If successful it also shares, at least to some degree, the consequences that signify entrepreneurial processes:

- it gives consumers new choice alternatives,
- it gives incumbent firms reason to shape up, and
- it attracts additional followers to enter the market, further reinforcing the first two effects (Davidsson, 2004).

Besides, imitative start-ups outnumber by far innovative ones (Reynolds, Bygrave and Autio, 2003; Samuelsson, 2004).

It is worth emphasising that the start-up of a new business activity is a process and not an event. Different types of research have shown that this process entails quite a number of behaviours or activities, which can take anything from a couple of months to several years to complete. Further, business start-ups do not all follow *one and the same* process. On the contrary, it has been shown that any sequence of events is possible, including having first sales before thinking of starting a business (Carter, Gartner and Reynolds, 1996). Neither is it likely that one particular set-up of the process is universally the *right* way to go. Being emergent and inherently uncertain phenomena, business start-ups typically involve a wrestling or tension between the planned, systematic, (pre)determined and rational(istic) on the one hand, and the serendipitous, creative, experimental and flexible on the other. This is a theme that will be returned to throughout this chapter.

It is possible, however, to bring some order to this chaos. One way of doing so is to conceptually distinguish between – and discuss separately – two sub-processes of the entrepreneurial process, *discovery* and *exploitation* (Shane and Venkataraman, 2000). The former refers to the conceptual and cognitive side of business creation, i.e. coming up with an initial business idea and the subsequent elaboration, adaptation and honing of it. Exploitation refers to the actual behaviours and activities undertaken to realise this idea, for example marshalling and combing resources, and convincing would-be customers. Another way to bring some order is to analyse under what circumstances which type of process is likely to work better. As shall be seen, certain characteristics of the *business idea*, the *environment*, the *individuals* involved and the *stage of development* of the venture are suggestive in this regard.

In this chapter these two ways of giving structure and direction to the exposition will be used. Before deepening the discussion of discovery and exploitation, however, the question of what particular actions or behaviours need to be undertaken in the entrepreneurial process will be explored further.

7.2 Learning objectives

There are four learning objectives in this chapter:

1 To understand the process nature of entrepreneurship.

2 To recognise the existence, core contents and interrelatedness of two entrepreneurial sub-processes – *discovery* and *exploitation*.

3 To appreciate the non-existence of a universally best approach to exploiting venture ideas.

4 To understand under what conditions a systematic, planned and linear process may be suitable, and when a more iterative and flexible process is appropriate.

Key concepts

- process ■ discovery ■ exploitation ■ business planning ■ effectuation
- uncertainty ■ venture idea ■ individual ■ environment

7.3 Steps in the entrepreneurial process

What, more precisely, is it that one has to do in order to get a business up and running? Gartner and Carter (2003) list no less than 28 'gestation behaviours' that have been investigated in empirical research, ranging from saving money through to listing a separate telephone number for the company, to having paid taxes on revenue from the firm. Davidsson and Honig (2003) expand a similar list to 46 possible steps to be taken. Although not even that list is an exhaustive account of what founders can and sometimes have to do in order to get a business up and running, such a detailed level will not be dwelt upon here. A more fruitful categorisation for the current purpose may be the eight 'cornerstones' of business development that Klofsten (1994; cf. Davidsson and Klofsten, 2003) arrived at after studying a number of start-up processes close up. In the list below other influential entrepreneurship researchers' support for the centrality of these cornerstones has been added:

1 *The business idea.* A clear idea should be developed concerning what the firm will offer the market; how and for whom this creates value; and how enough of that value can be appropriated so that the venture becomes profitable. The critical importance of the value creation and appropriation mechanisms is also emphasised by many other researchers (Alvarez and Barney, 2004; Amit and Zott, 2001; McGrath, 2002).

2 *The product.* A functional product or service has to be developed. Obviously the emerging business needs something attractive to sell and consequently the provision of new or 'future' products and services is what Shane and Venkataraman (2000) point out as the essence of entrepreneurship.

3 *The market.* The target market must be defined in geographical and/or demographic terms. Other scholars emphasise that when the product or service is innovative the market may need to be created before it can be defined (Sarasvathy, 2001).

4 *The organisation.* An organisation must be created, which coordinates the purchasing, production, marketing, financing, controlling and distribution activities that are needed in order to serve the market in a legal and profitable manner. The pre-eminence of organisation creation as the core outcome of the entrepreneurial process has been especially advocated by Gartner (Gartner, 1988; Gartner and Carter, 2003).

5 *Core group expertise.* The competencies most crucial for the business's success must be hired into or developed in the management team. Shane has used both in-depth and broadly based data to provide compelling evidence of the importance of the founders' prior knowledge (Delmar and Shane, 2003b; Shane, 2000).

6 *Core group commitment.* The key individuals must have sufficient commitment to the start-up. In support of this notion, Baum and Locke (2004) recently demonstrated the importance of passion and tenacity for the long-term success of the new venture.

7 *Customer relations.* In order to achieve first sales, trustful relationships with prospective customers have to be developed. For example, Bhave (1994) observes that most of the entrepreneurs he studied had their initial customers lined up well before product creation.

8 *Other relations.* Other key relations must also be developed, for example with suppliers, investors or government agencies. One of the most important insights from systematic entrepreneurship research is that it is much more a social game than merely an individual one. For example, Davidsson and Honig (2003) showed that social capital, or developing one's business network, is very important for making progress in the start-up process (cf. also Aldrich and Zimmer, 1986; Birley, 1985).

Klofsten (1994) emphasises the importance of reaching at least a minimum acceptable level on all cornerstones; excelling at a few may not help if others are severely underdeveloped. While Klofsten does not point out a particular sequence in which to develop the cornerstones, Delmar and Shane (2003c), based on interviews with expert entrepreneurs, suggest the following sequence of start-up behaviours is advisable.

- Write a business plan.
- Gather information about customers.
- Talk to customers.
- Make financial projections.
- Establish a legal entity (i.e. register a sole proprietorship, partnership or limited liability company).
- Obtain permits and licences (as needed).
- Secure intellectual property (e.g. patents, trade marks, industrial design protection, copyright, etc.) as far as possible.
- Seek financing.
- Initiate marketing.
- Acquire inputs.

One aspect particularly worth noting about this sequence is that it progresses from activities that require no or little financial commitment to those that are more demanding in this regard. This is an issue where there is widespread consensus among entrepreneurship scholars. In many cases it is advisable that the founders get their business up and running at very low cost through so-called *financial bootstrapping* (Bhidé, 1992; Winborg and Landstrom, 2001). This refers to all the smart ways founders can find to get ahead without financial outlays. Illustrations of this will be found in short descriptions of the Sports Bra and Nantucket Nectars cases later in this chapter. Far more controversial is the priority Delmar and Shane (2003c) give to the written business plan. This is a very tricky issue, and the fact is that researchers using the very same data arrive at different conclusions (Delmar and Shane, 2003c; Honig and Karlsson, 2001; Samuelsson, 2004). Delmar and Shane's research suggests that advance planning is beneficial (Delmar and Shane, 2003a). However, this does not necessarily mean that *sticking* to the plan is a good strategy. The business plan has several potential roles or uses:

1 It can be an *analysis tool* used internally to go through the strengths and weaknesses of the venture as well as the threats and opportunities potential customers, competitors and other environmental conditions present.

2 It can be a *communication tool* that explains the logic and goals of the business to other parties, such as banks, venture capital firms and the government agencies that issue required licences and permits.

3 Writing a plan may increase the entrepreneur(s)' own *commitment* to the realisation of the project (cf. Cialdini, 1988). As noted above, Klofsten (1994) points out commitment as one of the eight cornerstones.

4 Finally, the plan can be used as a blueprint, as a detailed *guide to action*. First you plan, and then you do what the plan states.

Few would argue with the first three points. In particular, it is widely acknowledged that a written business plan makes it easier to get investors to accept the business concept. In the light of extant research the more questionable part of the planning emphasis is (blind) use of the plan as a guide to action. When something new is launched on the market, customers' and competitors' reactions are very difficult to predict. The business environment is uncertain and rapidly changing. Under such conditions, sticking to the plan may blindfold the entrepreneur(s) not only to possible and necessary adaptations that can save the future of the venture, but also to positive deviations from the plan, for example that much bigger sales and profits than those originally predicted are attainable.

To sum up this section, a range of activities need to be carried out after a business idea is first conceived and before the business is steadily up and running. Some researchers, like Klofsten, emphasise the importance of not neglecting any critical dimension. Others, like Delmar and Shane, suggest that a certain sequence of activities leads to better results. Either way, it is clear that starting a business is a process; there is no way all the necessary activities could be conducted at once. The next section will take a closer look at the discovery part of this process.

7.4 The discovery process

As pointed out at the beginning of this chapter, 'discovery' is used for the ideas side of business development, as opposed to the realisation side, which is called 'exploitation'. It is important to point out that 'discovery' as used here does not imply that something exists objectively in the environment, ready to be discovered. Neither does it imply that the start-up will be successful. As conceived of here, discovery is about developing business ideas and business ideas are the creations of individuals' minds. They may or may not reflect external conditions that make them viable. If someone is working on a business start-up in vain because it is based on a completely incorrect conjecture, the idea development side of that start-up is still an example of a discovery process, eventually leading to the more or less costly insight that the idea will not work (Davidsson, 2003, 2004). Further, although some economic theorists conceptualise entrepreneurial discovery as instantaneous, i.e. as if in a flash of insight you had the ready-to-fly business concept rolled out before you (Kirzner, 1973), empirical research reveals this part of the story is also a process (Bhave, 1994; de Koning, 2003; Van der Veen and Wakkee, 2004). You start with a rough idea. Before the idea is converted into an up-and-running business it is likely to have been changed, refined and elaborated.

A hotly debated issue is whether or not it is possible to apply systematic search for entrepreneurial discoveries, i.e. for new business ideas. The theoretical argument against this can be summarised, in short, in this question: How can one search for that which one does not know what it is (Kirzner, 1973)? According to this view, entrepreneurial discovery always carries an element of surprise and all aspiring entrepreneurs can do is to subject themselves to a greater flow of information in general (through extensive networking and media use) in the hope that *something* valuable will turn up, although there is no way they can know in advance *what* specifically they are looking for.

Although there was some early support for successful entrepreneurs behaving in this way (Kaish and Gilad, 1991), common sense and later research suggest it is possible to apply a more directed search. For example, about half of Bhave's (1994) cases were people that had more or less stumbled over a business opportunity without having a strong prior intention to go into business for themselves. Consequently they did not search for or consider multiple business ideas; they encountered one and decided to go for it. The other half, however, first made their minds up that they wanted to become independent business persons and then started looking more or less systematically for opportunities until they eventually decided they had found one that was promising enough. Research on a large, representative sample has since shown that these two discovery processes are about equally common (Gartner and Carter, 2003). Researching emerging internal ventures in small, owner-managed firms, Chandler, Dahlqvist and Davidsson (2003) could confirm that business ideas were the result of three different search processes: *proactive search* (actively looking for new opportunities because you want to), *reactive search* (ditto, but because you have to in order to make up for, for example, lost market share for existing products, or unemployment in the case of independent start-ups), and *fortuitous discovery* (that is, stumbling over an unsought-for opportunity).

So systematic search for viable business ideas is possible. Research strongly suggests aspiring entrepreneurs do not search randomly, or even for the idea with the biggest world market, but for ideas in a domain where they have relevant prior knowledge, for example because of work experience or a hobby (Fiet, 2002; Shane, 2000; Vesper, 1991). It is in these areas that aspiring business founders are likely to have or be able to develop the *expertise* and *commitment* that Klofsten (above) points out as cornerstones in new business development. Research further suggests using existing networks to find and hone business ideas (de Koning, 2003; Kaish and Gilad, 1991). In order to illustrate the possibility of systematic ideas search, as well as excelling in network use, consider the following example:

> The entrepreneur in this vignette was already the founder of many companies based on his sophisticated technological knowledge. He travels frequently and during the trips he often arranges evenings out with management consultants that he knows. While he is quite happy to pick up the bill for an evening's entertainment, he will press the consultants to tell him about some problem that their clients are struggling with, and which requires a technical solution. One such problem had a robot as its logical solution. However, the work environment was such that contemporary robots did not like it any more than humans did. The entrepreneur then turned to his second network, consisting of university professors in engineering, to find out whether something like a 'robust robot' was technologically feasible. Having learnt that this was indeed the case, he again turned to his management consultant network in order to get in touch with the end users. He made these pay the development costs (which also ensured demand for the finished product) incurred by the company he set up together with his academic experts. In the end he cashed in a handsome profit – without having invested any significant means of his own in the project (McGrath, undated).

As Bhave (1994: 230) observes, the starting point for businesses that are not the result of systematic search is often that 'the prospective entrepreneurs experienced, or were introduced to, needs that could not be easily fulfilled through available vendors or means.' The non-existence of both entrepreneurial intention and current supply, however, does not mean that this is the realm solely for relatively insignificant products or firms. For example:

> Carin Lindahl, the inventor of the sports bra – now a world product – was a somewhat bosomy workout freak who had painful personal experience from the insufficient support and inconvenience of then existing bras, taping and bandaging. When years later she stumbled over a fabric that expanded in one direction while being completely stiff in the other

she saw the obvious solution, bought a few yards of the fabric, and sewed a few bras for herself. She also tried to make manufacturers adopt the product, but to no avail. She then decided to start her own firm to provide the market with sports bras (Davidsson, 2000; Lindahl and Skagegård, 1998).

In the late seventies, Bert-Inge Hogsved was the CEO of a medium-sized company. He also had some computing skills in his background. His wife was a chartered accountant. For serendipitous reasons they were among the first owners of a PC in Sweden. Bert-Inge decided to use his new toy to write some software that would unfetter his wife from some of the most repetitive and tedious number-crunching aspects of her work. Of course, not only she but also her colleagues loved what they saw, and they soon wanted to get a copy of the software. When demand had increased to a critical level the Hogsveds had to decide whether or not to go into business for themselves wholeheartedly. The result was to become the Hogia group, the biggest business software company group in Sweden, presently employing over 400 people in some 30 semi-independent firms that have diversified into related areas (Hogsved, 1996; www.hogia.com).

Tom Scott was 23 in 1988 when he started what was to become Nantucket Nectars – valued at around US$100 million in 2002. However, at that time he had no intention to make it big, nor become a juice producer. It all started with a business called Allserve, which involved going boat to boat in Nantucket Harbour, selling muffins and newspapers, taking trash, doing laundry. In Tom's words, it was 'like a floating 7-Eleven'. The second summer his partner Tom First joined in, but while the business became legitimate and grew, it was decidedly a lifestyle enterprise. The following winter they stayed on the island. They made making dinner for one another a competition, and one night, in Tom Scott's words: 'Tom made this juice for dinner, peach juice made fresh in the blender. Within five minutes we were saying, "Let's sell this off the boat next summer. We'll call it Nantucket Nectars." ' (*Food and Drink Weekly*, 2002; Nantucket Nectars, 2004; Scott, 1998)

Clearly, in these cases the facts that these ideas were not systematically searched for, and that nobody else had seized these opportunities, were not indications that these opportunities were in any sense small. Equally clearly, the discovery process was not completed in the moment these entrepreneurs first saw what they were already doing as a business idea. Innumerable steps remain between the end of the vignettes as described above, and the fully worked out business models these three firms serve their markets with today. This leads to the question: When does the discovery process end? The only defensible answer, arguably, is that it *never* does. There is every reason to continue to adapt and expand one's business idea, even long after initial commercialisation. When founder-owners of a business believe they do not need to re-examine their business ideas they are setting the seeds for their demise.

7.5 The exploitation process

Unless perhaps when the exploitation of the business idea consists of a one-off outright sale to another organisation, exploitation, like discovery, is a process. It evolves over time. As used here the concept of exploitation carries none of the negative connotations it has in certain other contexts. Neither does the term exploitation as used here necessarily imply success. What is being referred to is, simply, the attempted realisation of the value creation and appropriation potentials of the business idea.

Obviously, no entrepreneurial process is complete without exploitation. No matter how smart or revolutionary the ideas, no value is going to be created until someone acts upon them. Exploitation activities make the start-up effort tangible (Carter *et al.*, 1996) and stakeholders committed to it (Van der Veen and Wakkee, 2004). In Table 7.1 the cornerstones or process steps discussed above have been listed and commented upon as regards how they relate to discovery and exploitation, respectively. There are many ways one can, on this basis, summarise what exploitation entails. One way of making sense of the entries in the table is to emphasise the following, partly overlapping categories:

- Efforts to *legitimise* the start-up, such as creating a legal entity, obtaining permits and licences, developing a working prototype of the product and developing relations with various stakeholders.

- Efforts to *acquire resources*, such as core group expertise, financial capital, intellectual property, and other inputs.

- Efforts to *combine and coordinate* these resources through the creation of a functional organisation.

- Efforts to *generate demand* through marketing and the development of customer relations.

While all of the above are important, it may be argued that for the long-term success of an independent start-up the most critical aspect of the exploitation process is to

Table 7.1 Steps in entrepreneurial process as related to discovery and exploitation

Klofsten's cornerstones		Shane and Delmar's process steps	
1 *Business idea*	Discovery. Conceiving, elaborating and refining a business idea is the core of the discovery process	*Write a business plan*	Discovery. Developing a business plan is essentially the same as developing an elaborate business idea. Communicating the plan is part of exploitation, as is doing what the plan promises.
2 *Product*	Discovery and Exploitation. Conceiving of a product/ service is an important part of the business idea. Developing a working prototype is part of exploitation	*Gather information about customers*	Discovery. Although behavioural rather than cognitive, this activity largely affects the business idea rather than being part of its implementation.
3 *Market*	Discovery and Exploitation. Defining the market is an important part of the business idea. Actually approaching that market is exploitation.	*Talk to customers*	Discovery and Exploitation. Talking to customers gives input to idea development but is also a step towards convincing them to buy.

Table 7.1 (cont'd)

Klofsten's cornerstones		Shane and Delmar's process steps	
4 *Organisation*	Discovery and Exploitation. An organisational plan is an important part of the business idea. Hiring people, distributing tasks and implementing routines are parts of the exploitation process.	*Make financial projections*	Discovery. This exercise may lead to adaptations of the business idea but does not in itself take the emerging venture any closer to market exchange.
5 *Core group expertise*	Discovery and Exploitation. Matching the business idea with existing expertise is part of discovery. Cultivating or hiring management team expertise are aspects of exploitation of the idea.	*Establish a legal entity*	Exploitation. This is a necessary step in implementation. However, learning about particularities of the regulations for different legal forms may in some cases feed back on the business idea (i.e. discovery).
6 *Core group commitment*	This cornerstone does not really fit as part of either process. It can be an important input to either, or a result of good matching of the business idea and the people, as well as of the existence of an attractive plan for exploitation.	*Obtain permits and licences*	Exploitation. This for some businesses is a necessary step in implementation. However, learning about aspects of the regulations for the particular type of business may in some cases feed back on the business idea (i.e. discovery).
7 *Customer relations*	Exploitation. Developing customer relations is an indispensable aspect of the exploitation process. This exchange can, however, feed back on the discovery process.	*Secure intellectual property*	Exploitation. This for some businesses is a critical factor in value appropriation. Learning about the IP possibilities may feed back on the business idea (i.e. discovery).
8 *Other relations*	Exploitation. Developing relations with other stakeholders is an important aspect of the exploitation process. Again, this can feed back on discovery.	*Seek financing*	Exploitation. Having money is not necessary for dreaming up ideas, but often is for their implementation. Again, the activity can feed back on discovery.
		Initiate marketing	Exploitation. The core of exploitation is to get customers to buy. The more interactive aspects of customer relations have been covered above.
		Acquire inputs	Exploitation. Acquiring the resources is necessary for realising the value-creating potential of the business idea.

obtain resources and resource combinations that are *valuable*, *rare* and imperfectly imitable (Barney, 1997), thus providing some 'isolating mechanism' (Rumelt, 1991).

The implementation of these elements of the exploitation process seems rational and textbook-like enough. And often it is, for example when the founder is an experienced habitual entrepreneur setting up yet another venture in a mature industry (e.g. a new up-market restaurant) and/or when the start-up is backed with formal venture capital and the external control that follows. In other cases, however, the execution of these exploitation behaviours does not look textbook-like at all – and that is not necessarily a bad thing. As start-ups are often resource-starved they need to find smart and frugal ways to get ahead. As a bonus, these approaches are often impossible for large, established competitors to copy. Some examples are as follows:

> In order to reach her target group Carin Lindahl, the inventor of the sports bra, used an annual all-women running event that attracted some 15,000 participants. Early in the morning Carin and her friends broke into (without damaging, of course) all the mobile toilets that were set up for the event, and applied posters advertising the product on the inside of the doors. After the runners reached the finish line (although not immediately at it, where only official, paying sponsors could operate) they were handed a leaflet with further information. In order to get stores to carry the product Carin would visit them and show the product's functionality through a very intense and unforgettable workout session in front of the astonished shopkeepers. She would also send family and friends to the stores to ask for the product. In case they carried it they would ask for a different colour. When she needed a (thin) product catalogue she used herself and friends, among them a personal friend who happened to also be one of Sweden's most famous stage artists, as models and endorsers, and in addition she shot many of the pictures herself. In order to expand her product assortment she needed to cultivate other relations within the industry. The way she did this was to invest most of the first year's profits (which were short of £1,000 anyway) in a high quality coffee machine, and offer free coffee to fellow exhibitors at trade fairs (this was before the global Italian coffee revolution and really good coffee was a rare find in this type of context). This way she got to know 'everyone important' in the industry. (Lindahl, personal communication; Lindahl and Skagegård, 1998).

> As regards Nantucket Nectars, and again in Tom Scott's own words: 'We started making it fresh and sold it off our boat and out of a little storefront we'd opened. We figured out a way to get the product into recycled wine bottles. Through this period we made money off everything but our boat business. We were doing anything else on the side: painting houses, bartending. Sometimes I lived in my car; other times I lived in a group house where the heat was never turned on. In terms of making the business work financially, what we did was pay our bills slowly, collect our receivables as fast as possible, and pay ourselves nothing. That's how you finance a business . . . We found that being young was an advantage, too: no wives, no kids, no mortgages, no responsibilities. If we wanted to work 14 hours a day, we did; if we didn't have money for clothes, it was OK – we didn't need clothes. We didn't need a car. Also, when we went into the factories, when we met with distributors, there was definitely a sense that, Hey, here's a couple of young kids – give 'em a break . . . [W]e made the juice the way we liked it, and we didn't worry about the other stuff. We just sold it. Then we started considering mass production, and the factories told us, "You can't use that bottle. You're going to have to use high-fructose corn syrup, not cane sugar," and on and on. Now I see why the other juice companies are the way they are – the factories don't want to handle the business differently. Thankfully, we were stubborn. We didn't want to compromise our product just because the factory said so. Anybody who knew something we didn't know about the juice

or beverage business, we studied like a hawk. The business isn't high tech, although it's more complicated than people realise – or than we realised at the time. But it's learnable. People always ask, "How did you learn about those factories and all that?" You just do it. You make a lot of mistakes in the process. Nantucket Nectars is one big collection of mistakes. The fear of production, the fear of getting things mass-produced, is unfounded. Ultimately, Tom and I just operated from the shared belief that there are no rules in life; there are laws, there are ethics, but there aren't any rules. You don't have to make juice with high-fructose corn syrups, no matter how many people say that you do.' (Scott, 1998)

In many cases, however, capturing and sustaining a strong position in the market is a very difficult task for a new firm lacking resources and track record (Aldrich and Auster, 1986). More generally, regardless of where they originate, some business ideas are better exploited by independent start-ups while others fit better in existing organisations. This highlights the importance of *mode of exploitation* (Shane and Venkataraman, 2001). Combining the possibilities of discovery and exploitation by independent individual(s) and members of existing corporations yields the four cases outlined in Figure 7.1.

Although Shane and Eckhardt (2003) emphasise that sufficient research-based knowledge about the prevalence and success rates of these cases does not yet exist, it is possible to exercise informed speculation about the fit between type of idea and exploitation mode. The four cases are as follows.

Case one

This concerns discovery as well as exploitation by independent individuals; the *independent start-up* mode. Certain structural characteristics of small or emergent organisations give them discovery advantages (Acs and Audretsch, 1990; Arrow, 1983; Barker and Gump, 1964), but that does not necessarily make them the best vehicles for

Figure 7.1 Locus of discovery and locus of exploitation

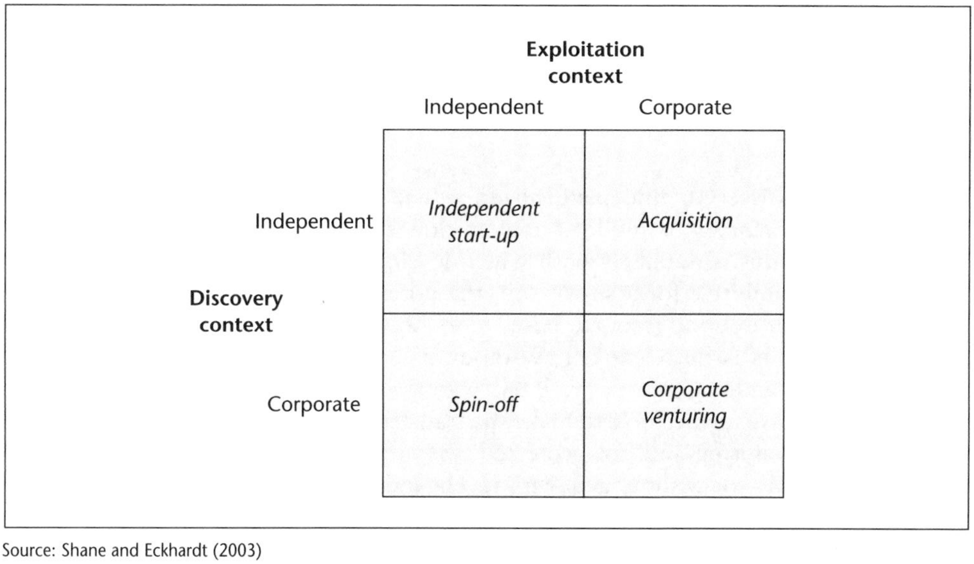

Source: Shane and Eckhardt (2003)

exploitation as well. It is likely that business ideas that originate outside corporate contexts can also be successfully exploited as independent start-ups when: a) development costs are not prohibitive and small-scale production is economically feasible; b) the potential market is not large enough to attract large actors; c) existing firms cannot use their existing resource base to exploit the idea in a superior manner; d) the new firm can successfully develop resources and resource combinations that are difficult to copy, i.e. create sustainable competitive advantage (Barney, 1991; 1997); and/or e) the new firm is able to stay ahead of the competition through continuous innovation.

Case two

This concerns both discovery and exploitation within a corporate context – the *corporate venturing* mode. This mode is particularly likely for incremental innovations that leverage established firms' existing knowledge-base, production technology and distribution networks. It is also a possibility for radical innovations that require substantial development costs and/or a combination of several highly specialised competencies that already exist in the firm and/or its network.

Case three

This concerns discovery within an existing corporation and exploitation by an independent start-up: the *spin-off* mode. This is likely when the new business idea, although it originated within the firm, does not make good use of the firms' existing resources and capabilities. As observed by Kogut and Zander (1992), when firms depart from their knowledge base their success probability approaches that of an independent start-up. In fact, for radical innovations the existing knowledge base and organisational routines can be liabilities relative to an independent start-up (Anderson and Tushman, 1990; Henderson and Clark, 1990). Another spin-off reason is that the new initiative addresses a small market niche (Christensen and Bower, 1996). Finally, referring to Bankman and Gilson (1999), Shane and Eckhardt (2003) observe that risk-taking propensity and other characteristics of the discoverer also influence whether an idea originating in a corporate context will be commercialised within the corporation, as a spin-off, or not at all.

Case four

This concerns discovery by independent individual(s) and exploitation by established corporations: the *acquisition* mode of exploitation. As a mirror image of the independent start-up case this is the likely path when development and/or small-scale production costs are prohibitive for a small firm, the potential market is large, and existing firms can use their existing resource bases to exploit the idea. The relation to intellectual property rights is not clear cut. Without such rights the originators would not have much to sell and might just as well try to go it alone. So it is rather in possession of such rights they have an incentive to make the transfer happen. On the other hand, when the concept is promising and not protected, the large actor can easily outmanoeuvre the small actor, with or without acquisition. The independent discoverer thus faces the 'prospector's paradox' (Alvarez and Barney, 2004) and may have to develop some other basis for sustainable competitive advantage – or give up. A final reason for transfer from independent to corporate context would be that the individual(s) involved do(es) not feel motivated or able to exploit the idea. For example, academic researchers whose research has commercial potential may not want to switch to a business career. Through licensing or outright sale they may still reap some of the financial benefit of their discoveries.

Further examples

In order to further illustrate the mode-of-exploitation problem, consider the following examples:

> The Solar Mower – a solar powered robotic lawn mower that uses random walk computer software and magnetic cord demarcations to walk and cut the garden little by little, like a modern sheep – was invented by an independent Belgian inventor who happened to have special competence within both of the two main technologies concerned. This is a radical innovation, unlikely to originate in an existing lawn mower manufacturing company (and reputedly a doomed one in the UK because it does not make stripes!). But think of the enormous hurdles this innovator would face in development costs, acquiring or ascertaining reliable production capacity for this new combination of technologies, building awareness about the product and confidence in the new brand, and getting into the available distribution channels without prior connections or proof of profitable demand. Wisely, the inventor decided to sell the idea to Husqvarna, an internationally established lawn mower manufacturer, and as the technology was new to them the company wisely decided to employ the inventor. However, the product never took off in a big way presumably because it did not make much use of Husqvarna's capabilities other than its brand name and distribution network. Apparently in an effort to bring it closer to the family, the Solar Mower became the Automower, without solar cells but with an ability to find its way back to the recharging pit when needed. Another problem remained, though: the risk of cannibalisation on Husqvarna's other lawn mower lines if the product achieved great success. Presumably in an effort to overcome this problem the Automower has recently been transferred to the Electrolux brand (within the same corporation) where it enjoys similar benefits of strong brand name and distribution, but without in-house competition with other technologies. As a bonus Electrolux got a cousin to its robotic vacuum cleaner, which was developed on the basis of a very similar idea and with some technological overlap as well (Bjenning and Bjärsvik, 1999; Davidsson, 1994; Electrolux, 2004).

> When you think of it, the sports bra could very well have originated within an existing underwear or sportswear manufacturer. You could even argue it should. But they failed to see this opportunity before Carin Lindahl did. Not only that, some established firms got the chance but refused to take it when Carin suggested they pick it up. Once she had proven the viability of the concept, however, it was very difficult for Carin to establish a sustainable competitive advantage. The manufacturer of the fabric had no reason to give her exclusive rights; the idea was not patentable, and industrial design protection would have been very easy to circumvent. Consequently, the big actors marched in and captured most of the world market. Through emphases on quality, differentiation and brand extension Carin has been able to build and sustain a healthy small business (called *Stay In Place*, as it were), but most of the value her idea created has been appropriated by other actors (Lindahl, personal communication; Lindahl and Skagegård, 1998).

These examples do not exclude the possibility that independent start-ups can successfully exploit opportunities and grow large in their own right. IKEA, McDonald's and

141

Starbuck's are spectacular examples of ideas that did not seem (initially) very difficult to copy; yet they managed to both create and appropriate enormous value out of seemingly simple ideas. Over time they have, of course, built brand equity, tacit knowledge, casual ambiguity and super-efficient business systems that now make them very difficult to challenge for an imitator.

7.6 The relationship between discovery and exploitation

Above it was noted that just because an idea originates with independent individual(s) it does not have to be exploited as an independent start-up, and just because an idea emerges in a corporate context it need not stay there forever, In this regard, then, the discovery and exploitation processes are separable. An examination of Table 7.1, however, suggests they are intricately entwined but if what is being referred to is the *entire* discovery and exploitation process then the latter process is the truer image in most cases. Importantly, it is usually *not* the case that ideas (or 'opportunities' as they are often called) are first discovered (i.e. conceptually completed) and then exploited (Bhave, 1994; de Koning, 2003; Van der Veen and Wakkee, 2004).

In an attempt to restore some order it has been suggested that the entrepreneurial process, while not linear, is at least directional: *existence* of opportunity is a precondition for *discovery*, which is a precondition for *exploitation* (Shane, 2003; Shane and Eckhardt, 2003). But not even that holds up empirically. People develop and hone ideas that do not reflect objectively existing, external opportunity, or ideas that become viable because of external events that occur *after* the idea was developed. In other cases they acquire and combine resources that *de facto* help exploit a business idea they have not yet conceived, or they successfully exploit a different opportunity from the one they thought they were pursuing, for example because it was a hit with completely different buyers and/or for other uses than the founders had imagined (Davidsson, 2003).

The interrelation of discovery and exploitation is what Figure 7.2 attempts to portray. For example, an entrepreneurial process may start with an individual perceiving what they think is an opportunity for a profitable business [discovery]. In the efforts to make this business happen, contacts with resource providers and prospective customers [exploitation] make it clear that the business as initially conceived will not be viable

Figure 7.2 The interrelation between discovery and exploitation

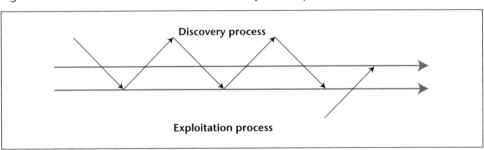

[feedback to discovery]. The individual changes the business concept accordingly [discovery] and continues efforts to marshal and coordinate the resources needed for the realisation of the revised business concept [exploitation] (Davidsson, 2004).

Importantly, considerable success is unlikely if either process is severely under-emphasised. Regardless of the degree of temporal separation or integration of the two sub-processes it is important that both receive adequate attention. The perils of lack of balance can be described as follows:

■ Where there is too much emphasis on discovery no value will ever be created or appropriated. For example, certain kinds of engineer-led high-tech firms are notorious for being eternal playgrounds for the development of the 'perfect' product rather than one for which a significant number of customers are willing to pay an above production cost price. Also in this vein, Carter et al. (1996) obtained results suggesting that those who did not do enough tangible exploitation activities were less likely to get the business up and running. Further, as observed by Singh (2001), failure is not evidence that the idea is wrong. It may have been the case that a faulty exploitation effort ruined a basically sound idea.

■ Where there is too much emphasis on exploitation there is the risk that not enough value is being created because the founders have not tuned in carefully enough to the customers' real needs and preferences.

■ Another type of overly strong emphasis on exploitation is when the founders try to appropriate (close to) *all* the value created by their product or service (or more), rather than sharing the benefits with the customers. The customers will then have incentives to look for other solutions instead. When the founders are unwilling to share the value created with external investors they may end up being sole owners of a very insignificant operation rather than substantial part owners of a multi-million pound business.

■ Finally, when entrepreneurs try to appropriate value without creating value on the societal level their activities are socially destructive rather than constructive (Baumol, 1990) and will be looked down upon and/or be subjected to legal counteraction. Examples here might include business activities that are typical for mafia organisations, but there are other examples as well. One real example is a graffiti removal business whose founder-owners used night time (and spray paint) to generate demand for their daytime business activity! While such activities can be short-term profitable they are often detrimental in the longer term and/or for entrepreneurs collectively.

7.7 The effectuation process: an alternative entrepreneurial logic?

A recurrent theme in this exposition has been the tension between the structured, planned and systematic on the one hand, and the emerging, iterative and somewhat chaotic on the other. Entrepreneurship researchers have long observed that what business founders do often has relatively little semblance to the conventional analysis-planning-implementation-control rationality of normative management textbooks. They have also suspected that since this is often true also for highly successful entrepreneurs the deviations from prescribed conventional rationality may in fact be well-founded.

Recently, Sarasvathy (1999; 2001) suggested an alternative entrepreneurial logic, which she calls 'effectuation', and which was based on conceptual forerunners as well as empirical observation of highly successful entrepreneurs. She defines causation and effectuation processes in the following way: 'Causation processes take a particular effect as given and focus on selecting between means to create that effect. Effectuation processes take a set of means as given and focus on selecting between possible effects that can be created with that set of means' (Sarasvathy, 2001: 245).

Causation and effectuation can work towards similar generalised goals. Sarasvathy (2001) takes 'making dinner' as an illustrative non-business example: either you start from a menu and then get the required ingredients (causation) or you rummage through the cupboards and create a dinner from whatever you find there (effectuation). To further expand on Sarasvathy's (2001) own examples it can be observed that either process could start with the same generalised goal ('I need to make a living for myself/I want to be my own boss/I want to get rich and control my own destiny') and arrive at the same result (e.g. an Indian fast-food franchising chain called 'Curry in a Hurry'). However, the processes would have very different origins and histories. In the causation case, it might start with any business-minded people perceiving a possible gap in the market. The business concept, the target market in terms of location and clientele, the menus, etc., would be carefully worked out before (and while starting to burn equity) a heavily advertised launch of the initial Curry in a Hurry outlets would be made in locations that were selected after careful strategic consideration. The expansion of the chain would follow a set plan based on market-related criteria.

The effectuation process Sarasvathy describes would most likely start from a person knowing how to cook Indian food. This person might try it out by starting a small lunch catering service in the lunchrooms of friends' employers; move on to a fast-food corner in an established restaurant; then upgrade to a first independent outlet; eventually expand to a second unit run by a relative in the town where he happened to live, and only thereafter, if ever, start to conform to a franchised fast-food chain as they are usually conceived of. Importantly, however, just as Nantucket Allserve took off in a completely different direction when the founders stumbled over the juice opportunity, Sarasvathy emphasises that her imaginary lunch caterer could, depending on the market response and after a series of incremental steps, end up building a business as travel agent, motivational consultant or just about anything else instead.

The effectuation process typically starts with the individual's given means (Who I am. What do I know? Whom do I know?) and works incrementally and iteratively towards any of the effects that can be created with these means (and the secondary resources that the initial means allows one to acquire). According to Sarasvathy (2001) the effectuation process is also characterised by the following principles:

Affordable loss rather than expected return

By taking incremental steps and avoiding financial commitments whenever possible, the entrepreneur(s) make sure the worst-case scenario does not lead to disastrous consequences. This implies the testable prediction that, when they fail, effectuation-based start-ups fail in a more minor way than causation-based counterparts. The affordable loss principle rhymes well with the bootstrapping behaviour that has been discussed and illustrated above. On the other hand, the principle implies income foregone in cases when market acceptance of the concept is high. Thus, an effectuation-based start-up may capture the market at a slower pace, or obtain a smaller market share, than a successful start-up based on causation logic.

Strategic alliances rather than competitive analysis

An effectuation strategy emphasises circumventing competition and building strength through alliances (e.g. 'Curry in a Hurry' as a fast-food corner of an existing restaurant) rather than building one's own muscles and trying to take on competitors directly (e.g. by raising large amounts of venture capital and launching heavily advertised outlets near the competitors).

Exploitation of contingencies rather than exploitation of pre-existing knowledge

In an effectuation process the actors stay open to influences rather than working towards firmly predefined goals. They can therefore exploit contingencies that arise unexpectedly as the process evolves, like Carin Lindahl when she happened to come across the right fabric, or the Nantucket Nectars founders when they thought others might appreciate fresh juice as much as they did – or later, when they sought expansion finance from one of the yacht owners they had become acquainted with through their company and who also happened to be a major risk capitalist.

Controlling an unpredictable future rather than predicting an uncertain one

The logic of causation is that if the future can be predicted one can control it. By contrast, the effectuation logic is that if one can control the future one does not need to predict it. Thus, effectuation seems to rhyme well with situations where human action counts while it is very difficult to predict what will happen in the future. Think, for example, of a game of chess. No doubt, the player's skill and strategies count. At the same time, chess is a complex game and it has turned out impossible even for high-powered computers to win the game by using their superior ability to analyse the consequences of possible future moves. Arguably, it makes a strong case for effectuation that although chess is a very complex and sophisticated game there is but one opponent who can only choose among a finite number of next moves. In business, there are innumerable other actors with innumerable options. To control one's future by predicting their moves may be too big a challenge to take on.

Sarasvathy's theorising builds on empirical input from successful entrepreneurs (Sarasvathy, 1999). It also concurs with observations other entrepreneurship researchers have made, and with some existing theories of organisation and strategy (Sarasvathy, 2001: 254–7). However, the theory has so far not been put to an acid test and consequently Sarasvathy (2001: 246) is careful to point out that effectuation is suggested as a viable and descriptively valid alternative, not as a normatively superior one.

Arguably, there is little doubt that both more and less successful entrepreneurs' behaviour often deviates from conventional, textbook rationality. At the very least, effectuation theory offers a systematic and logically coherent description of such an alternative approach to establishing new business activity. Interestingly, Sarasvathy's reasoning gives reason to qualify the first entry in both Klofsten's and Shane and Delmar's respective first steps in Table 7.1. The questions are:

- How early should the business idea really be carved in stone? and
- To what extent can one really plan in a game much more complex than chess?

Regrettably, there are no easy answers. In the next section, however, the analysis of when different approaches are likely to fit better will be pursued.

7.8 Which process is better?

So, which is preferable – the planned and systematic or the experimental and flexible? There is some evidence that directed and systematic search is possible and, on average, leads to more successful outcomes (Chandler *et al.*, 2003; Dahlqvist, Chandler and Davidsson, 2004; Fiet, 2002). On the other hand it is not difficult to find examples of spectacular successes based on serendipity and fortuitous discovery. Delmar and Shane (2003a; 2003c) have obtained results supporting that planning and following the 'right' sequence leads to better performance. However, these results are obtained from a sample dominated by imitative start-ups. Arguably, such start-ups should be characterised by less uncertainty and are thus possible to organise more successfully with a more analytical approach (Gustafsson, 2004). Samuelsson (2001; 2004) has at least demonstrated that the start-up processes are different for imitative and innovative start-ups, respectively.

One advantage of the less systematic 'effectuation' (Sarasvathy, 2001) and 'internally stimulated' (Bhave, 1994) processes are that they almost guarantee a high degree of *fit* between the founders and the business idea, as they start from one's own means and/or problems. Such fit has been strongly emphasised as a success factor by influential scholars (Shane, 2003; Timmons, 1999; Vesper, 1991). Another advantage of effectuation was mentioned above: if the venture fails, it fails affordably. In addition, Hmieleski and Ensley (2004a) recently found change of the original business concept – a sign of iterative incrementalism – to be positively associated with new venture growth.

So, the evidence is at best inconclusive. In all likelihood, it depends. The question is just what, more precisely, it depends upon. At least four prime suspects can be identified as reasons for differential effectiveness of different approaches to discovery and exploitation of new business activity: the characteristics of the *venture idea*; the characteristics of the *environment*; the *stage of development* of the venture; and who you are, i.e. the characteristics of the *individual(s)*. In the following the discussion of each of these sources of contingency effects will be expanded.

7.8.1 The characteristics of the venture idea

To some extent the above has covered the issue of how the *cost/value structure* of the intended product or service is related to what type of organisation can effectively exploit it. Figure 7.3 takes a somewhat different look at this problem, with a particular eye on the idea's potential for incremental and experimental exploitation.

Figure 7.3 Cost/value structures of different venture ideas

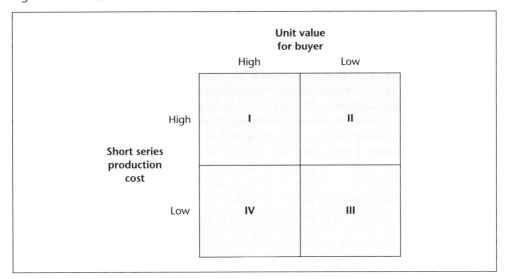

Quadrant I represents the situation where it is costly to produce short series and when each unit has high value for the buyer. This type of idea arguably requires more of a causation process; no incremental process governed by concerns for affordable loss would lead to this result, and no commercial actor would be willing to experiment haphazardly without knowing for which solution there is money-backed demand. In this situation one would have to know where one was heading (with the possible positive and negative exception of government-funded basic research at universities and the worst period of the Internet craze, respectively). The high value to the customer, however, implies a potential for strategic alliances, and this in turn reveals that despite the costs a small actor may play a key role. This was in fact precisely what the 'robust robot' case illustrated.

Quadrant II illustrates the case that is most difficult to exploit with small funds and an incremental strategy. Here, costs are substantial before a single unit has been delivered and yet the value per customer is low. Examples here are Federal Express and the freesheet *Metro*, which after its birth in Stockholm in 1995 has been launched in many major cities of the world. It is not possible to build this type of business gradually from a very mundane start. New concepts of this kind have to be introduced with a lot of fanfare to reach the volumes required to cover development costs and/or reach economically viable unit costs in production. They therefore require pre-launch investments of a size that only large organisations or venture capital consortia can come up with.

Quadrant III, where short series are economical and the value per unit is also low, is perhaps the best option for independent start-ups using an incremental strategy. Here both producers and customers can afford to experiment without much risk, and that makes it easier for a new actor to get established. Nantucket Nectars, Curry in a Hurry (if started as a lunch catering operation) and Stay-in-Place (Carin Lindahl and the sports bra) are cases that represent this category.

Quadrant IV is also characterised by low cost for short series, which makes room for incremental strategies. This would be true for used car dealers, but examples also include on-site construction of houses through to high-value, services-based specialised knowledge, such as being one of a few knowing how to repair a machine that has a critical role in a process industry. However, the high value to the customer will make it difficult for new and small actors to enter the market if there are other alternatives. Likewise, as illustrated by the sports bra case (quadrant III) a small actor that approaches the market incrementally will easily be outrun by larger, later entrants if the total market holds promise of being big enough to attract their attention. This may be even truer in quadrant IV to the extent that the high value to customer implies potential for high margins.

Another important aspect of the characteristics of the venture idea is its *degree of uncertainty*. Sarasvathy *et al.* (2003) discuss three types of venture ideas (or 'business opportunities' as they call them) as related to their degree of uncertainty (note that 'discovery' is here used more restrictively than earlier in this chapter):

- *Opportunity recognition*, which is low uncertainty because the sources of both supply and demand exist rather obviously. An example would be the opening of a new outlet in an existing franchising chain.

- *Opportunity discovery*, which is medium uncertainty because only one side of demand or supply obviously exists. The authors mention cures for diseases (demand with unknown supply) and applications for new technologies (supply with unknown demand) as examples.

- *Opportunity creation*, which is highest in uncertainty because neither demand nor supply exists in an obvious manner. The examples here are radical innovations that create new markets and new behavioural patterns.

Along this uncertainty dimension there is reason to believe that the higher the inherent uncertainty of the idea, the more questionable is Klofsten's (1994) emphasis on a clearly worked-on business idea and Delmar and Shane's (2003c) placing the writing of a business plan first in the process – at least if this is interpreted as suggestions for what needs to be done *before* any market-related action is taken. When the uncertainty surrounding the idea is high, experimentation may be the *only* way to find out what will or will not work, and hence may be the only way to home in on a viable business idea or obtain useful input for a business plan. Further, based on cognitive psychological research on expertise, which suggests that analytical rationality works best in low uncertainty situations, Gustafsson (2004) was able to show that the more uncertain the situation, the less expert entrepreneurs rely on analysis in making their decisions.

7.8.2 The characteristics of the environment

Continuing the uncertainty argument it may be assumed that causation processes, planning and the early carving out of a narrowly defined business idea are relatively more questionable practices in more dynamic and uncertain environments. In line with this, praise of improvisation, learning-by-doing, etc., is quite frequent in the literature on dynamic capabilities and organisational learning (see Zahra *et al.*, forthcoming). A

recent example of research that strongly supports the idea that more dynamic environments require more incremental and improvising approaches is Hmieleski and Ensley
(2004a). Their study indicated strong positive interactions between degree of change of
the business idea and environmental dynamism, and between improvisation behaviour
and environmental dynamism, with respect to new venture growth.

7.8.3 Stage of development

Not only the industry's stage of development but also the stage of development of the
venture itself may affect the viability of different approaches to discovery and exploitation. This also follows the uncertainty argument; as the venture matures its managers'
task environment typically becomes less uncertain. Consequently the argument is that
while effectuation strategies may work or even be superior in very early stages of a venture's life, a causation mode may have to be adopted later in order to secure continued
success (Read *et al.*, 2003). Sarasvathy *et al.* (2003) uses the Starbuck's case to illustrate the development from high uncertainty to low uncertainty for the same venture
over time, accompanied by a switch from effectuation to causation approaches. Also
in line with this reasoning, Hmieleski and Ensley (2004b) recently reported some
intriguing – albeit tentative – results. In short, according to their results analytical intelligence has no main effect on venture outcomes in the pre-formation and formation
stages, whereas this conventional form of intelligence has a strong positive effect on
performance in the presumably more structured and less genuinely uncertain growth
stage. For creative and practical intelligence, presumably conducive of early market
experimentation, the pattern is the opposite. However, the positive effects of these latter types of intelligence in the earliest stages are boosted if analytical intelligence is also
high. That is, the results suggest that people high *only* on analytical intelligence are not
helped by this in the early, highly uncertain stages of venture development. However,
for those who possess creative and practical intelligence a sound dose of analytical
intelligence helps guide these other talents in a more productive direction.

7.8.4 Characteristics of the individual

Finally, and importantly, who you are also matters. It has been noted above that
Klofsten (1994) made commitment and drive of the key actors one of his cornerstones
of successful business development. It has also been noted that many other researchers
emphasise the fit between the entrepreneur(s) and the business idea or, in more general, psychological language, between the individual(s) and the task. It cannot be ruled
out that fit between person and type of process is likely to be equally important. To
some extent people can put a straightjacket on themselves, control their impulses and
do what the situation requires even when their real preferences point in a different
direction. For example, Gustafsson (2004) was able to show that expert entrepreneurs
are able to adapt their decision-making style to the characteristics of the task. To some
other extent, however, it may be necessary for individuals to use the approach they
prefer and make that work regardless of what the situation 'objectively' calls for. Thus,
those who prefer a systematic, planning-based approach may be better off applying
this approach in high-uncertainty situations, and vice versa with people who thrive on

chaos, rather than adopting an approach one does not feel comfortable with. Even better ways to handle this matching problem may be to go for ideas that are a good match with the preferred type of process or to have a diverse founder team where different members' abilities and preferences complement each other in this respect.

7.9 Chapter summary

This chapter has propagated a process view of entrepreneurship, because entrepreneurship consists of an array of behaviours that cannot be completed all at once. More- and less-detailed examples of such concrete behaviours are given, such as Klofsten's eight cornerstones. The two sub-processes of discovery and exploitation are also distinguished. *Discovery* refers to the cognitive side of starting a new venture, i.e. the conception and further development of a venture idea. The literature shows that while some real-world entrepreneurs arrive at venture ideas through systematic search, it is also common for them to more or less stumble over ideas without any prior intention to strike out on their own and that such fortuitous discoveries lead to quite substantial businesses. However, there is no empirically based evidence that systematic search would be futile. The important thing appears to be that prospective entrepreneurs direct their search to domains where they have particular knowledge and interest.

The *exploitation* process consists of the concrete behaviours that are needed to realise venture ideas. This includes acquiring and combining resources, but also efforts to generate demand and to make the business legitimate in the eyes of others. A sub-section was set aside for a discussion of under which circumstances an independent start-up is a feasible mode of exploiting a venture idea. It was concluded that while other types of ideas may well be discovered in an independent start-up context, successful exploitation in that mode is difficult when development costs are high, the potential market is large, and when existing organisations can benefit from their existing knowledge base and resources. The independent start-up is in a good position when the idea makes incumbents' knowledge and resources obsolete; hard-to-copy resource combinations can be created, and/or the start-up can stay ahead through continuous innovation.

The chapter then discusses the interrelatedness of the discovery and exploitation sub-processes. Usually these processes are in part parallel rather than sequential. Feedback from the exploitation efforts leads to changes in the venture idea and these adaptations in turn affect how it can best be exploited. Further, it was emphasised that a balance is needed between the two processes. Excellent exploitation efforts of under-developed ideas often lead to failure, as does poor implementation of excellent ideas.

A central theme in the chapter has been that the behaviour of real-world entrepreneurs often deviates from the planned, systematic and linear process that is typical for normative management textbooks. The fact that this is true also for highly successful entrepreneurs leads to the suspicion that such deviations may, under certain conditions, reflect a sound strategy. Sarasvathy's (2001) identification of an alternative entrepreneurial logic, the *effectuation* approach, was discussed at some length. The final section of the chapter analysed under what conditions a more iterative, incremental and flexible strategy like that used in effectuation may be more successful than its opposite, the textbook-like *causation* approach. It was concluded that the higher the inherent uncertainty of the venture idea and the environment, the less likely it is that all relevant information can be collected and viable long-term strategies can be worked out as a desk assignment prior to market launch. It was further shown that the cost/value structure of the venture idea has a bearing upon what type of process is suitable. Finally, the fit between individual(s) and type of process should also be considered.

Questions

1 Why should the start-up of a new venture be thought of as a process?

2 What characterises the discovery and exploitation sub-processes, respectively?

3 What are the different possible uses of a business plan, and which of these uses are more and less controversial, respectively?

4 What characterises causation- and effectuation-driven processes, respectively?

5 Under what conditions can an effectuation-based process be more successful?

Web links

www.bibl.hj.se/ice
This is a library website with an excellent collection of searchable links to information on almost any aspect of entrepreneurship in a multitude of countries. The site also has searchable databases and journals dedicated to entrepreneurship research.

http://effectuation.org/
This website gives additional information and references regarding Sarasvathy's effectuation theory.

www.gemconsortium.org
Contains a range of reports on entrepreneurial activity from the Global Entrepreneurship Monitor project.

CHAPTER 8

The psychology of the entrepreneur

Frédéric Delmar

8.1 Introduction

In this chapter, evidence on the entrepreneurial personality and behaviour is reviewed. It begins by describing how this area has evolved until now, concentrating on different problems and criticisms related to the subject. Thereafter, entrepreneurial traits are reviewed such as the need for achievement, locus of control and risk-taking propensity. The chapter then continues with an overview of current research and results about entrepreneurial behaviour, with a focus on cognitive motivation models which have the ability to address individual differences in entrepreneurial behaviour and performance. This chapter also addresses the training and education of potential entrepreneurs.

8.2 Learning objectives

There are six learning objectives in this chapter:

1 To explore the development of the field.

2 To examine why the traits approach has previously been adopted to study the entrepreneur.

3 To understand why the traits approach has failed in understanding entrepreneurial behaviour.

4 To define and explore the major theoretical schools of the psychology of the entrepreneur.

5 To understand the practical as well as theoretical advantages of cognitive models.

6 To understand how entrepreneurship can be promoted from a psychological perspective.

Key concepts

■ personality characteristics ■ proximal and distal processes ■ cognition
■ motivation ■ entrepreneurial behaviour

8.3 The entrepreneurial personality

The personality of the entrepreneur is often perceived by students and practitioners as one of the most fascinating topics in the field of entrepreneurship. The reason for this is the human tendency to attribute great performances to a person's individual characteristics rather than to situational constraints. That is, there is a general tendency to explain the behaviour of others as a consequence of their personalities rather than as consequences of what the situation has to offer. This is often referred to as the 'fundamental attribution error' which suggests that it is often believed that a successful entrepreneur is the result of a special set of personal abilities and characteristics, rather than the results of either being in a favourable situation or through pure chance.

As a natural consequence of this belief, the psychological perspective in entrepreneurship research has for a long time concentrated on discovering stable individual characteristics such as personality traits. It is, as pointed out earlier, an attractive explanation and of direct practical relevance as most parties having a financial interest in entrepreneurship would like to find an easy test that could identify potential successful entrepreneurs.

As will be explained, psychology cannot offer (at the present time) such a valid test, but enterprises are made of men and women and there is a need to understand how they behave. The entrepreneur (and his ideas) often represents the only available information that various stakeholders such as venture capitalists, bankers or policy makers have available to make a decision on whether or not to grant finance to that individual or to create an infrastructure promoting entrepreneurship. In order to do that, these parties need to have information about what characterises entrepreneurial behaviour and how it can be understood.

Personality traits cannot explain more than a minor share of entrepreneurial behaviour and differences in business performance. As will be seen, these disappointing results can be explained by theoretical as well as methodological problems characterising the perspective (Carsrud and Johnson, 1989; Chell *et al.*, 1991; Delmar, 1996; Gartner, 1988; Herron and Robinson, 1993; Sexton and Bowman, 1985). The research field of entrepreneurial behaviour has instead turned its attention towards more sophisticated models where people's cognition and motivations are the explanatory factors behind entrepreneurial behaviour instead of personality traits (Baron, 2004; Baum and Locke, 2004; Baum *et al.*, 1998).

8.4 The development of the field of entrepreneurial personality and behaviour

Figure 8.1 illustrates the complexity and the inherent problems associated with the psychological perspective. It is composed of four boxes each containing a basic question relating to the research field and numbered from one to four. The numbers represent the approximate historical evolution of the field. In short, research started first with trying to find a personality profile describing entrepreneurs (Box 1) although it became clear that more conceptual work was needed to define what an entrepreneur really is

Figure 8.1 The field of applied psychology in entrepreneurship

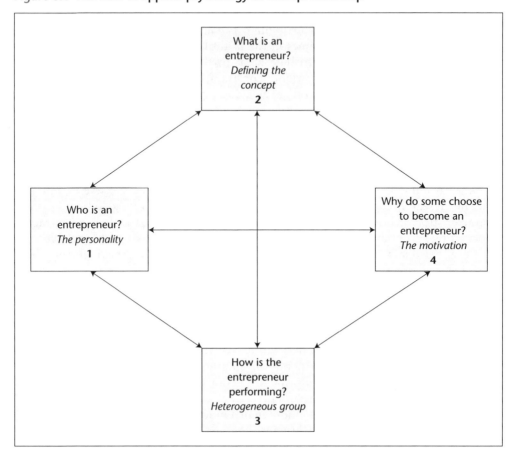

and what he or she is performing (Box 2). This conceptual work led to a greater aware-ness that entrepreneurs act at different stages in a business's development. Research then focused on relating different personality traits to the firm's performance (Box 3). However, trait theories were proven not to be a viable alternative in explaining entre-preneurial behaviour and cognitive motivation models have been adopted instead (Box 4). It is worth noting that the boxes are interrelated and that one question cannot be answered without taking the other questions into consideration.

8.4.1 Who is an entrepreneur? Understanding the concept of personality

Personality is often loosely defined in terms of regularities in action, feelings and thoughts that are characteristics of the individual (Snyder and Cantor, 1998). In other words, there is supposed to be a set of characteristics or traits that are stable across situations and time. This means that one hopes to find an entrepreneurial personality profile that can help to better understand which characteristics lead to success and which to failure. If it were possible to identify such personality characteristics, the financial risk exposure of venture capitalists and bankers could be limited by giving them an effective selection instrument. Furthermore, it would be possible to encourage those with the winning personalities and discourage those with failing personalities to engage in an entrepreneurial career. However, the search for the entrepreneurial personality stumbles upon several problems.

Inconsistency

The first problem of the perspective is the inconsistency of such an approach due to the large number and variants of traits. Furthermore, researchers have not reached consensus on the relevance of these individual characteristics, their importance and how they vary in different situations. For example, Hornaday (1982) identified more than 40 traits that have been associated with entrepreneurs, and the most popular identified by previous research include the need for achievement, internal locus of control, risk-taking propensity, tolerance for ambiguity, over-optimism and the need for autonomy. Thus, there is a rich abundance of different characteristics that are attributed to the entrepreneur, which will be explained in greater detail later in this chapter. For the moment, it is important to remember that it is difficult to reach a common frame of reference because of the large number of characteristics and their definitions.

The static nature of entrepreneurial characteristics

The second problem is the assumption that the variables characterising the entrepreneur and the environment are static. However, it is clear to all that the environment changes constantly and traits or characteristics alone have very little ability to explain behaviour. Thus, the external validity of the psychological trait approach can be questioned.

Obsolescence of current theory

The third problem is that the theory and methods in use are, in relation to modern psychological research, obsolete. The concept of personality is not one-dimensional (and measured with only one trait) but multi-dimensional. An individual's personality is now mainly measured in five broad dimensions called the 'Big Five' (cf. Goldberg, 1993; Hogan, 1991; Hogan et al., 1996). Hence, when measuring personality, the measures should include at least these five dimensions of interpersonal evaluation. The five dimensions are extraversion, emotional stability, agreeableness, conscientiousness and openness to experience. Indeed, recent findings in entrepreneurship research show that an entrepreneur's conscientiousness was positively related to long-term survival; the entrepreneur's openness was relatively associated with survival; and the other three measures were not related. Survival was measured as the ability to maintain the operations of the same firm for the minimum of eight years (Ciavarella et al., 2004). However, the results should be interpreted with caution, as it is only a first attempt to map the relationship between the Big Five and entrepreneurial performance.

Furthermore, it is not possible to state unambiguously that differences are due to predispositions (i.e. not yet having managed a venture) or are the results of having entrepreneurial expertise (i.e. already managing a venture) (Mitchell and Seawright, 1995).

155

In other words, the fact that entrepreneurs exhibit certain characteristics does not necessarily mean that they had them from the very beginning. These characteristics could have been developed during the time they have been entrepreneurs. It is therefore difficult to state clearly if the characteristics exhibited by entrepreneurs are causes of previous life experiences or the result of being an entrepreneur.

American bias

Finally, there is the problem that the research is mainly based on US samples. As a result, it has been argued that many of these characteristics (especially the need for achievement) are culturally dependent and as a consequence lacking of predictive power in other cultures (Spence, 1985). Research findings about entrepreneurs' attitudes in different countries give some support to this argument, at least when the US is compared with Asian countries (Stimpson *et al.*, 1990).

The inability to handle these five problems in the field of entrepreneurship has led to the abandonment of the attempts to identify a single trait. Instead, researchers have attempted to adopt increasingly complex approaches in the hope of more fruitful results. More specifically, social psychological models incorporating individual characteristics and social contexts have been proposed to understand better the psychology of the entrepreneur (Herron and Robinson, 1993; Katz, 1992; Krueger and Brazeal, 1994; Starr and Fondas, 1992). In addition, researchers are now increasingly developing studies which attempt to understand what entrepreneurship really is and how it can be better measured, i.e. defining entrepreneurship and understanding how an entrepreneur performs.

8.4.2 What is an entrepreneur? Defining the concept

Whilst defining an entrepreneur is beyond the scope of this chapter, it is enough to remind the reader of the diversity in definitions and the fact that there is no general agreement of what is and what is not entrepreneurship. However, the characteristics associated with entrepreneurship have mainly been examined by concentrating on differences between entrepreneurs and other groups (Low and MacMillan, 1988). Thus, previous research has tried to link the state of being defined as an entrepreneur to different personality traits. This is problematic as it assumes that entrepreneurs are a homogeneous group. However, it is clear that this is not the case as individuals will start businesses for different reasons. Whilst some are only interested in having an extra income in addition to their regular jobs, others only want to create a business large enough to support them and their families. In addition, there are a few individuals who want to create a fast-growing expanding business.

One of the first studies to differentiate entrepreneurs specifically was the work of Smith (1967), who examined the differences between the type of entrepreneur and the type of firm created by the entrepreneur, with the basic assumption that the way the firm was organised and performed was reflected by the personality of the entrepreneur. He identified two types of entrepreneur:

- the craftsman-entrepreneur
- the opportunistic-entrepreneur.

It was assumed that the craftsman type had a lower education, preferred manual work and wanted a stable income to support the family. On the other hand, the opportunist had a higher education, was more prone to be a leader and expand the business. Even if this may now seem an overly naive conception of entrepreneurship, it has the important advantage of highlighting the difference among entrepreneurs themselves. Therefore, it is a serious flaw of research not to acknowledge that entrepreneurs have totally different personal goals and, as a result of these, very different business goals.

It is therefore more accurate to assume heterogeneity and focus on differences between different types of entrepreneurs. More precisely, research has become more aware of the problem of defining entrepreneurship and now pays more attention to problems of definition and the need to examine entrepreneurship at different points of the dynamic process of business creation and expansion.

8.4.3 How do different entrepreneurs perform?

The previous two sections have described the development of the field from a simple assumption that entrepreneurs are all alike (but different from other people) to a more complex picture where entrepreneurship can be studied at various stages of a firm's development and that entrepreneurs as a group are very heterogeneous. One consequence of this is that research moved towards trying to explain the performance of the firm by examining the link between different personality characteristics of the entrepreneur and contingency variables such as age of firm, industry affiliation and organisational structure (e.g. Miller, 1987a; Miller and Toulouse, 1986). However, even if the models had evolved from simple trait-states models (as described previously) to more complex models taking into account the characteristics of the firm as well as the characteristics of the entrepreneur, the results were still weak. Two main explanations of this can be identified: namely the definition of performance and the link among personality characteristics, entrepreneurial behaviour and business performance.

To start with, what is meant by performance in this case? Three different measures are most often associated with the concept of performance:

- Survival of the firm – what factors influence the long-term survival of the firm?
- Firm growth – what factors affect the expansion of the firm?
- Firm profitability – what factors influence the firm's ability to generate profits?

These performance measures can then in turn be operationalised in a number of ways, thus adding to the confusion (Delmar, 1997; Murphy *et al.*, 1996). However, this is not the main problem, which remains one of linking traits to behaviour and then linking behaviour to business performance. When modelling behaviour and subsequent performance, psychologists tend to make a difference between distal and proximal factors affecting behaviour (Ackerman and Humphreys, 1990).

A *distal* factor is one that may explain general behaviours (such as eating, sex drives and sleeping) but which has little ability to explain how individuals act in a specific situation. For example, individuals have the need to eat and the explanation is that they have to refuel energy supplies in order to survive. However, the explanation that behaviour is driven by needs will not explain why one will have a preference to eat hamburgers instead of an *à la carte* dinner.

A *proximal* explanation looks at factors defining the situation in which individuals find themselves when choosing to go to a restaurant instead of a hamburger bar. For example, it is Friday night, they have just received a pay cheque and want to impress people. Therefore they choose to go to a fancy restaurant to eat instead of choosing a hamburger bar. The actual behaviour is then better explained by proximal factors (task characteristics) than by distal factors (traits and needs). Traits are, in general, distal factors and they therefore have little ability to explain actual behaviour and even less business performance.

Furthermore, the entrepreneurial venture can be characterised as highly complex, i.e. the demands on an individual in undertaking simple tasks such as playing pinball are very different from those of starting and maintaining a business. Campbell (2003) suggests business venturing is an example of one of the highest degrees of complexity, and these so called 'fuzzy tasks' (characterised by the presence of both multiple desired end-states and multiple ways of attaining each of the desired outcomes) are also characterised by uncertainty and conflicting interdependence. In such a case, the relation between behaviour and performance is weakened by the interactive effects between motivational processes, cognitive abilities and environmental factors. Not acknowledging this lack of correspondence between behaviour and performance has serious consequences for understanding the effects of motivation on entrepreneurial performance. For example, whilst motivation can yield high levels of cognitive effort, if it misdirected, then there will be a failure in performance (Kanfer, 1991). Thus, as McCloy *et al.* (1994) suggest, a successful entrepreneur will have to:

- possess the requisite knowledge;
- master the requisite skills;
- actually choose to work on the job tasks for some period of time at some level of effort.

To sum up, research examining the different traits or other psychological factors characterising the entrepreneur needs to take into account the complexity of the entrepreneur's situation. This is because trait theories are not sophisticated enough to account for the complexity of entrepreneurial behaviour. Therefore, research has evolved towards more proximal explanations where entrepreneurial behaviour and business performance are explained by more proximal psychological theories and where the effect of the situation is better controlled.

8.4.4 Why become an entrepreneur? The cognitive approach

The studies examined so far have concluded that the trait approach has not given any insight of great value. The assumptions behind entrepreneurial behaviour have been far too simplistic by trying to relate a trait to the state of being an entrepreneur or the performance of the firm. It is therefore impossible to say that entrepreneurs are characterised by traits predestining them to engage in business activities. Entrepreneurs are not, to a large degree, different from people in general. However, this does not explain why certain individuals still choose to undertake an entrepreneurial career. The reason for this probably lies in the fact that the same situation is perceived differently by different people depending on their previous experiences. Simple trait theories cannot account for that and the research field has now turned its attention towards theories that help us to understand how people perceive and understand the world and how it affects their behaviour. Theories trying to explain behaviour by individuals perceiving and interpreting the information around them are called *cognitive theories*.

Paralleling the development of social psychology, entrepreneurship research has moved from simple trait theories towards more cognitive theories that are better able to explain the complexity inherent in entrepreneurial behaviour. Cognitive theories assume that individuals do not possess a perfect knowledge of the world because there simply is too much information out there to handle. As a consequence they have to select information and interpret it, and thus based on their previous experience they tend to see and know the world differently (Taylor, 1998). For example, what is seen as business opportunity for one person is seen as an enormous problem impossible to solve by another. In short, individuals are actively involved in the construction of their own realities.

The use of cognitive theories enables a better understanding of why people engage in an entrepreneurial behaviour. The contribution of these theories is that they make it possible to understand better the interaction between the characteristics of the situation and characteristics of the entrepreneur. In other words, there is a movement from studying the personality of the entrepreneur to study the situations that lead to entrepreneurial behaviour (Baron, 1998; Carsrud and Johnson, 1989; Shaver and Scott, 1991). Behaviour is heavily based on how individuals perceive the situation or environment and how it is presented to them.

In other words, behavioural patterns are the products of two psychological processes. The first process operates through the selection of environments and the second through the production of environments. When people have gained certain preferences and standards of behaviour, they tend to choose activities and individuals who share the same set of preferences, thereby mutually reinforcing pre-existing personal inclinations and fixed courses of actions (Bandura, 1982; Deci, 1992a). More precisely, the individual characteristics leading to an entrepreneurial career are only activated when exposed to a favourable socialisation process, where an entrepreneurial career is seen as a viable possibility among others. Thus the social environment is of primary importance to foster future entrepreneurs. The general idea is that individual characteristics are precursor traits and in the context of a given 'cafeteria of experiences' help to determine both how experiences are weighted or attended to and how the individual reacts to those experiences. That is, individuals will only activate their entrepreneurial potential if:

- they have a certain specific ability and sensitivity,
- there are environmental possibilities,
- they have social support.

These three prerequisites must be fulfilled if actions are to be taken to become an entrepreneur. Thus the relation between intentions to act in a certain direction, the current situation and experience form the base used to better understand human and, of course, entrepreneurial behaviour. Actually, this interaction between ability or skills, environmental possibilities and social support is likely to lead to a positive reinforcing spiral where the entrepreneur is supported and therefore can further develop his specific set of skills. Hence basic intelligence coupled with an interest in becoming an entrepreneur leads the individual to develop the skills needed to become successful. These skills have been termed successful intelligence, which is a sort of intelligence that is truly task specific (Sternberg, 2004). Successful intelligence is the ability to succeed in life according to one's life goals, within one's environmental context. Hence, success is defined in terms of personal goals.

Thus, two questions arise from this section and the previous one on the characteristics of the entrepreneurial situation:

- How do people come to choose an entrepreneurial career?
- What does the entrepreneur need to learn in order to perform satisfactorily or successfully?

These are questions that are not easily answered without taking into account the complexity of human nature based on previous experience, abilities and intentions to act. The research field of entrepreneurial behaviour has, as a consequence, come to rely more and more on complex cognitive models, and especially cognitive motivation models, in order to better understand and explain the functioning of entrepreneurial behaviour, and the next step of linking actual behaviour to business performance. This is a very positive development, because the use of more sophisticated psychological models enables the research to make better sense of the findings in other fields of entrepreneurship.

Motivation theories provide a good support to understand the choices made by entrepreneurs and why they persist in doing what they are doing. They are easy to operationalise and have proven validity. Thus there is a good and reliable understanding of what motivates entrepreneurs. However, it is still problematic to understand the link between intention to do something and actual behaviour because motivational theories tend to focus on volitional behaviour, and a large part of entrepreneurial behaviour is dependent on available resources, the cooperation of others and skill. The interaction between motivation and the development of cognitive abilities represents an important avenue for future researchers interested in understanding entrepreneurship (Ackerman and Heggestad, 1997; Ackerman *et al.*, 1995; Sternberg, 2004).

8.4.5 The development of research in entrepreneurial behaviour

This section has shown that this research area has been dominated by four different basic research questions:

- Who is the entrepreneur?
- What is an entrepreneur?
- How does an entrepreneur perform?
- Why does an individual become an entrepreneur?

It was suggested that the elaboration of these four questions could explain the development of the research field from starting with a simple quest of trying to link single traits to the state of entrepreneurship to complex cognitive models taking into account the heterogeneity of entrepreneurial behaviour. In other words, the field has developed from examining personality traits in isolation to examining the interaction among the entrepreneur's perception, intention, ability and characteristics of the situation. Thus, the research field in general does not offer an easy answer to the question of who is an entrepreneur. Instead, it has evolved towards acknowledging entrepreneurship as a process that is created by entrepreneurs in cooperation with others. In short, entrepreneurial behaviour should be regarded as the consequence of person–situation interactions.

8.5 Individual characteristics of entrepreneurs

This section describes some of the individual characteristics that are supposedly related to entrepreneurs and the intention to pursue an entrepreneurial career:

- risk-taking propensity
- need for achievement
- locus of control
- over-optimism
- desire for autonomy.

The first four concepts are closely related to each other as they affect our decision making under risk and uncertainty (Mellers *et al.*, 1998). The fifth concept is closely related to the choice of becoming an entrepreneur as autonomy and freedom are often quoted as among the most important reasons to start a business. Whilst these five characteristics are often seen as positive characteristics of entrepreneurs, some research has also been undertaken on the more negative characteristics of entrepreneurs, and the section is concluded by an overview of the 'entrepreneur's dark side'.

9.5.1 Risk-taking propensity

According to economic theory, one of the important roles of the entrepreneur is the role of economic risk taker or risk bearer of the economic system (Buchanan and Di Pierro, 1980; Knight, 1921). Can it therefore be assumed that the entrepreneur is attracted to risk taking more than others are? The answer is clearly no, as a number of studies have found no significant differences between entrepreneurs and others when measuring general risk propensity (Brockhaus, 1980; Masters and Meier, 1988; Peacock, 1986). Scheré (1982) found, when examining tolerance for ambiguity, which is a concept related to risk taking, that entrepreneurs have a somewhat greater degree of tolerance than managers. Tolerance of ambiguity is an emotional reaction to ambiguity and uncertainty, and low tolerance results in stress and unpleasantness in a complex situation. Individuals with high tolerance, on the contrary, find such situations desirable and challenging. Therefore, individuals with high tolerance would expose themselves to higher risks than individuals with low tolerance who prefer well-understood situations.

Whilst these studies assume that risk taking is independent of the situation, it has been found that risk taking is extremely dependent on either a perception of the situation

(Hogarth, 1987; Mellers *et al.*, 1998) or if decision makers perceive themselves as experts in the field (Heath and Tversky, 1991). One of the most well-known studies in the field of decision making under risk is the work of Kahneman and Tversky (1979). In their book *Prospect Theory*, they suggest that a person's willingness to take risks is dependent on the perception of the situation. Individuals will be risk averse if they perceive themselves in a win situation, but will be risk seeking in a loss situation. Heath and Tversky (1991) have also suggested that individuals take considerably more risks in situations in which they feel competent.

Studies in entrepreneurship taking the context into consideration have found that risk taking was dependent on the entrepreneur's age, motivation, business experience, number of years in business and education (Schwer and Yucelt, 1984). In similar studies, Ray (1986, 1994) found that entrepreneurs are able to give up job security and take specific risks because they have the confidence that they will succeed. To sum up, results from research on risks and entrepreneurs are mixed, but apparently the perceived context (knowledge and situational characteristics) is a more important determinant of risk taking than personality.

Dickson and Giglierano (1986) propose another perspective on entrepreneurial risk taking. In their conceptual work they argue that the concept of risk can be divided into two separate components, namely the likelihood of a new venture failing and the likelihood of missing out on a strategic opportunity. According to this research, management and marketing research has mainly focused on the likelihood of failing and not on the search of new opportunities to explore. However, entrepreneurs may weigh the likelihood of missing out on a strategic opportunity higher than the likelihood of a new venture failing. Mullins and Forlani (2005) tested these hypotheses on a sample of 75 CEOs from fast-growing public firms in the US. They found that the entrepreneurs in the sample in general preferred the risk-averse choice. That is, when asked to choose between two ventures with different risks, they preferred the venture with the lower probability of losses. Furthermore, they would rather miss out on a strategic opportunity than jeopardise an existing venture. Das and Teng (1997) have also proposed a more detailed view on risk behaviour by proposing that risk is closely related to the time perspective, and an entrepreneur has to balance short-term risks against long-term risks. This has been empirically tested by Tsur *et al.* (1990) who found that risk-averse individuals were prepared to accept great risk in the short term if they believed it would minimise their long-term risk exposure. In other words, an entrepreneur will accept the risk of launching a new venture, if it is believed that the venture will minimise long-term risks (e.g. being unemployed and not having a satisfactory income).

8.5.2 Need for achievement

One of the most popular characteristics associated with entrepreneurs is McClelland's 'Need for Achievement' (1961, 1969). This characteristic is also closely related to risk taking as it takes into account the perceived risk of the situation as well as the perceived level of competence. According to McClelland, entrepreneurs are individuals who have a high need for achievement and that characteristic makes them especially suitable to create ventures. McClelland's theory identifies the situations preferred by individuals high in need for achievement, and which situations arouse the achievement motivation. Individuals who are high achievers will choose a situation characterised by:

- individual responsibility,
- moderate risk taking as a function of skill,
- knowledge of results of decisions,
- novel instrumental activity,
- anticipation of future possibilities.

It is the prospect of achievement satisfaction, not money, that drives the entrepreneur. Money is important primarily as a measure of how well one is doing in business. McClelland's theory has received consistent empirical support suggesting that there is a relationship between entrepreneurship and achievement motivation (Begley and Boyd, 1987; Bellu, 1988; Davidsson, 1989a; Delmar, 1996; Johnson, 1990; McClelland, 1961; Perry *et al.*, 1986).

Recently Miner and his associates have developed McClelland's achievement motivation theory by developing five motive patterns instead of the single achievement motive. This task motivation theory suggests that it is not possible to predict behaviour or performance on the basis of a single value, as is the case of need for achievement, but that performance can be predicted by a complex set of values or motive patterns. Miner's five motive patterns form an overall index of task motivation. They are:

- self-achievement
- risk-taking
- feedback of results
- personal innovation
- planning for the future.

Results show that the 'Miner Scales' have consistent validity, in that scores (especially total score on all scales combined) correlate significantly with entrepreneurial performance, particularly growth (Bellu, 1993; Bellu and Sherman, 1995; Miner *et al.*, 1989; Miner *et al.*, 1992; Miner *et al.*, 1994).

8.5.3 Locus of control

The concept of 'Locus of Control' can be traced back to Rotter's social learning theory (Rotter, 1966) of how individuals' perception of control affects their behaviour. The theory assumes that individuals categorise events and situations based on their underlying, shared properties. One such category concerns whether a potential end or goal can be attained through one's actions or follows from luck or other uncontrolled external factors. A person believing that the achievement of a goal is dependent on his own behaviour or individual characteristics believes in internal control. If, on the other hand, a person believes that an achievement is the result of luck and external factors, they believe in external control. Therefore, locus of control is conceived as one determinant of the expectancy of success (Weiner, 1992).

To date, some empirical results have found a low to moderate positive correlation between internal control and entrepreneurs, and there is a weak tendency that a high internal orientation is associated with better performance (Brockhaus, 1982; Miller and Toulouse, 1986). However, a number of studies have reported no significant differences between entrepreneurs and managers with respect to locus of control (Sexton and Bowman-Upton, 1985). In psychology, the concept and measurement of locus of control has been heavily criticised (Furnham and Steele, 1993), and the concept has been more or less abandoned in favour of attribution theory, which has a more complex view on causality orientation (Anderson and Strigel, 1981; Weiner, 1985). As a result, locus of control is a concept which should probably not be included in future empirical research on entrepreneurial behaviour.

8.5.4 Over-optimism

Over-optimism is closely related to locus of control, because both are related to expectancy of success. Cooper *et al.* (1986) have studied entrepreneurs' perceived chances of success shortly after they became business owners. Their responses were then compared with the actual success rate in the respective industries. When asked about the chances for a business resembling their own to survive, most of the entrepreneurs were optimistic (78% considered the chances of survival as 50:50 or higher). When asked about their own success chances the entrepreneurs were extremely optimistic (81% considered the chances of survival to be 70:30 higher). Egge (1987) also found that a majority of entrepreneurs were over-optimistic about their success rates.

This can be compared with the research undertaken on personal and general risk. *Personal risk* is defined as ratings made by the respondents of a risk as pertaining to themselves; ratings of a risk pertaining to people in general are called *general risk* ratings. Personal risks are often rated as lower than general risks as individuals have a tendency to believe that a risk (such as being hit by a car or abusing alcohol) is larger for others than for themselves. The difference between these two types of risk is related to perceived control (Sjöberg, 1993). Consequently, these differences between personal and general risk perception are of a general nature and not unique to entrepreneurship and the business setting.

8.5.5 Desire for autonomy

Entrepreneurs have been found to have a high need for autonomy (Sexton and Bowman-Upton, 1985) and fear of external control (Smith, 1967). Entrepreneurs value individualism and freedom more (i.e. the possibility to make a difference for oneself) than the general public or managers, even if those values imply some inequalities in society (Fagenson, 1993; McGrath *et al.*, 1992). This desire to manage one's own business is a central feature of entrepreneurship, but it is difficult to explain the causal order. That is, do individuals with a high desire for autonomy start a venture because they want autonomy, or do they want autonomy because they do not want others to take control of what they have once created? Differently stated, desire for autonomy can result in venture creation, but can also be a result of having created a business.

8.5.6 The dark side of entrepreneurship

Any review of the psychological approach would be incomplete without mentioning the contribution of Kets De Vries (1977) on the dark side of the entrepreneur. The reason Kets De Vries is included in this chapter is his psychoanalytical approach to entrepreneurship, despite the fact that the study was undertaken more than 20 years ago. When most researchers see entrepreneurial behaviour as the result of positive characteristics or drives, Kets De Vries takes an opposite stand-point. Entrepreneurial behaviour is the result of negative characteristics and drives. According to him entrepreneurial behaviour and its resulting financial benefits do not always lead to personal satisfaction and happiness. Quite the contrary, the entrepreneur is: 'an anxious individual, a non-conformist poorly organised and not a stranger to self-destructive behaviour' (Kets De Vries, 1977:41).

Furthermore, he suggests that financial success is often followed by personal crises and even poverty. Basically, what goes up must come down. This behavioural pattern is explained by experiences related to a troublesome and very disturbed childhood where the father is often absent. As a consequence, the entrepreneur becomes a person with low self-esteem and lacks self-critical reflections, always dreaming of becoming a person in total control and independent of everything and everyone. This would then explain why entrepreneurs become engaged in high-risk situations and choose to create their own organisation instead of working within an established one.

However, there are doubts about this research. Entrepreneurs are not more troubled than anyone else, and there is substantial evidence that entrepreneurs come from financially and emotionally stable families. For example, a substantial number of studies have pointed out that positive role models, and especially parents, are of central importance for fostering future entrepreneurs (Aldrich *et al.*, 1997; Matthews and Moser, 1995; Scherer *et al.*, 1991), which is obviously in conflict with Kets De Vries' study. His main contribution is the acknowledgement that entrepreneurs are not some kind of superhuman heroes, but that they are people like the rest of us with faults and merits, and that their behaviour can be explained by more or less noble goals. Furthermore, Kets De Vries points at the fact that entrepreneurs encounter problems they cannot solve and that they may therefore fail. Therefore, it is clear that the psychological perspective has been far too interested in success, and that behaviour in crisis and failure situations is an under-researched field.

8.5.7 Summing up individual characteristics of entrepreneurs

A large number of traits or characteristics have been proposed to describe entrepreneurs. With the exception of the need for achievement, the results have in general been poor and it has been difficult to link any specific traits to entrepreneurial behaviour. Nevertheless, recent research leads to more optimism; with more updated theories and better knowledge of when personality traits are expected to have an effect we tend to find some basic relationships. The reasons for this are complex but what can be seen is that these traits now seem to collapse into broader areas – risk taking, need for achievement, locus of control and over-optimism are all closely related to decision making under risk. Therefore, those researchers still interested in risk and entrepreneurship tend to rely more and more on cognitive decision theories. However, the problem with cognitive decision theories is that they do not take into account individual differences and this is still the main objective of the field. There is still a need to understand why some engage in entrepreneurial behaviour and others do not. Cognitive motivation models offer both the ability of explaining highly complex behaviour and differences in choices and performances. The next section of this chapter will discuss the most recent advances in the field.

8.6 Cognitive models of entrepreneurial behaviour

There is a need for an individual-level understanding of the processes leading to entrepreneurial behaviour that has not been met by studies of individual traits. Research, as stated earlier, has evolved towards more integrated and complex models that take into account not only psychological characteristics of entrepreneurs but also situational variables and personal background (e.g. age, sex). These models can be divided in two groups depending on their focus. As they are models of human behaviour they tend to overlap, but they tend to focus on different theoretical explanations of human behaviour.

The first group is mainly interested in how our attitudes to entrepreneurship (i.e. starting a business or expanding a business) shape our behaviour. This group is labelled *attitude-based models*. The second group is concerned with motivation in achievement contexts. That is, why do individuals engage and behave in situations where they have to compete with others and therefore risk failure? This group is labelled *achievement-context models*.

8.6.1 Attitude-based models

Attitude is one of the major concepts in motivation theories. An attitude is a valuation of an object or a concept, i.e. to what extent an object or concept is judged as good or bad (Eagly and Chaiken, 1993). In psychological language, traits such as 'Locus of Control' or 'Over-Optimism' are distal, i.e. weak determinants of specific behaviours. Attitudes, on the other hand, are proximal, i.e. more specific, and because of their specificity they are considered to be important determinants of behaviour. Furthermore, attitudes are interesting because of their applied relevance. It is believed that attitudes have an impact on behaviour. It is therefore interesting to understand how attitudes can be changed. Consequently, the impact of attitudes on entrepreneurial behaviour is worthy of closer examination because they are supposed to have a directive influence on behaviour and they are much easier to change than personality and other more distal traits or characteristics. This would mean that if the attitudes characterising entrepreneurs starting a new business were known, other people could be influenced to adopt these attitudes and, as a result, increase the number of people starting a business.

The drawbacks concern how well attitudes actually predict behaviours and explain when or why a specific action is engaged in. The importance of attitudes in predicting behaviour has been most debated, but recent research has now shown that attitudes can predict behaviour if certain conditions are met (Bagozzi and Warshaw, 1992; Doll and Ajzen, 1992; Kim and Hunter, 1993). Attitudes are tendencies or dispositions to behave in a generally favourable or unfavourable way towards the object of the attitude. For example, this means that it is difficult to say if a person will start a business because their attitudes are positive to the act of starting a business. It is only known that this person will act in a way that is in accordance with their attitudes. In this example, it means that this person will behave favourably to everything that is connected with business start-ups such as encouraging a friend or relative to start a business, finance a start-up effort, or even to individually establish their own business. A shortcoming of attitude theories is that they give no information about how an individual's evaluation of a concept is translated into action and outcomes. Differently stated, attitude theories help us understand how choices are made and why, but they give little guidance about the chosen level of effort and persistence (Locke, 1991).

Nevertheless, the advantages override the disadvantages. The possibility to closely examine attitudes towards different facets of entrepreneurship and the ability to easily communicate the results to a wider audience (such as policy makers) are strong arguments. Furthermore, even if attitudes are not perfect predictors of behaviours, they are still much better than distal personality characteristics. As a consequence, attitude theories have received a fair share of attention within the field of entrepreneurship. Two attitude concepts have been predominantly researched, namely attitudes to becoming self-employed or starting a business and attitudes to business growth. The research around these concepts is either based on formal attitude theory or on finding simple relationships among attitudes and the concept. The most used model is Ajzen's (1991) *Theory of Planned Behaviour* or adapted versions of it. Researchers such as Krueger and colleagues (Krueger and Brazeal, 1994; Krueger and Carsrud, 1993) have proposed the theory as a possible venue for explaining entrepreneurial behaviour, and especially the engagement in the start-up of a business.

The purpose of the theory of planned behaviour is to explain behaviour when actions are not under complete behavioural control. That is, when actions are dependent on something or someone else beyond one's control. Starting a business is an example of where actions are dependent on necessary resources and knowing the right people. The basic assumption is that people carefully assess the information they have about the behaviour and form beliefs about it, and then try to act in accordance with these beliefs or attitudes. The theory postulates that the tendency to engage in a particular behaviour is determined by the individual's intention to do so. Thus, behavioural intentions mediate the effect of attitudes on behaviour (Ajzen, 1995). This means that people will start a business if:

■ they have enough information to form an opinion,

■ the opinion is favourable to the behaviour of starting a business,

■ they have the intention to start a business.

Thus, behaviour is determined directly by one's intention to act, and intention in turn is influenced by attitudes. This is the first factor of the theory of planned behaviour.

The second factor is subjective or social norms which, in combination with attitudes towards the behaviour, determine intention and consequently actual behaviour. Social

167

norms as a concept are defined as the perceived social pressure (what other things the individual should do) to perform or not to perform the behaviour (Bagozzi and Kimmel, 1995). To continue the business start-up example, this means that a person will only try to start a business if they feel that people around them encourage or support that kind of behaviour.

However, these two factors (attitudes and subjective norms) are by themselves not enough to explain why people engage in specific behaviour when it is not under full behavioural control. Hence, a third factor is introduced in order to predict intentions and behaviour, namely perceived behavioural control. This is a concept of central importance in explaining entrepreneurial behaviour and is defined as the perceived ease or difficulty of performing the behaviour. Furthermore, it is supposed to reflect anticipated problems and obstacles as well as past experiences. Assuming somewhat favourable subjective norms and attitudes to a behaviour, a person's intention to perform the behaviour will increase with perceived behavioural control. Furthermore, if perceived behavioural control is in accordance with actual behavioural control, this can help to predict the likelihood that intentions will be realised into behaviour (Ajzen, 1991, 1995).

How does this theory then help further to understand entrepreneurial intentions? First of all it is a theory taking into account the complexity of human behaviour and it points out a central wisdom: 'You are not born an entrepreneur, you are made an entrepreneur.' That is, attitude models such as the theory of planned behaviour give us valuable instruments to understand how to change people's feelings and beliefs towards entrepreneurship, and consequently create a more supportive environment to entrepreneurship. Thus, the theory of planned behaviour is often referred to in entrepreneurship research, but few have actually tested the model. Most research is only based on measurement between the three different factors (attitudes, subjective norms and perceived behavioural control) and intentions. The link between intentions and actual behaviour is still a black box. Nevertheless, valuable results have been produced.

Whether business start-ups (Davidsson, 1995; Kolvereid, 1996a, 1996b; Krueger, 1993) or growth (Davidsson, 1989b; Kolvereid, 1992; Kolvereid and Bullvag, 1996; Wiklund, 1998; Wiklund et al., 2003) are examined, the same results tend to be repeated. First, attitudes have by themselves little ability to predict the intention to expand a business or to start one. Second, subjective norms have an even weaker predictive power. What others believe or feel is important does not particularly affect the entrepreneur's intentions. However, what is important and stands out as the strongest predictor is perceived behavioural control. In other words, people in general are rather positive towards entrepreneurship (starting or expanding a business), which means that perceived behavioural control does not discriminate very well between those that engage in a particular behaviour and those that are just favourable. What stands out instead is whether people feel that entrepreneurship is a feasible option for themselves. In other words, a person will try to start a business if they believe that they can do it in terms of having the ability and knowledge required to carry out the behaviour. Thus, perceived behavioural control or perceived feasibility is the key component to explain when a person will engage in entrepreneurial behaviour. Davidsson (1995) studied intentions to start a business in Sweden and found that men and women differed little in their attitudes, but women were low on perceived behavioural control. This could then explain why women are under-represented among entrepreneurs. They do not have enough confidence in their own ability and in know-how to start and operate a business, and therefore they abstain from doing so (see Chapter 9 for a more detailed discussion of gender).

To sum up, research on attitudes and entrepreneurship has yielded consistent findings. A number of studies found that perceived behavioural control was the single most important predictor of intentions. Both attitudes and subjective norms played a relatively minor role. However, attitude models, such as the theory of planned behaviour, offer little information on how and why certain behaviour is chosen by an individual.

8.6.2 Cognitive motivation models and entrepreneurship

The next section will review two cognitive motivation models of human behaviour and how they have been applied to the field of entrepreneurship. The common denominator of these models and the one presented in this section is the search for control. That is, individuals try to organise their lives in ways that give the level of perceived control. However, the following two models go a step further by incorporating moods and emotions in their structure. The theory of planned behaviour is concerned with preferences (what is and what is not important) rather than emotions (what we find enjoyable, boring or stressful to do), and human behaviour is dictated to a large extent by our moods and feelings. Furthermore, these models deal with both behaviour and actual performance and are therefore referred to as *achievement-contexts models*.

Perceived self-efficacy

The chapter has already concluded that perceived behavioural control is an important determinant of entrepreneurial behaviour. A closely related concept is the concept of perceived self-efficacy. It is a concept 'concerned with people's beliefs about their capabilities to produce performances that influence events affecting their lives' (Bandura, 1995:434). In other words, it is about a person's beliefs in their capabilities to mobilise the motivation, cognitive resources and courses of actions needed to control events in their life. Hence, it is concerned with how individuals' beliefs about their own capabilities shape the perceived control of their levels of functioning and over the events of their lives. A person's beliefs in their efficacy influence the decisions they make, their level of aspirations, how much effort is mobilised in a given situation, how long they persist at the task in the face of difficulties and setbacks, and whether their thought patterns are self-hindering or self-aiding.

Perceived self-efficacy has been proposed as a central concept in entrepreneurship (Boyd and Vozikis, 1994) because it is proximal in nature and has been proven to be associated with initiating and persisting in achievement-related behaviours such as business settings (Wood and Bandura, 1989). The perceived self-efficacy of entrepreneurs has been proven to affect the strategies and performance of their businesses (Westerberg, 1998), and it was found that entrepreneurs high in perceived self-efficacy in general achieved a higher performance for their firms than those low in perceived self-efficacy. Performance was measured here as profitability, customer satisfaction and ability to survive. Perceived self-efficacy is also positively related to the intention of starting one's own business and exploring new opportunities (Chen *et al.*, 1998; Krueger and Dickson, 1993; Krueger and Dickson, 1994).

The roots of self-efficacy can be traced back to the concept of locus of control discussed earlier although there is one large difference. Whilst an individual's self-efficacy depends on the situation, locus of control can be seen as generalised self-efficacy. In other words, self-efficacy is closely related to a situation or to an object, which means that we can have high self-efficacy in one situation and low self-efficacy in another. For example, individuals may perceive themselves as highly capable rock climbers, but with low capabilities in business matters, even if the two situations involve considerable risk taking.

Furthermore, perceived self-efficacy is part of a larger theory called social cognitive theory of self-regulation (Bandura, 1986, 1991; Wood and Bandura, 1989). The aim of this theory is to explain goal-directed behaviour and it assumes that most behaviours have a purpose regulated by forethought. More precisely, individuals tend to form beliefs about what they can do, they anticipate the likely consequences of prospective actions, they set goals for themselves, and plan courses of action that are likely to produce the desired outcome. In this theory, perceived self-efficacy is one of the most central mechanisms as it is the key to understanding how individuals function when setting goals and carrying out the actions needed to fulfil them. In comparison with the theory of planned behaviour (which focuses on predicting behaviour), it is more relevant to explain the functioning of perceived control and its effect on both behaviour and performance.

On the one hand, people with a high level of self-efficacy (i.e. with high assurance in their capabilities) approach difficult tasks as challenges to be mastered rather than issues to be avoided. They set themselves challenging goals and maintain strong commitment to them. They are persistent even in the face of failure and they maintain an analytical distance that guides effective performance. They also tend to attribute failure to insufficient effort and poor knowledge. On the other hand, people with a low level of self-efficacy shy away from difficult tasks which are perceived as personal threats. They have a low level of aspirations and commitment to the goals they have chosen to pursue, do not maintain any analytical focus, and they give up easily. Failure is attributed to external obstacles and personal deficiencies. As a consequence they rapidly lose faith in their own capabilities. A personal level of self-efficacy is often the result of previous successful or unsuccessful experience (both personal experience or by observing role models). Therefore, self-efficacy has the tendency to be a pattern of a positive or negative circle – success breeds success and failure breeds failure. In other words, if one has observed successful entrepreneurs or has personal positive experience there is a high probability that one might engage in the same behaviour again and be successful in it again. In the same manner, a person with low self-efficacy will not engage in a specific behaviour, and if that person still engages in this behaviour they stand a high probability of failure. However, a negative pattern due to low self-efficacy can be broken and self-efficacy enhanced through proper training (Bandura, 1986; Westerberg, 1998).

To conclude, self-efficacy is related to perceived behavioural control, but the present concept focuses more on the actual functioning of perceived capabilities. The role of self-efficacy has been researched within the field of entrepreneurship and received support. That is, how beliefs in one's capabilities to mobilise the motivation, cognitive resources and courses of actions needed to control events in life (such as starting and managing a business) affect our behaviour and subsequent performance. Self-efficacy is a proximal concept and closely related to a person's feelings towards a behaviour. This means that self-efficacy is malleable and (as with the rest of the cognitive models) it means that self-efficacy can be enhanced through proper training. The training and development of cognitive resources such as self-efficacy will be discussed separately when the impact of cognitive models on our understanding of entrepreneurial behaviour is summarised. The next model is also linked to the relationship between motivation, behaviour and performance, and focuses specifically on one of the positive effects of high self-efficacy: the feeling of intrinsic motivation.

Intrinsic motivation

Intrinsic motivation is closely connected to or even equated with interest and enjoyment. Intrinsic motivation is often determined as an action engaged in for its own sake, contrary to extrinsic motivation where external motivators play a central role to motivate behaviour (e.g. acting to get a reward and not because the task itself is attractive) (Amabile *et al.*, 1994; Deci, 1992b). In other words, intrinsically motivated behaviours are ones for which there is no apparent reward except for the activity itself. On the other hand, extrinsically motivated behaviours refer to behaviours where an external controlling variable can be readily identified by the persons acting. People focusing more on behaviours for their extrinsic benefits tend to perform worse than those who focus on behaviours for their intrinsic benefits. Compared with perceived self-efficacy which focuses on one's representation of capabilities and control of behaviour, theories of intrinsic motivation focus on one's representation of what one finds enjoyable (and self-fulfilling) and on control of behaviour. However, these are different sides of the same coin, and Bandura (1991, 1995) himself points out that intrinsic motivation is both an antecedent and a consequence of high self-efficacy.

Theories about intrinsic motivation or task interests have the capacity to integrate attitudes, goals and emotions. Interest is closely connected to the emotion of enjoyment and it is an important factor in achievement settings. Attitudes differ from interests, where the latter refers to what the individual likes/dislikes and the former to what the individual finds important/unimportant. Thus, certain events can be considered important but not interesting, and vice versa. Together, attitudes and interests can be assumed to form a set of preferences that guides our choices between different alternatives in decision making. Preferences are used when, through rank-ordering, assessments are made of the alternatives in choice situations. Interests, attitudes and preferences therefore reflect the emotional value of the cognitive representations of reality.

Interest functions primarily as an important positive emotion motivating cognitive and motor search, and exploratory behaviour, and is a significant determinant of selective attention and hence of the contents of perception and cognition. It not only determines the choices made, but also the intensity and strength of an experience. The direction of interest is highly personal and varies widely between different individuals. It probably has its background in personal development and is linked to an inborn ability and sensitivity and the possibilities and support given by the environment. Interest is a function of challenge and ability, which in its turn determines what is a moderately difficult challenge. It is therefore important that the challenge can stimulate an activity where the individual has a good chance of success but is not certain to succeed. Interest is also a prerequisite condition to a really creative contribution, as creativity on a high level demands great devotion to a certain kind of activity that one may be unwilling to undertake if one does not feel a great interest for the activity (Csikszentmihalyi, 1992; Izard, 1984).

Tasks or job interests have been shown to predict entrepreneurial behaviour (measured as business growth and profitability) and how it is manifested (Delmar, 1996). Interest plays a central role in entrepreneurial behaviour as it is closely connected to central entrepreneurial concepts such as achievement, autonomy and creation. Interest can also be assumed to be central to the entrepreneurial process, since an entrepreneur has, in some sense, to be interested in (or attracted to) some aspect of entrepreneurship. The entrepreneur's interests are important because they are related to which goals are chosen and how much effort will be expended in order to achieve them.

The relation between goal setting and interest and enjoyment is based on the fact that, when people are engaged in interesting activities, they often have goals for what they want to accomplish (Elliot and Harackiewicz, 1994; Epstein and Harackiewicz, 1992; Harackiewicz and Elliot, 1993). For example, an entrepreneur might start a business to expand into a larger business, find a pleasurable professional activity or escape unemployment. An entrepreneur may generate such goals on their own or the goals may be implicit in a particular situation. An achievement-orientated entrepreneur may strive to expand the venture in any situation or the situation itself may be structured to elicit achievement situations (e.g. in a highly competitive industry such as the computer hardware industry). These goals could also be influenced by other people, as family, friends or capital providers try to prompt the adoption of particular goals for performance. What is important is that when the entrepreneur's personal interests coincide with business goals such as expansion, they become more effective and successful in operating the business.

To sum up, the emotion of interest and its effect on entrepreneurial behaviour have been discussed. It was found that an entrepreneur's task interest (i.e. what kind of task they most enjoy doing) affected the development of the business measured in terms of profitability and growth. Entrepreneurs are more interested in marketing-related questions, are more growth oriented and had more profitable businesses. The explanation is that interest is a significant determinant of selective attention and hence of the contents of perception and cognition. Thus, when the entrepreneur's interests coincide with achievement goals such as business profitability and growth, they will have an easier and more enjoyable time, and behave in a way that results in higher performance compared with entrepreneurs not interested in the same goals. In short, interest leads to higher attention, better decision making and a feeling of enjoyment. As we have seen earlier in this chapter the interaction between motivations such as interest will affect both creativity and the development of cognitive abilities such as successful intelligence (Sternberg, 2004; Sternberg and Lubart, 1996).

8.6.3 Summing up cognitive models

This section has reviewed three different cognitive models or concepts (attitude models, perceived self-efficacy and intrinsic motivation) that have greatly enhanced our understanding of entrepreneurial behaviour. The theoretical value of cognitive models is that they offer a sophisticated theoretical frame of reference that incorporates the complexity of entrepreneurial behaviour and enables the actual test of the model. They are, in nature, more proximal than the more distal traits or personality characteristics. This leads to higher explanatory power as we have to understand what really is at the core of entrepreneurial behaviour. For example, Baron and Markman (2003) investigated the social competence (the ability to interact effectively with others based on discrete social skills) of entrepreneurs. Based on a sample of 230 entrepreneurs taken from both the cosmetics and the high-technology industries, they found that the accuracy of perceiving others (e.g. their traits, intentions and behaviour) was positively associated with financial success. Furthermore, they found that social adaptability (the ability to adapt or feel comfortable in a wide range of social situations) was important for entrepreneurs in the cosmetics industry, and expressiveness (the ability to express oneself clearly to generate enthusiasm in others) was important for entrepreneurs in the high-technology industries. This research indicates the importance of understanding situational constraints, that skills are developed over time, and that proximal measures are likely to generate important results in understanding the psychology of the entrepreneur. Finally, research can offer better explanations of how entrepreneurs behave because we are focusing on their cognition, i.e. how we organise and come to understand the information around us. This also leads to a number of practical consequences.

By focusing on how people think and react more than on who they are, there has been a shift in focus from stable traits that are not easily changeable to more easily changeable cognitive processes. Thus the practical value of this research is that there is an understanding of how entrepreneurs become who they are and this knowledge can be used to educate and train potential entrepreneurs. That is, in order to create an environment where more businesses are created and expanded we need to have favourable attitudes and feelings towards the object. However, what leads to actual behaviour is the individual's feeling of control and that they enjoy what they are doing. More precisely, an individual will engage in an entrepreneurial act if they believe they know how to do it and that behaviour is intrinsically rewarding. This knowledge and feeling can, according to Bandura (1995), be obtained in four different ways:

■ by mastery experiences – personal experience
■ by vicarious experiences – experience by observing others
■ by social persuasion
■ by reducing negative emotions towards the behaviour.

Mastery of experience is the most effective way of accomplishing a high feeling of control. The reason is that personal experience offers the authentic evidence that one can master what it takes to succeed. Successes tend to build a strong belief in one's personal capabilities and failures tend to undermine it, especially before a strong sense of one's capabilities have been rooted. The second way of creating and enhancing beliefs of capability and control is through vicarious experiences, for example observing role models. Seeing people similar to oneself succeed by sustained effort raises an individual's beliefs about his capabilities; observing others fail despite high effort lowers an individual's beliefs about his capabilities. For the experience to be effective, it is important that the individual can identify with the role model. A third, but less effective, way than the two previous ones is through social persuasion (i.e. convincing people that they have what it takes to succeed). The last way of modifying people's feeling of control towards a specific behaviour is to reduce the negative emotions such as stress and anxiety. The reason is that people rely to a large extent on their somatic and emotional state (such as having a gut feeling, nervousness or fatigue) in judging their capabilities. As a result, negative feelings are interpreted as having low capabilities.

Hence, it can be concluded that cognitive models such as the one presented here have several advantages compared with previous trait-based models. Instead of talking about a set of non-changeable traits, cognitive functions that can be altered should be discussed. Cognitive models have both a greater power to explain entrepreneurial behaviour and offer practical advice on how to train and educate future entrepreneurs.

8.7 Chapter summary

In attempting to present a review of research on entrepreneurial personality and behaviour this chapter has been divided into three major parts. The first part covered the development of the field until the present, while the second part examined the early research related to traits and personality characteristics that have dominated the field for a long time. Due to the inability to explain entrepreneurial behaviour, early research was abandoned in favour of more complex models that take into account the situation and the person's perception of the situation, known as cognitive models.

The development of the field from individual trait theories to cognitive models also represents a shift in how entrepreneurial behaviour can be understood and how knowledge can be utilised. Traits are supposedly stable over time, and can only offer grounds for selection of potential entrepreneurs. Cognitive models (such as those reviewed here) conceive human behaviour as directed by goals and motivation and perception of control. As a consequence, their practical value is that they are better at explaining entrepreneurial behaviour and can create instruments to better educate and train potential entrepreneurs.

However, the careful reader will notice that relatively little research has been achieved using models based on cognitive theories. There have been several conceptual papers advocating cognitive theories, but little empirical research has actually been carried out where different models have been systematically tested. Hence, much more work is still needed to fully understand the complexity of entrepreneurial behaviour.

Questions

1 Discuss the traits approach to the entrepreneurial personality and the reasons why it fails to properly predict the behaviour of entrepreneurs.

2 Discuss the differences between the major theoretical schools regarding the psychology of the entrepreneur.

3 What are the theoretical and practical advantages of the cognitive model in describing the behaviour of entrepreneurs?

Web links

www.babson.edu/entrep/fer/
Website of the Annual Frontiers of Entrepreneurship Research Conference that contains a range of papers on the characteristics of the entrepreneur.

www.businessballs.com/davidmcclelland.htm
An article that introduces David McClelland and his work on need for achievement.

www-unix.oit.umass.edu/~aizen
Homepage of Icek Ajzen who developed the theory of planned behaviour.

www.des.emory.edu/mfp/eff.html
An overview of social cognitive theory with links to the websites of the key researchers such as Albert Bandura.

CHAPTER 9

Gender and entrepreneurship

Sara Carter and Dinah Bennett

9.1 Introduction

Over the past 30 years two parallel trends have occurred. First, in almost every country in the world there has been growth in both the size and the relative importance of the small business sector. Second, female suffrage, achieved in many countries within the twentieth century, has been followed by a large-scale expansion in the economic participation of women in the labour market. Although there is as yet no country in the world where women constitute the majority of business owners, women's share of business ownership appears to be growing. Early research on gender and enterprise, initially undertaken in the US in the 1970s, but rapidly followed by analyses undertaken in a wide variety of country contexts, concentrated on developing descriptive analyses of women business owners. These studies portrayed women business owners as broadly similar to their male counterparts, but identified gender-specific barriers and constraints. Most recent research has attempted to empirically demonstrate the presence of gender-specific barriers and to assess the effect of these barriers on women-owned firms. This chapter reviews the development of the research literature on women's entrepreneurship and highlights some of the main themes that have emerged. Finally, the chapter assesses the likely future development of the women's entrepreneurship research field and specifies the need for greater theoretical engagement in order to unravel the causes and consequences of gender disadvantage.

9.2 Learning objectives

There are four learning objectives in this chapter:

1 To understand the personal and business characteristics of women entrepreneurs and the main management constraints that they may face.

2 To understand the similarities and differences in the characteristics of women entrepreneurs and the constraints they may face within differing country contexts.

3 To review the historical development and status of research investigating female entrepreneurship.

4 To understand the need for a greater theoretical engagement with the social sciences in order to unravel the causes and consequences of gender disadvantage.

Key concepts

■ women   ■ gender   ■ entrepreneurship

9.3 Gender and enterprise

Research investigating women's ownership of small businesses essentially dates from the mid-1970s. Prior to the pioneering studies of Schreier (1973) and Schwartz (1976), the contribution women made to the small firms sector either as business owners in their own right or, more commonly, as providers of labour to family-owned firms, was largely unrecognised. The growth in interest in the small business sector, coupled with a rise in the number of women moving into self-employment, triggered a number of important research studies investigating the issue of gender and enterprise. This research effort continues to this day, although the issues and themes being addressed by researchers have changed and developed over time. While many of the major studies have emanated from the US and Western Europe, research investigating the characteristics and experiences of women business owners has been drawn from a wide range of countries and socio-economic contexts. This chapter highlights some of the key themes which have emerged from these studies. Following this introduction, the chapter starts by documenting the increase in the numbers of women entering self-employment and business ownership. This is followed by an overview of the research studies that have explored women's business ownership, highlighting the early exploratory studies and more recent analyses drawn from a variety of country contexts.

More recent studies have focused on the broad issues of management in female-owned businesses, in particular the relative access to finance for female entrepreneurs. Increasingly sophisticated studies have attempted to explain the differing business financing profiles of male and female business owners. While most studies have focused on women's access to and usage of debt finance, in particular bank finance, increasing attention is currently being focused on private equity and venture capital. In a new development within the literature, research has not only focused on women's access to equity finance, but also on investigating women as providers of equity capital to other entrepreneurs. As a key theme within the literature, this chapter considers the main research evidence relating to the gender, entrepreneurship and finance nexus.

Despite the development of an important research literature on women business owners, some researchers argue that the study of female entrepreneurship remains a neglected area (Baker *et al.*, 1997). While the volume of research that considers gender is still relatively small, particularly in relation to that which considers the small business sector as a whole, there is evidence that the quality of the research has developed a greater sophistication and methodological maturity. In addition, key critiques from within the entrepreneurship subject domain (Ahl, 2002) and from the broader social sciences (Mirchandani, 1999) have outlined the need for future research to contain stronger theoretical engagement. The chapter concludes by considering the reasons why the study of female entrepreneurship has been relatively neglected and evaluating the benefits that can accrue from critical perspectives on the gender and entrepreneurship research literature.

9.4 The growth of female entrepreneurship

Over the past 30 years there have been increases in the number of women entering self-employment and business ownership, although the rate of increase has varied widely from country to country. In the US, it is estimated that there are currently 10.6 million firms that are at least 50% owned by a woman, accounting for 48% of all privately held firms. Women-owned firms in the US employ in the region of 19.1 million workers and generate $2.5 trillion (defined as a million millions) in sales (National Women's Business Council, 2004). Collectively, women-owned businesses in the US are estimated to spend $492bn per year on salaries and employee benefits, and in addition spend $38bn on IT, $25bn on telecommunications, $23bn on human resource services and $17bn on shipping (National Women's Business Council, 2004). The number of women-owned businesses in the US has expanded much more rapidly than in almost any other country. Between 1997 and 2004, the estimated growth in the number of women-owned firms (17%) was nearly twice that of all firms (9%) and the number of women-owned firms with employees grew by 28%, three times the growth rate of all firms with employees (National Women's Business Council, 2004).

A key issue in international comparative assessments of the numbers and trends relating to women's business ownership lies in the definitional differences of what constitutes a woman-owned business. In the US the term 'women-owned businesses' includes businesses solely owned by a woman or women, businesses that are majority (>51%) owned by a woman or women and businesses that are owned equally (50/50) by women and men. A more precise definition of women-owned businesses would include only those that are majority (>51%) woman owned. However, even this more careful definition still demonstrates the outstanding success of female entrepreneurship in the US. Businesses that are majority owned (>51%) by women comprise 63% of women-owned businesses, a total of 6.7 million firms that collectively employ 9.8 million people and generate $1.2 trillion in sales (National Women's Business Council, 2004). International comparisons may be more accurately assessed through the use of self-employment data. In 2002, the total number of self-employed in the US was 8,490,000 (6.4% of total employment). Of this, male self-employment accounted for 5,124,000 (7.3% total male employment) and female self-employment accounted for 3,366,000 (5.4% total female employment). While male self-employment still accounts for a larger proportion of the self-employed total (60.3%), the female share of self-employment, which currently accounts for 39.6% of the total, has expanded every year for the past 30 years. In 1976, women constituted 26.8% of total self-employment in the US, a figure that has increased gradually year by year to its present level of nearly 40%.

By comparison, within the UK, researchers have operated a more cautious definition of women-owned businesses, focusing their attention on businesses that are wholly owned by women. Survey data suggests that about 15% of UK businesses are women-owned, 50% are male-owned and 35% are co-owned by males and females (Small

Business Service, 2004). Women currently account for 26.7% of the self-employed total, a figure that has shown modest fluctuations but little change since 1984 when the female share of self-employment increased from 18% to 24% of the total (Labour Force Survey, 2005). Although remarkable increases in female self-employment have been seen within the US over the past ten years, the UK situation is marked by more modest attainment. In 1992, there were 899,000 self-employed women (7% of economically active women) accounting for 26% of the total self-employed population. In 2004, following growth in total UK self-employment, there were 963,000 self-employed women in the UK, but they accounted for the same proportion of economically active women (7%) and a similar share of the self-employed population (27%).

Across the EU (15), in comparison with men, there are fewer self-employed women in all age groups and across all business sectors. The EU (15) average level of self-employment in industry and services, as a percentage of total employment, is 15.5% for men and 8% for women. Self-employment in the UK is slightly below the average for the EU (15) (14% male, 6% female) and much lower than in the highest countries of Greece (31% male, 16% female), Italy (26% male, 15% female) and Portugal (20% male and 13% female). The EU (15) countries with the lowest levels of self-employment as a percentage of total employment are Luxemburg (8% male, 5% female), Denmark (10% male, 4% female) and Austria (10% male, 5% female). More female (30%) than male (23%) self-employment is within the retail and distribution sectors, while more male (30%) than female (13%) self-employment is within the industry and construction sectors. Across the EU (15) as a whole, with the exception of Greece, a much larger proportion of female self-employment is within distribution, community and personal services, and hotels and restaurants sectors. While the male and female self-employed population has similar levels of education, self-employed females are more likely to operate smaller enterprises/units (Franco and Winquist, 2002).

A recent study of female entrepreneurial activity rates undertaken as part of the Global Entrepreneurship Monitor (Acs *et al.*, 2005) shows that there is, as yet, no country in the world where there are more women than men participating in business ownership (Minitti *et al.*, 2005). The GEM research project also found that, despite the remarkable growth in the number of women entrepreneurs, the US lies only eighth out of 34 nations. The countries with the highest levels of female entrepreneurial activity rates are Peru, Uganda, Ecuador and Jordan. All of these countries also demonstrate correspondingly high levels of male entrepreneurial activity. While some researchers have drawn distinctions between the types of entrepreneurial activity apparent in developed and developing countries, tending to conceptualise the former as opportunity-driven and the latter as a function of necessity (Acs *et al.*, 2005), it is clear that many developing countries may offer rich insights into the experiences of women-owned businesses.

Global comparisons are not only constrained by definitional differences, but are complicated by the differing social and economic environments in which enterprises operate, the prevailing culture and the legal status of women (Marcucci *et al.*, 2001; Richardson *et al.*, 2004). Delmar and Holmquist (2004) point out that women's entrepreneurship depends on both the situation of women and the role of entrepreneurship in the society. The motivation and objectives for starting a business, education, individual levels of entrepreneurship as well as time management of home and community responsibilities all have an impact on levels of entrepreneurial participation and the types of enterprises established. A study undertaken by Richardson *et al.* (2004) of women-owned enterprises in Africa and Asia, for example, reported the situation in Bangladesh, a country in a lengthy recession, dependent on foreign assistance and where unexpectedly severe monsoon floods added a long-term risk to growth forecasts. Female economic participation was 73% of the male rate, while the share of earned income of women was 23.1% in contrast with the male share of 76.9% (UNDP, 1998). As a consequence of economic necessity, purdah (female seclusion) was becoming less rigid, allowing women to work outside the home. As Richardson *et al.* (2004) point out, the economic background and culture of Bangladesh is markedly different from western countries where most studies of female entrepreneurship have been conducted. Despite this, broad comparisons can be drawn. In all of the countries studied, the share of earned income of women was lower than that of men and the highest proportion of women-owned enterprises operate within traditionally feminised sectors such as retail and low-order services (Marcucci, 2001).

9.5 The characteristics and experiences of female entrepreneurs

Little was known about the female entrepreneur until the mid-1980s. Although many studies had been undertaken investigating small business owners, the bulk of the work concentrated upon the male-owned enterprise and there was an assumption that patterns of female behaviour conformed to those established using male samples. As Berg (1997: 259) states, theory building in the area of entrepreneurship has been 'based on studies of men'. The 1980s heralded the start of a new research interest in women's business ownership, reflecting both the rise in the number of women starting in business in many western economies and a growing academic interest in small business and the nature of entrepreneurship. Influenced by the existing small business literature, early studies of female entrepreneurship concentrated mainly upon the motivations for business start-up (Schreier, 1973; Schwartz, 1976; Goffee and Scase, 1985b; Hisrich and Brush, 1986) and, to a lesser extent, the gender-related barriers experienced during this phase of business ownership (Watkins and Watkins, 1984; Hisrich and Brush, 1986; Carter and Cannon, 1992). In Europe, researchers focused their attention on trying to establish links between motivations for female self-employment and the overall position of women in the labour market (Goffee and Scase, 1985b; van der Wees and Romijn, 1987; Cromie and Hayes, 1988; Carter and Cannon, 1992). As Berg's (1997: 259) critique highlighted: 'The aim of the majority of the studies [was] . . . mainly to make comparisons with male entrepreneurs and to make women entrepreneurs visible'. Overall, these studies presented a *prima facie* picture of business women with more similarities to than differences from their male counterparts. Like men, the most frequently cited reason for starting in business was the search for independence and control over one's destiny. The greatest barriers to business formation and success were access to capital and mobilising start-up resources. Few of the early studies developed sophisticated taxonomies, preferring to identify female proprietors as a homogenous group, and there was an implicit acceptance by researchers that, beyond the start-up phase, few significant differences existed between male- and female-owned and man-aged companies.

Many of the early studies concentrated on describing the characteristics of the female entrepreneur and their motivations for self-employment. Schreier's (1973) pilot study of female business owners showed that the female entrepreneur had much in common with her male counterpart, though tended to operate in industry sectors with traditionally high levels of female employment, mainly services and retailing. Schwartz (1976) also described a predominance of service-based businesses and concluded that female motivations for starting businesses were similar to those of men. Notably, Schwartz (1976) drew the earliest research attention to some specifically female bar-riers to business ownership, including financial discrimination, a lack of training and business knowledge, and generally underestimating the financial and emotional cost of sustaining a business. Hisrich and Brush (1986) continued these broad, exploratory themes by attempting a demographic profile of female entrepreneurs, examining their motivations for starting in business and their barriers to business success. The 'typical' female entrepreneur was described as being the 'first born child of middle-class parents . . . After obtaining a liberal arts degree, she marries, has children, and works as a teacher, administrator or secretary. Her first business venture in a service area begins after she is thirty-five' (Hisrich and Brush, 1986: 14). Motivations for start-up were described as being the search for job satisfaction, independence and achievement, while the major problems facing women were believed to be the initial under-capitalisation of new businesses and a lack of knowledge and training in business skills. As Hisrich and Brush (1986: 17) described: 'For a woman entrepreneur who lacks experience in executive management, has had limited financial responsibilities, and proposes a non-proprietary product, the task of persuading a loan officer to lend start-up capital is not an easy one. As a result, a woman must often have her husband cosign a note, seek a co-owner, or use personal assets or savings. Many women entrepreneurs feel strongly that they have been discriminated against in this financial area.' Highlighting issues of credibility that would recur in several later studies, Hisrich and Brush (1986) also reported that half of their respondents reported difficulties in overcoming social beliefs that women are not as serious as men about business.

Early British studies also focused on describing the motivations and characteristics of women starting in business. Comparing the experiences of 58 female and 43 male business owners, Watkins and Watkins (1984) found substantial differences. Men entering self-employment were more likely to have prior work experience related to their venture; self-employment provided an essentially similar occupation with the added attraction of independence and autonomy. Choice of business sector for women was largely determined by consideration of which areas posed the least obstacles to their success, where technical and financial barriers to business entry were low. As Watkins and Watkins (1986: 230) emphasised in a later article: 'choice of business can be seen in terms of high motivation to immediate independence tempered by economic rationality, rather than by a conscious desire to operate "female-type" busi-nesses'. Goffee and Scase (1985b) continued this theme with their analysis of the experiences of 54 female proprietors in the UK, developing a typology of female entrepreneurs based on their relative attachment to conventional entrepreneurial ideals in the form of individualism and self-reliance and their willingness to accept conventional gender roles, often subordinate to men. Four types of female entrepreneur emerged:

- 'conventional' entrepreneurs highly committed to both entrepreneurial ideals and conventional gender roles;
- 'innovative' entrepreneurs who held a strong belief in entrepreneurial ideals but low attachment to conventional gender roles;
- 'domestic' entrepreneurs who organise their business life around family and held low attachment to entrepreneurial ideals; and
- 'radicals' who held low attachment to both, often organising their businesses on a political, collectivist basis.

These pioneering studies provided valuable descriptions of a group of entrepreneurs who had, hitherto, been overlooked by the mainstream small business research effort, though critics drew attention to their descriptive nature, the small size and unrepresentative nature of the sample (Carter, 1993), the general lack of utility and rigour (Allen and Truman, 1988; Solomon and Fernald, 1988; Rosa and Hamilton, 1994) and the limited extent of their cumulative knowledge (Stevenson, 1983; Hamilton *et al.*, 1992). By the late 1980s it was becoming clear that the research debates surrounding the issue of gender and business ownership were continuing largely because of the difficulties for researchers in providing clear and unequivocal evidence, either through empirical investigation or through more theoretical approaches. While several studies had suggested that it was considerably harder for women both to start and run their own enterprises, others had argued that start-up problems tended to be equally great for men, and that many women 'far from being discriminated against, thought that being a woman gave them a positive advantage over men' (Birley, 1989: 36).

Though the research field as a whole has progressed to encompass some of the most interesting and controversial research themes, such as the existence and extent of female disadvantage in starting and running a business and the processes and practices of gender relations within entrepreneurship, it is also the case that many descriptive studies of female entrepreneurship are still being undertaken. Many replicate the exploratory approach seen in early studies, albeit in very different country contexts.

In an analysis of women business owners in African and Asian countries, Marcucci (2001) described women as being more often pushed by severe economic conditions to create survival income. Given the barriers to women in the formal sector and time constraints of domestic ties, many women start a business they can run from home using traditional skills. In such circumstances, entrepreneurship is seen less a choice than a 'desperate attempt by women with few alternatives' (Mayoux, 1995: 4), in contrast to men who are seen as pulled by the prospects of increased earnings, independence and the opportunity to directly benefit from their own work. Overall, however, the study found the gender differences to be not large, with both sexes 'pushed' into micro-enterprise creation. Women in Ethiopia, Tanzania and Zambia more often proactively decided to be entrepreneurs, rather than being driven by necessity arising from poverty. They also explicitly referred to their roles as mothers, wives and daughters and their need to generate income for the family as important motivations for business ownership. The study failed to find any evidence to suggest women were less committed to their businesses than male entrepreneurs and strong evidence of women successfully balancing their business and household demands (Marcucci, 2001).

In common with many descriptive studies emanating from more developed economies, studies of women entrepreneurs in Africa and Asia describe female-owned enterprises as being generally younger, smaller and requiring lower start-up resources than those owned by men (Marcucci, 2001; Richardson *et al.*, 2004). Women-owned enterprises are less likely to be registered, more likely to be located from home and to operate in low-remuneration, over-crowded sectors (Marcucci, 2001; Richardson *et al.*, 2004). Richardson *et al.* (2004) also reported that women started businesses with minimal social, human, financial, physical and natural resources, having low levels or no formal education, often illiterate, and having limited or no experience of employment and limited networks. Women's enterprises also tend to operate in restricted locally based markets, where access, mobility and networks were easier to negotiate, but with the consequence of excessive competition and under-pricing (Zewde and Associates, 2002). They are also constrained by household and community roles which restrict the time and acceptability of their travelling to conduct business. Richardson *et al.* (2004) found men were four times more likely to be members of employers' organisations, chambers of commerce and small enterprise associations, prompting concern within the International Labour Organization that women entrepreneurs were less able to express themselves through associations and decision-making forums. Access to information, in particular market information, may also be problematic for women entrepreneurs. In Bangladesh, for example, women found it difficult to interact openly with men and to sell their products at the market (Marcucci, 2001). Overall, these studies portray women-owned enterprises as being often under-capitalised and generating limited or no profits. However, as Downing and Daniels (1992: 2) noted in their study of women entrepreneurs in Southern Africa, 'when investments are made to increase profitability and decrease the labour intensity of the women's income generating activities, the activities are frequently taken over by men'.

9.6 The management and financing of female-owned businesses

In an attempt to refocus the research effort away from broad descriptions of the personal and business characteristics of female entrepreneurs, throughout the 1990s increasing attention was given to the attempt to understand the real nature of management differences in female-owned firms (Carter and Cannon, 1992; Rosa *et al.*, 1996). More recent studies have continued to explore the issue of management of female-owned businesses, but the field of study has developed to encompass more sophisticated methodologies, larger-scale samples, and more robust sampling procedures, in particular the use of both male and female samples. The focus of investigation has evolved to concentrate on the effect of gender on both the experience of self-employment and the relative performance of small businesses (Rosa and Hamilton, 1994; Rosa *et al.*, 1996; Berg, 1997; Carter and Allen, 1997; Marlow, 1997; Marlow and Patton, 2005).

A recurrent theme throughout this body of research has been the focus on gender differences in the access to and usage of entrepreneurial finance. Following initial work by Buttner and Rosen (1989) and Riding and Swift (1990) in North America and Fay and Williams (1993a) in New Zealand, researchers have highlighted differences in the financing patterns of male-owned and female-owned businesses (Brush, 1992; Coleman, 2000; Brush et al., 2001). Women-owned businesses tend to start up with lower levels of overall capitalisation (Carter and Rosa, 1998), lower ratios of debt finance (Haines et al., 1999) and much less likelihood of using private equity or venture capital (Greene et al., 1999; Brush et al., 2001).

As the most commonly used form of external finance, research has focused more on debt rather than equity finance (Greene et al., 2001). Studies investigating gender-based differences in debt financing have focused on two related themes. First, researchers have sought to unravel the complex relationship between gender of entrepreneur and bank finance with regard to the volume of finance lent, the terms of credit negotiated and the perceived attitudes of bank lending officers to female entrepreneurs (Fay and Williams, 1993a; McKechnie et al., 1998; Haynes and Haynes, 1999; Coleman, 2000; Verheul and Thurik, 2000). Second, researchers have attempted to demonstrate whether gender-based differences are a consequence of supply-side discrimination by bank lenders, demand-side aversion to debt or risk by women entrepreneurs, or simply the result of the structural dissimilarities of male-owned and female-owned businesses (Buttner and Rosen, 1989; Orser and Foster, 1994; Fabowale et al., 1995; Read, 1998; Watson and Robinson, 2003).

Research has exposed gender-based differences in patterns of finance usage, with women-owned firms using less external finance in the form of bank debt and private equity (Greene et al., 1999; Brush et al., 2001). Over the past 15 years, a number of studies have investigated the effect of gender on bank lending, though few have found any direct evidence of gender discrimination. Buttner and Rosen (1989: 256), for example, found 'no evidence that lending decisions were significantly affected by entrepreneur's gender', results endorsed by a range of increasingly sophisticated later studies (Fabowale et al., 1995; McKechnie et al., 1998; Haines et al., 1999). Despite the weight of evidence pointing away from gender discrimination by bank loan officers, a number of studies suggest that the relationship between gender, entrepreneurship and bank lending is complex and the question of why women-owned businesses fail to access and use external finance remains unresolved.

Several studies have attributed gender-based differences in finance usage to the 'structural dissimilarities' between male- and female-owned businesses (Read, 1998). In a large-scale survey analysing bank loan files, Haines et al. (1999) found initial differences between male and female entrepreneurs (lower sales levels and liabilities, lower levels of salary and drawings) to be a product of business size, age and sector. Fabowale et al. (1995), similarly, argued that structural factors accounted for differences in rates of loan rejections between male and female entrepreneurs. Examining 282 matched pairs of male and female business owners, McKechnie et al. (1998) found few substantial differences once structural factors had been taken into account, but a greater dissatisfaction among women entrepreneurs with regard to their treatment by bank lenders. Evidence from other studies has been less conclusive. A survey of 2000 Dutch entrepreneurs (Verheul and Thurik, 2000) found that most differences in the use of starting capital by male and female entrepreneurs were explained by 'indirect' effects (size, age, sector); however, some 'direct' gender effects survived.

In the absence of direct evidence of gender discrimination, researchers have suggested that differences in patterns of finance usage may be explained by the practices of individual lending officers or through the use of application procedures that inadvertently disadvantage women business owners. Buttner and Rosen (1988: 249), for example, reported that perceptions held by bank loan officers of the characteristics of successful entrepreneurs were 'more commonly ascribed to men than women.' In a study notable for its use of experimental protocols, Fay and Williams (1993a) presented bank loan officers with an identical loan application from male and female applicants. Gender-based differences were found when the applicant was described as having high school education, but not when the applicant was university educated. They concluded that their study 'demonstrate[d] experimentally that some loan officers do employ differing evaluative criteria for female and male applicants, and that these differences in evaluative criteria may act to female disadvantage' (Fay and Williams, 1993a: 304). Orser and Foster (1994: 16) questioned the use of the standard 5Cs model of bank lending (character, capacity, capital, collateral and conditions), suggesting that supposedly 'objective' criteria were applied in a 'subjective' manner to the detriment of female entrepreneurs. Coleman's (2000) analysis found women less likely to use bank debt, attributing this to the lower average size of women-owned businesses, a view endorsed by Mahot (1997). Rather than discriminating against women, Coleman (2000: 49) concluded that bankers 'discriminate on the basis of firm size, preferring to lend to larger and, one would assume, more established firms. This preference may put women at a disadvantage given that they are half the size of men-owned firms on average.'

A focus on supply-side discrimination has been countered by evidence of demand-side risk and debt aversion. A lower preference for risk among women has been a recurrent finding of comparative analyses of male and female entrepreneurs (Sexton and Bowman-Upton, 1990; Watson and Robinson, 2003). The greater risk aversion of women is seen not only in their reluctance to assume the burden of business debt, but also within their reluctance to engage in fast-paced business growth (Cliff, 1998; Bird and Brush, 2002). Debt aversion among women entrepreneurs, often conceptualised as a quasi-psychological characteristic, is as likely to be rooted in socio-economic factors: women's comparatively lower earnings in employment (Equal Opportunities Commission, 2005) are reproduced among the self-employed (Marlow, 1997; Parker, 2004).

Overall, the weight of research evidence considering gender, entrepreneurship and bank lending suggests that while the bank financing profiles of male and female entrepreneurs are distinctly different, much – but not all – is attributable to structural dissimilarities. The research evidence also suggests that while women entrepreneurs perceive that they are treated differently by bank lending officers (Fabowale *et al.*, 1995), there is almost no evidence of systematic gender discrimination by banks. Indeed, there is a growing recognition that women entrepreneurs constitute an important new market for banks, and it is difficult to argue that it is within the banks' interest to deliberately, much less systematically, exclude this growing market. The debate has continued largely because of dissatisfaction with existing explanations, coupled with the methodological difficulties facing researchers in providing clear and unequivocal evidence (Mahot, 1997; Haines *et al.*, 1999). While entrepreneurship researchers continue to debate the extent and causes of the gender, entrepreneurship and bank finance nexus, feminist

analyses may provide new insights. In a review of the entrepreneurship research literature, Mirchandani (1999) points to the essentialism inherent in the construction of the
'female entrepreneur' category and stresses that gender should not be seen simply as a
characteristic of individuals, but as a process integral to business ownership, a critique
developed by Ahl (2002) and Bird and Brush (2002). As Mirchandani (1999: 230)
argued, the practice of statistically equalising structural dissimilarities between men
and women in order to explain gender differences in bank borrowing suggests that 'it
is business structure rather than gender that is the prime determinant of access to credit'.

9.7 The performance of female-owned businesses

The performance of small businesses, that is their ability to contribute to employment
and wealth creation through business start-up, survival and growth, is an important
policy and academic debate. Comparatively little rigorous and in-depth research, however, has been undertaken on the issue of gender and business performance. Although
many studies have made some mention of it, most shy away from direct examination
of quantitative performance measures, preferring instead to engage in discursive debate
concerning gender differences in qualitative assessments of success. These studies suggest that women perform less well on quantitative measures such as jobs created, sales
turnover and profitability. This, it is argued, is usually because women do not enter
business for financial gain but to pursue intrinsic goals (e.g. independence, and the
flexibility to run business and domestic lives) and assess their success in relation to
their achievement in attaining these goals rather than on the more usual economic or
financial measures.

An example of this approach was seen in a study which linked the self-reported
motivations of women leaving organisations in order to start businesses and their subsequent success in achieving their goals (Buttner and Moore, 1997). Four related issues
were investigated in the study: first, the motivational influences which affect former
managerial or professional women's entrepreneurial decisions; second, the role family
concerns play in these former corporate women's entrepreneurial motivation; third,
how these female entrepreneurs measure success in their ventures; and finally, whether
the women's entrepreneurial motivation is related to the ways they measure success in
their own businesses. Using a sample of 129 American female entrepreneurs who were
all formerly managers in large organisations, the data was collected by focus groups,
interviews and structured questionnaires. In common with several previous studies of
female entrepreneurship both in Europe and in the US, the sample were both better-
educated and less likely to be married than the total population. Similarly, the profile of the businesses owned by respondents revealed a strong bias towards services
(81%).

Reasons for exiting organisations were measured using 32 items on a rated scale. Of
the five main reasons for leaving their former employment, the desire for 'challenge'
(*to gain more respect; to be in charge; to regain excitement; to get recognition*) and
'self-determination' (*to make it on my own; self-esteem*) were the most influential.
'Family concerns' (*to balance family and work; to control my time*) and 'blocks to
career advancement' (*discrimination; career barriers; didn't fit into corporate culture*)

were the next most influential reasons for exiting organisations. Of least importance was the influence of 'organisational dynamics' (*little motivation to produce; no urgency to finish; lack of shared information; low quality standards*). Success was measured using six items on a rated scale. Of these items, 'self-fulfilment' was found to be the most important measure of success. This was followed, in order of importance, by 'achievement of their goals', 'profits', 'growth', 'balancing family and work' and finally, making a 'social contribution'. Using correlation analysis, certain relationships emerged between reasons for leaving previous employment and how success was measured in their own enterprises. Women who had left employment for the 'challenge', for example, were found to measure entrepreneurial success in terms of 'self-fulfilment' and 'profitability', those who had left because of 'organisational dynamics' sought success in balancing work and family, while those who had left because of 'family concerns' measured success in balancing family and work and in making a 'social contribution'.

One methodological issue which emerged from this investigation was concerned with the attempt to isolate and rank measures of business success, particularly in studies which attempt to demonstrate differences between female and male respondents. Within the literature that deals with gender and performance, there is an implicit assumption that men measure business success using quantitative, 'external' criteria (i.e. profits, growth, etc.), while women use qualitative, 'internal' criteria (i.e. self-fulfilment, goal attainment, etc.) In this, there is a concern that researchers may be projecting particular value systems onto subjects and that the expectation of differences becomes a self-fulfilling prophecy. Assumptions such as these, which inadvertently result in trivialising women's entrepreneurial efforts, have generally been derived from studies using single-sex samples that lack the ability to pose identical questions to both genders.

The few studies that have used more sophisticated methodologies in pursuing issues of gender and performance have presented less clear-cut results. In a longitudinal study of 298 UK businesses, of which 67 were female-owned, Johnson and Storey (1993) found that women proprietors in their study had created more stable enterprises than had their male sample, although on average the sales turnover for women was lower than for males. Kalleberg and Leicht (1991) also found only slight and inconclusive differences in key performance measures in their sample of 400 businesses from three industrial sectors in Indiana. Fischer's (1992) study found that women's businesses tended to perform less well on measures such as sales, employment and growth, but concluded that determinants of gender differences in business performance were far more complex than had been recognised in earlier studies.

Rosa *et al.*'s (1996) study was one of the few large-scale studies specifically designed to investigate the impact of gender on small business management. In analysing the comparative performance of businesses by gender, the study outlined four different measures:

- primary performance measures (number of employees, growth in employees, sales turnover, value of capital assets);
- proxy performance measures (geographical range of markets, VAT registration);
- subjective measures (including the ability of the business to meet business and domestic needs); and

187

- entrepreneurial performance measures (the desire for growth, the ownership of multiple businesses).

The analysis of primary performance measures suggested that women's businesses employed fewer core staff, were less likely to have grown substantially in employment (more than 20 employees) after 12 months in business, had a lower sales turnover, and were valued at a lower level than male-owned businesses. The analysis of proxy performance measures also indicated that women-owned businesses were more likely to serve only local markets, although gender differences in export sales were non-significant. Male-owned businesses were also more likely to be registered for VAT. The subjective measures of performance, however, were less clearly divided by gender. In considering how well their businesses had performed in the previous two years, men and women gave comparable responses. Women did, however, appear to be less optimistic than men in their expectation of future business success. Women were also less likely to believe that their business created sufficient income to meet domestic needs. This result appears to stem directly from the fact that women's businesses tended to be substantially smaller than male-owned businesses in the sample. Male respondents whose businesses had a similar-sized turnover were equally dissatisfied with their ability to meet domestic financial needs. The final measure, entrepreneurial performance, also demonstrated marked sex differences. Men were significantly more likely to own other businesses (19.6% compared with 8.6%) and also to have strong growth ambitions in so far as they wanted to expand their businesses 'as far as they could (43% versus 34%)' (Rosa et al., 1996: 469).

Although these results appear to demonstrate marked gender differences in business performance, they should be treated with caution. Not only are conclusions potentially premature given the scarcity of previous research, there are a number of complicating factors (such as industrial sector, business age and presence of co-owners) which, depending on how they are treated methodologically, appear to produce widely differing results in business performance (Rosa et al., 1996). Moreover, Rosa et al. (1996) argue that, while the performance of women-owned businesses appears at first sight to be substantially lower than for their male counterparts, women have only recently emerged as an entrepreneurial group and their businesses are much younger and therefore less established. On this basis, they concluded that: 'If female business owners have started from a much lower tradition of achievement in business, then this trend is encouraging and may provide support for Birley's (1989) view that the gender gap in the UK is narrowing' (1996: 475).

Collectively, the results of the various studies which compare male and female performance differences offer mixed results. Overall, these studies suggest that the determinants of performance (i.e. the measures that are used by owners to assess their business performance) are similar by gender. Contrary to many of the earlier studies of gender and entrepreneurship, neither is there any evidence to suggest that men are more profit-orientated than women or less likely to value intrinsic goals. Although the Rosa et al. (1996) study found some marked sex differences in performance indicators, the complexity of the overall pattern of results suggests that a more complex interpretation is required than simply attributing differences to gender alone.

9.8 The neglect of female entrepreneurship

So far this chapter has concentrated on describing the research studies that have been undertaken in an attempt to understand the true dynamics of women's entrepreneurship. It has, however, been noted that, in comparison with the volume of academic research which has been undertaken on the small-firm sector, the female entrepreneur has been seriously 'neglected' by both the mass media and the academic community (Baker *et al.*, 1997: 221). For some, the lack of attention paid to women's experience of entrepreneurship is evidence of a wider problem of gender effects being omitted from mainstream research studies into social phenomena. Carter (1993: 151), for example, notes that 'historically women have been left off the small business research agenda or made invisible by research practices or in other ways written out of the analysis of self-employment'. Hamilton (1990) cites an example of how this is done, using Rees and Shah's (1986) analysis of self-employment in the UK. As Hamilton (1990: 6–7) points out, their study 'excludes a number of categories of people and then a whole gender "in order to obtain sharper results". Among those excluded are "those who are not heads of household" (mainly women); "those who worked for less than 30 hours a week" (mainly women); "females" (on the basis that "self-employment is predominantly a male preserve").' The neglect of female entrepreneurship is, therefore, part of a much wider problem which has resulted in the social sciences being structured in a manner which favours the male experience. Concepts of entrepreneurship are traditionally assumed to be gender neutral, but as Berg (1997: 261) points out: 'rely in fact on notions of humanity and rationality that are masculinist'. Dualities such as the rational–irrational distinction may appear to have no apparent gender bias, but in reality are 'thoroughly imbued with gender connotations, one side being socially characterised as masculine, the other as feminine, and the former being socially valorised' (Massey, 1996: 113).

Although many of the early studies which examined the demographic characteristics and motivations of female entrepreneurs were subsequently criticised for their small scale and their lack of rigour, their importance cannot be underestimated in identifying and clearly delineating a, hitherto, 'invisible' group (Baker *et al.*, 1997: 221). Although exploratory, these studies challenged for the first time the view that entrepreneurship is a gender-neutral activity. Their success can be judged in two main ways: first, by considering whether subsequent research has developed in a manner which addresses the methodological criticisms of the late 1980s; and second, by considering whether they have influenced the design and output of non-gender specific studies.

As this chapter has demonstrated, research investigating female entrepreneurship has expanded and matured considerably over the past 20 years. This has been demonstrated by the refocusing of attention away from early studies of women's business ownership which considered female experiences entirely in relation to male norms, and towards an increasing awareness of gender differences within entrepreneurship which are socially constructed and negotiated. As this chapter has attempted to present the research output in approximate chronological manner, developments in the methodological basis of many studies have been demonstrated. Where early studies were criticised for their use of small-scale samples and qualitative approaches, more recent research has moved towards large-scale, quantitative methods. Developments have not only occurred in the growing trend towards empiricism, however. Engagement with socio-logical approaches, in particular, has enabled a more insightful, qualitative analysis of the entrepreneurial principles and processes used by both men and women. On this basis, therefore, the field has matured to develop a cumulative knowledge.

Whether research investigating the effects of gender in entrepreneurship has been successful in influencing the remainder of the small business research field is less cer-tain. Although there appears to have been an increase in the number of studies that have included gender as a variable for analysis, there remains a pervasive assumption that female experience should be considered only in direct relation to male norms. Elsewhere, studies still assume a gender-neutral or androcentric position. As Shakeshaft and Nowell (1984: 187–8) point out in discussing the pervasive assumption of andro-centrism in the social sciences, this results in the: 'elevation of the masculine to the level of the universal and the ideal, it is the honouring of men and the male principle above women and the female. This perception creates a belief in male superiority and a value system in which female values, experiences and behaviours are viewed as inferior'.

9.9 Chapter summary

The past two decades have seen a growth in the number of women entering self-employment and business ownership. During the same period, the growing interest in the role and importance of small businesses within the overall economy has led to an increase in the volume of research studies that focus on the small firms sector. Although the experiences of female entrepreneurs have been only a minority interest, research investigating the influence of gender on small business ownership has developed con-siderably over the past 15 years. While early research into female entrepreneurship focused on describing women's characteristics, motivations and experiences, the field has progressed beyond these exploratory and rudimentary studies. More recent research has not only developed a degree of methodological sophistication, it has also focused on increasingly specialised issues, such as the role of gender effects on the financing and the performance of firms.

This chapter has attempted to provide an overview of the growing literature on female entrepreneurship, highlighting some of the key debates within the field. It has also attempted to highlight more recent concerns that the female experiences of entre-preneurship and the effects of gender in small business management are seriously neglected areas of study. Studies that have started to investigate key issues, such as the management and performance of female-owned firms, have revealed the extent of female disadvantage in business financing and the related and relative under-performance of women-owned firms. Although definitive results have yet to be attained, many recent studies unequivocally point to the same conclusion that as a relatively new group of entrepreneurs, operating significantly younger businesses, women-owned firms may not yet have attained the same level of achievement as those owned by men, but as a group they are catching up fast.

Questions

1 Discuss the possible reasons that could explain why growth in the numbers of women-owned enterprises varies so much between different countries.

2 Different definitions of women-owned businesses are deployed by researchers. Which, in your opinion, is the most accurate for the purposes of researching female experiences of business ownership? Give reasons for your choice.

3 Do women experience disadvantage in raising business financing? Explain the reasons that led you to your conclusion.

4 What factors should be taken into account when considering the performance of female-owned businesses?

5 Given the widespread emancipation of women, do you believe that researchers should continue to investigate gendered experiences of entrepreneurship? Explain your reasoning.

Web links

www.prowess.org.uk/
Prowess is a network of organisations and individuals who support the growth of women's business ownership.

www.onlinewbc.gov/
The Office of Women's Business Ownership and the Online Women's Business Center – an organisation established in the US to assist women achieve their dreams and improve their communities by helping them start and run successful businesses, regardless of social or financial disadvantage, race, ethnicity or business background.

europa.eu.int/comm/enterprise/entrepreneurship/craft/craft-women/
women-dgentr-activities.htm
A range of papers from the European Commission DG Enterprise on issues of female entrepreneurship across Europe.

www.sbs.gov.uk/SBS_Gov_files/services/female-entrepreneurship.pdf
The Promoting Female Entrepreneurship booklet highlights the contribution that female-owned businesses make to the UK economy and puts forward the case for additional proactive support for women-friendly business support services.

CHAPTER 10

Ethnicity and entrepreneurship

Monder Ram, Giles Barrett and Trevor Jones

10.1 Introduction

Ethnic minority-owned businesses are now an established and growing feature of many advanced industrial societies. In addition to fulfilling an important economic and social role for minority communities, ethnic minority-owned firms have become particularly conspicuous within the general small business population. This chapter reviews a number of the often contentious themes that have characterised this emerging field of enquiry. These include: the myriad explanations of the formation of ethnic minority businesses (EMBs), which range from 'culturalist' accounts to more structurally oriented responses; factors behind different levels of self-employment activity; the material basis of 'family' labour; the nature of the market environment; financial experiences; and issues for business support agencies.

10.2 Learning objectives

There are four learning objectives in this chapter:

1 To account for different levels of self-employment among Britain's ethnic minorities.
2 To understand the different explanations of the formation and development of ethnic minority firms.
3 To describe the dynamics of financing EMBs.
4 To identify the challenges facing policy makers in supporting ethnic minority firms.

Key concepts
■ opportunity structure ■ culture ■ ethnicity ■ diversity ■ family

10.3 Ethnicity and enterprise

Throughout advanced industrial societies, the last two decades have witnessed a significant increase in self-employment and small business activity among ethnic minorities

(Kloosterman and Rath, 2003; Ram and Jones, 1998; Waldinger *et al.*, 1990). Many of these businesses are embedded in immigrant-origin communities which grew out of post-war demand for low-skill and low-wage labour, particularly in labour-intensive manufacturing industry. Since the 1970s, de-industrialisation and the growing importance of the service sector have reduced traditional job opportunities for immigrant labour, while simultaneously creating openings for self-employment (Phizacklea and Ram, 1996; Sassen, 1997).

In Britain, EMBs have been the subject of growing interest from a variety of sources. The media have not been slow to publicise the 'rags to riches' stories of conspicuously successful South Asian entrepreneurs, even though more careful accounts of this community in business convey a more complex picture. Researchers continue to offer competing explanations for the apparent entrepreneurial flair of some ethnic groups, noticeably South Asians, and the below-average propensity for self-employment among other communities, in particular African-Caribbeans. To varying degrees, business support agencies have attempted to respond, on the one hand, to high levels of unemployment in Black communities and, on the other, to the increasingly significant phenomenon of ethnic enterprise in particular localities and economic sectors. These developments need to be set against a political context which, during the 1980s, was punctuated by civil disturbances in a number of British inner-city areas. A consensus among policy makers rapidly developed that exhorted the Black population to engage in 'productive pursuits' (Scarman, 1981): encouraging self-employment among ethnic minorities therefore emerged as a means of maintaining social harmony in urban areas.

This interest is testimony to the growing importance of the ethnic presence in the small-firm population. In this chapter, key aspects of EMB activity in Britain are assessed. These include explanations of the different patterns of self-employment among ethnic minority groups, particularly African-Caribbeans and South Asians; the contentious question of entrepreneurial motivation and the apparent impact of 'cultural' resources on the business-entry decision; the role of the often lauded 'family' in the ethnic minority firm; the constraining nature of the market environment; the relationship between ethnic enterprise and high-street banks; and the role of business support agencies in EMB development. However, since ethnic minority entrepreneurship is not a peculiarly British phenomenon, we begin with a brief assessment of EMB activity from an international perspective.

10.4 Ethnic minority enterprise: an international perspective

Throughout virtually the entire economically advanced world, immigration has increased steadily from the mid-twentieth century onwards and immigrant-origin ethnic minorities have emerged as a burgeoning presence among the entrepreneurial self-employed. Indicative of a tension that permeates the ethnic business literature, some observers have argued that particular groups are culturally predisposed to engage in these types of activities (see Werbner, 1984, for example), while other contributors have stressed the importance of wider structures in shaping the entrepreneurial activity of ethnic minorities (Jones *et al.*, 2000; Rath, 2000). For Rath (2003: 7), ethnic enterprise arises out of 'the intersection of rising immigration and the post-industrial transition', immigration coinciding with a shift towards services and flexible production, which has created conditions for new small enterprises to flourish.

In France, high levels of business activity among individuals of Moroccan, Tunisian and Chinese origin have been noted. These enterprises tend to offer the same product as indigenously owned firms but provide a different quality of service. Competitive advantage is achieved over their rivals through longer opening hours, easily available credit and the sale of produce in very small quantities (Ma Mung and Guillon, 1986; Ma Mung and Lacroix, 2003). The Tunisians are the smallest of the three groups originating in North Africa but they have the greatest affinity towards self-employment. Research has shown the concentration of approximately 180 Tunisian catering establishments in only a few neighbourhoods of Paris. Within these outlets strong traditions are fostered and the firm provides much needed work for family members and co-ethnics (Boubakri, 1985). Yet despite their numerical profusion, ethnic minority firms in France are very much restricted to a 'narrow path' (Ma Mung and Lacroix, 2003), concentrated very much at the lower, least-profitable end of catering and retailing. It is important to note that this clustering in ill-rewarded labour-intensive sectors is a hallmark of EMB, an internationally recurrent pattern recorded for the UK (Barrett *et al.*, 2003), the Netherlands (Rath, 2000), Germany (Wilpert, 2003) and Austria (Haberfellner, 2003). In the latter two countries especially, this narrow focus is attributed to tight legal regulation of migration, citizenship and employment, emphasising that ethnic business patterns are subject to politics as well as economics and ethnic culture itself.

Mention of culture reminds us that, for historical reasons, the ethnic origins of entrepreneurs are variable from country to country. In Germany it is Turkish entrepreneurs who occupy centre stage, with Turkish-owned businesses proliferating considerably since the 1980s. As elsewhere, this rise is explicable with reference to a combination of positive and negative factors. On the plus side, the Turkish community retains strong family traditions, with family members furnishing the valuable resource of labour power. Additionally, the presence of a large Turkish population creates a market demand for culturally specific products. At the same time, self-employment has also arisen as a means of material survival in the negative circumstances of rising unemployment. Over time, business activity has begun to break out of its reliance on the co-ethnic market towards providing such items as fast food and transport for the wider non-Turkish market (Wilpert, 2003). Turks in Belgium also appear to be following a similar trajectory, particularly in relation to restaurants (Kesteloot and Mistiaen, 1997).

The Netherlands too has witnessed growing EMB activity. Ex-colonial subjects constitute the largest ethnic minority in the country and the Surinamese are the largest single group (Blaschke *et al.*, 1990). Low levels of entrepreneurial activity have been officially noted for Turks, Moroccans, Chinese, Javanese and Creoles among other groups. However, recent attention has turned to examining the informal economic activities of ethnic minorities in the Netherlands (Kloosterman *et al.*, 1998; Rath, 1998). Informal activities, defined as income-generating activities which do not meet the requirements of regulatory frameworks, are a feature of post-industrial urban economies throughout the world (Pugliese, 1993). They not only provide income for the business owner but may also be instrumental in providing much needed income for other ethnic minorities who may be, for example, between regular jobs or have no regular source of income whatsoever.

The immigration of Surinamese to the Netherlands has been characterised by a stop–start process, with immigration peaking in 1974–75 and then declining sharply following the independence of Surinam in 1975. The entrepreneurial behaviour of the Surinamese in Amsterdam reflects this pattern of migration, with the first wave of businesses established in the 1960s concerned with serving the dietary needs of the early migrants. As the numbers of co-ethnics rose in subsequent years, there was both a proliferation in the number of these tropical food-stores and a diversification into other activities. According to Blaschke *et al.* (1990) there were, in 1983, approximately 250 Surinamese ventures in Amsterdam, mostly occupying the cheapest sites in the older parts of the urban centre, where Surinamese residents had settled (Byrne, 1998).

In North America, immigrant enterprise has historically been prominent for far longer than in Europe (Light, 1984) and often tends to be taken as a theoretical template for similar businesses elsewhere in the world. Business ownership has been repeatedly promoted as a self-help strategy through which oppressed American minorities can achieve economic advancement. Japanese Americans, Chinese, Jews, Middle Easterners, French Canadians and Cubans among others have all been the focus of research studies into the business activities of these diverse ethnic minorities (see respectively Light, 1972; Min and Bozogmehr, 2003; Razin, 1993; Light *et al.*, 1993; Langlois and Razin, 1995; Portes and Bach, 1985). Much of this interest in ethnic business has tended to focus on the question posed by Waldinger (1995: 62) of 'why some visibly identifiable and stigmatised groups make it through business and others do not'. A recent manifestation of this is the comparison between Koreans and African-Americans in business (as we shall see, this has echoes with the juxtaposition of South Asian and African-Caribbean entrepreneurship in Britain).

'Business-minded' Koreans have been presented as the archetypal role model for all disadvantaged minorities to aspire to in their logical quest for socio-economic advancement. Both Kim (1981) and Min (1991) discuss the propensity of Korean-owned businesses to become established in low-income Black areas of central cities. Their decision to service the population in these areas is twofold. First, there is a desire to exploit the vacant niche which has not been filled by African-American entrepreneurs who (allegedly) lack the necessary cultural and class-based resources conducive to small business formation. In New York City, the emergence of these niches has been precipitated by an ageing population of Jewish and Italian business owners whose fear of crime, their age and the reluctance of heirs to inherit businesses have prompted them to sell their businesses on. Second, Korean entrepreneurs perceive that the Black ghettos represent a relatively less hostile environment than predominately White areas. Whilst Korean entrepreneurs have brought much needed services to central city ghettos, their strong ethnic ties and cultural attachment has served to exclude others (Light, 1995). These exclusionary practices have prompted violent responses from inner-city Black communities angered by the failure of Korean-owned firms to employ African-American workers and contribute finance to African-American community organisations. The organised boycotts of Korean-owned outlets have also been a feature. Hence the entrance of Korean businesses into African-American locales is often viewed as risky because of simmering inter-ethnic tensions (McEvoy and Cook, 1993).

Bates (1994) questions whether the educational merits of Korean entrepreneurs are sufficiently rewarded in their business activities. Min (1991) notes that the vast majority of Korean immigrants have received a high school or college education in South Korea, hence their employment in retail and service activities represents an under-utilisation of their human capital. Across the Atlantic a similar argument has been proposed for South Asians in Britain (Aldrich *et al.*, 1981, 1985; Srinavasan, 1995). Hence self-employment has afforded the entrepreneur the opportunity to make their own decisions about the operations of the enterprise but the wider structures of society regulate access to the different types of activities. Moreover, despite the ethnic and economic solidarity exhibited by Korean enterprise and their heavy investment in their ventures, actual returns on their human and physical capital are very small and inferior to the returns accruing to African-American-owned ventures (per dollar invested in capital) (Asante and Mattson, 1992). This suggests that the appropriateness of the Korean entrepreneurship model as the benchmark for all marginalised minority groups to follow should be treated with caution.

As early as the 1880s some intellectual African-American leaders in the US, such as Booker T. Washington, propagated the rise and development of a Black (African-American) bourgeoisie (Asante and Mattson, 1992). This emerging strand of the middle classes would lead to the full emancipation of African-American people as business opportunities and property ownership became widespread and an accepted facet of African-American culture. These developments would be underpinned by the bond of shared values, racial cooperation and self-help.

However, Frazier (1957) points out that the capital mobilised within the African-American community was insignificant in relation to the American economy, and that African-American entrepreneurship provided very few jobs for co-ethnics. Hence to promote African-American business activity as a panacea for the deep-seated and intractable problems of disadvantage and institutionalised racism is highly problematic. Frazier (1957: 153) labels the belief that entrepreneurship represented an over-arching solution to the endemic problems of racism as a 'Social myth . . . [and] . . . one of the main elements in the world of "make-believe" which the black bourgeoisie has created to compensate for its feeling of inferiority in a white world dominated by business enterprise'.

The comparatively low rates of African-American business ownership are generally attributed to the lack of socio-cultural and class resources, which can be mobilised in the pursuit of entrepreneurship. Both Light and Bonacich (1988) and Waldinger *et al.* (1990) affirm that the fragmented nature of African-American communities militates against the development of group social networks and mechanisms of in-group attachment, which help to nurture business opportunities. The absence of petit bourgeois values is also a serious setback to encouraging new firms. Low educational attainments among African-Americans, small amounts of financial capital and the absence of resource-generating mechanisms such as rotating credit schemes are among the class-related factors that severely hinder the processes of business formation (Bonacich and Modell, 1980; Curran and Burrows, 1986; Light and Rosenstein, 1995).

However, a fundamental hindrance to Black progression is the persistence of racism. Unequal access to health, education, capital and labour market opportunities have stunted the growth of a Black entrepreneurial class (Marable and Mullings, 1994; Waldinger and Perlmann, 1998). The promotion of an 'enterprise culture' during the

1980s under President Ronald Reagan actually involved considerable cuts in welfare and health expenditure and the proclaimed belief that poverty was a self-induced state of being. Hence socially, politically and economically marginalised groups such as the homeless, un/underemployed and visible minorities were held responsible for their own plight (Murray, 1990). Neo-conservative thinking acted to create a pool of exploitable low-cost labour so that US industrial capital could begin to compete more readily with international competitors (Kasarda, 1989; Sassen, 1991). Whilst in the late 1990s some economic progress was detected for ethnic minorities in the US, this is extremely uneven. The recent founding of initiatives such as inner-city enterprise zones and Specialised Small Business Investment Companies (SSBICs) has failed to galvanise a new generation of Black entrepreneurs in the US (Bates, 1994b).

10.5 Ethnic minority business activity: the British experience

As in the US, one of the most debated features of the EMB population in Britain is the marked disparity between the circumstances of different groups, most clearly evident in the patterns of self-employment among ethnic minority communities. South Asians are particularly well represented in self-employment, with people of Pakistani or Bangladeshi origins three times as likely to be self-employed as West Indians or Guyanese. While there are inescapable transatlantic echoes here of the Korean/African-American gap, we shall see later that the picture has begun to change significantly. In the meantime, however, we shall concentrate on the 'Afro-Asian gap', the question of 'Why so few black businessmen?' (Kazuka, 1980), which has attracted an almost obsessive interest since the 1980s (Peach, 1996; Ward, 1991).

10.5.1 African-Caribbean experiences

Many of the explanations accounting for African-Caribbean 'under-representation' in self-employment appear to make reference to the apparent lack of cultural resources that are often documented in other ethnic minority groups. Unlike Asians, who are invariably portrayed as richly endowed with family resources, communal networks and other forms of social capital (Basu, 1998; Metcalf *et al.*, 1996), African-Caribbeans are argued to be under-endowed in various crucial respects. These include the different value base of the African-Caribbean family unit, which apparently does not predispose them to running a family business (Reeves and Ward, 1984); the legacy of slavery, which had a deleterious effect upon African-Caribbean culture (Fryer, 1984; Gilroy, 1987; Pajackowska and Young, 1992; Rex, 1982); and the absence of extended family and community networks (Blaschke *et al.*, 1990).

However, explanations that focus exclusively on the absence or otherwise of 'cultural' resources often fail to appreciate the impact that the opportunity structure can have on the facilitation of business opportunities. Basu (1991) in particular eschews culturalist interpretations and presents a cogent case for locating African-Caribbean under-representation in the socio-context of Black people in Britain. To this end, a number of factors need to be considered. First, many African-Caribbeans originally migrating to Britain were from a working-class background, essentially a 'replacement' workforce who came from working-class backgrounds to fill occupational and residential niches vacated by Whites.

'Class' resources (Light, 1984) are important in developing attitudes, beliefs, educational qualifications and social networks conducive to entrepreneurship. South Asian migrants in Britain appeared to have a broader socio-economic profile and, therefore, greater access to class resources. The greater entrepreneurial success of the more affluent Blacks that migrated to the US and Canada (Foner, 1979, 1987) would seem to bear out the importance of class background. Ethnic identity is cross-cut by class background in this as in many other instances.

Second, comparatively high levels of unemployment among the Black community (Jones, 1993) serve to induce self-employment in low-skill, highly competitive and poorly rewarded industrial sectors. Often such 'no-choice' businesses operate in the informal economy (and thus are not accounted for in official statistics) or remain marginal concerns with little prospect of real progress (Basu, 1991).

Third, negative stereotyping of African-Caribbeans in British society impinges upon their capacity to mobilise resources potentially useful in business. Less preferential treatment by the banks (Jones *et al.*, 1994a) and racist customer behaviour (Jones *et al.*, 1992) are important business processes where such stereotyping has been noted.

Fourth, residential settlement patterns appear to influence business development among minority groups. For example, Reeves and Ward (1984) argue that the relative dispersal of African-Caribbean settlement (compared with the concentration of South Asians), their numerically smaller population and the apparent lack of culturally specific needs combine to limit market potential for growth in small businesses.

Finally, African-Caribbeans are further constrained by their comparatively low levels of home ownership, which diminishes their capacity to offer collateral for business start-up funding (Basu, 1991). It appears, then, that this group is faced with a powerful combination of structural handicaps to entrepreneurialism, handicaps which in themselves have little directly to do with ethnic cultural attributes. This needs to be borne in mind in comparative assessments of ethnic minority entrepreneurship.

Also to be borne in mind are recent trends that threaten to undermine many of the stereotypical assumptions about an Afro-Asian gap. Since the 1990s, there are signs that the onward march of South Asian enterprise has gone into reverse, notably among Indians. Due in part to a supermarket-induced decline in small retailing and in part to young Asians shunning self-employment for professional careers, there is now a palpable reduction in Asian self-employment (Jones and Ram, 2003). With African-Caribbean self-employment continuing to rise, any inter-ethnic entrepreneurial gap can only diminish and even disappear. In any case, what matters in the final analysis is quality not quantity. Though diminishing numerically, the signs are that Asian business is shifting away from low-profit, labour-intensive sectors into human-capital-rich activities like information technology (Ram *et al.*, 2003).

10.5.2 The Asian entrepreneurs

A further recent line of enquiry focuses on emerging differences within the South Asian entrepreneurial population itself. According to such sources as Metcalf *et al.* (1996),

Indians and East African Asians are the real Asian entrepreneurial success stories in terms of business resources, good practice, positive motivations, earnings, profitability, growth and scale. Conversely, much Pakistani and Bangladeshi enterprise appears relatively weak in performance, economically marginal and arising out of a context of disadvantage. Once again caution must be urged, since other researchers have found much less of an inter-ethnic gap and have identified many Pakistani firms as outstanding high-flyers (Ram *et al.*, 2003).

10.6 The business entry decision

One of the most keenly debated issues within the ethnic business literature concerns the decision to become self-employed. Various explanations have been advanced outlining the processes that give rise to EMB ownership. Jenkins (1984: 231–4), for instance, has identified three basic explanatory models of ethnic involvement in business. The 'economic opportunity' model regards EMB activity as essentially no different from routine capitalist activity, relying on the market for its fortunes. The 'culture' model asserts that some cultures predispose their members towards the successful pursuit of entrepreneurial goals. Finally, the 'reaction' model views self-employment by members of ethnic minority groups as a reaction against racism and blocked avenues of social mobility, a means of surviving at the margins of white-dominated society. Waldinger *et al.* (1990) have developed a more interactive approach for understanding ethnic business development. Essentially, they argue that ethnic enterprise is a product of the interplay of opportunity structures, group characteristics and strategies for adapting to the environment.

A steady stream of studies since the 1980s has stressed the importance of external factors in their explanations of the proliferation of particularly South Asian-owned small enterprises (Aldrich *et al.*, 1981, 1982, 1984; Jones, 1981; Jones *et al.*, 1989; Mullins, 1979; Nowikowski, 1984; Robinson and Flintoff, 1982). According to this perspective, self-employment is a survival strategy borne out of the persistent discrimination that ethnic minorities face within the wider labour market. Compelling evidence for this view is presented by Jones *et al.* (1992) in their national study of 178 South Asian, 54 African-Caribbean and 171 White small business owners. More than a quarter of South Asian owners turned to self-employment because of blocked opportunities or unemployment. Furthermore, Jones *et al.* (1992: 186) believed this to be an underestimate: 'Since there were also many other Asian respondents who had experienced periods of unemployment or unsuitable employment even while giving positive entry motives like money or independence, we take this as a sure sign that Asians in Britain are no more culturally predisposed or voluntaristically oriented towards enterprise than any other group.'

In contrast, there are strong proponents from a more 'culturalist' tradition who privilege what they regard as distinctively ethnic resources in their accounts of business formation (Basu, 1995; Srinavasan, 1992; Werbner, 1980, 1984, 1990). For example, Werbner (1984) identifies a distinctive Pakistani ethos of self-sacrifice, self-denial and hard work that serves to fuel entrepreneurial activity. Basu (1995) also located a particularistic South Asian 'entrepreneurial spirit' in her survey of 78 South Asian retailers.

Basu (1995: 16) maintained that: 'It is difficult to support the hypothesis that the small businessmen in our sample were driven or pushed into self-employment as the only alternative to escaping unemployment.'

The controversy shows little sign of abating. But, nonetheless, it is clear that the simple concept of 'push' versus 'pull' (which has featured in some of the more quantitatively oriented studies of ethnic enterprise) are unlikely to grasp fully the complexity of entrepreneurial decision making. As Granger *et al.* (1995: 513) note in their study of freelancers in the book publishing sector, 'research designs which simply focus on the moment of transition from one labour market state to another, without exploring background career histories, are unlikely to grasp the real dynamics of self-employment career changes.'

This point is given added resonance by Ram and Deakins' (1996) study of African-Caribbean entrepreneurs. From a reading of employers' initial responses (using pre-set statements), the findings indicated that African-Caribbean entrepreneurs had in common with White small business owners largely positive motivations for entrepreneurship (Curran, 1986b). But more qualitative accounts from respondents were also elicited; this revealed that an unfavourable opportunity structure, in the guise of menial jobs or limited prospects at work, still had a bearing on the business-entry decision.

From this review of the evidence, then, it would seem that pure culturalist explanations are not adequate in accounting for small business formation in ethnic minority communities. Indeed, more recent studies of entrepreneurial motivations suggest that ethnic culture is often overridden by *class* culture, a set of values common to all small entrepreneurs (including Whites) in which independence and the desire to be one's own boss are paramount in the decision to enter and continue in business (Ram *et al.*, 2003). Where inter-ethnic differences do apply, what is of more significance is the nature of the opportunity structure and what Light (1984) has called *class resources*. This refers to tangible material resources like property and accumulated finance, which can be used to spin off new firms or branches, and less tangible properties such as contacts and information networks and the self-confidence that goes with the possession of all these assets together with a track record. As noted above, such resources are not evenly spread across ethnic minority groups, though the signs are that a more educationally qualified and professionalised British-born generation of business owners is steadily acquiring these resources (Ram *et al.*, 2003).

10.7 Family and co-ethnic labour

A further prominent characteristic of EMBs is the use made of family and co-ethnic labour. Such labour is often portrayed as a critical source of 'competitive advantage' for ethnic business, since it is often cheap and the problem of supervision is made easier (Mitter, 1986). It is widely held that their rapid expansion into such labour-intensive lines as clothing manufacture, catering and above all convenience retailing is enabled by their superior capacity to tap into a ready supply of labour power, thus equipping them to work long unsocial hours at their customers' convenience (Ward, 1991). South Asian-owned firms are often seen as the exemplars of the 'family business'. Very similar tendencies have also been attributed to Greek Cypriots and the Chinese. For the former,

Curran and Blackburn (1994) observe that because their entrepreneurs are intensely concentrated in the restaurant trade, they work very long hours boosted by ordering and collecting supplies. The Chinese are even more specialised in restaurants and take-aways and, consequently, exposed to extremely long hours of work in order to obtain a competitive cost advantage (Parker, 1994: 622). Among many factors, it is above all this competitive undercutting which has enabled the Chinese takeaway, in a large part, to replace the traditional English 'chippie' in many areas (Liao, 1992). The personal toll on the business families in question is often considerable, as Parker (1994: 622) notes: 'the whole of family life and the domestic economy [is] shaped by the takeaway'.

The facility of family labour does not appear to be as extensively utilised within African-Caribbean enterprise (Reeves and Ward, 1984). Explanations accounting for this include the more 'egalitarian' nature of the African-Caribbean family unit (Basu, 1991) and the lack of scope for enlisting unskilled family labour in the type of busi-ness sectors that the community tend to be involved in (Curran and Blackburn, 1993). Further corroboration is provided by Curran and Blackburn's (1993) study of Greek-Cypriot, Bangladeshi and African-Caribbean businesses; family labour was used least by African-Caribbeans. Curran and Blackburn explain this by reference not only to the nature of family culture, but also to the community's dispersed business activities. For instance, the type of unskilled or semi-skilled family labour that characterises many ethnic minority firms may not be particularly appropriate in sectors like personal or professional services, where African-Caribbeans are involved.

However, two points that question the conventional wisdom on labour intensiveness and family labour, particularly in relation to South Asian businesses, need to made. First, long working hours tend to be prevalent across the small firm population (Curran and Burrows, 1988a). When Jones et al. (1994b) examined this question with South Asian, African-Caribbean and White small business owners, they found that ethnic minority respondents did operate more labour-intensive practices than is customary, but these 'were as much a function of sectoral distribution and of external pressures as of spe-cific ethnic cultural and behavioural traits' (Jones et al., 1994b: 201).

Second, the tendency to view the 'family' as an unqualified resource for the ethnic entrepreneur also needs to be more closely scrutinised. A growing body of evidence argues that 'culturalist' portrayals of the family at work are often one-dimensional; they fail to appreciate the extent to which primacy often accorded to the family can con-strain business development (Barrett et al., 1996; Ram, 1992, 1994a; Ram et al., 1995; Phizacklea and Ram, 1996). In other words, over-reliance on the family can actually get in the way of economic rationality. Ram's (1994) ethnographic study of South Asian employers in the West Midlands clothing sector documents many instances where family members were retained in the business despite a lack of competence; where regular breaches of discipline were ignored; and where family workers secured equal remuneration despite varying contributions to the business. Hence the role of the family in ethnic minority enterprises is frequently 'double-edged', a point rarely given suffici-ent attention in the more celebratory accounts of minority business (see Chapter 11 for a fuller discussion of the role of family in enterprise).

The 'family' label also tends to mask the unequal nature of gender relations in ethnic minority firms (Dhaliwal, 1998; Mitter, 1986; Phizacklea, 1990). This is evident in terms of ownership; Barrett et al. (1996) speculate that many male-owned businesses conceal the extent of women's centrality to the enterprise. It is also clear that women's contribution in the day-to-day activities of the business is often unacknowledged. Recent studies on the internal management processes in ethnic businesses (Ram, 1992, 1994; Phizacklea and Ram, 1996) and, indeed, small firms *per se* (Fletcher, 1997; Holliday, 1995) illuminate the often critical contributions that women play in managing the business (see Chapter 9).

Often the scale of operation can be too large to be handled by family workers alone, as for example in many restaurants and clothing factories run by Asians in Britain. In order to maintain an essential degree of trust, such firms tend to restrict their hiring of non-family workers to members of their own ethnic community, using informal word-of-mouth methods of recruitment (Jones *et al.*, 1994b). Once again, it is often assumed that the bonds of common ethnic membership make for harmonious, mutually beneficial, working relationships, with paternalistic goodwill rendering unnecessary such practices as written contracts, formal wage bargaining and legal rights. However, evidence from employees themselves suggests that, in many instances, paternalistic benevolence provides a smokescreen for unacceptably low pay and long hours (Gillman *et al.*, 2002), especially for low-skilled workers subject to discrimination in the mainstream labour market, whose job choice and bargaining leverage is minimal (Ram *et al.*, 2001). More recently, too, researchers have highlighted a growing reliance on illegal immigrant workers on the part of struggling firms desperate to cut costs in order to survive (Ram *et al.*, 2002). Such workers represent the extremes of vulnerability, absolutely without any employment rights or bargaining power whatsoever (CARF, 1997; Staring, 2000).

10.8 Restricted spatial markets

Most EMBs are located within Britain's inner cities, which is perhaps a reflection of ethnic settlement patterns (Basu, 1991; Reeves and Ward, 1984). Labour Force Survey data indicate that 70% of the economically active ethnic minorities live in metropolitan county areas. This compares with 30% of the White population (*Employment Gazette*, 1994: 68). An inner-city location can have important implications for the viability and growth prospects for small businesses. It was often 'white-flight' from decaying inner-city areas that provided the opportunity for ethnic minorities to take over businesses, particularly in the retail distributive sector (Jones *et al.*, 1994b). But, despite providing this initial opportunity, the problems inherent in an inner-city location often temper the potential for the development of such businesses. For example, local environmental conditions like physical dilapidation, inadequate parking and vandalism are depressingly commonplace. They can often prove a major constraint in securing high-quality markets from outside the immediate locality (Basu, 1991). Moreover, they accentuate the problem of raising appropriate finance (Deakins, Hussain and Ram, 1994) and insurance cover (Patel, 1988).

Although co-ethnic consumer tastes may provide an initial opportunity for business activities, continued reliance acts a major constraint on business development. This is due to the comparatively small size of ethnic minority communities. Furthermore, minority entrepreneurs tend to cater for mainly local residents within inner-city areas where customers have relatively low spending power (Basu, 1991). Moreover, such 'community markets' are likely to be in long-term decline since successive British governments have made immigration progressively difficult and there is the likelihood of later generations of ethnic minorities being more integrated with the dominant White culture and economy (Curran and Blackburn, 1993). However, as Curran and Blackburn's own findings (1993: 60) show, break-out may be less of an issue for minority firms located in areas where there is still a large ethnic minority population. They found that businesses in London, where there is a very significance ethnic minority presence, were more dependent on co-ethnic markets for their sales than those in Sheffield and Leeds. Hence demographic trends are likely to have a bearing on the urgency of break-out for EMBs.

In the light of such unpromising trading circumstances, encouraging 'break-out' into majority markets has emerged as an issue of particular importance (Curran and Blackburn, 1993; EMBI, 1991; Jones *et al.*, 2000; Ram and Jones, 1998). But what actually constitutes break-out? Clearly, it is rather more than simply servicing White markets. For instance, a corner store in a White inner-city area may be in no better position than a similar business situated in an ethnic enclave; in both cases, highly competitive market conditions and geographic location militate against any real prospect of substantial growth. A recent study of African-Caribbean entrepreneurship in Britain (Ram and Deakins, 1996) remains cautions against simplistic notions of ethnic business development. Contrary to many previous studies, Ram and Deakins found that firms in their investigation had an average of 50% sales to the majority population. Hence, at a basic level, many entrepreneurs may have heeded the advice of commentators advocating the servicing of 'White' markets as the way forward for ethnic enterprise. But it was not uncommon for these mixed-market-oriented firms to remain low-yielding marginal concerns with little prospect for significant development in the future.

Curran and Blackburn (1993: 12) provide a rather more sophisticated view of break-out. They argue for the assessment of plans for expansion with evidence of preparation for growth; examples of the latter would include investigating sources of finance, planning for the re-fitting of premises to enhance potential for growth, and the revamping of existing products or services offered by the business to appeal to a wider market or achieve higher mark-ups. Precise measurement of these facets might be difficult, but, none the less, a genuine attempt at break-out would need to address such issues. However, given the sectoral and spatial confines of many ethnic minority firms, and their usually labour-intensive *modus operandi*, break-out in these terms is likely to be highly problematic.

10.9 Funding ethnic minority enterprise

There can be little doubt that under-funding remains one of the most intractable problems facing ethnic minority small business owners. The difficult task of securing finance for business start-up is the most documented problem facing both existing and potential ethnic minority business owners whether in Europe or North America (Barrett, 1997; Jones *et al.*, 1992; Jones *et al.*, 1994a; Woodward, 1997). Problems of under-capitalisation perpetually thwart the growth and threaten the survival of many EMBs

(Barrett, 1997; Basu, 1991). A major debate has been the extent to which the relationships between ethnic entrepreneurs and commercial banks serve to alleviate or exacerbate this problem. Recent research (Curran and Blackburn, 1993; Deakins *et al.*, 1994; Jones *et al.*, 1994a) presents a mixed picture. For some groups, including Greek-Cypriots and Indians, the acquisition of bank finance does not appear to be problematic and, indeed, the positive entrepreneurial image now often attached to such groups may even be an advantage. Even so, complacency is certainly not in order here, since research has thrown up countless instances of Asian funding applicants being turned down by banks in circumstances that raise suspicions of racist discrimination and negative stereotyping (Jones *et al.*, 1989, 1994a; Ram *et al.*, 2003).

In the case of African-Caribbeans the benefit of the doubt is even less in evidence, with negative experiences with mainstream financial institutions consistently reported ever since Ward and Reeves' (1980) initial report on the question (Barrett, 1999; Brooks, 1983; Jones *et al.*, 1989, 1994a; Ram *et al.*, 2003). Taking the sanguine view, this might be explained in purely technical terms with reference to 'business problems' (Curran and Blackburn, 1993), which can be addressed by training and greater professionalism. Less happily, it may reflect the rather more insidious problem of institutionalised discrimination (Brooks, 1983; Jones *et al.*, 1994a. Whatever view is taken, it continues to be a major constraint upon the development of African-Caribbeans in business.

In addressing these problems, some progress has been made by Black-led enterprise support agencies, who appear to have been very active in assisting with business plans, and even the provision of finance (Curran and Blackburn, 1993). But Deakins, Hussain and Ram (1994) suggest a number of further steps that the banks could take. These include the training of staff to appreciate more fully the dynamics of ethnic minority firms; employment of appropriately qualified ethnic minority staff in more influential positions within the organisation; greater involvement in the social and cultural activities of minority groups; ethnic monitoring of customers; and more extensive networking with Black-led support agencies. A recent large-scale study of finance and ethnic minority firms in the UK reiterated these recommendations (Ram *et al.*, 2003).

10.10 Ethnic minority business and enterprise support

Encouraging ethnic minority communities into self-employment has been a discernible feature of national and local policymaking since the early 1980s (see Chapter 4). There appear to be two particular reasons for this policy direction. First, the civil disturbances in many inner-city areas that occurred in the early part of the decade focused attention on the often dire position of Black racialised minorities (Cross and Waldinger, 1992). Following Lord Scarman's pronouncements in the wake of the disturbances in Brixton, promulgating self-employment among the Black population was seen as an important means of tackling disadvantage and maintaining social harmony in urban areas. Second, some minority communities, notably South Asians, Chinese and Cypriots, have come to dominate particular sectors and local economies. Often this position of prominence has been achieved without the assistance of business support agencies (Marlow, 1992).

A consistent finding of previous research on EMBs is their low propensity to use mainstream business support agencies, often relying instead on self-help and informal sources of assistance (see Deakins *et al.*, 2003; Ram and Jones, 1998; Ram and Smallbone, 2002 for reviews; and Chapter 4 for a fuller discussion of support agency usage). Of course, it could be that the low take-up of business support from formal agencies reflects a low level of perceived need or a lack of interest by ethnic minority business owners in receiving external assistance. However, growing evidence (Marlow, 1992; Deakins *et al.*, 2003) suggests that the low level of use of mainstream business support agencies cannot necessarily be put down to the lack of interest on the part of the business owners. 'Supply-side' issues – for example inability to reach out to firms, inadequate databases and the inappropriateness of the 'product-oriented' approaches used by many support agencies – are also pertinent factors.

The ostensibly low take-up of formal sources of business support draws attention to the capacity of mainstream business support agencies to cater adequately for the needs of ethnic minority firms. The 'equality of access' approach which professes to 'treat all businesses the same' seems to founder on the reluctance of many EMBs to utilise the services of mainstream agencies and is severely constrained on the practical grounds that such agencies often fail to capture the most basic data on the scale, dynamics and issues facing EMBs.

A key issue in the debate on appropriate policy support for EMBs is the extent to which their 'needs' are similar to, or different from, those of other SMEs. In practical terms, one of the distinctive characteristics of EMBs in the UK that has important potential implications for business support policy is their concentration in particular sectors, for example retailing, catering and personal services. This is important because the prospects for business development are heavily influenced by market and demand trends and the degree of competition in each of these sectors.

Size is another important characteristic of EMBs, which has implications for their access to finance and business support. Although the absence of comprehensive, large-scale business databases that include an ethnic variable makes it impossible to paint a totally accurate picture, it is widely accepted that most EMBs are not just small, but very small firms; this means they share many of the characteristics, problems and support needs of micro enterprises more generally. These include frequent problems in raising finance to start a business and/or expand (particularly in the early stages), as well as deficiencies in certain core management competencies, such as marketing and financial management skills. One of the consequences of their very small average size is that most EMBs fell outside the main target group of the mainstream business support agencies in England (i.e. Business Links) during the 1990s, when such organisations were mainly concerned with firms employing more than five (or ten) employees with growth potential (Ram and Smallbone, 2002) – see Chapter 4.

Location is a further characteristic of EMBs, which may influence their support needs. Most EMBs are located within Britain's inner cities, reflecting ethnic settlement patterns more generally. The negative consequences of such a location for trade has been documented since the first major study of Asian businesses in 1978 (Aldrich *et al.*, 1984), and reinforced in more recent studies of other minority groups (see Ram and Smallbone, 2002, for a review). Local environmental conditions such as physical dilapidation, inadequate parking and vandalism are commonplace in such settings.

Furthermore, locational factors can add to the difficulties faced in raising finance, which is compounded by the tendency for minority entrepreneurs to cater for local residents where customers have relatively low spending power.

In interpreting such findings about EMBs, it is important to recognise the reluctance of small firm owners *per se* to utilise external assistance. This resistance stems from doubts about value for money, scepticism of generalist advice (particularly where this is offered by advisers that lack detailed sectoral knowledge) and an emphasis on autonomy, which some owner-managers perceive is threatened by the use of external advice. This may result in a greater use of informal rather than formal channels of support, particularly in cases where managers lack formal management training or qualifications, reflecting the importance of trust-based relationships in the effective delivery of advice and consultancy to small firms, regardless of the ethnicity of the owner (Ram and Smallbone, 2001).

10.11 Chapter summary

The increasing importance of self-employment among ethnic minorities has been one of the marked features of labour market change internationally over the past 20 years. As in many advanced industrial societies, EMBs are now an established and growing feature of contemporary Britain. In addition to fulfilling an important economic and social role for the minority communities themselves, ethnic enterprise has also made a significant contribution to both the revival of the small business population and the revitalisation of depressed urban retail landscapes. There is little doubt that particular areas of economic activity, such as retailing, clothes manufacture and catering, have been transformed by the dynamic presence of minority communities. Groups like the South Asians, Chinese and Greek-Cypriots have been notably conspicuous in effecting such transformations in often adverse competitive environments. Although African-Caribbean 'under-representation' in self-employment has precipitated much speculation, there is little doubt that they are an emerging presence on the small business scene. Recent evidence on African-Caribbean entrepreneurship (Curran and Blackburn, 1993; Ram and Deakins, 1996) points to the promising growth potential of this community in business.

In this chapter, we have attempted to scrutinise the growing literature on ethnic minority enterprise with a view to assessing some of the key debates that have dominated this subject. The processes that underpin small business formation have been shown to extend beyond pure culturalist arguments that, for instance, depict South Asians as natural entrepreneurs and African-Caribbeans as uninterested in entrepreneurial activities. The influence of the socio-economic context, or 'opportunity structure', continues to affect the life-chances of Britain's ethnic minorities and its impact upon the decision to enter self-employment can rarely be detached.

Investigation of family and co-ethnic labour inside the ethnic small business further exposes the fragility of popular stereotypes. It is undoubtedly the case that in terms of hours worked, entrepreneurial rewards and commitment to the business, ethnic minorities (African-Caribbeans as well as the more commonly noted South Asians) are remarkably industrious. But it is equally evident that such practices are characteristic of the harshly competitive economic sectors that such minority groups trade in rather than a culturally specific work ethic. Moreover, when the capacity of family labour to constrain business development and the often unequal nature of gender relations is highlighted, the image of the cosy, consensus-oriented ethnic minority firm becomes even more illusory. This is not to deny the importance of particular ethnic resources, which can often serve as an important source of competitiveness. Rather, it serves to reinforce the importance of the context in which such firms operate. Hence, a comprehensive synthesis of the multi-faceted nature of ethnic minority business enterprise is incomplete without an elaborate understanding of the intricacies of economic change and how and why the proclivity to entrepreneurship in advanced market economies varies between ethnic groups.

An important part of this context is the relationship with external agencies crucial to small firm development, notably the high street banks. Debate continues on whether the reported problems between ethnic minority firms and the banks are business or 'race' related. However, there is little doubt that under-funding remains one of the most serious problems facing ethnic minority small businesses. In attempting to assist with these and other problems, the 'mainstream' business support agencies appear to be constrained by major obstacles that seem endemic to the burgeoning 'enterprise' industry. These include a lack of clarity over objectives, inter-agency competition, scarce resources, inappropriate services and a lack of networking.

Questions

1 How adequate are 'culturalist' accounts in explaining ethnic minority involvement in self-employment?

2 What factors account for the different levels of self-employment among ethnic minorities?

3 How feasible is 'break-out' for ethnic minority firms?

Web links

www.ethnicbusiness.org/
The Ethnic Minority Business Forum's (EMBF) remit is to provide independent advice to Government in relation to SME policy and practice as they relate to ethnic minority business.

www.bankofengland.co.uk/publications/financeforsmallfirms/ethnic.pdf
Special report by the Bank of England on the financing of ethnic minority firms in the UK.

http://business.kingston.ac.uk/research/kbssbs/ramsmall.pdf
The paper 'Ethnic Minority Enterprise: Policy in Practice' by Monder Ram and David Smallbone reviews recent research on ethnic minorities in business, focusing on those

aspects that have potential implications for policy and identifying the types of initiatives that have been implemented for EMBs, highlighting good practice principles.

http://europa.eu.int/comm/enterprise/entrepreneurship/craft/craft-minorities/minorities.htm
A range of papers from the European Commission DG Enterprise on issues in ethnic entrepreneurship across Europe.

CHAPTER 11

Family and entrepreneurship

Denise Fletcher

11.1 Introduction

This chapter provides a review of the different approaches that have been utilised to examine the link between family and enterprise. Definitional issues are addressed, as are rationalist and 'systems' ways of evaluating the relationship between family and enterprise. Criticism is made of the effects of rationalist thinking on studies of family businesses that have tended to create duality and polarity in our understanding of the family-enterprise relationship. It is argued that a developmental and integrated view of family and enterprise is more useful for understanding the *specific transactions* linking the institutions of 'economy' and 'family'. A range of approaches and theories that are being used to examine the *integration* of family and enterprise/business activities are outlined. The chapter concludes with a discussion of interpretive inquiry and its potential benefits or uses in explaining how family and enterprise issues 'come together' in small business creation and development.

11.2 Learning objectives

There are four learning objectives in this chapter:

1 To give the reader an understanding of the ways in which family issues and relations link to enterprise activities.
2 To explore the different approaches that have been utilised to examine the link between family relationships and enterprise.
3 To help readers identify key research themes and topics for further inquiry.
4 To encourage reflection on the value of interpretivist ideas and narrative analysis for investigating the dynamics of family and enterprise issues.

Key concepts
■ family ■ family enterprise ■ interpretivist approaches ■ narrative analysis

11.3 Family and enterprise

Throughout history the institutions of family and economy have always been broadly interrelated. In pre-industrial societies, for example, 'family' and 'working' life were highly integrated and the family unit was seen as important for imposing some control over daily tasks. The family unit was also seen as a valuable source of labour – a place where traditional values and skills were passed on to the next generation of workers. According to Kanter (1989a, referring to the work of Hareven, 1975, and Nelson, 1975), 'it was the family system that made possible the transition from pre-industrial to industrial ways of life . . . The family was an important work unit in city factories in England . . . Spinners in textile mills chose their wives, children and near relatives as assistants . . . [and] children entering the factory at eight or nine worked for their fathers, perpetuating the old system of authority and the traditional values of parents training children for occupations' (1989a: 79). Similar patterns are present in developing or transition economies where the family unit is (at best) seen as a vehicle for stimulating enterprise and initiative or (at worst) a resource to be exploited for enterprise profitability.

It is not surprising, therefore, that in Western Europe, the US and the Far East, many studies have reported the close relationship between work, family and small business development. Indeed, there is now a well-established literature concerned with examining notions of family – what it means in different cultures, and how families are sustained through social structures and psychological/social reproduction patterns or processes. As such, the study of families has a long history and tradition with roots not only in sociology and psychology but also social anthropology with its interest in communities, clans and kinship patterns, and economic history with its attention to family dynasties and their contribution to economic growth (Crossick *et al.*, 1996; Muller, 1996; Grell, 1996; Hareven, 1975; Nelson, 1975; Kanter, 1989; Cookson, 1997). But, in spite of this multi-disciplinary interest, it is rare to see interpretivist analyses that focus specifically on peoples' whole lives and the *relationality* between peoples' enterprise activities and their family relations. It is possible to argue, therefore, that there is still considerable authority and relevance in the argument put by Kanter (1989: 77) that 'the *specific transactions* linking the institutions of "economy" and "family" as "connected organizers" of experience and systems of social relations', whilst not ignored, provide scope for further study.

In the sections that follow in this chapter, a review of the different approaches that have been utilised to examine the link between family relationships and enterprise is provided. It is argued, however, that while many studies report on the interrelationship between family and enterprise, the *relationality* between peoples' whole lives, family lives, their biography and orientations to enterprise or work could be brought more fully to the surface and made more explicit in research accounts. The chapter concludes with a discussion of the value of interpretivist ideas and narrative analysis for investigating the relationality of family and enterprise issues. Finally, some potential research themes and topics for further inquiry are presented.

11.4 Family and business: an overview of key approaches

The broad relationship between family relations and work issues has, as referred to above, been widely studied from various perspectives. In this section an overview is given of the ways in which *family* and *business*, in particular, are interlinked and reported in research studies.

The relationship between family and business is frequently examined in the context of businesses defined as 'family firms'. The specific ways in which one might define a family firm are discussed more fully below. But, broadly speaking, the notion of 'family' in society refers to groups of people bound together by blood and marriage ties (Muncie and Sapsford, 1997) and can include the traditional nuclear form of family, extended families, kin groups and single-parent families. Business activity becomes related to family issues when family members are involved in the business in some way. This involvement can be in the form of a managerial role and/or it could be through the ownership of shares in a business. Given that the notion of family is complex – because of its different compositions, forms and meanings – so, also, is the complexity of family business forms. The monolithic concept of 'family business' cannot adequately describe the complexity of family-business practice (Holland and Boulton, 1984: 16). As these writers argue, the family-business relationship changes according to the structure and size of the business.

In its loosest form, family firms can be businesses where family members (such as spouses or siblings) do not have a formal role in the business but are involved 'at the periphery' by providing support of some kind. In these situations, the family unit often provides social capital (trust, network contacts and tacit knowledge) and emotional resources to support the business. Individuals can draw upon this social capital in the pursuit of economic advancement (Boissevain, 1974), whether this be to take advantage of unpaid flexible sources of labour, overcome market/environment obstacles, acquire emotional support or provide a safe retreat from the trials of business activity (Ram, 1994b: 51). This is because the family unit is a 'social organisation of production' – producing and reproducing an accumulation of mutual obligations amongst members which builds cooperation, solidarity, mutual dependence and further obligation' (Sanders and Nee, 1996: 233). To take account of the informal role of family resources, the 'household' is sometimes taken as the central unit of analysis (Whatmore, 1991; Wheelock and Oughton, 1996). Other researchers examine the complex nature of business-family relationship (Holland and Boulton, 1984; Gibb *et al.*, 1994; Wheelock and Baines, 1998; Poutziouris and Chittenden, 1996). Further studies consider how family ties and networks have contributed to the economic development of regions and European industries (Weidenbaum, 1996; Heuberger and Gutwein, 1997; Brogger and Gilmore, 1997; Muller, 1996; Lombardini, 1996).

In its more complex form, family businesses are those that have several family members involved in owning and managing a business. The complexity of family ownership and management is intensified in businesses that have passed from one generation to another. Building on Barry's (1989) categorisations, Litz (1995) identifies nine categories of family firms that are derived from two structural considerations: ownership and managerial control. In its more complex form, a family business is one where family members own *and* manage the business. But also, the Litz typology takes account of firms that have non-family ownership and where family managers are involved in the day-to-day management (e.g. in a situation where a business has gone public, or been sold to new owners, but where family members are still involved in senior management positions). This could also work the other way round where family members own a company but are not involved in managing the business (e.g. in situations where succession is planned and the family owners are either looking to keep shares in the business without having the responsibility of day-to-day management, or where the owners are planning to retire or sell the business in which case they may introduce a manager-director designate and/or initiate a management buy-out).

What is useful about the Litz (1995) framework is that it acknowledges that ownership and management structure is not static in that it can evolve from one 'type' to another. It takes account of a whole range of family-business related situations in between the looser and more formal definitions. This framing draws attention to the 'intentionality' within the business (i.e. to become, remain, erode or displace family involvement). In addition, it provides for analysis of the *behavioural* aspects of family firms (Chua *et al.*, 1999) and the ways in which family relations 'scale up' to influence outcomes such as business success, failure, strategy and operations (Astrachan *et al.*, 2002). It also highlights the problems, obstacles and opportunities involved as businesses make judgements about pre-family, family, adaptive family or post-family involvement (Holland and Boulton, 1984) as they move through a range of family and business life-cycles (Dyer and Handler, 1994; Gersick *et al.*, 1997).

In broad terms, therefore, taking account of all types of family involvement, family businesses (large and small) can be estimated to comprise between 15 and 81% of all businesses in Europe and the US (Westhead *et al.*, 1997; 2002). If, however, a more formal quantitative definition of family business is adopted, a more precise understanding of the extent of family firms within a particular economy can be achieved. Westhead *et al.* (2002) offer seven categories of family firms. Where businesses are defined as those in which 50% or more of the ordinary voting shares are owned by members of the largest family group related by blood or marriage *and* where one or more of the management team are drawn from the family, in addition to the business being perceived by the chief executive as a family firm then they report that 62.1% of their research sample constitute family businesses. If an inter-generational transition is added to the definitional criteria, then the number of family firms sampled in the Westhead *et al.* study is reduced to 28.6%.

Either way, family businesses constitute a substantial empirical phenomenon. And, perhaps not surprisingly, an extensive literature has evolved over the last 30–40 years concerned with emphasising the 'specialness' and 'distinctiveness' of family firms. Dyer and Sánchez (1998) and Chrisman *et al.* (2003) provide reviews of the range of topics published about family firms. Dyer and Sánchez (1998) argue that until the mid 1980s the field was focused largely on succession issues, and they claim that it remained 'shallow' in terms of theoretical rigour and systematic analysis. Since then, interpersonal family and business dynamics, firm performance, consulting to family firms, and gender and ethnicity in family firms have received more attention. In their 'strategic reflection' on the field, Chrisman *et al.* (2003) identified that topics had widened to include economic performance (15%), firm governance (10%), resources/competitive advantage and conflict (6% each), entrepreneurship/innovation, culture, goals/strategy formulation (5% each), internationalisation (3%), and professionalisation of the family firm (2%). (The figures in brackets represent the number of articles published on this topic between 1996 and 2003.) Most authors agreed that more 'rigorous' empirical studies began to emerge with a trend towards greater experimentation, a wider variety of analytical tools and efforts in theory building, and less emphasis on descriptive anecdotal accounts (Bird *et al.*, 2002; Chrisman *et al.*, 2003a; Chrisman *et al.*, 2003b).

In the following section a strategic overview is provided of how the relationship between family and enterprise/business has been reported on and developed over the last 30 years. It is to this that the discussion now turns.

11.5 Family business: a strategic overview

One approach to the study of family businesses has been to identify the characteristics and processes that differentiate family from non-family firms (Donckels and Fröhlich, 1991; Daily and Dollinger, 1993; Poutziouris and Chittenden, 1996; Beehr *et al.*, 1997; Westhead, 1997). In 1992 research undertaken by BDO Stoy Hayward and BBC Business Matters (Leach, 1994: 11) showed that family firms considerably outperformed non-family firms. The superior performance of publicly quoted family firms (relative to non-family firms) is also confirmed in a study sponsored by Grant Thornton and reported by Poutzioris (2005). However, Poutzioris *et al.* (1996) and Westhead *et al.* (1997) found that there was no significant difference (statistically and qualitatively) with regard to performance indicators and non-financial objectives between unquoted family and non-family firms. The only significant difference was that family firms tend to be more concerned with lifestyle and securing family jobs in the management team (Westhead *et al.*, 1997).

Differentiating family from non-family firms is important on a number of grounds. First, it is important for understanding what is unique or special about the organisational practice of family firms. Here, then, a body of knowledge and theorising can occur about this practice that can be drawn upon for research and to give guidance to family firms. Second, it is important for drawing policy attention to the specific needs of family firms (such as succession issues, leadership, work–life balance and training needs). But, also, because the evidence on the specialness of family firms has been contradictory, responses from the research community and other supporting bodies such as accountants or management consultants have been inconsistent. On the one hand, family businesses are upheld as financially stable, and long term in orientation and strategic planning and, therefore, good for the economy. On the other, they are chastised for nepotism and being governed by emotions rather than business-like principles – and needing, therefore, careful corrective management.

This latter and more negative view of family businesses has shaped much of the early academic writings and consultancy responses concerned with their support. For example, separating 'family' from 'business' issues was frequently espoused as the guiding principle for developing a successful business. Thus, the dominant approach adopted for studying the family firm was to view the 'family' and the 'business' as two 'systems' competing for power and control within the organisation. This was because family ties and emotional issues were seen to compete with the demands of the business and commitment to family clashed with the ability to be loyal, efficient and totally committed to the work organisation. As a result, therefore, the early studies of family businesses (Donnelley, 1964) tended to be highly normative, prescribing how the emotional issues involved in running a family business should be smoothed away by preventive or corrective strategies.

In the family business literature this 'corrective' approach to the study and support of family firms is referred to as a 'rational' view of businesses. According to Hollander and Elman (1988), this rational view sees two 'organisations' co-existing within the family business. One is the family organisation characterised by emotions, nepotism and the 'non-rational' dynamics between family members. The other is the business or 'rational' component characterised by efficiency, structure, functions, role clarity and purpose – the point being that when the two parts clash the 'business' side loses out to the power, sentiment and emotional issues of the family. Hollander and Elman (1988) suggest that early writers on family business (referring to Calder, 1961; Donnelley, 1964) 'lamented the fact that family firms were not operated in a more "business-like" way . . . and therefore the solution was to excise the family' (p. 146). Issues such as kinship ties, nepotism, hereditary management and emotionalism were seen to have a detrimental effect on the company in that the needs, goals and demands of the 'family' conflicted with the needs, goals and demands of the 'business'.

Kanter (1989a) ties this rationalist thinking to the rise of systematic or scientific management. A scientific management approach is concerned with ensuring equality and rewarding individual merit in order to secure the development of rational bureaucracies. A 'scientific management' approach is problematic in Kanter's (1989a) view because it tends to encourage a view of family influence as an *impediment* to the efficient and effective operation of a business. It also means that family relations and resources – influences which were highly integrated in pre-industrial societies – are best seen as isolated from the workplace, and the close relationship between work and family is disparaged and discouraged.

In approaching family firms from this rational versus non-rational perspective, this gave rise to the business and the family components of family businesses being conceptualised as two *systems* competing with each other inside the firm. A 'systemised' way of conceptualising the family firm is concerned with understanding the interrelationships of the different components that comprise the overall business system. Some authors (op. cit.) argue for the need to identify, separate and overcome the competing systems within the business in order to sustain a tidy and efficient business. Others suggest approaches for linking together the business, the founder and the family (Beckhard and Dyer, 1983). Here, aspects of the market-place, industry, technology, stakeholders, task system, founder and family issues interact to form a 'highly complex, open system of interactive elements' (Hollander and Elman, 1988: 157). The joint system operates according to rules that are derived from the separate components of the system but, at the same time, the conflicting needs and demands of the different components are continuously being adapted to the needs of the whole system (Davis, 1983). As a result of applying systems analysis, it is argued that boundaries can be drawn around the different components of the system in order to locate problems that need resolving.

The effect of rational and systems approaches to understanding the link between family and business has been twofold. First, more positively, these studies have highlighted the special needs and situations of family businesses (from which specific policy or consultancy responses can be tailored). Second (and perhaps less helpfully) these studies have led to a *dualist* understanding of family firms whereby they are smaller, less efficient, professional, entrepreneurial, formalised and growth oriented, and often showing tendencies of 'defender' (rather than entrepreneurial/proactive) strategic behaviour (Daily and Dollinger, 1993). This dualism is particularly evident in discussions about the need to: 'professionalise the business'; 'manage succession' (Dyer, 1989; Fox *et al.*, 1996; Kimhi, 1997); manipulate life-cycle changes (Davis and Stern, 1980; Gersick *et al.*, 1997) and encourage entrepreneurialism (Gibb *et al.*, 1994). An example here is Hoy and Verser's (1994) work in which they set up family and entrepreneurial domains as separate (albeit sometimes overlapping) ends of a continuum.

During the 1980s, however, a more 'developmental' approach to the study of family businesses began to emerge. This approach is distinctive because it takes account of the more positive ways in which business and family issues interrelate. A developmental approach was seen as important for taking account of the human element, the discretion possessed by key decision makers, and how values, beliefs and ideologies may influence decisions (Riordan and Riordan, 1993) – something neglected in the rational and systems view of family firms. Also, the rational view tends to ignore the potential 'ability of the owner-manager to allocate resources in non-economic ways to fulfill personal family goals' (Riordan and Riordan, 1993: 76). Instead researchers began to approach the family as integral to the efficient working of the business system (Kepner, 1983; Hollander, 1984; Ward, 1987). As a result, alternative theories have begun to emerge that take account of the interrelationship between family and business issues.

Some examples of theories, or approaches, are 'field theory', resource-based theory, agency theory and entrepreneurship theory. Field theory focuses on the psychological forces in the life space of the owner-manger (Riordan and Riordan, 1993). Resource-based theory takes account of the significance of the family in contributing resource variety (Chrisman *et al.*, 2003a; Cabrera-Suarez *et al.*, 2001; Habbershon *et al.*, 1999; Heck and Kaye, 2004; Zahra *et al.*, 2004). Here, studies link to the strategic management literature and concepts/theories are drawn upon with a view to proposing ways of strengthening the performance of family firms by harnessing family resources to enhance competitive advantages, organisational goals and objectives (Chrisman *et al.*, 2003c). Agency theory is also being utilised to assess the costs involved in aligning the interests and actions of managers (agents) with the interests of the owners of the business. In family firms where family members own and manage a business, it is sometimes assumed that these agency costs are much reduced. But many authors are now examining this assumption with studies on family businesses (Chrisman *et al.*, 2004; Corbetta and Salvato, 2004). Finally, entrepreneurship theory is also being drawn upon to examine the organisational practices of family businesses. Studies focus on the effects of family on entrepreneurship (Aldrich and Cliff, 2003; Rogoff *et al.*, 2003); the overlap between family and entrepreneurship domains of research (Hoy and Verser, 1994; Dyer and Handler, 1994); the link between entrepreneurial management and governance in family firms (Steier, 2003); and entrepreneurial activities in family versus non-family firms (Zahra *et al.*, 2004; Heck and Kay, 2004).

11.6 Integrating notions of family and enterprise

The 'developmental' approach to the study of businesses involving family members (and the assumptions underlying it) provided the basis for a significant shift in our understanding of the relationship between family and business. Instead of polarising family and business issues, a more *integrative* understanding of the dynamic relationship between family and business began to emerge. An integrative understanding is significant because it challenges the 'myth of separate family and business worlds' and provides for a means of critically reviewing the relationship between work and family (Kanter, 1989a). And, it takes more fully into account the interactive, dynamic (or coevolutionary) relationship between family and enterprise (Kepner, 1983; McCollom, 1988).

Family and enterprise are closely related because of the nature of enterprise activity. Enterprise activity is usually associated with new business venturing or starting up a small business. And many new ventures emerge from ideas, knowledge or experiences that reside or are cultivated in the family unit. In some cases this might be an enterprise (or self-employment) response to a family problem (such as unemployment or desire to work from home and/or balance work and family). In other cases, the new venture may arise as a family response to a business or enterprise opportunity that might then lead to the creation of a family business (and this is discussed in more detail below). This is particularly the case with occupations that lend themselves to family or spouse involvement (such as farming and craft activities).

As a result, many studies have drawn attention to the relationship between enterprise creation and social networks (Tichy *et al.*, 1979; Birley, 1985; Aldrich and Zimmer, 1986; Johannisson, 1987c; Lorenzoni and Ornati, 1988; Butler and Hansen, 1991; Larson, 1992). Other studies take account of how family, kinship and gender relations facilitate enterprise development (Whatmore, 1991; Stafford, 1995; Salaff and Hu, 1996). Some focus on the 'business as family' – an approach suggested by Kepner (1983), but taken forward in many studies since (Wheelock, 1991; Poutziouris and Chittenden, 1996; Ram and Holliday, 1993a). Others draw attention more directly to the household as the unit of analysis (Baines and Wheelock, 1998a, 1998b) in order to highlight the interrelationship between the household, the state and labour markets (Baines *et al.*, 2002). In addition, there is now extensive study and writings on the issue of work–life balance. Consideration is given to dual career families, how family relations shape work or career patterns, and how gender relations shape changing patterns of household employment (Barnett and Barnett, 1988; Marshack, 1993; Wheelock, 1990).

But what is distinctive about this integrative approach to the study of enterprise and family is the shift away from the dominance of individual entrepreneurial figures heroically leading new venture creation to an acknowledgement of the household or business family situations for facilitating enterprise. These studies tend to emphasise the relationships and interdependencies connecting family and enterprise and the ways in which these provide resources enabling the enterprise activity to occur.

In referring to this range of studies, which bring together more explicitly notions of enterprise and family, it is possible to see how a shift has occurred in our understanding. Not only has a move been made from closed and non-problematised views of family but, also, alternative views of family have been developed which conceptualise family enterprise in terms of 'mapped realities' (Levin, 1993) highlighting how people attribute meaning to the relations they assign as familial. It is this interpretive view of family and enterprise that brings this chapter to a close.

11.7 Interpretive inquiry of family and enterprise

As outlined in the preceding sections, the study of family and enterprise has roots in a range of disciplines from psychology and social anthropology to economic history. The study of the relationship between family and business is receiving widespread attention from a variety of audiences including academia, consultancy and policy support agencies. Family businesses represent a significant empirical phenomenon and the informal relationship between enterprise and family means that the 'field' is flourishing and growing in theoretical and methodological diversity. Having said this, however, there is a particular emphasis within the study of family and enterprise that is worthy of more widespread application: this relates to the application of interpretive lines of inquiry.

Interpretive inquiry has five key characteristics (Fletcher, 2005). First, there is a concern for 'interpretive awareness' and thinking or feeling oneself into the situation of the research subject through intuition and empathy (Alvesson and Skoldberg, 2000). Second, it aims to focus on the sharing, negotiation and interpretation of meanings that are, for example, associated with the notion of family. The researcher would, then, be concerned with the interpretation of peoples' interpretive processes. Third, interpretive inquiry takes account of processes – processes that are historically, culturally and politically situated. This means considering the social embeddedness of family/ enterprise activity in particular social/cultural/political contexts. Fourth, interpretive inquiry assumes that meaning creation is constructed inter-subjectively through exchange and interaction. Attention is drawn, therefore, to how meaning making, knowledge and understanding are constructed between people in the process of *relating* (Gergen, 1999). Fifth, language and discourse lies at the centre of interpretive inquiry because it is through talk, conversation and dialogue that meaning is constructed.

Interpretive inquiry is not particularly novel in the study of family and enterprise. Ram found in his studies of ethnic minority firms (1991, 1994a) that meanings of family were interpreted and negotiated within the firm (see Chapter 10 for further discussions of this issue). Central to the negotiation of racial constraints, for example, was the role of family. He comments that whilst, internally, family relationships were a flexible source of labour and means of imposing managerial discipline, externally family roles were important for overcoming racial obstacles in the market (1994b: 51). Fletcher (1997) discusses how interpretations of family were 'drawn upon' to block the strategic development of the small business in her ethnographic study. Also, McCollom (1992) discusses the role of 'organisational' stories in the family-owned business. She reveals how family and non-family employees experience membership in a family enterprise. Through the use of organisational stories, she is concerned with how people become aware of the relationship between the 'family' and 'business' in their daily work lives and how this relationship shapes organisational structures and processes. Hamilton (2002) also utilises story-like narrative accounts to draw attention to the political and gendered nature of leadership in family businesses. Likewise, Ainsworth and Cox (2003) adopt an interpretive style of analysis to examine the symbolic, material and ideological significance of the family in creating divisions and disunity in small organisations.

What is significant about interpretive lines of inquiry is that explicit attention is drawn to how the concept of 'family' is interpreted and constructed by those working in family-enterprise situations. From this perspective, the notion of family (and enterprise) is approached as something that is multi-dimensional and interpretively dynamic. Consideration could be given to family discourses in order to identify how such discourses help us to assign meaning to the 'actions we take on behalf of the social ties designated as familial' (Gubrium and Holstein, 1990: 14). This is because family discourses provide a means of talking about, assigning meaning to, and making sense of relations with others and this understanding also provides courses of action (as seen in the studies cited above). Or, the notion of 'family' could be seen as a 'realised category' in which understandings and interpretations of 'family' (and enterprise) are socially constructed and help to make sense of the reality that they describe (Bourdieu, 1996: 21). Also, the 'familial analogy' could be used to explain the attachments, inter-personal linkages, emotional bondings and affectionate ties that develop between and among its members – acting like 'glue', holding firms together (Kepner, 1983: 60) and accounting for why people working in small firms often refer to themselves as 'one big happy family' (Holliday and Letherby, 1993). It also signifies that 'family' culture is not simply a product of employing family members and that feelings of 'family' can be cultivated without blood ties (Ram and Holliday, 1993b: 165).

Finally, interpretive inquiry is important for examining the link between family and enterprise because it provides for a close and detailed understanding of the *relationality* between people's whole lives, family lives, their biography and orientations to enterprise or work. For example, through interpretive analysis the processes that connect and interrelate people – their lives and work activities – into enterprise/organisational structures, whether this be self-employment situations with loose links to family resources, or wife-husband teams, sibling partnerships, second generation or large family 'cousin consortiums', can be explored. Attention can be drawn to the ways in which this relationality is played out in everyday human or financial managerial practices and in strategic decision-making processes about growth, succession or 'passing the baton'. Also, the ways in which family-enterprise relationality helps to shape (or inhibit) business development, longevity and performance can be made more explicit. Herein lie possibilities for exploring more closely the *specific transactions* linking the institutions of 'economy' and 'family' as '"connected organisers" of experience and systems of social relations' (Kanter, 1979). Further, It is hoped that researchers utilise interpretive ideas to bring these understandings more fully to the surface in research accounts.

In addition to the topics reviewed in this chapter, further topics that would benefit from interpretive analysis are: agency theory discussions; ethics and family firms; women in family firms; gender issues and the link to enterprise; perceptions of venture capital; exit strategies; cross-cultural and comparative studies of family businesses; strategic management and planning practices; conflict and the family business; and internationalisation strategies.

218

11.8 Chapter summary

This chapter has reviewed the different approaches that have been utilised to examine the link between family and enterprise. The chapter started by exploring some definitional issues regarding family and enterprise, prior to evaluating the relationship between family and enterprise using rationalist and 'systems' approaches. The chapter has made an explicit attempt to criticise the effects of rationalist thinking on studies of family businesses that have tended to create duality and polarity in our understanding of the family-enterprise relationship. It was argued that a developmental and integrated view of family and enterprise is more useful for understanding the *specific transactions* linking the institutions of 'economy' and 'family'. Next, a range of approaches and theories used to examine the *integration* of family and enterprise/business activities were described. Finally, the chapter concluded with a discussion of interpretive inquiry and its potential benefits and uses in explaining how family and enterprise issues 'come together' in small business creation and development.

Questions

1 Summarise the key antecedents shaping definitions and studies of the family firm. Which do you believe are the most (or least) useful, and why?

2 In what ways do family issues impact on the small business workplace?

3 How and in what ways are interpretavist ideas and narrative analysis helpful in investigating the dynamics of family and enterprise issues?

4 Imagine you are planning a small research project on this topic. List a range of potential research questions. What key concepts may shape your theoretical framework? How would you design the research project (constructing a sample, gaining access, building relationships, collecting data)?

Web links

www.ifb.org.uk
The Institute for Family Business, an organisation aiming to help sustain a successful family business community in the UK.

http://www.familybizz.net
A website sponsored by Grant Thornton designed to provide an insight into the specific issues of concern to family businesses around the world.

http://www.coutts.com/familybusiness/survey.asp
The Coutts Family Business Survey that aims to deepen the understanding of the issues and challenges facing family business owners in the UK.

CHAPTER 12

Social entrepreneurship

Alex Nicholls

12.1 Introduction

This chapter explores the phenomenon of *social entrepreneurship*. Whilst the term is increasingly to be found in public discourse there is still considerable confusion about what it means and what it can achieve. This chapter begins by setting out the meaning of social entrepreneurship through a consideration of its manifestations at both an individual and organisational level. The problematic issues around its interpretation are elaborated and a definition is derived. Next the drivers behind the emergence of social entrepreneurship internationally are identified. The social enterprise model within the spectrum of social entrepreneurship is then discussed. The chapter ends with a brief consideration of the current and future challenges presented to social entrepreneurs across the world.

12.2 Learning objectives

There are four learning objectives in this chapter:

1 To understand what is meant by social entrepreneurship.
2 To understand how social entrepreneurship has developed internationally.
3 To understand the meaning of social enterprise.
4 To put social entrepreneurship in context.

Key concepts

■ entrepreneurship ■ civil society ■ social enterprise ■ welfare reform

12.3 Introducing social entrepreneurship

Once in a rare while, the fundamental architecture of a significant part of society shifts. Over the last two and one-half decades, the organisation of the social half of society, led by social entrepreneurs, has done so. It has passed irrevocably through the tipping point from bureaucratic and monopolistic to entrepreneurial and competitive – the same transition that transformed the business half of society over the prior three *centuries*.

Bill Drayton, Founder of Ashoka (2002: 120)

Social entrepreneurship is not a new phenomenon. Whilst it may represent a newly coined term, it is hardly a novel concept. Innovative individuals and enterprising groups have been addressing social issues for centuries, as is demonstrated by the activities of extraordinary public innovators such as Florence Nightingale, Susan B. Anthony and Mahatma Gandhi, as well as the collective efforts of groups like the Rochdale Pioneers, the Tolpuddle Martyrs and the National Association for the Advancement of Colored People. In these examples, the individuals or groups acted as change makers challenging the status quo by identifying an apparently insoluble social problem and tackling it with tenacity and vision. Their outstanding leadership towards a social end and their ability to see opportunities where others only saw hurdles further single out these charismatic figures. Today, the same distinguishing features are also present in a new breed of social entrepreneurs and, therefore, a direct line of descent can be discerned between these extraordinary public change agents of the past and such modern-day social pioneers as Muhammad Yunus (Grameen Bank, Bangladesh), Fazle Abed (Bangladesh Rural Advancement Committee or BRAC), Chief Fidela Ebuk (Women's Health and Economic Development Association, Nigeria), David Green (Project Impact, US), Liam Black (Furniture Resource Centre, UK) and Jeroo Billimoria (Childline, India).

However, in comparison with the past, what is notable now is that the number and range of social actors behaving entrepreneurially is far larger than at any previous point in history (Bornstein, 2004: 3–6). For example, a recent survey of socially entrepreneurial activity in the UK suggested that new 'social' start-ups are emerging at a faster rate than more conventional commercial ventures (Harding and Cowling, 2004: 5). Other research has also demonstrated that employment rates in social sector ventures are significantly outstripping those in the business sector in a number of developed countries (Salamon and Anheier, 1999). While all of these new social actors will not, necessarily, be social entrepreneurs *per se*, the overall picture painted by such data still underpins the proposition that social entrepreneurship is growing fast worldwide. Even more significantly, the impact that social entrepreneurs are aiming to achieve is also far more ambitious than ever before. Today, social entrepreneurs are reaching huge numbers of new stakeholders. For example, the Grameen Bank in Bangladesh now serves more than two million micro-credit customers and BRAC, in the same country, is the largest single employer in the region. Moreover, social entrepreneurs are also bringing about systemic change by influencing social behaviour on a global scale. For instance, the Fair Trade movement has seen its sales internationally grow at double-digit rates for more than a decade and has helped catalyse a revolution in the way many consumers view their relationship with producers (Nicholls and Opal, 2005). It seems fair to say, therefore, that we live today in the age of social entrepreneurs.

However, there still remains some lack of clarity as to what social entrepreneurship actually means and, perhaps more importantly, what it is capable of achieving. This chapter aims to overcome some of the confusion around this important concept and to demonstrate the significant impact that social entrepreneurs are currently having around the world. First, the meaning of social entrepreneurship is explored in some depth, since establishing the parameters of the term remains a highly contested process. Next the drivers behind the development of social entrepreneurship internationally are traced. Following this, the spectrum of social entrepreneurship activity is set out with particular reference to social enterprise. Finally, some of the future challenges facing social entrepreneurship are considered.

12.4 What is social entrepreneurship?

> Social entrepreneurship . . . combines the passion of a social mission with an image of business-like discipline, innovation, and determination commonly associated with, for instance, the high-tech pioneers of Silicon Valley.
>
> Professor J. Gregory Dees, Duke University (1998: 1)

The title 'social entrepreneurship' has been applied (often reflexively) to a startling range of organisations and activities from grass-roots campaigns to the 'social' actions of multi-national corporations. Despite widespread agreement among community activists, non-governmental organisations (NGOs), policy makers, the media, international institutions, leading thinkers, academics and commercial managers about the impressive growth in innovative social action globally (Leadbeater, 1997; Salamon and Anheier, 1999; Borzaga and Defourney, 2001; Bornstein, 2004), the boundaries of social entrepreneurship as a distinct model of effective social intervention remain highly contested.

Research into social entrepreneurship emerged from work on non-profit organisations that first developed in the 1970s. Etzioni (1973) suggested that neither the state nor the market would propel innovations and reforms of society but rather that the catalyst would be 'a third alternative' that could combine the efficiency of the entrepreneurial market-place with the welfare orientation of the state. However, Chamberlain (1977) first coined the term 'social entrepreneur' in the context of the putative emergence of a new breed of socially motivated business executives who would commit themselves and their corporations to constructive attacks on social problems by changing the rules under which the corporations operate.

Subsequent academic research into social entrepreneurship has largely been focused on defining what it is, and what it does and does not have in common with commercial entrepreneurial activity (Dees, 1994; Boschee, 1995, 2001a; Leadbeater, 1997, 1998; Dees, 1998a; Dees *et al.*, 2001, 2002; Brinckerhoff, 2000; Austin *et al.*, 2003; Drayton, 2002; Thompson *et al.*, 2000; Thompson, 2002; Sullivan Mort *et al.*, 2003). However, despite some promising work thus far, the research gaps remain considerable. Indeed, in a review of the available published research on social entrepreneurship, Johnson (2000: 5) commented that: 'Defining what social entrepreneurship is, and what its conceptual boundaries are, is not an easy task . . . in part because the concept is inherently complex, and in part because the literature in the area is so new that little consensus has emerged on the topic.'

In the absence of an established literature on the subject, the complexity at the heart of the socially entrepreneurial concept – embracing as it does both contextual flexibility and wide operational diversity – will be tackled here via an analysis of its two distinct constituent dimensions: the entrepreneurial and the social. Whilst both of these terms are problematic and contingent, particularly the latter, a careful consideration of each sets the boundaries of the socially entrepreneurial space. In essence, social entrepreneurship may be defined as ventures that address social issues as their prime strategic objective and do so in an innovative and creative fashion. However, the next three sections will provide a richer formulation of this broad-brush definition to draw out a more detailed set of meanings.

12.5 The entrepreneurial dimension

The entrepreneurial dimension of social entrepreneurship is often articulated in terms of the established conceptualisation of the commercial, private-sector entrepreneur. Research into the latter has typically focused on two analytic fields: the characteristics and personal traits of the entrepreneurial individual ('who the entrepreneur is' (McClelland, 1961; Brockhaus, 1980)); and the entrepreneurial activities of an individual, group or venture ('what the entrepreneur does' (Gartner, 1988; Kent *et al.*, 1982)). The two approaches are sometimes united in an entrepreneurial paradigm centred on unexpected opportunity recognition and its creative exploitation (e.g. Shane and Venkataraman, 2000: 18; also see Drucker, 1985).

At the individual level of analysis, there has been much written about the entrepreneur as a uniquely skilled leader and innovator – something of a 'business hero' – with outstanding personal traits (Venkataraman, 1997; Gartner, 1988) (see Chapter 8 for a discussion of entrepreneurial traits). Casson (1982: 23) defined the entrepreneur as 'someone who specialises in taking judgemental decisions about the co-ordination of scarce resources' and who has 'imagination and foresight and skill in organising and delegating work'. Much work to date on social entrepreneurship has also focused on the individual social entrepreneur as 'hero' via, at times, somewhat hagiographic biographical accounts of their life and works, often in case study format (Leadbeater, 1997; Alter, 2002; Boschee, 2001a; Bornstein, 2004). Drayton (2002) located the special creativity found in many social entrepreneurs at the level of personal traits, while other writers have highlighted their unique leadership skills (Henton *et al.*, 1997; Thompson *et al.*, 2000). Furthermore, two important support and connecting mechanisms for social entrepreneurs, Ashoka and the Schwab Foundation, also reinforce this individual level of focus by their international activities centred on identifying outstanding social leaders to join their networks as publicly celebrated 'fellows'.

Despite the socially entrepreneurial individual or group sharing much in common with the conventional paradigm, particularly leadership, vision, drive and opportunism, a focus on the individual social entrepreneur's traits reveals greater complexity. The most significant issue here is the inclusion *a priori* of a 'socio-moral motivation' or social mission focus in the entrepreneurial activity and ambition (Casson, 1994: 3). Emerson and Twersky (1996: 2–3) noted: 'Social entrepreneurs have their roots in the history of community service and development. This history of commitment to social justice and economic empowerment is what feeds their passion for the creation of social purpose business ventures.'

The presence of an over-riding mission focus is, therefore, the critical differentiator between conventional, commercial, models of entrepreneurship and social entrepreneurship. Bornstein (1998) highlighted the social entrepreneur's particular ethical make-up and passionate mission zeal as being key (see also Boschee, 1995). Catford (1998) also identified a strong commitment to social justice as being a defining characteristic. Finally, Dees (1998a) stressed the central importance of a social mission as the driving force behind social entrepreneurship. The boundaries of this social component are considered in more detail in the next section.

In the spirit of the second level of analysis of the commercial entrepreneur (the operational), there is also some literature that takes a more process-oriented approach to interpreting the socially entrepreneurial paradigm (Dees, 1998a; Dees and Elias, 1998; Dees et al., 2001, 2002; Dees and Battle Anderson, 2002; Dees et al., 2004; Alter, 2000; Boschee et al., 2000; Thompson et al., 2000). For example, Dees's (1998a) analysis specifically drew upon existing economic conventions of entrepreneurial activity to frame his research in operational terms. Thus, where Say (2001) noted that a successful entrepreneur often creates new value by shifting economic resources out of an area of lower yield and into an area of higher productivity and greater yield, Dees suggested that social entrepreneurs also create new (social) value by marshalling resources effectively to address key issues. This also reflects Osbourne and Gaebler's (1992: xix) assertion that 'an entrepreneur . . . uses resources in new ways to maximise productivity and effectiveness'. Similarly, where Schumpeter (1980) identified innovation as being central to the entrepreneurial approach, declaring that the function of entrepreneurs was, above all, to reform or revolutionise the patterns of production, Dees pointed out that social entrepreneurs relentlessly search for new and better ways of delivering social value. Finally, where Drucker (1985) believed that an entrepreneur typically acts as a catalyst for change searching for new paradigms and exploiting them as new opportunities, it is clear that many social entrepreneurs also generate systemic social change in order to ensure the sustainability of their innovative interventions (e.g. micro-credit).

In what is perhaps the most widely quoted definition of social entrepreneurship, Dees (1998a: 4) drew on both established approaches to entrepreneurship (the individual and the operational) when he combined a focus on process achievements and an individual level of analysis centred on the priority given to special mission. Thus, he summed up the research in these terms: Social entrepreneurs play the role of change agents in the social sector, by:

■ adopting a mission to create and sustain social value (not just private value);
■ recognising and relentlessly pursuing new opportunities to serve that mission;
■ engaging in a process of continuous innovation, adaptation and learning;
■ acting boldly without being limited by resources currently in hand;
■ exhibiting a heightened sense of accountability to the constituencies served and for the outcomes created.

Finally, a limited amount of work to date has specifically addressed the issue of opportunity creation and recognition in social entrepreneurship (Austin et al., 2003; Dees and Battle Anderson, 2002; Dees et al., 2004; Sullivan Mort et al., 2003; Thompson,

2002) – see Chapter 7 for a fuller discussion of opportunity creation and recognition. Much of this work has developed new theoretical models that bring together multiple contextual elements to provide frameworks for strategic growth planning in a social setting. For example, Austin *et al.* (2003) focused on an analysis of the key differences between commercial and social entrepreneurship across four components behind successful growth: people; context; deals; opportunities. Guclu *et al.* (2002), on the other hand, developed a two-stage model of opportunity creation for social ventures that combined personal factors (defined as individual 'social assets') with operational issues (namely, developing a viable operating model, a convincing social impact theory, and an effective resource strategy).

However, despite this useful work to date, the true nature of the social 'virtuous' entrepreneur is not so easily captured (e.g. Sullivan Mort *et al.*, 2003). The limits of the language and terminology of business when applied to social sector actors are revealed here. By attempting to adapt existing models of entrepreneurship to the new paradigm of social innovation, key features are sometimes left unexplored. For example, the pervasive neo-liberal conceptualisation of the 'market' often fails appropriately to capture the negotiated and democratic structures of a properly functioning civil society (see, for example, Spinosa *et al.*, 1997). Furthermore, theoretical approaches such as conventions theory (Wilkinson, 1997; Renard, 2002) and actor network analysis (Callon, 1986, 1999; Latour, 1993) have also challenged and reconfigured the economic market paradigm in a sociological context. Consequently, it is no surprise that established entrepreneurial models are only partial guides to understanding social entrepreneurship. Several key omissions can be seen.

First, while both commercial and social entrepreneurs are relentless networkers, highly skilled at building partnerships and valuable connections, the latter exploit networks in a far broader range of contexts (Dennis, 2000; Blundel and Smith, 2001; BarNir and Smith, 2002) (see Chapter 16 for a fuller discussion of entrepreneurial networking). Social entrepreneurs engage with network activity not only to leverage resources and strengthen their own venture but also to deliver impact and create new social value. Key to this mind-set is a stakeholder world-view that prioritises maximising positive impact across the web of external and internal actors connected to a social venture ahead of traditional strategic objectives such as organisational growth and maintaining competitive advantage. A deeper understanding of network models often informs social venture development, since effective mechanisms for social impact creation are rarely linear and purely transactional processes. A good example is Fair Trade where building social connections across a reconfigured value chain has delivered both a new trading model and a new consumption and marketing paradigm to deliver innovative social value (see Nicholls and Opal, 2005).

Secondly, social entrepreneurs operate in a more diverse and dynamic strategic landscape than conventional businesses (see Chapter 21). While aiming never to compromise social mission, social entrepreneurs will look for alliances and sources of resources wherever they may be found most easily. Thus, many engage simultaneously with government, philanthropic institutions, the voluntary sector and banks, as well as the commercial market, to secure funding and other support where necessary. Similarly, social entrepreneurs will often exploit a range of organisational forms from charity to not-for-profit to commercial venture to maximise social value creation. For a social entrepreneur efficient social impact is the central strategic issue not the delivery mechanism. As a result, social entrepreneurs often view growth in a strategically different light from conventional entrepreneurs. For example, since they are focused primarily on social impact, rather than profit maximisation, the drive to scale may not always be relevant: maximum impact may best be achieved by staying small and local, deepening rather than broadening activities. Social entrepreneurs also move easily across sectors, often diversifying from their core mission to expand overall social value and increase resource flows. For example, the Furniture Resource Centre in Liverpool began as a furniture recycling, removal, and employment training social venture engaged with 'social' landlords, but diversified into community waste collection and recycling (Bulky Bob's), retailing (among other things, partnering with Ben and Jerry's ice cream), and finally – as its profile grew – into social sector consultancy (Cat's Pyjamas).

Finally, in the spirit of Schumpeter, social entrepreneurs often search out the creative destruction that will change the terms of engagement with respect to social issues for the better. They seek out the social spaces that the conventional commercial and welfare markets have failed to address and create new formulations of social capital through institutional change and innovation. Social entrepreneurs are, therefore, highly political in outlook (though not necessarily aligned party-politically) and are effective activists, campaigners and catalysts of wider change. The urge to change the terms of engagement within their own sectors, not for their own benefit, but for the benefit of their stakeholders, marks social entrepreneurs out again as quite distinct from their commercial corollaries. Indeed, the ultimate (though often unattainable) aim of many social ventures is to be so successful in addressing a social need that they effectively put themselves out of business. For example, if, in an ideal world, Oxfam could end global poverty it would no longer have a *raison d'être*.

12.6 The social dimension

The second distinguishing element of social entrepreneurship, its 'social' dimension, is also problematic. Primarily, this is because there has yet to be sufficient critical analysis given to the underlying complexity inherent in many normative concepts of the social goods generated by social entrepreneurship. The conceptualisation of the 'social' in this context has often been dependent on an, at times tautological, acceptance of what actually constitutes a normalised and effective social mission combined with a subjective and often partial sense of what characteristics define a socially driven individual. Blau (1977) highlighted the implicit contingency of the social web in which all human actions occur, suggesting that to isolate specific 'social' actions is ontologically impossible. Granovetter (1985) supported this view noting that all actions are ultimately 'social' given that they are inevitably constrained by, and embedded in, social relations.

Consequently, there remains a lack of rigour in the, often monological, analysis of social action that presumes positive social value is its inevitable outcome and lacks any inter-subjective dimension (see Habermas, 1989; Fraser, 1992). These assumptions can also act as apologists for the poor performance of some social ventures masking operational shortcomings in worthy mission objectives. Interestingly, another key feature of

Table 12.1 Defining the 'social' in social entrepreneurship

Defining characteristic	Examples	Contested issues
Context of social venture	Public welfare; environmentalism; development and aid	Acts as privatisation of public goods; does not address underlying political issues; narrow focus can create dependency
Process of social venture	Close engagement with key stakeholders; employ and train disenfranchised; act as trade intermediary	Stakeholder selection criteria/exclusion from process; empowerment of stakeholders
Outcomes and impacts	Improved public welfare; individual empowerment; crisis alleviation	Social impact often unmeasured; short-termism

the successful social entrepreneur is a desire to address and reject such obfuscation through new metrics and accountability.

Nevertheless, even acknowledging a level of positivist spin within the construction of social entrepreneurship as a normative concept, the social element within it will be framed here by an analysis of three operational dimensions within a given venture:

- the operational context (typically the social or welfare sector),
- the process of the social venture (engaging key stakeholders in the operation),
- the outcomes and impacts of the social venture (articulating its social mission).

It could reasonably be observed that each of these criteria could also be applied to a range of actions associated with profit-maximising corporations, rather than exclusively to social sector ventures. Such activities range from the strategic implementation of a corporate social responsibility agenda to a more enterprising approach to corporate social innovation (Kanter, 1999). However, the discriminatory issue here is one both of degree of integration of the social venture into core activities and the nature of the overall commitment to a social mission. Few mainstream companies develop operations with social value creation as their first objective. Indeed, it could well be argued that it is not their business to do so. In the final analysis, therefore, the majority of socially focused corporations are unlikely to be confused with social entrepreneurs.

The next section will explore each of these three dimensions further. Such an approach allows social entrepreneurship to be clearly set apart from conventional private sector ventures, but also exposes a range of contested issues and multiple interpretations (see the summary in Table 12.1).

12.6.1 Operational context

Historically, the main operational areas in which social entrepreneurs have worked have been:

- poverty alleviation through empowerment (e.g. the micro-finance movement);
- healthcare, ranging from small-scale support for the mentally ill 'in the community' to larger-scale ventures tackling the HIV/AIDS pandemic;
- education and training, such as widening participation and the democratisation of knowledge transfer;
- environmental preservation and sustainable development, such as 'green' energy projects;
- community regeneration, such as housing associations;
- welfare projects, such as employment for the unemployed or homeless and drug and alcohol abuse projects;
- advocacy and campaigning, such as Fair Trade and human rights promotion.

Of course, these are not distinct categories in reality and work in one often overlaps with another (e.g. a project like the Kaleidoscope initiative in London working with drug users can span the health, community, employment and welfare fields simultaneously). Indeed, some of the most successful and innovative social entrepreneurs consciously develop cross-sector activity to maximise social impact (and resource availability) across their whole value chain.

Social entrepreneurship typically evolves in the intersections between the three estates of modern society – the public sector, the market and civil society – where social market failures emerge and new opportunities for social value creation may be discerned (see Figure 12.1). However, the societal context of social entrepreneurship is complex. A number of distinct, and sometimes conflicting, points of origin can be identified across the junctions of the three estates of society, each reflecting a range of contexts. These can be grouped as: grassroots; institutional; political; spiritual; and philanthropic. Further, a variety of entrepreneurial approaches appropriate to each – innovative 'means' to social capital generating 'ends' – can also be discerned (see Table 12.2).

Grassroots activity is often driven by a lack of institutional support at either a macro- or micro-level that generates the need for new community action. For example, the Coin Street Housing Association grew out of a community reaction to the lack of affordable public or private accommodation in a part of inner-city south London. By leveraging local social capital and building a new institutional structure within existing legal boundaries a social market failure in community housing was effectively addressed. Such activity also generated a replicable model for other communities.

Social entrepreneurship typically addresses serious social needs from an embedded community perspective. By mapping these two dimensions (level of social need and level of community involvement), social entrepreneurship can further be positioned in relationship to the other two estates of society: the private and public sectors (see Figure 12.2). In quadrant one lie ventures that have low community involvement and low strategic engagement with social need. The profit-maximising private sector firm sits here. The traditional public sector welfare model resides in quadrant two. This represents the paternalistic distribution of social goods still common across many nations that attempts to addresses serious social need but does not engage closely with the communities it aims to benefit. This is the model that is under review in the UK (and, in a different context, in the US) as public sector demand-side 'choice' and empowerment

Figure 12.1 **The three estates of society**

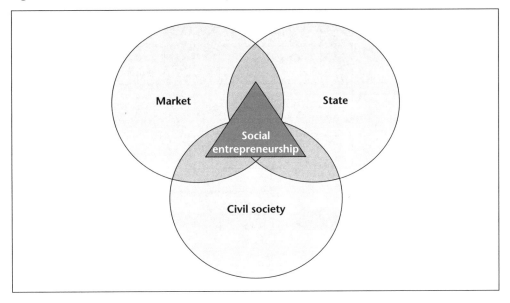

Table 12.2 **Contexts for social entrepreneurship**

Origins	Social market failure	Means	Ends	Example
Grassroots	Lack of institutional support	Critical social innovation	Coordinated creation of social capital through local/community action	Housing Associations
Institutional	Changing social landscape	Normative social innovation	Social entrepreneurship champions new social institution	Open University
Political	Retreat of centralised government control from society	Market socialism	Introduction of enterprise/private sector market philosophy into public sphere	Public–private finance initiatives (e.g. London Underground)
Spiritual	Decline of church influence in society	Commercialisation of congregation- and church-based activities	Revitalise role of faith in public affairs	CAFOD/Fair Trade Foundation
Philanthropic	Lack of finance for development of social capital	Foundations coordinating charity giving as social entrepreneurial start-up funding	Link business and social innovation	Skoll Foundation and community education

Figure 12.2 Mapping social need and community involvement

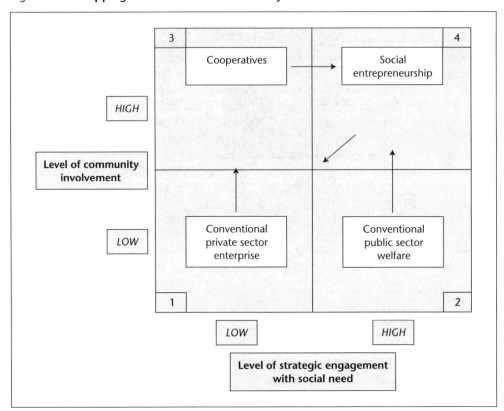

initiatives have become a key policy focus. Quadrant three contains ventures built upon a high level of community involvement but with low levels of strategic engagement with social need. The cooperative model can be placed here, although with important caveats. Namely, many cooperatives do, indeed, address serious social needs. For example, the crippling social effects of wholesaler monopsony in producer markets for coffee are being overcome by the Fair Trade movement's efforts to encourage producers to join together in cooperatives. However, many established cooperatives, particularly the retail cooperatives in developed countries, whilst continuing to generate valuable social capital through their membership structures, no longer address serious social need as their prime operating principle. At the intersection of high levels of community involvement and high strategic engagement with social need (quadrant four) sits the archetype of social entrepreneurship.

It should also be noted that these positions are not set but dynamic. For example, with the rise of a broad strategic acceptance of the corporate social responsibility (CSR) agenda across major corporations, many private sector firms are trying to reposition themselves towards quadrant three. This involves a greater acknowledgement of the significance of their relationship with all stakeholders, at least at a marketing, if not always operational, level (see Bakan, 2004, and *The Economist*, 2005, for a range of caveats around CSR). Similarly, the traditional public sector model of centralised delivery of social goods is increasingly aiming to move towards a more community focused format, hence the suggestion that social entrepreneurs have an obvious role to play here. The development of cooperative models across the globe, noted in the Fair Trade example above, is reflected in the dynamic range of applications that spans both quadrants three and four. Finally, the popularity of the social enterprise model of social entrepreneurship demonstrates a move by some social sector firms towards acknowledging some value in the discipline and efficiency of the better example of private enterprise.

The institutional approach to social market failure can be more resource hungry, but aims for significant impacts and has a broader social focus. Typically, this form of social entrepreneurship reacts to significant changes in the macro-social landscape that require large-scale solutions. The Tateni (a Nguni term of affection) project started by Veronica Khosa in South Africa (Bornstein, 2004: 183–99) provides a good example. In this case, the social entrepreneur reacted to the inadequacy of institutional support for victims of the catastrophe of AIDS/HIV by creating a homecare service that would both complement the existing welfare system and offer a new model of community-based training and action in healthcare. Between 1995 and 1999, the project's staff made over 200,000 home visits and trained over 1,000 new homecarers.

The astute political sensitivity of many social entrepreneurs has already been noted, but broader political contexts also exist. First, there has been a move towards 'reinventing' government in a number of countries (Osbourne and Gaebler, 1992). This entails bringing more entrepreneurial or 'business' thinking into public sector departments and operations in order to enhance their efficiency and impact. Second, as governments in Northern countries have increasingly retreated from their traditional role as providers of social goods, new models of provision have emerged. These have often taken the form of hybrid organisations that mix public and private agendas (the Public-Private Finance Initiatives in the UK are typical examples). In the UK this movement has been characterised as the 'Third Way' or 'market' socialism (Giddens, 1998, 2000). Finally, in developing countries in the south, other manifestations of the political agenda of social entrepreneurship can be seen. For example, in Brazil, the rationale behind the planning and execution of the extraordinary civic entrepreneurship embodied in the Curatiba community was entirely political (see, for example, Spengler and Ford, 2002; Leadbeater and Goss, 1998).

The political context of social entrepreneurship is, perhaps, the most fiercely contested of all. Often there is a perceived strategic conflict between addressing resources towards achieving institutional change for social impact and targeting the alleviation of immediate social crises. (This is considered further below as a part of the discussion of 'critical' and 'normative' social entrepreneurs.) Thus, the context in which social entrepreneurs operate may itself be the cause of social market failures. Consequently, the social good generated at an individual venture level may be seen as compromised by the very engagement with the problem. More productive would be an attempt to change the socio-political discourse around the need for such social goods. Failure to do this may result in stakeholder dependency and the maintenance of a socially dysfunctional *status quo*. The more politically entrenched social actors often level such critiques at social entrepreneurs, also accusing them of 'privatising' welfare provision by taking on government contracts to deliver public goods often in competition with private sector firms.

Recent policy discussions concerning the delivery of public sector welfare in the UK can be seen as part of a larger discussion concerning the wider societal role of social entrepreneurship. The New Labour government has increasingly promoted a role for social enterprises at the intersection between citizen and state to empower communities and generate choice in welfare provision. The ambitious aim is to extend the role of social entrepreneurship beyond addressing social market failures and into increasing the efficiency and legitimacy of the delivery of state supported social goods. Indeed, this has been a central policy initiative in the UK for the Social Enterprise Unit within the Department of Trade and Industry as well as Regional Development Agencies (Department of Trade and Industry, 2002, 2003b). Such thinking taps into the democratic principles of participation and empowerment that are inherent in many social ventures.

The decline of organised religion in some northern cultures has provided another context for new social entrepreneurship within religious institutions aimed at both reviving faith communities and mobilising faith-based resources towards wider social problems. The former is the commercialisation of some congregations where exploiting the money-raising possibilities of a parish to support and sustain it has become a strategic norm. The latter reflects the long tradition of faith-based solutions to social problems within civil society and is an emergent component of public sector policy in some countries, particularly the US. For example, the association between the Fair Trade movement and church groups has long been important in generating social and financial capital. Indeed, the bulk of sales for Traidcraft, one of the leading Fair Trade enterprises in the UK, still comes from retail activity rooted in Christian congregations across the country.

Finally, the philanthropic origin of some social entrepreneurship both reflects a longstanding convention of socially responsible giving and looks forward to new paradigms of social 'investment' through the emergent venture philanthropy market. These are social venture funds characterised by high levels of engagement with the social entrepreneur, long investment horizons, higher levels of risk taking, and a rigorous focus on auditing social impacts, where possible. Thus, venture philanthropy is, in essence, the philanthropic application of venture capital principles and practice. Moreover, in addition to funding, venture philanthropists typically provide networking, management advice and an array of other supports to organisations within their portfolio. The emergence of a number of significant venture philanthropy organisations in recent years, such as the Acumen Fund, New Philanthropy Capital, the European Venture Philanthropy Association, and New Profit Inc., demonstrates the growing interest in this model of social investment. However, it is important to note that the volume of funds currently under management by venture philanthropy groups still remains very small. Consequently, the most significant contribution being made by the venture philanthropy model currently lies in its 'engaged' approach to social investment rather than in the funds that it is directly contributing.

12.6.2 Process

In terms of process, social entrepreneurs are primarily focused on social innovation and the opportunity recognition of new social value creation. Thus, social entrepreneurs engage with a wide range of business and organisational models, both not-for-profit and for-profit, since it is not the mechanism by which social value is created that matters, but rather how to maximise their social impact. Furthermore, social entrepreneurs seek out opportunities to add social impact throughout their entire value chain, often employing and training disenfranchised groups as a part of delivering their social mission or revitalising depleted community resources such as housing stock. The process of social entrepreneurship, therefore, may typically be characterised by a range of social missions that are addressed at different points in the value chain.

However, such strategic complexity can be problematic. Addressing multiple stakeholder needs across a range of social missions in the context of often limited resources can lead to mission drift or strategic uncertainty as one set of social impacts is set against another. At the very least this can cause operational dysfunction. For example, Aspire was a successful social venture that employed homeless people to deliver Fair Trade catalogues and subsequent customer orders. However, significant sales growth at the UK end of the enterprise led the founders to be over-ambitious in their first social mission (employing the homeless) without planning carefully for their second (providing sustainable orders to Fair Trade producers). This lack of focus resulted in an over-commitment to orders that brought about a cash-flow crisis and ultimate bankruptcy. This was highly damaging to the Fair Trade producers reliant on Aspire's sales, although many of its UK employees found other work helped by the founders.

Social entrepreneurs often develop new transactional paradigms or organisational forms to solve social problems (e.g. Fair Trade). In this context, Leadbeater (1997: 8) noted that 'social entrepreneurs identify under-utilised resources – people, buildings, equipment – and find new ways of putting them to use to satisfy unmet social needs'. Thompson *et al.* (2000: 328) supported this view in their definition of social entrepreneurs as: 'People who realise where there is an opportunity to satisfy some unmet need that the state welfare system will not or cannot meet, and who gather together the necessary resources (generally people, often volunteers, money and premises) and use these to make a difference.'

The impact of the new social entrepreneurship model has been felt across the range of socially focused activities. On the one hand, the model has contributed to a reconfiguring of existing social ventures such as charities, not-for-profit organisations and NGOs. On the other, social entrepreneurs have helped catalyse the public sector to become more effective, accountable and flexible in its approaches to social provision.

For the former group, traditional measures of performance have been re-engineered to increase impact and accountability. Outputs have been recast as outcomes framed in terms of social value creation and impact, rather than simple numbers. For example, a charity would cease to be judged on its ability to raise money and remain solvent but rather on the effectiveness with which it addressed its social mission. Similarly, asset structures need to take increasing account of social, as well as financial and physical capital. Thus, measures of successful relationship building, trust, networks and co-operation become more important in strategic planning and assessment. This fits well with social ventures' typical ownership structures highlighting key stakeholders. Of course, all of this revolutionary thinking is contested and problematic, not least in terms of metrics. But what is patently clear is that social entrepreneurship is generating entirely new paradigms of social venture creation and development that are creating their own definitional terms and taxonomies as they emerge. This dynamic lack of clear terms of reference is one of the reasons behind the current discrepancy between resource allocation and socially entrepreneurial opportunities.

However, the normalising assumption that such approaches automatically maximise social value can be questioned. By some measures, individual social impacts can only ever be partial – some actors must be excluded by selection processes that are likely to be more pragmatic than needs based, if only because establishing a hierarchy of social need is invidiously difficult. Such issues inevitably question the empowerment of stakeholders by some social ventures and also raise issues of accountability and transparency.

12.6.3 Outcomes

Finally, in terms of outcomes and impacts a number of other contested issues are also apparent. Dees (1998a: 2) noted: 'For social entrepreneurs the social mission is explicit and central. This obviously affects how social entrepreneurs perceive and assess opportunities. Mission-related impact becomes the central criterion, not wealth creation.' Such activity blurs the traditional view that 'value' can be understood as either economic or social and that these two notions are quite separate, with for-profit business generating the former and non-profit social activism the latter. The commitment is not to the traditional model of profit accumulation and equity growth, but rather to the creation and maintenance of 'social capital' (see further, Putnam, 2001, 2004) through building communities around new nexi of connectivity that solve social problems. These key assets often take the form of relationships, networks, trust and cooperation that give access to physical and financial capital (Leadbeater, 1997). This conceptualisation is also present in Emerson's Blended Value proposition which combines fully monetised social impacts with more conventional financial data to judge the performance of a social venture (Emerson, 2003).

Fukyama (1995) defined 'social capital' as 'the ability of people to work together for common purposes in groups and organisations'. Leadbeater (1997) adapted this to suggest a further meaning embracing the building of something of real value to local communities or society. The social entrepreneur, then, exploits one form of social capital – relationships, networks, trust and cooperation – to access physical and financial capital that can be used to create something of value for the community. Whilst the outcomes of social entrepreneurship may be non-profit enterprises, they are also likely to be for-profit, particularly in the arena of public–private collaborations. Another important arena for social entrepreneurship has been in the 'reinventing of government' – namely applying 'professionalism' to the public sector (see Osbourne and Gaebler, 1992).

The main problematising issue here is metrics: measuring social impact and social value creation remains difficult and often highly contingent. A number of qualitative and quantitative measures have emerged recently, most notably the social return on investment (SROI) model pioneered by the Roberts Enterprise Development Foundation

(REDF) (Emerson, 1999a) and subsequently refined by the New Economics Foundation (2004). However, these metrics have yet to become fully accepted, let alone widely used (indeed, REDF itself has recently abandoned using SROI). Consequently, there are few agreed social impact benchmarks or best practices available to social entrepreneurs and their stakeholders. Establishing the success or failures of social entrepreneurship by outcomes and impacts alone will, therefore, remain open to criticism and dispute. Moreover, the narrow and targeted focus of many successful social ventures can lead to operational short-termism: namely, a failure to address more fundamental, systemic issues in planning and implementing strategy. This can both reduce long-term social impact and threaten overall sustainability.

12.6.4 Strategic focus

Finally, there is also complexity at the strategic level of socially entrepreneur action. As has already been noted, at the heart of the contested nature of social entrepreneurship is a sense that it encompasses two apparently contradictory trends in modern developed society: on the one hand, the supremacy of the neo-liberal consensus based on free market models (and on the 1980s conceptualisation of the entrepreneur as primarily a business champion) and, on the other, a return to valuing social justice as a nexus of public and private good (the driving force behind the emergence of corporate social responsibility as a board-level agenda item). In essence, social entrepreneurs reclaim the innovation and creativity of the entrepreneurial paradigm for the wider public good. They address social market failures left unaddressed by other institutions and identify opportunities for social value creation that the market ignores. This is their social mission and fulfilling it is the first strategic objective.

Within this definition, two types of social change agent may be discerned: the critical social entrepreneur and the normative. As has been noted above, social entrepreneurship typically addresses social market failures, namely gaps in (often state) provision for social sectors such as healthcare, education, sustainable development and community regeneration. In many cases, the commercial market puts little or no value on these social goods and, consequently, gaps in provision inevitably appear. The rise of 'critical' social entrepreneurs reflected these failures. These are social innovators aiming critically to improve the provision of social goods through new ventures spontaneously re-engineering social markets to satisfy communitarian needs. Such social action challenges the status quo and aims radically to rethink social value creation. A powerful example is the global micro-credit revolution of the past 20 years. On the other hand, 'normative' social entrepreneurs do not reject the social systems of the time by seeking structural change, but choose instead to offer new mechanisms within existing institutional frameworks for increasing social goods in general. The work of 'serial' social entrepreneur Lord Michael Young in the UK provides a number of good examples, namely the creation of the Open University and the Consumer's Association.

There is also evidence of an increasing blurring between these two types in public policy initiatives driven by the UK and US governments starting in the 1980s. The Thatcher and Reagan governments aimed to redefine the concept of social entrepreneurship as part of a political agenda to introduce private enterprise into the public sector by developing policies based on the new dogma of free market deregulation and the privatisation of state assets. This was coupled with a rolling back of taxation and, as a consequence, the boundaries of state provision were redrawn. At the same time a new 'enterprise culture' was encouraged through tax mechanisms that favoured the individual commercial entrepreneur. Such recasting of the entrepreneur marked a radical departure from either the normative or critical approaches that had gone before and signalled a retreat in governmental engagement with social goods. Ironically, it was the latter that unwittingly provided the template for much subsequent socially entrepreneurial activity.

In the 1990s as the social impacts of deregulated free markets became apparent in mass unemployment, huge rises in inequality and a jump in social deprivation, new models of welfare began to emerge that both decoupled 'enterprise' and 'business' and challenged the perceived conservatism and stasis of the public sector. This was most clearly articulated in the development of Third Way politics (Hutton, 1996; Giddens, 1998, 2000) within the Clinton and Blair administrations, which particularly reflected this dynamic societal change as well as a growing acknowledgement of the increasing failure of centralised public sector solutions. Institutional reform was typically linked to macro-level policy frameworks at a government level, spurred on by new 'think and do tanks' in the UK such as Demos and the New Economics Foundation. These policy interventions encouraged the growth of an enterprising social sector in both voluntary organisations and the public sector itself (cf. Osbourne and Gaebler, 1992). Interestingly, this agenda not only created a new breed of 'public–private' professional managing social institutions such as the National Health Service, but also generated further gaps in basic social provision thus heralding a new round of grassroots social entrepreneurship.

It is clear, then, that social entrepreneurship is a multi-faceted, dynamic and often highly contingent phenomenon. Nevertheless, for all these definitional challenges and caveats, it is still the case that a distinct paradigm of social entrepreneurship may be discerned by delineating the consistent features across a diverse range of social enterprises. Based on these, social entrepreneurship will be defined in this chapter as:

Innovative and effective activities that focus primarily on resolving social market failures both by creating new opportunities to add social value and consistently using a range of resources relentlessly to maximise social impact.

12.7 Drivers of social entrepreneurship

A range of diverse drivers behind the rise of social entrepreneurship in its modern form may be discerned (Bornstein, 2004: 6–10). On the demand side, these include a series of global crises ranging from the environment (global warming, mass extinctions and depleted resources) to health (the HIV/AIDS pandemic affecting over 100 million globally by 2010) to the economic (significant increases in inequality with the poorest 50% accounting for 5% of global income). These crises have been further compounded by social market failures that have seen mounting government inefficiencies in public service delivery across the globe at the same time as a strategic retreat from the public sector by many governments in face of free-market ideologies. At the same time there has been a significant increase in the scope of corporate power; for example, by 2003 the top 300 multi-national corporations accounted for 25% of total global assets.

According to Bornstein (2004) there have also been significant changes in the supply side of social entrepreneurship throughout the twentieth century, particularly in northern countries. For example, the century saw a 700% increase in per capita income in developed market economies that led to the emergence of a widespread middle class. Such growth was particularly marked in the 1960s and 1970s when the global economy grew, on average, at 5% per year. This rise in the spread of wealth combined with relentless technological innovation also increased productive life expectancy for many. In the richer countries, average life expectancy increased by 30 years between 1900 and 2000; in poorer countries the increase was an even more startling 40 years. The combination of these two factors generated significant new resources (i.e. more relatively wealthy people with more free time) to address social issues.

Societal changes across many countries also played an important part. For example, basic education was made available to millions of people in many countries for the first time from the 1970s onwards, such that from 1970 to 1985 adult literacy rates rose from 43% to 60% in developing countries (Salamon, 1994: 118). The number of universities in the world also doubled during this period. Thus, the number of people empowered with the knowledge and training to tackle social problems grew enormously. The rise in availability of affordable information technology and the communications revolution spurred by the Internet have also empowered individuals significantly and greater citizen self-confidence has been the result.

The number of citizens groups working across the public–private sectors has duly expanded dramatically. For example, in a study of eight developed countries, employment in the citizen sector was found to have grown at more than twice the rate of the overall economy between 1990 and 1995 (Salamon and Anheier, 1999). In 2003, the Global Entrepreneurship Monitor study (Harding and Cowling, 2004: 5) suggested that 6.6% of UK adults were engaged with social start-up activity (ahead of the level for commercial, entrepreneurial activity). Indeed, the global aggregate expenditures of the civil society sector amounted to £0.69 trillion by the late 1990s, making it the seventh largest global economy by GDP ahead of Italy in eighth place (Salamon *et al.*, 2003: 13). Whilst many of these NGO and not-for-profit ventures lack the innovation and risk-taking qualities of true social entrepreneurship they act, nevertheless, as a valuable bellwether of the structural shifts across societies that are generating many new social entrepreneurs.

The transfer of wealth from individuals to foundations resultant from the 1990s technology boom centred on Silicon Valley in the US has also played an important role in providing new funding resources for entrepreneurial social ventures. According to *The Economist* (2004) the number of charitable foundations registered in the US has risen from 22,000 in the early 1980s to 65,000 today. The same article noted that it has been estimated that the value of the wealth to be transferred in the US over the next 50 years will be more than the entire current global GDP (somewhere between £22 trillion and £72 trillion). Furthermore, new foundations such as that set up by Jeff Skoll the co-founder of eBay, often pursue a venture philanthropy approach that views giving as an investment and demands measurable social returns. Such an approach is highly congruent with socially entrepreneurial solutions to social issues.

Finally, there are several important institutional developments that have contributed to the growth in the supply side of social entrepreneurs. The most important of these has been the gradual spread of neo-liberal democracy across the globe. Since the early 1990s, most notably following the seismic shift in Eastern Europe after the collapse of the Soviet Union, there has been a steady increase in the number of democratically elected governments across the world. Whilst not all of these governments have proved to be effective, particularly in terms of economic policies, this shift towards a broad acceptance of the value of democracy has generally allowed social actors the space to operate in freedom and safety. For example, the inchoate Fair Trade movement in the Philippines had to function under severe military persecution throughout the 1970s and 1980s, with many of its organisers being jailed for their actions as 'subversives'. Today, happily, the movement is thriving in a more democratic, though still far from ideal, environment.

Internationally, the development of social entrepreneurship has also been given other institutional support, most notably by Ashoka, the Schwab Foundation and the Skoll Foundation. An ex-McKinsey and Company consultant, Bill Drayton, started Ashoka in 1982. Ashoka identifies 'fellows' around the world and provides a powerful network of supporting opportunities. The venture started in India and has subsequently expanded to the rest of Asia, Latin America, Africa and, more recently, to the US (in 2000) and in Continental Europe (in 2003). Today, Ashoka supports more than 1,400 fellows in 48 countries. The Schwab Foundation grew out of the World Economic Forum (WEF) in 2001 and aims to publicise social entrepreneurship while offering practical support to social entrepreneurs via a stipend and access to the business and political elite at its annual World Summit in Social Entrepreneurship and the WEF's annual meeting in Davos, Switzerland. Finally, the Skoll Foundation, based in California, also celebrates social innovation that challenges conventional paradigms to generate social value via a substantial grant programme.

12.8 Social enterprise

The organisational landscape of social entrepreneurship can best be conceptualised as a dynamic continuum ordered by the range of available funding structures (see Figure 12.3). The boundaries of this continuum are set, at one extreme, by voluntary activism (fully reliant on donations and volunteers) and, at the other, by corporate social

Figure 12.3 **Funding dimensions of social entrepreneurship**

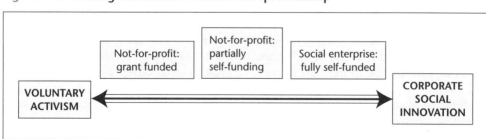

innovation (dedicated social ventures within the context of a private sector organisation; see Kanter, 1999). Lying along the continuum are alternative social organisational
types ordered according to the proportion of their operations that are self-funded. These
range from fully grant funded via those that are partially self-sufficient, having developed
some internal sources of income, to social ventures that are fully self-sufficient.

Globally, the pace of growth of social ventures has not been matched by a similar
advance in available resources. The result has been heightened competition for what
funding is available (Emerson, 1999b). One of the products of this mismatch between
resource supply and demand has been for social entrepreneurs to consider strategic
moves into new markets to subsidise their social activities either through exploiting
profitable opportunities in the core activities of their not-for-profit venture or via for-
profit subsidiary ventures and cross-sector partnerships with commercial corporations.
This new organisational model has attracted considerable public policy attention in
developed countries. It is widely known as 'social enterprise'.

Whilst social enterprise and social entrepreneurship are sometimes used as syn-
onyms (particularly in the US), the former is, in fact, a subset of the latter. Many social
ventures can be highly entrepreneurial without generating independent profit streams
(this could include innovation in the public sector, for example). Therefore, the primary distinction here lies in which funding model is adopted with respect to achieving a
social objective, namely social enterprises look to move away from grant dependency
towards self-sufficiency via the creation of income streams. Ultimately, the aim is to be
more sustainable (Boschee et al., 2000). Furthermore, they are unlike many traditional
not-for-profits, typically being more results driven and striving for accountability via
improved social impact metrics and audit mechanisms (Dees, 1998b; Pharoah et al.,
2004).

Alter (2002: 5) defined social enterprise as: 'a generic term for a non-profit business
venture or revenue-generating activity founded to create positive social impact while
operating with reference to a financial bottom line'. In 2003 Alter provided a more
holistic interpretation of the meaning of such ventures: 'the defining characteristic of
the social enterprise is that it uses market-based approaches to earn commercial
income and accomplish its mission' (2003: 4).

The social enterprise model has other key advantages aside from giving a social
venture greater independence, flexibility and sustainability (Dees and Battle Anderson,
2002). Most valuable, perhaps, is increased access to conventional financial markets that
allow the venture to leverage both public and private resources to respond to social
'demand' more quickly. This also frees up philanthropic funds and grants for non-profit
social ventures. The social enterprise model may also give access to a broader pool of
skilled personnel through supporting more competitive remuneration packages.

However, the social enterprise model is not suitable for all social ventures, nor is it
the only route to sustainability and maximum impact. The differences in funding structures evident across the social sector are often a product of the nature of the individual social mission. In situations where social entrepreneurs are effectively taking the
place of the public sector (say in health or education) the search for profit may be
undesirable or inherently unachievable, whereas in situations where the social impact
is directly linked to commercial success (e.g. employment or economic development
initiatives) the case may be quite different.

In comparison with grant funding, developing independent funding streams clearly does allow greater strategic flexibility and the opportunity for quicker growth. Nevertheless, the role of the social enterprise model within social entrepreneurship remains highly contested (see Boschee, 2001b; Dees, 2003). For example, Dees (2003) pointed out that the most important issue is not the funding structure of the social venture but its social impacts. From this perspective, the social enterprise is inherently neither better nor worse than any other social venture mechanism (i.e. not-for-profits that are grant maintained or donation driven).

Indeed, there may be a danger that focusing on generating earned income can distract a social venture from its true social mission. Furthermore, it is a false assumption to think that a reliance on selling to the commercial market for income is inherently more sustainable than reliance on grant funding. As Dees (2003) noted, earned income is only a means to a social end and it is not always the best means. It can even be detrimental, taking valuable talent and energy away from activities more central to delivering on the organisation's social mission. Though it is very popular right now, it is just one funding strategy among many and must be assessed on a case-by-case basis. The key is finding a resource strategy that works.

Within the social enterprise model there is further complexity. Dees (1996) identified two organisational types of social enterprise: the 'hybrid' form and the 'mixed' form. The former integrates social and commercial objectives within its core activities, whilst the 'mixed' format has its social activity linked to its commercial activity but maintains clear boundaries between each. This is often achieved through the development of two separate organisations with different reporting systems, governance structures, staff profiles and facilities, but with one providing funds for the other.

Alter (2003) developed Dees's analysis further and identified three organisational models for social enterprises:

- embedded (mission-centric social purpose enterprises),
- integrated (mission-related enterprises as profit centres for subsidising social purpose venture),
- complementary (unrelated to mission, leveraging tangible/intangible assets for income generation).

These she then further subdivided into 11 individual operational types.

The embedded social enterprise structure offers a number of social purpose options. The venture may offer entrepreneurial consultancy to other stakeholders, effectively 'selling' business support and training. Alternatively, the embedded organisation may act as a market intermediary offering product development or wholesale access to otherwise unavailable markets: this is the Fair Trade model. The venture could offer employment and job opportunities to the disenfranchised either as part, or all, of its social mission. The embedded model may also market a 'fee-for-service' approach that effectively commercialises its social services.

The integrated model typically develops a service subsidisation strategy with a strongly related commercial operation sustaining the core not-for-profit social venture. One manifestation of this model is a market linkage organisation that acts as a broker connecting producer and consumer, not as a wholesaler but as a provider of information and marketing/consultancy services. Another is the service subsidisation form that uses a for-profit business to provide funds for the (typically not-for-profit) social venture.

Finally, the complementary model spans a range of more complex organisational formats including social franchising and social sector–private sector partnerships that are mutually beneficial. The latter are often characterised by the exchange of market access and expertise (for the commercial partner) and new funding and capital (for the social venture). In the UK, there have been a number of high-profile examples of public–private partnerships (e.g. the London Underground) that have applied this social enterprise model to the public sector with mixed results.

12.9 Chapter summary

Social entrepreneurship represents a new paradigm of social value creation and reflects a dynamic revolution in the social sector. This changing agenda has seen a move away from the traditional charity/philanthropic/voluntary models of social venture towards new organisational forms including social enterprises, hybrids and social sector–private sector partnerships. The public sector in many countries has also undergone change towards a more enterprising culture. Institutional funders are increasingly shifting to outcomes-based, rather than needs-based, investment strategies, while social ventures are now more focused on impact and effectiveness rather than sustainability.

However, many challenges remain. At an individual venture level, the continuing organisational pressure caused by limited resources inhibits vital capacity building and can limit the managerial skills being brought into the sector. Succession planning remains a difficult issue for many social ventures built around the individual 'hero' social entrepreneur, as does effective and transparent governance. Furthermore, performance measurement and the associated productive resource allocation are also challenged by the lack of established social metrics and benchmark data currently in place. The tightening market for grants has further emphasised how many social ventures are under-resourced and highlights the urgent need for a social capital market with significantly more liquidity than is currently available.

There are also several inherent tensions within the social entrepreneurship model. First, the institutionalising of the social entrepreneur as hero can ignore vital community involvement in a social venture's development and governance. Second, social entrepreneurs have been accused of depoliticising social problems since their actions to address social market failures can ignore the role of campaigning and advocacy in bringing about more permanent social change. In a sense, effective social entrepreneurs can let governments 'off the hook'. In a similar line of argument, social enterprises that conceptualise social action as business process are accused of 'selling out'. Indeed, social entrepreneurs can also be criticised for their focus on impact and outcomes rather than on process which sometimes stands in sharp contrast to the tradition of community development projects. Finally, there is the danger that a constant strategic focus on innovation and change can lead social entrepreneurs to overvalue potentially short-term objectives. The tendency to seek high-impact interventions can also lead to a project-based approach that can ignore sustainability.

Nevertheless, social entrepreneurship is pioneering extraordinary changes in the social fabric of many communities across the world that offer sustainable paradigm shifts benefiting many people's lives. Social entrepreneurship generates benefits through the creation of social capital, improved and more efficient provision of public goods, and via the establishment of new 'hybrid' business forms that will ultimately both open up the markets of the future through new models of trade and credit and redefine the role of enterprise within the social sector. Thus, social entrepreneurship would appear to articulate much of the emerging zeitgeist of the twenty-first century.

Questions

1 What is meant by social enterprise? Describe the phenomenon using examples of theory and practice discussed within this chapter.

2 Describe how social enterprise has developed over time and within different cultural contexts.

3 How does social enterprise differ from for-profit enterprises described elsewhere within this book? Describe the differences and similarities between social and for-profit enterprises using practical examples of each to guide your views.

4 In what ways does social enterprise matter? Evaluate the phenomenon with reference to economic, social and ideological perspectives of social enterprise.

Web links

www.sbs.ox.ac.uk/skoll/
Website of the Skoll Centre for Social Entrepreneurship at the Said Business School, University of Oxford.

www.unltd.org.uk
UnLtd supports social entrepreneurs in the UK – people who have the ideas and the commitment to make a difference in their local communities. It does this by providing a complete package of funding and support to help these individuals start up and run projects that deliver social benefit.

www.sse.org.uk
The School for Social Entrepreneurs delivers a UK-wide programme for social entrepreneurs and is a growing network of schools and fellows meeting the needs of social entrepreneurs in local settings.

www.can-online.org.uk
CAN is a leading UK organisation for the development, promotion and support of social entrepreneurs.

CHAPTER 13

Technical entrepreneurship

Sarah Cooper

13.1 Introduction

This chapter explores some current issues in the field of technical entrepreneurship. Contrasting research approaches are discussed and issues that impact upon the entrepreneurial process are examined, focusing specifically on the key or lead entrepreneur. In concluding, a number of areas are identified that may be of relevance to policy makers wishing to encourage increased levels of entrepreneurship in order to benefit local, regional and national economic development.

13.2 Learning objectives

There are five learning objectives in this chapter:

1 To examine the growth in interest in technical entrepreneurship over the past 35 years.
2 To identify characteristics of entrepreneurs in high-technology sectors.
3 To highlight possible differences between entrepreneurs in contrasting technology-based sectors.
4 To identify aspects of technology-based industries that pose specific challenges for technical entrepreneurs.
5 To examine the role of the technical entrepreneur in economic development.

Key concepts
- technical entrepreneurship ■ typology of technical entrepreneurs
- cluster/agglomeration development ■ management experience

13.3 The development of technical entrepreneurship

Over the past 25 to 30 years many economies have experienced marked structural shifts. Developed, western economies have seen the decline of many traditional industrial sectors and a dramatic increase in the role played by services within the economy, with particular growth in the contribution of small firms to employment. While traditional manufacturing sectors have been changing fundamentally, expansion has occurred in technology-based fields that make an increasingly important economic contribution. The dramatic emergence and growth of high-technology-based areas in the US, such as Silicon Valley and Route 128 in Massachusetts, brought technical entrepreneurship under the spotlight some time ago in the US (see Chapter 5). However, it is only during the past 15–20 years that a burgeoning of technology-based entrepreneurial activity in Europe has occurred, exploiting existing and newly emerging technologies, bringing about a consequent growth in interest in the subject on the eastern side of the Atlantic. From an economic perspective local, regional and national governments and development agencies are focused on encouraging enterprise and are, understandably, eager to target their resources as effectively as possible into initiatives that will facilitate the emergence of new entrepreneurial business entities. Thus, they are keen to understand the entrepreneurial motives of founders and identify the needs of fledgling and established technology-based businesses to maximise economic growth and regeneration.

13.4 The study of technical entrepreneurship

Among studies in small business the investigation of firms in new-technology fields has been growing in popularity; while many of the early studies were conducted in the US, interest in the subject has risen in Europe over the past 15–20 years. A principal reason for the growth in interest is the increasing emphasis from government development and planning agencies on new forms of enterprise. Researchers examined the influences on industrial development and at an early stage turned their spotlight onto the entrepreneurs themselves. The number of North American technical entrepreneurship investigators grew steadily; however, outside the US research in the field was still in its infancy (Watkins, 1973). The past 15–20 years have seen the burgeoning of technology-based entrepreneurial activity in Europe, exploiting existing and newly emerging technologies, accompanied by a consequent growth in interest in technical entrepreneurship.

The impetus for research comes from two contrasting directions. Academics interested in the development of new technology-based sectors have focused their attention on the firm in general and, in particular, the role of the entrepreneur in its establishment and growth. Meanwhile, local, regional and national agencies with an economic development remit are concerned to identify ways in which the environment can be improved to facilitate the emergence and growth of new firms. They wish to target resources at initiatives that will bear entrepreneurial fruit and, thus, draw on in-house and academic research to help them understand the influences on founders and identify the needs of fledgling and established technology-based businesses to maximise economic regeneration and growth.

13.4.1 Methodological approaches

Research in the field of technical entrepreneurship is still at a relatively early stage compared with its 'big brother' of general entrepreneurship. Even so, a wide range of methodological approaches has been employed from those based upon quantitative approaches to those founded upon qualitative principles. A number of early US studies adopted quantitative approaches using questionnaires to samples hundreds of firms (Cooper, 1973; Roberts, 1991a). They generated aggregate trends and profiles of entrepreneurial types, but provided little contextual and anecdotal information available via 'softer' methodologies. The approach was used owing to the study of the high-technology industry being relatively advanced; aggregate entrepreneurship data were interpreted in the context of a broad understanding of the sectors concerned. Perhaps the most comprehensive research database on technology-based firms and their founders is that developed by Roberts. During well over a quarter of a century of research, he has conducted numerous studies of spin-off activity, particularly around Boston and MIT (Roberts, 1991b). This approach contrasts with that of Bygrave (1988) who advocates that an understanding of the entrepreneurial process will be found in the descriptive background of the entrepreneur. The use of qualitative techniques, such as participant observation and in-depth personal interviews, allows the generation of a more multi-dimensional view of the start-up and subsequent development of the organisation, the role of the founder within the process, and the influence of internal and external factors and actors.

European researchers have employed approaches ranging from large sample to case methodologies. Jones-Evans (1996a) suggests that research on the background of entrepreneurs should be largely exploratory but does not advocate the use of quantitative or quantitative approaches in isolation. Following quantitative survey work by in-depth exploratory interviews with a small number of survey participants can prove a powerful combination. Different approaches addressing similar themes sometimes yield contrasting results. Chandler (1996) used quantitative interviews to focus on the skills and degree of similarity between the founder's previous work and his new firm while Jones-Evans (1996a) favoured the softer, in-depth case approach for his research. Using a particular approach may influence the result: for example Cooper (1973) compares results of brief questionnaires and in-depth interviews. In the brief questionnaire a large number of respondents claimed socially acceptable 'pull' motives, such as 'desire for independence' as the reason for establishing their business; in interviews a large number cited push factors such as redundancy or serious unhappiness in their previous employment. No approach is optimal; it is necessary to understand the research aims and to design an appropriate methodology.

The sharp increase in the number of studies of new technology-based firms poses problems for researchers. Firms are receiving increasing numbers of 'invitations' to contribute to studies through the completion of questionnaires and participation in interviews and, while many managers wish to help, even the most tolerant find it increasingly difficult to respond positively to all requests. The firms most affected are those appearing in directories of organisations in specific sectors or in particular locations, such as science parks; they are 'sitting ducks' for researchers. In designing programmes and methodological approaches focusing on new technology-based sectors it is important to consider such wider issues and to be aware of potential 'research fatigue'.

The field of technical entrepreneurship technology-based firm research is highly dynamic; the rate of technological change is increasing, new sectors are emerging and as the costs of research and development (R&D) escalate firms are adopting innovative strategies. Large firms are developing partnerships, often with small firms whose specialist input complements their capabilities and resources, and the skills required on the part of technical entrepreneurs and their firms to work in this more corporate mode are changing. Given that there is still much to find out about the technical entrepreneur and the entrepreneurial process there is scope for purely quantitative and qualitative studies, and for those exhibiting a hybrid methodology, where trends identified using quantitative techniques are explored through softer, qualitative approaches. Having briefly considered the background to current technical entrepreneurship research, the following discussion considers what studies have revealed about this key economic actor.

13.5 The emergence of technical entrepreneurship

Technical entrepreneurship is not a new concept based on twenty-first century computer whiz kids. In the eighteenth and nineteenth century, British technical entrepreneurs such as James Watt and Alexander Graham Bell made significant scientific breakthroughs that built up vast industries and changed the lives of millions. Many of today's groundbreaking innovations were not developed by large multinational corporations but were based on the ingenuity and invention of individual entrepreneurial scientists. Such ideas which changed the world included:

- power steering (Francis Davis)
- Kodachrome (L. Mannes/L. Godowsky)
- zipper (W. Judson/G. Sundback)
- Polaroid camera (Edwin Land)
- ballpoint pen (Ladislao and George Biro)
- Cellophane (Karl Schroeter)
- air conditioning (Willis Carrier)
- insulin (Frederick Banting)
- FM radio (Edwin Armstrong).

During the past 30 years, with the dramatic growth of technology clusters, such as those in Silicon Valley, California and alongside Route 128 near Boston, technical entrepreneurship has been most prominent in the US, with the emergence of entrepreneurs such as Bill Shockley with the transistor, Steve Wozniak and Steve Jobs developing the personal computer at Apple, Bill Gates with his Microsoft empire and Jim Clark, who revolutionised the use of the Internet through Netscape.

The billions earned by such individuals within 'sexy' high-technology sectors have made all of them high-profile media celebrities and the resulting publicity has probably encouraged more scientists to take the step from the laboratory into the marketplace. However, one could also argue that perhaps too great an expectation has been placed on the development of high-technology industries. With the spectacular decline of the dot.com boom following a wave of large investments in Internet-based businesses, financial institutions, government and policy makers are perhaps now more wary of pushing technological entrepreneurship than they were a few years ago, although it is noteworthy that the creation of a knowledge-based economy, driven forward by entrepreneurs and innovators, still forms the cornerstone of national and regional economic policies in many parts of the world.

13.5.1 The rise of the technology-based firm

With the decline in many traditional sectors such as coalmining, steel manufacturing and textiles, many nations have realised that industries characterised by rapid technological advances can give competitive advantages in local, regional national and international markets, which can result in increased industrial output, employment and prosperity. As a result, policy makers have indicated that the future competitiveness of industry, and success in accelerating growth and increasing employment, depend upon the capacity of firms to innovate in response to changing external conditions, including the continuing rapid pace of technological development.

Given this, it is of little surprise that firms working in 'sunrise', high-technology sectors such as electronics, software and biotechnology have been hailed as vehicles for the creation of new jobs, for regional economic regeneration, and for enhancing national rates of technological innovation and international competitiveness. Whilst it was previously thought that only large firms could take advantage of technological innovation within global markets, focus has now moved towards the development of small entrepreneurial ventures. There are a number for reasons for this:

■ Small firms are more innovative than their large firm counterparts, being less bound by convention and are more flexible due to their organic and network-based structure, contrasting with the mechanistic and bureaucratic framework common in many large firms.

■ They make an important contribution to economic growth and vitality 'by offering alternative career possibilities to those engineers and managers who do not function most effectively in larger organisations.

■ In many respects, they are better able to deal with the volatility inherent in numerous technology-based sectors, especially when fast-moving technology life-cycles reveal market niches suitable for exploitation by enterprising small firms.

■ As firms are forced to innovate and develop new products and services on a continuous basis, and as competitors enter and overtake their market position, those working within such fields are forced to become acclimatised to a culture of instability and change, risk taking and dynamic action, which is best suited to the management and business style of technologically oriented, entrepreneurial small firms.

13.5.2 Characteristics of new-technology based sectors

The search for a definition of 'high technology' has occupied many writers and existing definitions are classified into those based upon purely subjective criteria, those drawing a distinction between product and process innovation and the final group using surrogate measures, such as the proportion of employees in R&D. Discussions regarding 'high-technology' industry and of sectors falling within the classification often imply that firms are similar; however, research on small firms in specific sectors suggests that theoretical and practical differences exist between 'high-technology' industries and that technology strongly influences the ability of founders to establish and grow firms (Oakey and Cooper, 1991; Oakey, 1995; Cooper, 1997a; Harrison *et al.*, 2004). The use of the term across a heterogeneous group of industries can lead to the mistaken assumption that all founders have similar entrepreneurial opportunities and experience similar problems.

Market entry by new technology-based firms depends upon barriers that may vary through time and between sectors (Oakey, 1995). Technological progress creates business opportunities for new, small, research-intensive companies offering products, services or a combination of activities. Competition is generally less severe in 'new' sectors and more commercial opportunities exist for small firms; as sectors become more mature larger firms tend to dominate and the remaining small firms are likely to occupy narrow niches, unattractive to larger firms. Collaboration between small and large firms often occurs as the activities of small specialist product and service firms complement those of large organisations, allowing large companies to focus on their core business (Cooper, 2001a)). An important factor in the growth and development of technology-based firms is the sectoral variation in the length of product life-cycle (Markusen, 1985; Malecki, 1981, 1991). In the electronics industry, for example, it is possible to take an idea from the drawing board to the market-place in a matter of months; by contrast, product-based firms in sectors such as biotechnology experience long lead-times. The result is that some businesses are established on the basis of contract research, which is a low-cost method of start-up, on which future product development is built using revenue from service activities (Oakey *et al.*, 1990).

Related to the question of timescales and development- and life-cycles is the issue of finance as the requirement for long-term funding is generally greatest where development cycles are the longest. For example, the capital required for the translation of an electronics idea into a viable product is likely to be significantly less than that required by a biotechnology firm to finance six years of laboratory/development work, two years of testing and clinical trials before revenue is forthcoming (Oakey and Cooper, 1991). The dilemma for firms working in fields where the outcome of R&D is uncertain is that while potential long-term financial gains may be very high, so are the risks. The requirement for up-front finance often prevents a firm from being established or sinks the firm whose ability to spend exceeds its ability to generate income. Wider issues of finance and the firm are discussed in Chapters 18 and 19.

13.5.3 The emergence of technology-based start-ups

The culmination of entrepreneurial activity is the appearance of a new firm and there are two principal routes by which new enterprises are established within a region. Spinning off, resulting from the outward movement of personnel from a firm in which they have worked, either as the owner or as an employee, is a particularly important method of new firm formation in areas of existing concentrations of high-technology industrial activity. The second method is the inward movement of individual and/or corporate capital into a region, often attracted by the quality of the local economic infrastructure or availability of incentives.

There is debate over whether entrepreneurs are born or made; whatever the case, some organisations appear to provide a greater stimulus to employees to be entrepreneurial and generate more spin-offs. Spin-off rates can vary dramatically between organisations; the spin-off rate from small firms is up to ten times greater than that of large organisations. Spin-off rates from business units within larger organisations tend to be greater than those where the activities of the organisation are not compartmentalised. Creating a culture supportive of enterprising behaviour within large organisations can bring performance improvements, which increase the feeling of achievement in staff and encourage individuals or groups to consider exploiting their capabilities through entrepreneurship. The decision to establish a business in the 'outside world' can, in turn, improve the prestige and social and professional standing of individuals. For this reason the culture both within the source organisation and in the local area is important in influencing the likelihood of entrepreneurial action.

Cooper (1973) identifies two types of organisation, generating above and below average numbers of new starts, which he categorises by their technical entrepreneur 'birth rates'. Low birth-rate firms produce below average numbers of entrepreneurs while high birth-rate organisations contribute more than their 'fair share' to the economy. Low birth-rate organisations employ large numbers of employees, are organised by function, recruit average technical people, are relatively well managed and are located in areas of little entrepreneurship. By contrast, high birth-rate organisations have small numbers of employees, are product-decentralised, recruit very capable ambitious people, are afflicted by periodic crises and are located in areas of high entrepreneurship, where the presence of role models stimulates prospective entrepreneurs to found enterprises. This model implies that the structure and strategic orientation of existing organisations within a region strongly influence the likelihood of new enterprise creation by indigenous entrepreneurs. Locations such as Silicon Valley have seen significant levels of new technology-based firm formation through local spin-offs, while regions populated by 'low birth-rate' organisations do not exhibit high natural levels of spin-offs, nor are they likely to do so without proactive intervention.

13.5.4 The environment for technology-based firms

Planners and agencies wishing to attract firms to their areas or encourage indigenous entrepreneurship need to understand what influences the founder of technology-based firms to select a location in the first place. In the mid-1980s, Galbraith (1985) commented that high-tech firms operate on the basis of factors different from those for other types of manufacturing, the one common element being the importance of a complex local infrastructure including universities, government research labs and mature companies, implying that the influence of materials and transport, so important in Weber's (1929) traditional location model, are less relevant in the context of new technology-based sectors. Porter (1998) defines clusters as 'geographic concentrations of interconnected companies, specialised suppliers, service providers, firms in related industries, and associated institutions (e.g. universities, standards agencies, and trade associations) in particular fields that compete but also cooperate'. In the context of technology firms the presence of institutions such as universities or research establishments plays a multi-dimensional role in encouraging and supporting new enterprise development (Keeble and Wilkinson, 2000). Institutions act as sources of entrepreneurs and of ideas on which firms are based and support innovation through the provision of specialist technical help to companies (Lindholm Dahlstrand, 1999). While technical links may be maintained over long distances, links are most readily maintained within a local area; enthusiasm for the university science park is predicated on the belief that inter-action will necessarily occur between firms on the park and academics in the univer-sity. There is debate between those who believe that universities and science parks play a role in stimulating industrial development (Monck *et al.*, 1988) and those who ques-tion the precise nature of the relationship between universities, science parks and the growth of agglomerations of technology-based firms (Oakey, 1985). While the level of interaction may vary, research-intensive organisations are viewed as an important part of the innovation infrastructure, improving the network to support and encourage new enterprise development and growth. A regional infrastructure rich in universities, research-active firms and other key actors in the innovation process provides an 'innovative milieu' within which to establish new ventures (Camagni, 1991). Such areas are characterised by high rates of learning and knowledge diffusion between organisations within the clusters (Castells and Hall, 1994; Keeble and Wilkinson, 2000). Researchers and policy makers are increasingly interested in the rich variety, in terms of both breadth and depth, of organisations (institutional thickness) in such areas (Amin and Thrift, 1995; Keeble and Wilkinson, 2000).

The tendency for firms to select similar locations results in the development of agglomerations or clusters of related firms and organisations, such as those in Silicon Valley and in the Silicon Glen of Scotland (Bell, 1991; Cooper, 1996). A location within an agglomeration frequently attracts higher costs, for example through high land, premises and wage rates, but yields benefits through ease of access to local customers, suppliers and financiers (Saxenian, 1996). In spite of this, a minority of firms establish themselves in relatively remote locations where the entrepreneur enjoys the quality of life and a pleasant working and living environment. Roberts (1991a) concludes that the supportive environment (including the presence of the Massachusetts Institute of Technology (MIT)) not only contributes to the high incidence of spin-off entrepre-neurs in the Boston area but also influences the degree of success of those ventures (BankBoston, 1997). Close proximity to a rich array of firms (including actual and prospective customers and suppliers), research institutions (such as universities and public sector R&D organisations) and resource providers, including venture capitalists and business angels, does not necessarily mean that cluster benefits will accrue. The contrasting fortunes of firms in Silicon Valley and those along Boston's Route 128 (Saxenian, 1996) illustrate the important fact that firms need to be culturally and institu-tionally as well as geographically proximate (Porter, 1998), otherwise effective inter-action will not happen.

The growth of industrial complexes leads to the development of specialist support infrastructure such as accountants, lawyers and financiers whose input can be vital, particularly in the pre-start and early days of the firm. A location providing ready access to those with the right skills/knowledge base should facilitate the establishment of the new business. Financial advisers with knowledge of technological sectors are not ubiquitous and locations with a strong presence of high-technology firms establish a reputation for the quality of local specialist support (Cooper, 1996). Universities are increasingly playing an important role in fostering the emergence of new firms through the provision of physical incubator infrastructure and business support. The availability of incubator space at preferential rates can provide new start-ups with appropriate and low-cost space in which to begin operations, often with mentoring or other business support from specialists. Initiatives such as the TOPS programme at the University of Twente in the Netherlands have been successful in supporting the development of new ventures through start-up into mature businesses.

The challenge for policy makers is that there is no easy recipe to develop a technology cluster, as a growing body of research suggests that all clusters do not follow a common path of development and do not operate in similar ways (Saxenian, 1996; Swann and Prevezer, 1996; Garnsey, 1998; Hendry and Brown, 2001): 'clusters come in many forms, each of which has a unique development trajectory, principles of organisation and specific problems' (Mytelka and Farinelli, 2000: 11).

13.6 The technical entrepreneur

In considering the resources necessary to establish a technology-based firm, labour, capital and land are important, but the key 'input' is the entrepreneur. Successful entrepreneurs of their day include Henry Ford, Alan Sugar and Bill Gates; however, while high-profile founders grab popular attention, the road to business ownership is less glossy for most technical entrepreneurs. Individuals require a combination of skills and expertise to accept the entrepreneurship challenge. Some learn 'by doing' while others adopt a systematic approach, developing the skills and knowledge base, culminating in the entrepreneurial step. Earlier contributions have considered aspects of the definition of what constitutes an entrepreneur. Definitions of the 'technical entrepreneur' range from that adopted by Jones-Evans (1995), where a technical entrepreneur is 'the founder and current owner-manager of a technology-based business, i.e. primarily responsible for its planning and establishment, and currently having some management control within the organisation', to that of Smith (1967) who suggests that an entrepreneur is an individual who is responsible for the setting up of a new venture but is not necessarily involved in its subsequent management.

In his early research focusing on the technical entrepreneur Cooper (1973) identified a number of influences on the entrepreneurship process including the founder herself, the organisation for which she worked previously and external factors relating to the locality of the new firm (see Chapter 7 for a fuller discussion of the entrepreneurial process). These elements interact to create a climate which is more or less favourable to entrepreneurial activity. In this highly dynamic environment the technical entrepreneur is the catalyst and leader (Collins and Lazier, 1993). Given that high degrees of uncertainty surround technology development, especially sectors with a scientific base such as biotechnology, the technical entrepreneur has to tolerate risk. In leading-edge technology firms he has to generate support for a technology about which few people know, imparting his philosophy, spirit, vision and enthusiasm for his enterprise to all concerned with it. Surrounded by uncertainty, financiers are persuaded to place their money over a 'black hole' capable of swallowing thousands or millions of pounds with no guarantee of a return, and personnel are recruited, often from positions within other organisations. Thus, the technical entrepreneur is a risk taker required to persuade others to put their faith, finance and careers in his hands. Risk may decrease as the sector matures, as the underlying knowledge base increases, thus improving the quality of decision making.

13.6.1 Motivations of technical entrepreneurs

Setting up a firm can be highly risky and it is logical to ask why entrepreneurs jeopardise their and their families' future stability to risk everything. Roberts (1991a) considers that a disproportionate number of technology-based firm founders had self-employed fathers and have, therefore, grown up in an enterprising environment. Some founders start their firm as a part-time activity while still employed; this provides the opportunity to judge whether the business is viable. A number of technology areas are characterised by long lead-times, meaning that significant time and resources are invested in research before any saleable result is produced. The part-time method of market entry means business ideas are developed in parallel with other employment. The ideas and concepts on which the firm is based evolve until research advances to the stage of producing workable product or service ideas – at this point the founder formally resigns and moves into business full-time.

A variety of 'pull' and 'push' factors stimulate technical entrepreneurs, whether acting on their own or in groups. The most commonly reported stimuli tend to fall into the 'pull' category with the desire to be one's own boss rating highly, followed by the wish to exploit a market opportunity (Oakey *et al.*, 1990; Roberts, 1991a; Oakey, 1995; Cooper, 1998; Harrison *et al.*, 2004). Market entry of a new firm implies that opportunities exist, either as a result of the technology-based sector being 'new' and, thus, competition less severe, or because the company is operating in a niche unattractive to larger firms. Start-up opportunities are dependent upon barriers to entry including capital requirements and the extent of large-firm domination (Oakey, 1995). Technological advances open up new business opportunities where small, research-intensive companies are able to flourish. Those reporting a negative or push stimulus have often become disgruntled and frustrated in their existing job, which prompts them to 'go out on their own'; others have little choice and are forced, as a result of redundancy and difficulty finding alternative employment, into being entrepreneurial (Harrison *et al.*, 2004). Principal motives are frequently supported by secondary factors; founders harbour latent thoughts of self-employment but do not explore it until redundancy converts it from a good idea into a solution to unemployment. It may take such a precipitating event to trigger this action.

The life-cycle stage of the sector may influence the formation stimulus (Cooper, 1998). A comparison of new firms in the electronics and software sector reveals greater numbers of founders in the relatively youthful software sector reporting, during in-depth interviews, the desire to work for themselves or exploitation of market/product opportunities as the primary motivator. The relatively mature electronics sector is affected by greater economic fluctuations, resulting in redundancy being a more common stimulus than in the software field. The pace and nature of change within a sector will influence the opportunities in the market suitable for exploitation by the new firm.

Self-employment offers entrepreneurs the opportunity to take control of their own destiny, and to control the direction and growth of their firm. Frequently, however, founders have little desire to grow their enterprises significantly, particularly when they have worked for large firms and in founding their own are trying to get away from that environment with its hierarchies, impersonality and lack of meaningful involvement (see Chapter 6 for a fuller discussion of business growth). Thus, many firms remain relatively small, limiting their contribution to employment generation. The optimal firm size will vary but a characteristic of the software sector is the strong representation of small firms. While there are high-profile firms such as Microsoft, employing thousands, the majority of software firms are small, occupying small niches, founded by people who have left other enterprises to capitalise on their skills and expertise; there is often little need to employ large numbers of staff, each with a different skill; and, as will be explored in more detail later, software founders commonly possess a composite of required skills. In addition, small firms often collaborate with each other if contracts are larger than one can manage on one's own.

13.6.2 Age and the technical entrepreneur

Bill Gates and Richard Branson both demonstrated entrepreneurial abilities at an early age, but there is no optimal age for 'going it alone' and some founders wait until they are in the twilight of their career. In general, however, new-technology firms tend to be established by relatively young entrepreneurs and a number of research studies have indicated that while technical entrepreneurs may range in age from their twenties to seventies when founding their firm, the median tends to be in the mid-thirties (Cooper, 1973; Roberts, 1991a; Cooper, 1997b). Roberts (1991a) suggests that the pattern of young high-technology founders is a result of the 'youthful age structure of the technical organisations at which they previously worked', pointing towards a self-perpetuating pattern. The entrepreneur makes numerous sacrifices, sinking significant amounts of time and money into a venture; younger individuals tend to have fewer financial and family commitments than those in their mid-forties and have greater flexibility to focus on a business. Increased age brings with it a maturity of approach and a greater depth of experience, but a potential drawback is that older people may be more set in their ways, a major barrier in a dynamic and rapidly changing environment. Someone who has been with an employer for a long time thinks seriously before moving from a job offering pension and other benefits; for older entrepreneurs redundancy is a more common stimulus than the desire to be self-employed as difficulties securing new employment result in their starting their own firm.

The sector or activity of the firm imposes certain constraints, for example the experience and level of skills that the founder requires to set up within it, and the consequent length of time required to acquire that grounding. A long period of study and work experience can help establish credibility. An electronics founder may study to degree level, followed by a long period of work experience in order to develop a thorough understanding of electronics in an applied environment; this scenario contrasts with that of a computer science graduate who works in a product development role with much client contact and is able to set up after a relatively short period of paid employment. The age of the founder influences the length of time which they have had to develop skills and expertise on which to draw in their own venture. Some sectors require higher levels of funding and prospective founders wait until they have amassed sufficient resources of their own in order to minimise borrowing from external sources. In software, for example, people are becoming entrepreneurs at an earlier age; those with the right skills are identifying opportunities and the relatively modest levels of investment required mean that financial barriers to entry are low. In other sectors, such as electronics and biotechnology, funding proves a greater barrier for potential founders who need to gather experience and finance; thus, some sectors offer a swifter route to entrepreneurship.

13.6.3 Education and the technical entrepreneur

Bill Gates is perhaps one of the best known Harvard 'drop-outs' but his is not the standard educational route. Many new-technology based sectors are highly competitive and a firm's competitive advantage is usually based upon the knowledge and expertise of the founder. Contrasting patterns are evident among the results of a number of studies. However, when the qualifications of technical entrepreneurs are compared with those held by non-technical entrepreneurs the level of attainment in the latter group tends to be more modest. Fewer than 5% of founders of non-high technology firms in Storey's (1982) study in Cleveland, UK, had a degree compared with high-technology science-park firms where 58% had a first degree and 38% a higher degree (Monck *et al.*, 1988). This relative position may change with an increasing number of people going on to further and higher education prior to moving into employment of all types. The majority of high-technology entrepreneurs hold degrees in science or engineering disciplines and most founders hold Bachelors and Masters degrees with a lower proportion having a PhD. Roberts (1991a) attributes the generally high 70–80% survival rate of new technology-based firms to the level of education of their founders.

While differences are apparent between high-technology and non-high-technology entrepreneurs, the pattern is not uniform between high-technology sectors. The proportion of degrees is higher in science park-based than off-park firms (Monck *et al.*, 1988), possibly as a result of the majority of science-park firms being at the R&D-intensive end of the spectrum. In addition, sectoral variations exist with founders of science-based firms in biotechnology commonly having a Masters degree and frequently a PhD (Oakey *et al.*, 1990). Vocationally orientated qualifications are more widespread in electronics with founders undertaking practical, technically based training within firms, backed up by study at local colleges. Hisrich and Peters (1992) consider that an important aspect of education is that people develop the ability to deal with people and communicate clearly.

The education system plays a role in mobilising entrepreneurial capital. Taking a degree or further education qualification frequently means moving away from home to attend university or college; thus, institutions attract bright individuals into their locality, a minority of whom spin off directly from university. Technology-based firms seeking able employees are drawn to university cities and towns to feed off the stream of graduates, as has happened in the Cambridge area. Ultimately, some employees spin off and set up their own firms in the locality, aiding the development of agglomerations of related firms.

13.6.4 Work experience and the technical entrepreneur

An entrepreneur needs to understand the environment within which his business operates, a process helped when he establishes his firm in a field with which he is familiar (Chandler, 1996) – see Chapter 21. Most entrepreneurs in technology-based start-ups work for other organisations prior to establishing their own enterprise and studies regularly report in excess of 80% of founders setting up within a similar market or using similar technology (Roberts, 1991a; Cooper, 1998). There are two aspects of the previous work environment that are relevant to the technical entrepreneur – the task environment, related to the market in which the firm operates, and the skills and abilities developed by the founder (Timmons, 1994).

A high degree of risk is associated with new venture creation; however, knowledge of the target sector helps to reduce some of that risk. Sectoral familiarity makes it easier to recognise opportunities offered by a technology and also the limitations which it can impose on firm development. The technological complexity of many sectors makes this aspect very important if the technical entrepreneur is to avoid jeopardising the future of their business by making elementary mistakes. Timmons (1994) considers that being able to recognise an opportunity is an important advantage of having worked in a sector previously. Sector knowledge facilitates the identification of small, viable niches and competitor-free areas of the market, and results in the entrepreneur having a broad understanding of the customer and supplier environment. Prior knowledge and experience, particularly commercial experience, are of key importance in the development of the entrepreneurial venture, particularly during the process of opportunity recognition (Shane, 2000; Shane and Venkataraman, 2000). The technical entrepreneur is better placed to understand aspects of the competition, allowing them to adopt a stronger position for their firm within the market-place. Knowledge of the task environment, resulting from business similarity, enables the entrepreneur to make more informed decisions.

Roberts (1991a) emphasises the role that the experience of the key founder plays in the business start-up since there is a strong dependence on him to lead the organisation in a highly competitive market-place. The lead entrepreneur may surround himself with capable managers and directors but there will be heavy reliance upon him to provide direction and motivation to those in the organisation. When persuading sceptical customers and financial backers of the viability of the business, technical and previous experience in the sector proves important in establishing credibility. In general, venture capitalists prefer technical entrepreneurs with experience in the field in which they intend to set up their own enterprise. Experience can be equated with the number of years spent in the sector; however, experience does not necessarily translate into success in the new venture (Chandler, 1996).

Time spent working within a similar field enables individuals to enhance their technical and managerial skills, depending on the positions they hold. Some entrepreneurs have held positions where they have developed specific skills similar to those required in their new business; useful skills include the ability to plan, organise and manage, all of which help an entrepreneur in the strategy implementation process. Oakey's (1984) entrepreneurial matrix represents the balance between business acumen and technical ability in which different entrepreneurial types are identified depending on the degree of business and technical experience that they possess. Technical skills are important in the early stages of the business development process but a lack of supporting management skills frequently proves a drawback in the longer term, implying that evolution of the management team is required to progress the business beyond the start-up and early growth stages.

The degree of sectoral similarity between the previous employer and the new enterprise may vary depending on the size and age of the sector. For example, most electronics spin-offs are generated from other electronics firms, while in a younger sector like software or biotechnology some new-starts originate from within the sector but a sizeable proportion come from organisations that share aspects of the underlying science/technology but are less closely related. At a practical level this implies that the number of related spin-offs generated within a particular sector is influenced by the profile of 'incubator' organisations. Recent work in Ottawa, Canada, highlighted that it is not only the organisation that the founder(s) worked for immediately prior to start-up that plays an important role in the development of a new venture. Many founders work for more than one organisation during their 'pre-entrepreneurial career' and draw upon this wider spectrum of knowledge and network connections when embarking on the creation of their own venture (Harrison et al., 2004).

The type of organisation for which the founder has worked may influence the breadth of knowledge that they develop (Harrison et al., 2004). Common source organisations are other firms, both large and small, and public sector institutions such as universities and government research establishments. Most provide a reasonable 'incubator' environment, allowing entrepreneurs to establish firms built upon their research and technical experience; what varies is the degree of exposure to commercial issues. Most entrepreneurs have experience primarily in technical areas since many have held mainly research and technical positions, providing limited management training; only a small minority have experience of functions such as finance and marketing. Cooper (1997b) revealed sectoral variations in expertise with the majority of founders in the electronics sector having mainly technical expertise, whereas, predominantly, software founders had a combination of technical and administrative/commercial skills. Many founders in the software sector had previously held technical/sales/commercial positions, involving product and service development, which resulted in their gaining a broad understanding of their sector and developing a wide range of skills. Electronics founders tended to have worked in relatively strict, usually technical, functional roles and so were less exposed to commercial issues. One area in which most technical entrepreneurs lack experience is marketing (Shanklin and Ryans, 1988; Oakey et al., 1993). This is most extreme where academic entrepreneurs set up in business; while strong on the technical side, they usually lack a strong commercial base to grow a business beyond the start-up stage. Some faculty members do not sever links totally with their universities but take on a part-time commitment to a new spin-off enterprise. Many 'academic' entrepreneurs have strength in project management and, from coordinating research teams, have relevant people-management skills (Jones-Evans, 1996a).

The commercialisation of public sector technology from universities and other research laboratories is a valuable way of exploiting and obtaining a financial return on the resources invested in its development (Cooper, 2001b; Smailes and Cooper, 2004). It is likely that the number of university and research centre spin-offs will increase over time as universities place more emphasis on the commercialisation of their knowledge base. Staff are being encouraged to identify licensing opportunities for in-house developed technology and, thus, are working more closely with commercial firms, gaining greater insights into the commercial world. In the long term a minority may be tempted into heading up a spin-off team or into taking part-time directorships with spin-off companies. Given their relative lack of commercial expertise the appropriate long-term role of academic entrepreneurs in the firm may be questioned.

13.6.5 Technical entrepreneurs: an occupational typology

Earlier in this chapter brief definitions of technical entrepreneurs were presented, indicating their general nature. In the context of the above discussion it is clear that technical entrepreneurs take a variety of routes when progressing along the path to self-employment. Founders differ in their educational, employment and skill base and yet all set up their firm alone or in consort with others. Each has a unique background which makes general classification difficult. It appears, however, that the occupational/work background is important for a number of reasons; the founder gains important sectoral and market knowledge and his occupation influences the extent of commercial and business expertise that he acquires. Authors have developed various entrepreneurial typologies. For example, Jones-Evans (1996b) divides technical entrepreneurs into four different types based on their occupational background; 'research entrepreneurs', 'producer entrepreneurs', 'user entrepreneurs' and 'opportunistic entrepreneurs'. Brief pen-portraits capture the essences of these entrepreneurial types, indicating the importance of occupational experience and educational background. Consideration of these types, in the light of the earlier discussion of broad influences on the technical entrepreneur, provides useful insights into the firms developed by these contrasting 'types'.

Research entrepreneurs

These have a knowledge-oriented, science and technology development background having worked in higher education/academia or in a non-commercial laboratory. They have relatively little management experience but are experienced in the management of research programmes and possess good personnel management skills. Most have a high level of technical expertise and experience coming from doctoral backgrounds and only a few have experience in a production environment, and even then only in a research capacity. Due to his technical strength the research entrepreneur provides the technical vision for the business; however, his lack of experience will often result in his forming a firm with others possessing commercial management skills. His level of links to suppliers, customers and other external parties is extremely limited. His long-term role in the firm is likely to be in the technical development area.

Producer entrepreneurs

These come from an industrial background having worked in production and development. They benefit from having direct commercial experience, combining both technical and management skills, often within the context of a large organisation. The majority of producer entrepreneurs have been educated to degree level, with a minority having served apprenticeships in technical subjects and moved into management later in their career, before themselves becoming entrepreneurs. Immediately prior to start-up some have worked in the technical environment while others have gained experience in management-intensive fields such as marketing. The producer entrepreneur is perhaps the best placed of all four types to found a business on her own as she has the most highly developed all-round skills. Her company-based experience makes it likely that she has extensive business-related contacts, enabling her to build upon relationships with suppliers, customers and service providers when establishing her firm. Her all-round perspective makes her the most able of all four types to retain a central role in the management of the business.

User entrepreneurs

This type have been users of technology but have not been involved in its design or manufacture. Some have worked in technical sales or marketing, selling technology, but their direct experience of technical design aspects is peripheral. The user entrepreneur is poorly placed to set up a firm on his own due to his lack of technical design and development expertise. His sales experience is highly valuable to the new enterprise and means that he is at ease working closely with customers.

Opportunist entrepreneurs

These entrepreneurs have no technical background but have spotted a gap in the market. They have little or no previous experience in the field and are entering into relatively unknown territory. Opportunist entrepreneurs are in the minority. Their lack of sectoral experience makes it important for them to team up with others to develop a business. Their knowledge of the market, of customers and suppliers is either acquired from their business partners or developed 'on the hoof'.

Technical entrepreneurs are acknowledged as playing an important role in economic development. It is apparent from this classification that entrepreneurs bring to the start-up situation a wide variety of skills. By considering these entrepreneurial types it is possible to see how an individual's background dictates the form and location of the enterprise which emerges. Such profiles also point to areas where entrepreneurs lack core skills and knowledge; many cooperate with others to compensate for their shortcomings but there are ways in which the development of technical entrepreneurship can be encouraged. Some implications for policy and practice arising from the above discussion are considered in the final section.

13.6.6 Developing the entrepreneurial team within technology-based firms

Many high-profile figures are known for their individual entrepreneurial actions; however, while some like Alan Sugar start a firm on their own many others establish a founding team. Even the lone entrepreneur usually draws on the support and expertise of others in respect of production, financial, commercial and marketing advice (Oakey *et al.*, 1988, 1990). The founder who builds a firm with substantial levels of support from others compensates for any shortcomings in their own skill and knowledge base. Given that only a minority of technical entrepreneurs have both technical and commercial experience the assistance of those with complementary skills is very important in many start-ups.

Entrepreneurial teams are important in helping to compensate for major weaknesses present in individuals and many technology-based firms result from such collective actions (Cooper, 1973; Roberts, 1991a; Cooper, 1997b). Team members perform a valuable psychological function providing mutual support and encouraging management to take the next step. Collins and Lazier (1993) stress that the development of a real team is essential to prevent the development of disparate agendas. Instances of institutional self-advancement are highly detrimental to the young firm as they smother the innovative spark that is vital in giving the organisation its competitive edge.

A variety of factors influence the composition of the start-up team. One is the need for particular sets of skills; the specialist knowledge on which products and services are based usually comes from the technical entrepreneur but the need for administrative, financial and marketing input causes the founder to seek collaborators. For this reason founding team members usually bring contrasting skills and expertise to the team. Cooper (1998) identifies sectoral variations in the size and composition of start-ups with the number of single founders being much higher in the software sector than in electronics. Founders in the software sector typically possess a range of skills, including programming and technical knowledge and market awareness, developed through direct client contact, that provides them with a sound base on which to found their own business. In addition, the capital investment required in software is relatively modest and is more readily raised by one person. An electronics start-up often requires a range of skills that are less commonly possessed by an individual and the greater level of capital investment frequently necessitates pooling financial resources. Oakey (1995) reveals that firms established by teams exhibit higher levels of growth; however, this does not imply a lack of business ability on the part of lone founders as some set up their own firm to escape from large organisations and have no major growth aspirations.

The previous workplace provides a fertile environment in which to identify possible business partners (Harrison *et al.*, 2004). It presents an opportunity to see how potential cofounders function within the business environment and means that team members bring appropriate skills and expertise, since the majority of technology-based start-ups are established within the field in which the lead entrepreneur has worked previously. Teams comprising former work colleagues tend to set up locally as, in all but the most extreme cases, it is uncommon for several households to relocate to establish a business. Lone founders have fewer constraints and are, thus, more footloose. The nature of the local, professional and social networks of potential entrepreneurs influences the composition of the start-up team; where networks are highly developed, aspiring entrepreneurs come into contact with potential entrepreneurial colleagues outside their workplace and immediate social circle (see Chapter 16 for a fuller discussion of networks). Highly developed networks in the Cambridge areas are considered responsible for high numbers of non-work-related start-up teams (Cooper 1997b). A small minority of teams comprise family members, for example a father with years of experience in a sector who teams up with a younger member of the family who has completed a university education and brief period of work. Wider aspects of family enterprise are discussed in Chapter 11.

13.6.7 Location and the technical entrepreneur

The processes of spinning off and the inward movement of entrepreneurial capital into an area govern the level of local new firm formations and, in turn, the size of the pool of firms from which future firms are generated. The *in situ* expansion of indigenous firms leads to industrial growth and increased sectoral employment in an area. These processes combine to result in the development of high-technology agglomerations like those that emerged in the US along Route 128, near Boston, in Silicon Valley, California, and in the UK along the M4 (Hall *et al.*, 1987) and M11–Cambridge corridors (Segal Quince and Partners, 1985) and in Scotland's Silicon Glen. Development agencies want to know where entrepreneurs come from, spatially, in order to ascertain the whereabouts of potentially enterprising types who can be targeted and encouraged into entrepreneurship.

Entrepreneurs setting up small firms are frequently influenced by the environmental quality of a region (Keeble, 1987; Harrison *et al.*, 2004)) and are attracted by the desire to live in a quiet and pleasant location, yielding not financial but psychic benefits (Tiebout, 1957). The location of customers and suppliers exerts a degree of influence on firms, particularly those collaborating closely over development and contract-based work. Some need to be in close proximity to suppliers and locate as near as possible to their key service or materials provider; others with input needs that can be serviced by post or carrier can locate at a greater distance from their suppliers (Oakey and Cooper, 1989). In a similar way some firms, such as sub-contract electronics component manufacturers, need to be located in close proximity to their main customers (Oakey, 1984; Oakey *et al.*, 1993). Other firms, such as those producing sophisticated specialised equipment, where potential customers are located in any part of the world, are not subject to such strong external influences on their location, so a degree of footlooseness is possible.

The principal founder's previous work-place frequently influences the start-up location, with inertia resulting in the entrepreneur not moving from his current location. Research indicates that the majority of entrepreneurs (often in excess of 70%) set up firms in the locality where they previously worked (Oakey *et al.*, 1988; Cooper, 1997b). Setting up in a location with which the founder is familiar reduces some of the risk, and the benefit of moving has to outweigh significantly the disadvantages. Anecdotal evidence points to an emphasis on minimising disruption to domestic life; starting a business is stressful enough without uprooting the family unnecessarily. Much information is required when establishing a business and setting up where the founder has been living and working means that numerous local contacts already exist and new ones are easily developed due to local knowledge. Some parts of the UK, especially agglomerations such as that around Cambridge, attract employees in to work for innovative organisations from which they spin off to form indigenous firms.

Studies examining the childhood home and previous work location of technical entrepreneurs indicate that many people are not native to the region in which they set up their firm (Oakey *et al.*, 1988, 1990; Cooper, 1998). They are drawn in to work for local firms from which they spin off, contributing to local economic development. The strong pattern of local spin-offs helps to increase the size of the agglomeration of related enterprises and intensifies the technology profile of a locality as many new-starts are in the same technological sector. The emergence of new firms supplying goods and services improves the quality of the local supply infrastructure. The rich supplier pool acts not only as a stimulus to enhance local spin-off activity but also as a magnet to attract footloose entrepreneurs from elsewhere into the area.

Entrepreneurial mobility may be related to the sector of activity, for example an electronics entrepreneur may be more likely to remain within the same locality than a software founder. Some electronics firms need to become highly integrated with local customers and/or supplier firms providing components and sub-contract services. As a consequence, the founder is reliant on their knowledge of the complex local inter-organisational network. The software founder trades information in its broadest sense and is less dependent upon the local environment. Knowledge of local suppliers and potential customers is, therefore, more important to new electronics than software firms, rendering the electronics start-up less mobile than the portable, software new-start.

To minimise costs many founders start up in their garage or spare room, with firms such as Apple and Hewlett-Packard growing from such humble beginnings. The home-based start is feasible where the process is 'clean', such as in software and some electronics firms. In sectors such as biotechnology the need for bespoke laboratory and factory space necessitates a rapid move into specialist facilities. These contrasting requirements pose differing barriers to start-up. In the longer term, even clean businesses need physical and 'emotional' space, as entrepreneurs find that synonymous home and work locations become too stressful; the temptation not to 'leave' work or to keep going back risks ruling and ruining families' lives. These sharply differing premises need to be addressed by private or public sector agencies attempting to encourage the development of technology-based entrepreneurship.

13.6.8 Continued entrepreneurial involvement and growth

For many founders of technology-based firms the organisation is their life. It develops from their idea, is based on their expertise, absorbs significant quantities of their personal and professional time, and allows them to pursue their interest and passion for a particular field of technology. Smith and Jones-Evans' definitions of the technical entrepreneur differ in respect of his ongoing business involvement. For those involved with the firm from the start it is often difficult to consider, with a rational eye, what their long-term role and level of involvement should be; from their perspective they are crucial to the continued existence of the business. It is sometimes the case, however, that the long-term involvement of the technical founder in a controlling position within the enterprise is detrimental to the sustainability of the firm.

The extent to which some technical entrepreneurs lack an understanding of commercial issues at start-up has been discussed; few entrepreneurs attempt to gain a detailed knowledge of management concepts as their firm develops and consequently learn only 'by doing'. In some cases the continued involvement of a technical entrepreneur in a key decision-making role risks thwarting the development of the organisation and jeopardising its future. Some entrepreneurs recognise their shortcomings as 'managers' and adopt a central role in research and new product and service development, acknowledging their technical strengths. Many are happy to exchange the grey suit of management for the white coat of the laboratory, handing over to those more skilled and able to move the business onto a strong commercial footing. Reflecting this, Rubenson and Gupta (1990) conclude that technical entrepreneurs tend to stay in control of their businesses for shorter periods of time than entrepreneurs in other activities.

Some technical entrepreneurs possess all of the required skills but make a conscious decision not to pursue a strategy of rapid business growth. Many set up their own business expressly to distance themselves from large, bureaucratic, mechanistic and impersonal organisations. The prospects for employment growth in many technology-based businesses may, consequently, not be as great as at first sight due to some entrepreneurs being economic satisficers rather than maximisers.

13.7 Chapter summary

Technology-based sectors have attracted the attention of policy makers because they are viewed as sunrise industries, capable of compensating for declining traditional activities. The emergence and growth of new sectors is inextricably linked with issues of entrepreneurship since the business founder drives the enterprise development process; thus, the encouragement of entrepreneurship has become a major focus for attention by development organisations. A first step towards a greater understanding of ways to encourage entrepreneurship is to learn from those already in business. All have followed a slightly different path and had varying needs; while it is not possible to develop an individual support programme there are some differences that agencies need to appreciate, which may influence the rate and direction of enterprise development. Oakey and Cooper (1991) caution politicians and government planners eager to capitalise on 'opportunities offered by emergent key technologies' not to assume automatically that 'the encouragement of any new technology will result in rapid and sustained industrial growth'.

A high proportion of technology start-ups result from positive stimuli, but a sizeable number still occur due to the entrepreneur being pushed by redundancy or frustration. There are numerous niches suitable for small firms and setting up a business should be encouraged as a positive action rather than a response to a negative occurrence. Most people spin off locally, suggesting that initiatives to increase levels of entrepreneurship will be more effective if they are targeted predominantly at local people. The use of local role models will encourage those with ideas to appreciate that not all technical entrepreneurs are like Bill Gates.

A large proportion of firms are established in the same field in which the founder worked previously. Given the preponderance of local spin-offs the strong pattern of indigenous new-starts results in the intensification of a region's technology profile. The prevalence of local spin-offs assists the development of agglomerations of businesses, adding new firms, potential new suppliers, customers, contractors and service providers, increasing the visible presence of the agglomeration, which in turn encourages the inward movement of entrepreneurs. For a location to remain attractive firms have to continue to innovate and adopt new techniques, otherwise the vitality of the agglomeration is reduced and competing clusters develop to become innovative centres, generating spin-offs and attracting inward investment.

Some organisations act as better entrepreneurial incubators than others and agencies need to analyse the composition of their indigenous organisations in order to ascertain the likely level of local spin-offs and innovative potential of an area. Traditionally, large organisations have not acted as major generators of entrepreneurs but more firms are organising their activities into smaller product/service based units, attempting to replicate the 'feel' of the small firm environment. This is likely to encourage the creation of more spin-off teams as communication between employees increases and individuals from different functional areas identify opportunities and skill synergies. Areas lacking in local spin-offs need to attract more technical entrepreneurs from elsewhere in order to establish an innovative base on which to build. Stimulating entrepreneurship in areas which are under-represented is a challenge for development agencies. The creation of centres based around particular technologies, similar to the *technopôle* concept in France, might encourage entrepreneurship. The provision of appropriate support infrastructure and incentives or concessions might kick-start the process of encouraging predominantly local, latent, aspiring entrepreneurs into business ownership.

While a minority of entrepreneurs move some distance to set up firms the majority spin off in the local area, aiding the development of agglomerations of technology-based firms. Many entrepreneurs are embedded within professional and social networks that influence the decision on where to locate; once established, the firm becomes a node within a complex arrangement of organisational and personal relationships. Those who have worked in an area previously, in broadly the same field, possess local/market knowledge and are some way up the knowledge curve; remaining within the known environment reduces risk. Subsequent spin-offs increase the stock of firms and improve the attractiveness of an area to mobile entrepreneurs seeking a new location. A small minority of founders seek a location offering a high quality of life, and remote locations are viable if firms are able to operate at a significant distance from customers, suppliers and other service providers. The extent of local linkages in the short term might not be great so firms will use distant contacts, but in the long term peripheral areas have the potential to develop self-sustaining clusters of indigenous expertise. Improvements in information technology are making remote locations increasingly viable for certain firms. While many entrepreneurs still choose a non-peripheral location, anything that relieves pressure on existing industrial/commercial centres is beneficial.

Many founders in technology-based sectors have little business background and there is a danger that some potential entrepreneurs lack an appreciation of the opportunities offered by self-employment; others lack the management know-how and confidence to found a business. A two-pronged approach could raise business awareness and whet the appetite of bright scientists and engineers. Both aspects revolve around education; one addresses the student while the other focuses on the prospective entrepreneur who is at a later stage in their career.

Many schools offer students the opportunity to study management subjects, and greater integration of business and enterprise into both the school curriculum and higher education programmes may prove fruitful. Gorman *et al.* (1997) advocate putting elements of entrepreneurship into formal education programmes, considering that entrepreneurs drive the economy. Courses socialise individuals into the idea of entrepreneurship as a viable and acceptable career path. Programmes incorporating entrepreneurship are relatively new in Europe, and until recently many 'would-be' technical entrepreneurs took a science/engineering degree that offered little exposure to management issues. Accreditation boards of professional institutes, such as those in civil and mechanical engineering, require that students on accredited degree programmes are exposed to management. Thus, management, accounting and legal concepts are becoming core elements in many college and university courses, ensuring that science and engineering graduates develop an understanding of the importance of management in organisations. In addition, increasing numbers of courses are incorporating industry placements. Hynes (1996) considers that 'non-business students have the talent of conceptualising new and original ideas'. This, promoting ideas of entrepreneurship and business by putting them into the syllabi of science and engineering courses, as has been happening in the UK context since 1999 through the Office of Science and Technology's Science Enterprise Challenge initiative, should reap benefits in the longer term.

In some technology-based fields a long 'apprenticeship' is not always required; the route to entrepreneurship is relatively swift. For example, in software, graduates are well placed to establish firms straight out of university. In other sectors prospective founders need to gather financial, intellectual and human resources on which to base their business. The lead time in some sectors is long and the provision of patient money will enable founders to start firms at an earlier stage in areas where significant development funding is required. To support the increased level of management exposure in education and work, specialist courses targeted at more mature prospective technical entrepreneurs would enable them to gain a general understanding of business management. Once convinced of the merits of self-employment, those with specific business ideas would work up their concept into a formal business plan; those requiring external funding would receive help to develop proposals for investors. Such initiatives might encourage entrepreneurs to start their firm proactively rather than as a response to a negative stimulus.

Technical people tend to remain in technical positions but through education may appreciate the pivotal role of business strategy and seek positions in which they can gain practical management experience. Ultimately, this may result in increased spin-off levels as founders develop a wider appreciation of the management function, making them better prepared for their role as founder. For those already running their own firms, communication of the benefits of expanding the management team to maximise growth potential and share the burden may increase the number willing to grow their enterprises, maximising their contribution to wealth and employment generation.

The technical entrepreneur is an important economic actor and the dynamic nature of most new-technology based fields means that there are numerous opportunities to further our understanding of what influences them to take that 'one small step'.

Questions

1 Identify the key characteristics of technical entrepreneurs and contrast them with those of entrepreneurs in general. Do they differ and if so how?

2 Select a technology-based business and develop a short case-study profile of the firm and its founder (or principal founder in the case of a team-based start-up). How and in which areas is the influence of their personal and employment background most apparent with regard to the firm?

3 Which areas within your country have the greatest concentrations of technology-based firms? Why do you think that such firms are so common there and what resource or factor advantages exist?

4 How easy is it for technical entrepreneurs to set up firms in your local area? What forms of assistance are available to help them? What types of infrastructure, support and finance are provided by local and national government bodies and regional agencies to help potential founders, and how supportive is the local business environment in terms of potential customers, suppliers and information providers?

Web links

www.fast50.co.uk
An objective ranking and celebration of the UK's fastest-growing high-technology companies, compiled by Deloitte.

www.netvalley.com/archives/mirrors/stanford-magazine-founding_fathers.shtml
The article 'Founding Fathers' by David Jacobsen (1998) epitomises the spirit of the high-tech garage start-up through tracking the history of Bill Hewlett and Dave Packard.

www.bankofengland.co.uk/publications/financeforsmallfirms/hightech2001.pdf
A Bank of England report 'Financing of Technology-Based Small Firms' that examines the financing environment for technology-based small firms in the UK.

www.sqw.co.uk
Homepage of Segal Quince and Wicksteed, the consultancy company that wrote the 'Cambridge Phenomenon' report. Under publications, there are a number of reports on academic entrepreneurship and technology transfer.

CHAPTER 14

Corporate entrepreneurship

Dylan Jones-Evans

14.1 Introduction

To compete effectively in dynamic and fast-changing world markets, many large organisations are adopting more innovative and enterprising approaches to management. One of these approaches is the development of entrepreneurship within a corporate environment, generally known as intrapreneurship. This chapter will define the concept of intrapreneurship, especially the difference between developing entrepreneurial practices in a large firm and a new venture. It will examine the barriers that exist in creating an intrapreneurial culture within a corporate setting and discuss some of the main factors that lead to the creation of a climate for intrapreneurship within an organisation. The specific characteristics of intrapreneurs will also be discussed and contrasted with corporate managers and entrepreneurs. Finally, the chapter will examine the importance of organisational learning to the development of a more entrepreneurial organisation and some of the key factors necessary to develop a learning business.

14.2 Learning objectives

There are six learning objectives in this chapter:

1 To identify the main differences between entrepreneurship and intrapreneurship.
2 To understand the key differences between a corporate and intrapreneurial culture within an organisation.
3 To understand the factors which can lead to intrapreneurship within the organisation.
4 To examine the barriers to intrapreneurship within a corporate setting.
5 To describe the personal and business characteristics of intrapreneurs.
6 To understand the importance of learning in encouraging entrepreneurship within organisations.

Key concepts

■ intrapreneurship   ■ corporate entrepreneurship   ■ organisations   ■ management

14.3 Intrapreneurship

In many economies, large companies are a result of the favourable trading conditions enjoyed in the immediate years after the Second World War, with corporate bureaucracies set up to manage large-scale businesses operating in stable global conditions. As with the development of self-employment and the small firm (see Chapters 2 and 3), the growth in interest in entrepreneurship at a corporate level is due to a combination of various internal and external factors (Jones, 2005; Thornberry, 2001; Gibb, 1990; Kanter, 1989b) including:

■ the blurring of boundaries between the formal and informal labour markets, with serious consequences for labour mobility and job security, especially for white-collar workers;

■ the change in attitudes towards entrepreneurship, with a higher degree of individualism, particularly among the middle classes who are the professional workers within many large organisations;

■ increasing rates of product and market obsolescence – as life-cycles become shorter and the rate of process and technology change faster, there is demand for a higher degree of innovation within the organisation (see Chapter 5);

■ the technological revolution, predominantly in computing and information science, which has had global consequences for industries as diverse as financial services and agriculture;

■ economic uncertainties leading to changing and unstable market conditions;

■ pressures on the manufacturing sector to discard unnecessary overheads and externalise previously internalised services.

To cope with these changes, large firms have increasingly adopted more innovative and enterprising approaches to management within their organisations (Sharma, 1999; Birkinshaw, 1997; Stopford and Baden-Fuller, 1994). One of these approaches is the development of entrepreneurship within a corporate environment, known as intrapreneurship, which is an attempt to integrate the strengths of small firms (such as creativity, flexibility, innovation and nearness to market) with the market power and financial resources of large companies. However, there have been doubts whether this can be achieved successfully and whether this may just be another management 'fad' adopted by large firms (Duncan *et al.*, 1988).

14.4 Defining intrapreneurship

As the previous chapters in this book have already demonstrated, there are a number of definitions of entrepreneurship. However, these tend to describe the activities of the owner-manager within a small organisation. With an increasing number of managers and professionals setting up new and small businesses within old and existing organisations during the 1970s, the term 'intrapreneur' was invented to describe those individuals who operated as entrepreneurs within existing organisations (Macrae, 1976).

During the 1980s, when entrepreneurs were again in favour, the concept was developed further to describe entrepreneurial behaviour within large organisations, rather than the establishment of small businesses within larger organisations. As Pinchot (1986) states: 'When I look at successful innovation in companies as diverse as Hewlett Packard, General Motors, Bank of California, 3M, General Mills, Du Pont or AT&T, I always find small independent groups of imaginative action takers working to circumvent or even sabotage the formal systems that supposedly manage innovation. These courageous souls form underground teams and networks that routinely bootleg company resources or "steal" company time to work on their own missions. They make new things happen while those trying to innovate by the official route are still waiting for permission to begin.' However, more recent work has also suggested that there is no reason why intrapreneurship cannot be initiated by employees working within established small firms (Carrier, 1996).

So what makes intrapreneurs different from entrepreneurs? Like entrepreneurs, intrapreneurs take personal risks to make new ideas and innovation happen. However, unlike entrepreneurship, where the time and capital of the entrepreneur are placed at risk, intrapreneurship will often take the large organisation into new products and markets, away from their established core businesses. This may risk the company's capital, credibility and market-share, and in so doing the intrapreneur's position within the company. Therefore, an intrapreneur is an employee of a large organisation who has the entrepreneurial qualities of drive, creativity, vision and ambition, but who prefers, if possible, to remain within the security of an established company (Gibb, 1988). A more detailed definition will be discussed later in this chapter.

As with entrepreneurship, the term 'intrapreneurship' has been used to describe a number of different organisational scenarios (Dess *et al.*, 2003; Coulson-Thomas, 1999; Gibb, 1990; Pearson, 1989; Knight, 1987), including:

- the development of an overall climate of entrepreneurship at a corporate level (Antoncic and Hisrich, 2003; Stopford and Baden-Fuller, 1994);
- intra-corporate venturing – the creation of new ventures within an existing organisation to stimulate or develop new products or product improvements, including autonomous business units established within the corporation to develop a new product and/or market (Block and MacMillan, 1993; Gee, 1994; David, 1993); venture groups or divisions set up for the cultivation of new ventures (Ginsberg and Hays, 1994) and independent spin-offs (Jones-Evans and Klofsten, 1997);
- initiatives by employees in the organisation to undertake something new, where an innovation is often created by subordinates without being asked, expected or even being given permission by higher management (Brazeal, 1996);
- rationalisation of the business, including management personnel (Fulop, 1991).

14.5 Entrepreneurial and intrapreneurial ventures

Therefore, intrapreneurship does not merely mean the development of a small business within a large organisation, and there are significant differences between creating a new independent venture and establishing a corporate venture through intrapreneurship

(McKinney and McKinney, 1989). These are most striking in the areas concerning the business environment, the decision to establish a new venture, sources and patterns of funding, and employment of staff.

14.5.1 The business environment

Whilst the entrepreneurial team within a new venture will gradually develop an understanding from which the right rules for running the business will evolve, staff within a corporate venture can be restricted by the parent corporation's existing 'rulebook', which has contributed to past corporate and managerial successes. As a result (and not always deliberately) the corporation can severely restrict the new venture by assuming that it must operate under the same old rules as other developments in the organisation. Therefore, for the intrapreneurial venture to succeed, its parent company must grant it the flexibility required to adapt to a previously unexplored and undefined market.

There can also be considerable differences in the degree of freedom each type of business has to develop its potential. Whilst corporate ventures – when part of a larger corporation – must subordinate themselves to the parent firm's goals, new independent ventures are usually free to compete in any market, develop any product and utilise any technology. For example, when an intrapreneurial venture wishes to compete in a market-place controlled by other parts of the firm, the intrapreneur, rather than being allowed to develop innovative advantages in any promising market, will, in the majority of cases, face severe resistance.

14.5.2 Establishing a new venture

One of the crucial resources for a new business is an adequate source of funding, both for start-up and further development as the business grows. Many independent entrepreneurs will approach sources of funding such as venture capital firms or business angels for this finance and, as Chapter 19 demonstrates, such funders will receive a high number of business plans from individual entrepreneurs each year, from which they will select only a few. On the other hand, the senior management of a large corporation will review only a few proposals for internal ventures every year. If the potential independent business is rejected by one source of funding, it can always apply to others who may understand their potential better. Within a corporate setting, rejected ideas have nowhere to go and thus a viable project may never realise its potential unless the intrapreneur takes the plunge, leaves the large organisation, and starts a new independent business.

Funding sources such as venture capitalists will tailor their criteria to the proposal when making the decision to invest in the independent new venture. However, internal corporate ventures will be subject to the same traditional corporate decision-making criteria as other projects, such as minimum sales volume, minimum acceptable return on investment and special restrictions on use of capital and personnel. Innovation, as a criterion for choosing the project, will usually have little significance. Whilst the entrepreneur has control of the business, with responsibility for its management and, ultimately, its eventual success or failure, the intrapreneur must share control with top management. Consequently, the intrapreneur will have to operate under managerial constraints that would not be present in many independent businesses. Indeed, any problems with the venture can result in top management taking ultimate control over its future.

14.5.3 Sources and patterns of funding

The amount of funding allocated to each type of venture can differ considerably. Within large organisations, the pressure for short-term gains can lead to too much early stage funding for intrapreneurial ventures. As a result, intrapreneurs may be tempted to commit resources before sufficiently understanding the new business area. (New businesses can take over five years to become established in the market-place.) This can lead to the corporate venture being terminated early, when top management does not receive the expected short-term results it expects. On the other hand, early-stage funding within independent new ventures is usually limited to the entrepreneur's personal finances. This is because entrepreneurs are less willing to let in vast amounts of early equity funding, which can dilute their share of the company and thus their control of the management of the venture. In fact, new small ventures tend to be funded on a 'milestone' basis, rather than through traditional budgeting and resource allocation processes, as is found in established corporations. For example, developing a new product or appointing a new director are 'milestones' that can attract additional capital.

The source of funds for business development also differs between independent and corporate ventures. The corporate venture is usually limited to one source of funds – the parent company. With no legal commitment the funds may appear or disappear and funding is mainly dependent on the parent's financial position. Within independent ventures, the entrepreneur negotiates a legal contract that guarantees initial funding with investors and sets guidelines for future funding. Should existing investors no longer wish to provide more funding, the entrepreneurial venture can seek additional funding from new investors.

14.5.4 Staff resources

A large organisation will recruit people to an internal venture on the basis of parent-company personnel in line for transfer or promotion, rather than on the basis of the needs of the venture. In contrast, an independent new venture is usually made up of eager qualified individuals who share the founder's vision. Therefore, an important reward for leadership of an independent venture is control over the resources and strategic direction of the firm. Additional incentives can include financial gain, which is usually linked to the profitability of the business. In corporate ventures, long-term success can be linked to that of the parent corporation, rather than the venture, and developing an adequate reward system for intrapreneurs is one of the issues that will be discussed later in more detail.

Most independent ventures have a board of directors, made up of outside directors, experienced venture capitalists from investing firms and other experts. These people provide valuable and wide-ranging experience in the technical or market areas related to the innovation. In most cases, the intrapreneurial venture does not have a board of directors and thus lacks a valuable source of advisors. If the intrapreneurial venture reports to its management in the traditional hierarchical manner, its interests often lack adequate representation in the top management circles.

14.6 Climate for intrapreneurship within an organisation

As with independent entrepreneurs, many managers in a corporation are not capable of being successful intrapreneurs. Being an intrapreneur is not something that can be assigned to individuals within an organisation, like other job descriptions such as financial controller or marketing manager. In many cases, intrapreneurs are self-selected, i.e. they come up with an idea that they will develop further, often in their own time (see Chapter 7). Intrapreneurship can only be developed within an organisation by creating the right climate for such individuals to flourish (Kuratko *et al.*, 1993).

14.6.1 Intrapreneurship sponsors

Within large companies where new innovations can often be lost in the bureaucracy and unresponsiveness of the organisation, intrapreneurs cannot sufficiently develop their ideas alone. A corporate environment favourable to intrapreneurship has sponsors and champions throughout the organisation who not only support the creative activity and resulting failures but have the planning flexibility to establish new objectives and directions as needed (Knight, 1987). Such sponsors can be at all levels of the organisation, from chief executive to project manager to other intrapreneurs.

The role of the sponsor should include:

■ overcoming the financial concerns of other managers regarding risky ventures, both in initial review and follow-up evaluations;

■ curing the need for resources by defending proposals in evaluation meetings, allocating initial exploration funding to new ideas and permitting flexibility in budgets in terms of money, people and equipment;

■ ensuring that corporate venturing develops quickly within an organisation by placing the rewards and initiatives in place for intrapreneurs;

■ fighting internal departmental issues, such as the hoarding of resources in one division and 'empire-building'.

14.6.2 Continuous involvement of the original intrapreneur

In many large organisations, it is usually the case that an innovator of a new idea will be forced to hand that idea to another team of individuals for its development. This is particularly the case where a member of a division working in one industrial sector has come up with an idea that is applicable in another industrial sector in which the company operates. The intrapreneur may also be left behind if the idea reaches a stage of development where the intrapreneur has no direct experience (e.g. from development to manufacturing).

In many cases, the removal of the original intrapreneur from a project can often result in that project not reaching fruition. This is particularly the case where an idea is new and innovative, and has been developed solely by the intrapreneur. In many cases, intrapreneurs are the driving force behind new ideas within the company. When they are removed from projects, the very driving force behind the project is lost, as the new 'project leader' tends not to have the same degree of enthusiasm as the intrapreneur, as he will be working on someone else's idea. As Pinchot (1986) states: 'Intrapreneurs cannot exist if their passionate commitment is ignored and their visions given to people who don't understand them. Without intrapreneurs, innovation flounders.'

There have been criticisms of using a single intrapreneurial team to take an idea from development to commercialisation, mainly because of the reluctance of companies to have intrapreneurial teams led by inventors or researchers with very little commercial experience. In such scenarios, the inventor should become a member of the intrapreneurial team, perhaps in the role of technical leader, or act as a consultant to the intrapreneurial management team while still working on the development of the idea. In other cases, the inventor of the idea has sufficient skills to become the leader of the intrapreneurial team. One of the more important factors is that the intrapreneurial team stays together throughout the duration of the project, even after commercialisation. This is often because if the idea is new to the market, then imitations will soon follow, often with significant improvements. In order for the company to be able to counteract these 'follower' strategies, it is important that the original intrapreneurial team stays together for subsequent product generations.

14.6.3 The autonomy of the intrapreneurial team

As entrepreneurs have a desire to be 'their own boss', with responsibility for the destiny of their company, intrapreneurs have a desire to have sole control over the destiny of their particular idea. In many cases, intrapreneurship is stifled within large organisations because the authority to develop innovation is often several management levels above that of the innovator, and with restricted access. If intrapreneurship is to work within large organisations, then intrapreneurs need the power to make decisions within their project remit (Garnsey and Wright, 1990). This may include having the necessary authority to source people and resources from outside the parent organisation.

14.6.4 Crossing boundaries in the organisation

In developing an idea from first principles to final commercialisation, the intrapreneur will have to cross a number of boundaries within the organisation. These may include:

- inter-functional boundaries, such as between research and development (R&D) and marketing;
- divisional boundaries between different business units within the company (e.g. an innovation may begin in the semiconductor division within a company, but may have more applicability in the instruments division);
- organisational boundaries between different levels of management in the hierarchy of the organisation (as mentioned earlier).

However, there is increasing evidence that managers within large organisations are recognising that vertically driven, financially oriented, authority-based processes, which for so long dominated company operations, are being overtaken by horizontal processes that cut across organisational boundaries (Goshal and Bartlett, 1995). For intrapreneurship to be effective throughout the whole organisation, willing individuals in the intrapreneurial team, regardless of functional specialism, must modify the traditional boundaries between different parts of the organisation to encourage multi-disciplinary teamwork and participation.

14.6.5 Tolerance of risks, failures and mistakes

Risk is a factor that is inexorably linked with entrepreneurship and innovation. However, large companies are risk adverse, as the concept of personal failure is anathema to the system of promotion and career development within traditional organisations, with managerial conservatism and performance measurement often inhibiting intrapreneurship (Schwab and Schwab, 1997). In contrast, many entrepreneurs in small firms see failure as a learning experience, from which new products, services and ventures can be developed. To foster an intrapreneurial climate, this tolerance towards risk and failure through experimentation should be encouraged (Sathe, 1989). If a large company wants to develop an entrepreneurial spirit, it has to establish an environment that allows mistakes and failures in developing new innovative ideas. While this is in direct opposition to the established promotion and career system of the traditional organisation, without the opportunity to fail few if any corporate intrapreneurial ventures will be undertaken

14.6.6 Long-term philosophy towards success

There is a danger that the creation of internal corporate ventures, which are externalised from the main functions from the company, could lead to considerable problems. Whilst such decentralisation may lead to researchers and product developers becoming closer to the market-place, it may lead to a focus on short-term market performance, in order to 'prove' the success of the new venture. Therefore, a company must be prepared to establish a long time horizon for evaluating the success of individual ventures as well as the overall intrapreneurship programme. An intrapreneurial climate should not be established within an organisation unless that company is willing to invest money with no expectation of return for five to ten years. It is also important that ideas are allowed to develop fully and that the resources allocated to such intrapreneurial projects are not withdrawn before the idea has progressed to commercialisation (Pryor and Shays, 1993).

14.6.7 Finding resources for ideas

Although intrapreneurs will often work on their new ideas in their own time, organisations need to make resources available to such individuals in order that these ideas reach the market-place more quickly. This can be done by allocating either time or funds to the intrapreneur. Often, if intrapreneurs cannot find time to make their ideas marketable to the company, then those ideas will remain in the intrapreneur's head rather than becoming a marketable product, process or service. Once the idea has been shown to be of some value to the organisation, then funds need to be made available to develop this idea to the point where it can be adopted by the organisation. In many companies, available resources are often committed to solving problems that have immediate effects on the bottom line, rather than the development of new ideas. If discretionary funds are not available, the intrapreneur may become frustrated to the point of abandoning the commercialisation of the idea altogether. More worrying for the company, the idea may be taken elsewhere to be developed by the intrapreneur, either to a competing organisation or a new small business.

14.6.8 An effective reward system

Although the attainment of commercialisation of their ideas is often sufficient, the energy and effort expended by the intrapreneurial team in the creation of the new venture needs to be appropriately rewarded (Brazeal, 1996). However, as intrapreneurship is a relatively new phenomenon, many companies have yet to develop an adequate reward system that is adequate in terms of pay and promotion.

In terms of pay, a study by Balkin and Logan (1988) has examined the different policies that organisations can develop to reward entrepreneurial staff. Their conclusions indicated that intrapreneurs should be paid below or at the market rate, with a significant portion of the individual's salary at risk in the form of pay incentives, which should be linked to individual and corporate venture's performance. Therefore, the fixed-package portion of an intrapreneur's reward package – salary and benefits – would be low. However, this should be compensated by a number of benefits including the following.

Short-term variable pay benefits

These include profit sharing, which can focus the intrapreneur's attention on the corporate venture's financial goals. This can also strengthen team spirit within the corporate venture, as all employees will receive a share of the profits proportional to their salaries. It is important within corporate entrepreneurship that a new internal venture does not imitate the reward policies of the corporation's other traditional business divisions, as these policies are usually designed for a complex bureaucracy and recognise the difference in pay scales according to an individual's status in the organisation.

Long-term variable pay benefits

Equity ownership is a means for rewarding intrapreneurs. As well as being an excellent retention tool for the large organisation (with employees likely to remain within the venture as it develops), it also gives intrapreneurs a sense of ownership and responsibility for their venture, distinguishing it from other projects that the intrapreneur may have previously undertaken in a corporate capability for the large firm. In addition, stock ownership may also create a grater entrepreneurial spirit within a corporate venture, as employees look for more innovations and opportunities that will increase the profits (and stock value) of the venture.

Education and health benefits

To pay for travel, tuition and supplies for job-related education and training. Entrepreneurial employees frequently, in the development of new ideas, discover gaps in their education and training, and must develop new skills to continue to be productive and innovative. This is crucial in high-technology industries where corporate entrepreneurship is prevalent. In addition, large firms initiating corporate venturing must be aware of the changes that will occur in the working lifestyles of intrapreneurs – as they assume 'ownership' for their ventures, their working hours will inevitably become longer (60–80 hours per week is not uncommon in these cases) and, as with entrepreneurs, the demands on their time will increase, as will the stress of the job. As a result, many companies are providing benefits in the form of health club memberships so that intrapreneurs can develop positive coping behaviours.

Therefore, pay policies within corporate ventures should recognise that individuals assuming the role of intrapreneur should be treated differently from the rest of the organisation. However, this could cause potential problems in the development of the intrapreneurial venture, especially in the attraction of staff from other divisions of the large firm. Indeed, corporate entrepreneurship should pay more attention to internal pay equity than independent small firms, because if it is to attract employees from other units of the large firm, it must be sensitive to the company's reward packages, and may have to match overall company pay and benefits levels, which may restrict its ability to design policies that reward innovation and creativity. However, this problem can be limited by:

■ physically separating the corporate venture from the rest of the organisation;
■ convincing possible transferees that the risk of greater long-term reward may be worth the short cut in pay;
■ not accepting transfers from other divisions in the large organisation.

The traditional reward within a corporate structure – promotion – is often not sufficient, as the motivation behind the development of the idea is often not career advancement. More importantly, intrapreneurs seldom make good corporate managers, as they rarely have the temperament for coping with the company's structure. This may cause problems in the organisation, especially with other corporate managers. 3M, for example, has developed a 'dual promotion system' where successful intrapreneurs can choose to be promoted either on the technical or the management hierarchy of the business (Fry, 1987). This recognises the needs of those intrapreneurs who do not wish to achieve more administrative responsibilities. Those intrapreneurs who wish to remain in technical development – and indeed are more valuable in the laboratory than in the office – are given a higher rank but are not constrained to purely administrative positions. On the other hand, some companies prefer to reward their intrapreneurs through giving them a position of freedom within the organisation to develop new ideas or even setting the intrapreneur up in a separate venture with suitable equity as motivation for success. For example, within both 3M and Johnson and Johnson, the intrapreneur who successfully develops a new product, market or service, and then builds a business on it, will become the head of that business (Drucker, 1985). This could be general manager or a division president, with the appropriate rank, bonuses and stock options.

14.7 Barriers to intrapreneurship within a corporate culture

The success of entrepreneurial practices within companies such as Apple and Microsoft in the US and Virgin and Marks and Spencer in the UK has resulted in attempts by many large companies to develop the positive side of small business and implement the spirit, culture and rewards of entrepreneurship into their organisations (Harris *et al.*, 1995). However, large companies have a problem in being entrepreneurial for one simple reason – they are too big. The size of such organisations means that managers have to structure the corporation in order to control it, and as the company grows bigger, even more structures of management are added in order to manage the whole operation. Consequently, a number of barriers to intrapreneurship may be created as there are considerable differences between a traditional corporate culture and an intrapreneurial culture, with the former having an emphasis on a culture and reward system that tends to favour caution in decision making.

For example, large businesses rarely operate on a 'gut feeling' for the market-place, as many entrepreneurs do. Instead, large amounts of data are gathered before any major business decision is made, not only for use in rational business decisions, but also for use as justification if the decision does not produce optimum results. Risky decisions are often postponed until enough hard facts can be gathered or a consultant hired to provide extra advice and information. As a result of such a culture, large firms will often face difficulties in attracting suitably entrepreneurial staff. Entrepreneurs will not be attracted to large organisations, preferring the risk and adventure associated with ownership of a small business, although there are exceptions such as John Harvey Jones of ICI, who develop an intrapreneurial style of management within a large organisation.

Moreover, large organisations may discourage the employment and advancement of entrepreneurial individuals. This is because the presence of entrepreneurs within a large company could possibly alienate other important managers within the organisation, especially if those individuals' career development is dependent upon conforming to the accepted structures and norms of the corporation. Other barriers to intrapreneurship within a corporate setting include the following.

14.7.1 Traditional corporate structures

The hierarchical nature of large corporations is not conducive to entrepreneurial behaviour, with considerable 'distance' between the top layers of management and the lowest level of the workforce, resulting in an impersonal relationship between management and staff. Multiple layers of management can also lead to many layers of approval between the potential intrapreneur and the person in charge of resources. For example, if a shop-floor worker in a manufacturing plant comes up with an idea to improve the production process, then the permission to develop the idea further usually comes from three or four levels of authority higher up, with each level having the potential to reject the proposal before it reaches someone with the responsibility and authority for funding.

14.7.2 Corporate culture

The nature of corporate culture itself – where job descriptions are rigidly enforced – may stifle innovation. The established procedures, reporting systems, lines of authority and control mechanisms of a traditional hierarchical organisation are there to support the existing management structure, and not to promote creativity and innovation (Krueger, 1998). For example, the reporting procedures of large firms are usually centred on the short-term needs of budget officers and performance measurements. Managers are therefore taught to think in terms of short-term cycles.

14.7.3 Large firm performance standards

The performance standards imposed by large businesses, especially in the short term, may adversely affect the development of intrapreneurial projects, many of which are long-term in nature. In many large organisations, short-term profits are generally used as the main measurement of a company's success. This is because increased short-term profits will support the company's share price and thus attract new investors. This will lead to pressure on managers to devise short-term strategies rather than look to long-term investment. Entrepreneurial activities, especially innovative new projects, will take time to develop sufficiently, and a short-term policy attitude will lead to problems with regard to financing such projects. Any mistakes may also be damaging to the personal reputation of the individual intrapreneur, who may be removed from the project prematurely and replaced with a less entrepreneurial corporate manager.

14.7.4 Planning procedures

The planning procedures within large organisations can stifle entrepreneurship. Generally, as companies get bigger the corporate environment will require more control and specific performance standards to exert this control. Thus paperwork and reporting standards on projects may take precedence over entrepreneurial and innovative behaviour. In some cases, this can lead to 'underground innovation', where intrapreneurs become involved in product innovations that are not authorised by the organisation (Abetti, 1997). Instead, they are carried out in secret in the intrapreneur's own time until they are so near market readiness that they cannot be stopped.

14.7.5 Ownership

Total ownership and the associated independence in decision making is one of the primary motivations in entrepreneurship. Within large companies, however, ownership of the assets of the intrapreneurial part of the business is rarely possible, except in the case of a management buy-out. Furthermore, the intrapreneur will have difficulty in retaining total ownership of the idea from its development stage to its final marketing due to the functional nature of management within a large organisation. As such, the influence of the intrapreneur on the innovative idea may be diluted by other individuals within the organisation.

14.7.6 Mobility of managers

Mobility of managers within large organisations may lead to a lack of commitment to specific projects, especially if those projects are of a long-term nature, as many intrapreneurial ones are. This may lead to a change in priorities by different managers for the project, thus losing the continuity associated with new product development within small companies. The flexibility to change the direction of projects may prove difficult if it impinges upon the activities of other departments within the company.

14.7.7 Inappropriate reward systems

In many large companies, there are often inappropriate methods to compensate creative employees. Rewards are normally based on improvements in strict performance measures laid down by management, with very little scope for a reward basis based on creativity and innovation. Promotion to management – the normal route for talented individuals within a large corporation – is seldom an attractive reward to intrapreneurs. This is because it normally takes them out of the job in which they have displayed their innovative talents and places them into a managerial position with increased administrative responsibilities.

However, despite these problems, there are a number of initiatives a large organisation can take which can create an environment that is conducive to innovation and entrepreneurship.

14.8 Intrapreneurial characteristics – who is the intrapreneur?

Studies have shown that managers and entrepreneurs vary considerably across a range of behavioural patterns. As Bouchard (2002) notes, their strategic orientation, the nature of their commitment, the way they access and consume resources and how they organise can be described as radically divergent. Indeed, what a corporate manager can accomplish well constitutes a major challenge for the entrepreneur, and vice versa. For example, corporate managers and their organisations are good at improving proven recipes while entrepreneurs are good at seizing opportunities and creating value through innovation and responsiveness. Given this, there have been doubts expressed as to whether large companies, through management education and action learning projects, can turn managers into corporate entrepreneurs (Thornberry, 2003).

However, various studies suggest that this may be possible if the best of both types of individual are brought together into one set of competences. Vandermerwe and Birley (1997) have suggested that intrapreneurial organisations often need a new type of person who can bridge the two worlds between the entrepreneurial and the corporate world. Indeed, the set of skills that define the intrapreneur are quite different from the skills needed by either the traditional corporate manager or the entrepreneur (see Table 14.1). For example, unlike entrepreneurs, intrapreneurs will need team-building skills and a

Table 14.1 Managers, entrepreneurs and intrapreneurs

	Traditional managers	Traditional entrepreneurs	Intrapreneurs
Organisational attributes			
Attitude to organisation	Sees organisation as nurturing and protective, seeks position within it	May advance rapidly in a firm – when frustrated, rejects the system and forms his/her own firm	Dislikes the organisational system
Managerial satisfaction	Pleases others (higher in the organisational hierarchy)	Pleases self and customers	Pleases self, customers and sponsors
Primary motives	Wants promotion and other traditional corporate rewards	Wants freedom. Goal-oriented, self-reliant and self-motivated	Wants freedom and access to corporate resources
Relationship with others	Organisational hierarchy as basic relationship	Transactions and deal-making as basic relationship	Transactions within organisational hierarchy
Managerial attributes			
Decisions	Agrees with those in power/delays decisions for superiors	Follows private vision. Decisive, action-oriented	More patient and willing to compromise than entrepreneur
Delegation of action	Delegates action – reporting and supervising takes most of time	Gets hands dirty and can upset employees by doing their work	Gets hands dirty – can do work but knows how to delegate
Management attention	Primarily on events inside the organisation	Primarily on technology and market-place	Both inside – management on needs of venture – and outside of firm – focus on customers
Market research	Has market studies done to discover needs and guide product/service concepts	Creates needs. Talks to customers and forms own opinions	Does own market research and intuitive market evaluation like the entrepreneur
Problem-solving style	Works out problems within the system	Escapes problems in formal structures by leaving to start own business	Works out problems within the system, or bypasses it without leaving
Skills	Professional management. Abstract analytical tools, people management and political skills	Knows business intimately. More business acumen than managerial skill. Often technically trained	Very like the entrepreneur, but situation demands greater ability to prosper within the organisation

▶

Table 14.1 (cont'd)

	Traditional managers	Traditional entrepreneurs	Intrapreneurs
Personal attributes			
Personal attributes	Can be forceful and ambitious – fearful of others' ability to harm career development	Self-confident, optimistic, courageous	Self-confident; courageous – cynical about system but optimistic about ability to outwit it
Educational level	Highly educated	Transactions and deal-making as basic relationship	Transactions within hierarchy
Failure and mistakes	Strives to avoid mistakes and surprises. Postpones recognising failure	Deals with mistakes and failures as learning experiences	Attempts to hide risky projects from view so can learn from mistakes without public failure
Family history	Family members worked for large organisations	Entrepreneurial small business, professional/farm background	Entrepreneurial small business, professional or farm background
Risk	Careful	Likes moderate risk. Invests heavily but expects to succeed	Likes moderate risk – unafraid of dismissal so little personal risk
Status	Cares about status symbols	Happy sitting on an orange crate if job is getting done	Dismisses traditional status symbols – covets symbols of freedom

Source: Adapted from Pinchot (1986)

firm understanding of both business and market realities, while also possessing the leadership and rapid decision-making qualities of successful owner-managers. Therefore, in developing intrapreneurs, the task for organisational managers is to identify those individuals that possess the managerial skills to manage a project within the boundaries of a large organisation *and* the entrepreneurial skills to be able to take the project forward (Jansen and van Wees, 1994).

14.8.1 Managerial skills

The managerial skills required by an intrapreneur are as follows.

The ability to adopt a multi-disciplinary role

At the beginning, it will only be the intrapreneur who will have a sufficient grasp of the concepts or ideas that they want to put forward within the organisation. Whilst intrapreneurs frequently have a background in one particular business discipline, such as development or marketing, they must be able to adopt a multidisciplinary approach when they become involved with the development of their own ideas into a viable business. This may often mean crossing boundaries between functions in the organisation.

Understanding the environment

The intrapreneur needs to understand the environment and its many aspects to establish a successful intrapreneurial venture. An individual must understand how their creativity can affect both the internal and external environments of the corporation.

Encouragement of open discussion

Open discussion must be encouraged to develop a good team for creating something new. A successful new intrapreneurial venture can only be formed when the team involved feels the freedom to disagree and critique an idea to reach the best solution. The degree of openness obtained depends on the degree of openness of the intrapreneur.

Creation of management options

The intrapreneur must challenge the beliefs and assumptions of the corporation and through this create something new in a largely bureaucratic organisation.

Building a coalition of supporters

Openness will lead to the establishment of a strong coalition of supporters and encouragers – the intrapreneur must encourage and affirm each team member, particularly during the problem times. This encouragement is very important, as the usual motivators of career paths and job security are not operational in establishing a new intrapreneurial venture.

14.8.2 Entrepreneurial skills

Some of the entrepreneurial skills required by the intrapreneur include the following.

Vision and flexibility

The intrapreneur must be a visionary leader, a person who 'dreams great dreams'. To establish a successful new venture, the intrapreneurial leader must have a dream and overcome all obstacles by selling this dream to others within the organisation, especially those in influential positions. However, whilst intrapreneurs are visionary, their dream is usually grounded in business experience, mainly because they realise that their dreams can only become reality if they themselves take action to turn an idea into a viable business proposition.

Action-oriented

Intrapreneurs tend to start doing immediately, rather than spending time planning the development of their idea in detail. Often, they do not wait for permission to begin their ideas. Instead, they will go ahead with the development of their ideas, often in their own time. Unlike managers, who often delegate responsibilities to subordinates, intrapreneurs will often be involved in a number of tasks associated with the intrapreneurial project, predominantly because of their affinity towards turning their vision directly into reality through their own efforts.

Dedication

Traditional product development systems cannot compete with intrapreneurship for one simple reason – they are too bureaucratic to enable or encourage dedication. Traditional managers will divide marketing and technology, vision and action, and a host of other responsibilities into separate jobs, which will deny intrapreneurs the commitment, responsibility and excitement that inspires total dedication. In some cases this dedication can be extreme, often to the extent of putting the priorities of the project before the people involved – intrapreneurs will prefer to get the job done on time rather than meeting people's needs.

Persistence in overcoming failure

The intrapreneur must persist through the frustration and obstacles that will inevitably occur during the creation of a new venture. Only through persistence will a new venture be created and successful commercialisation take place. More importantly, intrapreneurs (like entrepreneurs) tend to see failure as a learning experience – a temporary setback from which the idea can be improved.

Setting self-determined goals

The intrapreneur often sets personal goals for the project, rather than those corporate goals linked to short-term needs such as reporting procedures, etc. These goals are often related to high personal standards, as intrapreneurs gain little satisfaction from adhering to standards imposed by others.

14.9 Learning and the intrapreneurial firm

An increasingly complex business environment, where rapid changes in technology, competition, regulation and customer needs are the norm, has led to the search for new ways in which large firms can develop the right capabilities by which they can continuously anticipate the need for change. Therefore, organisational learning – which supports continuous adaptation and change – has captured the imagination of academics and managers who are trying to understand the increasingly chaotic environment in which organisations exist and operate.

Much of the recent literature on corporate entrepreneurship has indicated the importance of learning to the creation of an entrepreneurial culture within large firms (Baden-Fuller and Stopford, 1992; Zahra, 1999; Dess *et al.*, 2003), especially with regard to developing a learning organisation within an increasingly competitive business environment.

14.9.1 The learning organisation

The learning organisation can be defined as an organisation skilled at creating, acquiring and transferring knowledge, and at modifying its behaviour to reflect knowledge and insights (Garvin, 1993). New ideas are essential if learning is to take place and, whatever the sources, these ideas are the trigger for organisational improvement within the large firm. The development of such new ideas, and their implementation, is at the heart of intrapreneurial behaviour within large firms.

It is worth emphasising that all organisations are involved in a learning process, either as part of a corporate strategy or through their individual 'members'. Organisational learning is affected either directly or indirectly by individual learning, although organisational learning should not simply be counted as the sum of each member's learning (Kim, 1993). This is because organisations, unlike individuals, develop and maintain learning systems that not only influence their immediate members but are also then transmitted to others by way of organisational histories and norms (Fiol and Lyles, 1985).

Collective learning is therefore one of the major features that differentiate organisational learning from individual learning. Even when organisational members leave and leadership changes, knowledge and skills developed and shared among the members through learning can be accumulated and preserved in organisations' memories. Consequently, these routines and memories stored in the form of manuals, procedures, symbols, rituals and myths influence and determine the direction and scopes of individual and organisational learning (Romme and Dillen, 1997).

Although all organisations are assumed to be learning, the impacts derived from the learning differ according to the input and resources invested. Organisational learning starts with the intention and willingness to learn, which is articulated and supported by top management and shared by the members of organisations. Without providing appropriate tools and platforms for learning to be implemented in an organisation, effective learning will not take place.

Therefore, the development of an effective learning organisation requires a deliberate intervention by leaders to establish the necessary internal conditions for the growing firm to operate in a learning mode (Goh and Richards, 1997). Learning takes time and thus the early identification and assessment of the impact of the factors leading to learning within growing firms could help managers focus on specific interventions required to improve learning within organisations. An analysis of previous research into this area (Yoo et al., 2004) has shown that three major factors promote organisational learning, namely learning commitment, learning readiness and open-mindedness.

Learning commitment

Organisational learning requires a commitment by the organisation and whilst learning intent reflects the decision that the organisation intends to engage in learning, organisational commitment refers to the implementation of its intent. Therefore, whereas intention is the equivalent of vision and an antecedent to action, the firm's action in carrying out its intention is called learning commitment. Here the word 'commitment' is used in the sense of a firm's dedication to its learning intent and it is the firm's sincere and steadfast adherence to the goal of learning. Such commitment is action-oriented and would normally manifest itself in actions such as the setting aside and devoting a portion of its resources towards the learning infrastructure, systems, activities, training and development, policies and procedures needed for organisation learning. In undertaking such actions, the development of a more entrepreneurial culture will begin to manifest itself across the organisation.

Learning readiness

Although organisations may commit resources to address organisational learning, the difference between different organisations in their actual learning may be because of different levels of organisation readiness. In the same way that units in the military, with their training and preparation for mobilisation for war, may be at differing levels of operational readiness, organisations depending on activities, resources and commitment would also be at differing levels of learning readiness. Organisations that have yet to build the capabilities required for learning would be less ready than those that have. Such capabilities include appropriate and timely feedback and appraisal on learning, and shared values among the members of organisations.

Open-mindedness

This is the willingness to critically evaluate the organisation's operational routine and accept new ideas (Calantone *et al.*, 2002). In many instances, mental models (or deeply held images of how the world works) limit us to familiar ways of thinking and acting (Day and Nedungadi, 1994). When large businesses proactively question long-held routines, assumptions and beliefs, they are engaging in the first phase of what is known as 'unlearning', something many entrepreneurs will undertake on a regular basis to gain market advantage. Unlearning is at the heart of organisational change and intrapreneurial development, and open-mindedness is an organisational value that may be necessary for unlearning efforts to transpire (Sinkula *et al.*, 1997). Therefore, organisational learning starts with the intention and willingness to learn. Without providing appropriate tools and platforms for learning to be implemented within the organisation, effective learning will not take place.

14.9.2 Barriers to organisational learning

Prior to designing a learning culture within an organisation, it is necessary to recognise and identify the possible barriers to learning that are likely to occur. Early detection and elimination of the factors that inhibit the implementation of learning within an organisation is equally as important as building the platform for learning to occur. To date, only a few studies have attempted to identify the barriers to organisational learning.

For example, Bierly and Hamalainen (1995) suggested four impediments to organisational learning, namely environmental stability, structure of the organisation, organisational culture, and the need for the organisation to unlearn. According to their research, an open decentralised structure is typically more flexible, adaptive and responsive to external and internal stimuli. In turn, this not only affects inter-functional communication and learning within the organisational structure but plays a role in determining who communicates most frequently with, and influences, the top management.

An organisation's culture can also either facilitate or impede the different types of learning. A culture that emphasises risk-taking, openness in communication, and teamwork and that ensures that these values are shared and rewarded throughout the organisation will facilitate internal learning (Starbuck, 1992).

On the other hand, if the values of the organisation do not support and promote openness to outside knowledge sources, external learning can be impeded by the organisational culture. For example, a not-invented-here (NIH) syndrome will develop where alternative ideas and knowledge are rejected simply because it is thought that the organisation members' own ideas must be superior to outside sources. This attitude, combined with 'avoiding ambiguity' on information, can deter learning from external sources. Adams *et al.* (1998) state that organisations with a long history of stable practice have developed routines for filtering out ambiguous information because such information is anathema in a system that focuses on meeting standardised operating outcomes and maintaining stability (Nelson and Winter, 1982). People concentrate instead on codified information that fits into prevailing expectations, or they redefine ambiguous problem situations as standardised ones for which information is readily available. Thus, avoiding ambiguity is a major organisational barrier to information acquisition.

Another impediment to learning is 'compartmentalised thinking.' Many large, established organisations break tasks down into separate steps, and give people a clear role to play and set of requirements to meet. The shared mental models that develop in these organisations reflect different functional thought worlds (Dougherty, 1992). Thus, different groups in these organisations often have different targets and tend to evaluate the same outcome differently (Levitt and March, 1988). These routines lead to compartmentalised thinking and each department focuses on its own goals and, as a result, information either does not cross intra-organisational boundaries or is interpreted quite differently on 'the other side'. Poor communication between people and between organisations can be a major block to learning and quality improvement. Therefore, intra-organisational knowledge sharing refers to collective beliefs or behavioural routines related to the spread of learning among different units within an organisation (Moorman and Miner, 1997) and keeps alive the knowledge and information gathered from various sources, serving as reference for future action (Lukas *et al.*, 1996).

Finally, organisational 'inertia' is one of the greatest barriers to learning. Organisational change is difficult and inertia is resistance to change or, at least, resistance to changes that run counter to a fundamental existing orientation (Miller, 1993). An organisation's prior history (memory) constrains its future behavior in that learning tends to be premised on local processes of search (Levitt and March, 1988). Therefore, organisations often resist change even when their environments threaten them with extinction because a whole learning system is bound together by a theory of action. As a result, radically new situations require that theories of action be replaced, but organisations have difficulties doing this (Argyris and Schon, 1978). This is because organisational myths, norms and procedures that have worked well in the past are very difficult to change. Thus, many successful organisations tend to become complacent, learn too little and eventually fail (Nystrom and Starbuck, 1984). Unlearning is a prerequisite for generative learning to take place and is the process through which learners discard knowledge and make room for new responses and mental maps, although the process can take time and resources and lead to a temporary state of organisational paralysis. Organisations that have been poisoned by their success are therefore often unable to unlearn obsolete knowledge in spite of strong disconfirmation (Nystrom *et al.*, 1976) and unlearning is needed in order to make room for more adequate interpretative frameworks and responses in organisational memory.

14.9.3 External learning within intrapreneurial organisations

Intrapreneurial success among large firms has been largely described in the form of new product successes, such as the 3M *Post It* note (Brand, 1998). Therefore, for intrapreneurial organisations, the success of new products is also the dimension of performance that involves the organisation's ability to adapt to changing conditions and opportunities in the environment (Walker and Ruekert, 1987). In this regard, successful intrapreneurial organisations rely on external information to detect opportunities emerging in the environment and which enable them to respond with creative solutions. When such information is transformed through an internalising process and results in the creation of new knowledge, organisational learning can make a contribution to the development of novel products.

The knowledge-based view suggests that an organisation's most important resource is the knowledge embedded within it and the development and enhancement of this knowledge is critical in obtaining competitive advantage of an organisation (Grant, 1996). In particular, heterogeneous knowledge bases and capabilities of an organisation are the main determinants of performance differences, and organisations are therefore advised not only to use different knowledge bases and capabilities in developing knowledge but also to have access to externally generated knowledge (DeCarolis and Deeds, 1999).

In a world of increasing global competition and rapid technological change, organisational success depends on the ability to innovative consistently (Rosenkopf and Nerkar, 2001). As such, technological knowledge sourcing has become an important phenomenon as organisations have come to realise that they can no longer rely solely on in-house technological and knowledge capacity to generate new products, processes and services (Howells *et al.*, 2003).

As a result, innovative organisations are establishing greater linkages with other actors to access external knowledge and to benefit from the processes of knowledge interaction (Caloghirou *et al.*, 2004; Howells *et al.*, 2003). In many cases, this is due to an increasing recognition that competitiveness now depends not merely on the capabilities that an organisation can create and exploit internally, but on the effectiveness with which it can gain access and utilise sources of technological knowledge and capabilities beyond its boundaries (Howells *et al.*, 2003).

Organisations can either develop their own technologies through in-house R&D or source technologies via research cooperation or contracting arrangements such as licensing or outsourcing, and the learning attached to both types of technology development has advantages and disadvantages.

For example, internal knowledge development can make it difficult for other firms to imitate the competence and thus yield a sustained competitive advantage (Prahalad and Hamel, 1990), although focusing on internal development only may be high risk and involve major investments for the organisation. As a result, large amounts of organisational resources are typically required for an organisation to be successful at internal learning. However, these efforts may not produce results and could leave the organisation at a competitive disadvantage to those that are more efficient in internal learning (Bierly and Hamalainen, 1995).

In contrast, it is recognised that external learning is required to develop a broader knowledge base and to keep abreast of cutting-edge technologies. This approach increases flexibility and is critical to organisations operating within a dynamic environment (Grant, 1996). However, external knowledge typically takes longer to integrate into new products because it is harder to understand and interpret, as the external knowledge needs to be translated into a new language so that organisational members can understand and interpret its meaning. This is particularly the case if the new external knowledge is to be combined in a complex manner with existing internal knowledge. If the use of many different complementary technologies results in a new product, it may be very difficult to integrate new external knowledge that is based on different cognitive frameworks. Thus, product and process development may be slower for firms relying on external learning (Bierly and Hamalainen, 1995).

Although the organisation of innovation along the internal versus external sourcing dimension is considered to be a complex issue (Veugelers and Cassiman, 1999), both learning types are mutually interdependent and complementary processes. For example, Cohen and Levinthal (1990) suggest that firms must excel at internal learning and develop 'absorptive capacity' before they can learn from external sources. On the other hand, the internal learning process can be substantially improved by effective external learning, since there will be many new ideas generated outside the organisation. In addition, external learning will enable firms to view some issues from different perspectives, which may be difficult to do with only internal learning due to established organisational routines and biases. Thus, internal and external learning are both vital to success, and each organisation must determine how to balance the internal and external learning to maximise its overall learning (Bierly and Chakrabarti, 1996).

Indeed, high-technology sectors are more likely to be able to take advantage of complementarities between internal and external technology sourcing, and most organisations use a combination of both 'make' and 'buy' technology strategies, although smaller organisations have a higher probability of using an exclusive 'make or buy' strategy and are less likely to combine these technology-sourcing strategies compared with larger organisations. They may therefore use less combinatory strategies, but when they do so, they could use them more intensively and productively (Veugelers and Cassiman, 1999).

Certain types of organisational culture, such as underlying values and beliefs of organisations, are believed to impede learning from external sources. If the values of the organisation do not support and promote openness to outside knowledge sources, then external learning can be impeded by the organisational culture (Bierly and Hamalainen, 1995). For example, organisations that are intolerant of uncertainty tend to favour and rely on the well-articulated information and knowledge created internally and avoid ambiguous information available from external sources. Adams *et al.* (1998) state that organisations with a long history of stable practice have developed routines for filtering out ambiguous information, which is anathema in a system that focuses on meeting standardised operating outcomes and maintaining stability (Nelson and Winter, 1982). Hence, people concentrate instead on codified information that fits into prevailing expectations or they redefine ambiguous problem situations as standardised ones for which information is readily available.

As discussed earlier, the concept of organisational 'inertia' can be one of the greatest barriers to internal learning and can also impede external learning, especially as it has been argued that interaction is a key concept for knowledge creation and innovation. Thus the openness of organisations to external knowledge sources is an important element when evaluating their innovative potential (Caloghirou *et al.*, 2004). The organisation has to be constantly aware that it should try to avoid institutional lock-in as well as being flexible and responsive enough to be able to meet the demands of the future (Howells *et al.*, 2003). A lack of management comfort with learning from external sources tends to inhibit firms from making full of use of external developments (Tidd and Trewhella, 1997). Organisational inertia is resistance to change or, at least, resistance to changes that run counter to fundamental existing orientations (Miller, 1993) and the tendency to remain with the status quo (Huff *et al.*, 1992). Therefore, organisational inertia in external learning is similar to the concept of the NIH syndrome in the R&D community (Katz and Allen, 1982) that reflects a natural tendency in most employees to be somewhat resistant to change. Employees may feel threatened by new ideas and externally generated ideas may be devalued in an attempt to show support for, and endorsement of, internal projects (Bierly and Daly, 2004).

When an entrepreneurially oriented large business seeks to internalise new technology-based capabilities obtained from external sources, it must be sufficiently large to have considerable in-house technical expertise that can assist the organisation to understand, interpret and realise the benefits of a new idea from the external sources (Mowery *et al.*, 1998). Organisations are required to seek the knowledge and technologies to augment their current technology base and provide additional 'external capabilities' that can be deployed by them. External sources, in combination with the in-house generation of new knowledge, are then deployed to produce new and improved products and processes that are hopefully aligned with future market requirements (Howells *et al.*, 2003). Hence, without the intrapreneurial and learning capability to internalise the knowledge and skills sought from external sources, there is no guarantee that a diffusion of knowledge will occur within a large firm. Therefore, a large firm possessing a strong internalisation capability tends to know where and how to acquire the knowledge and skills required either to complement or advance its current competence base. Hence, the successful intrapreneurial large firm that has a strong capability to internalise knowledge and skills will not only pursue a strong in-house development but will also be actively involved in sourcing externally.

14.10 Chapter summary

This chapter has discussed briefly much of the general knowledge regarding the concept of intrapreneurship, i.e. entrepreneurship within a corporate environment. It has demonstrated that, under certain conditions in the large organisation, the enterprise, innovation and creativity of a small firm can be developed if specific barriers are overcome and certain policies and procedures put in place. It has also shown that the intrapreneur is quite different from the entrepreneur and the corporate manager, often possessing the competencies associated with both types of individuals.

In examining this phenomenon, the chapter has drawn predominantly on literature from the US to examine concepts such as the differences between an entrepreneurial and intrapreneurial venture; the barriers to intrapreneurship within a corporate environment; the climate for intrapreneurship; and, finally, the characteristics of an intrapreneur. To date, very little work has been carried out in the European context on this area. On the one hand, this may be due to the fact that much of modern and innovative management techniques could be described as falling within the sphere of 'intrapreneurship'; on the other hand, it could be that the general concepts of intrapreneurship have yet to penetrate the management of large European organisations in both the public and private sector. However, it is clear that more work needs to be carried out to examine the entrepreneurial practices of organisations that are not classed as SMEs. A clear research agenda needs to be drawn up to test some of the concepts presented in this chapter and to examine whether they exist in the UK and other European countries.

The chapter has also examined the key factors that both enhance and inhibit organisational learning as well as the issues that facilitate external learning within innovative organisations, thus leading to greater intrapreneurial behaviour. Three factors – learning commitment, learning readiness and open-mindedness – enhance organisational learning, which starts with the intention and willingness to learn. Without providing an appropriate platform for learning to take place, learning intent will never be realised. However, excessive reliance on internal learning may lead the organisation to a 'competence trap' by harnessing and focusing on 'core competence', which in turn may become 'core rigidities' and prevent entrepreneurial behaviour within the large organisation. Therefore, access to external sources of technology becomes important in ensuring the large firm's learning and, more importantly, enables it to continue to innovate and remain competitive. A number of key factors – most notably organisational culture and capability – can help to transform externally generated knowledge into a key competitive advantage for the organisation. More importantly, the capability to learn internally can enhance the learning from external sources of different organisations and enable a continuous culture of entrepreneurial behaviour within the firm.

Questions

1 Discuss the main changes that need to take place within a large organisation to ensure that it changes its corporate style to one that is intrapreneurial.

2 What are the main differences in establishing a new venture independently and a new venture within an existing large organisation?

3 What are the main characteristics of intrapreneurs and how do these differ from those of the 'traditional' entrepreneur?

4 In order to base decisions on the most up-to-date information, corporate entrepreneurs must put systems in place to increase their capability to better understand information in the external environment. In your opinion, what are the most important factors for intrapreneurs and policy makers in ensuring this approach is successful? What are the practical implications of firms utilising external sources of knowledge?

Web links

www.intrapreneur.com/
A site established by Gifford Pinchot III who established much of the original thought on intrapreneurship. Contains many articles on the subject.

www.usasbe.org/knowledge/proceedings/1998/18-Herbert.PDF
'The future of the corporation: corporate entrepreneurship on the fly' by Herbert and Brazeal (1998), which examines the factors that can affect the overall development of corporate entrepreneurship.

http://mba.tuck.dartmouth.edu/pdf/2002-2-0002.pdf
A case study of 3M and the policies it has put into place to develop an intrapreneurial culture.

www.lsda.org.uk/files/pdf/1685.pdf
A research report 'Learning without lessons – supporting learning in small businesses', which examines some of the challenges in installing a learning culture within small firms.

CHAPTER 15

Leadership, entrepreneurship and management of small businesses

David A. Kirby

15.1 Introduction

Before it is possible to consider leadership and the management of small businesses, it is necessary to examine the concept of entrepreneurship and its relationship to the small business. Although the term entrepreneurship is often equated with new venture creation and small business management, and the concepts of the owner-manager and self-employment (Gibb, 1996), it is contested here and elsewhere (Kirby, 2003) that the term is much broader than these concepts would suggest. Not all owner-managers can be regarded as entrepreneurs, nor are all small businesses entrepreneurial. This point has been recognised in the literature by Carland *et al.* (1984: 358) who have suggested that there is a clear distinction between the entrepreneur and the entrepreneurial venture and the small business owner and the small business venture. Indeed, they suggest that: 'An entrepreneur is an individual who establishes and manages a business for the principal purpose of profit and growth. The entrepreneur is characterised principally by innovative behaviour and will employ strategic management practices in the business. An entrepreneurial venture is one that engages in a least one of Schumpeter's four categories of behaviour: that is, the principal goals of an entrepreneurial venture are profitability and growth and the business is characterised by innovative strategic practices' (Carland *et al.*, 1984: 358).

This distinction between small firms and entrepreneurial ventures and the distinction between entrepreneurship, leadership and management is considered further in the work of Bjerke and Hultman (2003). Although they do not distinguish between the entrepreneur and the founder of a small firm, they do suggest that 'it is safe to state that whether a firm will start to grow or not depends mainly on the entrepreneur. The entrepreneur's attitude towards growth and his or her appreciation of the impact that successful growth will have on the new firm will be crucially determining factors.' They then go on to differentiate between the three concepts of management, leadership and entrepreneurship, suggesting that: management is an occupation requiring technical skills to be able to run a business; leadership is a role requiring 'social skills in order to make other people work' (op. cit.: 75); and entrepreneurship is the means to drive change requiring mental skills. These distinctions are necessary, they contest, in order to recognise that 'in different periods of a firm, a different combination of management, leadership and entrepreneurship are needed'. The contention here is that this is not necessarily the case but that there is a distinction between small firms that fail to grow and entrepreneurial ventures that do, and that the entrepreneur who drives these growth organisations will need to be, at all times, not just a good manager, but also a leader.

15.2 Learning objectives

There are four learning objectives in this chapter:

1 To appreciate the inter-relationship between entrepreneurship and leadership in the management of small firms.

2 To recognise the difference between transactional and transformational leaders.

3 To be aware of how owner-managers may be developed as transformational leaders.

4 To recognise the role of entrepreneurial leaders and how they achieve their objectives.

Key concepts

- leadership ■ entrepreneurship ■ management ■ transactional leadership
- entrepreneurial leadership   ■ small business

15.3 Concepts of leadership and entrepreneurship

To justify the contention proposed above, it is necessary, perhaps, to examine in more detail the concepts of leadership and entrepreneurship. This has been done, already, by Perren (undated) in a working paper prepared for the UK Council for Excellence in Management and leadership. In it he compares the conceptual building blocks between the two terms and concludes that 'entrepreneurship and leadership are similar notions and there are conceptual overlaps, but there are clearly still conceptual differences. Leadership tends to be more associated with the conceptual building blocks that relate to people (e.g. communication and social skills). Entrepreneurship, on the other hand, tends to be associated with the personal search for independence and identification of market opportunities' (Perren, undated: 6). In particular, he concludes that leadership and entrepreneurship share the same conceptual building blocks of personal drive, innovation and vision and risk acceptance.

Whilst this analysis does provide some extremely valuable insights into the two concepts, it is not without its limitations as he recognises. Not least it needs to be recognised that the aim of the study was to obtain the broadly accepted building blocks of the terms entrepreneur(ship) and leader(ship), rather than to discover all of the concepts that have been attached to these terms, and that in order to do this 'a certain level of interpretation of an author's intention is needed to stop the list of conceptual building becoming unwieldy'. Clearly, this filtering could impact considerably on the outcomes of the analysis. For example, it would no doubt be possible 'to find texts that have associated the conceptual building blocks in a different way', as the author recognises, or 'for other researchers to have different ideas about the terms'. Indeed, it may be for this reason that the research concludes, somewhat surprisingly perhaps, that a key distinction between entrepreneurs and leaders is in terms of their communication and social skills. In many works it is acknowledged that entrepreneurs are good communicators with networking skills that enable them not just to articulate their vision but to persuade others to share in it, thereby enabling them to harness the resources (both human and capital) needed to bring it about. This could, in fact, be a definition of entrepreneurship.

Although there is no standard definition of the term 'entrepreneurship', it should be recognised that the term entrepreneur is derived from the French verb *entreprendre* (to undertake). The entrepreneur is, then, an 'undertaker', someone who can make things happen. She may work for herself harnessing the resources to enable her vision to be fulfilled but, increasingly, she works as part of a team either as an owner-manager of a small venture or part of a larger organisation. It is here that the links with leadership emerge.

According to Adair (1986: 116), 'many of us tend still to believe that "a leader" implies one person dominating another or a group of people'. Indeed, this is implied in the Bjerke and Hultman quotation above where they suggest that entrepreneurs require the social skills to make people work. Good leaders do not do this and while such a strategy can be extremely effective in the short term, it is not sustainable long term. Employees quickly begin to feel exploited, resulting in high levels of staff absenteeism, turnover and even sabotage and aggression. The art of leadership is to hold employees accountable for results while, at the same time, maintaining morale and employee satisfaction. Indeed, according to Wickens (1999: 52) leadership 'is about getting people to do what you want them to do because they want to do it for you', and, perhaps, for themselves. This is what the truly successful entrepreneur excels at. He has a vision and is able to 'sell' that vision to others in order to ensure fulfilment. In a small firm context, it is contested that vision would be not just survival but growth and development for, as Timmons (1989: 1) has recognised, entrepreneurship is 'the ability to create and build something from practically nothing. It is initiating, doing, achieving, and building an enterprise or organisation'.

Having considered, then, the links between leadership, entrepreneurship and small firms, it is perhaps necessary to look at some of the traditional theories of leadership and how they might apply in an entrepreneurship/small business context.

Theories of leadership

theories are commonly grouped into four broad categories, as follows.

15.4.   of leadership traits

This is on   arliest approaches to the study of leadership. It assumes that leaders have certain   sonal characteristics such as sociability, persistence, initiative, know-how, self-confidence, perception/insight, cooperativeness, popularity, adaptability, good communication skills, etc. While it has been acknowledged that such traits are important, over the years it has become recognised that 'a person does not become a leader by virtue of the possession of some combination of traits, but by patterns of personal characteristics, activities and goals of the followers' (Stogdill, 1948: 64). Leadership is actually invested in a person by her followers based, as Wickens (1999) suggests, on their respect for her ability, their trust in her, their sharing of her goals and whether or not they are inspired by her.

15.4.2 Theories of leadership style

This is one of the most widely researched aspects of leadership. Generally, attention has focused on the emphasis that the leader places on the task and the people undertaking it. Essentially there is thought to be a continuum with concern for production at one end and concern for people at the other. Using this concept, Tannenbaum and Schmidt (1973) have suggested that leaders can be classified as:

- *autocratic* – they dictate what they want;
- *persuasive* – they sell their ideas;
- *consultative/participative* – they discuss with the team members before reaching a decision;
- *democratic* – they involve the team members in both the discussion and the decision.

How the leader manages these determines the kind of organisational climate that is created. However, it is generally accepted that the most effective leaders are open, candid and employee-centred, but the style of leadership depends on a range of situational factors.

15.4.3 Situational theories

These relate to the group environment, its physical setting, the size of the group, its technical abilities, the authority given to the leader by his superiors, etc. Perhaps the greatest attention has been focused on the role of communication in the group. The person at the centre of the communication system is often seen as the leader since group members come to him for information.

15.4.4 Integrative theories

These are the most comprehensive and realistic but least precise or conclusive. They embrace a wide variety of variables and from them it is possible to ascertain that the successful leader is aware of the great many forces affecting her effectiveness and is able to determine the most important forces operating at any particular time. Possibly two of the most significant contributions to this field are Fiedler's (1967) contingency theory and the work of Tannenbaum and Schmidt (1973), which identifies the factors or forces a leader needs to consider when deciding how to lead. The former suggests that the leader's performance can be improved by changing either her personality and motivation pattern or the favourableness of her situation. In contrast, the latter suggests that the way a leader should lead is decided by the forces invested in her (personal value system, confidence in her subordinates, own leadership inclinations, own feelings of security), her subordinates (their need for independence, their willingness to assume responsibility, their tolerance of ambiguity, their interest, their understanding of the group's goals and objectives, their knowledge and experience, their expectations with respect to the decision-making process) and the situation (the type of organisation, the effectiveness of the group, the problem and the urgency).

15.5 Leadership in practice

As mentioned earlier, the leader gets a task completed by developing good relationships with colleagues and harnessing their combined resources. According to Appell (1984: 173), it is the leader's task to 'arouse and unite followers towards a common goal. A true leader fulfills this function by being aware of changing group needs, by arousing these needs so that they become transformed into demands . . . and by organising the group so that these demands can be met through group action'. The leader 'arouses and unites' colleagues by:

- listening to them and gaining their respect and trust;
- being friendly and approachable but remaining sufficiently distant to exert authority;
- treating them as equals without losing the capacity to exert authority;
- paying attention to their individual as well as their collective needs;
- involving them in agreeing objectives, reviewing results, solving problems, etc.;
- representing their interests.

Colleagues' resources are harnessed by ensuring they:

- fully understand their goals and objectives and, as far as possible, are involved in determining them;
- know how they are going to achieve these objectives and are party to deciding and agreeing the course of action to be taken;
- are empowered to make decisions;
- know and agree the control to be exercised over them;
- are aware of the rewards and penalties of not achieving their objectives;
- trust and respect the leader's judgement.

15.6 Leadership development

As with entrepreneurship itself, there is considerable debate over whether leaders are born or made. While it is generally accepted that the natural, truly inspirational leaders are probably born, there is a growing acceptance that leadership capability, as in other areas, can be developed and/or enhanced. Indeed, Handy (1997) has suggested that leaders are grown, not made. Clearly, leaders need followers and in any organisation aspiring 'leaders' can secure the hearts and minds of their employees quite easily using a series of recognised 'currencies'. These include buying support with:

- economic currencies – rewarding loyal colleagues fiscally, with promotion and/or with perks;
- political currencies – rewarding loyal colleagues through protection or patronage;
- psychological currencies – using anger and threats to create a climate of fear that encourages loyalty;
- empowerment currency – rewarding desired behaviour with increased authority and power.

Such 'transactional' leaders exist within most organisations and, while they continue to have a role to play in many successful organisations, their long-term effectiveness is somewhat limited and their days are probably numbered. Their strength lies not in their true leadership abilities but in the power transferred to them, often by their positions in the organisation. These are not powerful people in their own right but people who have either acquired power through, usually, the control of budgets or/and the misuse of their positional power. They have 'led' through fear and patronage rather than through trust and respect. Often they have not been agents for change in organisations but enforcers of the status quo, seeing their subordinates not as an aid to achieving their goals but as a threat. However, not only are the needs of organisations changing, but the contemporary workforce is very different. In an era of very rapid change, increasingly organisations require leaders with vision, who can empower their colleagues and release the creativity within them to move the organisation forward. Also, the workforce is becoming more sophisticated. Employees are becoming more independent, they are more knowledgeable and they are far more mobile than previously. Hence, they have to be managed very differently from in the past and under such circumstances it is the transformational, rather than the transactional, leader that is required and needs to be developed.

Whereas the transactional leader is process or means oriented and uses transactions to maintain performance and, often, the status quo, the transformational leader is innovative, enthusiastic and concerned to empower others in order to create and achieve his vision. Transformational leaders provide a new sense of direction. They are the change agents – the true entrepreneurs. As McKenna (2000: 383) recognises: 'This type of leadership needs to be fostered at all levels in the organisation when the organisation faces . . . a turbulent environment where products have a short shelf life; greater international competition and deregulation of markets; technology becoming obsolete before it is fully depreciated; and demographic changes are anticipated.'

This is precisely the environment that most organisations (both large and small, private sector and public) find themselves in at the beginning of the millennium and it is for this reason that leadership training has emerged as a major growth industry, being provided by universities, private sector consulting organisations and specialist training centres. Numerous bodies have emerged to help create the leaders of the future. Perhaps the one most worthy of note here is the United Nations Institute for Leadership development based at York University in Canada (www.ildglobal.org). Founded in 1999, its mandate is to help define, shape and influence the critical issues concerning young professionals and young entrepreneurs (aged between 21 and 30) around the world. Using a variety of methods, it aims to develop positive attitudes, ethical understanding and a sense of responsibility in its participants, who come from diverse backgrounds, so that they become better decision and policy makers and socially responsible agents for change. Perhaps a more modest, but nonetheless valuable initiative is the UK's 'Common Purpose' programme (www.commonpurpose.org.uk) founded in 1988 by a mother of five young children, Julia Middleton.

15.6.1 Forms of leadership development

Essentially there are three forms of leadership development, as follows.

Formal training

Most formal training is conducted by training professionals, is time-fixed (e.g. a short course) and is away from the place of work. It includes such techniques as behaviour role modelling, case discussion, games and simulations which may be conducted inside or out. In recent years, outdoor challenge programmes have become increasingly popular but it is unclear how effective they are in improving leadership effectiveness.

Developmental activities

These are usually embedded within job assignments and the emphasis is on learning from experience. They can take many forms and include coaching, mentoring and multi-rater feedback, as well as special assignments and job rotation programmes that provide new challenges and the opportunity to develop the requisite skills. Although the research on developmental activities is inconclusive, 'the importance of learning from experience on the job is now widely acknowledged, and researchers have begun to map the relationships between specific experiences and specific leadership competences' (Yukl, 2002: 397).

Self-help activities

As the heading suggests, these are carried out by the individual on his own. The activities range from reading books, viewing videos, listening to audiotapes and using interactive computer programs. In some instances they are intended to be a substitute for formal training, while in others they are used either to supplement it or to facilitate learning from experience. Very little is known, unfortunately, about the effectiveness of such activities and there is scope for research into the extent to which such self-help activities can help individuals develop their leadership capability.

15.6.2 Acquiring skills

Interestingly, research conducted in the UK for the Council for Excellence in Management and Leadership (Perren and Grant, 2001) reported a wide variety of ways in which small firm entrepreneurs acquired their leadership and management skills, covering all three of the above methods. Most prominent, however, were informal methods, which ranged from observation to informal mentoring by business colleagues or a former lecturer. Examples were given of how more formal management courses had helped, though such courses were not portrayed as a substitute for the informal mechanisms. Again, when asked how the support for management and leadership could be improved, the respondents very much emphasised the need for informal fora, where experiences could be shared, and for mentoring and business coaching. On the basis of this evidence, the report concludes that while there has been an increase in the provision of formal support, there is little demand for such schemes from small firms, at least in the UK. It recommends, therefore, that leadership development activities should be an integral part of the entrepreneurial life and need 'to tap seamlessly into the activities that they (the entrepreneurs) would be undertaking as a normal part of running their business' (op. cit.: 16).

Although understanding is still very much in its infancy, contemporary thinking, therefore, is that leaders are best developed in their own work situations, where they can learn by doing. However, it is also recognised that if the leaders of the future are to learn from experience, they need skilled coaching and counselling as well as accurate feedback. Also, they need to be given the opportunity to widen their experience through broad job assignments, job rotation and lateral career moves and be put in positions where they have to move out of their comfort zones and take risks.

This suggests two things. First, perhaps the most appropriate form of leadership development is a formal programme of action learning (Revans: 1982). Essentially, action learning requires the learner to consider problems for which there are no obvious solutions but which can be resolved using prior experience. For Revans, action learning is a process that requires the learner to appreciate that the existing body of knowledge does not provide a solution to the problem under review and it is necessary, therefore, to rely on experience to provide questioning insights. Normally action learning programmes combine formal management training with learning from experience, the participants meeting periodically with a skilled facilitator to consider, and learn from, their experiences. Much emphasis is placed on developing cognitive and interpersonal skills rather than technical knowledge, though the value of action learning to the development of leadership skills is likely to be dependent on the project on which the learner is working. Unless the project involves considerable challenge, it is unlikely to provide much opportunity to develop the skills of leadership.

Second, the extent to which leadership competence is developed depends upon the conditions that prevail within the organisation. Leadership development needs, first of all, to be consistent with the strategic aims of the organisation and any developmental activity needs to be facilitated, supported and reinforced through a coherent and strong learning culture that emphasises the importance of continuous learning and development. According to Yukl (2002), numerous things can be done to create such an environment (see Figure 15.1).

15.7 The entrepreneurial leader

There are numerous definitions of what makes an entrepreneurial leader and, with reference to the work of Hitt *et al.* (1999), Kurakto and Hodgetts (2001: 516) have suggested that 'entrepreneurial leadership can be defined as the ability to anticipate, envision, maintain flexibility, think strategically and work with others to initiate changes that will create a viable future for the organisation'. While there is much in such a definition that is good, it lacks something of the emotional nature of leadership. As

Figure 15.1 Creating a climate for continuous learning

- Job assignments that allow people to pursue their interests and learn new skills
- Work schedules that allow sufficient free time to experiment with new methods
- Financial support for continuing education
- Specialist speakers and skill workshops
- Sabbatical programmes
- Career and self-awareness counselling
- Voluntary skill assessment and feedback programmes
- Pay increases linked to skill development
- Awards for innovation and improvements
- Symbols and slogans that embody values such as experimentation, flexibility, adaptation, self-development, continuous learning and innovation

Source: Yukl, Gary A., *Leadership in Organizations*, 5th Edition, © 2002. Adapted by permission of Pearson Education, Inc., Upper Saddle River, NJ

Tichy and Cohen (1998: 21) have recognised 'leadership is more about thinking, judging, acting and motivating than about strategies, methodologies and tools'.

Good entrepreneurial leaders care about their organisations and their people. They do not impose their solutions on their teams or exclude or suppress potential. Rather they encourage their staff to be creative and to find their own solutions to problems. In some ways, the modern entrepreneurial leader is like the leader of a jazz band. She decides on the music to be played, gathers around her the musicians to play it and then allows them to improvise and use their creativity to interact with each other to create the required sounds. In the process, they have much fun and it is the role of the band's leader to bring out the best in the group.

As in the world of jazz, the authority of entrepreneurial leaders comes from their expertise and values rather from their position and they lead by example, empowering their teams and nurturing leaders at all levels. By so doing, they ensure that the organisation is successful even when they are not around. They do this in the following way:

- Having a vision – entrepreneurial leaders constantly challenge the status quo to see whether they are doing the right things or if what they are doing can be done better or cheaper. They do not just identify the problem, they determine the solution and ensure the required actions are implemented. Thus they see both the problem and the solution.

- Setting the tone and determining the values of the organisation – they are careful to ensure that everything they do reflects the values they espouse and they encourage their people to examine their own values.

- Developing others – they have ideas that they can express and teach others about, coupled with well-developed coaching and teaching skills, as well as a willingness to admit to, and learn from, their mistakes.

- Exhibiting and creating positive energy – they work hard, with a determination that shows they care about the goal the organisation is attempting to achieve. While they never tire, they never use their energy to intimidate. Rather their enthusiasm enthuses others and encourages people to join them. To energise others, leaders:
  - create a sense of urgency – the problem is not going to go away unless something is done;
  - identify a mission worth achieving – the future looks better than the present;
  - set goals that stretch people's abilities – but are achievable;
  - develop a spirit of teamwork – risks are shared;
  - engender a realistic expectation that the team can succeed – they build confidence.
- Facing up to reality and making tough decisions, often with imperfect information. Frequently such decisions are not popular in the short term but the good entrepreneurial leader does not let the difficulty of the decision deter him from doing that which will improve the organisation, even though it may be frightening or painful.

Thus, they may be regarded as 'patient leaders, capable of instilling tangible visions and managing for the long haul. The entrepreneur is at once a learner and a teacher, a doer and a visionary' (Timmons, 1999: 221). However, if there is no immediate problem, entrepreneurial leaders will often 'stir things up' by breaking down established bureaucratic procedures or setting new stretch targets and goals.

According to McGrath and MacMillan (2000), the entrepreneurial leader will know she has succeeded when everyone in the organisation takes it for granted that business success is about a continual search for new opportunities and a continual letting go of less productive activities; feels that she has not only the right but the obligation to seek out new opportunities and make them happen; comes to work excited and is proud to be associated with it; and when the value created within the organisation translates into stakeholder wealth.

McGrath and MacMillan suggest that, to facilitate this, the entrepreneur needs to set the work climate, orchestrate the process of seeking and realising opportunities and become actively involved in identifying and developing new ventures. Setting the climate involves creating a pervasive sense of urgency to be working on the next new initiative. To achieve this, the entrepreneur has to model the sort of behaviour she requires 'consistently, predictably and relentlessly' and to dedicate a disproportionate share of her time, attention and discretionary resources to creating new business propositions. Orchestration involves defining the entrepreneurial directions that can be taken, minimising investment and launch costs until the returns have been fully demonstrated and implanting a discovery-driven philosophy into the organisation by which it is not a crime to fail, only to fail expensively and without learning. Getting involved in identifying and developing new ventures requires that the entrepreneur is not just involved in identifying entrepreneurial insights and converting them into business propositions, but that she:

- builds resolve (i.e. gets people to commit to the launching of a new initiative);
- practises leadership by setting realistic but challenging targets, absorbing uncertainty, defining what must and cannot be accepted, clearing away any obstacles that may arise and by underwriting the proposition;

- keeps a finger on the pulse to monitor progress;
- constantly checks for market acceptance;
- secures deals with key stakeholders;
- pushes the team to initiate revenue flows ahead of cost flows and be realistic in identifying skill deficiencies;
- orchestrates market entry;
- keeps the focus on learning;
- makes sure the team continues to monitor critical sensitivities.

Clearly not all initiatives will succeed and the entrepreneurial leader's role is as critical in failure as it is to success. According to McGrath and MacMillan, the leadership role in the case of failure is first to conduct constructive postmortems to distinguish projects that have failed through bad luck from those that have failed because of bad decision making. Second, the entrepreneurial leader needs to recoup all the benefits from the failed initiative, in particular emphasising to the team that it was the venture that failed not them. Finally, he may have to shut down a project if the team is entrapped in a 'welter of optimism' that prevents it from seeing that the project is doomed.

15.8 Chapter summary

In this chapter an attempt has been made to consider the relationship between entrepreneurship and leadership in the context of small business. It has been contested that there is a distinction between the owner-manager and the entrepreneur and that in order to deliver their vision, entrepreneurs need to possess the skills of the leader. While the role of the entrepreneurial leader is clearly not easy, it can be developed in small-firm owner-managers and, as a characteristic of the leader is that he develops other leaders, then it might be expected that entrepreneurs, through their networking activities, could be used to help develop leadership in others. Entrepreneurial leaders do not possess all of the answers and they are not dictators. Rather, they:

- develop their power by making the people around them more powerful;
- are truthful and sincere, thereby building trust and respect;
- provide direction, not the precise route;
- recognise that their colleagues may have some of the best ideas, especially if they are doing the job every day;
- support their staff when they 'fail' and celebrate their achievements when they succeed;
- learn from failure;
- facilitate change but protect fundamental values;
- broker people and harness the ideas that come from such encounters;
- build relationships through networking;
- expose their colleagues to reality but protect them from danger;

- lead by example and never ask their colleagues to do what they would not do themselves;
- educate and train their staff and create more leaders.

However, as von Bergen and Soper (2002: 71) have suggested, there are really no fixed rules. Rather than relying on one best way at all times, the successful entrepreneurial leader will use 'management techniques in a selective, situationally appropriate manner'. In other words, successful entrepreneurs adjust their management style to fit the situations in which they find themselves in order to maximise performance and achievement. That is the hallmark of good contigency leadership: knowing, possibly intuitively, how to get people to implement the vision because they want to, and that is precisely what entrepreneurs are good at, whether they are found in large or small organisations, in the private or the public sectors.

Questions

1 What are the differences between owner-managers and entrepreneurs, and small firms and entrepreneurial ventures?

2 How do transactional and transformational leaders differ?

3 How might owner-managers be developed into entrepreneurial leaders?

4 What characterises entrepreneurial leaders?

Web links

www.managementandleadershipcouncil.org
Website of the Centre for Excellence in Management and Leadership (CEML). Under publications, there is a report entitled 'Joining Entrepreneurs in their World: Improving Entrepreneurship, Management, and Leadership in UK SMEs'.

www.windsorleadershiptrust.org.uk
The Windsor Leadership Trust brings together top leaders from every sector to reflect on how they can use their influence, decisions and actions to benefit their organisations and wider society. There are a number of good articles on leadership in the publications section.

www.thesystemsthinker.com/PDFs/070101pk.pdf
Read the classic article by Peter Senge on leadership within the learning organisation.

PART 3

The small business

CHAPTER 16

Networking and the small business

Stephen Conway and Oswald Jones

16.1 Introduction

The study of entrepreneurship has often concentrated on either the personality traits of entrepreneurs or upon neoclassical views of rational economic activity. Critics have argued that both approaches are inadequate in explaining entrepreneurial behaviour that is embedded in networks of social relations (Aldrich and Zimmer, 1986). Indeed, research has highlighted the importance of social networks and networking as an entrepreneurial tool for contributing to the establishment, development and growth of small firms. Social networks, for example, have been found to assist small firms in their acquisition of information and advice (Birley, 1985; Carson *et al.*, 1995; Shaw, 1997, 1998), in their supplementing of internal resources (Aldrich and Zimmer, 1986; Jarillo, 1989; Hite and Hesterly, 2001), in their ability to compete (Brown and Butler, 1995; Chell and Baines, 2000; Lechner and Dowling, 2003), and in their development of innovative products (Birley *et al.*, 1991; Rothwell, 1991; Conway, 1997; Jones *et al.*, 1997; Freel, 2000). Gibson (1991: 117–18) contends that 'the more extensive, complex and diverse the web of relationships, the more the entrepreneur is likely to have access to opportunities, the greater the chance of solving problems expeditiously, and ultimately, the greater the chance of success for a new venture'. Thus, paradoxically, whilst entrepreneurs may be characterised by their autonomy and independence, they are also 'very dependent on ties of trust and cooperation' (Johannisson and Peterson, 1984: 1).

Johannisson (2000) argues that the concept of networking helps us focus on entrepreneurship as a collective, rather than an individualistic phenomenon. Similarly, Jones *et al.* (2001: 13) see networks as a way of understanding the 'embeddedness' of entrepreneurial activity; where 'embeddedness refers to the fact that economic action and outcomes, like all social actions and outcomes, are affected by actors' dyadic (pairwise) relations and by the structure of the overall network of relations' (Granovetter, 1992: 33). Jones and Conway (2004: 91) view the network perspective as providing a 'conceptualisation of the entrepreneurial process as a complex and pluralistic pattern of interactions, exchanges and relationships between actors'.

To demonstrate this perspective on entrepreneurship we draw upon the well-known UK case of James Dyson. At one level Dyson illustrates the traditional viewpoint that sees entrepreneurs as 'heroic' individuals who achieve success as a result of their motivation, persistence and hard work. However, a closer reading of Dyson's autobiography, *Against the Odds* (Dyson, 1997), reveals that at crucial stages in all of his business ventures he made extensive use of his wide and diverse social network. The autobiography, for example, highlights the important contribution of Dyson's personal network to his access to finance, legal advice, social and emotional support, marketing and public relations services, as well as to talented young design engineers. Drawing upon this example, as well as other empirical work, it is argued here that the personal or social network should be viewed as an important, and sometimes critical, resource of the entrepreneur. Indeed, for Leonard-Barton (1984: 113), 'entrepreneurs who, for geographic, cultural or social reasons, lack access to *free* information through personal networks, operate with less *capital* than do their well-connected peers'. However, as Birley *et al.* (1991: 58) warn, 'networks do not emerge without considerable endeavour'.

16.2 Learning objectives

This chapter has three learning objectives:

1 To understand the alternative foci of network research in the area of entrepreneurship.

2 To appreciate the social network perspective through examining the Dyson story and focusing on the role and contribution of Dyson's personal network to his entrepreneurial activities.

3 To be aware of the key findings from academic research on entrepreneurial networks.

Key concepts

■ entrepreneurship   ■ social networks   ■ small firm relationships

16.3 Alternative foci of network research in entrepreneurship

The study of 'the entrepreneur' and 'entrepreneurship' from a network perspective originates from the mid-1980s with the work of academics such as Howard Aldrich, Sue Birley, Dorothy Leonard-Barton and Bengt Johannisson. Over the last decade or so, there has been an increasing body of research concerning the role, nature and dynamics of the entrepreneur's network. However, within the entrepreneurship and small firm literature, the term 'network' has been used to describe a variety of phenomena. In particular, the notion of entrepreneurial or small firm networks has been employed with reference to industrial districts (e.g. Piore and Sabel, 1984; Pyke, 1992; Saxenian, 1985; 1990); support structures (e.g. Chaston, 1995; Chaston and Mangles, 1997) and the personal contacts of entrepreneurs and small business owner-managers (e.g. Birley, 1985; Aldrich and Zimmer, 1986). For example, studies have explored the networks of small firms within industrial districts such as Emilia-Romagna in Northern Italy (Piore and Sabel, 1984; Pyke, 1992), and Silicon Valley in California (Saxenian, 1985; 1990). This research has sought to develop an understanding of the networking patterns and collaborative arrangements present within such networks to inform policy makers of their impact upon the competitiveness of small firms. Similar interests have motivated research concerning the networks of support organisations, such as 'Business Links' in England and 'Local Enterprise Companies' in Scotland, which exist to support the creation and growth of small firms. Encouraged by government enthusiasm for collaborative relationships between small firms, this branch of research has sought to inform policy of the nature and extent to which umbrella organisations such as local chambers of commerce and business clubs serve as a catalyst for small firm networking activities, and thus indirectly assist in the establishment and subsequent development and growth of small firms (Chaston, 1995; Chaston and Mangles, 1997).

Research centred on the personal or social networks of the entrepreneur and the small firm owner-manager has been motivated more by an interest in understanding the impact that these networks have upon the ability of such individuals to create, develop and grow their small firms (Birley, 1985; Aldrich and Zimmer, 1986; Aldrich et al., 1986; Aldrich, 1987; Carsrud et al., 1987; Birley et al., 1991; Dubini and Aldrich, 1991). A number of these studies have focused on the impact of gender (Aldrich, 1989; Aldrich et al., 1989; Katz and Williams, 1997; Greve and Salaff, 2003) or ethnicity (Zimmer and Aldrich, 1987) on the nature and role of the entrepreneur's social network. Such research is interested in exploring the full breadth of relationships of entrepreneurs, rather than just the narrower set of 'business' relationships in which small firms are involved. Thus, in contrast to studies concerning industrial districts and support networks, this area of research does not separate or 'abstract' the business relationships of entrepreneurs and small firm owner-managers from the ongoing social relationships within which small firm activities occur.

16.4 An overview of the social network perspective

The 'network' metaphor is a powerful way of viewing social groupings; it changes the imagery from a focus on pairs of relationships to one of 'constellations, wheels, and systems of relationships' (Auster, 1990: 65) and of 'webs' of group affiliations (Simmel, 1955). It is perhaps not surprising then that the social network perspective has been employed extensively since the 1960s to reveal the patterns of relationships and interaction within a wide range of communities and organisations. Whilst the network perspective can and has been used to study the network of relationships between individuals, groups and organisations, for example (i.e. various units of analysis), the social network perspective focuses on the relationships between individuals.

It is useful to distinguish between 'networks' and 'networking'; the network is a social structure, comprised of a set of relationships between a set of individuals, which is viewed as being 'greater than the sum of its parts', while networking can be seen as the activity by which these network relationships are built, nurtured and mobilised, and the 'flows' through these relationships, such as information, money, power and friendship. However, there is also an interplay between a network and the networking that occurs within that social structure; on the one hand the network may constrain or liberate the patterns of interaction and exchanges between network members; on the other, networking behaviour may serve to either ossify the existing network membership and relationships or create a dynamic in the membership and relationships within the network. This interplay of network and networking, that is, structure and agency (i.e. action), is encapsulated by 'structuration' theory (Giddens, 1984).

Thus, when researching social networks and social networking activity, there are four key components that need to be investigated (Conway *et al.*, 2001: 355):

- *actors* – the individuals within the network;
- *links* – the relationships between the individuals within the network;
- *flows* – the exchanges between the individuals within the network; and
- *mechanisms* – the modes of interaction employed by the network members.

We will now introduce the various dimensions of each of these network components.

16.4.1 Dimensions of actors

There is a wide range of dimensions along which individuals can be categorised, from the generic, such as age, gender, family membership, nationality, ethnicity and educational level, to the more specific, such as functional background (e.g. finance, marketing and engineering) or sectoral background. The selection from this wide range of dimensions should be informed by the nature and objective of the research.

16.4.2 Dimensions of links and relationships

The nature of a link or relationship between network members may also vary along a number of dimensions, perhaps the most relevant here being the following:

- *formality* – distinguishes between informal or social linkages and formal linkages, embodied in a written contract, for example;
- *intensity* – is indicated by the frequency of interaction and the amount of flow or transactions between two actors over a given time period (Tichy *et al.*, 1979);
- *reciprocity* – refers to the balance of flow over time between two actors through a given linkage. The link is considered to be 'asymmetric' or 'unilateral', where the flow is unbalanced (i.e. largely one-way), and 'symmetric' or 'bilateral', where the flow is balanced (i.e. two-way). Asymmetric linkages tend to imply some form of inequality in the power relations between two actors (Boissevain, 1974);
- *multiplexity* – signifies the degree to which two actors are linked by multiple role relations (e.g. friend, brother and business partner); the greater the number of role relations linking two actors, the stronger the linkage (Tichy *et al.*, 1979). Boissevain (1974: 30) also argues that 'there is a tendency for single-stranded relations to become many-stranded if they persist over time, and for many-stranded relations to be stronger than single-stranded ones, in the sense that one strand role reinforces others';
- *origin* – this dimension refers to the identification of the events leading to the origin of a linkage. It is intended to incorporate factors such as the context in which the relationship originated and the initiator of the relationship; and
- *motive* – the functional significance of networking does not qualify as a convincing explanation of its occurrence. In addressing this issue, Kreiner and Schultz (1993:

201) argue that 'one must determine the motives and perspectives of the actors who reproduce such patterns'.

16.4.3 Types of 'flow' or 'transaction content'

Tichy *et al.* (1979) distinguish between four types of flow within a network, often termed 'transaction content' with the network literature:

- *affect* – the exchange of friendship between actors;
- *power* – the exchange of power and influence between actors;
- *information* – the exchange of ideas, information and know-how between actors;
- *goods* – the exchange of goods, money, technology or services between actors.

Individuals may 'exchange' any one of these types of transaction content for another, for example goods for money, or information for friendship, although in many cases, as with the latter, this may be implicit rather than explicit. It is also worth pointing out here that the perceived value of the flow or flows between two actors within a network may vary greatly between the 'sender'/'giver' and the 'recipient', and, indeed, by others in the network.

16.4.4 Mechanisms of interaction and network maintenance

There are a number of ways in which individuals can interact with one another, including telephone conversations, e-mails, documents and face-to-face meeting. Kelley and Brooks (1991) dichotomise these mechanisms of interaction into 'active', referring to those modes involving personal interaction, whether face-to-face or over the phone, for example, and 'passive', essentially referring to documents and other textual material, where there is no direct interaction between the 'sender' and 'receiver' of the information. As we noted in the introduction, 'networks do not emerge without considerable endeavour' (Birley *et al.*, 1991: 58), and thus we are not only interested in the mechanisms for the exchange of information and goods through the network, but also the mechanisms and forums by which entrepreneurs build and nurture their networks.

16.4.5 Dimensions of networks

The overall network may also be seen to vary along a number of dimensions. The most relevant network dimensions for our concerns include the following:

- *Size* – this dimension simply refers to the number of actors participating in the network (Tichy *et al.*, 1979; Auster, 1990). However, the size of the network under investigation is frequently influenced by some arbitrary boundary set by the researcher (see discussion below).
- *Diversity* – this network characteristic most frequently refers to the number of different types of actor (Auster, 1990), which as we discussed above may be measured along a number of dimensions, such as age, gender and education, etc.
- *Density* – the density of a network refers to the 'extensiveness of the ties between elements [actors]' (Aldrich and Whetten, 1981: 398). That is, the number of actual

linkages in the network as a ratio of the total number of possible linkages. This dimension is also sometimes termed 'connectedness' (Tichy *et al.*, 1979; Rogers and Kincaid, 1981). However, Boissevain (1974: 37) argues that: 'It must be stressed . . . that network density is simply an index of the potential not of the actual flow of information' (i.e. it is a measure of network structure and not networking activity). Boissevain (1974: 40) also argues that: 'There is obviously a relationship between size and density, for where a network is large the members will have to contribute more relations to attain the same density as a smaller network.' Furthermore, network density tells us nothing of the internal structure of the network itself and as Boissevain (1974: 40) points out '. . . networks with the same density can have very different configurations'.

■ *Openness* – in the entrepreneurship literature the distinction is often made between strong ties and weak ties. Strong ties are found in cliques and associated with dense networks (i.e. relationships with individuals who are also linked to each other), whereas weak ties connect to individuals outside a clique and thus create 'openness' in the network, that is, they are boundary-spanning relationships or links that span 'structural holes' (Burt, 1992).

■ *Stability* – Tichy *et al.* (1979: 508) define this dimension as 'the degree to which a network pattern changes over time'. Auster (1990) expands on this, referring to both the frequency and magnitude of change of the actors and linkages in a given network.

16.4.6 Setting boundaries for network research and network mapping

One of the key problems in undertaking a network study is the determination of the boundary of the network, since this establishes the sample of actors and links under investigation. Mitchell (1969: 12) distinguishes between the 'total' network of a society, that is, 'the general ever-ramifying, ever-reticulating set of linkages that stretches within and beyond the confines of any community or organisation', and the 'partial' network the researcher must abstract from the total network. This process of 'abstraction' (Scott, 1991) is problematic since social networks have little regard for formal or informal boundaries, whether defined by the network members themselves (e.g. teams, groups, and organisations) or by the network researcher. Thus, in setting a boundary, the network researcher must be aware of the potential limitations of their sample. Network researchers may focus either on a group of individuals, which is termed a 'socio-centred' network, since it centres on a group such as a team of scientists within an organisation, or the network of an individual, which is termed a 'focal' or 'ego-centred' network, since it centres on the network of a focal individual, such as an entrepreneur.

Network mapping, that is, the graphical representation of a network, is 'a powerful, though under-utilised, tool for the representation of relational data' (Conway and Steward, 1998: 223). It is particularly useful in allowing for the comparison of a network over time, such as at different stages of the life of an entrepreneurial firm; an excellent example of this is provided by Blundel (2002) who studied the network evolution of two small regional cheese-making firms in the UK.

16.5 Re-telling the Dyson story from a social network perspective

We believe that the Dyson case is important to the study of entrepreneurship for a number of reasons. First, James Dyson is an accomplished designer, innovator and entrepreneur, and all of his entrepreneurial ventures (the 'Sea Truck', 'Ballbarrow' and 'Dual-Cyclone') illustrate that creative thinkers can identify exceptional opportunities in very mature sectors. Second, Dyson is in some regards a modern reincarnation of the traditional inventor-entrepreneur, as exemplified by Richard Arkwright, Robert Stephenson, James Watt and Isambard Kingdom Brunel, who are such a feature of the UK's economic history (Mathias, 1969). Third, the case highlights the importance of self-belief, persistence and sheer hard work in the creation of new businesses. Fourth, and perhaps most importantly, the case illustrates the role played by informal or social networks in providing support, information and knowledge for even the most individualistic of entrepreneurs.

16.5.1 Case background and chronology of key events

After leaving school, where he studied humanities at 'A' level, James Dyson went on to art school in London, and later was accepted on to a Masters degree course in design at the Royal College of Art (RCA). He became particularly inspired by Buckminister Fuller, the American engineer dismissed by many as a 'dreamer', and the great Victorian engineer Isambard Kingdom Brunel, who was responsible for many of the railways, steamships and bridges that symbolised the UK's industrial power. Dyson's father had died when he was young and this he believes accounts for his own self-sufficiency and identification with 'external figures'. Dyson's subsequent business career can be roughly split into three major phases, which we shall address chronologically.

Phase I – Rotork and the Development of the Sea Truck

While still a student at the RCA, James Dyson began to work for an entrepreneur named Jeremy Fry who manufactured motorised valve actuators for pipelines. Fry encouraged him to adopt a 'hands-on' (practical) approach to design rather than one based on theory; this is an approach that has been the hallmark of Dyson's subsequent entrepreneurial ventures. Dyson was soon working on one of his innovative ideas – the 'Sea Truck' – and over the following months went on to build a prototype. He patented his idea and Fry set up a subsidiary of his company – 'Rotork' – to manufacture the product. More that 250 Sea Trucks were sold at a turnover of many millions, but Dyson soon began to feel he had been away from the drawing board for too long.

Phase II – Kirk-Dyson and the development of the Ballbarrow

While working for Rotork, Dyson and his family had moved from London to a 300-year old farmhouse in the Cotswolds. Undertaking most of the re-building work himself, he became familiar with the failings of the traditional wheelbarrow: unstable when fully laden, tyres prone to puncture, liable to sink into soft ground, and with a steel body that damaged door-frames and human limbs. He considered the problem for around a year, before hitting upon the idea of re-inventing the wheelbarrow by replacing the wheel with a ball. It was at this point that Dyson decided to set up his own manufacturing company – this was to become 'Kirk-Dyson'. Dyson's company launched the 'Ballbarrow' and it soon became a commercial success. However, owing to Kirk-Dyson's claim that a US company had stolen its idea, and the subsequent legal case that Kirk-Dyson lost, tension between board members due to the failed legal case resulted in Dyson's being voted out of the company.

Phase III – Dyson and the Development of the Dual-Cyclone Vacuum Cleaner

Undeterred, Dyson then decided to investigate why the performance of the household vacuum cleaner declined so rapidly after fitting a new dust bag. He found that it needed only a thin layer of dust inside the bag to clog the pores and reduce perform-ance to 'an enfeebled suck'. Experience with industrial cyclone technology provided Dyson with the idea for a cyclone vacuum cleaner. Using an old vacuum cleaner, card-board and industrial tape, he spent one evening constructing a fully working model of the world's first bagless cleaner – the prototype for the 'Dual-Cyclone'. After two years of trying to convince British and European companies of the Dual-Cyclone's potential, Dyson decided to try the US. Yet despite the optimism and the 'can-do' spirit of the US, which he found refreshing after the negativity he experienced in the UK, no com-pany was willing to manufacture the Dual-Cyclone. In November 1984, after five years of trying to gain interest in the Dual-Cyclone among European and US manufacturers, Dyson received an informal approach from a Japanese company, 'Apex', who agreed to produce the Dual-Cyclone for the Japanese market under the 'G-Force' brand name. He then once again turned to the US market and eventually set up a deal with 'Iona', a Canadian company, who agreed to produce the Dual-Cyclone for the US market under the 'Drytech' brand name. However, as the product was about to be launched onto the US market, Dyson discovered that 'Amway', a US company that had origin-ally rejected the Dual-Cyclone concept several years before, had unlawfully launched their own version. Reluctantly, Dyson once again found himself involved in a long-running and extremely expensive legal battle with a US company. Then in 1991, after almost five years of litigation, Amway agreed to a deal over its patent infringement and the haemorrhage of legal fees stopped. Finally, in July 1993, 15 years after his original idea, the first 'DC01' Dual-Cyclone vacuum cleaner rolled off Dyson's own assembly line, and the innovation was successfully launched in the UK.

Dyson's social network and the development of the Sea Truck and the Ballbarrow business ventures (Phase I and II)

Dyson's most significant and influential contact was Jeremy Fry who inspired and sup-ported his early ventures. While studying at the RCA Dyson had met Joan Littlewood, the theatre and film impresario, who invited him to design a new theatre that she was planning to build. Dyson, operating under the influence of Buckminster Fuller, created a 'mushroom-shaped auditorium built of aluminium rods'. He sought financial support from British Aluminium and during his first meeting a manager suggested he contact Jeremy Fry; this was the start of a career-long relationship:

> I had shown Fry my model of the proposed theatre, and I think he rather liked it, if not enough to cover me with gold. What he *did* offer me, however, was to prove far more useful in the long run: work [at Rotork], and the first of many collaborations'.
>
> (Dyson 1997: 47)

Having developed the Sea Truck at Rotork, Dyson describes his mistakes in attempting to market the Sea Truck by conveying a message that was too complicated for potential buyers. At the same time, he makes reference to the support of his wife in overcoming this problem:

> For each function Deidre designed a brochure, and they began to sell. And it all seemed so obvious: you simply cannot mix your messages when selling something new.
>
> (Dyson 1997: 62)

Dyson eventually left Rotork to set up his own company to manufacture and market the Ballbarrow, which he had been working on over the previous year. Although he had made money from the Sea Truck he needed financial support to establish a company to manufacture the Ballbarrow. Perhaps not surprisingly, as with many entrepreneurs, he turned to his family:

> I went to see a lawyer friend of my brother-in-law . . . Andrew Phillips not only helped with the formation of the company, but fell in love with the Ballbarrow and persuaded said brother-in-law (Stuart Kirkwood) to invest in it. Stuart was the son of one Lord Kirkwood, former chairman of the mining company RTZ. He and his brother . . . as a result, inherited some family money. Which is always nice.
>
> (Dyson 1997: 79–80)

These contacts were fundamental to the setting up of Kirk-Dyson as they provided legal advice on forming the company, and funding to develop the Ballbarrow and invest in production equipment. Even with this support things did not progress smoothly and the new entrepreneurs had considerable difficulty in finding a market for their revolutionary barrow. Help was at hand:

> I had a friend called Gill Taylor whom I had met at Badminton and just so happened to have been Miss Great Britain in 1964. She was blond, attractive, curvaceous and a typical 'travel around the world and help people' beauty queen. She was also at a loose end and quite prepared to tour the garden centres of the West Country touting Ballbarrows.
>
> (Dyson 1997: 82)

Gradually, the partners managed to make the Ballbarrow a success and began considering ways in which they could expand the business. They wanted to increase output by acquiring a 'proper' factory and invest in some injection-moulding equipment. George Jackson, a local property developer, was approached and subsequently sold a third share in the company. Dyson does not explain how this particular contact was made nor why he was judged to be an appropriate member of the board (other than having the required £100,000). In addition, his social network was important in providing industrial expertise:

> I brought in an old friend of my father's, Robert Beldam, to have a bit of moral support on the board. He was chairman of the CBI small companies section, and though his presence created a little, never expressed, resentment on the board, having him there made me feel somewhat better.
>
> (Dyson 1997: 87)

Eventually, tension between Board members meant that James Dyson was voted off the Board and out of the Kirk-Dyson company.

Dyson's social network and the development of the Dual-Cyclone business venture (Phase III)

Following his departure from Kirk-Dyson, Dyson decided to concentrate his efforts on developing the Dual-Cyclone vacuum cleaner. However, he needed finance to proceed, and thus sought a partner to invest in the setting up of the Air Power Vacuum Cleaner Company:

> Fry . . . was always likely to be my best hope. And so it proved. With £25,000 from Jeremy, and £25,000 from me, £18,000 of which I raised by selling the vegetable garden at Sycamore House and the rest borrowed with my home as security . . . I was in the vacuum cleaner business.
>
> (Dyson 1997: 120)

Dyson eventually built around 5,000 prototypes over a three-year period, and by 1982 he had a Dual-Cyclone that was 100% efficient, but debts of more than £80,000. He had also spent a considerable amount of time trying to persuade various European companies, including Hoover, Hotpoint, Electrolux, AEG and Zanussi, to manufacture his vacuum cleaner, but to no avail. The Fry connection once again proved invaluable, as Rotork's Chief Executive, Tom Essie, was persuaded by Fry to provide further funding:

> Together we drew up a business plan for the production of an upright Dual-Cyclone vacuum cleaner, and the *Rotork* board of directors, swayed presumably by Jeremy's dual involvement, approved it. We thrashed out an agreement that paid me £20,000 and gave me a 5% royalty, and I went off to develop the vacuum cleaner.
>
> (Dyson 1997: 138)

Ultimately, Tom Essie was replaced by what Dyson describes as a 'money man' and Rotork did not proceed with manufacture of the Dual-Cyclone. The company did, however, provide Dyson with financial support at a crucial time in the development of the Dual-Cyclone. A new opportunity was soon at hand; it was not only his extensive social network that proved of value to Dyson, serendipity also seemed to play a part in the story. A key element in the ultimate success of the Dual-Cyclone was the deal he established with a Canadian company that took over responsibility for the North American market. The company was run by an Englishman:

> Jeffery Pike, with whom I had become friendly quite by chance after we sat next to each other on an aeroplane in May 1986, and both turned out to be reading the same novel by Fay Weldon. Having flunked English A Level all those years before, my fortune looked as if it was about to be made by a novel.
>
> (Dyson 1997: 175)

In 1991 Dyson decided that he would set up production in the UK himself, but once again he was hampered by the lack of capital. As usual in times of crisis he was able to make use of his extensive network as a way of resolving the problem:

> When I started with the Ballbarrow I had approached a man called David Williams, whose plastics company, WCB, built all our tooling and then recouped the money in instalments as we began to sell . . . He was now running a company called Linpak which, quite handily for me, was Britain's biggest plastic producer.
>
> (Dyson 1997: 186)

As plans for the manufacture of the Dual-Cyclone in the UK progressed Dyson was keen that it embody the very latest technological developments. By this time he had a healthy stream of royalties from Japan and the US and could afford to hire designers from his Alma Mater:

> The team consisted of four design engineers straight out of the RCA – Simeon Jupp, Peter Gammack, Gareth Jones and Mark Bickenstaffe – all in their twenties, a marvellous bunch, whose presence made me feel as if I was freshly sprogged from the Royal College myself. . . .
>
> (Dyson 1997: 192)

Even when Dyson's business venture was well-established he still retained links with the RCA, which illustrates the importance of utilising long-standing social networks:

> Round about the time I was planning the DC-02, I was at the RCA degree show – for I had since become an internal examiner on their product design course – and I went around offering one or two of the graduates jobs, as is my habitual wont.
>
> (Dyson 1997: 239)

The RCA connection continued to be of value to Dyson after the company became highly successful; by 1995 demand meant that he had to move out of the Chippenham factory because it had a limited capacity of 30,000 units per week.

> A fantastic new factory was designed for us by my old tutor Tony Hunt, and a whizzkid architect called Chris Wilkinson, but we expanded so fast that we had outgrown it before it was even built . . . Wilkinson and Hunt were back though in the Autumn of 1996, drawing up plans to treble the 90,000 square foot factory space by extending over more of our twenty-acre site.
>
> (Dyson 1997: 246)

By 1996 Dyson was considering ways in which he could extend into the increasingly global market for consumer products. After considering the attractions of Germany and France as the first step in his expansion he eventually settled on Australia:

> I got a call from a man called Ross Cameron. Cameron was an Australian who had seen a presentation of mine at Johnson-Wax in Racine, Wisconsin. 'Why not start up in Australia?' I asked. A couple of days later Ross rang back to say 'OK'. He was that sort of man, not one to mess about.
>
> (Dyson 1997: 252–3)

Yet again, Dyson's social network (see Figure 16.1) proved to have a major impact on the direction and fortunes of his business venture.

16.5.2 Case summary

Through a 're-telling' of Dyson's autobiography *Against the Odds* from a social network perspective, we have sought to demonstrate that the creation of Dyson's various business ventures was heavily dependent upon both family and friends (strong ties), as well as acquaintances and serendipitous meetings (weak ties). Dyson's large and diverse social network incorporates relationships that originate from various stages and facets of his life and career; many of these relationships are long-term and multiplex in nature. We see from the case, for example, that Dyson's family and friends provided him with

315

Figure 16.1 The social network of James Dyson

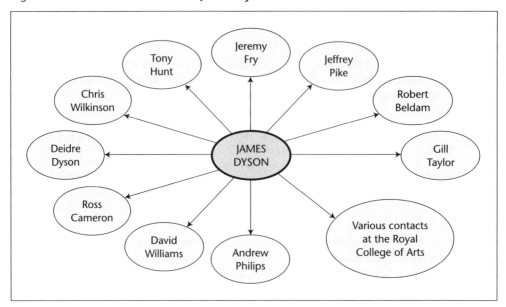

financial and knowledge-based resources that helped ensure that he was able to turn his various novel ideas into successful business ventures. Of course, not every potential entrepreneur will be fortunate enough to be able to call upon an ex-Miss Great Britain to sell their products or a senior member of the CBI to provide business expertise, but perhaps what distinguishes entrepreneurs is their ability to maintain and make use of their strong ties, as well as their effectiveness in initiating, nurturing and mobilising, weaker ties. As the case illustrates, contacts made on aeroplanes, and in business meeting and seminars, can eventually become an extremely important element in business success.

The point of these examples is not to suggest that Dyson over-emphasised the importance of his own contribution to the success of his various business ventures, rather what we are trying to illustrate is that it is all to easy to attribute the success of entrepreneurial ventures to the sole efforts of the man or woman responsible for founding a new business. In Dyson's case, persistence, hard-work and self-belief obviously made a massive contribution to his ultimate success. At the same time, it is important to recognise that at crucial points in the Dyson story his extensive and diverse social network provided him with considerable financial, legal, business and emotional support. Without these networks it is unlikely that Dyson would have overcome what were no doubt formidable odds.

16.6 What has research told us about entrepreneurial networks?

Following seminal studies in the mid- to late-1980s, there has been an increasing interest in the social networks of entrepreneurs from both academics and policy makers.

Academic research has sought to reveal the nature of the actors, relationships and flows within the entrepreneur's network, as well as overall features such as network size, diversity, openness (incidence of weak ties) and stability. We will discuss some of the findings of this research in the subsequent sections of this chapter.

Whilst a number of studies have been cross-sector (Birley, 1985; Conway, 1997; Greve and Salaff, 2003), research has also focused on a wide variety of business sectors, such as computing and IT (Saxenian, 1985, 1990; Collinson, 2000; Lechner and Dowling, 2003), wine (Brown and Bulter, 1995), specialist cheese (Blundel, 2002); business services (Chell and Baines, 2000); and oil (MacKinnon *et al.*, 2004). This research has highlighted the importance of entrepreneurial networks across a broad range of business sectors.

Over the last decade or so, research has also indicated the importance of social networks to entrepreneurial activity across a wide range of countries, including the US (Saxenian, 1985), the UK (Conway, 1997), Japan (Aldrich and Sakano, 1995), Greece (Dodd and Patra, 2002), Norway, Sweden and Italy (Greve and Salaff, 2003), Germany (Brudrel and Preisendorfer, 1998), Russia (Rehn and Taalas, 2004), Belgium (Donckels and Lambrecht, 1997), Slovakia (Copp and Ivy, 2001) and Sri Lanka (Premaratne, 2001). However, these studies also reveal some degree of variation in the social networking patterns of entrepreneurs from different countries; these will be discussed in the following sections. Similarly, differences between the social networking patterns of female and male entrepreneurs will also be highlighted in the following discussion (Aldrich, 1989; Aldrich *et al.*, 1989; Katz and Williams, 1997; Greve and Salaff, 2003).

16.6.1 Network size and network diversity

A number of studies have sought to reveal the size and membership of the networks of entrepreneurs and small firms. Some of these have focused on specific activities, such as innovation (e.g. Rothwell, 1991; Conway, 1997; Freel, 2000), though most are more general in nature and look at the overall composition of the entrepreneurial network (e.g. Birley *et al.*, 1991; Donckels and Lambrecht, 1997). What is common among the findings of such studies is the importance of the diversity of actors within the network of the entrepreneur or small firm (Beesley and Rothwell, 1987; Dodgson, 1989; Conway, 1997; Shaw, 1997, 1998). This network diversity allows small firms to draw upon a range of external resources, such as technical knowledge, market information and finance, to supplement the internal resources of the organisation.

In the more general studies of entrepreneurial and small firm networks, the importance of family and friends has been highlighted, particularly during the early phase of entrepreneurial activity. However, as the enterprise evolves, the network grows and the entrepreneur increasingly develops and utilises more formal business relationships (Birley and Cromie, 1988; Jarillo, 1989; Birley *et al.*, 1991; Larson and Starr, 1993; Donckels and Lambrecht, 1997; Hite and Hesterly, 2001; Greve and Salaff, 2003). This pattern is articulated clearly by Birley *et al.* (1991: 59), who note that: 'entrepreneurs, at an early stage of enterprise development, rely heavily on an informal network of friends, family members and social contacts from the local neighbourhood to gather relevant data. At a later stage, entrepreneurs rely increasingly on professional bankers, accountants, lawyers, suppliers, government agencies, etc. to gain access to requisite business information.'

The diversity of the entrepreneurial network is highlighted by Conway (1997) in a study of the relationships mobilised in the development of a sample of successful technological innovations. The networks revealed were often found to be large, predominately informal, localised and diverse, stretching 'upstream' along the supply chain to suppliers, 'downstream' to various users and distributors, and incorporating other individuals such as university academics. Of particular importance to the innovation process were linkages with users and suppliers. The research also revealed that the 'ego-centred' network of entrepreneurs frequently plugged into a series of important and extensive 'secondary' networks (i.e. the networks of those to whom they were linked). These weak ties allow them to tap into knowledge, information and resources from a wider set of relationships than those to whom they are directly connected. Five broad categories of 'secondary' network were identified:

- *Scientific and technical networks* – these are organised around scientific or technological domains, and include academic and corporate researchers.
- *Profession networks* – these are comprised of individuals within a given profession, such as medicine or education, and bound by 'professional ethics of cooperation'.
- *User networks* – these evolve with the end-users of a firm's products.
- *Friendship networks* – this refers to the personal networks of individuals based predominantly on friendship.
- *Recreation networks* – this is a particular type of friendship network whose cohesion arises from the mutual sense of attachment to some recreational activity, such as sailing, mountaineering or rugby, where the feelings of challenge, achievement and comradeship through participation create and maintain personal bonds.

Research has also highlighted a number of factors that promote the geographical 'reach' of the network of an entrepreneur. For example, a study by Donckels and Lambrecht (1997) revealed that highly educated entrepreneurs were significantly more likely to have personal networks that spanned national boundaries into the international arena, and that the bias towards local contacts in the network was lower for small businesses of more than ten employees and for growth-orientated small firms.

However, work comparing the networks of entrepreneurs of different nationalities has suggested that variations exist in their size and membership. In their study of US, Norwegian, Swedish and Italian entrepreneurs, for example, Greve and Salaff (2003) found that US entrepreneurs had the largest networks, followed by the Swedes and Italians, with the Norwegians having the smallest networks. They also found that US entrepreneurs had a significantly smaller proportion of family within their networks compared with the other three nationalities in their study (6% compared with 22–25%). Studies of Northern Irish entrepreneurs (Birley *et al.*, 1991) and Greek entrepreneurs (Dodd and Patra, 2002) indicate that their social networks are relatively small, being similar in size to those of Italian entrepreneurs, although Dodd and Patra (2002) also found that Greek entrepreneurs had extremely extensive 'secondary' networks, that is, they combined small yet strong circles of contacts with weak ties to the networks of others. Greek entrepreneurs also have a large percentage of family members in their networks, accounting for approximately a third of the network (Dodd and Patra, 2002).

The evidence regarding differences in the network size and membership of male and female entrepreneurs is more limited. Greve and Salaff (2003), for example, found some evidence that female entrepreneurs had slightly larger networks than their male counterparts, and that these often included a higher proportion of kin. This ties in with the contention of Renzulli *et al.* (2000) that female entrepreneurs often find it difficult to expand their networks into male-dominated business circles.

16.6.2 The nature of network linkages and relationships

Research has also focused on the nature of the linkages between actors within entrepreneurial networks. A key distinction is made between informal or personal relationships and formal relationships, such as joint ventures, licensing agreements and supply-chain linkages with either suppliers or users. The importance of informal or personal relationships, and the role of trust, is frequently cited (Birley, 1985; Dubini and Aldrich, 1991; Conway, 1997). Informality would appear to play an important role in allowing entrepreneurs to resolve the apparent paradox raised earlier in this chapter: that while on the one hand 'the entrepreneur personifies individualism and independence', on the other 'he is . . . very dependent on ties of trust and cooperation'.

Johannisson and Peterson (1984: 3) argue that the individual linkages of an entrepreneur's social network 'are multi-stranded involving unique syntheses of instrumental, affective [friendship] and moral [bonds]', in contrast to the bureaucratic desire 'to separate the strands and in particular to focus in on instrumental [bonds] only'. For Freeman (1991: 503), 'behind every formal network, giving it the breath of life, are usually various informal networks . . . Personal relationships of trust and confidence . . . are important both at the formal and informal level.' Indeed, in reviewing existing research concerning the evolution of the network relationships of entrepreneurs, Hite (2005: 116) notes that 'work-related ties may evolve . . . as social exchanges are layered over the business relationship'. Conway (1997) in his study of successful small firm innovation also found evidence of multiplex relationships, although, while in some cases friendships emerged from formal relationships, in others, friendships spilled over into more formal joint projects. Although comparative research has indicated that informal relationships are important to entrepreneurs of different nationalities, some variations have been revealed. For example, Leonard-Barton (1984) found that US entrepreneurs were more likely to draw upon informal personal relationships, as opposed to more formal channels, than their Swedish counterparts. Similar variations are implied by research that we discuss next, concerning the mechanisms and venues for interaction.

16.6.3 The nature of flows through the network and mechanisms of interaction

We saw in the Dyson story that an extensive and diverse social network provided James Dyson with considerable financial, legal, business and emotional support. A number of studies have shown that such a diversity of flow and transactions through the entrepreneur's network is important to successful entrepreneurial activity. Birley (1985), for example, found that the social networks of entrepreneurs, incorporating family, friends and contacts, were more important than formal relationships in sourcing raw materials, equipment, premises, employees and finance. In her study of the innovative behaviour of a sample of small service firms in the UK, Shaw (1998) highlights the variety of flow through their networks, such as information, advice, friendship, economic and bartering exchanges. She also found that each of these flows had an important impact on the innovation processes of these small service firms. Similarly, in his study of successful technological innovation by small entrepreneurial firms, Conway (1997) revealed the importance of a variety of flows, including technical knowledge and solutions, market information and prototype feedback, for example, from contacts in universities, suppliers, customers and even competitors.

We noted earlier in this chapter that considerable effort is required to create, nurture and maintain network relationships. Indeed, research indicates the importance of 'active' modes of interaction and, in particular, face-to-face interaction in the development, nurturing and utilising of entrepreneurial networks (Conway, 1997; Donckels and Lambrecht, 1997; Dodd and Patra, 2002). Research by Donckels and Lambrecht (1997) found that the educational level of the entrepreneur and the growth orientation of the firm can positively impact the use of certain forums of interaction, such as tradefairs and business seminars. Conway (1997) noted that relationships with users, in particular, tended to be informal, with the principal mechanisms for interaction being customer site visits, chance meetings at exhibitions and contact over the phone.

There are, however, some differences in the networking patterns of entrepreneurs of different nationalities. In their study of US, Norwegian, Swedish and Italian entrepreneurs, Greve and Salaff (2003) found that Italian entrepreneurs spent significantly more time both developing and maintaining their relationships, while Norwegian entrepreneurs were found to spend significantly less time maintaining their relationships. Research by Dodd and Patra (2002) found that Greek entrepreneurs spent substantial time developing and maintaining relationships, some 44 hours per week; this is much higher than that spent by Italian entrepreneurs. They also found that roughly 40% of this networking activity by Greek entrepreneurs occurred in a social setting, with roughly 40% in a business office and 20% over the phone. In sharp contrast, Japanese entrepreneurs reported very low levels of networking activity compared with other nationalities (Aldrich and Sakano, 1995). Once again, research concerning the networking activity of male and female entrepreneurs is mixed; whereas Aldrich (1989) found lower networking levels for female entrepreneurs, Greve and Salaff (2002) found no significant difference.

16.6.4 The function or role of the network

The personal or social networks of entrepreneurs can be seen to play a number of important roles: they generate social support for the actions of the entrepreneur; they help extend the strategic competence of the entrepreneur in response to opportunities and threats; and they supplement the often very limited resources of the entrepreneur, allowing the resolution of acute operating problems (Johannisson and Peterson, 1984). For Donckels and Lambrecht (1997: 13), 'the fragility which accompanies small size can be offset by the supportive environment provided by resilient networks'. Thus, the function or role of the social network can range from the more general (e.g. supporting firm development or competence building) to the more specific (e.g. supporting the development of particular instances of innovation).

Johannisson (2000) argues that all start-up firms need an 'organising context' that helps structure exchanges with the broader environment. This context helps the entrepreneur cope with ambiguity, provides a shelter against uncertainty and aids with reactions to unexpected changes in the market-place. In this regard, entrepreneurial networks can be particularly important during the start-up phase of a new venture (Birley, 1985; Aldrich and Zimmer, 1986; Larson and Starr, 1993; Johannisson, 2000). With reference to university 'spinouts', a particular type of new venture, Nicolaou and Birley (2003) argue that the nature of the networks of the key academics involved in the spinout can have profound impacts on the future relationship between the new venture and the university, and hence may be associated with different growth trajectories. There is substantial evidence to indicate that entrepreneurial networks are also important to the growth of a firm, since they open up new opportunities and resources (Aldrich and Zimmer, 1986; Jarillo, 1989; Brown and Butler, 1995; Shaw, 1997, 1998; Chell and Baines, 2000; Hite and Hesterly, 2001; Lechner and Dowling, 2003; Hite, 2005). However, in her study of small service firms, Shaw (1997, 1998) reveals that social networks may play both positive and negative roles in the development of the firm depending on network membership and on the nature of what flows through the network. Specifically, it was found that the more heterogeneous or diverse the social network in which the small firm was embedded, and the greater the variety of information and advice flowing through the network, the more positive the impact the social network was found to have on the firm's development. In an interesting longitudinal study of two regional specialist cheese-makers in the UK, Blundel (2002) demonstrates how stable entrepreneurial networks may evolve to enable the firm to adapt to major changes in their environment, what he terms 'episodes'.

Research has also highlighted the role that networks play in the building of technological competence within small firms. In their study of the influence of networks on new biotechnology firms in the UK and France, Estades and Ramani (1997) develop a typology of three technological competence trajectories:

- *competence 'widening'* – a diversification of the technological competence of the firm;
- *competence 'deepening'* – an improvement of existing technological competencies of the firm;
- *competence 'narrowing'* – an abandoning of a set of existing projects, processes or products, without the development of new technological competencies.

Estades and Ramani (1997) also found that the decisive networks associated with the deepening or widening of technological competence in these small firms were scientific (i.e. those linking them to scientific communities) and inter-firm networks (i.e. those linking them to large firms).

The importance of networks to the innovation process has already been noted. This holds true for both small and large firms, although small firms are more reliant on such boundary-spanning networks to overcome internal resource constraints (Conway, 1994). However, the importance of the small-firm network, and of particular actors within it, will vary depending on the task at hand (Conway, 1997; Freel, 2000). In his study of small-firm technological innovation, introduced earlier, Conway (1997) distinguished between the nature and importance of the contribution of the network towards different stages or activities in the innovation process, that is:

■ *project stimuli*;

■ *concept definition*;

■ *idea generation* regarding features and functionality of innovation;

■ *technical problem solving*; and

■ *field testing* prior to commercialisation.

Users were found to be a major source of inputs in the idea-generation phase, and this was particularly evident during 're-innovation', that is, the modification of earlier models (Rothwell and Gardiner, 1985). In addition, users were also seen to represent a major source for the pre-commercialisation field testing of the innovations. This adds support to Habermeier's (1990) hypothesis that product characteristics and user requirements can often only be discovered if the innovation is actually used, sometimes for long periods of time. Field tests were seen not only as an important test bed for the technical performance of the innovations, but also for the suitability of the embodied features and functionality. The study also highlighted the key role played by suppliers in providing inputs into the technical solutions embodied in the commercialised innovations, sometimes developing critical components in response to specific requests from the small-firm innovators. The cases in the study provide clear illustrations of both the 'complementary' and the 'substitutive' nature of external sources of knowledge and technology in relation to indigenous innovative activity in small entrepreneurial firms.

16.7 Chapter summary

The study of entrepreneurship from a social network perspective is an important contribution to our understanding of entrepreneurial behaviour, supplementing more long-standing psychological approaches that emphasise the sources of individual motivation (McLelland, 1961; Manimala, 2000), and economic theories that concentrate on the economic rationality of those starting their own businesses (Casson, 1982, 1990). Indeed, the contention of Aldrich and Zimmer (1986: 9) that 'comprehensive explanations of entrepreneurship must include the social context of (such) behaviour, especially the social relationships through which people obtain information, resources and social support', is now broadly accepted in the entrepreneurship literature. For some, perhaps, the concept of networking takes us a step further; it helps us move away from the traditional view of entrepreneurs as resourceful individualists to an image of entrepreneurship as a collective phenomenon (Johannisson, 2000). We are, however, not suggesting that the motivation of individual entrepreneurs can be discounted in explaining the creation of new business ventures. Rather, we agree with Wickham (1998: 39) that the characteristics of successful entrepreneurs include: hard work, self-starting, goal-setting, resilience, confidence, assertiveness and comfort with power. It is certainly the case that James Dyson demonstrated all of these characteristics over a considerable length of time. At the same time, we have illustrated how Dyson's entrepreneurial activities were heavily embedded in an extensive network of family, friends and casual acquaintances. Clearly this network would not have developed in the way that it did without Dyson's ability (agency) to maintain and utilise existing strong ties while at the same time initiating, nurturing and mobilising a range of weaker ties.

Since the seminal work on entrepreneurial networks in the mid- to late-1980s by the likes of Howard Aldrich, Sue Birley, Dorothy Leonard-Barton and Bengt Johannisson, there has been an increasing interest and burgeoning body of empirical work in the area. This work has provided insights into the size, diversity, stability and morphology of entrepreneurial networks, and has highlighted the range of important roles and functions for which it is nurtured and mobilised. Research has also informed us of the variety of the flows through the network, the mechanisms and forums for interaction, and the often informal and multiplex nature of many of the network relationships. More recent empirical work has highlighted differences in the nature of the network and networking activity between entrepreneurs of different nationalities and, to a lesser extent, between male and female entrepreneurs.

Questions

1 Why might entrepreneurship be considered to be a 'collective' phenomenon?

2 If entrepreneurship is to be considered a 'collective' phenomenon, then what would you view to be the key roles, skills and resources of the entrepreneur?

3 In what ways might an entrepreneur's social network be mobilised during the entrepreneurial process?

4 What characteristics of an entrepreneur's social network are likely to promote successful entrepreneurial activity?

Web links

www.unc.edu/~healdric/
Homepage of Howard Aldrich, containing a range of articles and publications.

www.socialnetworks.org/
Contains a range of references on social networking.

www.dyson.co.uk
The corporate website for Dyson, with information on the entrepreneur, his products and his company.

CHAPTER 17

Marketing and the small business

David Stokes

17.1 Introduction

This chapter considers the role that marketing plays in the fortunes of small businesses and their owners. Although marketing is a key factor in their survival and development, small firms share a number of characteristics that cause marketing problems. These include a restricted customer base, limited marketing expertise and impact, variable, unplanned effort and over-reliance on the owner-manager's marketing competency. However, entrepreneurs and small business owners interpret marketing in ways that do not conform to standard textbook theory and practice. This chapter presents evidence suggesting that they tend to be more 'innovation-oriented' than customer-oriented. They target markets through 'bottom-up' self-selection and recommendations of customers. They shy away from formalised research, relying more on informal networking. They prefer interactive marketing methods to the mass communications strategies of larger companies. In summary, it is more useful to characterise 'entrepreneurial marketing' using 'I's' rather than the 'P's' of traditional marketing models. As a strategic process it involves innovation, identification of target markets, informal information gathering and interactive marketing methods – methods that can be summarised as a marketing mix of influence (word-of-mouth communications), image building, incentives and involvement ('four + four I's' rather than 'four P's' of the conventional marketing mix).

17.2 Learning objectives

This chapter has four learning objectives:

1 To understand the importance of marketing to small firms and their owners.

2 To appreciate the typical marketing problems that small firms face.

3 To gain insight into how entrepreneurs and owner-managers interpret the marketing function.

4 To understand the characteristics of entrepreneurial marketing and the processes and methods that are typical of its implementation.

Key concepts

■ **entrepreneurial marketing**　■ **marketing competencies**　■ **networking**

17.3 Marketing and the small firm

There has been a tendency among both marketing theorists and small business owners to associate marketing with large, rather than small, organisations. Marketing theory was developed from studies of large corporations, and most textbooks (e.g. Kotler, 1997) still reflect these origins in the concepts and case studies that they present. Even owner-managers of small firms seem to give marketing a low priority compared with the other functions of their business, often regarding marketing as 'something that larger firms do' (Stokes *et al.*, 1997). Yet there is considerable evidence that marketing is crucial to the survival and development of small firms. Research findings are summarised below indicating that marketing is particularly important to smaller organisations because it represents a) a vital interface between a small firm and an uncertain, fast changing external environment, and b) a key internal management skill that differentiates between surviving and failing firms.

17.3.1 Marketing as the interface between a small firm and the external environment

A key feature that distinguishes small from large firms is the much higher closure rates of small firms (Storey, 1994). Businesses are at their most vulnerable when they are very young and very small. Only a small percentage stay in business in the long term; over two-thirds close in the decade in which they opened. Businesses exist in fast-changing environments, and the youngest and smallest are particularly exposed in this unpredictable world (Hall, 1995). Their lack of market power and dependency on a relatively small customer base make their environments more uncontrollable and more uncertain than that of larger organisations (Wynarczyk *et al.*, 1993).

How can small firms best cope in this hostile business environment? Marketing is certainly important in the early, vulnerable years, because it provides a vital interface between the organisation and its external environment. Research involving case studies of surviving and non-surviving small manufacturing firms by Smallbone *et al.* (1993) indicated that *adjustment* is the key. The most important adjustment both for survival and growth was active market development – a continuous search for new market opportunities and a broadening of the customer base of the business. Those firms that are most active in making adjustments in what they do, and how they do it, particularly in relation to the market-place, seem to have a greater chance of survival than those who carry on as before. As the function that supplies the necessary information and direction to guide such adjustments, marketing provides a key interface between a small business and its external environment.

17.3.2 Marketing management and small firm survival

It is not surprising therefore that research has identified marketing management as a key internal function that influences survival (Berryman, 1993). The judgement of individual investors in small business, or so-called 'business angels', is interesting in that it indicates what they have discovered to be critical factors that make a venture more likely to succeed or fail (see Chapter 19). According to Harris (1993) the principal reasons given by business angels for *not* investing are:

- lack of relevant experience of entrepreneur and any associates;
- deficiencies in marketing;
- flawed, incomplete or unrealistic financial projections.

Cromie (1990) interviewed 35 manufacturing and 33 service firms, which had been trading for four to five years, and asked each of them open-ended questions on the major problems they had encountered and the mistakes they had made. His overall conclusion was that: 'Small, young organisations experience problems particularly in the areas of accounting and finance, marketing and the management of people' (Cromie, 1990: 58–9). Hills and Hultman (2005) cite a survey of venture capitalists who rated marketing management as important to the success of new ventures at 6.7 on a seven-point scale.

There is some consensus in this literature on why firms close that indicates the centrality of what has been referred to as the 'three Ms' of 'Marketing, Money and Management of people' (Stokes, 1998a). Marketing represents a key management discipline, which differentiates between survival and failure of small firms.

17.4 Characteristics of small firms and marketing problems

However, small organisations tend to suffer from a number of distinctive marketing problems. Certain characteristics, which differentiate small from large organisations, lead to marketing issues that are especially challenging for small business owner-managers.

17.4.1 Limited customer base

A number of studies have shown a relationship between size of firm and number of customers, with a high percentage of small businesses dependent on less than ten customers and some on only one buyer (Storey, 1982; Hall, 1995). As well as depending on a small number of customers, small businesses tend to trade only in a limited geographical area (Curran and Blackburn, 1990). This ties their fortunes closely to the cycles of the local economy, with limited opportunities to compensate for any downturn.

17.4.2 Limited activity

Lack of access to financial and human resources restricts marketing in small firms. A small enterprise has less to spend on marketing as a percentage of income because of the impact of fixed costs which take up a higher proportion of revenues; financial constraints also restrict their ability to employ marketing specialists (Weinrauch *et al.*, 1991). Carson (1985) concluded that the marketing constraints on small firms took the form of restricted resources, lack of specialist expertise and limited impact.

17.4.3 Lack of formalised planning and evolutionary marketing

As we have already discussed, small firms have to cope with an ever-changing environment, meaning they have to continually adapt and adjust as a business to survive (see Chapter 16). It would seem that those firms that do survive adjust to the new conditions in a continual process of evolution (Smallbone *et al.*, 1992). The marketing implication is that short-term considerations take priority over longer-term planning. Research has confirmed that planning is a problem for small firm management, which tends to be reactive in style (Fuller, 1994). Cromie (1990) characterised this as an operational, as opposed to a strategic, orientation. However, just as the firm must evolve to survive, so marketing evolves to reflect the owner-manager experience and the needs of the firm. Carson (1985) has suggested four stages in the evolution of marketing in small firms:

- initial marketing activity in the set-up stages;
- reactive selling as demand grows;
- a DIY marketing approach under the direction of the owner-manager as the firm realises the need for a more positive marketing stance; and finally
- integrated, proactive marketing as the firm adopts longer-term marketing strategies usually involving the recruitment of specialist marketing management.

17.4.4 Innovation, niches and gaps

Small firms today are often seen as playing a key role in the innovation of new products and processes because of their flexibility and willingness to try new approaches. However, innovation is neither a unique nor a universal characteristic of small firms; large organisations are also important innovators and not all small firms can be considered innovative. Nevertheless, innovation is an important characteristic of small firms in certain industry sectors (Rothwell, 1986).

Niches or market focus can help small firms overcome their inherently lower profitability compared with larger firms. But the marketing problem that arises for smaller firms is not only how to develop innovative products and services, but also how to defend their competitive advantage and exploit innovations to the full with limited resources. Cannon (1992) saw this as important weaknesses of small firms because of their lack of access to the resources to realise fully the potential of the gaps in the market they identify. He warned of what he called 'poisoned apple marketing' in which it is not unusual for large firms to wait for smaller enterprises to open up markets and make the mistakes before they use their resource base to capitalise on the opportunity (Cannon, 1992: 473). Exploiting niche markets to the full can be as big an issue as developing them in the first place.

Figure 17.1 Small organisations: characteristics and marketing issues

Small organisation characteristics	Marketing issues
Relatively small in given sector	Limited customer base
Resource constraints	Limited activity, expertise and impact
Uncertainty	Little formalised planning; intuitive, reactive marketing
Evolutionary	Variable marketing effort
Innovation	Developing and defending niches
Personalised management style	Dependent on owners' marketing competency

17.4.5 The owner-managers' marketing competency

Scholhammer and Kuriloff (1979) recognised a personalised management style as a distinguishing feature of small enterprises. This is typified as personal knowledge of all employees, involvement in all aspects of management and lack of sharing of key decisions. The dominant influence of the owner-manager has led to a large literature that seeks to establish relationships between the psychology, type and background of owners and the performance of their firms (Chell *et al.*, 1991).

If the personal characteristics of the owner-manager are the dominant internal management influence, then the marketing management of a small enterprise will be much affected by the marketing competency of the owner. Carson *et al.* (1995) describe entrepreneurial marketing in terms of the experience, knowledge, communication abilities and judgement of the owner-manager, key competencies on which marketing effectiveness depend. As the competency of SME owners varies widely in these areas, so does the marketing performance of their firms (Carson *et al.*, 1995: 12–13). These characteristics of small organisations and the marketing issues and problems that typically arise are summarised in Figure 17.1.

17.5 Is marketing different in small organisations?

Advisors, educators and policy makers attempting to overcome these marketing problems have met with little success. Curran and Blackburn (1990) concluded that small business owners are not 'joiners', with only a minority having contact with Training and Enterprise Councils (TECs) and Business Links, and they often reject approaches from advisers and consultants because of a 'fortress enterprise' mentality. But there is also a danger that notions of best practice among larger firms are automatically assumed to be appropriate for small businesses providing they can be given the resources to adopt them. For example, there is evidence that SMEs implement the concept of market orientation less fully than larger companies (Brooksbank *et al.*, 1992; Liu, 1995). However, there is little to suggest that traditional marketing concepts such as this are relevant to smaller firms. Too often, marketing as practised by larger firms is automatically assumed to be what is required for smaller businesses, providing they can be given the necessary resources.

17.5.1 Marketing defined

One of the problems in investigating small business marketing is the lack of clarity over what 'marketing' actually means in any context. Even marketing in larger firms is not clearly defined; for example Crosier (1975) compiled a list of 50 different definitions of marketing in the literature, an indication of the difficulties marketers have had in defining their own discipline. In order to investigate and describe marketing in smaller organisations we will adopt Webster's (1992) classification of marketing into three distinct elements: as an organisational philosophy or culture, as a strategic process, and as a series of tactical functions or methods.

- *Marketing as an organisational philosophy* – This relates to a set of values and beliefs concerning the central importance of the customer to the success of the organisation. This has been refined as the concept of market or customer orientation, which requires that an understanding of customer needs should precede and inform the development and marketing of products and services (Kotler, 1997). Most definitions of marketing relate mainly to this level of meaning; for example the definition of the (UK) Institute of Marketing states that marketing is 'the management process responsible for identifying, anticipating and satisfying customer requirements profitably'.

- *Marketing as a strategy* – This defines how an organisation is to compete and survive in the market-place. Most marketing textbooks (e.g. Kotler, 1997) review marketing strategy through the stages of market segmentation, targeting and positioning. This involves: first, research and analysis of the market-place in order to divide it into meaningful groups or segments of buyer-types; second, one or more segments are chosen as the most appropriate targets for marketing activities; third, an appeal is made to this target group through an appropriately positioned product or service.

- *Marketing tactics* – These use specific activities and techniques, such as market research, product development and advertising to implement the strategy. These are referred to as elements in the 'marketing mix', commonly summarised as the four 'Ps' of product, pricing, promotion and place.

17.5.2 Marketing defined by small business owners

Entrepreneurs and owner-managers of small businesses tend not to see marketing this way. They define marketing in terms of tactics to attract new business – in other words, at the third level of meaning in the definitions list above. They are less aware of the other, philosophical and strategic meanings of the term. Research by Kingston University's Small Business Research Centre (Stokes *et al.*, 1997) indicated that most small business owners equated marketing with selling and promoting only. Unprompted definitions of marketing focused on customer acquisition and promotions whilst identifying customer needs, and other non-promotional aspects of marketing, such as product development, pricing and distribution, were largely ignored. Many owners suggested that their business was reliant on word-of-mouth recommendations and therefore 'they did not have to do any marketing'.

This does not necessarily mean that they overlooked other aspects of marketing, only that they were unaware of the terminology. The business owners' narrow view of marketing was not borne out by what they actually did. Their activities indicated a strategic marketing awareness, particularly in areas such as monitoring the market-place, targeting individual market segments and emphasising customer service and relationships. When asked to rank their most important marketing activities, 'recommendations from customers' was first in all sectors and sizes of small firms. However, this reliance on recommendations was not necessarily an indication of minimal marketing effort, as such recommendations were often hard won. To an outside observer, it is all too easy to accept the owner-manager's comment that they 'do not have the time or resources for marketing', when those same owners do indeed devote much of their time to building relationships with satisfied customers who then recommend the business to others. In other words, they spend considerable time and resources on marketing, but they call it by another name.

17.6 Entrepreneurial interpretations of marketing

Marketing in small firms is not the simplistic, promotional activity that it appears at first sight; nor is it marketing according to the textbook. If we examine each of the three elements in the definitions of marketing as described earlier, we discover distinct variations between what successful small business owners actually do and what marketing theory would have them do.

17.6.1 Customer orientation versus 'innovation orientation'

Marketing as an organisational philosophy indicates that an assessment of market needs comes before new product development. Entrepreneurial business owners frequently do it the other way round. They start with an idea, and then try to find a market for it. Creativity and innovation in product or service development are the hallmarks of successful entrepreneurship (Drucker, 1985), not careful research into customer needs. Well-known entrepreneurs such as Roddick and Branson did not found their early businesses on market analysis, but on an intuitive feel for what was required. Innovation is a key entrepreneurial activity, taking new ideas and turning them into useful products or services that customers need (Adair, 1990). But often this is achieved through a zeal for the development of new concepts and ideas – an 'innovation orientation' – rather than through a dedication to the principles of customer orientation. According to Hill and Hultman (2005), growth entrepreneurs place a strategic emphasis on exceptionally high-quality products and services, and pursue a balance between product orientation and market orientation. Entrepreneurs have a propensity to act on potential opportunities rather than evaluating them thoroughly.

17.6.2 'Top-down' versus 'bottom-up' strategies

Marketing as a strategy involves the processes of segmentation, targeting and positioning, so that products and services are focused on appropriate buyer groups. Entrepreneurial owner-managers identify closely with a specific group of customers whose needs are well known to them, in accordance with these theories of strategic marketing (Hill and Hultman, 2005). However, most marketing textbooks advocate a 'top-down' approach to the market in which the strategy process develops in the following order:

- The profiles of market segments are developed first using demographic, psychological and other buyer-behaviour variables.

- An evaluation of the attractiveness of each segment concludes with the selection of the target segment.

- Finally, the selection and communication of a market position differentiates the product or service from competitive offerings.

This process implies that an organisation is able to take an objective overview of the markets it serves before selecting those on which it wishes to concentrate. This usually involves both secondary and primary market research with evaluation by specialists in each of the three stages.

Although successful entrepreneurs do seem adept at carefully targeting certain customers, the processes they use in order to achieve this do not seem to conform to the three stages described above. Evidence suggests that successful smaller firms practise a 'bottom-up' targeting process in which the organisation begins by serving the needs of a few customers and then expands the base gradually as experience and resources allow. Research into 'niche marketing' approaches indicates that targeting is achieved by attracting an initial customer base and then looking for more of the same (Dalgic and Leeuw, 1994). The stages of entrepreneurial targeting are as follows:

- *Identification of market opportunities* – matching innovative ideas to the resources of a small enterprise identifies possible opportunities. These opportunities are tested through trial and error in the market-place, based on the entrepreneur's intuitive expectations that are sometimes, but not often, backed up by more formal research.

- *Attraction of an initial customer base* – certain customers, who may or may not conform to the profile anticipated by the entrepreneur, are attracted to the service or product. However, as the entrepreneur is in regular contact with these customers, she gets to know their preferences and needs.

- *Expansion through more of the same* – the entrepreneur expands the initial customer base by looking for more customers of the same profile. In many cases, this is not a deliberate process as it is left to the initial customers who recommend the business to others with similar needs to their own. A target customer group emerges and grows, but more through a process of self-selection and some encouragement from the entrepreneur, rather than through formal research and proactive marketing.

This bottom-up process has advantages over the top-down approach. It requires fewer resources and is more flexible and adaptable to implement – attributes that play to small business strengths. It has corresponding disadvantages. It is less certain of success and takes longer to penetrate the market to full potential – weaknesses that characterise many small firms.

17.6.3 Four P's versus one-to-one marketing tactics

Marketing strategies are implemented through marketing activities of various types, which have been summarised as the marketing mix – the set of tools at the marketer's disposal. As these tools are numerous, various attempts have been made to categorise them into a manageable form, including the four-P's, as discussed earlier. Entrepreneurial marketing activities do not fit easily into these existing models of the marketing mix. Owner-managers do not define their own marketing mix in terms of product, pricing and place decisions, although they usually include promotions.

Instead, a different theme seems to run through the marketing methods preferred by entrepreneurs: they involve direct interchanges and the building of personal relationships. Entrepreneurs prefer interactive marketing. They specialise in interactions with their target markets because they have strong preferences for personal contact with customers rather than impersonal marketing through mass promotions. They seek conversational relationships in which they can listen, and respond, to the voice of the customer, rather than undertake formal market research to understand the marketplace. Interactive marketing methods imply one-to-one contact through personal or telephone selling and perhaps direct or electronic mail. In smaller firms, the ability of the owner-manager to have meaningful dialogues with customers is often the unique selling point of the business.

17.6.4 Market research versus networking

In each stage of the traditional marketing process, whether strategic or tactical, formal market research plays an important part. Market orientation relies on research to determine customer needs. Strategic segmentation and targeting is determined by market research. The success of adjustments to the marketing mix is tracked by consumer research. Successful entrepreneurs shy away from such formal research methods (Hill and Hultman, 2005), instead preferring more informal methods of gathering market information, usually through networks of contacts involved in the industry or trade (Carson *et al.*, 1995).

17.7 Entrepreneurial marketing

So what does entrepreneurial marketing consist of? We have described a marketing process common among entrepreneurs and successful small business owners that encompasses innovation, identification of a target market, interactive marketing methods and informal information gathering. We will examine each of these further to uncover more about how a typical entrepreneur carries out this marketing process.

17.7.1 Innovation

We have already echoed the views of several commentators who have stressed the importance of innovation to entrepreneurship (Drucker, 1985; Adair, 1990). However, we should not assume that entrepreneurial innovation consists of major breakthroughs and inventions. It is more likely to consist of incremental adjustments to existing products and services or market approaches, rather than larger-scale developments (Henry and Walker, 1991). Whilst a few small firms may make the big innovative breakthrough and grow rapidly as a result, the majority that survive do so by growing more slowly through making small but regular improvements to the way in which they do business. This may mean stocking new lines, approaching a new market segment with a particular service, or improving services to existing customers – in other words incremental, innovative adjustments that together create a competitive edge.

17.7.2 Identification of target markets

We have described how the identification of a market for new products often comes after the development of the idea, when customers are found through a bottom-up process of self-selection and recommendation. In this way, many successful small firms occupy 'niche' markets in which they supply specialised products or services to a clearly identified group of customers. Others find a gap in a particular market-place for the provision of more general services. Either way, success is dependent on identifying a particular group of customers who need the product or service on offer.

However, target markets need not be solely concerned with customers in the conventional sense of the term. Small businesses survive in their changeable environment not only by successfully marketing to those who buy their products or services, but also by developing important relationships with other individuals and organisations. Suppliers, bank mangers, investors, advisors, trade associations, local government and public authorities may be as vital as customers to a small business's success. Entrepreneurs may target marketing strategies at these other markets that go beyond conventional definitions of the term 'customer'. In this sense, entrepreneurial marketing resembles relationship marketing, which defines the need to develop a supportive framework around the organisation: 'Marketing can be seen as relationship management: creating, developing and maintaining a network in which the firm thrives' (Gummesson, 1987). In other words, entrepreneurial marketing can target any organisation or individual, which can have a positive or negative effect on the small firm.

17.7.3 Interactive marketing methods

A selling point for a small business often lies in its ability to stay in touch with customers. Owner-managers themselves usually spend a considerable part of their working day in contact with customers (Orr, 1995). This allows them to interact with their customer base in a way which large firms, even with the latest technological advances, struggle to match.

Interactive marketing for small firms implies responsiveness – the ability to communicate and respond rapidly to individual customers. Entrepreneurs interact with individual customers through personal selling and relationship-building approaches, which not only secure orders but recommendations to potential customers as well. These interactive marketing methods have some common themes too. They rely on the influence of word-of-mouth marketing, which can be stimulated by image building, involvement and incentives, as discussed below.

333

The influence of word-of-mouth marketing

Entrepreneurial marketing relies heavily on word-of-mouth marketing to develop the customer base through recommendations. Research studies inevitably cite recommendations as the number one source of new customers for small firms. Such recommendations may come from customers, suppliers or other referral groups. Word-of-mouth marketing has been defined (Arnt, 1967) as: 'Oral, person-to-person communication between a perceived non-commercial communicator and a receiver concerning a brand, a product or a service offered for sale.' This definition makes two crucial distinctions between word-of-mouth and other forms of marketing activity:

■ it involves face-to-face, direct contact between a communicator and a receiver; and

■ the communicator is perceived to be independent of the product or service under discussion.

The importance of such communications is well documented in the marketing literature, which suggests that word of mouth is often crucial to purchase decisions in many consumer and business-to-business markets. For many small firms, reliance on recommendations is no bad thing as it is more suited to the resources of their business. Referrals incur few, if any, additional direct costs; most owner-mangers prefer the slow build-up of new business that word-of-mouth marketing implies because they would be unable to cope with large increases in demand for their services. Word-of-mouth marketing has two major disadvantages:

■ It is *self-limiting*: reliance on networks of informal communications restricts organisational growth to the limits of those networks. If a small business is dependent on recommendations for new customers, its growth is limited to those market areas in which its sources of recommendations operate.

■ It is *non-controllable*: owners cannot control word-of-mouth communications about their firms. As a result, some perceive there to be few opportunities to influence recommendations other than providing the best possible service.

In practice, however, successful entrepreneurs find ways of encouraging referrals and recommendations by more proactive methods.

Image building

Successful owner-managers recognise the importance of building favourable images of their business in the market-place in order to encourage the influence of positive word-of-mouth marketing. Image building is particularly important for the great majority of small businesses, which are involved in selling services rather than tangible products. Prospective buyers cannot easily test or sample services so their perceptions of the selling organisation become even more important in the purchase decision. A number of factors influence such perceptions including the ethos or atmosphere of the place of work, the physical appearance of anything associated with the business from letter-heads to lorries, and the attitudes of people who have customer contact – which is usually everyone in a small firm. As a result, growth entrepreneurs more often possess an excellent reputation compared with non-growth entrepreneurs (Hills and Hultman, 2005).

Incentives

Like most organisations, owner-managers promote their business by offering a variety of incentives including reduced prices and promotional offers. However, some incentives can be used not only to generate immediate business but also to encourage the development of supportive networks in which the business owner can operate. For example, Shaw (1997) demonstrated that small graphic designers used bartering, hospitality, flexible pricing and differential handling of work to help in the development of their networks. Entrepreneurs use such incentives not only to encourage existing customers but also to develop new markets by expanding their networks.

Involvement

A feeling of involvement or participation with a small business can also encourage customer loyalty and recommendations. From a study of lawyers' practices in the US, File *et al.* (1992) suggested that the intensity and variety of client participation during the service delivery process was predictive of positive word-of-mouth and referrals. Stokes (1997) found that the more parents became involved with their children's school, through helping in class or fund-raising activities, the more they were likely to become strong advocates of the school. This reinforces the need for owners who wish to improve word-of-mouth communications to adopt interactive marketing practices that encourage involvement of some sort with the business, so that customers feel an added sense of commitment to it.

17.7.4 Informal information gathering

Successful entrepreneurs maintain an external focus to their activities, which alerts them to opportunities and threats in their environment. Their informal information-gathering techniques allow them to monitor their own performance in relation to competitors and react to competitive threats. They are also open to new ideas and opportunities through a network of personal and inter-organisational contacts. This process restarts the marketing cycle by forming the basis for further innovative adjustments to the activities of the enterprise. The four main elements of entrepreneurial marketing, together with the four types of interactive marketing methods, can be conceptualised as the 'four + four I's' of entrepreneurial marketing, as shown in Figure 17.2.

17.8 Chapter summary

This chapter has shown that marketing is particularly important to very small, young firms as it represents the interface between a small firm and its external environment. In particular, the marketing competency of owner-managers is a key discriminator between survival and failure of small firms. It has also been demonstrated that the inherent characteristics of small firms lead to distinctive marketing problems, although this can be due to the owner-managers' conceptualisation of marketing being narrow and concentrating largely on promotions. Successful owner-managers and entrepreneurs are active in marketing, although they may not call it that. Indeed, entrepreneurial

Figure 17.2 The entrepreneurial marketing process: four + four I's

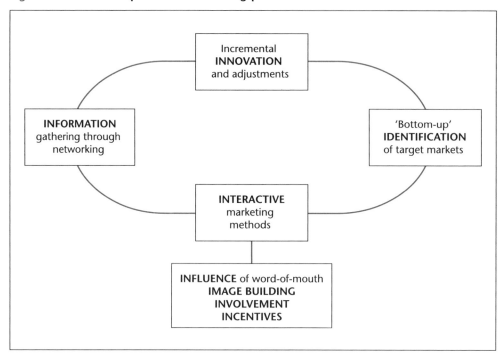

marketing is innovation-oriented, rather than customer-oriented, and entrepreneurs target customers through bottom-up rather than top-down approaches. They also gather information informally through networks of contacts and prefer interactive marketing methods, relying on the influence of word-of-mouth communications, supported by image building, incentives and the involvement of customers. Therefore entrepreneurial marketing can thus be simplified as four process stages – innovation, identification of markets, information gathering and interactive methods – and four elements of the marketing mix – influence, image building, incentives and involvement (four + four I's rather than four P's).

In summary, entrepreneurial marketing can be conceptualised as a process and as specific activities typical of entrepreneurial business owners. Innovative developments and adjustments to products and services are targeted at identified customer and other influential groups. Interactive marketing methods work through the influence of word-of-mouth communications, stimulated by image building, incentives and involvement. Information gathering through informal networks monitors the market-place and evaluates new opportunities, which may, in turn, lead to further innovations, to begin the entrepreneurial marketing process over again. In this way successful owner-managers have overcome the inherent marketing problems in running a small business.

Questions

1 Why do many owners of small firms seem to be wary of marketing?

2 How can entrepreneurs market their business effectively with the limited resources at their disposal?

3 As entrepreneurs rely on word-of-mouth marketing to promote their business, how can they stimulate recommendations and referrals?

4 Is it possible for a business to be both innovation-oriented and customer-oriented?

Web links

www.cim.co.uk
Website of the Chartered Institute of Marketing, the world's leading professional marketing association.

www.womma.org
Website of the Word of Mouth Marketing Association.

www.marketing-society.org.uk
The Marketing Society is a professional association dedicated to raising the stature of marketing in business.

www.academyofmarketing.info
The Academy of Marketing is the leading association in the UK catering to the needs of marketing researchers, educators and professionals.

CHAPTER 18

Finance and the small business

Robin Jarvis

18.1 Introduction

The information available on how small firms are financed is limited because little is in the public domain. However, through a careful search of the literature a picture emerges indicating that small firms use different types of finance compared with large firms. Large firms benefit from established markets where they can raise funds. There are no similar markets for the vast majority of small firms. Therefore, the proportion of equity invested in small firms is much less than that of large companies. In general, small firms tend to rely on bank lending and other types of financial products.

The question of whether a finance gap exists for small firms has been examined and debated over many years and much has been written on the subject. Through government initiatives and the introduction of new products by the financial institutions much has been done to bridge this gap. However, many argue that the gap still exists, particularly for firms starting up or wishing to grow. The influential variables in the capital structure decision of large firms are not as critical in small firm decisions. The markets in which the small firm operates, the firm's life-cycle and the preferences and desires of the owner(s) are influential. The research also shows that there is an important link between small firms' annual report and accounts and the providers of finance. A number of studies have identified that this information is used by providers in their decisions to grant credit and to monitor the firm's progress.

18.2 Learning objectives

This chapter has five learning objectives:

1 To understand the arguments as to whether or not a finance gap exists for small firms.

2 To appreciate the types of finance used by small firms.

3 To recognise that capital structure theory is not influential when small firms make capital structure decisions.

4 To appreciate the importance of small firms' annual report and accounts to the providers of finance.

5 To understand the reasons why small firms and large firms are financed differently.

Key concepts

■ finance gap   ■ capital structure decision   ■ the separation of ownership and management   ■ the importance of annual reports to finance providers

18.3 Finance and the small firm

It is important, when examining the financing of small firms, to recognise that there are distinct differences between the financing of large quoted companies and small firms. Most of the literature, however, relating to finance focuses on large quoted firms and to a great extent implies that it is relevant to small firms. This reflects the commonly held notion that small firms are only smaller versions of large firms.

From a financial-economic perspective, the main difference lies in the lack of availability of capital markets where small firms can raise funds compared with their larger counterparts who have established markets such as the London Stock Exchange. The differences from a socio-economic perspective are primarily associated with the relationship between the finance provider and the enterprise. In the case of small firms the owner normally represents the enterprise in the capacity of both the owner and manager. In large firms, which are invariably quoted companies, the relationship is between the providers of finance (the shareholders who are the owners of the company) and the directors (the managers) who are invariably separate from the owners (shareholders). The significance of these differences will be a theme running throughout this chapter.

Although much has been written about the different types of finance employed by small businesses, only limited information is available on the extent to which each type is actually used. This is because not all the information relating to the financing of small businesses is in the public domain. By contrast, information relating to the different types of finance used by large companies is publicly available from a variety of sources including these companies' own annual reports and accounts. The annual reports 'Finance for Small Firms' published annually by the Bank of England has, however, over the last 11 years made an important contribution to giving helpful insights into the types of finance used by small firms. This Report brought together academic research and surveys from trade and professional bodies to formulate an authoritative picture of small firm finance. Unfortunately, the Bank of England's eleventh report published in April 2004 (Bank of England, 2004) was its last.

The research and the surveys examining the financing of small firms should be interpreted with caution for two reasons. First, there is no universal definition of a 'small' business; the second is connected to the aggregation of the data. This is particularly important when examining how small businesses are financed because it is likely that the extent and source of funds will depend upon the size of business. For example, small firms with a turnover of £50,000 are likely to have very different capital structures from small firms with a turnover of £1m. Another important factor that tends to

339

affect the type of finance employed by a small enterprise is the industrial sector in which it operates. For example, a firm which has tangible assets such as land and buildings that can be offered as security, such as a firm in the property sector, is likely to find it easier to obtain funds than a firm in a sector whose assets are intangible in nature, such as a firm in the advertising industry whose main assets tend to be creative, reflecting the skills of the personnel they employ. These problems will result in reducing the validity of a comparative analysis between research and surveys.

This chapter begins by examining what is referred to as the 'finance gap'. The importance of this gap is reflected in the significant proportion of small business literature devoted to the subject, as well as the number of government committees that have been set up to investigate it. This is followed by a review of the main sources of finance employed by small enterprises and an examination of the relative risk from the perspective of the providers of the finance and the owner-managers of the firms receiving the funds. Next, the capital structure of small enterprises is examined and this focuses on the critical issue of the choice of financing the firm with equity only or with both equity and debt. This section looks at some theoretical models, followed by some evidence of practice. Finally, the role of financial information is considered, with specific reference to financial reporting, and comparisons are made between the users of large company financial reports and how these are used.

18.4 The finance gap

The finance gap refers to a situation where a firm has profitable opportunities but there are no, or insufficient, funds (either from internal or external sources) to exploit the opportunity. In finance theory this situation is known as hard capital rationing, as opposed to soft capital rationing which, to a great extent, is a self-imposed restriction. Hard capital rationing occurs when there is a mismatch between the supply and demand for finance from equity and debt sources. The term 'equity gap' is also commonly used and specifically refers to the gap between funds that can be profitably employed by the firm and its inability to raise equity as opposed to debt. Similarly, the inability to raise debt finance is commonly referred to as the debt gap. Clearly, if a gap in the funding of small businesses exists, it may seriously curtail the growth of such enterprises, which could adversely affect the economy. Not surprisingly, therefore, the subject has attracted much attention from government, policy makers and academia.

Historically, the existence of a 'finance gap' was formally recognised nearly 70 years ago. In 1931 the government-sponsored Macmillan Committee reported that the financing needs of small business were not well served by the then existing financial services institutions. The committee consisting of such eminent academics as John Maynard Keynes and politicians such as Ernest Bevin illustrates the importance given to the subject of financing small firms by government in the 1930s. Since then this criticism of financial institutions has been echoed by other important inquiries (Bolton, 1971; Wilson 1979). In response to this criticism successive governments have introduced a number of initiatives with varying success. For example, the Small Firms' Loan Guarantee Scheme is a guarantee scheme for firms that have limited security to act as collateral for bank loans (this scheme is examined in more detail later in the chapter). In recent years financial services institutions have broadened their scope and for commercial reasons have introduced new products that have made access to funds easier for smaller firms. It has been argued that, if a finance gap still exists, it has been substantially narrowed because of these initiatives and subsequent responses by the market since the 1930s (Deakins, 1996). However, others dispute this claim on both empirical and theoretical grounds (e.g. Harrison and Mason, 1995). The following examines the nature of the gap and some of the evidence of whether it exists and whether it is a constraint on the financing of small enterprises.

In terms of equity capital, most small firms depend on the capital the owner or owners put into the business at the start-up stage, together with a proportion of the profit retained to develop the business. There is a very limited opportunity for small firms to raise funds in the equity markets. The main market for small businesses in which to raise funds is the Alternative Investment Market (AIM), but only a very small proportion of small businesses in the UK are eligible for listing. In addition, there is some evidence to suggest that a large proportion of owner-managers of small firms are reluctant to seek equity finance from external sources (Cowling *et al.*, 1991; Binks *et al.*, 1990b). This reluctance is primarily due to the owner-manager's desire to maintain his independence and control of the business (Keasey and Watson, 1993). AIM will be discussed later in this chapter.

In terms of debt finance (e.g. bank loans) financial institutions should assess the application for funds from small firms applying the principle of risk-return trade-off. Figure 18.1 illustrates the relationship between risk and return. Simply, the economic rationale of the principle dictates that the higher the risk, the higher return that can be expected. With reference to Figure 18.1, point 'a' on the graph is the base rate and the gradient from points 'a' to 'b' represents the increase in interest rates as the risk increases. The point X on the horizontal risk axis represents the risk associated with Firm X; X1 indicates the interest rate (the return) relating to that level of risk. In contrast, point 'Y' on the horizontal axis indicates the risk associated with the much riskier Firm Y and point 'Y1' on the vertical axis the interest rate relating to this higher level of risk. Risk is conventionally measured by the variability in returns of a firm; the higher the variability of returns, the higher the risk and vice versa. The variability in a firm's returns and thus risk is a function of the type of business, the structure of the industry and other similar businesses characteristics.

Whilst this explanation of the relationship between risk and return is blessed with sound economic logic and is widely used for assessing large firms, it suffers from one major problem when applied to small firms since it is impossible to measure risk with any reasonable accuracy. At first sight, this is not necessarily apparent because the word 'risk' in this context is very much a part of institutional financiers' rhetoric, whether referring to large or small firms; for example, the phrase 'well it all depends upon the risk' is commonly heard from clearing bankers when considering business loans. The inability of financial institutions to measure risk and make some assessment of the debt interest that should be charged has resulted in the use of secured lending and crude credit scoring systems to control exposure to risk. Security is normally based on the assets of the borrower or a personal guarantee. The amount of security available is clearly a constraint on borrowing by small business owners. Credit scoring is a system of analysing information for making lending decisions. Points are allocated based on

Figure 18.1 The relationship between risk and return

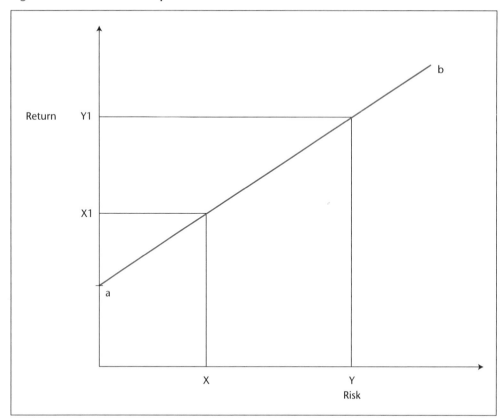

the characteristics of the applicant. The sum of the points is the credit score, which indicates the degree of risk (Berry *et al.*, 1993a: 202). Security and credit scoring both limit the extent to which small firms can borrow and therefore contribute to the finance gap.

Since 1997 deposits have exceeded total lending to small and medium-sized enterprises (SMEs) which suggests that small firms, in general, are not finding it difficult to access debt finance (Bank of England, 2004). This conclusion can also be extended to all sources of finance from the evidence of recent surveys where the small firm respondents have not raised access to finance as a concern (Wilson, 2004; CBI, 2004; Small Business Research Trust, 2003). This suggests that, in general, a so-called 'finance gap' does exist for small firms. However, there is evidence that a number of groups and sectors, categorised within most definitions of a small firm, face distinct challenges when accessing finance. Some of the firms who are subject to these challenges will be discussed below.

It would appear that a subset of small businesses who wish to grow have more acute financing problems because of their need for development finance (Buckland and Davis, 1995). The Wilson Committee some 28 years ago, for example, recognised that the finance gap was a particular problem for such firms. Research shows that only around 10% of firms want to grow (Hakim, 1989a) and of these only approximately 10% will actually do so. However, this subset of small firms has attracted much attention (e.g. Buckland and Davis, 1995) because of their significant actual or perceived contribution to the economy. A particular problem for growth firms is their lack of access to equity capital. The problem is that businesses can only increase loan capital in proportion to assets held and the equity interest prevailing. Therefore, the only way the firm can increase capital is through injections of equity capital. In recognition of the difficulties faced by small enterprises the capital markets have introduced AIM and financial institutions have developed products known as venture capital. Venture capital normally takes the form of equity in high-risk small firms. These firms are characterised by high growth and are often in the high-tech industries.

The shortage of start-up and early-stage equity capital in general, not necessarily in growth firms only, has also been cited as a particular problem for small enterprises (e.g. Robson Rhodes, 1984; ACOST, 1990). The problem often relates to insufficient start-up capital (the amount owner-managers initially invest in the enterprise) and subsequently this affects the ability to raise loan capital.

Women setting up in business have been identified as a particular group who face challenges in raising finance to start up businesses. Women achieve one-third of the funding compared with men when starting up in business (Carter *et al.*, 2001). The reasons for this are not fully understood. Female entrepreneurship is a key issue on the UK government's small business agenda. It is claimed by the UK government that if women set up businesses at the same rate as men in the UK, there would be another 150,000 businesses created every year and if women set up businesses at the same rate as they do in the US there would be another extra 750,000 businesses. Under-capitalisation at the start of the business may lead to long-term under-capitalisation problems and put women at a disadvantage in terms of being able to grow their businesses.

Another group facing challenges in raising finance to set up businesses are university graduates. Graduates are one of the most entrepreneurial groups of people (Global Entrepreneurship Monitor, 2001) and research shows that nearly half of undergraduates would consider setting up their own businesses after university. However, average levels of student debt currently stand at £12,000 (Ward, 2004). This is increasing year on year and is predicted to reach levels of £33,000 per student in 2010 (Ward, 2004). New graduates with significant levels of student debt may be more inclined to enter paid employment. Lending institutions may not be able to provide funds to new graduates to start up in business, given the levels of debt. This could have a significant detrimental effect on the economy.

Much attention in recent times has been given to informal risk capital provided by investors, known as business angels, as a means of providing small amounts of equity capital to close the gap. A number of initiatives have been developed to make this form of finance more accessible. However, the main problem is one of matching potential investors with the firms that need the funds. Business angels are considered in more detail in the next section.

Research into the finance gap has also highlighted an 'information gap'. It is claimed that the reason why small enterprises have problems raising finance is because owner-managers are insufficiently informed of funding opportunities with regard to both equity and loan capital, the quality and cost of information which can drive and sustain bank lending decisions (Bovaird *et al.*, 1995; Binks and Ennew, 1995). In recent years, however, the information flows and the advice available have improved substantially with the setting up of government agencies, such as Business Links, and the growing amount of literature on the range of sources of finance available to small firms.

It would appear that the evidence from research on whether or not there is a finance gap is inconclusive. However, the attention of successive governments to the problems faced by small businesses with regard to raising finance has resulted in a number of initiatives that have improved matters for some owner-managers. At the same time financial institutions have developed a number of products to increase the range of options for financing small enterprises.

18.5 Sources of finance

In this section empirical evidence is drawn upon in order to provide an overview of the nature and usage of varying types of finance employed by small businesses. Usage, it is assumed, is a reasonable surrogate for importance. As already mentioned, the results of the surveys reviewed must be interpreted with care due to the problems associated with the lack of a standard definition for what constitutes a 'small' business and other limitations of survey methods. The main sources of finance are reviewed below.

18.5.1 Banks

The importance of bank lending as a primary source of small business finance is widely acknowledged (Berry *et al.*, 1993a; Binks and Ennew, 1995; Cruickshank, 2000; Keasey and Watson, 1993). Indeed, the Bank of England (2001) quotes the work of Cosh and Hughes (2000), which showed that bank finance accounted for an estimated 61% of external finance in 1997–99 compared with 48% in 1995–97. This is perhaps not surprising as small firms do not have access to the capital markets to raise finance.

The pattern of bank lending to small firms has changed dramatically in recent years. Just over two-thirds of lending by the UK clearing banks is on a fixed-term basis; only less than a third is in the form of overdrafts. This can be contrasted with the situation in 1994 when there was an even split between overdrafts and fixed-term loans. An overdraft is a short-term loan that banks grant customers giving them the right to overdraw their bank account by an agreed amount and is normally repayable on demand.

The term of any loan should ideally be matched with the life of the investment for which the loan is required. For example, if finance is required to purchase a printing machine, the term of the loan ideally should match the commercial life of the printing machine. This ensures that monies generated from the use of the machine are available to repay the loan. The life of the assets used by business to generate funds should be for periods commensurate with long- or medium-term loans that are fixed term. However, if finance is required to fund working capital, a short-term loan, perhaps in the form of an overdraft, is likely to be more appropriate.

Although matching the term of the loan with the life of the investment makes commercial sense, this does not always take place in practice because time is associated with uncertainty and therefore risk. The longer the time period, the greater the uncertainty and the risk associated with predicting outcomes. This notion of uncertainty due to the passing of time is therefore extremely relevant in the lending decision. The length of the loan, in terms of the period of repayment, will be strongly influenced by the other perceived risks associated with the applicant for the loan and the purpose of the loan. Therefore, in the case of most (but still acceptable) applications the lending banker is likely to lend only for a short period, ignoring the matching principles relating to the life of the investment and the repayment of the loan.

Smaller businesses are generally perceived as being more risky than their larger counterparts and this has tended traditionally to lead to banks lending short-term rather than long-term. A survey of small firms by Binks *et al.* (1988) found that 25% of the fixed assets (i.e. long-term investments) were funded by overdraft rather than by fixed, longer-term forms of funding. This strategy, it is argued, was one of the major causes of the liquidity crisis when banks called in overdrafts during the credit squeeze in the early 1990s. The banks suffered considerable criticism for this policy. More recent moves towards increased fixed-term lending may be a reflection of the banks' sensitivity to these criticisms, since such a policy means that they are more exposed to risk.

The provision of finance and other services offered by the clearing banks to small firms has been subject to much criticism since the early 1970s. In 1979 the Wilson Committee concluded that bank managers tend to be overly cautious in their lending decisions, finding evidence of banks demanding a high level of security as collateral for loans, which constrained the financing of small firms in the economy. More recent research (Binks *et al.*, 1988, 1990b, 1993) provides evidence that banks have continued to demand high levels of security. However, some relief has come from the introduction of behavioural scoring and the Small Firms Loan Guarantee (SFLG) Scheme, examined below. Behavioural scoring is a type of credit scoring which monitors customers' credit risk in the light of the activity in their bank accounts. This type of scoring is concerned with helping banks to decide specific terms for individual accounts, based on their risk assessment. For example, if a customer goes into overdraft on his account without previous agreement with the bank then this is likely to go against the customer in terms of his future relationship with the bank. It is claimed that greater reliance on these schemes has tended to lead banks to move away from secured lending, but it seems that collateral is still a major consideration in successfully accessing finance (Graham, 2004).

There has been a concern for many years regarding the lack of competition for bank lending to small firms in the UK. Cruickshank (2000) estimated that the big four UK clearers have 89% of this market. Some commentators have suggested that such concentration levels are detrimental to competition. In the large corporate lending market, the effects of deregulation created an open and competitive environment for UK clearers owing to competition from overseas financial institutions based in London (Berry *et al.*, 1987). With the advent of the European internal market as well as the number of overseas banks in the UK there was an expectation that at least the European banks based in the UK would compete in the UK small business lending market, which would enhance competition. However, to date only a very small proportion of these European banks have entered the small business market (Berry *et al.*, 2003).

18.5.2 Loan Guarantee Scheme

The Small Firms Loan Guarantee (SFLG) Scheme was introduced in 1981 by the government. It stemmed originally from a recommendation of the Wilson Committee 1979 to counter criticism of the high levels of security required by small enterprises to provide as collateral for a loan. Initially, there was a lower than expected take-up and there have been many critics of the scheme. The main criticism is that it is costly (because of the premium). In addition, banks are reluctant to use the scheme because it is excessively bureaucratic and expensive to administer (Robson Rhodes, 1984). For these reasons it had been described as a scheme of last-resort lending for small business owners who have limited security.

The scheme is aimed at small firms that have a viable business proposal, but have tried and failed to obtain a conventional loan from a bank, because of lack of security or business track record, or both. The provision by government to guarantee against the potential default by borrowers enables banks to reduce their exposure to risk and addresses market failure. Currently the government guarantees 75% of the loan, the other 25% being taken on by the banks. The maximum amount of the loan is currently £250,000 for a maximum term of ten years.

The scheme is intended to be in addition to normal commercial finance and is not available if a conventional loan can be obtained. Under the scheme the applicant applies initially to a bank. Once the loan officer has decided that the applicant has a viable business proposal and is eligible for a loan under the scheme, the bank applies to the Department of Trade and Industry (DTI) for a guarantee. The intention is for the scheme to be self-financing and a premium is charged on top of the normal interest rate to recover bad debts. The premium currently stands at 1.5% variable rate and 0.5% fixed-rate lending. In 2003, however, the scheme had a deficit of £60m due to a 35% default rate.

Recently the scheme has been reviewed and recommendations were published in September 2004 (Graham, 2004). These recommendations have been accepted by the government and the scheme will now be focused on start-ups and young businesses, the two groups identified who suffer the most from their inability to raise finance due to lack of collateral and business track record. One of the main criticisms of the scheme is that it is excessively over-regulated. In future, lenders will be able to make decisions without reference and approval from the Small Business Service.

18.5.3 Leasing and hire purchase

Leasing and hire purchase (HP) are often considered together in surveys and, excluding equity, studies show that after bank loans and overdrafts, leasing and HP represents the second most important source of finance to small firms. In this section, further evidence is considered with regard to the use of leasing and HP by small firms, the nature of leasing and HP and the main reasons why it is an attractive source of finance to small firms.

Leasing can be described as a form of renting. The ownership of the asset rests with the lessor who allows the lessee the use of the asset for an agreed period. There are two types of lease: an operating lease and a finance lease. Under an *operating lease*, the asset is leased for a period that is substantially shorter than its useful economic life.

The responsibility, in this case, for servicing and maintenance normally rests with the lessor. Typically, equipment such as photocopiers, computers and cars are acquired by firms under operating leases. Such leases are very attractive to small businesses not only because they are convenient, but because by leasing instead of buying, small firms can insure against the risk of future uncertainty as to the asset's value (e.g. changes in technology) as the risk is transferred to the lessor.

A *finance lease* is a lease that transfers substantially all the risks and rewards of ownership to the lessee (Hussey, 1995). It is a contractual commitment to make a series of payments for the use of an asset over the majority of the asset's life, which normally cannot be cancelled. The lessee therefore acquires most of the economic value of the ownership although the lessor retains the title. Finance leases are long-term and are very similar, apart from the question of ownership when purchasing an asset with a bank loan.

HP is a method of buying goods in which the purchaser takes possession of them as soon as an initial instalment of the price (known as the deposit) has been paid. Ownership of the goods passes to the purchaser when all the agreed number of subsequent instalments, which include an interest charge, have been made. Purchasers have the use of the goods over the period that they are making the payments and, as with leasing, benefit from being able to use the asset without incurring a large capital outlay. It is because of this similarity that HP and leasing are often grouped together when considering sources of finance of firms, as discussed next.

A survey of 90 small businesses (Berry *et al.*, 1990) found that 70% had some assets financed by leasing or HP with 12% of the total value of assets leased and 65% acquired via HP. Of 238 different assets acquired by the sample businesses in a year, 45% were financed by leasing or HP. The sample comprised firms in printing, computer services and professional services, and some significant variation was found in the relative importance of leasing compared with HP. In the printing industry only 9% of the total value of the assets were leased, while 77% were acquired using HP. The main reason for this difference was because the assets acquired (in this case printing machines) tend to appreciate in value and there is a very active second-hand market for them. Therefore, printers preferred to use HP as a source of finance since the ownership of the asset eventually transferred to them. If firms in the printing industry are excluded from the analysis because of this particular preference for HP, the percentage of the value of the assets leased by the remaining sample would be just above 20%.

The study demonstrated that the use made of leasing and HP was related to certain characteristics of both the business and the asset. The larger the size of the firm, the more likely it was to use both leasing and HP. The firm's past experience of various sources of finance in negative or positive terms was also found to affect the firm's future preference for a particular source of finance. Of the sample firms, 21% expressed negative attitudes towards leasing while only 4% of the sample responded negatively to HP. The type of asset was found to influence the type of finance used; for example, assets such as photocopiers and cars have traditionally been marketed via leasing. Finally, the study found that the number of firms using leasing appears to increase with the upward growth rate of the firm, although the number using HP does not.

Previous research, which was mainly focused on large firms, indicates that the influence of tax is the most significant factor influencing the decision to lease. This relates to tax benefits via capital allowances that are obtainable when using finance leases as opposed to operating leases (e.g. Drury and Braund, 1990). A study by Jarvis *et al.* (1994) gathered the views of owner-managers of small firms on the perceived advantages of leasing. The findings showed that tax was not important in the leasing decision and suggested that few owner-managers could undertake the complex tax computations necessary to establish the cost of leasing compared with other forms of finance. The main advantages to owner-managers in leasing is that it avoids a large capital outlay; it is cheaper; it helps cash flow; and it is easier to arrange.

18.5.4 Equity

The term *equity* is used here to mean the finance contributed by the owner(s) of the enterprise. This definition ignores whether the enterprise is a company, a partnership or a sole trader. Although funds from business angels and venture capital could be included within this definition, these forms of finance are considered in detail separately. Individuals starting a business normally need to invest a certain amount of their own money in the business whether they are a sole trader, partnership or a company. After the start-up, owners can choose whether to withdraw profits from the business or to re-invest these funds. Funds retained in the business are another form of equity finance, which together with start-up funds are often referred to as *internal equity*. Finally, during the life of the business, owners may make further investments from their own personal funds to finance the business.

The amount of equity invested by the owners in the business depends on a number of factors, the most influential of which are the owners' wealth and the profitability of the business's activities. From a survey of small firms, Keasey and Watson (1992) estimated that internal equity contributed approximately 30% of the capital structure. This suggests that the amount of equity contributed to the business after start-up from owners, and funds derived from the retention of profits, is relatively low compared with other sources of finance. A more recent survey (Cosh and Hughes, 1996) estimated that only 6% comes from this source. The Keasey and Watson study also found that approximately 70% of operating income is withdrawn by the owners of small firms leaving a relatively small residue to re-invest. This evidence has alerted policy makers to the need to develop strategies to encourage owner-managers, through tax incentives, to retain a greater proportion of profits in the business.

Access to sources of equity other than that contributed by the original owners (external equity) is limited to formal venture capital and informal venture capital (business angels) and raising finance from the Alternative Investment Market (AIM). All of these sources will be discussed separately. However, it should be borne in mind that, as already mentioned, the overriding evidence is that many owner-managers resist any form of external involvement and therefore do not seek external equity sources.

The extent of a small firm's overall funding generally depends on the owner-manager's wealth and the equity in the business. Other forms of finance, such as bank lending, normally depend on the security provided by the business. Such collateral usually takes the form of a charge on the firm's assets or on the personal assets of the owner-manager, or a combination of the two. The limitations of equity sources of small firms therefore constrain the assets acquired by the business and the wealth of the owner-manager further limits their ability to raise finance elsewhere. Binks (1990b) argues that this reliance on collateral effectively creates a 'debt gap'.

18.5.6 The Alternative Investment Market (AIM)

When AIM was established in 1995, Michael Heseltine (then President of the Board of Trade in the UK) said: 'Smaller and growing firms are critical to Britain's long-term economic prosperity and that a market which will enable them to raise capital for investment and have their shares more widely traded can only help to strengthen this sector of the economy.' The support of the government was an important factor in the initial success of the market, but perhaps more important was the timing of its launch in the middle of a bull market when investors had been lured by easy profits made from the sensational share price gains. For example, the shares of ViewInn were placed at 100p and in June 1996 were traded at 650p.

In the first 12 months of its existence, 162 companies obtained a listing on AIM and by 1998 the number had grown to more than 260. This high volume of companies joining AIM in its short lifetime provides strong evidence of the need for an alternative market for small companies. However, during 1998 a series of companies crashed shortly after they were listed on AIM and this has made companies wishing to join the market a little cautious. Generally, prospective companies considering joining, in particular computer and high-tech companies, are looking for a higher profile and a wider source of funds. A survey by Kidson Impey, a firm of accountants, found that potential users of AIM felt that the market is less accessible than a year ago and argue that this is attributable to the increase in due diligence required by nominated advisors as a result of well-publicised failures.

Conditions for listing on AIM are that companies must have a nominated advisor, broker and reporting accountant in order to give investors some degree of reassurance about the quality of the company. Once listed, the company must appoint, and retain at all times, a nominated advisor and nominated broker. The nominated advisor is selected by the corporation from a register of firms approved by the Stock Exchange. The advisor and broker are required to ensure that the company has complied with the listing rules for AIM. The reporting accountant is required to ensure that the company complies with the rules regarding the publication of price-sensitive information and the quality of the interim and annual reports. A prospectus must be produced, but not necessarily a trading record.

A listing currently costs between £200,000 and £400,000, plus around 3% funds raised. The annual cost of listing is at least £25,000. It is generally claimed that AIM is suitable for companies wishing to raise between £1m and £50m. Therefore, only the larger small companies tend to be listed. At this stage in its life, it would appear that AIM makes very little contribution to the overall funding of small enterprises in the UK.

18.5.7 Venture capital

Venture capital is finance provided to companies by specialist financial institutions. Venture capitalists tend to be very selective, concentrating on fairly risky investments typically in the form of backing for entrepreneurs, financing a start-up, developing business, or assisting a management buy-out (MBO) or management buy-in (MBI). Usually the venture capital is represented by a mixture of equity, loans and mezzanine finance. *Mezzanine finance* is usually provided by specialist institutions and is neither pure equity nor pure debt. It can take many different forms and can be secured or unsecured. It usually earns a higher rate of return than pure debt but less than equity, yet carries a higher risk than debt although less than equity. It is often used in the financing of MBOs (Hussey, 1995) and for medium- to long-term investments where the venture capitalist is looking eventually for an exit route.

Although much is written about venture capital as a major source of funds for small enterprises, the evidence is that the majority of firms that receive funds from this source are relatively large enterprises. The average investment of a venture capitalist is £1m to £2m and the smallest investment £100,000. A large and an increasing proportion of capital has been invested in MBOs. Although Murray (1995) contends that venture capital 'represents a small but important part of the finance for new firm formation and industrial restructuring in both the UK and continental Europe', earlier in the same paper he graphically shows start-ups and other early stage finance as representing 6% of UK venture capital investments as opposed to MBO/MBI investments of over 50% in 1991. Arnold (1998) claims that 75% of venture capital in 1995 went into MBO/MBI investments, with only 4% being placed in early stage companies. The Cosh and Hughes (1997) survey shows that between 1% and 2% of small firms used venture capital to finance their business.

Other more recent research has suggested (HM Treasury/SBS, 2003) that the reason why venture capital plays a very little part in the financing of small enterprises is largely because of the high fixed transaction costs associated with the provision of small amounts of capital, a shortage of available exit routes and historically lower returns from early stage finance. In addition, there is also evidence that small business owner-managers do not want equity for fear of dilution of ownership and control (Bank of England, 2002).

In recent years a number of schemes have been introduced by the public sector to inject venture capital funds into the small business economy in an attempt to bridge the equity gap. It is too early to come to any reasonable conclusion relating to the performance of these funds (Bank of England, 2004).

18.5.8 Informal venture capital (business angels)

Business angels are a source of informal venture capital. They are wealthy individuals, rather than financial institutions, who tend to have considerable business experience and are willing to invest in start-ups, early-stage or expanding enterprises. Another description of *business angels* or, more precisely, *informal venture capitalists*, that focuses on the nature of the capital is: 'equity or near equity risk finance invested by private individuals directly into businesses which are not listed on a stock exchange' (Gaston, 1989). The term 'informal' venture capital derives from the fact that it is individuals rather than financial institutions who invest venture capital in a more controlled environment. Although informal venture capital is well developed in the US and could also be a significant source of finance in the UK, it has only been in the past ten years that this type of finance has attracted much attention from academics and policy makers (Mason and Harrison, 1992).

It has been argued (Harrison and Mason, 1995) that the use of informal venture capital provides an appropriate resolution for the new small business equity gap because it lowers the information and monitoring costs that are incurred in borrowing from external sources and there is less likelihood of owner-equity value dilution. Loans and other forms of finance from external sources normally involve the preparation of detailed credit reviews and the collection of information for formal reviews and monitoring of the progress of the enterprise. However, informal venture capitalists normally have prior knowledge of the industry, which is a crucial factor in their investment decision. Information is also disclosed to private informal investors on a more informal and informative basis.

Harrison and Mason claim informal venture capitalists are more patient than venture capitalists and are willing to invest smaller amounts of capital in line with the needs of the owner-managers of small firms. Business angels tend not to look for quick exit routes and typically invest sums up to £10,000. Only a small proportion of angels invest more than £50,000. Very few business angels have high incomes or are millionaires. They tend to have an average income of less than £50,000 p.a. and their worth, excluding their own residence, rarely exceeds £100,000. Business angels sometimes join together to become investment syndicates and, in such cases, the sums invested can be relatively large.

The major problem associated with informal venture capital is that of matching investors with smaller firms seeking finance. The main way in which firms and business angels find one another is through friends, family and business connections. In recognition of the importance of this source of income, formal networks have been set up to aid this matching; for example, most Business Links maintain databases of interested parties. However, it would appear that only a small proportion of proposals are attractive to business angels since between 90% and 97% of proposals are rejected.

The extent to which business angels contribute to the pool of finance available to small enterprises is extremely difficult to determine. There does appear to be an acknowledgement, however, that informal venture capital contributes considerably more funds to financing small enterprises than venture capital does. A survey estimated that in 1997 some 4% of funds for a sample of small firms was derived from business angels (Cosh and Hughes, 1996). Therefore, business angels play an important role in the financing of small enterprises, but not so significantly to claim that this source of funds will address market failure and resolve the finance gap.

There is more detailed discussion of informal and formal venture capital and its role in the development of entrepreneurship and small firms in Chapter 19.

18.5.9 Factoring

Factoring is the purchase by a factor of the trade debts of a business, usually for immediate cash. The sales accounting functions are then provided by the factor who will manage the sales ledger and collection accounts, under terms agreed by the seller. The factor may agree to take the credit risk within certain limits or this risk may be retained by the seller. This source of finance is, to a certain extent, dependent upon the nature of the business (i.e. where the business has a reasonably high debtors' balance). In the right circumstances, factoring can provide a significant source of finance on a continuing basis to firms.

An interesting paper published by the Policy Unit of the Institute of Directors in 1993 examining the late payment of debt argued convincingly that the 'majority of overdue debts could be reduced by better credit management' (Institute of Directors, 1993). Good credit management itself is, of course, a source of finance. Research shows that small firms in particular suffer from late payment and tend to have weak credit management. Factors employ specialist credit controllers and tend to use state-of-the-art computer software, which enables them to manage efficiently the credit given to the customers of small firms. The effectiveness of factors in credit management is demonstrated by figures published by the Factors and Discounters Association (FDA) in 1995: the average waiting period for payment was 75 days as compared with the factoring industry's own average of 58 days.

Over the past 20 years factoring has increased in popularity. For example, turnover in the factoring industry rose from £4.4m in 1984 to £47.2m in 1997. Ignoring currency fluctuations this still represents a significant increase. However, it would appear that only 8% of small and medium-sized enterprises (SMEs) in the UK currently use factoring (Grant Thornton, 1998). A survey of the perceptions of accountants (Berry and Simpson, 1993) identified three main reasons why SMEs do not use factoring: the high cost, reduced customer relations and the issue of confidentiality. There is, however, very little independent evidence on the perceptions of owner-managers of small enterprises since much of the literature in this area tends to be anecdotal and speculative.

Invoice discounting is normally classified as a form of factoring; however, it simply relates to the raising of finance from customers and excludes all the credit management functions normally associated with factoring. With invoice discounting, therefore, invoices are pledged to the finance house in return for an immediate payment of up to 90% of the face value. It will then be the responsibility of the finance house to collect the debt. Invoice discounting has grown significantly over the years and in 2003 invoice financing provided just under £1b of finance for firms with an annual turnover of less than £1m.

18.6 The capital structure decision

Finance theory assumes that the firm is a vehicle for shareholders to maximise their wealth and ignores other stakeholders. Much of the finance literature also assumes there is a separation of ownership and control by directors/managers. Therefore, it is not surprising that the main question when deciding how the firm should be financed is whether there is an optimal capital structure that will maximise the value of the firm and hence shareholders' wealth.

Traditionally, the starting point for examining the capital structure decision is the seminal paper by Modigliani and Miller (1958). Modigliani and Miller demonstrated that assuming a perfect capital market with no information costs, the value of the firm is independent of its capital structure. Thus, there is no optimal capital structure, therefore the financing decision is irrelevant and the value of the firm is solely dependent upon the firm's ability to generate profits (cash flows) from operations. Their assumptions importantly include a world with no taxes. Since this paper, a number of researchers have examined the effect on the capital structure decision by the relaxing of one or more of the market imperfections which Modigliani and Miller in their 1958 paper assumed did not exist (e.g. Ross, 1977; Myers, 1984). Perhaps the most influential research that allowed for one of these market imperfections was in a paper by Modigliani and Miller themselves in 1963 which considered the effect of corporate and personal taxes on the capital structure decision. Modigliani and Miller in this later paper demonstrate that, when other things are held constant, firms with high tax rates should use more debt than firms with low rates, because the value of debt financing is tax deductibility *vis-à-vis* equity, and the value of this benefit increases with the tax rate. Therefore, financing the firm using debt rather than equity implies that firms should obtain as much debt finance as possible. Clearly this does not happen in practice, primarily because of the countering effects of other market imperfections such as bankruptcy. However, this is not to say that this tax effect is not influential to some extent in the overall capital structure decision.

Despite these developments in finance theory it does not yet fully explain the different capital structures that firms adopt in practice nor do we know how firms choose the debt, equity or hybrid securities they issue (Myers, 1984). Nevertheless, from a careful inspection of real-world market imperfections we get a good idea of the factors that will affect the capital structure decision (Higson, 1993). However, large firms have been the main focus of the research on capital structure decision (Michaelas *et al.*, 1996) and thus the literature relating to small firms' capital structure is less well developed and restricted to a few papers (Keasey and Watson, 1993).

Small firms, of course, are subject to very different financial, economic and socioeconomic structures compared with large firms. For example, as previously mentioned, there tends not to be a separation between ownership and control of firms and large firms are listed and quoted on markets. These are two significant characteristics of small firms that are likely to influence the capital structure decision. Therefore, capital structure decision theory related to large firms has very limited applicability to small firms.

Norton (1990, 1991a and 1991b) is one of a few researchers who have examined the capital structure decision from the perspective of small firms. In examining a number of market imperfections, which it is claimed are influential in the capital structure decision of large firms, Norton argues that bankruptcy costs, agency costs and information asymmetries seem to have very little effect on a small firm's capital structure decision. He also highlights the importance of certain factors relating to the market in which the firm operates, and the preferences and desires of the owner(s). Small firms, Norton concludes, are less likely to have target debt ratios and there is a preference to use internal finance to external finance.

Michaelas *et al.* (1996) conducted a study of the financial and non-financial factors that determine the capital structure of small privately owned firms. Their findings show that the life-cycle of a small firm is influential in determining its capital structure. When firms start up, and as they grow, they use debt finance. However, as they mature the reliance on debt declines. A positive relationship was found between gearing and the collateral value of the assets and this emphasises the importance of security in the bank lending decision. The research also found that tax and bankruptcy costs were not influential in the decision and no relationship was found between gearing levels and profitability, growth, risk and the level of debtors. Firms in different industrial sectors seem to differ in their capital structure preferences and it was found that economic conditions also had a bearing on the capital structure decision.

Research to date from a small firm perspective does highlight that financial theory related to large firms, and particularly that related to the theory of the capital structure decision, is not necessarily appropriate to smaller enterprises.

18.7 Financial reporting considerations

An important link between the sources of finance for a business, particularly for small firms, are the financial reports produced periodically by firms which primarily give an account of the performance for a stated period, normally a year (the profit and loss account), and the financial position of the business on a stated date (the balance sheet). The evidence is that this information is required by the providers (creditors) of finance when assessing the applicant firm requiring the finance (Berry *et al.*, 1993a). Also there is evidence that some creditors, such as banks, require financial reports to monitor the progress of the business to which they provided finance (Berry *et al.*, 1993b).

Sole traders and partnerships are not required by statute to disclose such information, but may do so in order to satisfy the needs of creditors. In contrast, companies are required by statute to file annual accounts (whether or not they are seeking external finance) with the Registrar of Companies and give copies to their shareholders. However, it is the legal requirements and accounting regulations that influence and drive the form and nature of the annual accounts produced by small enterprises who are outside the scope of these requirements. In the main, the legal and regulatory requirements have been designed for large quoted companies where there is a separation of ownership and management. The primary concern of the regulations is one of stewardship; that is, the annual financial report forms an integral information liaison between the managers (directors) of the company, who run the operations of the business on the one hand, and the owners (shareholders) of the business on the other. Of the total companies in the UK, only 0.8% are quoted; the other 99.2% are unquoted, and 99.5% of these companies are small. Therefore, the way in which these small companies report has very little to do with their needs. Consequently, it may be the case that the financial reports for small businesses would look very different if standard setters considered what they are used for and who uses them.

In a review of the literature (Jarvis, 1996) on the users and uses of the financial statements of small businesses, banks were identified as a major user (e.g. Berry *et al.*, 1987, 1993b; Deakins and Hussian, 1994b). Within the bank-lending process, it is recognised that financial reports play a significant role (Berry *et al.*, 1993b). In fact, the 'excessive' use of financial reports and other financial information in this process has been heavily criticised by some; for example, Deakins and Hussian (1994a) argue: 'we find that there is an excessive reliance on financial information such as forecast balance sheets and profit and loss accounts and standard financial ratios.'

The findings of research into bankers' use of financial reports recognise that the use of financial information is dependent upon a number of contingent variables (Berry and Waring, 1995). An influential factor in the use of financial information is whether or not the applicant is currently a customer with the bank and whether the business in question is new or existing (Berry *et al.*, 1993b). For example, if the application is from an owner-manager of a new business no financial reports would be available. There is also evidence that this user group can obtain additional information in support of figures in financial statements (e.g. management accounting information and valuation reports commissioned by the business). Banks are able to successfully demand this information because they are in a relatively powerful position within the relationship.

In the literature review identified earlier (Jarvis, 1996) a study by Mitchell *et al.* (1995) examined venture capitalists' use of financial reports in investment decisions. The financial statement was seen as an important source of information in the process of making decisions.

Recent research (Collis and Jarvis, 2000) provides evidence of owner-managers' use of financial reports. It is clear that managers recognise the importance of financial statements to creditors of the enterprise. In that context it is likely that owner-managers will monitor the reports to ensure that everything looks correct in respect of creditors, otherwise this may cause concern (Jarvis, 1996).

Although there is no further evidence of other creditors' (e.g. business angels) use of financial reports it is generally assumed that these investors in small companies are significant users of financial reports of SMEs, even though they may not necessarily reflect the needs, as previously mentioned, of users of the reports.

18.8 Chapter summary

This chapter examined the types and sources of finance used by small firms and three important related issues: the finance gap, the capital structure decision and financial reporting. Small firms use different types of finance compared with large firms. Large firms have established markets where they can publicly raise funds but there are no similar markets for the majority of small firms. The proportion of equity invested in small firms tends to be less and there is more reliance on bank lending. Over the years the question as to whether a finance gap exists has been debated. Although the finance gap is never likely to disappear completely, through the introduction of government initiatives and new products by financial institutions it has become much less of a constraint for the majority of firms.

Finance theory relating to the capital structure decision was found not to be wholly applicable to small firms. A significant influential variable is the life-cycle of small firms. When firms start up, and as they grow, they tend to rely on debt, but when the firm matures this reliance on debt declines. The amount of security available, however, restricts the extent to which the firm can obtain debt financing. The concept of stewardship (reporting to the owners of the business on the performance of the firm's management) is irrelevant in the reporting of the financial affairs of small businesses. However, financial reports are an important source of information for financial institutions in making credit decisions and monitoring the client's progress. Therefore, it is clear that from a number of perspectives the financing of small businesses differs significantly from the way in which large firms are financed.

Questions

1 Are small enterprises constrained in their operations by the lack of finance?

2 Why do large companies use different types of finance compared with small firms?

3 From a financial perspective compare businesses where there is a separation between the owners and the managers, and where the owner is also the manager.

4 What are the influential variables in the capital structure decision of businesses? Do they differ according to the size of the business (i.e. whether it is small or large)?

5 Small businesses invariably have higher gearing levels than large businesses. Discuss.

6 Why are the financial reports of small businesses used by banks in making lending decisions?

Web links

www.acca.co.uk/smallbusiness/
The Association of Chartered and Certified Accountants (ACCA) site for small business policy.

www.bankofengland.co.uk/publications/financeforsmallfirms/
A range of reports, published by the Bank of England between 1991 and April 2004, which monitored the availability of finance to SMEs in the UK.

www.dti.gov.uk/sflg/
Details of the UK Government's Small Firms Loan Guarantee (SFLG) Scheme.

CHAPTER 19

Venture capital and the small business

Colin Mason

19.1 Introduction

Firms pursuing significant growth opportunities are likely to find that their financial needs exceed their capability to generate funds internally while their ability to attract bank loans is restricted by their lack of collateral and negative cash flows. Indeed, the faster a firm grows the more voracious is its appetite for cash – investments in research and development (R&D), product development and testing, recruitment of key team members, premises, specialised equipment, raw materials and components, sales and distribution capability, inventories and marketing all add up (Bygrave and Timmons, 1992). These firms will need to turn to venture capital in order to achieve their growth ambitions. *Venture capital* can be defined as finance that is provided on a medium- to long-term basis in exchange for an equity stake. Investors will share in the upside, obtaining their returns in the form of a capital gain on the value of the shares at a 'liquidity event', which normally involves a stock market listing, the acquisition of the company by another company or the sale of the shares to another investor, but will lose their investment if the business fails. Venture capital investors therefore restrict their investments to businesses that have the potential to achieve rapid growth and achieve a significant size and market position because it is only in these circumstances that they will be able to achieve both a liquidity event and a capital gain. However, very few businesses are capable of meeting these demanding investment criteria. So, as Bhidé (2000: 16) observes, venture capital-backed firms 'represent an out-of-the-ordinary phenomenon'.

Although the number of companies that are successful in raising venture capital is small they have a disproportionate impact on economic development in terms of innovation, job creation, R&D expenditures, export sales and the payment of taxes (Bygrave and Timmons, 1992). The injection of money and support enables venture capital-backed companies to grow much faster than the proceeds from sales revenue alone would allow. Moreover, this superior growth rate is sustained over the long run (Gompers and Lerner, 2001b). Venture capital-backed companies are faster in developing products and bringing them to market, pursue more radical and ambitious product or process innovation, and produce more valuable patents (Hellman and Puri, 2000). It is because venture capital-backed companies play such an important role in economic

357

development that venture capital attracts the attention of both scholars and policy makers.

As a final introductory point, it needs to be acknowledged that this chapter takes an 'Anglo-Saxon' perspective focusing largely on the US and UK literature. Venture capital was pioneered in the US immediately after the Second World War and it was not until the early 1980s that it began to develop in Western Europe, initially in the UK and subsequently on the Continent. During the 1990s embryonic venture capital industries began to appear in emerging markets such as Asia and central Europe, and these regions are now beginning to attract attention from researchers (e.g. see Lockett and Wright, 2002, and Wright *et al.*, 2002). However, venture capital in Europe and Asia is rather different from its namesake in the US, being less technology-oriented and focused on more mature and later-stage deals rather than young, rapidly growing entrepreneurial companies. These differences are reflected in terminology. In Europe the term 'venture capital' and 'private equity' are often used interchangeably to cover all types of equity investment from start-up through to management buy-outs (MBOs) and buy-ins (MBIs), that is, the funding of incumbent or incoming management teams to buy companies from their owners to run as independent businesses. However, in the US the venture capital and MBO/MBI investments (termed leveraged buy-outs, or LBOs) are regarded as entirely different industries, with the term 'venture capital' restricted to investments in new or recently started companies (Campbell, 2003). This chapter follows the US definition of venture capital, focusing on the financing of the seed, start-up and early-growth stages of business development.

19.2 Learning objectives

This chapter has three learning objectives:

1 To consider the demand side in order to highlight the sources of finance available to companies at different stages in their development

2 To understand the role of business angels (or *informal* venture capital) and venture capital funds (or *formal* venture capital) as they are potentially available to any firm that offers the promise of rapid growth.

3 To consider the characteristics of investors, their investment activity, sources of deals, investment criteria, deal characteristics, post-investment involvement and harvest.

Key concepts

■ finance for small firms ■ business angels ■ venture capital

19.3 Financing entrepreneurial companies: a demand-side perspective

Entrepreneurial companies typically evolve through multiple stages of growth and development, with attendant changes in their capital requirements and the source of the finance (Roberts, 1991a). At the *seed stage* (or zero stage) a business will be in the process of being established, is undertaking R&D, solving key product development issues and moving to an operating demonstration prototype of the initial product. This phase typically occurs in the founder's home while the founder is working full-time. There may not be a formal business plan at this stage. Financial needs are likely to be fairly minimal and will be met by a combination of the founder's own personal savings, family and friends (the three F's) and 'bootstrapping' techniques – where bootstrapping can be defined as strategies for marshalling and gaining control of resources at minimal or no cost (see Bhidé, 1992; Freear *et al.*, 1995a; Winborg and Landström, 2001; Harrison *et al.*, 2004).

Commercial investors will regard such 'pre-ventures' as being too high risk. However, government support may be available in the form of R&D and proof-of-concept grants for technology-based firms. The *start-up stage* begins with the founding of the company, demonstration of commercial applicability, securing of initial sales and seeking new sales channels. The financial needs increase as the company invests in capital equipment, begins to employ staff and for working capital. Investment in businesses at this early stage is very high risk – the management is unproven and the product or service has yet to demonstrate widespread acceptance – and any return may not materialise for five to ten years. Thus, businesses are likely to continue to rely upon a combination of 'love money', bootstrapping and government support, although those with growth prospects may be able to raise finance from business angels. Particularly in Europe, few venture capital funds will be interested in investing at such an early stage unless they have been established with an economic development mandate. Companies that come through the start-up stage with a product or service which is in demand enter the *initial growth stage*. The business will be seeking to improve product quality and lower its unit costs and develop new products. The business may be reaching profitability but this is insufficient to fund the growth that is required to expand plant and equipment and obtain bigger premises and additional staff to fill out each of the functional areas and increased working capital requirements. Risk and uncertainty have declined. By this stage the business will no longer be reliant on 3F money. The main source of funding will be business angels but they typically make relatively small investments (less than £250,000), so larger funding requirements and follow-on financing are likely to be met by venture capital funds. Companies that continue to grow enter the *sustained growth stage*. These companies are often termed 'gazelles', and can expect to grow to beyond £10m/$20m in sales and 100 employees. Profits and cash flow are sufficient to meet the majority of their capital requirements but additional finance may be required to grasp new growth possibilities (including acquisitions). Such companies will look to venture capital funds specialising in development capital and even to more esoteric financing instruments, and ultimately to a stock market listing where shares are available to the public (Roberts, 1991a; Sohl, 1999).

Thus, there are a variety of potential funding sources available to finance new businesses through these stages of growth and development.

19.3.1 Personal savings of the entrepreneur or team

This is typically the primary source of initial funding. Even though the amounts involved are usually quite small, this funding is important for two reasons. First, subsequent investors will expect to see that entrepreneurs have committed themselves financially to the business. Second, the effect of raising outside capital will be to dilute the proportion of the business owned by the original entrepreneurs. Thus, the bigger the amount that they are able to invest, and the longer that they can survive on this and other non-equity sources of funding and bootstrapping, then the less dilution they will experience when they come to raise external capital. The entrepreneur is also likely to contribute 'sweat equity' by working for no salary or at a level below what could be obtained by working for someone else until the business is on a solid financial footing.

19.3.2 Family and friends

Recent research by the Global Entrepreneurship Monitor (GEM) consortium, an international consortium of 38 countries that collect data on entrepreneurial activity on a consistent basis by means of large-scale household surveys, reports that close family members, friends and neighbours are by far the biggest source of start-up capital after the founders themselves (Bygrave *et al.*, 2003). Such investments typically take the form of short-term loans which may be converted into equity at a later stage. This form of finance is relatively easy to obtain, although the amounts involved are relatively small. The providers are unlikely to regard their investment as a commercial one and, indeed, may not expect it to be repaid. However, entrepreneurs may be reluctant to 'take advantage' of kinship and friendship ties and may feel under emotional pressure not to lose the money (Roberts, 1991a).

19.3.3 Business angels

These are wealthy private individuals, generally with a business background, and often cashed-out entrepreneurs, who invest their own money – either on their own or with a syndicate of other angels – in new or recently started businesses with growth potential. Their motives are economic but not totally so. Non-economic motivations include the fun and enjoyment that come from an involvement with a young, growing company and social responsibility. Their investments are typically at or soon after start-up and range from under £10,000 to over £250,000, although the norm is £50,000 to £100,000. These investors do not normally seek a controlling interest or management position in the business but it is usual for them to perform an advisory role and they would expect to be consulted on major management decisions.

19.3.4 Venture capital firms

Venture capital firms are financial intermediaries that attract investments from financial institutions (banks, pension funds, insurance companies), large companies, wealthy families and endowments into fixed life investment vehicles ('funds') with a specific investment focus (location, technology, stage of business development). The money is then invested in young, growing businesses that offer the prospects of high reward. The function of the fund managers (the general partners) is to identify promising investment opportunities, support them though the provision of advice, information and networking and ultimately exit from the investment. The proceeds from the exit – or liquidity event – are returned to the investors (the limited partners). Most venture capital firms are independent organisations. Some are subsidiaries of financial institutions (termed 'captives'). A few large non-financial companies, particularly technology companies, have their own venture capital subsidiaries that invest for strategic reasons to complement their own internal R&D activities (corporate venture capital). Venture capital firms rarely invest in basic innovation. Rather, venture capital money assumes importance once the business model, product and management capabilities have been proven, market acceptance has been demonstrated and uncertainties about the size of the market and the profitability of the business have been reduced (Bhidé, 2000). Companies at this stage are looking to commercialise their innovation and need funding to create the infrastructure to grow the business (Zider, 1998). Thus, venture capital firms tend to invest significantly larger amounts than business angels and invest at later stage in business development.

19.3.5 Government-backed investment organisations

In most countries governments have created investment vehicles to fill what are perceived to be gaps in the supply of venture capital that results in funding difficulties for particular types of company. In the past it was common for governments to use their own money to provide the investment funds. However, it is now common practice for governments to create investment funds under private management by leveraging private sector money by using the tax system or other financial incentives to alter the balance of risk and reward for the private investor. Examples of venture capital funds that have been created as a result of tax incentives are Venture Capital Trusts (VCTs) in the UK and Labor-Sponsored Venture Capital Funds in Canada (Ayayi, 2004). Examples of investment funds created as a result of government co-investment alongside private money but on less favourable terms, thereby improving the investor's return, include Small Business Investment Companies (SBICs) in the US, the KfW and DtA programmes in Germany and the Regional Venture Capital Schemes in England (Sunley et al., 2005).

Gaining a listing on a public stock market may be the logical final step for a fast-growing company to fund its ongoing growth. Further shares in the company can be sold to institutional and private investors to raise additional finance. Raising debt finance also becomes easier with a public listing. Public companies can also use their shares to make acquisitions. And a listing is also an important way in which existing shareholders – notably the founders and their families, business angels and venture capital funds – can realise their capital gains. However, the costs of obtaining and maintaining a stock market listing mean that it is only an option for larger companies.

Amazon.com provides a good example of a company that has drawn on these various sources of finance as it has grown (Table 19.1). However, while most companies will utilise 3F money, only a minority will go on to raise second- and third-round funding from external sources. For example, in Manigart and Struyf's (1997) study of young, high-tech Belgian companies, all had relied on funding from the founder or founding team for start-up capital. Most had also raised funding from other sources, notably family, banks and private investors, whereas only two firms had raised venture capital. Eight firms went on to raise a second round of finance: six firms attracted investments by venture capital funds (including the two firms that had raised venture

Table 19.1 A financial chronology of Amazon.com, 1994–99

Date	Price per share ($)	Source of funds
7/94–11/94	0.001	Founder: Jeff Bezos starts Amazon.com with $10,000 of his own money and borrows a further $44,000
2/95–7/95	0.1717	Family: father and mother invest a combined $245,000
8/95–12/95	0.1287–0.3333	Business angels: two angels invest a total of $54,408
12/95–5/96	0.3333	Angel syndicate: 20 angels invest $46,850 each on average for a total of $937,000
5/96	0.333	Family: siblings invest $20,000
6/96	2.3417	Venture capitalists: two venture capital funds invest $8 million
5/97	18	Initial public offering: three million shares are offered on the equity market raising $49.1m
12/97–5/98 (exercise price on loan warrants)	52.11	Loan and bond issue: $326m bond issue is used to retire $75m in loan debt and to finance operations

Source: van Osnabrugge and Robinson (2000: 59)

capital at start-up, which raised larger amounts of funding from venture capital syndicates), and two firms raised finance from corporate venture capital sources. None of the firms raised further finance from founders or family.

The remainder of this chapter examines the two main sources of external equity finance – business angels and venture capital firms. Agency theory provides a framework to study their investment process. An agency relationship is said to exist when one individual (the principal) engages the services of another individual (the agent) to perform a service on their behalf (Jensen and Meckling, 1976). This involves the delegation of a measure of decision-making authority from the principal to the agent. Both are assumed to be economic-maximising individuals. The central concern of agency theory is opportunism – the separation of ownership and control creates the risk that the agent will make decisions that are not in the best interests of the principal. This creates two types of risk for the principal (i.e. the investor). The first is adverse selection, which arises as a result of informational asymmetries: the agent is better informed than the principal about his true level of ability. However, agents may deliberately misrepresent their abilities to the principal. The second risk is moral hazard. In situations where it is not possible for the principal to observe the behaviour of agents the latter may shirk, engage in opportunistic behaviour that is not in the interests of the principal or pursue divergent interests that maximise their economic interests rather than those of the principal. Fiet (1995) argues that every investment decision also includes market risk – the risk that the business will perform less well than anticipated on account of competitive conditions (e.g. competition, demand, technological change). A key theme running through the remainder of this chapter is how business angels and venture capital fund manage these sources of risk.

19.4 Business angels

19.4.1 Definition and characteristics

Business angels are conventionally defined as *high-net-worth individuals who invest their own money directly in unquoted companies in which they have no family connection in the hope of financial gain and typically play a hands-on role in the businesses in which they invest.* Several aspects of this definition need to be emphasised. First, having wealth is a prerequisite for becoming a business angel. Business angels invest upwards of £10,000 per deal (sometimes in excess of £100,000) and typically have a portfolio of between two and five investments. However, because this is high risk most business angels will only allocate between 5% and 15% of their overall investment portfolio to such investments. Second, the fact that business angels are investing their own money means that they do not have to invest if they are unable to find suitable investment opportunities. They can also make quick investment decisions and have less need for specialist professional input so their transaction costs are low. It also means that they can have idiosyncratic investment criteria. Third, investing directly means that business angels are making their own investment decisions rather than investing in a pooled investment vehicle in which investment decisions are made by a manager. This implies that people who become business angels have both the networks that will provide a flow of investment opportunities and the competence to undertake the appraisal of these opportunities. Indeed, the majority of business angels are successful cashed-out entrepreneurs, while the remainder either have senior experience in large businesses or have specialist professional expertise. Fourth, business angels are active investors in unquoted companies, playing a hands-on role in supporting their growth. Fifth, business angels are investing for a financial return.

However, psychic income is also important. Business angels derive considerable fun and enjoyment from being involved with entrepreneurial businesses. Indeed, for successful entrepreneurs becoming a business angel is a way in which they can recapture this experience and use the skills and intuition that they have developed as entrepreneurs to the benefit of their investee companies.

The typical business angel therefore has the following profile:

- *Male*: typically around 95% of business angels are males. This reflects the fact that relatively few women have built up successful companies or hold senior positions in the corporate sector.

- *Successful cashed-out entrepreneurs*: most business angels have had experience of business start-up and growth. This provides them with the skills and competence to evaluate investment opportunities and add value to those business that they invest in.

- *In the 45–65 year age group*: this reflects the length of time required to build significant personal net worth, the greater discretionary wealth of this age group and the age at which successful entrepreneurs may choose, or be forced, to disengage. Becoming a business angel is often a way in which such individuals remain economically active. Indeed, some cashed-out entrepreneurs become business angels because they find that a life of leisure is boring.

These characteristics are remarkably consistent across countries. However, this typical profile masks considerable heterogeneity in the business angel population, notably in terms of their motivation, the size and frequency of their investments, and their involvement with their investee companies (Coveney and Moore, 1998; Kelly and Hay, 1996; 2000; Sørheim and Landström, 2001). What this underlines from the entrepreneur's perspective is that angel funding is a differentiated commodity and that they must identify the appropriate type of investor who is both willing and capable of contributing the financial and other resources that they require.

19.4.2 Size of the market

It is impossible to be precise about the number of business angels, the number of investments made and the amount invested. This is because there is no obligation for business angels to identify themselves or register their investments. Indeed, the vast majority of business angels strive to preserve their anonymity and are secretive about their investment activity, not least to avoid being inundated by entrepreneurs and other individuals seeking to persuade them to invest or provide financial support for other causes (Benjamin and Margulis, 2000). Thus, measures of the size of the informal venture capital market are only crude estimates. Sohl (2003) suggests that there are 300,000 to 350,000 business angels in the US, investing approximately $30bn in almost 50,000 ventures. Venture capital funds, in contrast, invest $30–$35bn in fewer than 3,000 entrepreneurial ventures. The equivalent estimate for the UK is 20,000 to 40,000 business angels investing £0.5bn to £1bn in 3,000 to 6,000 companies. They make eight times as many investments in start-up companies as venture capital funds (Mason and Harrison, 2000). However, these calculations of the amounts invested by business angels are an underestimate of the size of the informal venture capital market. First, most business angels have further funds available to invest (Coveney and Moore, 1998; Mason and Harrison, 1994, 2002a) but cannot identify appropriate investment opportunities. This uncommitted capital is substantial: one study reported that it exceeded the amount invested by the respondents in the three years prior to the surveys (Mason and Harrison, 2002a). Second, there is a substantial pool of potential, or virgin, business angels who share the characteristics of active angels but have not entered the market (Freear et al., 1994a; Coveney and Moore, 1998). Sohl (1999) has estimated that in the US these potential angels exceed the number of active investors by a factor of five to one.

19.4.3 Investment characteristics

We have already noted that business angels occupy a crucial place in the spectrum of finance available to growing businesses, providing amounts of finance that are beyond the ability of entrepreneurs to raise from their own resources and from family, and below the minimum investment threshold of venture capital funds. Business angels, investing on their own or in small *ad hoc* groups, will typically invest up to £100,000, while the larger angel syndicates will make investments of £250,000 and above. This investment is usually provided in the form of equity or a combination of equity plus loans. However, all-loan investments are by no means unusual. (As Gaston (1989) notes, the financial needs of new and young businesses are not neatly boxed into separate loan and equity categories. Their capital needs frequently shift between these types. Angels make their investments in the form of loans (usually unsecured), loan guarantees, equity and combinations of these types of finance.) In terms of *stage of business development*, investments by business angels are skewed towards the seed, start-up and early-growth stages whereas venture capital funds focus on business expansion.

The geographical characteristics of business angel investments are also important. This has two dimensions. First, 'angels live everywhere' (Gaston, 1990: 273). Gaston's research suggests that the proportion of business angels in the US adult population is fairly constant at around four angels in every 1,000 adults. Certainly, research has documented the presence of business angels in various economically lagging regions, such as Atlantic Canada (Feeney *et al.*, 1998; Farrell, 1998; Johnstone, 2001). Second, however, there is a greater chance of a mismatch between the needs of the entrepreneurs and the preferences and value-added skills of potential investors in such regions. Johnstone (2001) notes that, in the case of Cape Breton, demand for angel finance is concentrated among IT businesses and they want investors to provide marketing and management inputs whereas the investors typically have no knowledge of the sector and so have limited ability to add value.

In contrast, institutional sources of venture capital are disproportionately concentrated in leading economic regions, such as Silicon Valley and New England in the US, and south east England in the UK (Mason and Harrison, 1999). Second, various studies indicate that the majority of investments by business angels are local. This reflects both the localised nature of their business and personal networks through which they identify most of their investments and their hands-on investment style and consequent need for frequent contact with their investee businesses. Two implications follow. First, in most areas outside major financial centres and technology clusters business angels are the only source of risk capital (Gaston, 1989). Second, the informal venture capital market is an important mechanism for retaining and recycling wealth within the region that it was created.

19.4.5 The investment process

Following Riding *et al.* (1993) and Haines *et al.* (2003) a number of discrete stages in the investment process can be identified:

- deal origination;
- deal evaluation: this can, in turn, be sub-divided into at least two sub-stages: initial screening and detailed investigation;
- negotiation and contracting;
- post-investment involvement;
- harvesting.

As we will see later, this sequence is similar in most respects to the investment decision-making model of institutional venture capital funds (Tybjee and Bruno, 1984; Fried and Hisrich, 1994). However, the approach of business angels is less sophisticated.

19.4.6 Deal origination

The evidence is consistent in suggesting that business angels adopt a relatively *ad hoc* and unscientific approach to identifying investment opportunities. Informal personal contacts – business associates and friends – are the most significant sources of deal flow. Professional contacts are much less significant: of these, accountants are the most frequent source whereas few business angels receive deal flow from lawyers, bankers and stockbrokers. Those angels who are known in their communities also receive approaches from entrepreneurs. Information in the media is another source of deal flow for a significant minority of business angels. Some business angels also undertake their own searches for investment opportunities. Those business angels who are members of Business Angel Networks (BANs), which provides a mechanism for entrepreneurs who are looking to raise finance and investors who are looking for deals to connect with each other, also report that these organisations are significant sources of deal flow (Mason and Harrison, 1994, 2002a). In some cases, especially in the case of *ad hoc* investors, the entrepreneur is not a stranger but a business associate who is known to the angel (e.g. client or supplier) (Atkin and Esiri, 1993). Kelly and Hay (2000) observe that the most active investors rely less on 'public' sources (e.g. accountants, lawyers, etc.) and place more emphasis on 'private' sources that are referred by individual and institutional sources in their extensive and long-standing networks of relationships.

However, these various sources of information differ in their effectiveness. Freear *et al.* (1994b) have calculated yield rates for different information sources (i.e. comparing investments made against deals referred for each information source). This points to the informal personal sources of information – business associates, friends and approaches from entrepreneurs – as the ones that have the highest probability of leading to investments whereas non-personal sources such as accountants, lawyers and banks have a low likelihood of generating investments. These findings are largely corroborated by Mason and Harrison (1994) for the UK. However, in their study the highest yield rates are recorded by some of the infrequently used professional contacts, notably banks and stockbrokers. This study also notes the low yield ratio for BANs.

Investing in businesses that are referred by trusted business associates and friends is an obvious way in which business angels can minimise adverse selection problems. As Riding *et al.* (1995) comment, 'even if the principals of the firm are unknown to the investors, if the investor knows and trusts the referral source risk is reduced.' Deal referrers are passing judgement on the merits of the opportunity and so are putting their own credibility and reputation on the line.

19.4.7 Deal evaluation

The process of evaluating investment opportunities involves at least two distinct stages – initial screening and detailed evaluation (Riding *et al.*, 1993). The initial step of business angels is to assess investment opportunities for their 'fit' with their own personal investment criteria. The investment opportunity will also be considered in terms of its location (how close to home), the nature of the business, the amount needed and any other personal investment criteria (Mason and Rogers, 1997). Business angels will then typically ask themselves two further critical questions: 'Do I know anything about this industry, market or technology?' and 'Can I add any value to this business?' Clearly, the ability to add value is very often a function of whether the angel is familiar with the industry. If the answer to either of the questions is no, then the opportunity is likely to be rejected at this point.

Angels then undertake a quick review of those opportunities that fall within their investment criteria to derive some initial impressions. Although most business angels expect a business plan, they are unlikely to read it in detail at this stage. Their aim at this point in the decision-making process is simply to assess whether the proposal has sufficient merit to justify the investment of time to undertake a detailed assessment. This stage has been the subject of a detailed analysis by Mason and Rogers (1996, 1997) using verbal protocol analysis, an experimental-type technique which asks subjects (in this case business angels) to think out loud as they perform a task (in this case evaluating a real investment opportunity). They observe that angels approach this stage with a negative mindset, expecting that the opportunity will be poor (because of the opportunities that they have previously seen) and looking for reasons to reject it. This approach has been termed 'three strikes and you're out' (Mason and Rogers, 1996, 1997) and is supported by evidence that the rejection of opportunities is generally based on several factors rather than a single deal killer (Mason and Harrison, 1996a). The market and the entrepreneur are the key considerations at this stage. Less significant are the product/service and financial factors. Indeed, angels exhibit considerable scepticism about the value of financial information in the business plan of start-ups (Mason and Rogers, 1997). Nevertheless, investors want to see that there is the potential for significant financial return, that the principals are financially committed and what the money that is invested will be used for. Some angels will be flexible, willing to treat some of these criteria as compensatory (e.g. a strong management team would compensate for a distant location), whereas others will regard them as non-compensatory (Feeney et al., 1999).

The purpose of the initial screen is to filter out 'no hopers' in order to focus their time on those opportunities that appear to have potential, which are subject then to more detailed appraisal. The investor will read the business plan in detail, go over the financial information, visit the premises, do some personal research to gather additional information on market potential, competition and so on, and assess the principals. Indeed, getting to know the principals personally (by a series of formal and informal meetings) is the most vital part of the process (May and Simmons, 2001). Most angels emphasise their intuition and gut feeling rather than performing formal analysis (Haines et al., 2003) – although more experienced angels, and angel groups adopt more sophisticated approaches (e.g. see Blair, 1996).

Once the opportunity has passed from the initial screen the importance of 'people' factors becomes critical (Riding et al., 1995), with investors emphasising management abilities, an understanding of what is required to be successful, a strong work ethic, integrity, honesty, openness and personal chemistry (Haines *et al.*, 2003; Mason and Stark, 2004). This reflects the long and personal nature of the angel–entrepreneur relationship. Rewards, realism of the projections and potential also assume greater importance while 'investor fit' becomes less of a consideration (Riding *et al.*, 1995).

This stage ends when the investor has decided whether or not to negotiate a deal with the investor. In their Canadian study Riding *et al.* (1993) found that 72.6% of opportunities were rejected at the initial impressions stage, a further 15.9% were rejected following more detailed evaluation, and as this stage proceeded another 6.3% were eliminated, a cumulative rejection rate of 94.8%. Thus, business angels proceed to the negotiation stage with only 5% of the investment opportunities that they receive.

The key role of the entrepreneur/management team in the decision whether or not to invest is confirmed in other studies. Using conjoint analysis – a method to measure quantitatively the relative importance of one decision-making criterion in relation to another (see Shepherd and Zacharakis, 1999) – Landström (1998) found that business angels attach the greatest importance to the leadership capabilities of the principals, followed by the potential of the firm's market and products. Feeney *et al.*'s (1999) approach was to ask business angels, 'What are the most common shortcomings of business opportunities that you have reviewed recently?' This highlighted shortcomings in both the management (lack of management knowledge, lack of realistic expectations, personal qualities) and the business (poor management team, poor profit potential for the level of risk, poor fit, undercapitalised/lack of liquidity, insufficient information provided). Asking investors, 'What are the essential factors that prompted you to invest in the firms that you have chosen?' Feeney *et al.* (1999) highlighted three management attributes – track record, realism and integrity and openness – and four attributes of the business – potential for high profit, an exit plan, security on their investment and involvement of the investor. However, while the primary deal killer is the perception of poor management, the decision to invest in an opportunity involves a consideration of management ability, growth and profit potential. In other words, angels are looking for businesses that show growth potential and have an entrepreneurial team with the capability to realise that potential (Feeney *et al.*, 1999). Both these studies also emphasise that investment criteria are personal, with angels using different criteria in their assessment of investment proposals. For example, Feeney *et al.* (1999) suggest that the decision processes of more experienced investors differ from that of less experienced investors.

This emphasis on the entrepreneur reflects the view of angels that agency risk is more of a threat than market risk. Fiet (1995) argues that business angels lack information or the tools and resources to evaluate market risks effectively. As a consequence, they specialise in evaluating agency risk – assessing whether or not the entrepreneur can be relied upon as a venture manager – while relying upon competent and trustworthy entrepreneurs to manage market risk. This contrasts with venture capital funds which, as we will see later, attach more importance to market risk than agency risk because they have learnt how to protect themselves using stringent boilerplate contractual provisions that allow them to replace an entrepreneur who is not performing or is found to be incompetent (Fiet, 1995).

19.4.8 Negotiation and contracting

Having decided, in principle, to invest, the business angel must negotiate terms and conditions of the investment that are acceptable both to themselves and also to the entrepreneur. There are three main issues – valuation, structuring of the deal (share price, type of shares, size of shareholding, timing of the exit) and the terms and conditions of the investment, including the investor's role. In agency theory terms, deal structuring – mechanisms for allocating the rewards to the investor and entrepreneur – are an attempt to align the behaviour of the entrepreneur with that of the investor, while the terms and conditions attempt to control the behaviour of the entrepreneur.

In the study by Riding *et al.* (1993) half of the investment opportunities that reached this stage were not consummated. The most frequent reasons for not making an investment were associated with valuation, notably 'inappropriate views by entrepreneurs (in the opinion of the investors) regarding the value of the firm as a whole and, within the firm, the value of an idea compared with the overall value of a business. Most investors note that potential entrepreneurs overvalue the idea and undervalue the potential contributions (both financial and non-financial) that are required to grow and develop a business' (Haines *et al.*, 2003: 24). Putting a value on the 'sweat equity' of the entrepreneurs is also problematic.

There is no universally agreed method of valuing a small company. Market-based valuations are inappropriate because small businesses are not continually valued by the market and appropriate comparator stocks are unlikely to be available. Asset-based valuations are more commonly used although finance theory prefers earnings or cash-flow based valuations because they value the business in terms of the future stream of earnings that shareholders might expect from the business. However, these approaches are complex. Valuation of new and early-stage businesses adds further complications because they may only have intangible assets (e.g. intellectual property). It is therefore not surprising, especially since most angel investments are concentrated at start-up and early stage, that methods of pricing and calculating the size of shareholdings is remarkably imprecise and subjective (Mason and Harrison, 1996b), based on rough rules of thumb or gut feeling. As investors May and Simmons (2001: 129) note, 'the truth about valuing a start-up is that it's often a guess.' Where an attempt is made to price the investment on a more rigorous basis, then the earnings-based approach is the most common (Lengyel and Gulliford, 1997).

Angels draw up contracts as a matter of course to safeguard their investment, although their degree of sophistication varies. Contracts specify the rights and obligations of both parties and what will be done, by whom and over what time frame. Their objective is to align the incentives of the entrepreneur and the investor by means of performance incentives and direct control measures. Kelly and Hay (2003) note that certain issues are non-negotiable: veto rights over acquisitions/divestments, prior approval for strategic plans and budgets, restrictions on the ability of management to issue share options, non-competing contractual commitments required from entrepreneurs on the termination of their employment in the business, and restrictions on the ability to raise additional debt or equity finance. These issues give investors a say in material decisions that could impact on the nature of the business or the level of equity holding. However, there are also a number of contractual provisions to which angels attach low importance, and which might be considered to be negotiable, for example forced exit provisions, investor approval for senior personnel hiring/firing decisions, the need for investors to countersign bank cheques, management equity ratchet provisions and the specification of a dispute resolution mechanism in writing up front. Less experienced investors place relatively greater emphasis on the need to include a broad array of contractual safeguards to protect their interests. However, experienced investors are more likely to include specific provisions that can impact on the level of their equity stake (share options, ratchets) and the timing of exit (forced exit provisions). In other words, with experience business angels become more focused on those elements that can impact on their financial return.

Investors recognise that the investment agreement must be fair to both sides (May and Simmons, 2001): contracts that favour the investor will be detrimental to the entrepreneur's motivation. In Mason and Harrison's (1996b) study, two-thirds of investors and entrepreneurs considered that the investment agreement was equally favourable to both sides, and half of the investors reported that this was their objective. Indeed, a significant minority of investors believed that the agreement actually favoured the entrepreneur. Thus, the available evidence suggests that in most cases entrepreneurs are not exploited by investors when raising finance.

The inclusion of contractual safeguards does not indicate whether investors will be willing to invoke them to protect their interests. Moreover, contracts are, of necessity, incomplete by their very nature. This is because it is costly to write complete contracts, it is impossible to foresee all contingencies and because of the presence of asymmetric information (van Osnabrugge, 2000). Thus, in practice, investors place a heavy reliance on their relationship with the entrepreneur to deal with any problems that arise (van Osnabrugge, 2000; Kelly and Hay, 2003). Indeed, Landström *et al.* (1998) argue that one of the purposes of establishing a contractual framework at the outset is to provide a basis for the development of a relationship between the parties to develop. In other words, the contract is less a protection mechanism *per se*; rather, it is a means by which mutual behaviour expectations of all parties in the transaction can be clarified.

Most angel investments involve input from professional advisers, although this is relatively limited compared with their involvement in venture capital fund transactions. For example, lawyers would normally review, and might draw up, the investment agreement, but would not be involved in the negotiations. Similarly, accountants may be consulted for advice but would rarely play a more prominent role. Thus, transaction costs are low (Mason and Harrison, 1996b). In Lengyel and Guilliford's (1997) study the entrepreneur's costs amounted to an average of 5.1% of the funds raised (and 29% reported no costs) while for the investor the average costs were 2.8% of the amount invested (and 57% reported no costs).

The time taken by business angels to make investments is much shorter than that of venture capital funds (Freear *et al.*, 1995b). Mason and Harrison (1996b) report that in their study the entire investment process rarely extended over more than three months, and often takes less than a month. Most negotiations took less than a week to complete whereas the evaluation could take up to three months or more. Thus, in nearly half of the investments less than a month elapsed between the entrepreneur's first meeting with the investor and the decision to invest; in 85% of cases the elapsed time was under three months.

19.4.9 Post-investment involvement

From an agency perspective, monitoring is the main way in which principals attempt to mitigate the risk of opportunistic behaviour on the part of the agent going undetected. In line with this expectation, most business angels play an active role in their investee businesses. However, in contrast to agency theory the involvement of angels in their investee businesses is not motivated by monitoring considerations. First, as noted earlier, angels derive psychic income from their involvement in their investee businesses in the form of fun and satisfaction from being involved with new and growing businesses and their belief that their experience, know-how and insights can 'make a difference'. Second, angels see themselves as 'offering help' rather than 'checking up' on their investee businesses by acting as mentors, providing contacts, guidance and hands-on assistance (Haines *et al.*, 2003). Third, as Kelly and Hay (2003: 309) comment, 'from the outset, the relationship between the business angel and the entrepreneur appears to be more positive and trusting in character than the inherently adversarial one implied by agency theorists.'

There is a spectrum of involvement: at one extreme are passive investors who are content to receive occasional information to monitor the performance of their investment while at the other extreme are investors who buy themselves a job. However, most angels do not want day-to-day involvement hence the typical involvement ranges from one day a week (or its equivalent) to less than one day a month (Mason and Harrison, 1996b). Nevertheless, Sætre (2003) emphasises that some angels are so involved, and involved so early, that they are indistinguishable from the entrepreneurs, and are seen by the entrepreneurs as being part of the entrepreneurial team. In similar vein, Politis and Landström (2002) see angel investing simply as a continuation of an entrepreneurial career.

Madill *et al.* (2005) identify a number of roles that business angels play in their investee businesses: advice about the management of the business, contacts, hands-on assistance (e.g. legal advice, accountancy advice, provision of resources), providing business and marketing intelligence, serving on the board of directors or advisory board, preparing firms to raise venture capital and providing credibility and validation. The nature and level of involvement is influenced by geography. Landström (1992) notes that frequency of contact between angels and their investee companies is inversely related to the geographical distance that separates them. It will also be influenced by the performance of the business, with angels more involved at particular stages of business development and in crisis situations.

A majority of entrepreneurs and angels regard their relationships as productive and consensual – although entrepreneurs have a more favourable view of their productiveness than angels (Freear *et al.*, 1995b; Mason and Harrison, 1996b). However, there has been no rigorous study to assess whether this involvement of business angels has a favourable impact on the performance of their investee businesses. Such research has formidable methodological difficulties and Harrison and Mason (2004) propose critical incident analysis as an alternative way in which to assess the contribution of investors.

One study reported that half of the entrepreneurs who had raised finance from business angels regarded their contributions as being helpful or very helpful (Mason and

Harrison, 1996b). Another study reported that entrepreneurs considered that the most valuable contribution of their business angel has been as a sounding board (Harrison and Mason, 1992). There is a suggestion that entrepreneurs want their investors to be more involved in certain areas, especially financial management (Ehrlich *et al.*, 1994). Criticisms by entrepreneurs who have raised finance from angels are mainly concerned with those who lack knowledge of the product or market (Lengyel and Guilliford, 1997). Finally, most business angels report that they have derived fun and enjoyment from their investments, often more than expected, in cases where the investment is still trading, but not when the business has failed. Psychic income returns are therefore related to business performance rather than compensating for financial loss (Mason and Harrison, 1996b).

19.4.10 Harvesting

Investing in unquoted companies is regarded as being high risk. Diversification is the main strategy for reducing risk. However, this is not an option for most business angels. First, typically they have just a handful of investments in their portfolios. Second, they often restrict their investments to sectors which they know and understand, so their portfolios are unbalanced. Third, as the first external investor in a business, and generally lacking the financial resources to make follow-on investments, they are vulnerable to being diluted in the event that further funding rounds are required.

A UK study of the investment returns of business angels (Mason and Harrison, 2002b) highlights the highly skewed distribution of returns, with 40% of investments making a loss (34% a total loss), and another 13% only breaking even or generating bank-level returns. However, there was a significant subset of investments, some 23% in total, which generated returns in excess of 50%, although it is important to note that these studies only measure multiples achieved on the amounts invested. However, many angels also attempt to draw back at least part of their investment in the form of a director's fee or interest on loans provided, either now or at some stage in the future when the business is financially stronger. This could be quite a significant proportion of the investment in smaller deals (Mason and Harrison, 1996b; Lengyel and Guilliford, 1997).

A Finnish study, in contrast, sought to identify differences between the most, and least, successful *investors*. The most successful investors were more likely to be motivated by the fun and interest of making such investments, have a large deal flow and have a lower estimation of the value of their hands-on involvement. The least successful investors were more likely to be motivated by altruism, have a low deal flow and make few investments, rely to a greater extent on friends for deal flow and were more likely to make investments in friends' businesses and have a different pattern of hands-on involvement, over-emphasising contributions that other research has suggested are least important in adding value (Lumme *et al.*, 1998).

Business angels are thought to be relatively patient investors, willing to hold their investments for up to seven years or more (Wetzel, 1981; Mason and Harrison, 1994). In reality, angels hold their investments for a much shorter time. The median time to exit in the UK is four years for high-performing investments and six years for moderately-performing investments, while failures appear, on average, after two years

(Mason and Harrison, 2002b). In Finland, investments that had a positive outcome were five years old whereas those that failed had an average holding time of 2.8 years. In both studies a trade sale (i.e. sale of the company to another company) was the most common exit route for successful investments, with an IPO only accounting for a small minority of cases. Trade sales, along with sale to existing shareholders, were the most common exit routes for investments with little or no value.

19.5 Venture capital funds

19.5.1 Definitions and characteristics

Venture capital firms are professional investment organisations that raise finance from financial institutions (e.g. banks, insurance companies, pension funds) and other investors (e.g. wealthy families, endowment funds, universities, companies) attracted by the potential for superior returns from this asset class to invest in businesses with high-growth prospects. These funds are established with a fixed life and will normally have a specific investment focus, for example in terms of stage of business, industry and location. The investors in the fund (termed 'limited partners') lack the resources and expertise to invest directly in companies, and are only allocating a small proportion of their investments to this asset class (typically a maximum of 1–2%) and so find it more convenient to invest in funds managed by venture capital firms (or general partners) who have specialist abilities that enable them to deal more efficiently with asymmetric information than other types of investor (Amit *et al.*, 1998, 2000). The following points apply:

■ The potential for adverse selection is reduced by investors' information-gathering skills, specialist knowledge of particular industries and expertise in selection, which enables them to identify and select projects with the potential for high returns.

■ Moral hazard problems are minimised by their skills in structuring the transaction and monitoring the investment.

■ Their skills in providing value-added services to their investee businesses and securing an exit for the investment maximise returns.

Under this limited partnership model the venture capitalists have discretion over the management of the fund, which is normally established with a ten-year life. The major part of the cash is invested over the initial three years, with the rest held back for follow-on investments. These investments are then harvested in the later years so that by the end of the fund's life it can be liquidated and the proceeds (initial sum and profits) returned to the limited partners. For performing this role the venture capital firm normally receives an annual fee (2–3% of the value of the fund), which covers running costs, and a 'carried interest', or profit share (normally 20% of the profits generated), which is distributed among the general partners (Zider, 1998; Campbell, 2003). The general partners would normally seek to raise a new fund some two to four years into the life of an existing fund so that they always have at least one fund that is in investing mode.

Across Europe there are over 900 specialist venture capital companies (www.evca.com), of which around 170 are in the UK (www.bvca.co.uk). The National Venture Capital Funds Association (www.nvca.org) in the US has 450 members. There are also venture capital associations covering Asia, Australasia and Latin America. Although the limited partnership model is the most organisational form in the venture capital industry it is not the only one. Some venture capital firms are public companies quoted on stock markets; others, termed 'captives', are the in-house venture capital subsidiaries of financial institutions (e.g. banks), and some have been established by public sector agencies.

19.5.2 Source of investment opportunities

Venture capital firms receive investment opportunities from two main sources. The first source is unsolicited deal flow. Venture capital firms are very visible, being listed in various directories and websites. Indeed, most countries and regions have venture capital associations that publish membership directories. The second source of deal flow comes through the personalised networks of venture capitalists from intermediaries such as bankers and lawyers, entrepreneurs and other venture capital funds (Florida and Kenney, 1988). Not surprisingly, most venture capitalists ignore the unsolicited deal flow and focus on those investment opportunities that come through their networks of trusted intermediaries. The quality of this deal flow is superior because it has been filtered by these intermediaries who know what kinds of deals will be of interest and to eliminate poor quality. A recommendation from such a source is seen by the venture capitalist as a positive signal about its quality. Steier and Greenwood (1995) highlight the need for an investment proposal to attract endorsement from one or more key players in a venture capitalist's network if it is to be seriously considered. Roberts (1991b) also emphasises the importance of trusted sources of referral on the prospects of a deal attracting finance. From an analysis of one firm's files he was able to conclude that: 'the more projects a source had brought to Atlantic Capital's attention, the more likely its new project would get accepted. Similarly, and even more strongly, the source of the accepted company had significantly higher percentage acceptance rates in their previous referrals than did the sources of newly rejected companies'.

19.5.3 Deal evaluation

Venture capital funds operate a two-stage evaluation process similar to the approach of business angels, comprising an initial screening process followed by a detailed evaluation process for those deals that pass the initial screening. Most of the research on the investment criteria of venture capital fund managers relies upon questionnaires and surveys. However, Shepherd (1999) argues that these approaches have significant limitations on account of their retrospective nature and the biases and errors inherent in self-reporting. Specifically, they tend to overstate the least important criteria and understate those that are most important. Zacharakis and Meyer (1998) further argue that venture capitalists are poor at introspecting about their own decision processes. A further limitation of questionnaires and surveys is that they also fail to differentiate between the criteria used at different stages in the evaluation process (Elango et al., 1995). Shepherd (1999) (see also Shepherd and Zacharakis, 2002) therefore argues that studies should use real-time methodologies such as conjoint analysis (Muzyka *et al.*, 1996), verbal protocol analysis (Hall and Hofer, 1993; Zacharakis and Meyer, 1995) and participant observation (Silva, 2004).

However, this second stage is much more exhaustive, time-consuming and, for the entrepreneur, expensive than the equivalent process in the business angel's investment evaluation. The initial screening, which is undertaken quite rapidly and intuitively, has two purposes: first, an investor specific-screens to ensure that the investment proposal fits the investment focus of the fund (e.g. location, stage, sector, size) and second, a generic screen is applied to search for features in the proposal that would indicate closer investigation is likely to be worthwhile (Tyebjee and Bruno, 1984; Fried and Hisrich, 1994; Boocock and Woods, 1997). Entrepreneurs can improve their chances of getting funding if they are able to send credible signals to potential investors about the likelihood of success of their business. This can assist the venture capitalist in overcoming the asymmetric information that surrounds a deal (Busenitz *et al.*, 2005). Financial analysis is not important at the initial screening stage (Dixon, 1991). However, the amount of equity held by the entrepreneurial team and the amount of their personal wealth committed to the business are examples of signals that might influence a potential investor (Busenitz *et al.*, 2005). Boocock and Woods (1997) note that missing information in the business plan is a major reason for rejection at the initial screening stage.

Those deals that pass the initial screening stage will be scrutinised in detail in a process involving the gathering of information from both inside and outside sources, a series of meetings with management, a review of the financial statements, and may also involve interviews with suppliers, customers, bankers, other investors and industry experts. Financial analysis will also be undertaken, first to come up with a valuation for the business (although in practice this is often quite subjective: O'Shea, 1995), and second to assess whether the investment is likely to generate the required rate of return. The minimum return would be around 30% but venture capitalists would apply an additional risk premium to more risky investments, notably the stage of the business and whether it is technology-based (Dixon, 1991; Murray and Lott, 1991; Lockett *et al.*, 2002). Dixon (1991) argues that the risk premium is mainly related to the financing stage whereas Lockett *et al.* (2002: 1023) argue that 'technology remains a more important risk factor than the stage of investment.'

Venture capital funds invest at a later stage than business angels – when the risks and uncertainties have been reduced – and commit larger amounts. The business model and the product will have been proven and exhibited market acceptance, and uncertainties about the size of the market, the profitability of the business and the quality of the management team have been reduced. Hence, 'even the founders of companies . . . who eventually turn to venture capitalists to secure the funds and management expertise they need to grow, start out on credit cards and sweat equity' (Bhidé, 2000: 16). Venture capitalists are also looking for higher returns and so are even more selective than business angels. Their key considerations are the size of the opportunity and the time to cash-out (ideally no longer than five years). Consequently venture capitalists will favour investments addressing large, growing markets and that have proprietary technology or processes and seasoned management teams (Bhidé, 2000).

Fried and Hisrich (1994) suggest that an attractive investment proposal will rate highly on three components:

- *The concept*: a project that has significant potential earnings growth, where the idea has already been demonstrated to work and so can be brought to the market quickly or, better still, has already demonstrated a degree of market acceptance (Fried *et al.*, 1993), where there is a substantial competitive advantage and with reasonable capital requirements.
- *Management*: who possess personal integrity, have done well in previous jobs (although failure is not an automatic disqualification – see Cope *et al.*, 2004), are realistic, are hardworking and flexible, and exhibit leadership.
- *Returns*: the project has to have an exit route and offer the potential for both a high rate of return and also a high absolute rate of return.

However, Zider (1998) argues that because it is difficult to distinguish between the eventual winners and losers (their financials look similar at an adolescent phase) the critical challenge for venture capitalists is to identify competent management that can execute. Empirical studies of venture capital decision making similarly emphasise that it is the quality of the entrepreneur that ultimately determines the investment decision (MacMillan *et al.*, 1985; Dixon, 1991; Muzyka *et al.*, 1996). As Macmillan *et al.* (1985: 119) note: 'there is no question that irrespective of the horse (product), horse race (market), or odds (financial criteria), it is the jockey (entrepreneur) who fundamentally determines whether the venture capitalist will place a bet at all.' Smart (1999) explores how venture capitalists actually appraise management teams.

Most businesses do not meet the investment criteria of venture capital funds – they have limited revenue potential because they do not have proprietary products, are not the first or second entrant into a market, are offering a 'me-too' product or service, operate in niche markets, and their management teams lack the experience that is thought to be necessary to build and manage a growing company (Bhidé, 2000). Thus, it is not surprising that rejection rates are high. In one study it was noted that 75.5% of opportunities were rejected at the initial screening stage, a further 21.1% were either rejected or withdrawn at the evaluation stage and only 3.4% attracted investment (Dixon, 1991). Lockett *et al.* (2002) found that the acceptance rate for generalist funds was 3.6% and for technology funds was 2.6%. Boocock and Woods' (1997) case study of an English regional venture capital fund in its first two years of operation found that its acceptance rate was even lower, at 1.46%.

One consequence of the venture capitalist's search for high-growth ventures is that it can lead to 'investment bubbles' characterised by over-investment in attractive industries as exemplified by the recent dot.com boom and bust. Investment decision making by venture capitalists occurs within an environmental context of competitive and co-operative behaviour with other venture capitalists. Venture capitalists are aware of the investments pursued and made by other investors and of the relative success of these investments (Valliere and Peterson, 2004). However, what Sahlman and Stevenson (1985) term 'myopia' is fuelled when investors fail to consider the wider implications of their individual investment decisions and so end up investing in too many companies in these sectors. The process starts with the success of some early investments in an emerging (and hence unfamiliar) sector. This creates a 'hype' that drives other investors to invest in the same sector and attracts new capital and new investors. The consequence is that too many companies are started and this drives up valuations.

Many of these new companies will subsequently fail both because of lax investment appraisal induced by the 'hype' (or the perception that normal risk assessment is inappropriate for this new technology) and because the market is not sufficiently large to support all of the new companies that have been started. The bubble eventually bursts at high cost to investors. This has the effect of driving valuations down and encourages investors to return to making more rigorous investment appraisals. Sahlman and Stevenson (1985) describe this process in the hard-disk-drive sector in the 1980s while Valliere and Petersen (2004, 2005) develop a model of 'irrational' investment behaviour during the Internet bubble.

19.5.4 Deal structures

Having decided to invest, the next stage is for the venture capitalist and the entrepreneur to negotiate the terms and conditions of the investment. The venture capitalist's key consideration is to minimise risk. A typical investment agreement for a venture capital fund will involve the following elements (Sahlman, 1990). First, it will give the investor control over key decisions, notably to replace the management team and to approve any expenditure above a certain limit. However, in practice venture capitalists may be reluctant to use their power because of the adverse impact that it will have on the relationship with the entrepreneurial team. Second, it will give the investor involvement in the company, typically in the form of one or more seats on the board of directors. Third, it will specify a compensation scheme for the management team to align their interests with that of the investor, typically by means of a combination of low salaries and stock options. Fourth, the investor will use investment instruments that give downside protection and a favourable position to make additional investment if the company is successful. In practice this means that they will invest in preferred shares rather than ordinary shares (Norton and Tenenbaum, 1992) because this creates a mechanism for deriving some income from the investment if it is only marginally successful. (Preference shares (of which there are several types) command a higher priority over ordinary shares in the event of a liquidation. Since the entrepreneurs (and other early investors) invest in ordinary shares the effect of the venture capitalist taking preference shares is that it pushes risk to the entrepreneur.)

This mechanism will include a liquidation preference, which gives the investor first claim to all of the company's assets and technology, and anti-dilution clauses, which protect against equity dilution if subsequent rounds of financing occur at lower valuations (Zider, 1998). Finally, rather than providing the entire sum of money at the outset, it will be staged over time as various milestones are met. This provides the investor with the option to revalue or abandon the investment if new information emerges which suggests that the business appears unlikely to be successful, thereby reducing losses from bad investment decisions. (Birmingham *et al.* (2003), however, suggest that venture capitalists are actually rather poor at disengaging, noting that they continue to make investments in companies that subsequently are shown to be on a failing trajectory.) However, milestones also enable the investor to increase the capital committed in the light of positive information on the company's prospects. Equally it enables the entrepreneur to raise capital at a higher valuation and thereby minimise dilution. Staging also keeps the entrepreneur on a 'tight leash'. The prospect of running out of money creates strong incentives for the management team to meet targets and create value (Sahlman, 1988, 1990).

The venture capitalist therefore adopts a much more sophisticated approach to the investment agreement and deal structures than business angels. This provides protection against agency risk and enables venture capitalists to focus on market risk which they have the skills to assess (Fiet, 1995). Business angels, on the other hand, are less able to protect themselves from agency risk by means of boilerplate contractual terms and conditions because of the cost. Consequently, they place greater emphasis on becoming personally acquainted with the entrepreneur (Fiet, 1995; Mason and Stark, 2004).

Another aspect of venture capital investments is that they are likely to be syndicated with other funds, especially in second and subsequent funding rounds. There are several reasons for this. First, this strategy avoids over-committing the fund to a small number of investments in situations where large follow-on funding rounds occur and so enables diversification. Second, it provides the original investor with a second opinion and helps to establish a fair price for the next round. Third, it provides complementary sources of value-added. For example, in the case of Canadian technology companies, it is quite common for Canadian investors to fund the initial funding round but to bring in US investors at subsequent rounds because of the perception that they can provide valuable contacts to help the company gain market share in the US (Mason *et al.*, 2002). Finally, it decreases the load on individual partners as they will only play a significant hands-on role when their fund is the lead investor (Bygrave 1987, 1988; Lockett and Wright, 1999).

19.5.5 Post-investment involvement

Venture capitalists spend around half their time monitoring and supporting the companies in their portfolio through a combination of telephone and e-mail conversations, video-conferences and on-site visits, with the remainder of their time allocated to sourcing and evaluating potential new investments (Gorman and Sahlman, 1989; Zider, 1998; Gifford, 1997). Sahlman (1990) reported that a typical venture capital investment executive would be responsible for nine portfolio companies and sit on the boards of five of them. He (or, more rarely, she, as Brush *et al.* (2002) have found fewer than 10% of women professionals in the US venture capital industry) would visit each company 19 times per annum and spend 100 hours in contact. This is very similar to Zider's (1998) estimate of 80 hours per year with each portfolio company – equivalent to just two hours per week. Venture capitalists use their expertise and networks to make a variety of contributions to their investee companies (Sahlman, 1990):

- They help recruit and compensate key individuals in the firm.
- They work with suppliers and customers.
- They help establish tactics and strategy.
- They play a major role in raising capital.
- They help structure any transactions (e.g. mergers and acquisitions) that the company might make.

Steier and Greenwood (1995) emphasise the emotional support that a venture capitalist can provide to an entrepreneur, and to make this point they provide the following quote from a venture capitalist: 'Who can an entrepreneur talk to about his problems? He can't talk to his wife – she'll leave. He can't talk to his employees – they'll quit.'

Venture capital funds place more emphasis on control and reporting requirements than business angels (Ehrlich *et al.*, 1994). MacMillan *et al.* (1988) add an important caveat, noting that venture capital firms have *variable* patterns of involvement with their investee companies and that this is related to choice of investment 'style' rather than investment focus. However, other studies suggest that the degree of involvement is related to contingent factors, notably stage, degree of technology innovation, distance, experience (Manigart and Sapienza, 2000) and the performance of the investee business. Venture capitalists may change the management if the performance of the business is unsatisfactory (Bruton *et al.*, 1997) and, in extreme situations, may even take over day-to-day control of the business (Sahlman, 1990).

Various studies have sought to explore the importance of this hands-on involvement by venture capitalists in their investee businesses to determine which types of contribution are the most significant. According to Sapienza and Timmons (1989), the high importance roles are as a sounding board and business consultant; of medium importance are coach/mentor, financier and friend/confidant roles; while the least important roles are as management recruiter, industry contact and professional contact. However, even the low-importance contributions score near the middle of a five-point scale. Macmillan *et al.* (1988) also identify 'serving as a sounding board' as the most important contribution of venture capitalists but find that 'obtaining alternative sources of equity finance' is the second most important value-added contribution. Other studies suggest that the provision of strategic support is the most important value-added contribution of venture capital funds (Sapienza *et al.*, 1996; Busenitz *et al.*, 2004). However, Rosenstein *et al.* (1993) report that entrepreneurs did not value the venture capitalists on their board higher than any other board members, although the boards of venture capital backed firms are generally more active than those of non-venture capital backed firms (Fried *et al.*, 1998).

However, there is no evidence that greater involvement is a necessary condition for adding value nor whether involvement produces enhanced business performance (Fried *et al.*, 1998; Sapienza and Gupta, 1994). This may be because the involvement of venture capitalists is with their poorly performing firms, determining whether and how they can be turned around, or even whether continued support is desirable (Zider, 1998). This is the view of Higashide and Birley (2002) who argue that the involvement of venture capitalists starts to increase when they perceive the performance of the business to be unsatisfactory and where they feel that they can make a contribution. This analysis therefore suggests that venture capitalist involvement is negatively associated with performance, with the direction of causality going from firm performance to involvement and not the other way. In contrast, Sapienza *et al.* (1996) argue that venture capitalists adopt a 'home run strategy' of focusing their attention on likely winners rather than those businesses in their portfolio that are likely to yield little return.

There is a recognition that studies that have sought to find a direct link between the venture capitalists' involvement and firm performance are too simplistic. Attention has therefore turned to the nature of the relationship between the venture capitalist and the entrepreneurial team as an important intermediary variable influencing the impact of the venture capitalist's involvement. Various studies have observed the value of cooperative behaviour in successful investing, as opposed to an agency perspective that emphasises control (Cable and Shane, 1997). Cooperative behaviour leads to perceptions of fairness, the creation of mutual trust, thereby mitigating the fear of opportunistic behaviour, and open and frequent communication. These are prerequisites if the involvement of venture capitalists is to have a favourable impact on the performance of their investee businesses (Sapienza and Korsgaard, 1996; Sapienza *et al.*, 1996; Busenitz *et al.*, 1997, 2004; Shepherd and Zacharakis, 2001).

19.5.6 Harvesting

As noted earlier, venture capital involves investing for capital gain and not for dividend income. Thus, the end-game is to secure profitable exits for venture capitalists' investments. However, this highlights an important difference between venture capital funds and business angels. The objective of venture capitalists is to maximise the returns of the fund rather than seeking every investment to be successful. Indeed, there is a rule of thumb in the industry that anticipates two or three investments will fail, between four and six will be economically self-sustaining but fail to achieve expected levels of growth or exit opportunities (the so-called 'living dead') (Ruhnka *et al.*, 1992), and a further two or three investments will be spectacular successes. It is the presence or absence of these winners that determines the performance of the fund. However, most business angels make too few investments to be able to adopt this portfolio approach and so have to seek a positive return from every investment that they make. There are three other key influences on venture capital returns:

- *The stage of investment focus* – in Europe, the average returns have been higher for funds specialising in later-stage and, in particular, management buy-out funds than early-stage funds (which typically have a technology focus), whereas in the US the pattern is the exact opposite.
- *The timing of the fund's launch* – as venture capital returns are cyclical, the returns are sensitive to the year in which the fund was launched.
- *The type of fund* – Manigart *et al.* (2002) suggest that in Europe independent funds have higher rates of return than either captive or government funds.

There are three main mechanisms for harvesting:

- A *public offering* in which the shares of the venture capitalist, and potentially other shareholders, are sold on the stock market. A public listing generally produces the highest returns but this is not unconnected with the fact that only the best companies in a venture capitalist's portfolio go down this route (Bygrave and Timmons, 1992). However, public markets are cyclical and so cannot be relied upon to produce the most profitable exit. Being a publicly listed company brings prestige to the company, enables the company to raise further amounts of finance by issuing new shares, and provides liquidity for employees who have been given shares to compensate for a low, or no, salary in the early stages of the business. However, there are constraints on how soon and how quickly existing shareholders can sell their shares. Specifically, there is normally a 'lock-up' period that prevents existing shareholders from selling their shares for a pre-specified period after the flotation (usually six months). The share price would collapse if existing shareholders sold most or all of the shares as soon as the company obtained a listing because the market would assume that as insiders they had negative information about the future prospects of the company. There are also concerns about whether the stock market fully values the firm. Publicly listed companies are also subject to much greater public attention. Other disadvantages include the costs of maintaining a listing and the need for investor communications and relations (Bleakley *et al.*, 1996).

■ A *trade sale* in which the business is sold to another company. This type of exit has the advantage that investors can sell all of their shares immediately (indeed, are likely to be required to do so) and get paid straight away (in cash or shares of the acquiring company). However, it is likely to require the entrepreneurs to exit alongside the venture capitalist and so is inappropriate if the entrepreneur wants the business to retain its independence and to continue to run it. A trade sale may also be an option for companies in distress since their assets may have value to a competitor.

■ A *private placement* involving the purchase of the venture capitalist's share by another investor. This is less common although there are some secondary purchase funds that specialise in buying the portfolios of existing venture capital funds rather than making their own individual investments.

The previous section discussed the value-added contribution of the venture capital fund, and specifically whether it has an effect on the firm's performance. Some studies have examined the venture capitalist's value-added contribution from the perspective of the harvest, suggesting that the venture capital firm plays a certification role during the IPO process resulting in a higher price compared with non-VC backed companies. However, the evidence is mixed (Megginson and Weiss, 1991; Brav and Gompers, 1997; Espenlaub *et al.*, 1999; Lange *et al.*, 2001).

19.6 Chapter summary

A consistent theme running through this chapter has been that the informal venture capital market and the institutional venture capital market play complementary roles in supporting entrepreneurial activity. This is evident in terms of the size and stage of investments made by business angels and venture capital funds (Freear and Wetzel, 1990). The boundary between business angels and venture capital funds was around $500,000: business angels dominated when the size of round was under $500,000 but their involvement fell away rapidly as deals got bigger and were replaced by venture capital funds. Business angels also dominated at the seed round but declined rapidly from the start-up stage when venture capital firms took over. A further dimension of this complementary relationship is that venture capital funds often provide follow-on funding for firms that were initially funded by business angels (Harrison and Mason, 2000; Madill *et al.*, 2005).

However, these complementarities are now breaking down because venture capital funds in North America and Europe have raised their minimum investment size to more than £1m in the UK and $5m in the US, and continued to shift their investment focus to later-stage investments (Jensen, 2002; Sohl, 2003). This stems from the growing popularity of venture capital as an asset class, which has resulted in an increase in the size of funds under management. As there has not been a commensurate increase in the number of venture capital executives each one is managing more money but with the same time scale in which it has to be invested. The inevitable outcome is that deals have become larger. Moreover, at least in Europe, the shift to making later-stage deals has increasingly drawn venture capitalists into corporate finance and away from fostering entrepreneurial businesses.

These trends have several potential consequences. First, they create a funding gap for projects that are too large for business angels but are still too small for venture capital funds. As a result, some businesses may be constrained in their growth, others that have raised initial funding but whose investors are unable to provide further funding might fail, and some entrepreneurs may be deterred from starting. Second, business angels are forced to undertake more follow-on investing, thereby reducing their ability to make new investments.

However, in response to these trends there has been the emergence of angel syndicates which Sohl *et al.* (2000) claim are 'the fastest growing segment of the early stage equity market' in the US. There are currently estimated to be around 200 angel syndicates located throughout the US and growing evidence of specialisation by industry sector (e.g. healthcare angel syndicates) and type of investor (e.g. women-only angel syndicates) (see May and O'Halloran, 2003, for some case studies). The same trend is also clearly evident in the UK although at an earlier stage, and it has not attracted the same degree of attention from researchers or commentators.

Angel syndicates have emerged because individual angels found advantages in working together, notably in terms of better deal flow, superior evaluation and due diligence of investment opportunities, and the ability to make more and bigger investments, as well as social attractions. They operate by aggregating the investment capacity of individual high-net-worth individuals. Some groups are member-managed while others are manager-led (May and Simmons, 2001; May and O'Halloran, 2003; Preston, 2004).

The emergence of angel syndicates is of enormous significance for the development and maintenance of an entrepreneurial economy. First, they are helping to address this 'new' funding gap – roughly the £250,000 to £2m+ range in the UK and the $500,000 to $5m range in the US, which covers amounts that are too large for typical '3F' (founder, family, friends) money but too small for most venture capital funds. Indeed, angel syndicates are increasingly the only source for this amount of venture capital in this range. Second, angel syndicates have the ability to provide follow-on funding. With the withdrawal of many venture capital funds from the small end of the market individual angels and their investee businesses have increasingly been faced with the problem of the absence of follow-on investors. Because angel syndicates have got greater financial firepower than individual angels or *ad hoc* angel groups they are able to provide follow-on financing, making it more efficient for the entrepreneur who avoids the need to start the search for finance anew each time a new round of funding is required. Third, their ability to add value to their investments is much greater. The range of business expertise that is found among angel syndicate members means that in most circumstances they are able to contribute much greater value-added to investee businesses than an individual business angel, or even most early-stage venture capital funds. Fourth, angel syndicates have greater credibility with venture capitalists. Venture capital funds often have a negative view of business angels, seeing them as amateurs whose involvement in the first funding round of an investment could complicate subsequent funding rounds because of their tendency to over-price investments, use complicated types of investment instruments and make over-elaborate investment agreements (Harrison and Mason, 2000). Venture capitalists may therefore avoid deals in which angels are involved because they are too complicated. However, because of the professionalism and quality of the membership of angel syndicates venture capital funds hold them in much higher esteem. Finally, syndicates reduce sources of inefficiency in the angel market. They are visible and easier for entrepreneurs to identify and approach, and have stimulated the supply side, enabling high-net-worth individuals who want to invest in unquoted companies but lack the time, referral sources, investment skills or ability to add value. Other attractions of syndicates for investors are the ability to reduce risk by spreading their investments more widely, the ability to participate in investments that they could not have invested in as individuals, access to group skills to evaluate opportunities and add value and the opportunity to learn from more experienced investors (Mason, 2006).

Angel syndicates are therefore increasingly becoming the only source of finance, other than government-supported funds and schemes, for growing businesses that have exhausted '3F' funding. In this sense, venture capital is returning to its 'classic' roots. Many of the early venture capital funds in the US started on the basis of investing funds supplied by wealthy individuals and families (Gompers, 1994). Indeed, Bygrave and Timmons (1992) argue that it was the flow of institutional money into venture capital that has led to its shift to bigger and later-stage deals. The emergence of angel syndicates and the boost that it gives to classic venture capital therefore augurs well for future level of entrepreneurial activity.

Questions

1 How are different sources of funding important to businesses at different stages of growth?

2 What is the role of business angels in the development of growth firms?

3 Describe the process by which venture capitalists enter and exit into financial relationships with businesses?

Web links

www.bvca.co.uk
Website of the British Venture Capital Association, which contains a range of articles on the industry in the UK.

www.evca.com

The European Venture Capital Association undertakes a range of studies into areas such as venture capital, corporate entrepreneurship and management buy-outs across the continent.

www.eban.org

Website of the European Business Angel Network, established to encourage the exchange of experience among business angel networks, to encourage 'best practice' and to promote recognition of business angel networks.

www.bbaa.org.uk/

The British Business Angels Association (BBAA) is the National Trade Association for the UK's Business Angel Networks.

CHAPTER 20

Labour management and the small business

Susan Marlow

20.1 Introduction

Evidence indicates that the majority of people currently employed in the private sector work in small firms (DTI, 2003a). Yet until quite recently, we knew relatively little about the terms and conditions of such employment when compared with that in larger enterprises (Marlow, 2002). In the early 1970s, the Bolton Report (1971) reflected upon the harmonious nature of employment relations within the small firm. This pronouncement was based on the assumption that proximity between owner and employee within the workplace would create a team environment, a sense of shared rewards and challenges which, in turn, successfully overcame the tensions evident between capital and labour that fuelled industrial relations problems in larger firms. It was taken as read that given the axiomatic nature of this proposition further investigation into the employment relationship in smaller firms was superfluous. It has only been relatively recently that this assumption has been questioned with a growing body of evidence emerging to challenge the harmony thesis while drawing attention to heterogeneity within the sector.

Progress in both conceptual and empirical terms has been notable, with Ram and Edwards (2003: 719) arguing that the growing complexity of the literature exploring labour management in small firms is 'a key exemplar of analytical advance'. From the expanding base of evidence regarding employment relations in small firms, it is apparent that it is inappropriate to presume that firm size alone will determine a specific type of labour management. Whilst there are some qualified generalisations that can be applied, it is recognised that there are a variety of policies and practices that firm owners utilise to manage their employees; moreover, it is essential to place these practices into the wider context of the market. Consequently, this chapter will offer an overview of contemporary evidence regarding employment relations in British small firms drawing attention to common themes and trends while being sensitive to heterogeneity. In recognition of the influence of differing policy and practice within other nations, an overview of evidence from the European Union (EU) is explored to consider the degree to which particular social and economic agendas regarding labour management shape the employment relationship in smaller enterprises.

20.2 Learning objectives

1 To understand the role of small firms as employers within the UK economy.

2 To critically evaluate contemporary accounts of labour management in small firms.

3 To appreciate the internal and external influences upon small firms that generate specific approaches to labour management.

4 To be able to comment upon and critically assess the extent to which the management of people in the small firm accords with the regulatory approach of the current government.

5 To be able to comment upon labour management practices in small firms in the EU.

Key concepts
- employment relations ■ labour management in small firms
- terms and conditions of employment

20.3 Employment relations and the small firm

Given the challenges of establishing a consensual definition of a small firm (Storey, 1994) and the evident heterogeneity of the sector, it is with caution that comment will be made upon the management of labour in small firms. Added to the general difficulty of definition and variety is the fact that it is only recently, since the early 1990s, that a body of evidence has grown to explore the specificity of employment relations in smaller firms. Scase (2003: 470) comments upon this issue, noting that: 'our knowledge of industrial relations in small firms is highly limited for two major reasons. First, small businesses have received little attention in academic social research. Second, issues of employer-employee relations have been considered to be non problematic.' Traditionally, there has been a tendency for academics and policy makers to focus on industrial relations in larger firms as they were deemed to be indicators of national trends in policy and practice and, accordingly, used as the basis for theoretical construct. This is evident from the Workplace Industrial Relations Survey's time series data (since 1999, the Workplace Employment Relations Survey – WERS) collected periodically to assess the changing nature of labour management in the UK (Daniel and Milward, 1983; Milward *et al.*, 1992; Milward and Stevens, 1986). Not until the late 1990s (Cully *et al.*, 1999) were smaller enterprises included in this survey data that allegedly offered a detailed picture of labour management policy and practice throughout the economy. Even when this omission was addressed in 1999, only firms with more than 25 employees were included and, moreover, they were not studied as independent entities but in comparison with small multiples (firms owned by larger organisations). In the next edition of this series, labour management practices of firms with more than ten employees will be considered in their own right but it is worth considering that it has taken from the early 1980s until the twenty-first century to recognise the specificity of the employment relationship in small firms.

It should be noted that such omissions are difficult to justify given that DTI statistics indicate that, in 2002, 99.1% of private sector enterprises employed less than 50 employees, that 43% of the work force were employed in such firms and they contributed to 36% of domestic turnover (DTI Small Business Service, 2002). Some of the explanation for this lack of interest in smaller firms lies in the notion of academic elitism, by which it is suggested that there has been a certain dismissal of the importance and credibility of investigating and commenting upon the employment relationship in smaller firms. Such a dismissal is premised on reasons other than a failure to recognise the contribution of small business to contemporary labour management policies and practices. As Curran and Burrows (1986: 274) commented, 'the small firm has been taken up as the articulating principle of *right wing* reaction to economic crisis' (italics inserted). As such, there is a sense that industrial relations research and theory formulation will be diminished by association with smaller firms, whose development and ethos reflect an academically unpopular political and economic philosophy articulated in an era that saw savage attacks upon the traditional elements of established industrial relations practices in larger firms. Closer examination of existing research does, however, suggest that such views are blinkered and are, in fact, ensuring continued ignorance of a critical area of employment.

A further problem for this particular research agenda is the prevailing presumption that employment relations in smaller firms are relatively unproblematic and still reflect the Bolton Report's (1971) superficial analysis of homogeneous harmony and unitarism across the sector. This presumption is supported once again in 1983 by the Conservative Government whose 'Moving Forward' pamphlet declared that a major advantage that small businesses enjoy is the generally good state of relations between owners, managers and employees, the notion being that absence of overt conflict is positively correlated with harmonious employment relations and a sense of partnership, made possible because of small group interaction. However, the growing body of research emerging since the late 1980s (Rainnie, 1989; Goss, 1991; Ram, 1994b; Holliday, 1995; Moule, 1998; Marlow, 2002) indicates that a blanket presumption of equanimity in employment relations in smaller firms is both simplistic and inaccurate. Therefore, there is considerable scope for investigation regarding the varied experiences of employment in smaller firms and any implication this has for national trends and policy development.

It is not always easy to undertake research in small firms; as Buchanan (1988: 67) notes the art of good research is 'getting in, getting on and getting out'. To fulfil this seemingly simple formula requires gaining the trust of small firm owners and taking their time and that of employees: in a small firm where human resources are scarce, time is a significant issue. Moreover, it has been established that the terms and conditions of employment in smaller firms are generally more informal, less regulated and subject to greater owner idiosyncrasy than those found in larger firms (Marlow *et al.*, 2004). This being the case, there is often reluctance to allow outsiders access to the privileged space of the work-place. So, in terms of research credibility, sample identification, contact and access, it is apparent that undertaking research into the employment relationship in smaller firms is problematic. However, despite such problems, as noted above, a growing body of evidence has emerged over recent years exploring the particularistic nature of labour management in small firms.

The picture that emerges is one of heterogeneity and complexity with some broad agreement regarding greater informality (Ram, 1994b; Moule, 1998; Marlow *et al.*, 2004). To explore these issues in greater detail this chapter will offer an overview of the evidence pertaining to labour management in small firms and consider the implications of the literature. To undertake this task, it is necessary to place employment management practices in small firms within the wider context of the growth of academic and political interest in smaller firms. Existing studies pertaining to employee relations in smaller firms will then be outlined and discussed. Although the main focus of this chapter will be upon studies undertaken in the UK, it is noted that smaller firms play a key role as employers, across Europe in general. In recognition of this, brief comment will be offered upon the employment environment in smaller firms in other European countries but given the complexity of each particular case, this will be an overview.

20.4 The changing economic context, 1979 onwards

The mandate of the 1979 Thatcher administration firmly rejected the post-war consensus of corporatism between state, employers and trade unions. In its stead, a combination of free markets, monetarism, entrepreneurialism and individualism would address the economic, social and industrial challenges of the late twentieth century. Each individual was deemed responsible for their own needs, encapsulated in the claim that there is no such thing as society; rather, we live among a complex collection of individuals pursuing their own ends. Hence the role of the state was to be constrained to facilitate individual freedom and choice (Hutton, 1996). Thus, inequality was considered the motor of enterprise while unemployment an individual failing and necessary evil to control inflation (Rose, 2003). A key element in the realisation of Conservative policies and philosophies was the reform of industrial relations in large firms, along with the creation of a buoyant, entrepreneurial small firm sector where the employment relationship would constitute the exemplar of harmony (see the Conservative Pamphlet, 'Small Firm, Big Future', 1983).

In keeping with the Austrian school of economic thought (Hayek, 1979), it was argued that a free market was critical to encourage individuals to act independently and entrepreneurially while enabling them to fully benefit from their actions. So, it was necessary to deregulate markets for goods and services in society. Regarding the labour market, this entailed a supply-side approach, removing protective legislation, extending periods of employment before claims for unfair dismissal could be registered, disbanding wages councils and making it altogether easier to hire and fire labour. As state regulation, influence and protection declined, public spending savings would be transformed into tax concessions, further enhancing disposable income for individuals who had greater freedom and choice in the free market for goods and services. A key element of this new approach involved privatisation and competitive contracting initiatives in the public sector whereby previously state-owned monopolies and public sector provision were now placed within the private sector. Through the adoption of such strategies, the government effectively reduced the level of publicly owned stock and introduced price competition into that which remained. Such initiatives, coupled with mass unemployment in the 1980s, stimulated a growth in self-employment and to a lesser extent new small firm foundation (Storey, 1994; Stanworth and Purdy, 2003).

Overall, during the 1980s and early 1990s, the employment relationship was deregulated and subject to market discipline; for many employees this has resulted in greater job insecurity, loss of union protection, greater flexibility, a move from larger to smaller employers or venturing into self-employment or small firm ownership (Edwards, 2003). Such a focus on the individual in a deregulated labour market, within the rhetoric of an enterprise society, facilitated self-employment and the start-up of new small firms. Successive governments during that period hoped that developing policy and practice to support greater individual enterprise would contribute towards creating new wealth and reducing unemployment.

Investment in policy to support the creation and sustainability of smaller enterprises has also been a feature of Labour governments elected since 1997. However, the emphasis has shifted away from free-market individualism to one of fairness for all. Although there has been no move to repeal employment relations legislation enacted by previous Conservative governments (particularly that which constrained and controlled the power of trade unions) Labour administrations have recognised the European social agenda and introduced, if rather cautiously, a raft of employment regulation legislation (McKay, 2001). This legislation has offered some support for trade unions through statutory recognition procedures but, in the main, focuses upon creating 'fairness at work' for the individual. Such regulation has, for the most part, been applicable to firms with more than 20 employees (although exceptions for discrimination and information and consultation regulations are noted). Hence, the employment relations environment has been shaped by such regulation and the manner in which this has actually impacted upon smaller firms will be explored further in the discussion below.

In summary, the post-war industrial relations consensus constructed upon collective *laissez faire*, Keynesianism, voluntarism and collective bargaining articulated through a pluralist analysis was challenged in the 1970s by crises of capital accumulation and labour resistance to government policies. Since 1979, Conservative governments promoted individualism and free-market policies aiming to create wealth, choice and competition, but there is little evidence for such – rather, a growth in insecurity, poverty and poor quality employment (Hutton, 1996; Noon and Blyton, 1997). However, there can be little doubt that one outcome of contemporary conservatism has been the expansion of self-employment and a focus upon smaller firms as economic regenerators (see Chapters 2, 3 and 4). Unemployment, redundancies, a positive image of the entrepreneur, some financial inducement and an expansion of opportunity in the service sector where entry costs are low, have all combined to 'push' and 'pull' people into individual enterprise. It is questionable, however, whether these market shifts have had the desired effect with, for example, Stanworth and Purdy (2003) arguing that whilst individual self-employment grew during the 1980s, the number of small and medium-sized enterprises (SMEs) within the economy changed relatively little. Moreover, given the high level of churning within the sector (new start-ups versus failures) and the propensity for a very few smaller firms to grow into large enterprises, the case for wealth and new job creation has not been proven. As Curran (1997: 34) observed: 'small businesses, on any realistic assessment of their role in the UK economy, are not likely to transform it by themselves into a major player in the global economy though they will play a part in that process'. However, regardless of the shifting parameters of the small firm sector, undoubtedly it does create more new jobs than its larger counterpart with a considerable number of employees depending upon such firms for their livelihood. Accordingly, the manner in which labour is managed in such firms is of critical importance to the understanding of employment relations in the broader sense.

20.5 Managing people in small firms

As noted above, over the past 15 years greater attention has been focused upon the terms and conditions of employment in smaller firms and, from the emerging evidence, it is possible to identify some common trends and themes that underpin the employment relationship while remaining sensitive to heterogeneity. To explore these issues in more depth, the now infamous quote from the Bolton Report (1971: 21) will be noted from which the discussion will take its departure point:

> In many aspects, the small firm provides a better environment for the employee than is possible in most large firms. Although physical working conditions may sometimes be inferior in small firms, most people prefer to work in small groups where communication presents few problems: the employee in a small firm can more easily see the relation between what he(sic) is doing and the objectives and performance of the firm as a whole. Where management is more direct and flexible, working rules can be varied to suit the individual. Each employee is also likely to have a more varied role with a chance to participate in several kinds of work . . . turnover of staff in small firms is very low and strikes and other kinds of industrial dispute are relatively infrequent. The fact that small firms offer lower earnings than larger firms suggests that the convenience of location and generally the non-material satisfactions of working in them more than outweigh any financial sacrifice involved.

Thus, an image of harmonious employment relations in small firms was portrayed where the antagonism between labour and capital was successfully overcome through partnership and shared ambition. The very scale of operations enabled individual employees to identify their contribution to the organisation, thus overcoming the anomie associated with working for the larger bureaucracy. This was an image which was presented during a period when focus was renewed upon small-scale activity with the 'small is beautiful' thesis generated by Schumacher (1974) becoming increasingly influential. Further support for individual job satisfaction was offered by Ingham (1970) who argued that small firm employees self-select themselves to such enterprises precisely because the identification with the firm, its owner and other employees is sufficient compensation for lower wages and a restricted career path. Emphases on small-scale enterprise also emerged in the early 1980s with theoretical debates surrounding the emergence and existence of post modernism.

20.5.1 Flexibility

In post modernist society, Piore and Sabel (1984) argued, a second industrial divide would emerge with skills as a defining feature. Production would be focused on SMEs with a core group of multi-skilled employees working with advanced technologies. The emphasis was upon *flexibility* in that the size of the firm would facilitate a rapid flexible response to changing market demand; the polyvalent nature of the employee would enable a quick response to such changes while advanced technology would make such flexible production possible. Core employees in smaller enterprises would be highly valued and rewarded – thus collective protection such as that offered by unions would be needless, whilst secondary or peripheral labour, utilised casually where and when necessary, would be too weak to resist either individually or collectively. When such theoretical considerations were aligned with an ideology of harmonious labour relations, an image of the entrepreneur as pioneer of risk and uncertainty with rewards shared by all, and the individualistic free market philosophy of the newly elected Conservative government in the early 1980s, the advantages of supporting small firm development were strong and convincing.

However, challenging such a presumption of harmony, a number of studies emerged questioning the role of smaller firms as the leaders of a new epoch in respect of the relations of production. As early as 1979, Curran and Stanworth questioned Ingham's (1970) view of self-selection pointing out that it was, in fact, employers who had greater prerogative in terms of recruitment and selection (which then extended into determining the nature of the employment relationship). Moreover, it was argued that a blanket presumption of harmonious employee relations could not be applied to such a heterogeneous sector as that of small firms, an issue that formed the basis of many subsequent studies (Goss, 1991; Ram, 1994b; Marlow, 2002).

20.5.2 Harmony

During the 1980s, further critical analysis emerged regarding the *harmony* thesis. Rainnie and Scott (1986) argued that as part of the market economy small firms still have to address the tension inherent within capitalism. From a Marxist perspective, the researchers argued that it is necessary for small firm owners to purchase labour and extract surplus value (profit), through exploitation, so the challenge is to identify how exploitation is experienced and how it is made effective. Rainnie and Scott rejected the notion that the absence of trade unions in small firms facilitates harmony but argued instead that whilst there may be a positive correlation between non-unionism and an absence of overt dispute, this does not denote a causal relationship (given that a wide range of variables will impinge upon union presence such as sector, age, locality, labour characteristics, any inference must recognise and adjust for complexity). Rather, further attention needed to be focused on other channels for articulating discontent such as turnover, absence and industrial (now employment) tribunal referrals. Hence, attention is drawn to the importance of class relations, the limited opportunities small firm employees have for expressing overt discontent and the necessity of analysing the complexity of intervening variables underpinning any such assertions.

In a more comprehensive study of labour management in small manufacturing firms, Rainnie (1989) also critically assessed the notion of independence of small firm owners and managers. When considering their position in the wider labour market, Rainnie argues that labour management styles of small firm owners are constrained by the demands and competitive position of their larger counterparts (as customers or suppliers) and by the market for goods itself. To demonstrate this, Rainnie offers a typology of relations between small firms and the market:

- *Dependent* – where survival is totally dependent on a relationship with a larger firm (e.g. as a subcontractor).
- *Competitive dependent* – competition is directly with larger firms, therefore survival depends on the ability to cut costs and is likely to result in extreme exploitation of labour.
- *Old independent* – niche market firms where growth is constrained due to market demand.
- *New independent* – new or developing markets where larger firms may invade if the opportunities for profit and expansion are attractive.

To fully comprehend the manner in which labour is managed, the market conditions under which the firm operates must be analysed and so awareness of heterogeneity and labour markets is critical. These studies were useful in identifying the heterogeneity of small firms and locating them in the wider economy – in particular Rainnie draws attention to the falseness of the 'dual' approach where small and large firms are deemed as being separate spheres without overlapping confluence. There are some problems with the analysis, which depends on a deterministic presumption that external pressures will fully dictate labour management strategies. It must also be questioned whether typologies and taxonomies can realistically be applied to markets or whether they can only exist as generalised overviews or conceptual examples. Finally, the empirical work which Rainnie utilises to illustrate his theory is based largely upon manufacturing firms whereas the majority of small firms are located in the service sector (Curran, 1991), so a question of representation remains. However, despite a number of issues regarding this study, it was of considerable importance in articulating a comprehensive and theoretically grounded critique of the harmony thesis.

In his study of social harmony in smaller firms, Goss (1988) criticises the reliance on employer perception of the quality of employment relations which leads to positive reporting. To evaluate such perceptions, Goss argues that conflict is submerged beneath 'intergroup credibility' (p. 116), which emerges from the pragmatic response to powerlessness by small firm employees. It is argued that the proximity of owner, managers and labour when at work ensures that 'trouble makers' can be identified or removed and conflict is masked. Goss (1988: 116) states that 'small firms provide an environment in which contradictions implicit in the labour/capital relation can be relatively effectively contained or neutralised by employers'. In his critique of the social harmony thesis, Goss focuses upon the ability of employers, combined with market pressures to limit opportunities for employee resistance to labour management tactics. Using evidence from a small study of printing firms, Goss found that owners identified good and bad employees according to their willingness to tolerate labour process changes, demands for overtime and flexible working. Those deemed bad were denied pay bonuses and had their jobs threatened – thus, compliance with the owner was based on powerlessness, not identification. So, Goss reiterates Rainnie's (1989) findings that harmony and conflict are complex issues that cannot be presumed from the presence or lack of overt conflict.

In a later work, Goss (1991) develops this debate further by developing a typology to demonstrate the manner in which employers exert control over both employees and the labour process itself but also how employees might resist such control. A number of categories are identified:

- *Fraternalism* – where there is a shared sense of skill and effort, owners tend to work alongside employees (e.g. in construction). There is a reliance on negotiation between employer and employee with a realisation that all are needed for the firm to survive; thus the circumstance of mutual reliance and close working generate a form of partnership.

- *Paternalism* – there is a differentiated power relationship between employer and employee but an effort is made to generate an identification from labour with the ethos of the enterprise (e.g. in agricultural communities). Other forms of employment may be scarce but employers still need commitment from labour to undertake unsupervised work, unscheduled overtime and display other forms of flexibility. Identification with the work-place extends into the community with some evidence of mutual obligation. (For more discussion, note the concept of the 'deferential worker', Newby, 1977.)

- *Benevolent autocracy* – there is a clear identification of the role of employer and the power this commands but this is based solely within the work-place. There is a tendency towards informality with a pragmatic acceptance of labour/capital inequality but some evidence of joint identification of organisation needs.

- *Sweating* – again a clear imbalance of power but the employer makes no effort to cultivate employee identification and there is a critical focus on cost containment.

Goss notes the complexity of managing employee relations in smaller firms and, importantly, notes that there is potential for some employees to influence social relations at work. This analysis again underpins the complexity of the employee relationship and the need to consider carefully definitions of harmony, but the dependence of typologies is not always useful (see above) and the study is, again, overly dependent upon manufacturing firms for conclusions.

Reflecting the critical analyses developed by Rainnie (1989) and Goss (1991) that recognised heterogeneity and complexity, a number of studies have emerged over the intervening years drawing largely upon the case study approach to explore such issues in more depth. Such studies, with their detailed exploration of the dynamics of daily life in smaller firms, exposed the complex web of relations between the external and internal environment of the firm. So, for example, the work by Ram (1994b) explored labour management issues in three family-owned textile firms. Through the adoption of the case study approach, Ram was able to build a picture of the employment relationship that enabled the influences of market constraints, ethnicity, gender and family tensions and allegiances to be acknowledged and incorporated. From this research, Ram argued that the employment relationship within many small firms is underpinned by a complicated system of social negotiation between owners and employees and, indeed, between the workers themselves. In drawing attention to the importance of the social relations of production, Ram (1994b: 150) argued that theories based upon deterministic market relations, such as those outlined by Rainnie (1989), did not fully 'convey the bargained nature of life on the shop floor, the extent of mutual dependency between workers and management and the importance of informal accommodation'.

20.5.3 Social negotiation

Holliday (1995) offered further support to the social negotiation thesis; her study focused upon family firms where she found that family priorities strongly influenced the approach towards labour management. In particular, the notion of paternalism – the idea of a father figure making key decisions in the interest of all – was evident. More recent work by Dundon *et al.* (1999) also draws attention to the manner in which family dynamics are influential upon small firm management. Focusing upon non-unionism in smaller firms, Dundon *et al.* commented upon the background to their case study firm where there had been a 'long history of familial control in which "walking the shop floor" had been the main way owner-managers engaged with employees. Traditionally, family members had always occupied strategic positions . . . there are few personnel policies and no formal method of involving employees other than a familial culture of friendly relations' (1999: 255). Indeed, this case is apposite as the introduction of non-family managers and other changes were being undertaken to improve competitiveness in an increasingly tight market environment. The resulting move from what Dundon *et al.* describe as traditional paternalism to autocratic pater-nalism had created disquiet among staff and prompted some interest in unionisa-tion, but this had not on the whole prompted formal resistance or notably increased labour turnover. Rather, the research team found a high degree of satisfaction with the informal social relations of production between the employees themselves; also the level of positive customer interaction was appreciated and enjoyed by employees. So, despite considerable dissatisfaction with pay, worries over job security and poor pro-motion prospects, very few employees stated that they would leave the firm if offered work elsewhere. It was argued that family paternalism transposed into the setting of the firm blurred and camouflaged the reality of exploitation within the employment relationship but, with the introduction of a professional tier of management, such ten-sions were exposed.

The manner in which social relations underpin the employment relationship in a complex and varied fashion is further illustrated by the work of Ram *et al.* (2001) exploring the Indian restaurant sector. In analysing this sector, Ram *et al.* note that it is defined by very poor terms and conditions of employment but the influence of wider labour market discrimination, family reciprosity, social pressures and informal work-ing meant that employees were drawn to such work on the basis of a wide range of social and economic elements, themselves embedded within the local community. The interaction of location, social expectations and reduced economic prospects else-where generate a particular working environment that reflected market, community and familial issues and pressures. As such, the employment relationship was embedded within the norms of local community values which bounded both employer and employee behaviour (Granovetter, 1985).

Acknowledging the influence of social negotiation upon the employment relation-ship in smaller firms, Taylor (2004) generates a conceptual analysis focused specifically upon the discourse of human resource management (HRM) and particularly how this approach 'fits' the smaller organisation. HRM strategies and policies emerged in both theory and practice in the 1980s as a new managerial strategy to increase the value added to the production process by employees (Beardwell *et al.*, 2004). As such, most large organisations have now adopted the rhetoric, if not the reality, of HRM (Legge, 1995) based upon the presumption that it is an effective and efficient economic and functional approach to labour management. However, within the HRM discourse there is little sensitivity to the context of the firm size. Again, using detailed case study material Taylor considers the 'building blocks' of HRM – recruitment, selection, training, development, appraisal and reward – finding that the interaction of management norms, state regulation and organisational culture within small firms critically affects the manner in which the HRM discourse is articulated. It is noted that: 'cultural barriers (related to firm size) are also cited when commentators suggest how to "improve" managerial practice within smaller organisations. Lack of resources to train specialists, lack of complexity . . . lack of familiarity with management theory, disinclination to seek or take advice on management . . . mitigate against the adoption of modern best practice in analysing why smaller organisations remain stubbornly rooted in an alternative way of thinking' (Taylor, 2004: 35).

Taylor goes on to argue that the smaller organisation is then presented as the 'other' in terms of an inability or unwillingness to adopt best practice employment relations as demonstrated by their larger counterparts. This, it is suggested, completely fails to recognise the specificity of the small firm context and the mediating role of firm culture that does not offer a ready home to HRM policy and practice. In essence, Taylor is arguing for greater sensitivity to heterogeneity and, once again, recognition of the manner in which employment relations are socially embedded within the culture of the organisation such that there cannot be one best practice example. From this brief snapshot of contemporary analyses of labour management in small firms, a number of themes are emerging. Clearly, empirical evidence would indicate that the social relations of production in small firms are shaped by firm size and the ensuing proximity between employers and employees, which is itself founded upon the notion of informality.

20.5.4 Formality and informality

There is some temptation to view formality and informality in labour management as a dichotomy. However, it is more appropriate to consider these concepts as existing along a continuum. As Ram *et al.* (2001: 846) note, 'informality is, therefore, a matter of degree not kind'. Marlow (2002) explores these notions in some detail and observes that large firms have a foundation of formal policy and practice that bounds the employment relationship even if issues of custom and practice dominate regarding the daily management of work. Smaller firms, however, are less likely to employ professional HR or personnel managers (Wynarczyk *et al.*, 1993) and so the employment relationship is more likely to reflect the idiosyncrasies of the owner's priorities and interests. This lack of professional, in-house skill ensures that it is unlikely that formal policy and practice will be put into place and/or observed upon a daily basis. Furthermore, the proximity of owner, manager and employee positively encourages informal consultation, supervision, grievance and discipline articulation. Added to such internal pressures for informality, Ram *et al.* (2001) also argue that this preference is a response to shifting labour and product market demands, and contributes to the much lauded flexibility of smaller firms.

Accordingly, it would appear that, as Marlow *et al.* (2004: 6) argue, there are differentiated degrees of informality and formality in both large and small firms but, 'that within larger firms, the dynamic of control and consent is bounded by formality in that if, and when, line managers have to overtly assert authority, they have the channels by which to do so'. On the other hand, in small firms, owner prerogative is more likely to shape the parameters of the employment relationship without any fall-back position of formal policy and practice. Axiomatically, it would seem appropriate for smaller firms to adopt informality given the proximity between employers and employees, team-working ethos and paternalistic management practices. However, this approach has inherent problems, particularly regarding the development and application of fair, objective and clear employment rules and regulations. Where individual managerial prerogative dominates, there is obvious scope for spontaneous subjective action and discrimination.

So, although there is little firm evidence regarding labour turnover in smaller firms, that which does exist finds higher levels of quitting than within larger firms and, moreover, a greater tendency for tribunal applications for unfair dismissal (Earnshaw *et al.*, 1998). It would therefore appear that whilst informality may be advantageous for those who fit well in the firm, it does not accommodate those who either do not accord with the norm or who might wish to raise objections to labour management practices. Further to these implications regarding individual employee management, a preference for informality also raises a range of issues regarding regulatory compliance.

20.6 Employment regulation and smaller firms

Since their election in 1997, successive Labour governments have regulated the employment relationship through a series of Acts that have recognised the European social agenda, extended individual rights at work and, to some degree, offered limited support to strengthen trade union rights and offer a statutory recognition process. This has been evident by the enactment of two Employment Acts (1999 and 2002), a National Minimum Wage Act and the adoption of a number of EU Directives (if, in a minimal fashion) (McKay, 2001). Evidently, firms that favour informality will find it difficult to incorporate formal employment regulation into their very limited policy and practice regime and so demonstrating compliance will be challenging. Contemporary research that has considered employment regulation compliance in smaller organisations has, to date, found a less severe impact upon their performance than had been prophesised by both representative pressure groups (Federation of Small Business, 2000) or media commentators (Oldfield, 1999). Blackburn and Hart (2001) found pessimistic predictions regarding deteriorating performance to be unfounded; it appears that the perception of potential problems does not seem to have been borne out in reality.

Moreover, in a study of regulatory compliance focused specifically upon the Employment Relations Act 1999, Marlow (2002) found a high degree of ignorance concerning the details of the Act. Over a third of her sample of firms, all of whom employed more than 20 employees (the base line figure for compliance), did not even issue formal contracts or offers of employment letters and, as a group, this sample had but a basic knowledge of new legislation. Moreover, the firm owners demonstrated little concern regarding lack of compliance as they could not foresee how this would ever be a problem where the only sanction might be a tribunal application. Those who had been subject to tribunal claims had certainly given some attention to policy and practice or had contracted the HR function to a professional agency, but had been irritated by the tribunal process rather than deeply affected. Similarly, Ram *et al.* (2001) and Gillman *et al.* (2002) found a very fluid, negotiated approach to National Minimum Wage compliance with some owners again ignoring regulation while others adopted a range of practices that reflected both the owner's idiosyncrasies and external market conditions.

It is argued that the current approach to employment regulation does not fully recognise the peculiarities of the small firm context (Marlow, 2002; Hart and Blackburn, 2004). The very proximity of employer and employees, plus the social ties between them, makes the adoption of formality in policy and practice incongruous and unlikely. However, the problem with this stance, as noted above, is the lack of objectivity in the fair application of uniform standards for all employees. Moreover, given the lack of formal trade union recognition within smaller firms there are few opportunities for employees to voice concerns other than a direct approach to the owner or line manager (Dundon *et al.*, 1999). The lack of opportunity to voice dissent is again apparent in the statistics on employment tribunal applications where smaller firms dominate in issues of unfair dismissal and cases relating to redundancy (DTI, 2002).

20.6.1 New legislation

The forthcoming Information and Consultation for Employees Act (ICE) which (from 2008) will apply to firms with more than 50 employees aims to offer opportunities for employee consultation and voice. Again, however, drawing upon existing evidence regarding regulatory compliance, which indicates patchy acknowledgement at best, it is unlikely that the forthcoming ICE Act will be the solution to the lack of employee voice in smaller firms. As Marlow and Gray (2005) suggest, in the case of the ICE there will be differentiated levels of compliance as evidence indicates (Wynarcyzk *et al.*, 1993; Storey, 1994) that, as firms grow, so they adopt more formalised management functions (although HR is usually of low priority). Given that the key provisions of the ICE are:

■ the identification of employee representatives for consultation purposes and as conduits for information dissemination;

■ consultation regarding changes to terms and conditions of employment; and

■ information regarding terms and conditions of employment, firm performance and prospects;

it is unlikely that in the firms within the smaller size bands, where owners, managers and employees work in close proximity so that interaction is direct and immediate, specific representatives will be appointed or formalised consultation adopted. Furthermore, given the context of the smaller firm, there are some dangers in focusing upon formal employee representation: 'there would be some question regarding how frank the representative may want to be with the firm owner who is also the direct employer . . . in an environment where there are a small group of employees working in proximity with management, some doubt must be expressed in regarding the ease of maintaining the anonymity of employees expressing dissatisfaction' (Marlow and Gray, 2005).

20.6.2 Implementation of legislation

In this short consideration of employment regulation, it is evident that firm context is highly influential in shaping labour management; there are real difficulties in ensuring the uniform application of regulation. Indeed, as noted above, interest groups such as the Confederation for Business and Industry and the Federation of Small Businesses have strongly criticised regulatory regimes but this does beg the question regarding the protection of those who work for smaller firms. Atkinson and Storey (1994) and Earnshaw *et al.* (1998) have largely supported the overall view that there is a problem with the durability and quality of work in the small firm sector. Such employment, on the whole, commands lower pay, offers fewer opportunities for training and development, small internal labour markets constrain career progression, and hours worked are either longer to enhance wages or are more likely to be part-time. However, it is interesting to note that there is some indication that employees are not necessarily discontented in such work or that employers fear external regulation that would improve conditions, such as that from trade unions (Curran, 1997; Dundon *et al.*, 1999).

Regarding pathways to encourage compliance, the government is committed to a voluntary approach but, as noted above, this is likely to have a limited impact upon smaller firms in general. In considering alternative options to encourage or compel compliance, it would seem inappropriate to give trade unions, for instance, greater powers as regulatory enforcers for a number of reasons. It is difficult to force employers to grant union recognition and even more challenging to ensure bargaining occurs in good faith. Employers cannot be forced to welcome trade unions so it is questionable whether they could be forced to even tolerate them where they were unwanted. It is debatable to what extent private service sector employees, in particular, would support union regulation having little experience of union benefits and no tradition of union affiliation. So, unions would require some official status and funding to 'police' workplaces where they were not recognised – and this is unlikely. Also, it must be questioned whether unions would be up to such a task in the short or even medium term as policing regulation would require coherent strategies and significant numbers of well-trained organisers. This is clearly not beyond the scope of unions given time, resources and official encouragement. However, given the distant relationship that currently exists between trade unions and the Blair government, this is not a very likely scenario. Alternatively, existing bodies such as the Health and Safety Executive could be further empowered or new regulatory organisations pertaining to wages and conditions could be formed. These bodies would require substantial funding, professional advisers and powerful sanctions to be effective – all of which is perfectly possible and would ensure greater professional management and uptake of advice.

So, it is clear that, on the balance of existing evidence, the argument for greater regulation to improve employment conditions in small firms is persuasive. Yet it is difficult to imagine how focusing on one particular sector of the economy, which is noted for its heterogeneity, could be adequately justified given the criticisms this would elicit. Also the effect on production costs and consequent implications for firm survival must be recognised. Moreover, whilst the Labour government has made a pledge to promote fair employment through a flood of regulation, in keeping with traditional UK approaches the emphasis is on voluntary regulation with some sanctions available through the employment tribunal system. So, whilst formal regulation might be the most effective manner to address inequality and exploitation in employment, the social and market context of many smaller firms will ensure that compliance is uneven across the sector.

For voluntary regulation to be effective, it must offer sustainable benefits for all interested stakeholders. This might be obtained through extending and developing the system which in the past pertained to local government contracting whereby tenders were considered on not just cost but also issues such as employment standards. Given the dependency of many smaller firms upon such contracts within the private and public sector, this would encourage a review of standards while offering the benefit of contracts. This type of requirement is already evident in some cases where larger firms require sub-contractors to attain Investor in People status or other quality standard indicators (Marlow, 2002). Whilst this would necessitate larger firms extending their remit for tenders, given the formality/bureaucracy of such organisations this would not be excessively demanding.

20.6.3 Critical themes summarised

From this overview of labour management in small British firms, a number of critical themes have emerged. As recognised at the outset, generalisations are made but the heterogeneity of sector is noted; Scase (2004), for example, explores labour management strategies within a number of sub-sectors of small firms noting how the employment relationship in high-tech firms will differ markedly from that in a traditional craft-based business. However, recognising differences in degree concerning style and approach, there are still common themes that can be identified. So, for instance, it appears that size, owner and employee proximity combined with market situation is likely to favour an informal approach to managing labour. Whilst there are undoubted benefits to this in terms of promoting team working, shared goals and aspirations while enabling flexibility, there are also disadvantages.

Where owner prerogative dominates there is clear scope for subjectivity in the manner in which employees are managed; moreover a lack of professional HR knowledge mitigates against engaging with the most efficient and effective employment policy and practice. Of course, as noted in detail above, informality is a barrier regarding regulatory compliance. A number of case study explorations (Ram, 1994; Holliday, 1995; Moule, 1998) have all drawn attention to the degree of social negotiation that surrounds the employment relationship in smaller firms where the close working relationship between owner and employees creates, to some extent, a sense of mutual dependence and shared interest, particularly regarding the survival of the firm. However, again these cases reveal how certain employees have greater leverage regarding the ability to negotiate their conditions; such leverage might be gained by the possession of valued skills but it was evident that issues such as seniority, gender, family affiliation and friendships also swayed this relationship. While recognising the importance of negotiated employment relations, it also emerged that owner prerogative was still highly evident and could be called upon whenever required to reassert managerial authority.

Having ascertained that employment relations in small firms are complex, the 'problem' of regulation emerges as one of uniform application and compliance. From one perspective, the problem focuses upon the desirability and possibility of introducing greater regulation into the fluid employment relationships that can be found in small firms. By attempting to introduce an element of uniformity and formality, the competitive edge gained from flexibility, team working and mutual interests will be compromised. However, if the government is to achieve its wish to promote fairness at work for all, smaller firms cannot be excluded from this policy, particularly as evidence would indicate that employees in the sector have poorer terms and conditions across a range of measures compared with their counterparts in larger organisations. Yet the government has excluded firms with fewer than 20 employees from much of the contemporary regulation (discrimination issues being a notable exception) and those with fewer than 50 are exempted from the ICE. With no effective strategy to impose regulation, however, evidence would indicate that compliance is at best partial and uneven (Hart and Blackburn, 2004). Having outlined issues regarding labour management in small firms in the UK, the discussion is now broadened to include some examples from the EU.

20.7 Labour management in small firms in Europe

Managing labour is a key task for any organisation regardless of place, context or sector so, it can be argued, all firms must address the problem of the effort-wage bargain (Burawoy, 1979) – that is, how much work will be undertaken for what level of reward. To some extent it is accepted that there is a universal element to the employment relationship but it is also axiomatic that differing economic, social, legal and political regimes within nations will create specific contextual environments that will shape the employment relationship. In the case of smaller firms throughout Europe, despite their economic and social importance to the EU, in-depth comparative studies are rare. However, in 2002 the European Foundation for the Improvement of Living and Working Conditions (EFILWC) produced a report detailing key elements of the employment relationship in a range of European countries including those of Eastern and Central Europe such as Bulgaria. From these collective findings, the report reflects many of the points made above in relation to the UK and notes a number of distinctive characteristics pertaining to labour management in micro and small enterprises as follows:

- a central role for the firm owner;
- a close relationship between owner and employee;
- employees are more visible to employers and vice versa;
- family involvement within the firm and its employment;
- informality of management and a lack of procedures;
- distinctive employment characteristics in terms of gender, education, skills;
- the sector is heterogeneous and generalisations are thus cautious.

20.7.1 Unionisation

Looking in more detail at specific issues, the report notes that overall collective representation opportunities are limited (EFILWC, 2001). Recognising that very little precise data is available, some examples were identified. For example in Germany small firms with fewer than five employees are not obliged to recognise a works council. In fact, Backes-Gellner (2000) found that only about 14% of firms with fewer than 50 employees had any form of works council. In Finland, where collective representation through voluntary shop stewards is highly developed, firms with fewer than 30 employees were unlikely to have such representatives. It is recognised that 'legal provisions in most EU Member States explicitly establish minimum enterprise size thresholds that exclude smaller enterprises from the possibility to set up formal employee representation structures. Notwithstanding this, irrespective of existing regulations, most micro and small enterprise employees never exercise these collective representation structures' (EFILWC, 2001: 7).

The report also finds that unionisation rates among smaller firms are generally low, again reflecting the situation in the UK. However, there are some exceptions with Denmark, Finland and Norway having up to 88% density in firms with more than one employee, reflecting broader economic and social trends towards union membership and recognition in such countries. This is an interesting finding as it indicates that where there is consistent state sponsorship of wider employee representations and employees themselves gain substantive benefit from such, allegiance is strong. Moreover, despite sentiments expressed within the UK, for example, it also illustrates that small firms can operate productively while tolerating a union presence. When considering the EU as a whole, what is notable is that data on unionisation are not available for Austria, Belgium, France, Greece, Ireland, Italy, Portugal or Spain but it is suggested that this is because density is so low. In a closer examination of the French case, Lepley (2000) argues that the benefits of union membership are not appreciated by employees; in fact they are perceived as disruptive, generating conflict and creating rigidity. However, it is argued that such opinions are based on a very poor knowledge of the role and activities of unions.

Similar to the case in the UK (Stanworth and Gray, 1991), trade unions themselves have not developed strategies to recruit small firm employees in many European nations; so for instance in France there are no specific branches for small and micro firms whereas in Spain attention is focused upon large firms (Costa and Duffy, 1991). The EFILWC report also draws attention to the informality in smaller firms, finding that this is a barrier to union representation. In Germany there are recognised informal structures such as 'Monday Roundtables' where owner and employees meet to discuss problems and issues but these are subject to limitations as the owner generally dictates the agenda. Overall, when considering employee representation across Europe, it was found that all formal representation, councils and committees are less likely to be present in small firms as informality mitigates against these structures, the proximity between employers and employees makes them rather superfluous and employers perceive formal representation as a stimulating resistance to owner prerogative.

20.7.2 Terms and conditions

It is generally agreed that the terms and conditions of employment improve as firms grow (Atkinson and Storey, 1994). This assertion was examined by EFILWC in relation to a number of key constituents of the employment relationship, i.e. wages, fringe benefits, working time, labour turnover and training within the broader context of Europe. Taking the case of wages and salaries, in all the cases where data was examined in some detail – Germany, Finland, France and Spain – it was found that there was a positive correlation between increasing reward and firm size. It is noted that firm size is not the only influence upon wages as, for example, employee productivity and skills tend to be greater in larger firms whereas smaller enterprises draw a disproportionate number of employees from the most vulnerable and least skilled sectors of the workforce (older workers, younger workers, temporary workers, ethnic minority employees, women). Moreover, even where minimum wage legislation is in place, similar to the UK experience, compliance among smaller firms is poorer than within their larger counterparts and compounding this issue, as noted above, such firms have a higher dependence upon minimum wage labour. So, for example, it was found that in France approximately 26% of micro-enterprise labour was drawn from minimum wage employees compared with 12% in larger firms (CFDT, 1998). Not surprisingly, given this evidence regarding wages and salaries, when other fringe benefits were considered by EFILWC, they were lower in smaller enterprises; whilst little detailed evidence is available, that from France, Germany and the UK indicates that pensions, productivity bonuses and management benefits are generally poorer than those in large firms.

Regarding working time and flexibility, detailed information is again generated for France, Germany and Spain. From official data collected from firm owners in France, it emerged that the smaller the enterprise, the longer the working hours; in 1997 it was found that whilst only 2% of employees in larger firms worked more than 41 hours per week the comparative data in micro enterprises indicated that this figure was more than 23%. In Germany, it was found that, overall, statutory holiday entitlement was less likely to be observed in smaller firms with notable deviations from the normal five-day working week. Evidence from Spain (Ortega, 1999) also found long hours to be a feature of small-firm employment with Spanish employees obliged to work overtime hours and weekends; furthermore, holidays often fell below collectively agreed minima. Given that the German and French economies, in particular, are perceived as having fully embraced the EU agenda for employee regulation and protection, and the latter has a 35-hour working week, it might be supposed that in the case of smaller enterprises they would be demonstrating best practice. This would indicate that even if data for other EU members is scarce, it is unlikely that provision will be superior to that of the countries described.

Perhaps not surprisingly, evidence linked to labour turnover indicates higher levels in smaller firms. In Finland for instance, unemployment arising from 'churning' (new jobs created versus jobs lost through downsizing or failure) is greater in smaller businesses while such firms have not complied with policies to employ long-term unemployed or difficult-to-place labour (Saari, 1996). In Spain, it emerges that greater numbers of temporary and casual employees are employed in smaller enterprises to adapt to peaks and troughs in demands and to avoid complex and costly dismissal procedures. Hence, such firms utilise insecure forms of employment to create greater flexibility within labour markets (Ortega, 1999). Finally, in respect of training and development there is a considerable body of extant evidence indicating that opportunities increase with firm size so, for example, the IKEI and ENSR survey (1997) of training initiatives within SMEs demonstrates a positive relationship between firm size and propensity to train. Drawing upon survey data from 840 smaller firms in Austria, Belgium, Finland, France, Greece, Iceland, Italy, the Netherlands, Norway, Portugal and Spain, it was found that slightly more than a quarter of micro firms undertook some training activity whereas this rises to 84% for firms with between 50 and 249 employees. Moreover, the formality and sophistication of training initiatives increased with firm size.

The EFILWC report offers an overview of its findings in relation to labour management in smaller firms across Europe which they represent as follows:

- In general, working conditions deteriorate as firm size decreases.
- Wages and salaries are generally poorer in smaller enterprises.
- Fringe benefits are less common and generally poorer.
- Working hours are longer and more weekend work is involved.
- Employment is more insecure and more likely to involve temporary or casual work.
- Training and development opportunities improve as firms grow.

The reasons for such outcomes are summarised as:

- higher presence of family members;
- blurred boundaries between labour and capital;
- informal, multi-task approach to work;
- lack of professional HR management;
- more jobs without formal contracts;
- greater job insecurity leading to workers accepting worse conditions.

To this list should also be added the element of volatile markets and uncertain competitive environments.

As has been noted in the introduction to this chapter and is reiterated in this European report, although common trends and themes can be identified for the purpose of debate and discussion, there is heterogeneity within and between small firms. EFILWC draw attention to the differences between the service and manufacturing sector particularly, noting the importance of craft enterprises in countries such as Germany and Italy where the employment relationship is subject to institutional frameworks. It is also recognised that those working in sectors that depend on highly skilled labour, such as high-tech firms, have greater leverage to negotiate preferential terms. For instance, in Germany such employees are more likely to benefit from the observation of collective agreements and wage settlements for the whole branch of the industry.

Meanwhile, in France location is influential as networks across communities and locales facilitate the development of minimum local standards and employment practices across the region. Moreover, French employees must have a written contract specifying hours, tasks, wages and working conditions. Indeed the French labour market is highly regulated with most of these provisions applicable to smaller firms. This might be compared with the case in Bulgaria, for instance, where employment contracts are rare and, given the difficult competitive environment, profits are marginal so there is little investment in individual training, development or collective forms of social insurance

(National Statistical Institute, 2000). Hence, there are clearly discrete influences arising from specific national contexts upon the employment relationship but there are also a number of common themes that span these borders. Firm size, sector and the tendency for individually negotiated employment relationships in an environment of informality appear to be widely influential upon labour management policy and practice in smaller enterprises. The manner and extent to which these trends emerge will clearly be influenced by the national agenda regarding social and economic policy.

20.8 Chapter summary

This chapter has offered an overview of labour management practices in small firms in both Britain and Europe. It is evident that the extant evidence and conceptual analysis regarding the employment relationship in smaller organisations has advanced substantially over recent years. In a recent critique of academic progress, Barrett and Rainnie (2002) argued this debate had, in fact, stagnated, with the 'small is beautiful' hypothesis still evident. This stagnation arose largely from the ongoing ignorance of structural forces and uncertainties by key researchers. However, in a robust response to this argument, Ram and Edwards (2003: 720) point to the increasing recognition given to the analysis of labour management in small firms within leading employment relations texts, research monologues (Marlow *et al.*, 2004) and critical empirical research (Workplace Employment Relations Survey, 1998) as a discrete and crucial area of study. This focus has been made possible by the expanding body of debate, analysis and empirical evidence afforded to employment relations practice and policy within smaller firms. As noted by Ram and Edwards, the theoretical approach has become increasingly sensitive to the manner in which the tensions surrounding managerial control of labour are articulated in the smaller organisations; moreover this analysis recognises both market imperatives and internal managerial strategies. The use of qualitative methodologies to explore and illustrate those processes that shape the employment relationship has substantially advanced the understanding of concepts of informality, negotiation and the prevailing social relations of production. In focusing upon the creation and recreation of the employment relationship upon a daily basis, this detailed evidence has also enabled a detailed exploration of the differentiated approaches to regulatory compliance.

It is recognised that there remains much to do in this area, particularly in the analysis of heterogeneity; although common trends such as informality have been identified, it is now essential to explore how this is influenced with respect to specific contexts. Moreover, although the arguments presented by Barrett and Rainnie (2002) regarding analytical progress are disputed, it is accepted that the interplay between structure and action in terms of market constraints and firm context merits further attention. Moreover, the issue of how firms change in respect to labour management practices, particularly as they grow, is an area of considerable interest. In the case of European countries again, commonalities were identified but, equally, the influence of differing national policy and practice was recognised. Questions arise regarding the impact of regulation upon smaller firms in France and Germany, why trade unions are influential in Finland and Scandinavia and, of course, the implications for small firm performance and standards of employment in these differing cases.

As such, this chapter has provided a flavour of the differences and similarities that define the employment relationship in smaller firms. Since the 1990s, a growing body of empirical evidence and a distinct conceptual analytical framework have emerged to illustrate and explore key issues and it is expected that this extant literature will continue to grow in future in terms of both depth and sophistication.

Questions

1 Discuss how and why the management of labour in small firms differs from approaches in larger organisations.

2 Evaluate whether the size of an enterprise can critically affect the tension inherent in the labour-capital relationship in modern market economies

3 Examine the reasons why the majority of small firm owners and their management teams adopt an informal *ad hoc* approach to the management of employees.

4 Outline the approach of your current government to the management of people at work and discuss how contemporary attitudes towards managing people in small firms will accord with such an approach.

Web links

www.ilo.org
The International Labour Organization is the UN specialised agency that seeks the promotion of social justice and internationally recognised human and labour rights.

www.eurofound.eu.int
The European Foundation for the Improvement of Living and Working Conditions provides information, advice and expertise on living and working conditions, industrial relations and managing change in Europe.

www.tuc.org.uk/smallfirmmyths
Report by the Trade Union Congress in the UK on some of the myths surrounding the small firm sector and contains some policy recommendations on the small business work-place.

CHAPTER 21

Strategy and the small business

Colm O'Gorman

21.1 Introduction

This chapter introduces the concepts of strategy and competitive advantage and their relationship to the management of small firms. Within the study of organisations the strategy concept is typically considered in the context of large firms. Do the concepts of strategy discussed in the literature apply in the context of small firms? We might expect them not to as small firms typically have fewer resources and are often organised differently from large firms. Small businesses also differ from large businesses in their perception of opportunities and their commitment of resources to new opportunities (Stevenson and Gumpert, 1985). Large organisations are typically characterised by an administrative management style. The resources that the business controls drive the growth and development of the business. Large businesses consider investment pay-off in the medium to long term. In making strategic moves, the large business will typically analyse the opportunity and make a one-off commitment of resources. In contrast, the small business is typically characterised by a lack of resources and management skills and by an entrepreneurial form of management. Small businesses can respond quickly to opportunities but may not be able to commit large amounts of resources to a new opportunity. Therefore, the small business manager tends to commit small amounts of resources, in a number of different stages, as opportunities emerge.

However, small need not be a competitive disadvantage. Small size can increase the flexibility of the business in responding to customer requests and to market changes. Small size can mean that the business can be more flexible in terms of production systems (Fiegenbaum and Karnini, 1991) or in terms of price. Small size may mean that the business is faster to respond to changes in the market. Small businesses may be less risk adverse and more inclined to initiate competitive actions (Chen and Hambrick, 1995).

The differences between small and large firms mean it is often inappropriate to compare them in terms of the strategy-making process or in terms of the strategies associated with success. Therefore it is important to consider strategy specifically in the context of the small firm and to consider how the characteristics of the small firm impact on how strategy is made and what strategies are associated with success. So, in reading this chapter bear in mind the following questions: What does strategy mean in the context of a small firm? Is it realistic for the small business to define its strategy and its strategic position? Should a small business have a formal strategy? Should a small firm 'plan' its strategy? What strategies should a small firm pursue? Can a small business reposition itself strategically?

The first part of this chapter outlines the strategy-making process in small businesses, highlighting the fact that this is a highly informal and *ad hoc* process in most small businesses. The advantages of a formal strategy-making process are then discussed. The second part of the chapter reviews research on the success strategies of small businesses. This review suggests that successful small businesses pursue 'focused' strategies and emphasise competitive advantages such as flexibility, fast response times and closeness to the customer. Innovation can also provide the small business with an important competitive advantage. The chapter concludes by highlighting structural and strategic weaknesses that impact on the choice of strategy and the strategy-making processes of small businesses. These weaknesses make it difficult for the small business manager to develop a clear competitive advantage. One of the most significant structural characteristics of small businesses that influences the strategy-making process is the centrality of the owner-manager. Strategic weaknesses include the lack of financial and managerial resources, reliance on a small customer base and poor technological competence.

21.2 Learning objectives

1 To appreciate the strategy-making process in small businesses.
2 To recognise the importance of focused and differentiated strategies for small businesses.
3 To understand the strategies that are associated with success in small businesses.
4 To introduce the strategic weaknesses of small businesses.

Key concepts
■ Strategy   ■ competitive advantage   ■ focus strategy
■ the strategy-making process

21.3 What is strategy?

Strategy is about two questions: 'What business(es) should we be in?' and 'How do we compete in a given business?' (Hofer, 1975). Drucker (1977) referred to these two challenges in terms of effectiveness and efficiency. Efficiency means doing things right – ensuring that day-to-day operations are managed well; effectiveness refers to ensuring that the business is doing the right things – that the focus of the business is correct in the context of customers, competitors and industry trends. Efficiency ensures short-term survival by producing a profit from existing activities, while effectiveness ensures long-term survival by focusing the business on activities that will continue to produce profits in the future. The essence of a good strategy is that it is feasible, that is, it is consistent with the resources and skills of the business; that it provides a clear competitive advantage; and that there is a 'fit' between the business and its external competitive environment (Rumelt, 1991).

The outcome of a strategy should be a clear competitive advantage. A competitive advantage is an advantage that is valued by customers and which distinguishes the business from competitors. The source of a competitive advantage can be conceptualised in terms of the strategic positioning of the business or in terms of its resources and skills. The positioning approach emphasises the need for the business to achieve 'fit' with the external environment. To develop a strategy the business must have a clear understanding of its market and of its competitors. The ongoing success of the business is dependent on its ability to maintain the 'fit' between itself and a changing environment.

The resource-based perspective argues that the source of a competitive advantage is the resources and capabilities of the business (Barney, 1991). By developing or acquiring resources the business can develop sustainable competitive advantages. Resources confer competitive advantage if they are hard to imitate, if they are heterogeneous (i.e. different from the resources that other businesses have) and if there is uncertainty as to the value of the resource. However, the value of resources can only be understood in the context of the market in which the business is operating and in the context of a particular moment in time. Of particular advantage to firms are having what are referred to as superior core competences and capabilities (Prahalad and Hamel, 1990). Core competences and capabilities refer to areas of activities within the firm that deliver added value to customers or allow the firm to operate more efficiently. In the context of small firms it is necessary to consider both superior competences and areas where the firm might have inferior competences and capabilities relative to competitors (Almor and Hashai, 2004).

The concept of strategy has different meanings in different contexts. Mintzberg proposed that strategy can be defined in five different ways, that is as a plan, as a ploy, as a pattern, as a position and as a perspective (Mintzberg and Quinn, 1991). Strategy as a plan refers to the intended actions that management have developed. When these plans refer to a specific decision they can be described as ploys. Mintzberg argues that not all strategies are planned but that in many situations strategy can be inferred from a pattern in a stream of decisions that management have made over time. Strategy can also refer to the position that the business has adopted in the external environment. This position can be defined in terms of the market that the business serves and the position that competitors have adopted. Finally, strategy can be conceptualised in terms of how a business perceives itself and its external environment; that is, in terms of the shared values and beliefs that guide the decisions made by the business.

21.4 Strategy making in the small business

In many cases the owner-manager of a small business may not formally articulate the business strategy or engage in any formal planning. However, there is a strong relationship between the owner-manager and the strategy pursued by the small firm. The strategy chosen by the owner-manager is likely to reflect the personal priorities and goals of the owner-manager (Kisfalvi, 2002). In turn, the owner-manager's personal priorities are likely to be determined by their own life experiences and prior work experiences. Furthermore, it is widely argued that the entrepreneur places a lasting 'stamp' on their company that influences the choice of strategy, organisational culture and managerial behaviours within the firm (Mullins, 1996). However, over-reliance on industry experience can result in a 'me-too' or 'copy-cat' strategy and no clear competitive advantage. In many industries with low barriers to entry, the cycle of 'me-too' new start-ups results in low profitability and high failure rates for small businesses.

Others have argued that strategy making in new and small firms is characterised by improvisation (Baker, Miner and Eesley, 2003). Improvisation describes a process whereby design and execution of a strategy occur simultaneously. Bhide (1994) argues that new ventures typically lack a planned strategy. Strategy in the ventures he studied emerged over time, with entrepreneurs responding flexibly to customer requirements. The ventures he studied typically faced significant capital constraints at start-up. Therefore, Bhide (2000) argues that in the context of new firms the key strategic challenge is the acquisition of resources. So rather than focusing on market position and competitive advantage Bhide suggests that the entrepreneur engages in creative ways of attracting resources and in generating sales. He argues that this process is unplanned and is typically characterised by 'guess work'.

One approach to developing a strategy is to engage in a formal planning process. However, there is evidence to suggest that formal and comprehensive planning systems are rare in small businesses. The planning processes observed in most small businesses have been described as 'informal, unstructured and sporadic' (Cohn and Lindberg, 1972) and as 'a passive search for alternatives' (Bracker, 1982). The structure of the small business and the centrality of the entrepreneur mean that all 'strategic planning' is typically concentrated in the owner-manager. The owner-manager may see no advantage in formalising the planning process that they use to develop the strategy of the business. Often the owner-manager will see disadvantages such as the potential loss of control, the loss of secrecy and the loss of flexibility.

The reality of strategy making and planning in the new venture context is that it is opportunistic and informal rather than formal. Founders analyse ideas parsimoniously and they integrate analysis and implementation (Bhide, 1994). However the lack of formal planning does not imply the absence of strategic thinking. Planning can be thought of as any reflective activity that precedes the making of decisions (Foster, 1993). Strategy change in new and small businesses may reflect a process of experimentation (Nicholls-Nixon et al., 2000). As such, the owner-manager seeks to determine the nature of the competitive environment and how best to compete in this environment by engaging in a process of trial and error learning.

21.4.1 The arguments in favour of adopting a formal planning system for a small firm

While formal planning systems may be uncommon in small firms there are some reasons for advocating that owner-managers engage in more systematic planning. Planning is generally perceived as a crucial element in the survival of new and small businesses (Kinsella et al., 1993; Hisrich and Peters, 1992; Jones, 1991). The models of planning suggested for small businesses have been adopted from the strategic management literature. However, small businesses differ from large businesses with regard to their planning needs and processes (Curtis, 1983). Small business generally do not have the resources to plan and purchase external advice and support; they are very susceptible to small environmental changes; owner-managers may not have the necessary experience for managing all aspects of a small business; and owner-managers cannot devote a lot of time to consciously working through plans because of day-to-day work pressures. A consequence of this is that owner-managers tend to have a shorter and more functional emphasis on planning. The essential components of a successful planning process in a small business are that the owner-manager is central to the planning process; the owner-manager and, where relevant, managers, must have sufficient time to devote to the planning process; and effective planning will only be possible if sufficient internal information is available. This means that an adequate financial record keeping and financial control system should be in place in the business. Financial information must be timely and accurate.

Business plans are essential if entrepreneurs are to acquire external financial support. By planning, the chances of success are increased as the right battlefield to suit one's skills is chosen (Hay *et al.*, 1993). Timmons (1994) argues that plans give the new business a results orientation that it would otherwise not have; that they force the new business to work smarter so that goals can be attained in the most effective and efficient manner possible; and that planning results in the consideration of alternatives that may not otherwise have been thought of and this allows planners to choose the optimum way of approaching a problem and, at the same time, it also makes them think ahead.

There are two main roles and uses of plans. Plans are used as communication devices and as aids to controlling the business's factors of production (Mintzberg, 1994; Baker *et al.*, 1993). The preparation of a business plan by an owner-manager is often seen exclusively as an external communications device. For some owner-managers a plan is written merely to improve legitimacy and satisfy demands from external agencies in order to acquire funding (Frank *et al.*, 1989). A clear description of how the entrepreneur will exploit the business opportunity allows investors to decide whether the project is a worthwhile investment and assess the risk attached to it. The second role of a plan is as a control device. Plans provide benchmarks against which subsequent performance can be evaluated. This is particularly important in small businesses as the owner-manager's time tends to be consumed by day-to-day management issues. The benefits of formal planning for small businesses are as follows:

- *A Statement of goals and objectives* – a formal planning system will require key managers and promoters to state the goals and objectives of the business. Essential to planning is the choice of a future direction, for, 'if you do not know where you are going, any road will take you there' (The Koran). By clearly specifying objectives, promoters and staff should be more focused in their daily work activities.

- *Efficient use of time* – by engaging in a planning process the owner-manager and, where appropriate, the directors of the business should make better use of their own management time. Planning should result in the identification and monitoring of a small number of key success factors.

- *Consideration of alternatives* – a formal planning system allows the small business to explicitly consider alternatives for its development. This may include addressing issues such as succession planning in family businesses.

- *Better internal management and staff development* – by focusing on the future development of the business a planning system should highlight the need for internal systems and processes and the future staff and managerial requirements of the business. The owner-manager should be able to develop these processes and systems in advance of the actual need. In many cases the development of these internal systems and structures will facilitate the strategic development of the business.

- *Better financial management* – planning systems are closely tied to financial systems. In order to plan, the small business will need a basic financial system that provides timely information on current performance. This should improve the financial control of the business and result in better decisions.

21.4.2 Planning and financial performance in small business

Within the literature on small business, research on planning has concentrated on establishing a link between planning and performance. Many researchers make the inference that the ultimate survival of a small business is dependent on the presence of formal planning activity (Bracker and Person, 1986). There is evidence that small business failure is linked to a lack of planning activity (Bracker and Pearson, 1986). However, this research on the significance and impact of planning in small businesses has proved to be inconclusive (Stone and Brush, 1996; Schwenk and Shrader, 1993; Cragg and King, 1988).

Schwenk and Shrader (1993) reviewed studies on the relationship between planning and financial performance and found conflicting results. In a comparative study between planners and non-planners, Cragg and King (1988) found no correlation between planning activities and financial performance. They also found a negative correlation between planning and size of sales and marketing team. Within this sample, however, younger firms performed better than older ones. Bracker and Pearson (1986) compared small mature firms in terms of age, size and planning history. They concluded that level of sophistication of planning had a positive impact on financial performance; younger firms performed better than older firms, as did firms with a longer planning history.

In many cases, the act of planning cannot necessarily be correlated with the success of a business venture (Robinson and Pearce, 1984). It is possible that the contribution of planning to new and small businesses cannot be measured quantitatively. Rather than compare planning and financial performance a more useful measure of planning might be the amount of vicarious experience that the owner-manager acquires by undertaking the planning process. Planning helps focus owner-managers on their resources, their market and their product; in this way, it could be argued that the main contribution of planning to a business is an increased level of environmental awareness. Similarly, the absence of planning cannot be used as the sole explanation of business failure. In fact, it has been argued that a higher proportion of unsuccessful firms coordinate written plans and performance, set goals and monitor goal achievement (Frank *et al.*, 1989).

21.4.3 Reasons for the absence of formal strategic planning in small businesses

Research suggests that most new and small businesses do not plan (Bhide, 1994; Stratos Group, 1990; Robinson and Pearce, 1984; Curtis, 1983). In many cases the structure of the small business is such that the owner-manager is intimately linked to all day-to-day activities. This allows the entrepreneur to control the direction of the business on a day-to-day basis. Where there is a planning process, it is often seen as a separate activity from the day-to-day management of the business rather than as a tool for improving day-to-day management. There are several barriers that inhibit the practice of planning in new and small businesses:

- *Clear sense of strategic direction/position* – most owner-mangers have a clear sense of the strategic position and direction of their business. Management activity is typically focused on striving to implement more effectively the strategy chosen at start-up.

- *Centrality of the owner-manager* – The close proximity of the entrepreneur to environmental issues often makes objective judgement difficult (West, 1988).

- *Environment context* – Many small businesses operate in highly turbulent environments. Formal planning may be counter-productive in such environments as it reduces the strategic flexibility of the business (Chaffee, 1985; Fredrickson and Mitchell, 1984).

- *Rigidity of formal systems* – Formal planning systems may be too rigid for a small business (Mintzberg, 1994). The small business often relies on its flexibility and speed of response as a competitive strength and a formal planning system with tight financial controls may restrict the responsiveness of the small business. Once a plan is developed, there are so many links between issues and areas that one change can upset the whole plan. In addition, some goals are planned in 'lock step immutable order', which means that the entire plan can be ruined by one unexpected difficulty (Timmons, 1994).

- *Lack of time* – the owner-manager is typically involved in the day-to-day management of the business and may not have the time to invest in formal planning. Many owner-managers have to complete administrative and record-keeping activities outside work hours.

- *Lack of experience* – owner-managers typically have little formal management training and little exposure to budgeting, controlling or planning systems.

- *Lack of openness* – owner-managers typically are sensitive about their business plans and performance. They are slow to share this information and key decisions with staff or external advisers.

- *Fear of failure* – the explicit statement of goals and objectives, an essential element to a planning process, may result in a failure to achieve these goals and a sense of overall failure by the entrepreneur. By avoiding stating the goals and objectives of the business the entrepreneur can avoid commitment to any one direction or goal.

21.5 Success strategies in small firms

The owner-manager must choose where to compete and then, given a particular environmental or industry context, how to compete (McDougall and Robinson, 1990). These choices have a significant and lasting effect on the organisation and its performance (Mintzberg and Waters, 1982; Quinn and Cameron, 1983). The choice of competitive strategy within a market determines the financial performance of the organisation: if the 'wrong' market is chosen performance may be low. However, most owner-managers of small businesses adopt a 'me-too' or 'copy-cat' strategy – replicating what has been done before.

Small firm performance can also be explained in terms of other factors such as industry structure and the entrepreneurial orientation of the owner-manager. Industry structure impacts on the success of new ventures and has a critical impact on the choice of strategy (Sandberg and Hofer, 1987). Periods of high-demand conditions, such as industry growth and industry maturity, offer better opportunities for the small business than do periods of low demand such as the emergent stage of the product life-cycle (Carroll and Delacroix, 1982; Romanelli, 1989). However, while market choice is a critical managerial decision, it is not a choice that is, or can be, subject to frequent change. The choice of environment is constrained by the owner-manager's past experience and by previous choices made, and is therefore not an active decision variable (Eisenhardt and Schoonhoven, 1990).

Recently, research has argued that firms characterised by an 'entrepreneurial strategic orientation' have higher levels of performance (Covin and Slevin, 1991). An entrepreneurial strategic orientation means that the firm is more willing to innovate, is more prepared to take risks and is more proactive than competitors. As such, entrepreneurial orientation captures aspects of the firm's decision-making styles, methods and processes (Wiklund and Shepherd, 2005).

More commonly, researchers focus on the strategic attributes of successful small businesses. Success is typically measured in terms of existing competitive position and the change in this position over time. Measuring success in a small business context is inherently difficult, as success should be related to the owner-manager's objectives rather than measured in terms of competitive, financial or market success. Studies on the strategies pursued by small businesses typically focus on some measure of success in terms of these latter criteria rather than in terms of the owner-manager's personal definition of success.

21.5.1 Choosing 'where' to compete: a broad or narrow focus?

The small firm might choose to appeal to a narrow market niche, hoping to capture a relatively high market share, or to compete by appealing to a broader range of customers. That is, the firm can choose to be a specialist or a generalist. The appeal of focusing on a narrow segment is that the small firm's resources can be targeted or concentrated and the firm can build a strong reputation and customer loyalty with this targeted customer base. The prescriptive advice from the strategy literature is typically that the small business should focus on market niches; that is, it should be a 'specialist'.

413

Porter (1985) argues that a focus strategy is most appropriate for smaller businesses. According to Porter, the business pursuing a focus strategy competes by selecting a segment or group of segments in its industry and by tailoring its strategy to serving these segments to the exclusion of others. By optimising its strategy in the target segments the business with a focus strategy achieves a competitive advantage even though it does not possess a competitive advantage for the whole market.

Some research suggests that small firms that focus achieve superior performance. For example, research studies of microbreweries and of local wineries suggest that small firms that compete more narrowly are more successful. Other research suggests that high-growth small businesses pursue market niche strategies. The essence of a market niche strategy in the context of many small businesses appears to be the avoidance of direct competition with both larger and smaller competitors. The evidence from the studies of fast-growth businesses in Ireland and the UK suggests that, despite attempts in the research to control for sector influences on growth by choosing 'matched pairs', high-growth companies rarely competed directly with low-growth companies (Storey, 1994; Kinsella and Mulvenna, 1993).

Research on low market share competitors has suggested a number of strategies that the smaller share business can successfully employ. The most common conclusion of these studies is that the smaller business should avoid head-to-head competition by seeking out protected market niches (Cooper *et al.*, 1986; Buzzell and Wiersema, 1981). Combined with this strategy of segmentation, the smaller share competitor should seek to differentiate its product offering and should offer a high-quality product.

Studies of successful medium-sized companies have suggested that a market niche strategy is an important characteristic of these companies. Cavanagh and Clifford (1983: 10) concluded that 'most winning companies are leaders in market niches, often in markets they have created through innovation'. Research evidence from the UK suggests that market position is an important characteristic of fast-growth businesses (Macrae, 1991; Solemn and Stiener, 1989). This research suggests that while the choice of overall sector may influence profitability and growth, the choice of specific market position is more important to the performance of an individual enterprise.

The empirical identification of a market niche strategy in small businesses is fraught with operational and definition difficulties. It is difficult for researchers to define precisely the product market a business is competing in. How does a small food manufacturer producing speciality frozen deserts for supermarkets define their product market arena? Such a business could define its business very narrowly, 'a producer of premium frozen deserts for supermarkets', or broadly, 'a desert producer'. The classification of its competitive strategy will be a function of the choice of business definition and more importantly this definition may broaden as the business seeks to grow and expand. Neither Kalleberg and Leicht (1991) nor Westhead and Birley (1993) were able to provide conclusive evidence of market niche strategies among fast-growth small businesses in the UK. Biggadike (1976) compared the relative attractiveness of a niche strategy and an aggressive market-share-seeking entry strategy and suggested that the latter is more appropriate for new ventures seeking to establish themselves. He suggested that the poor performance of many new ventures is the direct consequence of limiting market focus at the time of entry.

The dangers of pursuing a focus strategy are that the business may incorrectly identify a market niche. Unless the business gains a competitive advantage by focusing on the niche then it should pursue a more broadly based strategy. An additional problem of pursuing a focused strategy is that the chosen market niche may be too small for the business to survive or may require that the small business become involved in export markets at a stage when they lack the resources to support these markets.

Rather than focusing on a market niche the entrepreneur might try to gain a large share of the market. Some new businesses must pursue a broad entry strategy because of the large capital investment required at start-up. These businesses are only viable if they achieve high utilisation of their large capital investment. The advantage of a broad market strategy is that if the business is successful it will be on a large scale. Additionally a broad strategy might be more attractive to distributors, retailers or consumers. It suggests that there will be continuity in the business and it might include a more comprehensive service for the customer. Most new businesses do not have the resources to pursue such a strategy and therefore start on a small scale. Despite inconclusive empirical evidence, the prevailing wisdom in the strategy literature is that small businesses should optimise the use of their limited resources by competing in a limited market niche. In the literature on small businesses the prescriptive advice is that the best way to avoid direct competition with larger competitors is to pursue a niche strategy (Vesper, 1990).

21.5.2 Choosing 'how' to compete: cost or differentiation

Having chosen what market to compete in the small firm must choose how it is going to compete within this market. Porter (1985) identified two types of competitive advantage, which he termed cost leadership and differentiation. Based on these two advantages and on the competitive scope of the business, which he classified as either industry wide or focused, he developed three generic competitive strategies, namely cost leadership, differentiation and focus. According to Porter, businesses must choose one of these generic strategies; failure to do so results in below-average profitability.

Research suggests that a differentiation strategy is the most appropriate strategy for small businesses. The limited resources of small businesses suggest that the owner-manager should focus resources and pursue a differentiation strategy. A large number of firms pursuing different differentiation strategies may be successful in the same environment (Eisenhardt and Schoonhoven, 1990; McDougall and Robinson, 1990; Porter, 1980).

Product quality was the most important competitive advantage identified by SMEs across a number of European countries (Bamberger, 1989); in addition, factors such as 'reliability of delivery', 'reputation of firm' and 'competence of the workforce' were ranked as important competitive advantages. Interestingly, pricing factors were only rated 16th out of the 26 factors important to the development of competitive advantage. New ventures pursuing undifferentiated strategies performed less well than new ventures pursuing differentiated strategies (Sandberg and Hofer, 1987).

There are many ways in which a business may have a better product/service. These include superior product/service performance, faster delivery service, better location, wider product range, personal advice and after-sales service, longer credit terms, more flexible service, personalised attention, etc. It is important that the entrepreneur tries to maximise the number and the extent of advantages that the product/service has. This strategy is often not successful because the 'better' service/product that the business is offering is not of value to customers. Another reason why this strategy is unsuccessful is because the small business fails to communicate its better service/product to their customers. This may be because of the financial investment and time required for promotion, advertising and sales support, activities and areas of expenditure that most small businesses consider a luxury.

Porter (1985) proposes that a business differentiates itself from competitors by being unique at something which is of value to buyers. To be sustainable a business's differentiation must perform unique activities that impact on the customers' purchasing criteria. Porter (1985: 152) identifies several methods that a business can employ to enhance its differentiation. These are:

- to enhance its sources of uniqueness;
- to make the cost of differentiation an advantage;
- to change the rules of competition to create uniqueness; and
- to reconfigure the value chain to be unique in entirely new ways.

Intuitively most owner-managers believe that a low-cost strategy will be successful – customers should be willing to pay less for the same product/service. However, this strategy is not so easy to pursue and many owner-managers fail to pursue it successfully with the result that their business performs poorly. To pursue a low-priced strategy the new business should have a lower cost base than competitors. Many small businesses pursue this strategy of lower costs by ensuring that they have lower overheads, by operating outside the tax system, or by using low-cost labour and not costing their own time at the market rate. The danger with this approach is that the entrepreneur may not have identified all the overheads that the business will incur and that as the business develops overheads will increase. The advantage of a low-price strategy is that the new business should be able to attract customers. Lower prices should encourage customers to try the new business and may encourage new customers.

However, this strategy does not always work for small businesses. Often the net effect of lower prices is lower profits for the entrepreneur rather than increased sales. There are a number of reasons why this strategy may not work for the small business. The first is that for many products the price charged is assumed by customers to be a reflection of the quality of the product. Customers may interpret low prices as a sign of lower quality service rather than as a more efficient supplier. To overcome this problem it might be necessary for the entrepreneur to inform customers why they are cheaper, for example 'cheaper because we buy direct from the factory'.

The second reason why this strategy may not work is that the owner-manager fails to invest in promotion and advertising. The owner-manager may incorrectly assume that a low-cost strategy means not investing in marketing and selling costs. The net effect of this is that the customer is unaware of the lower-cost alternative and the new business remains small. Many small businesses fail to generate revenues to invest in advertising and promotion because of their low prices and turnover.

21.5.3 Innovation as a source of advantage

Within the literature on innovation, researchers have sought to establish a relationship between business size and the level of innovation. An alternative perspective is to compare the level of innovation with business profitability, growth and survival. To the extent that this has been done, mostly indirectly by studies examining the characteristics of better-performing companies in a particular size/industry sector, it appears that there is a relationship between better performance and higher levels of innovation. Scherer (1980: 422) concluded that 'what we find . . . is a kind of threshold effect. A little bit of bigness – up to sales levels of $250m to $400m at 1978 price levels – is good for invention and innovation. But beyond the threshold further bigness adds little or nothing and it carries with it the danger of diminishing the effectiveness of inventive and innovative performance'.

Innovation may manifest itself in terms of the introduction of new products. Research suggests that the ability to introduce new products is positively related to performance in small businesses (Murray and O'Gorman, 1994; Kinsella *et al.*, 1993; Wynarczyki *et al.*, 1993; Cambridge Small Business Research Centre, 1992; Woo *et al.*, 1989). Other evidence suggests that those businesses that are technically more sophisticated or technologically more innovative are likely to grow faster (Boeker, 1989; Philips and Kirchhoff, 1989). However, it may be that these technically more sophisticated sectors are experiencing faster growth.

Buzzell and Wiersema (1981) used the PIMS database to test which strategies were characteristic of businesses that were increasing their market share position. They found that the strategic factors generally involved in market share gains included increases in new product activity, increases in relative product quality and increases in sales promotion, relative to the growth rate of the served market.

Small businesses face a number of disadvantages in trying to be innovative. Most small businesses lack the financial, technical and human resources needed to innovate. The lack of time by the owner-manager for long-term thinking prevents the development of both technical and market-led innovations. The absence of a marketing function and marketing expertise restricts the development of customer-driven innovations. Even those small businesses that are technologically competent, for example small engineering or software firms, face problems in the management of technology. The competitive strength of these small businesses, their specialist technical knowledge, exposes them to the possibility of being exposed to technical developments outside their area of expertise. This problem is particularly apparent in sectors where developments have been driven by the fusion of two or more existing technologies. The small business typically does not have the expertise or the financial resources to cope with external developments. The solution to this problem often necessitates cooperation with other businesses or with universities or technical institutes. However, small businesses are reluctant to cooperate with other businesses. While universities may provide technical assistance they seldom provide access to investment and therefore can only partially solve the problems facing the small business.

21.5.4 Exporting and internationalisation strategies

Exporting or internationalisation can provide the small business with access to larger and more attractive markets (see Chapter 24). However, most small businesses do not engage in any exporting or international activities; in particular, small businesses in the service sector have very low levels of direct international activity. Small firms face significant barriers in trying to internationalise their activities. Of particular significance are a lack of knowledge and resources (Johanson and Vahlne, 1984). However, it is important to note that many small businesses are involved indirectly in international markets through their sub-supply activities with larger indigenous and multinational companies. The globalisation of some new high-technology sectors facilitates small companies internationalising at an earlier stage of development than is typical among small businesses (see Chapters 13 and 24).

21.6 The strategic problems of small businesses

Developing a sustainable competitive strategy entails not only developing superior competences and capabilities in some aspects of the business but also in minimising the impact of areas of the small firm where there are inferior competences and capabilities (Almor and Hashai, 2004). The strategic weaknesses that characterise most small businesses are the consequence of the managerial deficiencies of the owner-manager and the resource deficiencies of the small business.

21.6.1 Lack of financial resources

Most small businesses are undercapitalised and are inappropriately capitalised, in terms of both a high debt–equity ratio and an over-reliance on short-term debt (Davidson and Dutia, 1991). Inadequate and inappropriate capitalisation is a significant contributory factor to the high levels of failure among new businesses. Poor capitalisation may be the result of the difficulties that new businesses face in raising capital (Hall, 1989) and the low levels of profitability in small businesses (Davidson and Dutia, 1991). When capital is available entrepreneurs may choose debt capital in preference to equity capital due to its perceived lower cost (Brigham and Smith, 1967).

However, the capital structure decision is not purely a financial decision. Strategic factors also determine debt–equity ratios (Chaganti *et al.*, 1995). The desire to maintain control of the business may increase the use of personal equity investment. The level of personal equity investment by the entrepreneur may reflect the entrepreneur's 'insider' knowledge of the business and his evaluation of the likelihood of success, with low levels of investment resulting in non-value maximising behaviours such as higher chief executive salaries. Entrepreneurs may substitute financial capital with cheaper 'sweat equity'.

21.6.2 Marketing problems and customer concentration

Small businesses engage in little marketing activity. Most small businesses have few resources to devote to marketing and many owner-managers have no experience of marketing, preferring to devote their time to activities that are more familiar (e.g. production), with the result that little time is spent on either marketing or selling activities. Some of the marketing problems of small businesses relate to their lack of product differentiation. This makes it difficult for the owner-manager to position the product or service as a distinctive offering. A distinguishing characteristic of small businesses is their high dependency on a small number of customers. Research evidence suggests that as many as one-third of all small businesses are dependent on one customer for 25% or greater of their sales (Cambridge Small Business Research Centre, 1992). This is a high-risk strategy for the small business as the loss of one customer may result in business failure. Finally, owner-managers tend to have very little knowledge of export markets.

21.6.3 Management resources and human resources

By their nature most small businesses are owner-managed. The owner-manager is required to manage all functions of the business, including operations, finance, staff and marketing. However, the narrow expertise of the owner-manager and the lack of management skills mean that the small business is deficient in a number of these functional areas. Most small businesses do not have the resources to hire outside managers to strengthen functional areas of the business. Where resources are available the pervasive involvement of the entrepreneur in the business may make it difficult for outside managers to function in the business.

Small firms have difficulty in attracting good staff. For many potential employees, a small business will not offer the scope for training and development. Additionally, potential employees perceive working in a small business as a risky career move owing to possible business failure. Due to a lack of resources and low levels of profitability, small businesses often pay lower salaries than competing larger ones.

21.6.4 Over-reliance on the entrepreneur

Most small businesses are characterised by what Mintzberg refers to as a 'simple' structure (1979). This structure reflects the personality traits of the owner-manager (Miller and Droge, 1986). Typically the owner-manager is actively involved in the day-to-day management of the business and is often involved in the direct production of the product or the provision of the service. The customer base of the business is typically limited and is known directly to the entrepreneur. The entrepreneur relies on informal communication channels to communicate internally and externally. Due to a lack of time many entrepreneurs keep incomplete and out-of-date financial records and/or spend 'out of work' hours updating financial accounts. The benefits of this 'simple' structure are that the entrepreneur is in close contact with the key issues of the business and is 'on the spot' to deal with problems; quality standards are maintained through direct supervision by the entrepreneur; and staff are involved in the business and engage in frequent informal communication with the entrepreneur. These advantages allow the business to respond to the needs of customers in a quick, innovative and flexible manner. It is these latter qualities that many larger bureaucratic organisations are now trying to emulate through de-layering, down-sizing and team work (Kanter,

1984). Others argue that small firms exhibit diversity in how they are organised; that is, in how jobs are divided, grouped and coordinated (Barth, 2003).

However, in many cases it appears that the management style of the owner-manager is the antithesis of good management practices. The skills, competencies and behaviours necessary for successful new venture creation become barriers to the growth and development of a business (Kazanjian 1988; Churchill and Lewis, 1983). Traits such as a strong need for control and a high sense of distrust can result in owner-managers engaging in behaviours that prevent the organisation growing (Baumback and Mancuso, 1993; Kets de Vries, 1985; Churchill and Lewis, 1983). Such behaviours might include the centralisation of control and 'scape-goating' when activities are not successful (Kets de Vries, 1985). The pervasive involvement of the entrepreneur in the business means that it is difficult for them to attend to important, though non-urgent, issues. Finally, the high need for achievement that drives the entrepreneur may result in the centralisation of decision making (Miller and Droge, 1986).

21.6.5 Lack of systems and controls

Small businesses are characterised by informality and poor information systems. Specifically, small businesses are characterised by poor formal control systems (Huff and Reger, 1987). During the start-up period informality dominates in many aspects of the new business, including its control system (Walsh and Dewar, 1987; Quinn and Cameron, 1983). The lack of information results in poor decision making.

21.6.6 Technological skills

The majority of small businesses can be classified as technology contingent – having no influence on the technological trends and innovations that impact on the business. Most small businesses lack the capacity to investigate and assess new technical developments that might impact on their competitive position. In many cases, a small business operates in sectors that have a stable technological trajectory, allowing it to pursue a reactive strategy, that is, to respond to external changes as they happen. However, with technological developments the technical demands on many small businesses have increased significantly and technological competence has become a prerequisite to survival in many sectors.

21.7 Chapter summary

This chapter outlined research that explores how strategy is formed in a small firm, success strategies in small firms and the strategic weaknesses that characterise small firms. Most small businesses face significant strategic and structural weaknesses. In particular, small businesses lack the managerial skills necessary to develop and implement a strategy. The strategy-making process is typically *ad hoc* and informal, and frequently the entrepreneur's personality prevents the sharing of information about the business's strategic position. There is some evidence to suggest that some strategies, such as a focused market position and a differentiated competitive advantage, are positively associated with success in small businesses. In addition, the importance and significance of innovation as a means of developing competitive advantage was discussed. Strategic weaknesses also prevent the implementation of a strategy. Small businesses are typically characterised by insufficient financial and managerial resources. The lack of financial resources prevents investment in activities such as product development and marketing. The owner-manager's lack of financial skills means that the information necessary for managerial decisions is not available.

The implications of the research presented in this chapter for the owner-manager are that the development of a clear competitive advantage is essential to both short- and long-term survival. The owner-manager must understand that choices in relation to 'where' they compete and 'how' they compete impact on the viability and performance of the business. In addition, the owner-manager needs to understand that the structural characteristics of the business and their own managerial style may restrict the development of both an effective strategy-making process and an effective strategy.

Implications for the policy maker are that most small businesses are characterised by significant strategic and structural weaknesses. For individual small businesses to develop and prosper these deficiencies must be reduced. Clearly, the role of the policy maker is to help the owner-manager in the development of a strategy and competitive advantage. It is important that policy makers appreciate that the problem is not with the strategy formulation process but rather with the development of a clear competitive advantage. Pressurising owner-managers to produce formal plans does not assist them in addressing the strategic and structural deficiencies of the small business. Policy makers need to address systematically the strategic and structural deficiencies of small businesses by providing the owner-manager with the opportunity to develop the skills and acquire the resources that are needed for the development and implementation of an effective strategy.

Questions

1 What strategic and structural weaknesses affect the development and implementation of effective strategies in small businesses?

2 What strategies are associated with success in small businesses?

3 How appropriate is it for policy makers to require owner-managers of small businesses to prepare formal business plans prior to receiving any financial assistance?

4 Given the strategic and structural weaknesses of small businesses do the concepts of 'strategy' and 'competitive advantage' have any relevance to small businesses?

Web links

www.entrepreneur.com
The website of 'Entrepreneur' magazine containing a range of information for small businesses, including strategic planning.

www.usasbe.org/knowledge/proceedings/1999/Naffziger.PDF
'Strategic Planning in Small Businesses: process and content realities' by Douglas Naffziger and Carolyn Mueller details a study examining how entrepreneurs in the US are involved in the strategic planning process within their organisations.

www.eim.net/pdf-ez/N200416.pdf
'Strategic Decision-making in Small Firms' examines different types of decision makers within small firms and their impact on growth.

CHAPTER 22

E-commerce and the small business

Nigel Lockett and David Brown

22.1 Introduction

This chapter looks beyond the extraordinary developments in information and communication technology (ICT), particularly e-commerce and e-business, to the opportunities and challenges presented to small businesses by the emerging digital economy. E-commerce is but one, albeit high-profile, element of the e-business revolution in which small and medium-sized enterprises (SMEs) are able to utilise modern technologies to conduct business in new and innovative ways. Whilst business to consumer (B2C) e-commerce attracts much attention, over 85% of e-commerce revenues are generated within the business to business (B2B) sector. Furthermore US B2C e-commerce retail sales, whilst rapidly approaching $20bn per quarter, still represent only 2% of US retail sales across all sectors. Figure 22.1 shows the threefold rise in sales over the past four years.

Clearly there is considerable variation across market sectors with some sectors dominated by online sales, such as low-cost European airlines where over 95% of ticket sales are online. E-business, however, is more than e-based transactions and extends to new business models and new processes, both internal and external, many of which are collaborative. Dealing with such ICT-led change requires any company to constantly evaluate and respond appropriately. However, the strategic, organisational and financial impact on small businesses can present particular challenges. Unlike large firms they are unlikely to have the human and financial resources to appreciate fully the threats and the emerging opportunities from new ICT, such as broadband or 3G mobile technologies.

To discuss the implications of these radical developments the chapter is divided into three main sections. First, the context for e-business in small businesses is developed, including: definitions, government policies, nature of e-business engagement and the barriers and drivers to adoption. Second, three main strands of theory relating to e-business in small businesses are reviewed, namely: ICT adoption, inter-organisational networks and e-business models. Recent research into the role of aggregation and intermediaries is also discussed since this is likely to prove to be highly significant for small businesses and their engagement in e-business. Finally, the importance of trusted third parties is considered.

Figure 22.1 **US online sales by quarter**

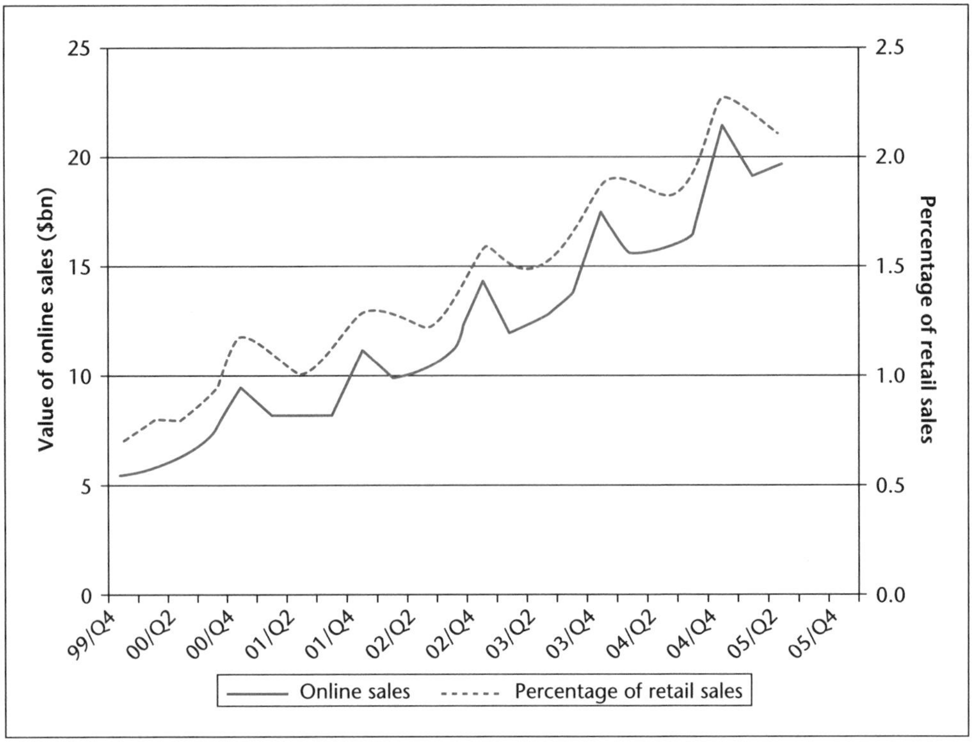

Source: US Commerce (2005)

22.2 Learning objectives

1 To understand the challenges and opportunities of e-business for small businesses.
2 To appreciate the current levels of engagement of small businesses in e-business.
3 To understand the strategic context and impact of e-business in small businesses.
4 To appreciate the role of aggregation and intermediaries in e-business adoption by small businesses.

Key concepts

■ e-business ■ e-commerce ■ ICT adoption ■ networks ■ intermediaries
■ aggregation

22.3 E-commerce in context

Governments in many leading economies, including the UK, have established national policies to encourage small businesses to adopt ICT, particularly e-business, and have set benchmarked targets to monitor their progress. Research between 1999 and 2004, within the UK government's authoritative Department of Trade and Industry (DTI) series of International Benchmarking Studies, suggests that this adoption is proving more problematic then anticipated:

> the trend of smaller businesses 'clicking off' is unmistakeable. It is particularly marked in the UK, and has been sustained for the last three years . . . smaller businesses face a real hurdle in moving beyond simple e-commerce to becoming true 'e-businesses' . . . smaller businesses, more than any, need someone to help them exploit the technology, but no one's set up to do it.
>
> (DTI, 2004: 14)

However, the DTI's most recent study suggests some improvement with the UK's micro and small businesses showing significant gains in the uptake of websites and trading online (DTI, 2004: i). Other studies looking across various industrial sectors in Europe (European Commission, 2004b) present a more varied and complex picture. Clearly the use of ICT in large companies tends to be more complex and sophisticated than that in small businesses. This often translates into more intensive and advanced e-business practices. Even in those sectors, such as the automotive and chemical industries, that are international leaders in e-business adoption, there remains a significant 'digital divide' between the large companies and the many small businesses within their supply chains.

It is within this context of the relative low engagement by small businesses in the more complex e-business technologies, resulting in a perceivable 'digital divide' between large and small firms, that this chapter seeks to explore how individual firms and groups of firms approach engagement in e-business.

22.3.1 Definition of e-business and e-commerce

E-business and e-commerce have been variously defined to mean the same, or different, concepts. Kalakota and Whinston (1996) defined e-commerce from four perspectives, namely:

- *Communication* – as the delivery of information, products/service or payments over telephone lines, computer networks or any other electronic means.
- *Business process* – as the application of technology towards the automation of business processes and workflows.
- *Service* – as a tool that addresses the desire of firms, consumers and management to cut service costs while improving quality and increasing the speed of service delivery.
- *Online* – as the capability of buying and selling products and information on the Internet and other online services.

Turban *et al.* (2004) in their widely cited book state: 'we use the term electronic commerce in its broadest scope, which is basically equivalent to e-business.' In the important UK Cabinet Office's *e-commerce@its.best.uk* report, which became the early reference point for much of government policy, it is stated: 'what the government describes as e-commerce is recognised in industry as e-business' (Cabinet Office, 1999). The report, however, made a distinction between process and transactional e-commerce, namely:

425

Figure 22.2 Elements of e-business activities

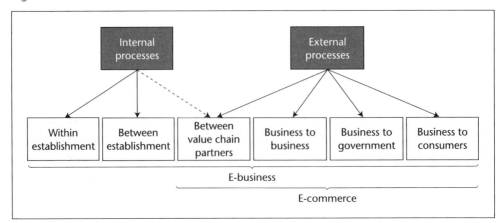

Source: European Commission E-Business Watch initiative (2004)

- *process* – B2B activity for intermediate goods and a wide variety of information.
- *transaction* – both B2B and B2C activity for final products and services.

Currently, the DTI defines e-commerce as 'any form of business transaction carried out electronically over public telephone systems' and uses a progressive model of e-adoption. In this model e-commerce is defined as ordering and paying online, thus reducing transaction costs, whereas e-business is seen as supply chain integration, so that manufacture and delivery become seamless. This is a helpful distinction.

Confirmation of this distinction can be seen in the recently introduced European Commission E-Business Watch initiative (European Commission, 2004b), which tracks e-business activity in Europe and states 'e-commerce will be taken to cover external transactions, and it therefore may be seen as a sub-group of e-business activities' (Figure 22.2).

The E-Business Watch benchmarking programme also went further and proposed a detailed scoreboard of e-business technologies and applications (Table 22.1).

Over time the clear trend has been towards using e-business as the broad term for all ICT-supported activities and e-commerce to be more directly concerned with transactions. This chapter adopts that convention and *e-commerce* is taken to be transaction focused and defined as: *selling or buying of goods or services using electronic communication networks*. Similarly *e-business* is viewed as transaction, process and collaboration focused and defined as: *the use of electronic communication networks to transact, process and collaborate in business markets*. Hence in this definition e-business incorporates e-commerce.

Within these definitions there is a broad spectrum of applications from simple e-mail and websites to the more complex applications of customer and supplier integration, which are collaborative in nature. It is the latter higher-complexity applications that may provide the major economic and competitive benefits; yet in 2004 UK small businesses were typically four times less likely than larger firms to be engaged in these higher-complexity collaborative applications (DTI, 2004).

Table 22.1 **Scoreboard of e-business technologies and applications**

Area	Number	Indicator
ICT infrastructure	1	Internet access
	2	Broadband Internet access
	3	Intranet
	4	Extranet
	5	Employee's access to e-mail
E-commerce	6	Website
	7	Online selling
	8	Online procurement
	9	B2B e-marketplace
E-business processes	10	Online collaboration
	11	eCRM
	12	IT-supported ERP
	13	Online working hours tracking
	14	E-learning

Source: European Commission E-Business Watch initiative (2004) (www.ebusiness-watch.org)

22.3.2 Nature of e-business engagement

The recent and rapid emergence of e-business applications has been primarily as a result of the availability of a low-cost, ubiquitous electronic communication network – the Internet. Telecommunication, technology and service companies have emerged or evolved to provide a range of e-business services or web services designed to exploit existing and emerging communication infrastructures. Typically these companies are known as application service providers (ASPs) and variously defined as:

■ 'third-party entities that manage and distribute software-based services and solutions to customers across a wide area network from a central data facility' (Webopedia, 2005);

■ 'provides a contractual service offering to deploy, host, manage and rent access to an application from a centrally managed facility, responsible for either directly or indirectly providing all the specific activities and expertise aimed at managing a software application or set of applications' (Gillan *et al.*, 1999);

■ 'a secure, flexible and integrated approach to delivering differentiated business value by combining the systems and processes that run core business operations with the simplicity and reach made possible by Internet technologies – IBM' (Amor, 2000).

The technology used by ASPs to deliver services relies on 'thin-client' application server products, such as Microsoft's terminal server and Citrix's WinFrame applications, addressing client devices, such as PC and Windows terminals. The use of web browser technologies on the client devices both reduces the sophistication of the client device (thus reducing purchase and support costs resulting in a lower total cost of ownership) and increases the interoperability of devices (as more devices incorporate web browsers). Whilst ASPs are external to organisations, larger enterprises can use these technologies to provide 'in-house' services, which effectively moves applications off PCs on to application servers, resulting in central control over application cost, usage and support. The provision of these hosted applications, by ASPs, on a rented basis is viewed as of particular relevance to small businesses.

The new (*hosted*) applications that facilitate e-business are very different from traditional (*resident*) applications in one main regard, namely that the user interface, application software, data processing and data storage can be located on different and multiple software and hardware platforms, and can be provided and supported by different entities (Figure 22.3).

They are, in essence, hosted services accessed by the user via a simple interface, such as a web browser, over electronic communication networks, such as the Internet. This is a fundamental change in the relationship between user, hardware and software and presents opportunities for new business models for service provision. Typically these hosted applications are offered on a rental or fee basis, rather than the traditional purchase model. The fee typically includes the use of the software and the provision of the processing and storage platforms, but not the provision of the electronic communication network. Importantly, these electronic communication networks are increasingly being considered as ubiquitous and are rapidly evolving from the public Internet through virtual private networks to grid computing and 3G mobile platforms. They provide the communication platforms on which ASPs can deliver hosted services. Service providers, however, come in many guises including ASPs, storage service providers (SSPs), network

Figure 22.3 **Architecture for e-business applications**

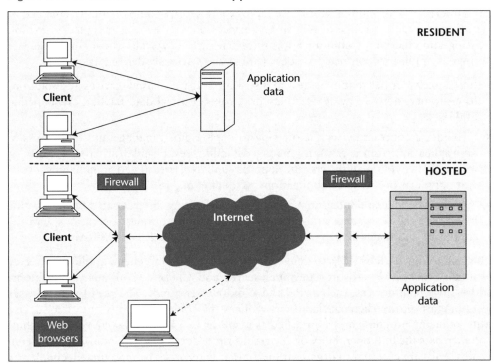

Table 22.2 Classification of e-business application complexity

Proposed classification	Examples	Complexity
Communication	E-mail, web access	Very Low
Marketing	Website	Low
Productivity	Microsoft Office, intranet	Low
E-commerce	Buying and selling online	Medium
Collaborative	Extranet	Medium
Enterprise	Financials, sales for automation, vertical applications	High
Market-place	E-marketplaces	High
Collaborative enterprise	Supply chain management, customer relationship management	Very High
Collaborative platform	Emerging platforms	Very High

Source: Adapted from Gillan *et al.* (1999)

service providers (NSPs), content service providers (CSPs) and wireless application service providers (WASPs).

To begin to understand the issues involved in e-business engagement we need to classify e-business applications, as there are significant differences between e-mail and e-marketplace applications both in terms of complexity and added value. The introduction of the EC E-Business Watch synthesis report represented an important move towards tracking e-business engagement across 15 industry sectors and over a range of e-business applications throughout all EU Member States (European Commission, 2004b). The report concluded that *access* to ICT was no longer a barrier to e-business uptake with connectivity at 84% for small businesses. It stated: 'the use of e-mail and the www has become nearly ubiquitous in the business world' (European Commission, 2004b: 7). However, this indicates an oversimplification evidenced by the tendency to equate e-business with e-mail usage and web access. A classification for e-business applications based on application complexity is shown in Table 22.2.

Importantly, this classification of application complexity stresses the roles of collaboration and interaction as key features of e-business applications, and recognises the resultant increase in complexity. This taxonomy of e-business complexity incorporates both technical and organisational factors. For example, both the security technology issues underpinning higher complexity hosted applications, and the perceived commercial risk of storing sensitive client information in third-party data centres increase with higher complexity. In this way application complexity provides a meaningful framework in which to consider, compare and analyse e-business engagement. Using this classification recent survey data (EC, 2003b; DTI, 2004) is analysed to show the level of e-business engagement by small businesses in terms of application complexity (Figure 22.4).

In summary, Figure 22.4 suggests that most small businesses appear comfortable with e-mail and web access (lower complexity, about 80%), are tentative with the use of the Internet for online buying and selling (medium complexity, about 30%), but have little or no engagement in the high or very high complexity applications, such as e-marketplaces, supply chains or inter-organisational collaborative networks (less than 10%). This is despite the early promise of ASPs facilitating such access to complex

Figure 22.4 E-business engagement by small businesses

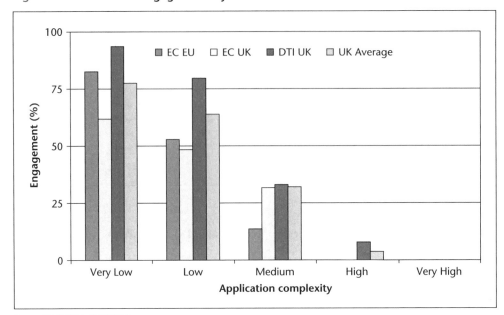

Source: EC (2003b); DTI (2004)

applications. Hence the trend in Figure 22.4 is not merely surprising in terms of the early expectations of engagement, but raises the important question of what this relative lack of engagement will mean not only for small businesses but also the larger organisations that have significant numbers of small businesses in their supplier networks.

This 'digital divide', which is evident in the widely differing rates of e-business adoption, has crucial theoretical and policy implications. Regarding theory, our understanding of ICT adoption by small businesses is largely characterised by the single firm as the unit of analysis and by a user perspective. Less well understood theoretically is the impact on adoption of other factors including the 'provider' perspective, the significance of 'application complexity', the role of aggregation and not least the behaviour of small businesses within networks such as supply chains. Regarding policy, the central belief that Internet access *per se* would be the key to increasing adoption of higher complexity applications for all firms has been shown to be inadequate as over 90% of UK businesses now have access to the Internet, but without a corresponding increase in their use of the more complex e-business applications.

23.3.3 Drivers and barriers for e-business engagement

The reasons why businesses, both small and large, choose to adopt e-business technologies are important in order to identify the value and benefits businesses have either achieved or believe they will achieve. Recent DTI studies (2003c) have highlighted a number of drivers or enablers to ICT adoption, including: increasing business turnover; increasing customer base in existing markets; communicating better with customers;

more efficient operations; communicating with workforce; enabling better financial management; operating more effectively with suppliers; improving delivery of goods and services; and better integration of business processes. Increase in turnover is consistently identified as the main driver to adoption. Drivers highlighted by other authors include: cost reduction; business partnership development; providing quality service; meeting customer/supplier demands; and creating/gaining competitive advantage (Hawkins and Prencipe, 2000; Clegg, 2001).

In terms of barriers to engagement many studies have been conducted in order to identify the barriers to ICT adoption by all enterprises, and small businesses in particular (DTI, 2003c). These highlighted a number of barriers to adoption, including: security; risk of fraud, concerns about confidentiality, set-up costs; running costs; not enough customers with online access; employees without IT skills, lack of information or knowledge. Security is consistently identified as the main barrier to adoption.

The broad theme of e-business engagement by small businesses, central to this chapter, is developed further below through a review of the relevant theory and later by considering recent research initiatives.

22.4 Understanding e-business within small businesses – theory and practice

In terms of informing our understanding of e-business and small businesses three main strands of theory are relevant. The first is the adoption of ICT by small businesses, including the diffusion of innovation. The second is the concept of aggregation and of inter-organisational networks as an organisational form. The latter provides the wider context within which the third strand of theory dealing with the emergent e-business model literature is discussed, with particular attention focused on the role of new intermediaries.

22.4.1 ICT adoption by small businesses

The broad antecedents for a theoretical appreciation of ICT adoption by small businesses are studies of technology transfer and the diffusion of innovations. Technology transfer can be seen as largely purposeful and is characterised by planning and deliberate actions. In contrast, innovation through diffusion is seen more as a natural process. In reality both mechanisms of technology transfer and diffusion are likely to coexist. However, this distinction, highlighted by Chakrabati and Rubenstein (1976) in their study of interorganisational technology transfer, is helpful since policy makers need to delineate the areas of intervention for facilitating e-business engagement, while recognising that other mechanisms will be at play.

Although studies on the adoption of e-commerce by small businesses are relatively recent, research antecedents are well established. Rogers' work on the diffusion of innovations (1962, 1995, 2003), whilst initially neither ICT nor SME-focused, has evolved to incorporate diffusion networks and critical mass in order to appreciate the adoption of interactive innovations, such as the Internet (1995: 313). The early work of Rogers took a provider (or supplier) perspective and identified the characteristics of innovation, which would impact on its rate of diffusion including such factors as compatibility, complexity, observability, relative advantage and trialability. In particular Rogers highlights the important roles of change agents (intermediaries) in influencing innovation decisions, including developing a need, establishing communication, diagnosing problems, creating an intent to change and then action. Theoretically the role of the intermediary as a means of facilitating the diffusion of complex ICT has been observed by a number of other authors, most notably Swan and Newell (1995) and Newall *et al.* (2000).

Within the specific domain of ICT adoption by small businesses, recent studies utilising Rogers' model of innovation include Kendall *et al.* (2001) and Mehrtens *et al.* (2001). These two studies provide support for the applicability of the model when related to e-business engagement by small businesses. Many other authors have contributed and three themes of work can be identified which, although overlapping, can usefully be separated, namely technological, strategic and organisational. All three strands can be interpreted within the long-established technology-push and need-pull models of technology innovation adoption in information systems (IS) (Zmud, 1984; Chau and Tam, 2000). These models typically identify 'push' factors, such as Government initiatives or technological drivers, and 'pull' factors, such as organisational crises or market opportunities.

The first literature theme, and arguably the most prolific, is the technological theme that views adoption as an outcome of a complex process of evaluation, frequently informal, by small businesses of multiple factors both external and internal. These factors are frequently cast as enablers or barriers to adoption (Lefebvre *et al.*, 1991; Cragg and King, 1993; Walczch *et al.*, 2000; Mehrtens *et al.*, 2001; Windrum and Berranger, 2003). Iacovou *et al.* (1995) focused on the single technology of electronic data interchange (EDI) and identified perceived benefits, organisational readiness (resources) and external pressures (competitive and non-competitive) as the critical factors in adoption. Since EDI is a complex application (but not necessarily Internet-based) these findings may be particularly relevant in the adoption of similar, higher-complexity e-business applications.

The second theme is that which emphasises the strategic logic in the decision to adopt ICT (Blili and Raymond, 1993; Kowtha and Choon, 2001; Sadowski *et al.*, 2002). In this context small businesses can be both victims and beneficiaries depending on their degree of proactivity. Blili and Raymond (1993) showed that IS planning was increasingly critical for SMEs as technology became more central to their products and processes, and they concluded that IS planning needed to be integrated with business strategy. Hagmann and McCahon (1993), however, concluded that in reality few small businesses plan their adoption of IS and that the limited planning that was evident was focused on operational improvements and was not concerned with competitiveness. The notion of strategic information systems planning in small businesses is further developed in Levy and Powell (2000, 2003) and Levy *et al.* (2001). This strand of research has resulted in frameworks, such as Levy's 'focus domination model', to help position and integrate ICT investments – some of which could be e-business applications. A model of the strategic use of IS by small businesses was proposed by Levy and Powell (2000, 2003) consisting of three interdependent factors, namely strategic content, business context and business process.

The third theme is that which takes an explicit organisational stance, and frequently that of the owner-manager and the social parameters within which the firm operates. As such, the approach counters the strategic or technological emphasis of the first two strands (Blackburn and McClure, 1998; Fuller and Southern, 1999; Poon and Swatman, 1999; Southern and Tilley, 2000; Quayle, 2002). An important observation of Southern and Tilley is that 'when small firms use IT complex relations unfold. It is by no means a simple linear development whereby observers can expect an incremental build up of knowledge and expertise on ICT to be established within the firm' (1999: 152). In the context of the adoption of increasingly complex e-business applications this view appears highly pertinent. Indeed this explicit organisational stance is very important in the context of the 'technology-push/need-pull' models applied to small businesses, since the analysis of social factors can identify the antecedents that need to be satisfied before the initial decision to adopt can be made.

22.4.2 Inter-organisational networks and aggregation

Since the medium- and higher-complexity e-business applications are essentially collaborative in nature the theoretical perspective of organisational networks is particularly relevant for explaining firm behaviour. Although 'networks' have always existed the recognition of networks as a distinct organisational form, amenable to analysis and theoretical development, is more recent (Granovetter, 1985; Thorelli, 1986; Miles and Snow, 1986; Provan and Milwood, 1995). As products have become increasingly modular and knowledge distributed across organisations, firms have recognised an increasing requirement to collaborate with other firms both formally and informally (Baldwin and Clark, 2000). Consequently, the locus of innovation and adoption is no longer the individual or the firm but increasingly the network in which a firm is embedded (Jarillo, 1998; Ebers, 1997; Powell et al., 1996; Furtardo, 1997). The importance of the strength of ties in the supplier network for productivity has also been demonstrated (Perez and Sanchez, 2002) and the standards necessary for a technology to function across different markets depend increasingly on networks of firms (Munir, 2003). For smaller firms the ability to gain access to new technologies is one of the principal reasons for engagement (Grandori and Soda, 1995) and cross-industry networks have been shown to play an important role in the diffusion of complex technologies (Erickson and Jacoby, 2003). These theoretical developments have been complemented by other advances on many different fronts: strategy, competition and collaboration (Doz and Hamel, 1998); network structure and embeddedness (Granovetter, 1985; Shaw and Conway, 2000); trust and governance (Johannisson, 1986a; Ring and Van de Ven, 1994); classification and evaluation (Cravens et al., 1996; Sydow and Windeler, 1998). What all these above theoretical contributions have in common is that they were developed outside a specific e-business context (i.e. offline). Nevertheless they provide many of the antecedents for the later emerging concepts of e-business networks (i.e. online).

The concept of business aggregations is well understood. These emerging, stable, non-equity based collaborative arrangements have become increasingly important as a means of reducing cost (Contractor and Lorange, 1998; Zajac and Oslen, 1993) or to increase revenue (Contractor and Lorange, 1998) or to mitigate risk in response to

Figure 22.5 **Taxonomy of aggregations for SMEs**

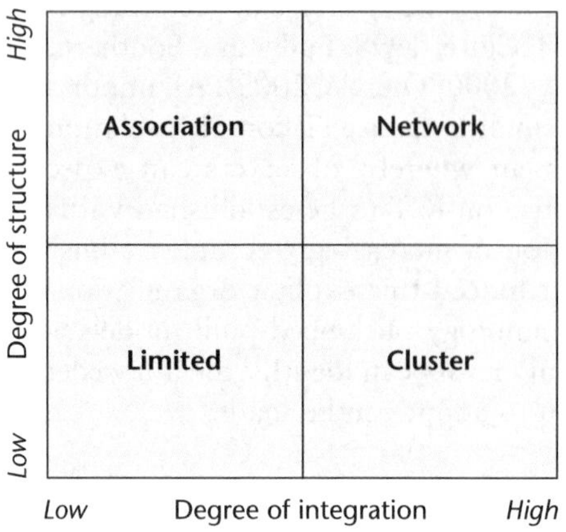

Source: Brown, D. and Lockett, N. 'The Potential of Critical Applications for Engaging SMEs in E-Business', 2004, *European Journal of Information Systems*, Vol.13 No.1, Palgrave Macmillan, reproduced with permission of Palgrave Macmillan

economic factors (Ebers, 1997). Such aggregations have generally been termed strategic networks and Jarillo's definition has been widely adopted:

> Strategic networks are long-term purposeful arrangements among distinct but related for profit organisations that allow those firms in them to gain or sustain competitive advantage *vis-à-vis* their competitors outside the network.
>
> (Jarillo 1988: 32)

Even within the above definition there are many possible manifestations of the network form and many ways of classifying them. In short, all inter-organisational networks (IONs) are aggregations but not all aggregations are networks. This presents potential difficulties in comparing ION research. Grandori and Soda (1995) differentiate networks by the extent to which the links between organisations are formalised and networks are termed bureaucratic, social or proprietary. A further classification from Cravens *et al.* (1996) links the type of network relationship (from short-term, transactional to long-term, collaborative) to the degree of unpredictability, and hence risk, in the environment. In the context of small businesses, Brown and Lockett's (2004) classification draws on the above, particularly Grandori and Soda, and links the degree of structure (informal to formal) to the degree of integration (independent to integrated) – see Figure 22.5.

Within the broad concept of aggregation this taxonomy locates 'networks' as one form of strong or complex aggregation that can be contrasted with other weaker or simpler aggregation forms – a distinction useful when considering the nature of a small business's engagement in an aggregation and the role of any intermediaries. Whilst online aggregation, at small business or industry level, was seen as a way of engaging the small business, consideration needs to be given to existing offline aggregations or groupings. Small businesses operate in business markets comprising relationships within their supply chain or industry sector, which can range from simple to complex in nature. The degree of structure (informal to formal) and degree of integration (independent to integrated) provides a taxonomy suitable for both online and offline aggregations and comprises four types:

- *Limited* – any relationships are loose and participants are independent, characterised by little or no aggregation. Intermediaries range from local business groups to more sophisticated organisations.
- *Association* – including trade associations and professional bodies, where reputation is enhanced by membership and structure is high, but businesses remain largely independent.
- *Cluster* – forming part of an identifiable business market, business cluster or economic cluster (Porter, 1998) where small businesses are increasingly dependent on complex linkages within a sector, but structure is low.
- *Network* – represents a more highly developed form of cooperation that exhibits both relatively high structure and integration. In the literature these networks are often implicitly described from a large business perspective.

The reality of practice challenges our theoretical understanding of both the adoption by small businesses of e-business and the emergence of aggregations as a meaningful development within the context of adoption. Here *aggregation* is defined as *any grouping of enterprises where there is evidence of inter-organisational relationships that go beyond simple transactions*. These aggregations can range from local retail traders campaigning for improvements to their local infrastructure to the highly developed supplier-based networks of the aerospace industry.

22.4.3 E-business models

The final strand of theory is the emergent e-business model literature, which includes insights into alternative business models and changing industry structures as a result of Internet-based technologies. A number of authors have offered broad conceptualisations of e-business models (Amit and Zott, 2001; Timmers, 2000; Hamel, 2000; Alt and Zimmermann, 2001; Afuah and Tucci, 2001; Weill and Vitale, 2001; Currie, 2004). Other authors have developed models specific to particular situations. Examples include: business-to-business (B2B) vertical supply chains (Kalakota and Robinson, 2000) and value adding intermediaries (Earle and Keen, 2000).

The need to encourage e-business engagement by small businesses has been readily acknowledged by industry and government but just how this was to be achieved, particularly with the more complex e-business application areas, remained unspecified. When examining the uptake of e-business among small businesses the concepts of collaborative networks, interdependence, power and trust provide important contributions. For example, whether owner-managers use adversarial or collaborative approaches to purchasing relationships may impact on their adoption of ICT (Cox and Hines, 1997). Similarly, the scope for intermediaries to play a crucial role in the support and provision of SME-orientated e-business applications has been noted (Currie, 2002, 2004; Smith and Kumar, 2004; Mazzi, 2001). In the specific context of ASP models and small businesses, several critical and reflective analyses have recently emerged (Kern *et al.*, 2002; Susarla *et al.*, 2003). In the main, all the above contributions reinforce the

Figure 22.6 eTrust Platform

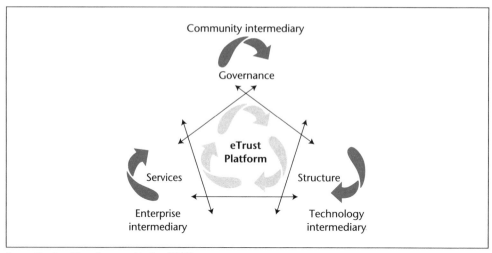

Source: Developed from Brown and Lockett (2001)

general significance of intermediaries as trusted third-party facilitators of IT diffusion, as noted by Swan and Newell (1995) and Newell *et al.* (2000), and cited earlier. However, the setting for these latter authors' works was not SME-specific. A conceptualisation that is small business grounded and focuses on intermediaries and their role in facilitating e-business engagement by small businesses is the eTrust Platform (Figure 22.6).

22.4.4 Aggregation and intermediaries in e-business adoption

The eTrust Platform conceptualisation of the role of intermediaries in the digital economy discussed above highlights the relationships between multiple small businesses and the intermediaries necessary for online aggregations of small businesses to function. There are three kinds of intermediary. The role of the *technology intermediary* is to provide the ICT infrastructure on which services can be provided and could include hardware, security and communications. The role of the *enterprise intermediary* is to provide the services including applications software, hosting and consultancy. The technology and enterprise intermediaries can be considered as generic. In reality these functions could be provided by one or more organisations. The *community intermediary*, however, is specific to a particular aggregation. It has a critical role in gaining the commitment of potential participants to enter the e-aggregation and can be considered as a trusted third party. It is the community intermediary, providing a broad governance function, which is a distinguishing characteristic of the eTrust Platform conceptualisation. A trade association would be an example of a potential community intermediary.

Three major findings have emerged from recent research, which focused on the role of aggregation and intermediaries in engaging small businesses in the more complex, high value-adding e-business applications (Brown and Lockett, 2004, 2005; Lockett and Brown, 2006). The research serves as a guide to how small businesses, through aggregation and the support of intermediaries, can access in a cost-effective way sophisticated applications. Given the growing trend towards hosted applications outlined earlier in the chapter more small businesses are likely to follow the trusted platform route. The findings are summarised below.

22.4.5 Emergence of critical e-aggregation applications

Community intermediaries, such as trade associations, confirmed the importance of SME-focused applications that attempted to meet a specific, important and common need by the group of small businesses. In some cases community and enterprise intermediaries collaborated in order to identify both the initial business needs of the small businesses within the aggregation and any subsequent desirable modifications to the critical e-aggregation applications. Early examples of critical e-aggregation applications developed in this collaborative way included:

- *project management* – for the construction industry (www.biwtech.com/)
- *dairy herd management* – for dairy farmers (www.milknet.sac.ac.uk/)
- *community management* – for knowledge-based workers (www.pcg.org.uk/)
- *advertising artwork management* – for artwork agencies (www.adfast.co.uk/)
- *field management* – for the organic farming industry (www.organicecology.com/),

where a *critical e-aggregation* is defined as: *an e-business application, promoted by a trusted third party, which engages a significant number of small businesses by addressing an important shared business concern within an aggregation.* In the main these critical e-aggregation applications were relatively new and in the early stages of development but already they appeared to be successfully measured by the level of uptake. Community intermediaries reported that some service providers of critical e-aggregation applications took the lead and developed the applications without a guaranteed market for the product. These service providers had identified community intermediaries early in the application's development and sought to establish collaborative arrangements that mitigated the risk and developed trust.

Critical e-aggregation applications are characterised as offering new functionality that was valued by aggregation members, was developed by interaction with community intermediaries and used a 'one-to-many' business model. On this basis these e-aggregation applications can be seen as 'critical' both in terms of functionality and perceived importance. The innovative nature of these 'critical e-aggregation applications' was the single most important factor for using the application.

22.5 Importance and role of trusted third parties

Trusted third parties proved to be key in establishing the confidence necessary for small businesses to engage in the more complex e-business applications. There was recognition by many community intermediaries that existing trusted offline relationships, be they a lead company in a business network or a trade association, could be important in recruiting small businesses to online services. Trade associations, in particular, identified a new role for themselves as a sponsor or facilitator, rather than a direct provider of e-business services.

The trusted third parties in e-aggregations exhibited several characteristics. First, they deliberately worked with service providers (enterprise intermediaries) to appreciate the business needs within the aggregation and develop the e-business applications to meet these needs. Second, they were aware of the accumulation of valuable information about the aggregation resulting from interaction with the e-business application. Third, they participated in activities that attempted to increase e-business application engagement of small businesses in the aggregation. These activities included: shaping users' perceptions; identifying and introducing the innovation to sub-groups within the aggregations; promoting (targeting) it to and through key actors; and providing incentives to early adopters.

In addition to the contribution made by the community intermediaries to the development of specific applications and to facilitating access to small businesses they had two further roles that derived directly from their trusted third-party status. First, as negotiators of the service fees charged either directly to users or themselves, and second, they acted as negotiators for the service level agreement with the service providers. Considering the importance of these agreements in the context of hosted applications, this implies a high level of trust on the part of the users, but also for many of them an indication of their dependence.

22.5.1 Evidence of increased structure and integration

From the research it appears that small businesses engaged in aggregation-based e-business applications had a propensity for further integration. This observation indicates that the impact of critical e-aggregation applications could be of strategic importance as it changes the very nature of these inter-organisational networks. First, the critical e-aggregation applications increased the degree of structure by standardising the format of information in order to facilitate information exchange. Second, the degree of integration was increased by the use of these critical e-aggregation applications. Significantly, the general effect of the critical e-aggregation applications was to move the inter-organisational networks towards the 'network' type shown in Figure 22.4.

In terms of the future outlook for small businesses' engagement in e-business the role of critical e-aggregation applications and of trusted third parties appears to be pivotal. Despite this, however, there is little evidence of national or regional agencies having identified this as one possible method of achieving their stated objectives of increasing e-business engagement by small businesses. One notable exception is the Australian government's Information Technology Online (ITOL) programme which acts as a catalyst by funding projects to existing aggregations dominated by small businesses and offering strong supporting evidence of the emergence of e-aggregation applications (NOIE, 2005). There have been 13 rounds of funding since 1996 resulting in the selection of over 100 collaborative e-business projects that encourage the adoption of e-business solutions by small businesses across a broad range of industry sectors and geographic regions. Recent examples include: Beef Industry Genetics, which sought to provide Internet delivery of modern breeding methods through collaboration with beef producers (www.breedobject.com); and Flinders Ranges Online Reservations for the tourism accommodation industry, which enabled customers to book and pay for accommodation over the Internet in a secure manner and receive immediate confirmation (www.frabs.com.au).

22.6 Chapter summary

This chapter presented three main areas relating to e-business and the small firm. First, the context was developed for e-business in small businesses including: definitions, government policies, nature of e-business engagement and the barriers and drivers to adoption. Second, three main strands of theory relating to e-business in small businesses were reviewed, namely: ICT adoption, inter-organisational networks and business models. Finally, recent research into the role of aggregation and intermediaries was discussed since this is likely to prove to be highly significant for small businesses and their engagement in e-business, and has policy implications.

In terms of e-business adoption, recent surveys indicate high levels of connectivity and usage of very low complexity applications, such as e-mail and web browsers, among small firms in the UK, Europe and North America. One recent study concluded that connectivity was no longer a barrier to e-business engagement. This suggests that most small businesses appeared comfortable with e-mail and web access (lower complexity). However, as application complexity increased levels of engagement declined significantly, indicating that small businesses are tentative about use of the Internet for online buying and selling (medium complexity), but had little or no engagement in the high or very high complexity applications, such as e-marketplaces, supply chains or inter-organisational collaborative networks. From a theory perspective there are a number of important issues. A particularly important one is the relevance of network theory for understanding firm behaviour, including small businesses, and the fact that the introduction of new cost-effective ICT can create new partnerships and relationships. Viewed in this way firms are members of aggregations and the final part of the chapter visited recent research that highlighted the particular benefits to small businesses acting within aggregations. In direct contrast to firms acting alone, the evidence is that small businesses acting as part of an aggregation with a trusted intermediary are more likely to be engaged in higher complexity e-business applications. These critical e-aggregation applications are both sophisticated and meet the particular needs of both the small businesses and the service providers in a cost-effective way.

Questions

1 What are the recent and current trends in e-business adoption by small businesses?

2 How might advances in mobile communication platforms (such as 3G) affect small firms? Might small firms be better placed to exploit opportunities that large ones?

3 Discuss an example of the strategic impact of e-business applications in small businesses. What are the potential risks and advantages to small businesses of such applications?

4 Compare and contrast the different approaches governments are taking to promote e-business in small businesses. In your view are some initiatives more successful than others and if so why?

Web links

www.ebusiness-watch.org
The e-business w@tch observatory monitors e-activities and their implications in different sectors across Europe.

www2.bah.com/dti2004/
The report 'Business in the Information Age – International Benchmarking Study 2003 – Executive Summary', undertaken by the DTI in the UK.

www.electronicmarkets.org/
Website of 'Electronic Markets – The International Journal'.

www.ecommerce.ac.uk/
Website of the E-Commerce Innovation Centre at Cardiff University.

CHAPTER 23

Franchising and the small business

John Stanworth and David Purdy

23.1 Introduction

At its best, franchising is an avenue into self-employment offered by franchisors (owners of a 'tried-and-tested' business format) to franchisees (typically aspiring small business-men and women), in exchange for payment of a one-off front-end fee followed by an on-going royalty (Hoy and Stanworth, 2003). Based on the principle of 'cloning' success, a principal tenet of the franchise fraternity is that franchise failure rates are low.

From the viewpoint of small business researchers, franchising has been argued to be of particular importance, since most franchisors still are, or have recently been, small businesses themselves and most of their royalty-paying franchisees are also small businesses. Thus, in principle, franchising offers a route to growth for the would-be franchisor and small business opportunities with limited risk for would-be franchisees.

This chapter examines the advantages and disadvantages of franchising from the viewpoints of franchisor, franchisee and the wider society. It also examines growth rates, internationalisation, job creation, management challenges, future trends and, not least, risk levels. What emerges here is a striking similarity between the failure rates of young franchise systems and conventional small businesses at the same stage of development.

23.2 Learning objectives

This chapter has four learning objectives:

1 To gain a basic understanding of the nature of a business format franchise.

2 To gain an understanding of the symbiotic nature of the franchisor–franchisee relationship.

3 To illustrate that franchising may be viewed as a growth strategy for small businesses or, alternatively, as a strategy for large businesses penetrating what have conventionally been recognised as small firm markets.

4 To demonstrate the potentially contentious nature of statistics issued by commercial bodies with an interest in promoting their particular business sector.

Key concepts

■ franchising ■ enterprise ■ growth ■ symbiosis ■ survival rates
■ service economy

23.3 Franchising and enterprise

A franchise can be defined as comprising a contractual relationship between a franch-isee (usually taking the form of a small business) and a franchisor (usually a larger business) in which the former agrees to produce or market a product or service in accordance with an overall 'blueprint' devised by the franchisor. The relationship is a continuing one with the franchisor providing general advice and support, research and development, and help with marketing and advertising. In return, the franchisee usu-ally pays an initial franchise fee and also an ongoing royalty or management service fee, normally based on the level of turnover and/or a mark-up on supplies purchased from the franchisor. The franchisee provides the capital for the outlet and is a legally separate entity to the franchisor.

Though the franchisor is usually a 'larger' business than the franchisee, in only a handful of cases does the franchisor truly meet the description of 'large'. Most franch-isors remain very much small and medium-sized enterprises (SMEs) with no more than a small handful truly qualifying as large and these are almost inevitably American in origin (e.g. McDonald's, ServiceMaster, Coca-Cola, Pepsi-Cola, Holiday Inn, Burger King, Kentucky Fried Chicken, Pizza Hut, Kwik-Kopy, Budget Rent-a-Car). Overall, in the UK, the average franchise involves around 30–40 outlets according to the British Franchise Association's statistics and could thus still certainly be considered an SME, if not a small business *per se*.

23.4 The nature of franchising: entrepreneurship or dependence?

At one extreme, it has been argued that the franchised enterprise is, in reality, a man-aged outlet featuring in the larger marketing pattern of another truly independent business – that of the franchisor (Rubin, 1978: 223–33). This distribution strategy has certain advantages for the larger enterprise but, just because the manager of the outlet has a capital stake in the business dressed up in the language of entrepreneurship, that is no reason to confuse a franchise outlet with a genuinely independent business. This is not to say that the arrangement cannot be highly beneficial to both parties but illusion should not be substituted for reality in a rigorous analysis of the status of the franchised outlet.

At the other extreme, the franchised small business may be viewed as an emerging form of independent small business in advanced industrial societies whose distinguish-ing characteristic is its overt and close relationship with another, usually larger, enter-prise. This association might be seen as being little different, except in degree and the explicit form it takes, from that now found between many small businesses and other firms with whom they do business. In an increasingly interdependent economy, such a close association may simply be seen as a reflection of the fact that 'no firm is an island entire of itself'.

The independence of the small firm can never be absolute and is often difficult to assess accurately in practice. Any small enterprise, whatever its form, is part of a wider network of economic interaction summed up in the economist's notion of 'the market' and, arguably, it is from this source that the main limitations on independence are derived. Whilst, economically, franchise relationships may appear to render franchisees highly dependent at a contractual level, at an operational level higher levels of independence may manifest themselves than appear likely at first sight (Stanworth, 1984).

The pioneering Bolton Committee researchers in the UK were attracted to the idea of classifying the roles of small firms according to the type of market they supply (Bolton, 1971: 31–32). Accordingly, they located small firms along a typology of reliance upon large firms:

- *Marketeers* – those firms that actually compete in the same or similar markets as large firms (e.g. computer software companies, fashion merchandise manufacturers and restaurants).

- *Specialists* – those firms that carry out functions that large firms do not find it economic to perform at all, though they may include large firms among their customers (e.g. repair and maintenance in the building industry, jobbing engineering and specialised retail outlets such as bookshops).

- *Satellites* – where the small firm is highly dependent upon a single larger business for the majority of its trade. The degree of dependence may be even greater if the large customer actually designs the product or service and merely sub-contracts its manufacture or supply, as appears to be the case with a franchise. Franchisees would appear to fall under this category.

Product franchises, embracing the fields of car and petroleum distribution, the soft drink bottlers (Coca-Cola, Pepsi-Cola, Seven-Up, etc.) and, in the UK, tenanted public houses, are often categorised as 'first generation' franchises and almost totally sidelined from most mainstream debates on modern franchising. The terms *franchising* and *business format franchising* are now used practically interchangeably in the franchise industry generally.

The relevance of business format franchising is perhaps best illustrated by US statistics, which apportion just $200bn of a total of over $600bn franchise industry sales turnover to business format franchising. However, something in the region of 3,000 from a total of 3,500 franchisors and 400,000 from a total of 500,000 franchisees reside in the business format sector (Sen and Lee, 1994).

In a nutshell, business format franchises are typically SMEs. However, given that the franchisor levies a royalty-based charge on the franchisee's level of turnover rather than profit, pressures to achieve market penetration and growth are institutionalised rather than optional. This can be achieved by expansion within a given franchise outlet or by expansion of the overall population of outlets – often involving multiple outlet ownership by more successful franchisees. For instance, this is particularly common in the field of fast-food franchising where, in the US, it is not uncommon for

50% of a franchise company's outlets to be owned by less than 20% (and sometimes less than 10%) of its franchisees. A single large franchisee may own several hundred outlets (Bradach, 1994). Multiple ownership in other sectors appears less common and, in the UK, it is estimated that 82% of franchisees operate just a single unit (The NatWest Bank/British Franchise Association Franchise Survey, 1993, published March 1994).

Previous research has shown that approximately one-in-three of franchisees has prior experience of independent self-employment and that levels of prior educational attainment and previous earnings tend to correlate with the buy-in costs of particular franchises. Thus, individuals taking relatively high-cost franchises in a field such as fast print are more likely to be graduates and have professional backgrounds than, say, individuals taking up relatively low-cost carpet-cleaning franchises.

23.5 The advantages and disadvantages of franchising

The following section is assembled from three main sources, namely the published literature on franchising, previous research and discussions with key figures in the industry, and will be presented under four headings dealing with the franchisor, the franchisee, the consumer/local economy and, finally, the national economy.

23.5.1 Advantages and disadvantages to the franchisor

Advantages

- Franchising enables the franchisor to increase the number of distributive outlets for their organisation's product or service with limited capital investment. It is the franchisees who provide much of the capital with their stakes in the business.

- Since the franchisee owns their own business, they are assumed to be highly motivated to maximise growth and profitability. This situation may be compared with that of a manager of a retail outlet who is a direct employee of the parent company. Generally, such a manager earns a fixed salary (with possibly an element of bonus incentive incorporated) and lacks the extra incentive to succeed, which may result from a personal financial investment in the business. A successful franchisee, with increasing profits, can be expected to contribute to the success of the franchisor.

- A franchise unit, being locally owned, is claimed to be readily accepted by the community as being a local business. It is not clear how far this is true, however, since very often local people may not be aware that a franchised unit is in fact owner-managed.

- The franchisor has limited payroll, rent and administrative overheads, because the very nature of the operation requires franchisees to be self-employed. Franchisees are themselves responsible for the staffing arrangements and operating costs of their particular outlets.

- As well as franchisors achieving a wider distribution network for their product or service, the nature of most franchise contracts ensures that franchisees are in some measure 'tied' to the franchisor. They are often obliged to purchase equipment from or through the franchisor plus, as in the case of fast-food franchise restaurants, the necessary ingredients that go to make up the final product.

Disadvantages

- It may be difficult for the franchisor to exercise tight control over the franchisee simply because they are not a direct employee of the franchisee and cannot be closely supervised. In turn, the poor reputation of one outlet, in terms of product quality or service, can be damaging to the general trade name and reputation of the franchisor and, in turn, the whole franchise organisation.

- A franchisor cannot always be certain that a franchisee is declaring their true level of business activity. Many franchisors employ a central accounting system to combat this though no system can be expected to be totally successful in this respect.

- If the franchisor believes that a franchisee has become demotivated and is not running their outlet efficiently, there is relatively little that can be done in the short term as long as the franchisee is operating within the terms of the contract.

- The management of a franchising company is limited in its flexibility. Conventional companies can move more quickly to exploit market potential when a modified selling strategy is required. However, to bring about changes can be a lengthy and cumbersome operation when dealing with individually owned franchised outlets. Any changes need to be carefully handled to avoid conflicts stemming from perceived threats to the franchisee's independence.

- There may be problems of information feedback from the franchisee to the franchisor. This can result from the franchisee's desire for independence or simply from channels of communication not being as well developed as they might be in company-owned and managed outlets.

- The franchisor is faced with a paradox. The franchise method of business tries to capitalise on the personal attention and service that characterise the owner-managed business. However, the franchisor's need for a standardised product or service, together with a uniform presentation, needed to give customers a sense of reliability and dependability, clashes with the former.

- The franchisor may have difficulty in recruiting suitable franchisees who: see franchising as an attractive method of doing business; are motivated towards self-employment; and have the necessary capital available for investment.

23.5.2 Advantages and disadvantages to the franchisee

Advantages

- It is possible for an individual to run their own business yet gain the advantages and economies of scale of a larger company. Here the advantages range from initial and ongoing training to centralised buying, ongoing product/service and market research.

- If the product or service has already achieved brand awareness, this relieves the franchisee of many of the normal demands of the sales and marketing function and allows them to concentrate on other aspects of the business. Most franchisors undertake both national and local advertising campaigns to keep franchisees' products or services firmly in the public mind.

■ It is claimed that franchisees require less capital than would be the case to equip a business independently. The franchisor can help with raising bank loans, site-selection, head leases on properties, and getting the business open and running smoothly. However, franchise investment levels tend to be fairly high and it could be argued that one could start a business successfully for a similar investment (or less perhaps) without the obligations imposed by a franchisor.

■ Many franchisees operate within a defined territory, which involves the franchisor giving an undertaking not to set up another competing outlet within a given geographical radius. However, there is nothing to stop another franchisor, or other conventional competition, moving into the same area if it appears attractive and lucrative.

■ There are other franchisees in the same network with the same challenges and problems and so any individual franchisee can use them as a source of non-threatening help and advice.

Disadvantages

■ The tight control exercised by the franchisor in order to regulate the way in which the product or service is presented to the consumer may leave little opportunity for the franchisee to impose their personality on the business.

■ Should the trade name of the franchise become tarnished, perhaps through mismanagement by the franchisor, or the shortcomings of other franchisees, then it is possibile that the franchisee may suffer simply because they are seen by the public as a representative of the franchise organisation in question.

■ The service provided by the franchisor may constitute a heavy expense to the franchisee. The franchisee may be obliged to purchase equipment and ingredients from the franchisor that they could have bought more cheaply from other sources. Also, management service fees and charges may be high.

■ There is the possibility that the franchise agreement may not fulfil the franchisee's expectations, both in terms of anticipated sales and profits and also possibly in terms of the franchisor not fulfilling their obligations.

23.5.3 Advantages and disadvantages to consumers and the local economy

Advantages

■ Consumers may have the convenience of an extended-hours service. Many franchises operate on the basis of long hours of service in order to maximise their markets and many independent businesses, not bound by agreements to provide such service, may choose not to do so or may lack the resources.

■ Franchisees, as owner-managers, should be able to offer a highly personal service.

■ Although all franchised outlets are independent and separate, consumers can locate them under a single trade name and apply their knowledge of one outlet to all others because of uniform presentation and consistent standards of quality. Conversely, if a consumer is dissatisfied, they need not waste time with other outlets.

■ If a conventional small business fails, dissatisfied customers may not get satisfaction. In the case of a franchise, failure rates may be lower and, in any case, customers can, in the final analysis, contact the franchisor.

■ Franchisees receive training from their franchisors, usually ranging from between 2 and 12 weeks. A portion of this will usually involve hands-on training in existing outlets run by other franchisees. Such training can be expected to add to the stock of business training and knowledge in the local economy.

Disadvantages

■ Franchising may reduce levels of diversity in local economies due to their stress on standardisation.

■ Franchising may 'export' money out of the local regional economy in terms of payments made to franchisors and may 'import' goods and services from the franchisor rather than from small suppliers locally.

23.5.4 Advantages and disadvantages of franchising to national economies

For individuals seeking self-employment opportunities but lacking the necessary experience and know-how, franchising can offer an avenue of opportunity. For others, already in business on a modest scale, a franchise as an addition, or alternative, to their existing business may offer the possibility of growth levels unlikely to be achieved by their existing business.

The role of the industry as a 'shop window' of business formats appears to have been recognised by leading franchisors who, over time, appear to have become generally less informative in response to early-stage enquiries. This has occurred in response to instances of individuals searching out information, under the guise of a potential franchisee, only to subsequently emerge in competition rather than in partnership.

The high level of publicity generated by the franchise industry, plus the steady flow of books and seminars, magazines and manuals, on the topic all act to reinforce this role. Overall, the franchise industry almost certainly plays a positive role in publicising and popularising the notion of self-employment.

23.6 Franchising in the US: history and more recent trends

Franchising is more developed in the US than in any other country. Also, research and data gathering are far more advanced in the US than elsewhere. Thus, much of what is known about franchising tends to be American in origin and other countries look towards the US experience as heralding the nature and scale of future developments in their own economies.

As a result of the large-scale development of franchising in the US, it is the major exporter of franchising on a global scale and American experience is invariably quoted

Figure 23.1 **Trends in total US franchising sales, 1975–90**

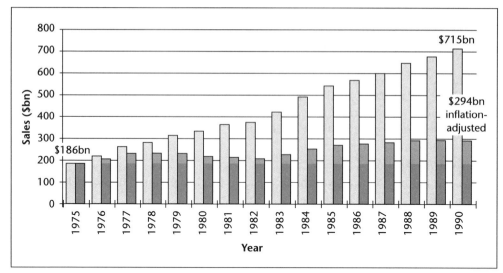

Source: Trutko, Trutko and Kostecka (1993)

(or misquoted) in justification of franchising in the UK and elsewhere. Three US statistics are quoted above all others:

■ Franchising accounts for approaching 35% of all retail sales in the US.
■ Franchising accounts for 10% of GDP in the US.
■ Franchising expanded by around 300% between 1975 and 1990.

Allied to these claims is an assumption that franchising is both a low-risk business option and a largely recession-proof business strategy. All of the above statistics appear essentially true. However, as Figure 23.1 illustrates, inflation-adjusted figures for the growth of franchising in the US over recent years pull down the overall growth figure for 1975–90 dramatically from 284.6% to 58.5%, and the average annual growth rate from 9.4% to 3.1%. Moreover, in six years of this 16-year period, franchise growth in the US was either zero or negative (Trutko *et al.*, 1993). The franchise industry in the UK appears completely unaware of the existence of the latter adjusted statistics. (The data terminate in 1990 due to the abandonment of an annual survey of US franchisors and franchisees by the US Department of Commerce.)

Although academics, researchers and bodies such as the International Franchise Association (America's franchise association) use the terms 'franchising' and 'business format franchising' almost interchangeably, the fact remains that, for statistical purposes, 'product' and business format franchises are usually grouped together in the US. In 1990, 48.4% of all franchising sales stemmed from the automobile and truck sector and a further 18.0% from franchised gasoline service stations.

Whereas product franchising grew by only 42.4% in inflation-adjusted (constant) dollars in the US between 1975 and 1990, against an overall sector figure of 58.5%, business format franchising grew by 115.5%, or around 5.1% in real terms per annum.

The expansion and contraction of franchising in the US seems to have closely followed general economic trends (Trutko *et al.*, 1993: 3–19). Between 1975 and 1989, GNP in the US grew by 52.7% in real terms against a comparable growth in franchise sales of 58.5%. The decline in franchise sales (in real terms) between 1979 and 1982 again closely reflected the wider economic situation. As the US economy recovered during the mid-1980s, franchise sales reflected the upturn, as they did the subsequent downturn towards the end of the 1980s.

Interestingly, however, whilst franchise sales performed relatively well between 1975 and 1990, the number of franchise establishments in the US grew by only 13.3% compared with a 48.4% increase in the number of establishment units in the US as a whole. It is predicted that this trend will continue with franchisors concentrating on generating higher profits per establishment in the future rather than expansion via increased outlets (Trutko *et al.*, 1993: 9–12). In this sense, franchising could be said to be limiting the number of small business outlets.

The largest 88 US franchisors had more than 500 franchise units in 1986 and accounted for two-thirds (65.0%) of all franchise sales and establishments. By way of contrast, one-third (33.9%) of all franchising systems had ten or fewer establishments and accounted for about 1% of sales and establishments.

Despite the overall dominance by large systems, there is some evidence that smaller systems have played an increasing role in recent years. Also, earlier thoughts that franchising might simply represent a temporary phase in a company's growth plans appear largely unfounded since the level of franchisee-owned stores appears to have been virtually unchanged since 1975 at 81.5%.

Women and minorities appear to have increased their representation in franchising in recent years though both groups are less visible than might be expected in terms of their general participation in the labour force at large. The evidence indicates that around 10% of franchise units are owned outright by women plus another 20% owned by women in alliance with men. Around 5% of franchise units were owned by minorities in 1986 compared with an 8.8% ownership level of US firms generally. This is despite government schemes targeted specifically at increasing the level of minority representation. Although there are no comparable figures collected for the UK, the position appears broadly similar, albeit with a heavy concentration of minority franchisees in the field of fast-food franchising.

It is felt by many that the help afforded by franchisors in setting up new franchisees, particularly those with no prior business experience, renders franchising user-friendly for women and minorities.

23.6.1 Franchise growth factors

A number of factors in particular are considered to have aided the general growth of franchising in the US in recent decades. First, the growth of the US economy since World War II. Second, 'downsizing' policies exercised by large corporations that have released corporate executives with the necessary financial resources, experience in business management and a reduced faith in corporate security, often willing to consider self-employment.

Further, the post-war 'baby boom' increased both consumer spending levels and the numbers of potential franchisees during the 1970s and 1980s. At the same time, the number of women in the US civilian workforce increased from 27.5 million in 1970 to 47.4 million in 1989 – a participation rate up from 42.6% to 57.2%. The growth in the numbers of working women and dual-income families led to increased needs for support services such as day care services, educational products and services, home cleaning, fast-food, home-delivery food and other services.

In addition, technological changes heralded a revolution in electronic data processing and materials handling. Technological benefits have often been made more available to small franchise outlets than small conventional small firms due to the economies of scale delivered by the franchisor. Retailing in particular appears to have benefited from technological advances.

23.6.2 Franchising in the UK: current trends

According to trade association data, the experience of franchising in the UK is of appreciable growth for several years prior to 1990, when it dipped. Thereafter, in real terms, the trend in combined sales turnover was one of modest recovery, stabilising from 2000 onwards (see Figure 23.2 and Table 23.1).

Figure 23.2 Trends in UK business format franchising, 1984–2004

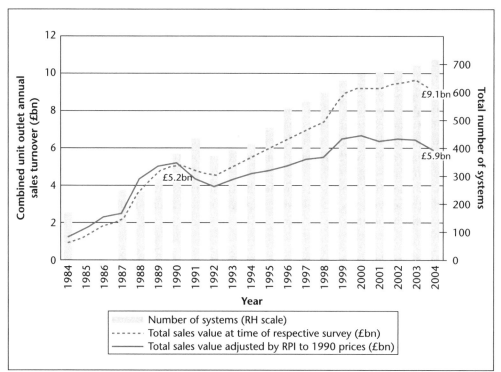

Source: NatWest/BFA Annual Surveys (Franchise system data N/A for 1985 and 1986); Office of National Statistics

Table 23.1 Key indicators for business format franchising in the UK, 1993–2004

Year of data collection (reported in following year)	1993	1994	1995	1996	1997	1998	1999	2000	2001	2002	2003	2004
1. Number of franchise systems												
Building Services	49	39	48	45	47							
Catering, Hotels	64	55	58	58	65							
Cleaning Services	15	15	19	23	27							
Commercial and Industrial Services	49	55	60	68	81							
Direct Selling, Distribution, etc.	32	51	72	75	78							
Domestic and Personal Services	25	25	24	39	40							
Employment Agencies, Training	11	15	19	22	24							
Estate Agents, Business Transfer Agents	15	16	16	21	20							
Parcel and Courier Services	12	13	15	19	21							
Quick Printing, Copying, Graphic Design	7	8	8	13	12							
Retail	84	86	92	110	106							
Vehicle Services	25	28	35	39	39							
Dairy (as reported or deduced)	8	8	8	9	8							
Total number of UK franchise systems	*396*	*414*	*474*	*541*	*568*	*596*	*642*	*665*	*672*	*677*	*699*	*718*
Change on 1993 value		+4.5%	+19.7%	+36.6%	+43.4%	+50.5%	+62.1%	+67.9%	+69.7%	+71.0%	+76.5%	+81.3%
1998 onwards: European Franchise Federation categories adopted (p. 19, March 1999 report)												
Hotel and Catering						97	100	116	114	113	117	112
Store Retailing						91	94	91	86	86	89	91
Personal Services						94	111	114	113	111	110	131
Property Services						111	114	125	140	147	152	165
Transport and Vehicle Services						66	68	75	76	72	76	64
Business and Commercial Services						130	148	141	140	145	152	152
Dairy (as reported or deduced)						7	7	3	3	3	3	3
						596	*642*	*665*	*672*	*677*	*699*	*718*

The 'headline' number of franchise systems quoted in the source reports for 2001 (671 systems) and 2003 (695 systems) data do not fully reconcile with the corresponding sector analyses.

451

Table 23.1 (cont'd)

Year of data collection (reported in following year)	1993	1994	1995	1996	1997	1998	1999	2000	2001	2002	2003	2004
2a. Estimate of franchised units/outlets by sector												
Building Services	1,015	925	1,000	960	1,080							
Catering, Hotels	3,380	3,095	3,070	3,245	3,675							
Cleaning Services	1,520	1,510	1,625	1,510	1,775							
Commercial and Industrial Services	845	1,085	1,105	1,115	1,595							
Direct Selling, Distribution, etc.	2,030	2,910	3,315	3,730	3,995							
Domestic and Personal Services	675	1,110	880	1,655	1,680							
Employment Agencies, Training	505	530	600	765	830							
Estate Agents, Business Transfer Agents	505	435	405	435	430							
Parcel and Courier Services	675	1,095	1,120	1,395	1,520							
Quick Printing, Copying, Graphic Design	675	635	570	560	600							
Retail	3,385	4,515	4,355	4,500	4,785							
Vehicle Services	1,690	1,555	1,655	1,630	2,035							
Dairy	8,000	7,000	6,000	5,300	5,100							
Total number of UK franchisee units/outlets	*24,900*	*26,400*	*25,700*	*26,800*	*29,100*	*30,000*	*35,150*	*35,600*	*34,500*	*34,395*	*33,815*	*31,363*
Change on 1993 value		+6.0%	+3.2%	+7.6%	+16.9%	+20.5%	+41.2%	+43.0%	+38.6%	+38.1%	+35.8%	+26.0%
1998 onwards: European Franchise Federation categories adopted (p. 19, March 1999 report)												
Hotel and Catering					4,725	6,015	6,395	7,120	5,655	5,800	6,394	6,381
Store Retailing					4,290	4,275	4,275	4,200	3,760	4,260	4,391	4,578
Personal Services					3,660	4,295	5,060	3,315	3,435	4,125	4,540	4,282
Property Services					3,540	3,570	3,960	4,440	5,560	5,260	5,545	6,174
Transport and Vehicle Services					3,280	3,105	3,365	3,470	3,520	2,700	2,554	2,408
Business and Commercial Services					4,505	4,240	7,845	8,655	8,570	8,650	8,591	4,740
Dairy					5,100	4,500	4,250	4,400	4,000	3,600	1,800	2,800
					29,100	30,000	35,150	35,600	34,500	34,395	33,815	31,363
2b. Franchise units/outlets – average number per franchise system	*63*	*64*	*54*	*50*	*51*	*50*	*55*	*54*	*51*	*51*	*48*	*44*
Change on 1993 value		+1.4%	−13.8%	−21.2%	−18.5%	−19.9%	−12.9%	−14.9%	−18.4%	−19.2%	−23.1%	−30.5%
3a. Combined franchise unit sales turnover (1990 'peak' = £5.2bn)	*£5.0bn*	*£5.5bn*	*£5.9bn*	*£6.4bn*	*£7.0bn*	*£7.4bn*	*£8.9bn*	*£9.3bn*	*£9.2bn*	*£9.5bn*	*£9.65bn*	*£9.1bn*
Change on 1993 value		+10.0%	+18.0%	+28.0%	+40.0%	+48.0%	+78.0%	+86.0%	+84.0%	+90.0%	+93.0%	+82.0%
U.K. Retail Price Index: 'All Items' January 1987 = 100	137.9	141.3	146.0	150.2	154.4	159.5	163.4	166.6	171.1	173.3	178.4	183.1
U.K. Retail Price Index: Rebased to January 1990 = 100	115.4	118.2	122.2	125.7	129.2	133.5	136.7	139.4	143.2	145.0	149.3	153.2

3b. Combined franchise unit sales turnover – 1990 RPI-adjusted values	£4.3bn	£4.7bn	£4.8bn	£5.1bn	£5.4bn	£5.5bn	£6.5bn	£6.7bn	£6.4bn	£6.6bn	£6.5bn	£5.9bn
Change on 1993 value		+7.4%	+11.5%	+17.5%	+25.0%	+28.0%	+50.2%	+54.0%	+48.3%	+51.2%	+49.2%	+37.1%
4. Direct employment in business format franchising												
Total franchise unit/outlet employees (excluding Dairy)	152,300	149,400	187,200	227,100	235,200	257,500	*no disaggregated details shown from 1999 onwards*					
Franchisees (allowing for multiple unit ownership)	11,000	12,300	11,700	12,100	11,500	18,300	*ditto...*					
Spouse/partners if active and not included in employee total	3,500	4,200	4,800	6,600	6,800	6,600	*ditto...*					
Employees at system HQs + system locations elsewhere	9,700	16,400	10,500	10,800	13,100	14,900	*ditto...*					
Dairy employment	12,000	10,000	8,500	7,500	7,200	6,000	*ditto...*					
Total	188,500	192,300	222,700	264,100	273,800	303,300	316,900	316,000	324,900	326,000	330,000	327,000
Change on 1993 value		+2.0%	+18.1%	+40.1%	+45.3%	+60.9%	+68.1%	+67.6%	+72.4%	+72.9%	+75.1%	+73.5%
NB 1993: No data shown for system employees 'elsewhere'												
5. Franchisee employment – average per franchisee unit/outlet (Total No. UK Employees ÷ Total No. UK Franchisee Units)	7.6	7.3	8.7	9.9	9.4	10.1	9.0	8.9	9.4	9.5	9.8	10.4
Change on 1993		–3.8%	+14.5%	+30.2%	+24.3%	+33.5%	+19.1%	+17.3%	+24.4%	+25.2%	+28.9%	+37.7%
6. Franchisee unit/outlet sales turnover – average per employee (Total UK Sales ÷ Total No. UK Franchise Employment) (‡)	£26.5k	£28.6k	£26.5k	£24.2k	£25.6k	£24.4k	£28.1k	£29.4k	£28.3k	£29.1k	£29.2k	£27.8k
Change on 1993		+7.8%	–0.1%	–8.6%	–3.6%	–8.0%	+5.9%	+11.0%	+6.8%	+9.9%	+10.2%	+4.9%
7. Franchisee unit/outlet sales turnover – average per franchisee outlet (Total UK Sales ÷ Total No. UK Franchisee Outlets) (‡)	£200.8k	£208.3k	£229.6k	£238.8k	£240.5k	£246.7k	£253.2k	£261.2k	£266.7k	£276.2k	£285.4k	£290.2k
Change on 1993		+3.8%	+14.3%	+18.9%	+19.8%	+22.8%	+26.1%	+30.1%	+32.8%	+37.5%	+42.1%	+44.5%
8. Franchise unit/outlet sales turnover – average per franchise system (Total UK Sales ÷ Total No. UK Franchisee Systems) (‡)	£12.6m	£13.3m	£12.4m	£11.8m	£12.3m	£12.4m	£13.9m	£14.0m	£13.7m	£14.0m	£13.8m	£12.7m
Change on 1993		+5.2%	–1.4%	–6.3%	–2.4%	–1.7%	+9.8%	+10.8%	+8.4%	+11.1%	+9.3%	+0.4%
9. Proportion of franchisees claiming to be profitable	87.5%	87%	90%	94%	92%	89%	90%	95%	93%	91%	95%	88%

(‡) *Unadjusted financial values (i.e. using the values in 3a., as contained in the original reports)*

Source: *RP02 Retail Prices Index (RPI) all items*, Office for National Statistics (April 2005); *Annual Franchise Surveys*, NatWest/British Franchise Association (February/March 1995–2005)

23.6.3 Franchising worldwide

A survey of franchise associations undertaken in 1995 by Arthur Andersen revealed some marked differences between the number of franchise systems in the respondent countries and regarding the corresponding number of franchisees (see Figure 23.3). At the forefront is the US (population 266 million at the time), but Canada (29 million) and Australia (22 million including New Zealand) – each also a 'land of opportunity' – have relatively large numbers of franchisees compared with their total population. All three of course had strong colonial ties to the UK. Some large-population countries were not included in the survey data – such as China (1210 million), India (952 million), Indonesia (207 million) and Russia (148 million) – but data collection can be problematic in emerging markets, especially where there is no franchise association. Each of these missing countries is known to have a small number of franchise systems.

In the UK, the franchise industry has been strongly influenced by developments from the US. In the mid-1970s, the British Franchise Association was formed by eight franchise companies:

- Budget Rent-a-Car (vehicle rentals)
- Dyno Rod (drain cleaning and hygiene services)
- Holiday Inn (hotels and motels)
- Kentucky Fried Chicken (fast-foods)
- Prontaprint (fast-print services)
- ServiceMaster (carpet and furniture upholstery cleaners)
- Wimpy International (fast-foods)
- Ziebart (vehicle rust-proofing services).

Only two of the above (Prontaprint and Wimpy) were distinctly British and even the latter was based upon an imported US idea, albeit developed by a British company. This dominant representation of US involvement in franchising has continued with US companies exporting to Britain largely via the medium of granting 'master licences' for an individual or company in Britain to develop their format nationwide.

This situation of high-profile US involvement in international franchising is one that wins favour at the highest levels in the US, as summarised in a recent analysis by Eroglu (1992: 19):

> From a balance-of-payments perspective, international franchising is considered (in the US) as a safe and speedy means of obtaining foreign currency with a relatively small financial investment abroad. It is notable in that it neither replaces (American) exports nor exports (American) jobs, all these reasons making this business arrangement one of the most preferred and government-supported forms of international involvement.

The attitude of the US government here appears plain and one which recommends itself to other governments – the message is that home-produced franchises, particularly those with export potential, can be fruitfully considered for targeted support.

Figure 23.3 Country franchisee populations: number of franchisees vs total population

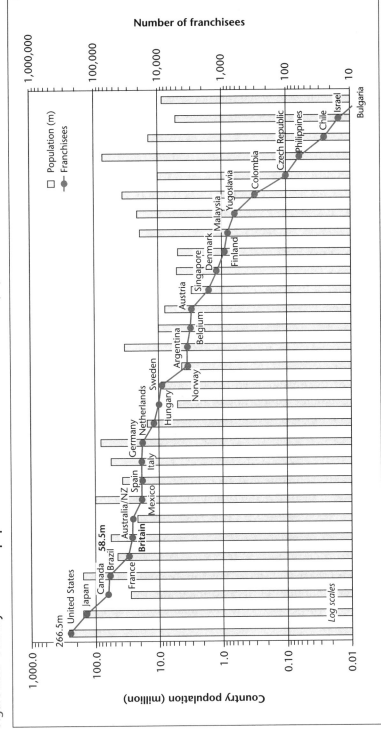

Notes: The above franchise data was derived from a survey of the franchise associations in 40 countries, which achieved a 90% response rate. The population and GDP values are estimates (1996 and 1995, respectively).

Source: Swartz (1995); Central Intelligence Agency (1996)

23.7 Ease of entry into franchising

The franchise industry is not without members who are regarded by their peers as having staged an entry into franchising by other than 'textbook' methods. Usually, this has involved selling franchises to members of the public before the business involved had been properly tried and tested. In fact, on such occasions, it has been literally tried and tested on its early franchisees. When this happens, it is not necessarily the case that the franchisor in question has deliberately set out to defraud the public by selling franchises prematurely. Rather, the explanation may lie in ignorance or over-enthusiasm. In the author's own past career as a small business trainer, there were occasions when an individual would attend a start-up course with the intention of selling franchises in the new business idea within weeks or months of starting up in business.

The conventional wisdom in the industry is that any completely new small business will need at least two years in order to establish itself in terms of testing out sales, marketing, product/service, pricing and staffing strategies. After all, every small business start-up plan inevitably requires considerable modification during the initial months of its implementation. High failure-rate figures, particularly during the first 30 months of operation, verify this fact.

Having established a basic business formula, the owner should then, ideally, establish an identical outlet in another location. The process of finding new premises, hiring personnel, organising a launch and all the other tasks accompanying a new outlet opening is an essential test of the owner's ability to replicate the success achieved in the founding unit. Again, there will be a steep learning curve here and the process could well take a further two years.

Finally, three key documents need to be drawn up prior to beginning franchising. First, an operating manual committing to paper detailed instructions for the guidance of franchisees when running an outlet for themselves; second, a franchise contract, stipulating the legal obligations of both parties – franchisor and franchisee – and, finally, a franchise prospectus as a marketing tool for use in recruiting franchisees. All three documents require a great deal of time, hard work and, usually, expensive external help from consultants, solicitors and accountants. Then begins the process of recruiting and training new franchisees and this, again, is liable to prove time-consuming and expensive since the business involved has no previous experience or public awareness to draw upon.

Overall, adopting a 'textbook' approach, a business starting up from nothing may well find itself involved in five years of hard work before it recruits its first franchisee. The founder(s) will find that they are not simply involved in testing out one business idea but two – a conventional business configuration plus an allied franchise format. Obviously, the final package has to be one capable of yielding notably better financial returns than the average small business since these must satisfy the franchisee's income needs, service banks loans and pay off loan capital, plus sustain the franchisor's needs for management services fees, amounting to usually around 10% on sales turnover.

Once a franchise company is well established, it will find a range of specialist services and advice on offer from bodies such as the British Franchise Association and specialist units in the clearing banks. The weakest link in the chain of development is almost certainly at an earlier stage – between establishing a conventional small

business with franchise potential and launching it as a fully-fledged franchise operation, without short-cuts being taken that could prove disastrous later.

Obviously, the above timetable can be safely reduced in the case of an already well-
established SME wishing simply to convert to a franchise format by cloning its previous
success, but the risks are still high. A report commissioned by the US Small Business
Administration estimates that initial franchise development costs can exceed $500,000
(Trutko *et al.*, 1993: 7):

> The development of a business from a proven concept through to the sale of its first franchise
> is typically a long, expensive and risky process for the franchisor. Even excluding the costs of
> direct management involvement, the franchisor bears sizeable 'upfront' costs for developing
> a programme before it can be marketed to franchisees.

They also similarly identify the early stage of entry into franchising as a difficult time
for the franchisee since: 'Prospective franchisees are often reluctant to use professional
advisers to evaluate franchise offerings because of the cost and/or difficulty of identifying an attorney in the area of franchising.' Without doubt, most specialist franchise
advisers see their principal area of vested interest as that of undertaking work for franchisors rather than franchisees.

23.7.1 Franchise contracts

The franchise relationship is governed, in the legal sense, by a written contract which
commonly spans 30–40 pages in length and can be even longer. These contracts usually run for a specified period of time though are usually renewable. The most typical
contract length is five years followed by ten years.

The most detailed comparative work on franchise contracts is that undertaken by
Professor Alan Felstead of the Centre for Labour Market Studies at the University of
Leicester, England. He compared 83 different franchise contracts on six main compon-
ent elements:

- guarantees granted to franchisees of territorial exclusivity;
- franchisor's rights to unilaterally imposed changes to their operating manuals;
- post-termination restrictions on competition;
- franchisor's stakes in franchisees' businesses via ownership of sites, telephone lines
  or equipment;
- franchisor's rights to police the quality of the franchisees' output; and
- the franchisor's imposition of output targets.

Felstead (1993: 115) constructed an Index of Contractual Control (Figure 23.4). Each
element of control is allotted a score of zero if absent, 1 if present and, where appropriate, 2 if present in a stronger form. Although this scoring mechanism does not 'weigh'
each of the components against one another, it does enable identification of 'hard'
franchise systems (where the degree of contractual control is high) from 'softer' forms
systems (where the degree of contractual control is low and franchisees enjoy greater
degrees of autonomy).

Figure 23.4 **Index of contractual control**

COMPONENT ELEMENTS		Score
a) Non-exclusivity:		
Exclusivity guaranteed in territory	0	49.4%
Qualified exclusivity	1	16.9%
Non-exclusive franchise	2	33.7%
b) Performance targets:		
None	0	62.7%
Turnover targets/expansion triggers	1	37.3%
c) 'Stake' in tangible business assets:		
No 'stake' evident in contract	0	33.7%
'Stake' in telephone lines/sites/equipment	1	66.3%
d) Operations manual:		
No rights to unilateral change	0	12.0%
Rights to unilateral change by franchisor	1	88.0%
e) Post-termination restrictions:		
None	0	13.3%
Non-compete or non-solicitation	1	25.3%
Both non-compete and non-solicitation	2	61.4%
f) Monitoring of output quality:		
No rights to police system	0	41.0%
Rights to inspect/communicate with clients on reasonable notice	1	10.8%
Rights to inspect/communicate without notice	2	48.2%
INDEX OF CONTRACTUAL CONTROL		
'Soft' franchising (0–3)		13.3%
'Medium' franchising (4–6)		65.1%
'Hard' franchising (7–9)		21.7%

Source: Felstead (1993)

Around two-thirds of the systems examined fell in between the two extremes, with the overall distribution 'scores' skewed towards the 'hard' end. Felstead (1993: 116) feels that franchisees occupy an ambiguous position of being neither fully in control of 'their' business nor fully controlled:

First, despite operating without close and direct supervision, franchisees are required to operate within procedures laid down and often subject to unilateral change. Moreover, franchisees are sometimes committed to adhere to franchisor-set performance targets, and, in any case, to give the aim of the franchisor (turnover maximisation) primacy in the running of the business. Secondly, while they appropriate the profits (and losses) of the business, they do so only after they have made turnover payments to the franchisor. Thirdly, although franchisees buy or lease much of the physical business apparatus, some parts remain in the hands of the franchisor, and some have franchisor-imposed restrictions on their use both during and after the currency of the agreement. Furthermore, franchisees have no ownership rights in the intangible business assets – they simply 'borrow' the business idea, trading name and/or format.

Felstead also traces a number of instances of franchisor–franchisee litigation. One particularly interesting case involved a Prontaprint franchisee in the UK who declined to renew his contract but continued to trade in the identical line of business and in the same premises, albeit under a different name. He lost a legal judgement on the grounds that:

- he was still drawing benefit from the Prontaprint name via repeat business and, for some time at least, being listed in local directories as 'Prontaprint'; and
- the franchisee was deemed to have had little understanding of the print business prior to being trained by Prontaprint.

The latter fact may explain the frequently expressed franchisor preference for franchisees without prior experience in the operational line of the franchise.

23.8 Franchisee success and failure rates

Research results (Stanworth and Purdy, 1993) identify quite clearly two principal appeals that franchising holds for 'potential franchisees'. One is 'independence/chance to be your own boss' and the other access to a 'proven business system'. Whilst both were chosen frequently and almost to the exclusion of other possible appeals of franchising, the precise ordering varied, depending upon whether or not respondents had prior experience of self-employment (see Figure 23.5).

Some causes of SME failure are seen as being due to 'generic' causes and should actually be remedied or reduced by franchising (Cross and Walker, 1987). These are:

- under-capitalisation,
- absence of economies of scale,

Figure 23.5 **Main appeal of franchising: by current employment status**

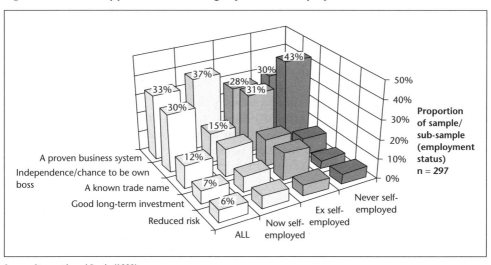

Source: Stanworth and Purdy (1993)

- lack of business acumen,
- inability to survive intense competition in sectors (such as retailing) where barriers to entry are low.

Franchising should reduce the probability of failure among franchisees due to such 'generic' causes, on condition of course that the franchisor's responsibilities are met and that the appropriate back-up services expand at a rate sufficient to cope with any growth of the franchise network. Thus, attempts by the franchisor to expand too quickly or, alternatively, to simply generate profits through the accumulation of once-and-for-all front-end fees, will act to the detriment of franchisees.

Failures due to 'franchising-related' factors, as opposed to 'generic' factors, are cited by Cross as falling essentially into five key categories:

- Business fraud, such as the use of celebrities to attract franchisees to ill-founded franchise schemes in the US during the 1960s and 1970s.
- Intrasystem competition, involving franchise outlets being located too close together and cannibalising each other's sales while maximising the franchisor's sales-based royalties. Also, company-owned outlets may be sited close to franchisee-owned outlets.
- Insufficient support of franchisees, encompassing advertising support, pre-opening programmes and management assistance.
- Poor franchisee screening (possibly fuelled by a drive to maximise front-end fees), resulting in a mismatch between franchisee's attributes and criteria for success.
- Persistent franchisor–franchisee conflict.

Mittlestaedt and Peterson (1980) have conducted work in this area that suggested franchise failure rates running at around 5% and turnover at around twice that level. Padmanabhan (1986) concluded that franchise operations fail generally less often than independents but that the opposite may be true of business services and automotive franchises. Ozanne and Hunt (1971) identified an annual failure rate of 6.7% among fast-food franchise systems but concluded that the actual failure rate could be two or even three times as high. The same went for franchisee failure rates that were lower on a percentage basis, suggesting that franchisee failures tended to be concentrated in smaller franchise systems.

In summary, we still lack any harmonised methodology for assessing failure rates and the differences between franchised business failures and independents is almost certainly much less than the impression given by promotional books and franchisee recruitment packages. However, the most honest and accurate statement that can be made on the issue of comparative failure rates probably remains that made by Housden (1984: 226):

> It has been claimed that as well as helping in the creation of new businesses, franchising substantially reduces the subsequent rate of failure in such businesses . . . No firm evidence has yet been produced to support this contention, but it seems probable to assume that franchised outlets of a reputable system are less likely to fail than independently-owned outlets, because of the franchisor's vested interest.

Statistics published in the US appear to underline the possible effects of franchisor fees and market saturation in influencing franchisee failure rates and profit returns. Bates (1994a: 4) drew up a sample of 7,270 small businesses started between 1984 and 1987 drawn from the US Census Bureau's Business Owners Database. Using 1987 as a baseline (year 1), he tracked these businesses through to 1991. Bates found that 34.9% of franchise businesses failed compared with 28.0% of non-franchise businesses. Pre-tax income levels were also higher for independent businesses. Bates concluded that the difference in performance rates between franchised outlets and other small businesses was based in part on differences in industry distribution, with franchises over-represented in retailing and under-represented in services. Among other possible reasons for these findings, he includes:

- the recruitment by franchise companies of candidates poorly qualified to become franchisees;
- the saturation of key franchise markets;
- the high level of franchisor fees and royalties.

He hypothesises that what might once have been a prudent route to small business success may now be undermined by excessive competition and/or fees relative to the value of franchisor services.

It should be remembered that, whilst a franchisee should, and hopefully will, receive the kind of professional managerial help and advice that is not normally available to SMEs, this is only delivered at a price and often a substantial one at that – typically an on-going rate of around 10% levied on sales turnover (in addition to front-end start-up fees and charges). Many SMEs would almost certainly not make total profits of this magnitude and, by any measure, this kind of royalty regime is likely to take in the region of half the total profits of even a well-run franchised outlet. In short, the royalty regime is a heavy burden for outlets to bear, particularly where conditions of recession and market saturation also take their toll.

23.9 The quality of jobs created in franchising

Very little research has been undertaken concerning the quality of jobs provided by the franchise industry in terms of pay, training and job satisfaction levels. However, most franchised businesses tend to involve a limited range of products and services and appear to lend themselves to low-skill/low-pay human resource strategies. After all, franchise company outlets are essentially non-unionised small firms operating on the basis of human resource strategies devised by the franchisee. This is a fruitful area for future research and there are already movements on the part of researchers interested in becoming involved in this as aspect.

Felstead (1993: 200) has presented some evidence that is, in all probability, fairly typical of the industry and thus generalisable. He makes the point that franchisees, in attempting to improve their profits, may be more motivated to save money on their payroll bills than by increasing turnover levels since the latter attracts a 10% (or thereabouts) levy by the franchisor whereas the former does not. Felstead conducted a comparison of franchised and non-franchised high street printers in the East Midlands (Felstead, 1988). He found that those who worked for franchisees were more likely to be young, government-sponsored (i.e. on training schemes) women workers in receipt of payment levels and non-pay benefits (such as holiday pay) substantially below those paid by the industry's more traditional employers.

Felstead says that these findings are corroborated by a survey of American fast-food restaurants, indicating that, despite the common characteristics that employees of company-owned and franchise restaurants exhibit, wages and especially fringe benefits (paid holidays, sick leave, uniform allowance, free meals, etc.) are greater for workers employed in company-owned stores than those employed by franchisees (Krueger, 1991; Katz and Krueger, 1992).

23.10 Chapter summary

The worldwide growth of franchising appears set to continue on a long-term basis. The growth of franchising overall (in real terms) is strongly dependent on the performance of the economy as a whole. Against this, business format franchising, concentrated upon more service-oriented activities, is likely to experience growth rates notably faster than those applying for franchising as a whole.

A number of factors appear likely to promote future growth. First is the general worldwide decline of traditional manufacturing industry and its replacement by service-sector activities. Franchising is especially well suited to service and people-intensive economic activities, particularly where these require a large number of geographically dispersed outlets serving local markets.

A second factor is the growth in the overall popularity of self-employment. Most governments throughout the world are looking towards self-employment and small business as an important source of future jobs. As franchising becomes increasingly well known and understood, it is likely to appeal to a growing number of people. Alongside this trend, we may expect to see an increase in the number of franchise opportunities. This process will be assisted, not least, by large companies following the current trend towards divestment from centralised control of an increasing propor-tion of their business activities. A notable example in the UK has been the franchising of domestic milk-delivery. Increasing female workforce participation will continue the current trend towards dual-career and dual-income families, resulting in both the need and the resources to purchase services. Home service franchises (cleaning, maiding, lawn-care, house-minding, etc.) are likely to feature here, as are childcare and child development services.

The demands of an ageing population in many countries will also create opportun-ities, ranging from the need for special diets to special needs in the fields of leisure and care. In the US, the healthcare industry is turning to franchised medicine, ranging from private-duty nursing agencies to the provision of alternative medicine. Greater aware-ness of health issues generally will also throw up opportunities in sectors ranging from food to exercise and counselling services. Entertainment and leisure activities will also offer additional franchise opportunities, ranging from travel agencies to ventures such as miniature golf courses, dance studios, specialist movie theatres, etc. American experience suggests that growth levels in the number of franchised outlets are unlikely to match growth levels in sales turnover figures, since franchise outlets tend to be larger than the average conventional small business in turnover terms.

On balance, it does not appear that franchise operations substantially displace conventional small businesses. Where they do challenge them, it is often because they act as a new force in the field with the flexibility to respond rapidly to changes in technology and market demand. They themselves may then subsequently be threatened by exposure to similar market forces, thus rendering their businesses and their profit margins more vulnerable than they and their franchisees would have expected or hoped. However, it is obviously untrue that those who eat at McDonald's do so without any measure of substitution concerning their former eating habits, or that customers of Kall-Kwik or Prontaprint still place their customary orders with traditional print firms. Encroachment and additionality appear to have developed hand-in-hand, usually aided by developments in technology, customer tastes and consumer spending power.

If we look at the quintessential icon of the industry – fast-food franchising – it is unlikely that it has not in some measure diverted trade away from more traditional providers in the field (many of them almost certainly small independents). However, the conditions fuelling a market restructuring here were almost certainly the development of technology capable of producing food quickly on a standardised basis, and a growth generally in trends towards convenience foods and eating out. Similarly, in the field of fast print franchising, new technology reduced the training and skill levels required to produce print copy and final product from years to weeks. The result is that print products can now be produced in hours rather than days, using cheaper and less skilled labour, while relocating from manufacturing premises off the high street to 'business service' premises on the high street. An additional key factor assisting the growth of fast print franchising was the trend of large firms in the 1980s to divest themselves of many internal services, and 'buy in' instead.

When a franchise first comes into being, it ideally requires some 'unique selling point', giving it an advantage over its competitors. Over time, however, competition arrives to challenge its market position. This may come in the shape of new franchise operations but may, equally, take the form of conventional small business operations.

Women and minorities appear to have increased their representation in franchising in recent years in the US. Although both groups are less visible than might be expected in terms of their general participation in the labour force at large, the evidence indicates that around 10% of franchise units in the US are owned outright by women plus another 20% owned by women in alliance with men. Around 5% of franchise units were owned by minorities in the US in 1986 compared with an 8.8% ownership level of US firms generally. This is despite government schemes targeted specifically at increasing the level of minority representation.

The help afforded by franchisors in setting up new franchisees, particularly those with no prior business experience, renders franchising a potentially fruitful route for increasing female and ethnic participation in small business. Thus, any government assistance to franchising is best advised to be targeted at indigenous franchises – particularly those with export potential and the facility for spreading jobs and enterprise among ethnic groups where opportunities might otherwise be lacking.

Questions

1 Which is more logically consistent – to consider franchising as small businesses colonising territory that is usually the preserve of large firms, or vice versa?

2 In what ways can franchising combine the strengths of both small business and large business?

3 Why are US franchises such a success on the global platform and UK franchises so relatively unsuccessful?

4 Consider why franchise trade associations routinely overstate industry achievements and the ethical implications of this stance.

5 Consider the following analysis and forecast for UK business format franchising made in 1998, along with the prior trend of the average number of franchised units per system (see Table 23.1 earlier), and assess whether or not the assumptions behind the forecast were reasonable.

> By the year 2002 franchisors believe that they will be operating more than double the number of franchised units than the 42.9 operated now [excluding dairy systems], that is on average 92.6 per system. This figure suggests that organic growth alone will lead to over 50,000 units by 2002. Again it is worth noting the apparent lack of suitable franchisees which may well temper such ambitious plans. Of course, economic conditions generally will undoubtedly influence the relative success of franchising over the next few years. Nevertheless such predictions indicate that those in franchising can expect to reap even greater rewards than are currently being experienced.
>
> (Annual Franchise Survey, NatWest/British Franchise Association, March 1998: 12)

Web links

www.franchise.org
The International Franchise Association is a membership organisation of franchisors, franchisees and suppliers.

www.wmin.ac.uk/IFRC
Website of the International Franchise Research Centre at the University of Westminister which contains a range of research reports and studies into franchising.

www.franchise500.com
List of the world's most successful franchises, as compiled by Entrepreneur magazine.

www.franchise411.com
This website – Franchise Profiles – has been created as an online library and resource centre to provide a comprehensive source of franchise information.

CHAPTER 24

Internationalisation and the small business

Kevin Ibeh

24.1 Introduction

This chapter is concerned with internationalisation of small and medium-sized enterprises (SMEs). It starts with some reflections on the now-established status of SMEs as international market actors and the economic and technological imperatives that have driven policy making and research on SMEs' internationalisation since the 1970s. It next considers theories of smaller firm internationalisation, covering such relevant approaches as the incremental internationalisation models, the network theories, and the arguably integrative resource-based perspectives. Further discussions centre on the factors that stimulate SMEs' internationalisation; the range and variety of barriers that impede them from so doing; the decision-maker and firm-specific characteristics that enhance the likelihood of successful internationalisation among SMEs; and the policy initiatives for assisting the internationalisation of SMEs across OECD countries.

24.2 Learning objectives

This chapter has five learning objectives:

1 To explain internationalisation and discuss the various ways in which it can be attained.
2 To appreciate the changing face of SME internationalisation, including its underlying dynamics.
3 To present the major theories for explaining SME internationalisation and identify the critical decision-maker, firm and environmental influences on the phenomenon.
4 To examine the major barriers and problems that impinge upon SME internationalisation.
5 To review the policy measures and institutional mechanisms commonly employed to assist SME internationalisation and make relevant recommendations.

Key concepts

■ internationalisation process   ■ 'stages'   ■ networks   ■ resource base   ■ barriers
■ policies

24.3 Internationalisation

Firm-level internationalisation has witnessed a phenomenal level of growth since the latter part of the twentieth century. Driven largely by the remarkable, and even revolutionary, changes in their external environments, companies, large and small, have increasingly embraced the international growth path as a way of leveraging technological, organisational and inter-organisational resources, and reducing business costs and risks (Ibeh, 2000; Royer, 2004). SMEs are not insignificant actors in this changing landscape. As recent OECD findings suggest, internationalised SMEs account for about 25–35% of world's manufactured exports, with their export contribution to GDP representing 4–6% for OECD countries and 12% for Asian economies (OECD, 1997a).

This seems very different from the period, not too long ago, when internationalisation was regarded as the domain of large corporations. Based on their presumed lack of internationalisation potential, small firms were largely ignored by most governments, policy makers and researchers, seeking to promote national economic position through greater firm-level internationalisation. This explains why the dominant theories and models of internationalisation – product life-cycle, market imperfection, internalisation/transaction cost and the eclectic paradigm – have an essentially multinational enterprise (MNE) focus, explaining the conditions under which MNEs extend and establish their activities, particularly production, overseas.

The serious difficulties experienced by western MNEs during the 1970s and early 1980s, and the knock-on effects on their national economies, however, served to expose the weakness of this exclusive reliance on the large firm. Assailed by such developments as the oil crisis of 1973–74, depressed global demand, intense international competition from Japan and the newly industrialising countries, and revolutionary new technologies, western MNEs lost their grip on world trade and were forced into plant closures, down-sizing and process re-engineering. Their governments soon reacted with massive programmes of de-regulation and privatisation. From the ashes of resulting redundancies, however, emerged many new small firms – their formation fuelled by rising trends in outsourcing, greater demand for services, and microelectronics (Bell, 1995). Subsequent evidence of the small-firm sector's economic contribution was reported in a number of studies, notably the Bolton Commission's (1971) in the UK; Birch's (1979, 1981) in the US; and Storey and Johnson's (1987) in the European Community.

Concerns were, however, expressed about the disproportionate under-representation of small firms in the international market. Cannon and Willis (1983), for example, observed that while small firms accounted for nearly 25% of the UK's gross national product, they contributed less than 10% of all manufactured exports. Even more insightful was the indication that a significant proportion of SMEs with exporting potential had restricted themselves to domestic operations, in the erroneous 'belief that size is an insuperable disadvantage' in internationalisation (Bolton, 1971). It was hardly surprising, therefore, that policy makers, faced with burgeoning trade deficits and an inert large firm sector, would begin to focus on developing the little-tapped export potential of smaller firms (Bell, 1995). This favourable policy climate transformed SME internationalisation into an important area of inquiry – a situation that has continued to date.

24.4 Concepts, context and extent

The term 'internationalisation' commonly refers to the process of increasing involvement in international operations (Welch and Luostarinen, 1988; Bell *et al.*, 2004). It describes the continuum that stretches from the firm's first import activity or extra-regional expansion or domestic internationalisation to full globalisation (Wiedersheim-Paul *et al.*, 1978; Luostarinen, 1994). Full company globalisation is characterised by the establishment of manufacturing plants and marketing affiliates across major international regions; extensive outsourcing of inputs and marketing of outputs across borders; and worldwide integration and coordination of resources and operations in pursuit of global competitiveness. Sometimes used interchangeably with globalisation (its most evolved form), internationalisation is attained through a variety of international market entry and development modes (Young, 1990). These include: direct and indirect exporting; licensing; franchising; management contract; turn-key contract; contract manufacturing/international sub-contracting; industrial cooperation agreements; contractual joint venture; equity joint venture; strategic alliances; mergers and acquisitions; and wholly owned subsidiaries.

A number of authors have tried to classify internationalisation modes. This chapter employs Luostarinen's (1980) approach, whose distinctions between home and overseas production, and direct and non-direct investments, offer useful insights into understanding SME versus large firm internationalisation. In general terms, the progression from home-based internationalisation modes to overseas production modes, and from non-direct investment modes to direct investment modes, is marked by increased resource commitments/transfer and risks. Given their obvious resource (financial and managerial) and attitudinal (to risk/control) differences, small and large firms have tended to adopt divergent internationalisation modes. Indeed, SMEs are more likely to supply their international markets from domestic production bases (through indirect and direct exporting, and sales/service subsidiaries). This explains why the bulk of the literature on SME internationalisation originates from exporting research.

According to a recent report (OECD, 1997), SMEs' share of export in each of the surveyed OECD and Asian economies ranges between 15% and 50%, with 20% and 80% being active exporters (Table 24.1). In general, SME internationalisation is greater in small, open economies and less in larger, more self-contained economies. This, however, is not always the case. France and Italy still have 30% and 70% of exports respectively contributed by SMEs, while internationalisation in small, open economies like Australia, Malaysia and Greece is less than might be expected (OECD, 1997).

That SMEs are not restricting their internationalisation forays to exporting, however, is evident in the rising trend towards small firms' adoption of more direct forms of international marketing, including low-level foreign direct investments (FDI), strategic alliances, licensing, joint ventures and similar cooperation-based modes (Young, 1987; Dimitratos *et al.*, 2003). A recent study (OECD, 1997) indicates the extent of SME internationalisation thus:

> About 10% of SMEs are engaged in FDI and about 10% or more foreign investment appear to be attributable to SMEs. Around 10 to 15% of SMEs have licences, franchises or other arrangements with firms outside their home country . . . It is estimated that about 1% or less

Table 24.1 Estimates of the extent of SME internationalisation

	Exports from SMEs (%)	Percentage of SMEs exporting	Notes
Australia	n.a.	5 to 10	0–100 employees
Belgium		20	0–500 employees
Canada		14	5–200 employees
Denmark	46		<500 employees
Finland	23		
France	M 26		
Greece	n.a.	n.a.	SME exports as % of industry turnover = 15–20%
Ireland		25	
Italy	52.7		<500 employees
		68	51–100 employees
		80	101–300 employees
		83	301–500 employees
Japan	13.5		<300 direct
	30–35		<300 indirect
Netherlands	26		<100 indirect + direct
		17	0–9 employees
		43	10–99 employees
		67	100+ employees
Portugal			No figures available
Spain		18	<20 employees
		50	51–100 employees
		70	101–200 employees
Sweden	36		<200 employees
Switzerland	40		
UK		16–20	
US	11	12	
China	40–60		
Republic of Korea	40		
Indonesia	10.6		
Chinese Taipei	56		
Thailand	10		
Malaysia	15		
Singapore	16		
Vietnam	20		

Source: OECD (1997a)

of SMEs (30,000 to 40,000) can be said to be global, in the sense of being active in multiple countries and/or across several continents, or having the ability to operate wherever they see fit . . . another 5 to 10 % of SMEs in manufacturing . . . can be said to be extensively internationalised . . . (with) a further 10 to 20% . . . active in up to three foreign countries.

These internationally active SMEs are growing faster than their domestic counterparts. Those in niche markets and new (including high-tech) industries constitute the fastest-growing segment (20%), while those in traditional industries (around 50%)

internationalise incrementally via exporting. It would, indeed, appear that most SMEs now see internationalisation as not only fashionable but imperative. This is based on the realisation that pressures from inward internationalisation are likely to be most unkind to firms that stand still and are not internationally active. As the OECD (1997) reports, probably less than 40% of SMEs are insulated from any effects of globalisation and the proportion of such firms (mainly small service providers) is expected to contract further to 20%. This does not imply that service firms are not active internationally. Many play an increasingly important international role (Erramilli and Rao, 1990; Sharma, 1993; Hellman, 1996), although measurement difficulties prevent an overall picture of the extent of service SMEs' internationalisation. It should be noted, nevertheless, that the easily measured physical manufactured exports are often accompanied by significant international SME service activity, including customer service, design, distribution, marketing, etc. (OECD, 1997).

24.5 Explaining SME internationalisation

Firm internationalisation has been studied from both the perspective of export development (involving mostly SMEs) and the emergence of the MNEs (Bell and Young, 1998). Focusing on SME internationalisation, four theoretical approaches can be identified:

- incremental internationalisation (or stage of development) models,
- network theory,
- resource-based perspectives (incorporating business strategy, contingency and international entrepreneurship perspectives).

24.5.1 Incremental internationalisation (or stage of development) models

A number of 'stage' models have emerged to explain the process of a firm's development along the internationalisation route. Common to all these models is the view of export development as a sequential, 'staged' process. All have their roots in the behavioural theory of the firm (Cyert and March, 1963) and Penrose's (1959) theory of the growth of the firm. According to the 'stage' theorists, firms adopt an incremental, evolutionary approach to foreign markets, gradually deepening their commitment and investment as they gain in international market knowledge and experience (Johanson and Vahlne, 1977, 1990). Firms are also believed to target neighbouring, 'psychically close' countries initially, and subsequently enter foreign markets with successively larger psychic distance. Psychic distance refers to extent of proximity in geography, language, culture, political systems and business factors like industry structure and competitive environment (Zafarullah et al., 1998).

Pioneering this approach was Johanson and Vahlne's (1977) model of knowledge development and increasing foreign market commitment, which built on Johanson and Wiedersham-Paul's (1978) study of the internationalisation behaviour of four Swedish firms from their early beginnings. They found that the internationalisation process was the consequence of a series of incremental decisions, rather than large, spectacular foreign investments. Four different stages were identified in relation to a firm's international involvement: no regular export; export via independent representation (agents); sales subsidiaries; production/manufacturing. As Johanson and Vahlne (1990) stated: 'the firm's engagement in a specific foreign market develops according to an establishment chain, i.e. at the start no export activities are performed in the market, then export takes place via independent representatives, later through a sales subsidiary, and, eventually manufacturing may follow'.

A further dimension was added to the internationalisation process model by Wiedersheim-Paul's *et al.* (1978) work on pre-export behaviour, which extended the establishment chain backwards to include a pre-export stage. Export start was found to be influenced by the interplay between 'attention-evoking factors' and the individual decision maker, and the environment and history of the firm, including experience in extra-regional expansion (domestic internationalisation). Thus, the establishment-chain model attempts to explain the whole process of a firm's internationalisation, from the pre-export stage to post-export stage, including FDI.

Cognisance should be taken of the differences in perspectives adopted by these 'stage theorists'. Anderson (1993) for example, distinguished between the 'Uppsala internationalisation (U) models' and 'innovation-related (I) models'. While the former clearly refers to the models that emerged from a Swedish school of that description, the composition of the latter is not so clear. It seems appropriate, however, to include as innovation-related models those works that present export development as an innovation-adoption cycle (Lee and Brasch, 1978; Reid, 1981) and those that see it as a 'learning curve', influenced by external attention-evoking stimuli (e.g. unsolicited orders or enquiries) and internal factors, such as managerial ambitions and excess capacity (Bilkey and Tesar, 1977; Cavusgil, 1980; Czinkota and Johnston, 1982; Crick, 1995). The actual number of 'stages' undergone by internationalising firms also differs according to models, but this, as observed by Anderson (1993), 'reflects semantic differences rather than real differences concerning the nature of the internationalisation process'. Anderson's (1993) major criticisms, however, are 'the lack of proper design to explain the development process', the absence of clear-cut boundaries between stages, and the lack of 'tests of validity and reliability'.

The incremental internationalisation models have also been faulted on grounds of limited applicability. Indeed, many studies involving firms from small domestic markets, service firms, high-technology firms, knowledge-intensive firms, entrepreneurial firms, subcontractors and international new ventures have reported evidence that counter the incremental approach (e.g. see Bell, 1995; Etemad, 2004). As Bell (1995) explains, stage theories use linear models to explain dynamic, interactive, non-linear behaviour. Clark *et al.* (1997) observed that the establishment model was one of several paths to FDI, noting that 'firms often bypass the intermediate stages to FDI'. The remarks by Bell and Young (1998) that the incremental internationalisation models merely identify the internationalisation patterns of certain firms, but not of others, and that they fail to explain adequately the processes involved seem to reflect the consensus position on the topic. Madsen and Servais (1997) sought to clarify the situation by categorising internationalising firms into three. First, the traditional exporters whose internationalisation patterns largely reflect the traditional stages model; second, firms that leapfrog some stages, for example late starters that have only domestic sales for many years, but then suddenly invest in a distant foreign market; and third, the born global firms. Suffice it to say that 'the stages theory has merit in its use as a framework for classification purposes rather than for an understanding of the internationalisation process' (Turnbull, 1987).

Findings supportive of the 'psychic distance' concept have been reported in a variety of studies, including Styles and Ambler's (1994) research, which concluded that 'firms should focus on those countries which are closest in 'psychic distance' for early export endeavours'. There have, however, been refutations of the psychic distance concept, most notably by Czinkota and Ursic (1987) and, to a lesser degree, by the 'network school' (Johanson and Mattsson, 1988). The latter ascribes limited relevance to the concept in the face of vastly improving global communications and transportation infrastructures, as well as increasing market convergence. Evidence of 'client follower-ship' has also been reported (Bell, 1995), which is inconsistent with the 'intuitive logic' (Sullivan and Bauerschmidt, 1990) of the psychic distance concept. O'Grady and Lane's Canadian study further identified a 'psychic distance paradox': operations in psychically close countries are not necessarily easy to manage, because assumptions of similarity can prevent executives from learning about critical differences (O'Grady and Lane, 1996).

Despite valid criticisms, the stage of development perspective remains a significant contribution to the understanding of SME internationalisation. Prior to its emergence, internationalisation was essentially theorised and discussed in terms of the MNE. It is also the case that its focus on initial internationalisation attracted considerable research attention and illumination to SME internationalisation, extending even to the pre-export stage. The postulations on psychic distance may now appear dated, given recent advancements in IT, but few would disagree that they resonate with the market selection pattern intuitively associated with exporters (Madsen and Servais, 1997). Criticisms of the model, based on its failure to reflect the internationalisation beha-viour of entrepreneurial, high-technology, knowledge-intensive and service firms, are acknowledged. Nevertheless, most studies involving firms in mature industries have been consistent in supporting the model's basic propositions.

24.5.2 Network theory

Another significant strand of internationalisation research was the development, from international industrial marketing, of the network or interaction and relationship con-cepts. The basic tenet is that internationalisation proceeds through an interplay between increasing commitment to, and evolving knowledge about, foreign markets, gained mainly from interactions in the foreign markets. These interactions – dynamic, evolving, less-structured – yield increased mutual knowledge and trust between international market actors and, subsequently, greater internationalisation commitment. In summary, 'a firm begins the export process by forming relationships that will deliver experiential knowledge about a market, and then commits resources in accordance with the degree of experiential knowledge it progressively gains from these relationships' (Styles and Ambler, 1994).

In network theory, markets are seen as a system of relationships among a number of players including customers, suppliers, competitors, family, friends and private and public support agencies. Strategic action, therefore, is rarely limited to a single firm, and the nature of relationships established with others in the market influences and often dictates future strategic options. For example, firms can expand from domestic to international markets through existing relationships that offer contacts and help to develop new partners and positions in new markets. At the same time, network relationships may restrict the nature of a firm's growth initiatives.

Internationalisation driven by customer/client followership, or what Hellman (1996) referred to as 'customer driven internationalisation', has been seen in service, high-technology and knowledge-intensive sectors (Bell *et al.*, 2004; Ibeh *et al.*, 2004). As observed by Johanson and Mattsson (1988), a firm's success in entering new international markets is more dependent on its relationships with current markets, both domestic and international, than it is on the chosen market and its cultural characteristics. This subtle shift from the core Uppsala internationalisation model (the psychic distance concept) was further endorsed by Johanson and Vahlne's (1992) remarks that many firms enter new foreign markets almost blindly, propelled not by strategic decisions or market research, but social exchange processes, interactions, and networks.

A growing body of evidence exists on the role of network relationships in SME internationalisation. Coviello and Munro (1995, 1997), for example, found that successful New Zealand based software firms are actively involved in international networks, and that they outsource many market development activities to network partners. As they observed, 'the network perspective goes beyond the models of incremental internationalisation by suggesting that firm's strategy emerges as a pattern of behaviour influenced by a variety of network relationships'. Coviello and Munro's evidence, while supportive of network theory, recognised the occurrence of internationalisation stages, *albeit* in a much condensed and accelerated form. This attempt to reconcile the network perspective with the work of the stage theorists and the 'international new venture' scholars also formed the substance of Madsen and Servais' (1997) theory-building effort.

There is no doubt that the network perspective has brought immense value to the understanding of the internationalisation process, particularly among SMEs. It presents a view of SME internationalisation that should be seen more as a complement than an alternative to the incremental internationalisation model. More importantly, it moves discussion away from the largely sterile debate, which, until recently, raged for and against the Uppsala model. It can, arguably, be credited with stimulating recent efforts being made towards a more holistic view of small firm internationalisation (Madsen and Servais, 1997; Bell and Young, 1998; Ibeh, 2001; Bell *et al.*, 2003). It is to this emerging perspective that the discussion now turns.

24.5.3 Resource-based perspectives (business strategy, contingency and international entrepreneurship perspectives)

A major recent development in the SME internationalisation research has been the increasing adoption of the resource-based theory as an integrative platform for explaining firm-level internationalisation (Bell and Young, 1998; Peng 2001; Ibeh, 2001, 2005). As Bell and Young (1998) explained, 'the resource-based perspective presents a holistic view of the firm', such that decisions on country market choice, mode of entry, and product strategies are made not on a stand-alone basis, but within a coordinated framework of resources and capabilities (whether internal or externally leveraged), as well as environmental (including competitive) realities. They elaborated that 'firms will have a different mix of resources/competencies and resource/competence gaps, and their strategic responses to these allow for the possibility of different paths to growth and internationalisation'. It could be argued that the resource-based theory of internationalisation is actually a more grounded restatement of the business strategy and contingency frameworks. It would appear to have met the need 'to root contingency frameworks within an underlying theory'. As its proponents observe, there is a close relationship with contingency approaches, which are designed to show the influence of a range of internal and external variables. This perspective is equally implicit in the business strategy frameworks and the recent work on international entrepreneurship.

The business strategy perspective proposes a strategically planned, rational approach to internationalisation, such that decisions on foreign-market entry and servicing strategies (entry mode) are made in the context of the firm's overall strategic development, and guided by rigorous analysis of relevant internal and external environmental factors (Young, 1987; Young et al., 1989). This is consistent with Chandler's (1962) view that 'structure follows strategy'. It also reflects the Turnbull et al. (1987) conclusion that a company's stage of internationalisation is largely determined by the operating environment, industry structure and its own marketing strategy. The business strategy perspective is implicit in much of the mainstream export literature, notably Aaby and Slater's (1989) model (widely referred to as the 'strategic export model'); Namiki's (1994) taxonomic analysis of export marketing strategy; Cavusgil and Zou's (1994) path analysis of export marketing strategy and performance, as well as Reid's contingency framework (Reid, 1983a).

The contingency approach to internationalisation views foreign expansion and export mode choice as severally influenced and situation-dependent. Reid (1983a) argued that: 'since exporting results from a choice among competing strategies that are guided by the nature of the market opportunity, firm resources and managerial philosophy, it represents a selective and dynamic adaptation to the changing character of the foreign market . . . Market factors and requirements are, therefore, closely intertwined with deciding whether to go international and what form this expansion should take'. Reid (1983b, 1985) further employed the economics-orientated transaction cost theory to explain firms' export mode decisions as dependent on the costs involved in initiating, negotiating and coordinating export transactions, reflecting Williamson's (1975) observation that transactional considerations are 'typically decisive in determining which mode of organisation will obtain in what circumstances, and why'.

International entrepreneurship researchers have generally sought to explain the behaviour of such recently identified firm categories as 'born globals', 'global start-ups', 'international new ventures', 'born internationals', 'rapidly internationalising firms', 'committed internationalists' and 'micromultinationals', by highlighting the quality of their knowledge assets (including the knowledge and experiential resources embedded in their top management), internationally focused entrepreneurial orientation, privileged access to network resources, social capital, and other market-based assets, among others (Oviatt and McDougall, 1994a, 1994b; Bell, 1995; Knight and Cavusgil, 1996; Madsen and Servais, 1997; Jones, 1999; Dimitratos et al., 2003; Etemad, 2004; Ibeh,

Young and Lin 2004; Ibeh, Johnson, Dimitratos and Slow, 2004; Zahra, 2004). According to this emerging literature, firms, including SMEs, would seem to have become more entrepreneurial and sophisticated with regard to their appreciation of international growth opportunities and feasible entry mode options; this has, thus, resulted in a faster pace of internationalisation (rapid internationalising firms) and more ambitious entry mode selection behaviour (micromultinationals).

A common denominator of these frameworks is the recognition that internationalisation is affected by multiple influences and that a range of the firms' internationalisation decisions, incorporating products, markets and entry modes, are made in a holistic way. There appears to be an increasing realisation of this extended base of internationalisation parameters. This is apparent in the emerging trend towards a more inclusive and holistic explanation of firm (particularly small firm) internationalisation. Having identified partial and situational relevance for each of the existing internationalisation models, Bell and Young (1998) invited more attention to their 'potential complementarities'. Researchers seem to have accepted this challenge. For example, Coviello and Munro's (1997) study of New Zealand software SMEs reported evidence of incremental internationalisation, network-driven internationalisation, as well as accelerated internationalisation (international new ventures), similar to the range of propositions offered by Madsen and Servais (1997) in their conceptualisations on 'born globals'. It will be interesting to see what other explanatory frameworks will emerge in the growing area of small firm internationalisation. Of more immediate relevance, however, is the role of internal (firm/decision maker) and external (environmental) factors that stage theorists, network scholars, resource-based theorists, business strategy and international entrepreneurship scholars have identified as significant to SMEs' initial internationalisation decisions.

24.6 Stimulating internationalisation

To initiate and subsequently develop international activity, a firm must first be influenced by stimulating or 'attention evoking' factors. The nature of these stimuli may offer invaluable insights into why some SMEs successfully internationalise while others do not. Building on previous typologies of internationalisation stimuli, Albaum *et al.* (1994) identified the following four categories:

- *internal-proactive* – factors associated with the SME's own initiative to exploit its unique internal competencies (e.g. potential for export-led growth);
- *internal-reactive* – responding to pressures from the internal environment (e.g. accumulation of unsold goods);
- *external-proactive* – active exploitation by management of market possibilities (e.g. identification of better opportunities abroad);
- *external-reactive* – reaction to factors from the external environment (e.g. receipt of unsolicited foreign orders).

Nevertheless, research on initial internationalisation suggests that stimuli are not sufficient on their own. They need to be supported by facilitating factors associated with the decision maker, the organisation and the environment. These factors constitute the real impetus behind the firm's decision to go international.

24.6.1 Decision-maker characteristics

Decision-maker characteristics are generally considered to have, in Brooks and Rosson's (1982) words, 'a decided impact on export decision'. All the major review articles on empirical exporting research have similarly concluded on the decisive importance of decision-maker characteristics. As Reid (1981) noted, 'empirical evidence points exclusively to the decision makers' attitude, experience, motivation and expectations as primary determinants in firms engaging in foreign marketing activity'. This is particularly so 'in small firms, where power, particularly decision-making power, is generally concentrated in the hands of one or very few persons'. According to Miesenbock (1988), 'the key variable in small business internationalisation is the decision maker of the firm. He or she is the one to decide starting, ending and increasing international activities'. Empirical findings on the specific decision-maker characteristics that increase the likelihood of SME internationalisation have, however, been inconsistent. This is particularly true of findings on decision makers' age and level of educational attainment. Garnier's (1982) remarks that it was not possible to ascertain whether there were statistically significant differences between managers of internationalised and non-internationalised firms with respect to age and level of education would appear to reflect the available evidence.

With regard to international orientation, variously defined as foreign education or work experience, travel, foreign birth or world-mindedness (Boatler, 1994), the balance of empirical evidence is that decision makers of internationalised SMEs are likely to have spent part of their lives abroad, and are generally less affected by foreign business-related uncertainties. Miesenbock (1988) concluded, from an extensive review of the literature, that 'the external contacts of the decision maker seem to be the most important objective characteristic'. Closely related to international orientation is another characteristic that may be referred to as international ethnic ties or contact networks. There is growing evidence that decision makers whose contact networks (see Chapter 16) are internationally spread are more likely to exploit international market opportunities than those who lack such ties. Jackson (1981), indeed, found the Zionist links of British Jews to be significant in explaining the flow of Israeli exports into Britain. Further supportive evidence has been reported by Crick and Chaudhry (1995) and Zafarullah et al. (1998) in their respective studies of British-Asian and Pakistani SMEs (see Chapter 10).

Decision makers' psychological traits are a further set of variables that have been widely studied. A large number of empirical findings have associated decision makers of internationalised SMEs with such characteristics as: favourable perception of exporting risks, costs, profits and growth; more positive attitudes towards exporting; aggressiveness and dynamism; flexibility; and self-confidence. As observed by Ford and Leonidou (1991), 'firms with a decision maker perceiving risk in the export market as being lower versus risk in the domestic market, profits in the export market as being higher versus profits in the domestic market, and costs in the export market as being lower versus costs in the domestic market are more likely to become exporters'.

Nevertheless, as Miesenbock (1988) stated, 'the explanatory power of psychologically-oriented research in internationalisation . . . (is) controversial'.

24.6.2 Firm characteristics and competencies

Very few issues in SME internationalisation research have as much empirical support as the positive link between management support, commitment, perceptions and attitude, and internationalisation behaviour. As Aaby and Slater (1989) remarked, 'management commitment and management perceptions and attitudes towards export problems and incentives are good predictors of export (behaviour)'. Studies have also found a much higher propensity to internationalise (export) among firms with market (or organisational) planning or exploration. As Aaby and Slater (1989) concluded, 'the implementation of a process for systematically exploring, analysing, and planning for export seems to be a very powerful discriminator between . . . exporters and non-exporters'.

Findings on the impact of firm size (whether measured by employee number, sales, ownership of capital equipment, financial capability or a combination of criteria) on internationalisation behaviour have been mixed, if not outright controversial. The balance of evidence, however, suggests the importance of size, particularly in initiating international activity. As a general rule, larger firms are more likely to internationalise than small firms. Beyond some point, however, exporting would appear not to be correlated with size, a view corroborated by Withey's (1980) critical mass of 20 employees for crossing the internationalisation threshold. Reid (1982) explained it thus: 'absolute size using traditional indicators (assets, employees, functional specialisation and sales) predominantly affect . . . (small firms') export entry'. The above standard does not, however, apply to SMEs in high-technology, knowledge-intensive and service sectors (Bell, 1994). Indeed, the use of e-commerce and online marketing via the web and Internet is increasingly removing whatever deterrence size brings to internationalisation of SMEs, even in traditional industries (see Chapter 22).

The SME's industry or product type has also been found to influence international market entry. As Tybejee (1994) remarked, industry membership, or the structural characteristics of the industry determine the conditions in which a firm competes and consequently its internationalisation. Garnier (1982), for example, in a study of Canadian printing and electrical industries, reported that 'the most immediate cause of export(ing) . . . is the nature of the product or service offered by the exporting firm'. While SMEs in industries characterised by low skill level, low intrinsic value, bulkiness and high transportation costs are less likely to internationalise, those in sectors marked by short life-cycles are 'motivated to accelerate their entry into the international markets' (Tybejee, 1994; McGuinness and Little, 1981). Another firm characteristic that appears to influence an SME's internationalisation is its history, including previous experience of extra-regional expansion, importing experience or 'inward internationalisation'. Such experiences and attendant (networks) relationships have been found to be significant precursors of internationalisation.

Empirical studies on SME internationalisation have also underscored the importance of firm competencies. It has, indeed, been suggested that 'firm competencies are probably more important than firm characteristics' (Aaby and Slater, 1989). The specific dimensions of firm competency which, on balance, have been empirically supported include: technology intensity; research and development (R&D); systematic market research; product development; unique product attributes and quality; distribution, delivery and service quality; and advertising and sales promotion.

24.6.3 Characteristics of the firm's environment

Relative to larger firms, SMEs tend to lack the necessary resources and political clout to control their operating environment. Empirical findings can broadly be categorised into two: those related to the firm's domestic environment and those concerned with foreign (target) market attractiveness.

As observed by Miesenbock (1988), 'the home country of the firm also determines the performed export behaviour'. The legal system 'may facilitate (e.g. tax advantages in exporting) or complicate (e.g. foreign exchange regulations) international business. The same holds for infrastructure (e.g. distribution facilities or impediments).' The Wiedersheim-Paul *et al.* (1978) model of pre-export behaviour and Garnier's (1982) theoretical model of the export process in a small firm both reflect the impact of the domestic environment. The former suggests that firms' location within an 'enterprise environment' facilitates an efficient exchange of information as well as creating 'possibilities for "contagion transmission" of ideas from other firms, in different stages of expansion'. Garnier (1982) also sees general characteristics of the environment as well as industry in which small firms operate as affecting their decision 'to export or refrain from so doing'. Bilkey (1978) and Pavord and Bogart (1975) identified 'adverse home market conditions' as a push factor in export initiation, one example being 'home market saturation'.

With respect to the foreign (target) market environment, studies have reported foreign government-imposed barriers and poor infrastructure – road and telephone systems – to be significant impediments to export market choice. Ford and Leonidou (1991) concluded that 'firms producing products which have to be modified in order to conform with the rules and regulations of foreign governments . . . are less likely to become exporters'. Further discussions on these and related issues are undertaken in the next section on internationalisation barriers and problems.

24.7 Barriers in SME internationalisation

This section reviews empirical evidence on the obstacles that confront SMEs at different stages in the internationalisation process, including the export initiation stage. Leonidou (1995) defined export barriers as 'all those attitudinal, structural, operational and other constraints that hinder the firm's ability to initiate, develop or sustain international operations'. Different classificatory schemes have been used in the literature with respect to these problems. In an extensive review of export barrier research, Leonidou (1995) combined his earlier framework with Cavusgil's (1984) into a 'two-dimensional export barrier schema' (Kaleka and Katsikeas, 1995). This identified four categories of problems:

- internal-domestic
- internal-foreign
- external-domestic
- external-foreign.

24.7.1 Internal-domestic

These problems encompass obstacles emanating from within the firm, and relating to its home country environment. They include: the lack of personnel with requisite information and knowledge about export marketing, including expertise in handling such problems as foreign government regulations; negative perceptions of risks involved in selling abroad; and management emphasis on developing domestic market activities, particularly large-sized domestic markets.

24.7.2 Internal-foreign

These problems arise mainly from the SME's limited marketing ability and are experienced in the foreign (target) market environment. For some SMEs, international market entry is inhibited if product modifications are required to meet foreign safety or health standards or customers' specifications. As Moini (1997) remarked, 'adapting a product to foreign standards may require a large initial investment which many non-exporters lack'. Similar difficulties have also been reported with regard to providing repair and technical services, pricing as well as communicating with overseas customers. Other typical obstacles here include both high transportation cost and transportation, service and delivery-related difficulties.

24.7.3 External-domestic

These problems emanate from the SME's domestic environment, but are typically beyond its control. Among the most cited obstacles in this category are the vast amount of time and complex documentation involved in international marketing. Also often reported is the absence of adequate government support – incentives and infrastructural – to overcome internationalisation barriers and the lack of reasonable access to (or prohibitive cost of) capital needed to finance internationalisation.

24.7.4 External-foreign

These problems originate from outside the SME and are typically experienced in the international markets. Several studies have reported on the inhibiting impact of foreign government-imposed restrictions, including exchange rate, import and tariff regulations. Equally problematic for the SME is the development of reliable overseas contacts/distributors/representatives, including the overcoming of language and cultural differences. Other often-cited internationalisation barriers in this category are the intensity of competition in international markets or SME's lack of price competitiveness and the difficulties of getting payments.

The nature of a firm's response to these obstacles depends broadly on the background decision-maker and firm characteristics, specifically organisational size, international business experience, international market research orientation and export involvement. Inexperienced exporters, relative to regular exporters, perceived strict import quotas and confusing import regulations as much more important in hindering their entry into the Japanese market (Namiki, 1988). Marginal exporters, compared with their more active counterparts, have significantly different perceptions of shipping complexity, uncertainty of shipping cost and complexity of trade documentation. Similar conclusions were reached by Tesar and Tarleton (1982) in respect of passive and aggressive exporters among their Wisconsin and Virginia sample; and Bell (1997) with regard to occasional, frequent and aggressive exporters.

It appears, also, that firms at different stages of internationalisation face problems of differing types and severity (Bell, 1997; Bilkey, 1978; Bilkey and Tesar, 1977). A three-nation study by Bell (1997), for example, reported that while 'finance-related problems often intensify with increased international exposure . . . marketing-related factors tend to decline as firms become more active in export markets'.

24.8 Policy and institutional support for SME internationalisation

This section highlights the existing policy frameworks and support programmes that underpin SME internationalisation in most OECD countries. Currently used measures can be classified into direct and indirect, in terms of whether they are specifically designed for export development, or with a general aim of enhancing SME overall competitiveness – internationalisation benefits being only implied (Bell, 1994). As observed by Seringhaus and Rosson (1991), direct assistance encapsulates 'an array of programmes that range from awareness-creating, interest-stimulating, research support, export preparation, export market entry, to export market development and expansion-focused activities'. These have been categorised broadly by Crick and Czinkota (1995) into export service programmes (e.g. seminars for potential exporters, export consultancy and export financing) and market development programmes (e.g. dissemination of sales leads to local firms, participation in trade shows and preparation of market analyses). Indirect assistance extends to those aspects described as economic infrastructure (Owualah, 1987), whether hardware (financial, fiscal, and plant and machinery leasing) or software (training, advice and information). They are generally aimed at effecting structural and process change within companies (Seringhaus and Rosson, 1991) and are often integrated into the industrial policy implemented by various governments at central and/or regional levels (Bell, 1994). Such programmes also, increasingly, seek to facilitate the adoption of innovative new technologies and best practices (including networking) among firms. Programmes of direct and indirect support include

- providing access to foreign market information;
- providing some form of financial assistance (export credit or foreign investment guarantees, venture capital, grants and subsidies);
- improving SMEs' capability through management advisory services and help with R&D and technology;

- providing SMEs with a better business environment, by facilitating networking and sub-contracting arrangements and offering simplified, one-stop assistance units, industrial parks and arbitration assistance.

Importantly, the extent of involvement of the government and the private sector in actual support provision varies between countries. While government involvement appears to be dominant in countries such as the UK, Ireland and Canada, others like Finland, Denmark and Germany tend to emphasise private sector leadership in support provision. Yet, a few others, notably France, The Netherlands and Austria, seem to provide highly rated support at both public and private sector levels. Granted that no firm conclusions have been reached regarding the relative merits of public versus quasi-public sector support mechanisms (Bell, 1997), it is safe to suggest that 'delivery systems that make use of existing and potential private sector activities are more likely to be cost-effective' (OECD, 1997a).

Despite the sophistication and comprehensiveness of policy measures available in advanced (as well as developing) economies, empirical findings on SMEs' level of awareness, usage and satisfaction with these programmes have been generally negative. This highlights the challenging nature of the task of seeking to improve SME internationalisation policy – a task the concluding section attempts to address.

24.9 Chapter summary

It would appear from the unremitting pressures of globalisation drivers that the trend towards SME internationalisation can only intensify. The OECD's (1997a) prognosis of a continuing shrinkage in the percentage of SMEs insulated from (inward) globalisation effects implies also that SMEs that ignore internationalisation realities risk losing their competitiveness. This makes it even more imperative that as many SMEs as possible are given whatever support is necessary to encourage their internationalisation.

A consensus appears to have emerged among academic researchers and policy makers that SMEs negotiate varying paths to internationalisation. Having been extensively and successfully challenged, the 'stage' approach would seem to have lost its traditional hegemony to a more inclusive, integrative view of SME internationalisation. This perspective, recently articulated by Bell and Young (1998), presents extant frameworks – incremental models; network-driven, including the accelerated 'born internationals' perspective; and the rationalistic strategy/resource-based models – as complementary rather than competing explanations. It is now clear that while some SMEs internationalise in an incremental manner, others accelerate through the process, driven possibly by their existing network relationships or entrepreneurial factors, and yet others adopt a rational, strategy-based process involving some consideration of relevant internal and external factors. Thus, it behoves policy makers to seek greater understanding of SMEs as the objects of their policy measures. Such an understanding should inform the segmentation of these SMEs for policy-making purposes and subsequently lead to needs-based targeting of appropriate assistance and support.

The idea of segmenting assistance targets is not new in the literature and is integral to the much-criticised stage models. What should, perhaps, be new is the rethinking of the segmentation framework, such that the 'stage-by-stage' approach is seen, not as *the way*, but as one of the ways to internationalise – across a spectrum that includes network-driven, including accelerated internationalisation as well as strategy/resource-based internationalisation. Hopefully, this perspective would translate to a broadening of the focus of programmes supporting SME internationalisation beyond their traditional exporting emphasis (Bell, 1994). Whatever the approach taken, policy makers should recognise the existence of different internationalisation pathways. For incrementally inclined firms, usual methods of assistance targeting based on stages of internationalisation may be appropriate. SMEs at lower stages may need intensive information support and one-to-one counselling to nudge them along their learning curve, while those at more advanced stages may require more experiential-type knowledge and perhaps assistance aimed at easing the financial obstacles facing foreign target customers (Crick and Czinkota, 1995). Proper acknowledgement of the reality of accelerated internationalisation should imply, for example, programmes of support for network building and activation among SMEs. Existing efforts in this direction, at industry, national and regional levels, should be strengthened. It seems appropriate, also, to widen the assistance programmes on offer to reflect a more diversified mix of internationalisation possibilities than is currently the case, such that SMEs who wish to establish joint venture operations overseas or engage in strategic alliances, or even acquire a production plant abroad, would find requisite support and encouragement. Given also the widely appreciated opportunities offered by e-commerce and online marketing, SMEs should be sensitised and supported with appropriate training and consultancy to optimise the benefits of Internet-based internationalisation.

To target SMEs and their decision makers effectively with the appropriate competence-enhancing support, it may be useful to employ a classification scheme built around their current characteristics and competencies, thus: internationalised entrepreneurial firms; internationalised less entrepreneurial firms; non-internationalised entrepreneurial firms; and less internationalised non-entrepreneurial firms (see Figure 24.1).

For the non-internationalised, less entrepreneurial SMEs, the focus should be on improving the entrepreneurial and international orientation of their key decision maker(s) through seminars and workshops, export information provision, sponsorship to trade fairs, and 'experiential knowledge assistance programmes' (Knight *et al.*, 2003). This should also involve introducing an external agent (Wiedersheim-Paul *et al.*, 1978) on a part-time or consultancy basis. Ideally, non-internationalised SMEs, lacking in entrepreneurial orientation, should be assisted in the search for, and employment of, managers with requisite profiles: experienced, internationally orientated and connected decision makers. Other measures that may be useful here include encouraging networking and linking them with foreign customers. The latter could be particularly crucial given the strength of empirical evidence on the impact of unsolicited orders from abroad in stimulating initial internationalisation.

As the name indicates, non-internationalised entrepreneurial SMEs have not yet internationalised but appear to have the right entrepreneurial disposition to do so. This category of firm, by definition, is likely to have top management or key decision makers with the requisite characteristics. Their resource gap may arise from any areas of firm competencies – product quality and technology, market intelligence or intermediaries' network. These areas of resource slack would have to be addressed in order to

Figure 24.1 Recommendations to assist SME internationalisation by SME categories

	Entrepreneurial	Less entrepreneurial
Internationalised	[IV] Encourage best practices – R&D, IT, innovation Facilitate participation in network structures Mitigate operational problems: assist foreign customers, ease market access, etc.	[III] Seek positive reinforcement Deploy liaison officer/problem-solver Encourage networking; export clubs Establish mentoring scheme
Non-internationalised	[II] Assist to redress competency gap Provide consultancy support and training Ease access to available support Introduce mentoring scheme Encourage best practices – R&D, IT, innovation, networking	[I] Introduce change agents Provide training/information support Help with foreign market contacts Encourage networking Establish and utilise international market brokers

Source: Adapted from Ibeh (1998)

enable these firms to internationalise, as they apparently wish to do. Potentially useful support measures may comprise providing access to market survey reports, assisting with consultancy and foreign market contacts and networks, including mentoring relationships.

Internationalised, but less entrepreneurial SMEs are those that have found themselves in the international market, but appear to lack a strong motivation for so doing. Such firms may have started exporting accidentally, through the receipt of unsolicited foreign orders or allied external-reactive stimulus (Albaum et al., 1994). The policy focus here should be on ensuring that such SMEs receive positive reinforcement from their international market experience. Suggested measures include: providing requisite assistance – information, training, counselling; easing operational problems; seconding 'change agents' or helping them to employ more decision makers with requisite qualities; and encouraging private sector organisations to draw them into their networks, hence giving them opportunities for sharing of experiences and learning.

Finally, the policy focus in respect of internationalised entrepreneurial SMEs should be on shoring up their key competencies and renewing their international and entrepreneurial vision. Such firms should be equipped to continually respond to the inevitable competitive challenges of an increasingly globalised market through appropriate adjustments and innovations in products, processes, organisations, markets and technology (Hyvarinen, 1990; OECD, 1997a). Increased attention needs to be given to relationships with key market actors (regular market visits and so on), particularly given the strength of empirical support on the potential benefits of so doing (Styles and Ambler, 1994, 1997; Bell, 1994). SMEs in this category, relatively speaking, need less assistance from the government and its relevant agencies. The direction in which government assistance would, nonetheless, be most appreciated is the minimisation of operational or access problems in foreign markets (Katsikeas, 1994; Morgan and Katsikeas, 1995). This is the standard service provided by government to its businesses, the most notable example, arguably, being the US government's deployment of their might in favour of their international companies. Policy makers can also make a real difference by facilitating sectoral and/or industry-level export cooperative arrangements among SMEs to assist them in meeting the increasingly stiff competition from other regions (Arnould and Gennaro, 1985). The potential benefits of this initiative may be quite immense, extending to cost-sharing in R&D and technology sourcing, more innovative and quality products, better reputation of a country's products in export markets, better leverage in relationships with distributors, agents, government officials (domestic and foreign) and, indeed, a whole lot of other network-related spin-offs (Ibeh, 2000).

Questions

1 An SME can be exposed to relevant stimuli but constrained from internationalising owing to barriers or lack of requisite managerial, organisational and environmental back-up. What implications has this statement for government policy making and support provision?

2 Discuss the following statement: a fuller understanding of SME internationalisation can be gained by focusing on the potential complementarities of existing explanatory frameworks as opposed to the current practice of viewing them as competing alternatives (Bell and Young, 1998).

3 Internationalised SMEs have progressed from being a rarity to a significant exporting presence and are now serious contributors to direct foreign investments, especially the cooperation-based modes. Explain this statement, focusing on the internal (within the firm) and external developments that have furthered SME internationalisation.

4 How do you perceive the future of SME internationalisation over the next five years?

Web links

www.uktradeinvest.gov.uk
Official website of the UK government organisation promoting international trade, jointly operated by the Foreign Office and the DTI.

www.oecd.org
The Organisation for Economic Co-operation and Development has published a number of reports on the impact of globalisation on the small firm sector.

www.export.org.uk/
Website of the Institute for Export, whose mission is to enhance the export performance of the UK by setting and raising professional standards in international trade management and export practice.

www.globalstartups.org
Global Start is a research project that is introducing new tools and mechanisms geared to helping nascent firms develop within the global market.

References and further reading

Aaby, N. and Slater, S. F. (1989), 'Management Influences on Export Performance: A Review of the Empirical Literature 1978–1988', *International Marketing Review*, 6(4): 7–23.

Abell, P., Khalif, H. and Smeaton, D. (1995), 'An Exploration of Entry to and Exit from Self-Employment', Centre for Economic Performance, LSE Discussion paper No. 224.

Abetti, P. A. (1997), 'Underground innovation in Japan: the development of Toshiba's word processor and laptop computer', *Creativity and Innovation Management*, 6(3): 127–39.

Ackerman, P. L. and Heggestad, E. D. (1997), Intelligence, personality, and interests: Evidence of overlapping traits, *Psychological Bulletin*, 121(2): 219–45.

Ackerman, P. L. and Humphreys, L. G. (1990), 'Individual differences theory in industrial and organizational psychology', in M. D. Dunnette and L. M. Hough (eds.), *Handbook of Industrial and Organizational Psychology* (2 ed., 1, 223–82), Palo Alto: Consulting Psychologists Press, Inc.

Ackerman, P. L., Kanfer, R. and Goff, M. (1995), 'Cognitive and noncognitive determinants and consequences of complex skill acquisition', *Journal of Experimental Psychology: Applied*, 1(4): 270–304.

ACOST (1990), *The Enterprise Challenge: Overcoming Barriers to Growth in Small Firms*, Advisory Council on Science and Technology, Cabinet Office, London: HMSO.

Acs, Z. J. (1999), 'Public policies to support new technology-based firms (NTBFs)', *Science and Public Policy*, 26(4): 247–57.

Acs, Z. J., Arenius, P., Hay, M. and Minniti, M. (2005), *Global Entrepreneurship Monitor 2004 Executive Report*, Babson Park, MA: Babson College.

Acs, Z. J. and Audretsch, D. B. (1989), 'Entrepreneurial Strategy and the Presence of Small Firms', *Small Business Economics*, 1: 193–213.

Acs, Z. J. and Audretsch, D. B. (1990), *Innovation and Small Firms*, Cambridge, MA: MIT Press.

Acs, Z. J. and Audretsch, D. B. (1991), *Innovation and Technological Change: An International Comparison*, Ann Arbor: University of Michigan Press.

Acs, Z. J. and Audretsch, D. B. (eds.) (2003), *Handbook of Entrepreneurship Research*. Volume 1: An Interdisciplinary Survey and Introduction, Dordrecht: Kluwer.

Acs, Z. J., Audretsch, D. B. and Carlsson, B. (1991), 'Flexible Technology and Firm Size', *Small Business Economics*, 3: 307–19.

Acs, Z. J., Audretsch, D. B. and Feldman, M. P. (1994), 'R&D Spillovers and Recipient Firm Size', *Review of Economics and Statistics*, 100(2): 336–67.

Adair, J. (1986), *Effective Team Building*, Aldershot: Gower Publishing Co. Ltd.

Adair, J. (1990), *The Challenge of Innovation*, Guildford: Talbot Adair Press.

Adams, E. M., Day G. S. and Dougherty, D. (1998), 'Enhancing new product development performance: An organizational learning perspective', *Journal of Product Innovation Management*, 15: 403–22.

Afuah, A. and Tucci, C. (2001), *Internet Business Models and Strategies*, New York, NY: McGraw-Hill.

Ahl, H. (2002), *The Making of the Female Entrepreneur*. JIBS Dissertation Series No.015, Jönkoping: Jönkoping International Business School.

Ainsworth, S. and Cox, J. W. (2003), 'Families Divided: Culture and Control in Small Family Business', *Organization Studies*, 24(9): 1463–85.

Ajzen, I. (1991), 'The theory of planned behavior', *Organizational Behavior and Human Decision Processes*, 50: 179–211.

Ajzen, I. (1995), 'Attitudes and behavior', in A. S. R. Manstead and M. Hewstone (eds.), *The Blackwell Encyclopedia of Social Psychology*, Oxford, UK: Blackwell Publishing Ltd, 52–7.

Albaum, G., Strandstov, J., Duerr, E. and Dowd, L. (1994), *International Marketing and Export Management*, 2nd ed., Wokingham: Addison-Wesley.

Aldrich, H. E. (1979), *Organisations and Environments*, Englewood Cliffs, NJ: Prentice Hall.

Aldrich, H. E. (1987), 'The Impact of Social Networks on Business Founding and Profit: A Longitudinal Study', in *Frontiers of Entrepreneurship Research*, Wellesley, Mass: Babson College.

Aldrich, H. E. (1989), 'Networking among women entrepreneurs', in O. Hagen, C. Rivchum and D. Sexton (eds.), *Women owned businesses*, New York: Praeger, 103–32.

Aldrich, H. E. and Auster, E. (1986), 'Even Dwarfs Started Small: Liabilities of Age and Size and their Strategic Implications', in *Research in Organizational Behavior* 8, ed.: B. M. Staw, L. L. Cummings. Greenwich: JAI Press, 165–98.

Aldrich, H. E., Cater, J., Jones, T. and McEvoy, D. (1981), 'Business Development and Self-Segregation: Asian Enterprise in Three British Cities', in C. Peach, V. Robinson and S. Smith (eds.), *Ethnic Segregation in Cities*, London: Croom Helm, 170–90.

Aldrich, H. E., Cater, J., Jones, T. and McEvoy, D. (1982), 'From Periphery to Peripheral: The South Asian Petite Bourgeoisie in England', in I. Simpson and R. Simpson (eds.), *Research in the Sociology of Work*, 2: 1–32.

Aldrich, H. E., Cater, J., Jones, T. and McEvoy, D. and Velleman, P. (1985), 'Ethnic Residential Concentration and the Protected Market Hypothesis', *Social Forces*, 63: 996–1009.

Aldrich, H. E. and Cliff, J. (2003), 'The Pervasive Effects of Family on Entrepreneurship: Toward a Family Embeddedness Approach', *Journal of Business Venturing*, 18(5): 573–97.

Aldrich, H. E., Jones, T. and McEvoy, D. (1984), 'Ethnic Advantage and Minority Business Development', in R. Ward and R. Jenkins (eds.), *Ethnic Communities in Business*, Cambridge: Cambridge University Press, 189–210.

Aldrich, H. E., Reese, P. and Dubini, P. (1989), 'Women on the Verge of a Breakthrough: Networking Among Entrepreneurs in the United States and Italy'. *Entrepreneurship and Regional Development*, 1: 339–56.

Aldrich, H. E., Renzulli, L. and Laughton, N. (1997), *Passing on privilege: resources provided by self-employed parents to their self-employed children*. paper presented at the American Sociological Association.

Aldrich, H. E., Rose, B. and Woodward, W. (1986), 'Social Behaviour and Entrepreneurial Networks', in *Frontiers of Entrepreneurship Research*, Mass: Wellesley, 239–40.

Aldrich, H. E. and Sakano, T. (1995), 'Unbroken Ties: How the Personal Networks of Japanese Business Owners Compare to Those in Other Nations', in M. Fruin (ed.), *Pacific Rim Investigations*, New York: Oxford University Press, 17–45.

Aldrich, H. E. and Whetten, D. (1981), 'Organisation-Sets, Action-Sets, and Networks: Making the Most of Simplicity', in P. Nystrom and W. Starbuck (eds.), *Handbook of Organizational Design*, Volume One, New York: Oxford University Press, 385–408.

Aldrich, H. E. and Zimmer, C. (1986), 'Entrepreneurship Through Social Networks', in D. L. Sexton and R. W. Wilson (eds.), *The Art and Science of Entrepreneurship*, Mass: Ballinger, 154–67.

Allen, J. (1992), 'Fordism and modern industry', in *Political and Economic Forms of Modernity*, Cambridge: Polity Press.

Allen, S. and Truman, C. (1988), *Women's work and success in women's businesses*, paper presented to 11th UK National Small Firms Policy and Research Conference, Cardiff Business School.

Almor, T. and Hashai, N. (2004), 'The competitive advantage and strategic configuration of knowledge-intensive, small- and medium-sized multinationals: a modified resource-based view', *Journal of International Management*, 10(4): 479–500.

Alt, R. and Zimmerman, H. (2001), 'Introduction to Special Section – Business Models', *EM: Electronic Markets*, 11(1).

Alter, K. (2000), *Managing the Double Bottom Line: A Business Planning Reference Guide for Social Enterprises*, Washington: PACT Publications.

Alter, S. (2002), *Case Studies in Social Entrepreneurship*, Washington: Counterpart International.

Alter, S. (2003), *Social Enterprise: A Typology of the Field Contextualized in Latin America*, Washington: IDB.

Alvarez, S. A. and Barney, J. B. (2004), 'Organizing Rent Generation and Appropriation: Toward a Theory of The Entrepreneurial Firm', *Journal of Business Venturing*, 19(5): 621–35.

Alvesson, M. and Skoldberg, K. (2000), *Reflexive Methodology: New Vistas for Qualitative Research*, London: Sage.

Amabile, T. M., Hill, K. G., Hennesey, B. A. and Tighe, E. M. (1994), 'The work preference inventory: Assessing intrinsic and extrinsic motivational orientations', *Journal of Personality and Social Psychology*, 66(5): 950–67.

Amin, A. (1989), 'Flexible Specialisation and Small Firms in Italy: Myths and Realities', *Antipode*, 21(1): 13–34.

Amin, A. and Thrift, N. (1995), 'Globalisation, institutional "thickness" and the local economy', 92–108 in P. Healey, S. Cameron, S. Davoudi, S. Graham and A. Madani-Pour (eds.), *Managing Cities: The New Urban Context*, Chichester: John Wiley.

Amit, R., Branser, J. and Zott, C. (1998), 'Why do venture capital firms exist? Theory and Canadian evidence', *Journal of Business Venturing*, 13: 441–66.

Amit, R., Brander, J. and Zott, C. (2000), 'Venture capital financing entrepreneurship: theory, empirical evidence and a research agenda', in D. L. Sexton and H. Landström (eds.), *The Blackwell Handbook of Entrepreneurship*, Oxford: Blackwell, 259–81.

Amit, R. and Zott, C. (2001), 'Value Creation in eBusiness', *Strategic Management Journal*, 22: 493–520.

Amor, D. (2000), *The E-Business (R)evolution: Living and Working in an Interconnected World*, Upper Saddle River, NY: Prentice Hall.

Anderson, J. (1995), *Local Heroes*, Glasgow: Scottish Enterprise.

Anderson, O. (1993), 'On the Internationalisation Process of Firms: A Critical Analysis', *Journal of International Business Studies*, Second Quarter, 209–31.

Anderson, O. and Strigel, W. H. (1981), 'Business Surveys and Economic Research – A Review of Significant Developments', in H. Laumer and M. Ziegler (eds.), *International Research on Business Cycle Surveys*, Munich, 25–54.

Anderson, P. and Tushman, M. (1990), 'Technological discontinuities and dominant designs: a cyclical model of technological change', *Administrative Science Quarterly*, 35: 604–33.

Antoncic, B. and Hisrich, R. D. (2003), 'Clarifying the intrapreneurship concept', *Journal of Small Business and Enterprise Development*, 10(1): 7–24.

Appell, A. L. (1984), *A Practical Approach to Human Behaviour in Business*, Columbus Ohio: Charles E. Merrill Publishing Co.

Argyris, C. and Schon, D. A. (1978), *Organizational learning: A theory of action perspective*, Reading, MA: Addison-Wesley.

Armington, C. and Acs, Z. J. (2002), 'The Determinants of Regional Variation in New Firm Formation', *Regional Studies*, 36(1): 33–45.

Arndt, J. (1967), 'Word-of-Mouth Advertising and Informal Communication', in Cox, D. (ed.), *Risk Taking and Information Handling in Consumer Behaviour*, Boston, MA: Harvard University.

Arnold, G. (1998), *Corporate Financial Management*, Financial Times Pitman Publishing.

Arnould, O. and Gennaro, E. (1985), 'Enhancing the market for new products and services by export co-operation between innovative SMEs', in *Developing markets for new products and services through joint exporting by innovative SMEs*, Commission of the European Committee Report EUR 9927, 27–32.

Arrow, K. (1983), 'Innovation in small and large firms', in J. Ronen (ed.), *Entrepreneurship*, Lexington, MA: Lexington Books, 15–38.

Arthur Andersen/Singapore Trade Development Board (1997), *Franchising in Asia-Pacific*.

Asante, M. K. and Mattson, M. T. (1992), *Historical and Cultural Atlas of African Americans*, New York: Macmillan Publishing Company.

Astrachan, J. H., Klein, S. B. and Smyrnios, K. X. (2002), 'The F-PEC Scale of Family Influence: A Proposal for Solving the Family Business Definition Problem', *Family Business Review*, 15(1): 45–58.

Atkin, R. and Eseri, M. (1993), *Informal investment – investor and investee relationships*, paper to the 16th National Small Firms Policy and Research Conference, Nottingham, 17–19 November.

Atkinson, J. and Storey, D. (1994), *Employment, the Small Firm and the Labour Market*, London, Routledge.

Atuahene-Gima, K. (1992), 'Inward technological licensing as an alternative to internal R&D in new product development: A conceptual framework', *Journal of Product Innovation Management*, 9(2): 156–67.

Audit Commission (1989), *Urban regeneration and economic development: The local government dimension*, London: HMSO.

Audit Commission (1999), *A Life's Work: Local Authorities, Economic Development and Economic Regeneration*, Audit Commission, London.

Audretsch, D. B. (1995), *Innovation and Industry Evolution*, Cambridge: MIT Press.

Audretsch, D. B., Thurik, R., Verheul, I. and Wennekers, S. (2002), *Entrepreneurship: Determinants and Policy in a European–US Comparison*, Boston, Dordrecht, London: Kluwer Academic Publishers.

Auster, E. (1990), 'The Interorganizational Environment: Network Theory, Tools, and

Applications', in F. Williams and D. Gibson (eds.), *Technology Transfer: A Communication Perspective*, Sage, 63–89.

Austin, J., Stevenson, H. and Wei-Skillen, J. (2003), *Social Entrepreneurship and Commercial Entrepreneurship: Same, Different, or Both?*, Harvard Business School Working paper.

Ayayi, A. (2004), 'Public Policy and Venture Capital: The Canadian Labor-Sponsored Venture', *Capital Funds, Journal of Small Business Management*, 42(3): 335–45.

Backes-Gellner, N. (2000), Wettbewerbfaktor Fachkrafte – Rekrutierungschancen und probleme von kleineren und mittleren Unternehmen, (Skilled Employees as a Competitive Factor), Garbler Edition Wissenschaft: Schriften zur mittelschandsforschung, Institut für Mittelstandsforschung, Bonn.

Baden-Fuller, C. and Stopford, J. (1992), 'Organisational Strategies for Building Corporate Entrepreneurship', in P. Lorange, B. Chakravarthy, J. Roos and A. van den Ven (eds.), *Implementing Strategic Processes: Change, Learning and Co-Operation*, Oslo Conference volume.

Bagozzi, R. P. and Kimmel, S. K. (1995), 'A comparison of leading theories for prediction of goal-directed behaviours', *British Journal of Social Psychology*, 34: 437–61.

Bagozzi, R. P. and Warshaw, P. R. (1992), 'An examination of the etiology of the attitude-behavior relation for goal-directed behaviors', *Multivariate Behavioral Research*, 27(4): 601–34.

Baines, S. and Wheelock, J. (1998a), 'Working for Each Other: Gender, the Household and Micro-Business Survival and Growth', *International Small Business Journal*, 17(1): 16–35.

Baines, S. and Wheelock, J. (1998b), 'Reinventing Traditional Solutions: Job Creation, Gender and the Micro-Business Household', *Work, Employment and Society*, 12(4): 579–601.

Baines, S., Wheelock, J. and Oughton, E. (2002), 'A Household Based Approach to the Small Business Family', in Fletcher, D. (ed.), *Understanding the Small Family Business*, London: Routledge, 168–79.

Bakan, J. (2004), *The Corporation: The Pathological Pursuit of Profit and Power*, New York: Constable and Robinson.

Baker, E. B. and Sinkula, J. M. (1999), 'The synergistic effect of market orientation and learning orientation on organizational performance', *Journal of the Academy of Marketing Science*, 27(4): 411–27.

Baker, T., Aldrich, H. E. and Liou, N. (1997), 'Invisible entrepreneurs: the neglect of women business owners by mass media and scholarly journals in the USA', *Entrepreneurship and Regional Development*, 9(3): 221–38.

Baker, T., Miner, A. and Eesley, D. (2003), 'Improvising firms: bricolage, account giving and improvisational competencies in the founding process', *Research Policy*, 32: 255–76.

Baker, W. H., Adams, L. and Davis, B. (1993), 'Business Planning in Successful Small Firms', *Long Range Planning*, 26(6): 82–8.

Baldwin, C. Y. and Clark K. B. (2000), *Design Rules, Volume 1, The Power of Modularity*. Cambridge. MA: MIT Press.

Baldwin, T. F., McVoy, D. S. and Steinfield, C. (1996), *Convergence – Integrating Media, Information and Communication*, Thousand Oaks: Sage.

Baldwin, W. L. and Scott, J. T. (1987), *Market Structure and Technological Change*, London and New York: Harwood Academic Publishers.

Balkin, D. B. and Logan, J. W. (1988), 'Reward policies that support entrepreneurship', *Compensation and Benefits Review*, 20(1): 18–25.

Bamberger, I. (1989), 'Developing competitive advantage in small and medium-sized firms', *Long Range Planning*, 22(5): 80–8.

Bandura, A. (1982), 'The psychology of chance encounters and life paths', *American Psychologist*, 37(7): 747–55.

Bandura, A. (1986), *Social Foundations of Thought and Action: A Social Cognitive Theory*. Englewood Cliffs, NJ: Prentice-Hall.

Bandura, A. (1991), 'Social cognitive theory of self-regulation', *Organizational Behavior and Human Decision Processes*, 50: 248–87.

Bandura, A. (1995), 'Perceived self-efficacy', in A. S. R. Manstead and M. Hewstone (eds.), *The Blackwell Encyclopedia of Social Psychology*, 434–36. Oxford, UK: Blackwell Publishers Ltd.

Bank of England (1996), *Finance for Small Firms: A Third Report*, Bank of England, London.

Bank of England (2001), *Finance for Small Firms – An Eighth Report*, Domestic Finance Division.

Bank of England (2002), *Quarterly Bulletin*, Spring.

Bank of England (2004), *Finance for Small Firms – An Eleventh Report*, Domestic Finance Division.

BankBoston (1997), *MIT: The Impact of Innovation*, Boston, BankBoston Economics Department.

Bankman, J. and Gilson, R. (1999), 'Why start-ups?' *Stanford Law Review*, 51: 289.

Bannock, G. (1981), *The Economics of Small Firms*, Oxford: Basil Blackwell.

Bannock, G. (1990), *Taxation in the European Community: The Small Business Perspective*, London: Paul Chapman.

Bannock, G. and Peacock, A. (1989), *Government and Small Business*, London: Paul Chapman.

Barker, R. G. and Gump, P. V. (1964), *Big School, Small School*. Stanford, CA: Stanford University Press.

Barkham, R., Gudgin G., Hart M. and Hanvey E. (1996), *The Determinants of Small Firm Growth: an Inter-Regional Study in the UK 1986–90*, London and Bristol, Penn.: Jessica Kingsley Publishers.

Barnett, F. and Barnett, S. (1988), *Working together: entrepreneurial couples*, Berkeley, CA: Ten Speed Press.

Barney, J. B. (1991), 'Firm resources and sustained competitive advantage', *Journal of Management*, 17(1): 99–120.

Barney, J. B. (1997), *Gaining and Sustaining Competitive Advantage*. Menlo Park, CA.: Addison Wesley.

BarNir, A. and Smith, K. (2002), 'Interfirm alliances in the small business: the role of social networks', *Journal of Small Business Management*, 40(3): 219–32.

Baron, R. A. (1998), 'Cognitive mechanisms in entrepreneurship: why and when entrepreneurs think differently than other people', *Journal of Business Venturing*, 13: 275–94.

Baron, R. A. (2004), 'The cognitive perspective: a valuable tool for answering entrepreneurship's basic "why" questions', *Journal of Business Venturing*, 19: 221–39.

Baron, R. A. and Markman, G. D. (2003), 'Beyond social capital: the role of entrepreneurs' social competence in their financial success', *Journal of Business Venturing*, 18: 41–60.

Barrett, G. (1999), 'Overcoming obstacles: Access to bank finance for African-Caribbean enterprise', *Journal of Ethnic and Migration Studies*, 25(2): 303–22.

Barrett, G., Jones, T. and McEvoy, D. (1996), 'Ethnic Minority Business: Theoretical Discourse in Britain and North America', *Urban Studies*, 33(4/5): 783–809.

Barrett, G., Jones, T. and McEvoy, D. (2003), 'United Kingdom: severely constrained entrepreneurialism', in Kloosterman R. and Rath J. (eds.), *Immigrant Entrepreneurship: Venturing Abroad in the Age of Globalisation*, Oxford: Berg.

Barrett, R. and Rainnie, A. (2002), 'What's so special about small firms? Developing an integrated approach to analysing small firm industrial relations', *Work, Employment and Society*, 16(3): 415–33.

Barry, B. (1989), 'Development of Organization Structure', *Family Business Review*, II(3): 293–315, Autumn 1989.

Barth, H. (2003), 'Fit among competitive strategy, administrative mechanisms, and performance: A comparative study of small firms in mature and new industries', *Journal of Small Business Management*, 41(2): 133–47.

Bartlett, J. (2000), *The Four Horsemen of the New Economy*, fastcompany.com

Basu, A. (1995), 'Asian Small Businesses In Britain: An Exploration Of Entrepreneurial Activity', paper to the Second International Journal Of Entrepreneurial Behaviour and Research Conference, Malvern, 18–20 July.

Basu, A. (1998), 'An Exploration of Entrepreneurial Activity among Asian Small Businesses in Britain', *Small Business Economics*, 10(4): 313–26.

Basu, D. (1991), 'Afro-Caribbean Businesses in Great Britain: Factors Affecting Business Success and Marginality', unpublished PhD Thesis, Manchester Business School.

Bates, T. (1994a), reported in: *The Franchise Update Report*, Issue 94-1.

Bates, T. (1994b), 'An analysis of Korean immigrant-owned small business startups with comparisons to African American and nonminority-owned firms'. *Urban Affairs Quarterly*, 30(2): 227–48.

Baum, J. R. and Locke, E. A. (2004), 'The relationship of entrepreneurial traits, skill, and motivation to subsequent venture growth', *Journal of Applied Psychology*, 89(4): 587–98.

Baum, R. J., Locke, E. A. and Kirkpatrick, S. A. (1998), 'A longitudinal study of the relation of vision and vision communication to venture growth in entrepreneurial firms', *Journal of Applied Psychology*, 83(1): 43–54.

Baumback, C. and Mancuso, P. (1993), *Entrepreneurship and venture management*, London: Prentice Hall.

Baumol, W. J. (1990), 'Entrepreneurship: Productive, unproductive and destructive', *Journal of Political Economy*, 98(5): 893–921.

Beardwell, I., Holden, L. and Claydon, T. (2004), *Human Resource Management: A Contemporary Approach*, London: Prentice Hall.

Beckhard, R. and Dyer, W. G. (1983), 'Managing Change in the Family Firm – Issues and Strategies', *Sloan Management Review*, 24: 59–65.

Beehr, T. A., Drexler, J. A. and Faulkner, S. (1997), 'Working in Small Family Businesses: Empirical Comparisons to Non-Family Businesses', *Journal of Organizational Behavior*, 18(3): 297–312.

Beesley, M. and Rothwell, R. (1987), 'Small Firm Linkages in the UK', in R. Rothwell and J. Bessant (eds.), *Innovation, Adaptation and Growth*, Amsterdam: Elsevier.

Begley, T. M. and Boyd, D. P. (1987), 'Psychological characteristics associated with performance in entrepreneurial firms and smaller businesses', *Journal of Business Venturing*, 2: 79–93.

Bell, C. G. (1991), *High-Tech Ventures: The Guide for Entrepreneurial Success*, Reading, Massachusetts: Addison Wesley.

Bell, J. (1995), 'The Internationalisation of Small Computer Software Firms – a further challenge to "stage" theories', *European Journal of Marketing*, 29(8): 60–75.

Bell, J. (1997), 'A Comparative Study of the Export Problems of Small Software Exporters in Finland, Ireland and Norway', *International Business Review*, 6(6): 585–604.

Bell, J. and Young, S. (1998), 'Towards an Integrative Framework of the Internationalisation of the Firm', in Hooley, G., Loveridge, R. and Wilson, D. (eds.), *Internationalisation: Process, Context and Markets*, London: Macmillan.

Bell, J., Crick, D. and Young, S. (1998a), 'Holistic Perspective on Small Firm Internationalisation', Proceedings of the AIB (UK Chapter) Conference, April.

Bell, J., Crick, D. and Young, S. (1998b), 'Resource Dependency Theory and Small Firm Internationalisation: An Exploratory Approach'.

Bell, J., Crick, D. and Young, S. (2004), 'Small Firm Internationalisation and Business Strategy: An exploratory study of knowledge intensive and traditional manufacturing firms in the UK', *International Small Business Journal*, 22 (Issue 1): 23–54.

Bell, J., Mcnaughton, R., Young, S. and Crick, D. (2003), 'Towards an Integrative Framework of Small Firm Internationalisation', *Journal of International Entrepreneurship*, 1(4): 339–62.

Bell, J. D. (1994), 'The Role of Government in Small-Firm Internationalisation: A Comparative Study of Export Promotion in Finland, Ireland, and Norway, with Specific Reference to the Computer Software Industry', Unpublished PhD Thesis, Department of Marketing, University of Strathclyde, Glasgow.

Bellu, R. R. (1988), 'Entrepreneurs and managers: are they different?', in B. A. Kirchhoff, W. A. Long, W. E. McMullan, K. H. Vesper and W. E. J. Wetzel (eds.), *Frontiers of Entrepreneurship Research*, 16–30, Wellesey, MA: Babson College.

Bellu, R. R. (1993), 'Task role motivation and attributional style as predictors of entrepreneurial performance: female sample findings', *Entrepreneurship and Regional Development*, 5: 331–44.

Bellu, R. R. and Sherman, H. (1995), 'Predicting firm success from task motivation and attributional style: A longitudinal study', *Entrepreneurship and Regional Development*, 349–63.

Benjamin, G. A. and Margulis, J. B. (2000), *Angel Financing: How to Find and Invest in Private Equity*, New York: Wiley.

Bennett, M. (1989), *Managing Growth*, NatWest Small Business Shelf, London: Pitman, 85–114.

Bennett, R. J. (1995), *Meeting business needs in Britain*, London: British Chambers of Commerce.

Bennett, R. J. (1997a), 'SMEs, Business Associations and their contribution to business competitiveness', paper presented to the 20th National Small Firms Policy and Research Conference, Belfast, November.

Bennett, R. J. (1997b), 'The Relations Between Government and Business Associations in Britain: An evaluation of recent developments', *Policy Studies*, 18(1): 5–33.

Bennett, R. J. (1999), 'Business associations: their potential contribution to government policy and the growth of small and medium-sized enterprises', *Environment and Planning C: Government and Policy*, 17: 593–608.

Bennett, R. J. and Errington, A. (1995), 'Training and the rural small business', *Planning, Practice and Research*, 10(1): 45–54.

Bennett, R. J. and Krebs, G. (1991), *Local economic development: Public-private partnership initiatives in Britain and Germany*, London: Belhaven.

Bennett, R. J. and Krebs, G. (1994), 'Local Economic Development Partnerships: An analysis of policy networks in EC-LEDA Local Employment Development Strategies', *Regional Studies*, 28: 119–40.

Bennett, R. J. and McCoshan, A. (1993), *Enterprise and Human resource development: Local capacity building*, London: Paul Chapman Publishing.

Bennett, R. J. and Payne, D. (2000), *Local and Regional Economic development: Renegotiating power under Labour*, Aldershot: Ashgate.

Bennett, R. J. and Robson, P. J. (1999a), 'The use of external business advice by SMEs in Britain', *Entrepreneurship and Regional Development*, 11: 155–80.

Bennett, R. J. and Robson, P. J. (1999b), 'Business Link: use, satisfaction and comparison with Business Connect', *Policy Studies*, 20(2): 107–32.

Bennett, R. J. and Robson, P. J. (2000), 'The Small Business Service: business support, use, fees and satisfaction', *Policy Studies*, 21(3): 173–90.

Bennett, R. J. and Robson, P. J. (2003), 'Business Link: use, satisfaction and the influence of local governance regime', *Policy Studies*, 24(4): 163–86.

Bennett, R. J. and Robson, P. J. (2004), 'Support services to SMEs: does the "franchisee" make a difference to the Business Link Offer?', *Environment and Planning C: Government and Policy*, 22: 859–80.

Bennett, R. J. and Robson, P. J. (2005), 'The advisor – SME client relationship: impact, satisfaction and commitment', *Small Business Economics*, forthcoming.

Bennett, R. J., Robson, P. J. and Bratton, W. J. (2001), 'Government advice networks for SMEs: an assessment of the influence of local context or Business Link use, impact and satisfaction', *Applied Economics*, 33: 871–85.

Bennett, R. J., Wicks, P. J. and McCoshan, A. (1994), *Local Empowerment and Business Services: Britain's Experiment with TECs*, London: UCL Press.

Berg, N. G. (1997), 'Gender, place and entrepreneurship', *Entrepreneurship and Regional Development*, 9(3): 259–68.

Berry, A. and Simpson, J. (1993), 'Financing Small and Medium Sized Businesses and the Role of Factoring – The View of Accountants and User Companies', Brighton Business School Research papers, Brighton University.

Berry, A., Citron, D. and Jarvis, R. (1987), 'The Information Needs of Bankers dealing with Large and Small Companies', The Chartered Association of Certified Accountants Research Report No. 7, London.

Berry, A., Faulkner, S., Hughes, M. and Jarvis, R. (1993a), *Bank Lending: Beyond the Theory*, London: Chapman and Hall.

Berry, A., Faulkner, S., Hughes, M. and Jarvis, R. (1993b), 'Financial Information: The Banker and the Small Business', *British Accounting Review*, 25(2).

Berry, A., Grant, P. and Jarvis, R. (2004), *Can European Banks Plug the Finance Gap for UK SMEs?*, ACCA Research Report No.81, ACCA, London.

Berry, A., Jarvis, R., Lipman, H. and Macallan, H. (1990), *Leasing and the Smaller Firm*, ACCA Occasional paper No. 3, The Chartered Association of Certified Accountants, London.

Berry, M. (1997), 'Government objectives and the "model" trade association', in R. J. Bennett (ed.) Chapter 9, Trade Associations in Britain and Germany: responding to internationalisation and the EU, Anglo-German Foundation, London and Bonn.

Berry, R. H., Crum, R. E. and Waring, A. (1993), *Corporate Performance Appraisal in Bank Lending Decisions*, London: CIMA.

Berry, R. H. and Waring, A. (1995), 'A user perspective on "Making Corporate Reports Valuable"'. *British Accounting Review*, 27: 139–52.

Berryman, J. (1993), 'Small Business Failure and Bankruptcy: a Survey of the Literature', *International Small Business Review*, 1.

Better Regulation Task Force (2000), *Helping small firms cope with regulations*, Cabinet Office, London.

Better Regulation Task Force (2002a), *Annual Report*, Cabinet Office, London.

Better Regulation Task Force (2002b), *Local Delivery of Central Policy*, Cabinet Office, London.

Better Regulation Task Force (2003), *Government: Supporter or Customer?*, Cabinet Office, London.

Better Regulation Task Force (2004), *The challenge of culture change*, Cabinet Office, London.

Bhave, M. P. (1994), 'A process model of entrepreneurial venture creation', *Journal of Business Venturing*, 9: 223–42.

Bhidé, A. V. (1992), 'Bootstrap finance: the art of start-ups', *Harvard Business Review*, 70: 109–17.

Bhidé, A. V. (1994), 'How Entrepreneurs Craft Strategies that Work', *Harvard Business Review*, 72(2): 150–62.

Bhidé, A. V. (2000), *The origin and evolution of new businesses*, New York: Oxford University Press.

Bierly, E. P. and Chakrabarti, A. (1996), 'Generic knowledge strategies in the U.S. pharmaceutical industry', *Strategic Management Journal*, 17 (Winter Special Issue): 123–35.

Bierly, E. P. and Daly, P. (2004), 'Sources of external organizational learning in small manufacturing firms'. Babson-Kauffman Entrepreneurship Research Conference, Glasgow, Scotland.

Bierly, E. P. and Hamalainen, T. (1995), 'Organizational learning and strategy', *Scandinavia Journal of Management*, 11(3): 209–24.

Biggadike, R. (1976), 'Corporate Diversification: Entry, Strategy and Performance', Division of Research, Graduate School of Business Administration, Harvard University, Boston, MA.

Bilkey, W. J. (1978), 'An Attempted Integration of the Literature on the Export Behaviour of Firms', *Journal of International Business Studies*, 9 (Spring/Summer): 33–46.

Bilkey, W. J. and Tesar, G. (1977), 'The Export Behaviour of Smaller-sized Wisconsin Manufacturing Firms', *Journal of International Business Studies*, 8(1): 93–8.

Binks, M. R. and Ennew, C. T. (1991), 'Banks and the provision of finance to small businesses', in J. Stanworth and C. Gray (eds.), *Bolton 20 years on: The small firm in the 1990s*, London: Paul Chapman Publishing, 50–75.

Binks, M. R., Ennew, C. T. and Reed, G. V. (1988), 'The Survey by the Forum of Private Business on Banks and Small Firms', in G. Bannock and E. V. Morgan (eds.), *Banks and Small Businesses: A Two Nation Perspective*, London: Forum of Private Business/National Federation of Small Business.

Binks, M. R., Ennew, C. T. and Reed, G. V. (1990a), *Small Business and their Banks 1990*, Knutsford: Forum of Private Business.

Binks, M. R., Ennew, C. T. and Reed, G. V. (1990b), 'Finance Gaps and Small Firms', paper presented to the Royal Economics Society Annual Conference, Nottingham.

Binks, M. R., Ennew, C. T. and Reed, G. V. (1993), *Small Business and their Banks*, 1992, Knutsford: Forum of Private Business.

Birch, D. (1979), 'The Job Generation Process', MIT Programme on Neighbourhood and Regional Change, Massachusetts, USA.

Birch, D. (1981), 'Who Creates Jobs?', *The Public Interest*, 65: 3–14.

Birch, D., Haggerty, A. and Parsons, W. (1997), *Who's Creating Jobs*, Cambridge, Mass.: Cognetics, Inc.

Bird, B. and Brush, C. (2002), 'A Gendered Perspective on Organizational Creation', *Entrepreneurship Theory and Practice*, 26(3): 41–65.

Bird, B., Welsch, H., Astrachan J. H. and Pistrui, D. (2002), 'Family Business Research: The Evolution of an Academic Field', *Family Business Review*, 15(4): 337–50.

Birkinshaw, J. (1997), 'Entrepreneurship in multinational corporations: the characteristics of subsidiary initiatives', *Strategic Management Journal*, 18(3): 207–29.

Birley, S. (1985), 'The Role of Networks in the Entrepreneurial Process', *Journal of Business Venturing*, 1: 107–17.

Birley, S. (1989), 'Female entrepreneurs: are they really any different?', *Journal of Small Business Management*, January: 32–36.

Birley, S. and Cromie, S. (1988), 'Social Networks and Entrepreneurship in Northern Ireland', paper Presented at the Enterprise in Action Conference, Belfast.

Birley, S. and Macmillan, I. (eds.) (1995), *International Entrepreneurship*, London: Routledge.

Birley, S. and Stockley, S. (2000), 'Entrepreneurial Teams and Venture Growth', in D. Sexton and H. Landstrom (eds.), *The Blackwell Handbook of Entrepreneurship*, Oxford: Blackwell.

Birley, S., Cromie, S. and Myers, A. (1991), 'Entrepreneurial Networks: Their Emergence in Ireland and Overseas', *International Small Business Journal*, 9(4): 56–74.

Birley, S., Myers, A. and Cromie, S. (1989), 'Entrepreneurial Networks: Some Concepts and Empirical Evidence', paper Presented at the 12th National Small Firms Policy and Research Conference, The Barbican, London.

Birmingham, C., Busenitz, L. W. and Arthurs, J. D. (2003), 'The escalation of commitment by venture capitalists in reinvestment decisions', *Venture Capital: an international journal of entrepreneurial finance*, 5: 218–30.

Bjenning, B. and Bjärsvik, A. (1999), En marknadsundersökning av en innovationsprodukt: en studie av de potentiella konsumenterna till Husqvarna AB: s automatiska gräsklippare, Auto Mower (Market Research for an Innovative Product: A Study of the Potential Buyer's of Husqvarna's Robotic Lawn Mower, Auto Mower). Bachelor's thesis, Jönköping International Business School, Jönköping.

Bjerke, B. and Hultman, C. M. (2003), 'A dynamic perspective on entrepreneurship, leadership and management as a proper mix for growth', *International Journal of Innovation and Learning*, 1(1): 72–83.

Black, J., DeMeza, D. and Jeffreys, D. (1996), 'House Prices, the Supply of Collateral and the Enterprise Economy', *Economic Journal*, 106(434): 60–75.

Blackburn, R. A., Curran, J. and Jarvis, R. (1990), 'Small Firms and Local Networks: Some Theoretical and Conceptual Explorations', paper

Presented at the 13th National Small firms Policy and Research Conference, Harrogate, November.

Blackburn, R. and Hart, M. (2001), 'Ignorance is bliss, knowledge is blight? Employment rights and small firms', paper to the 24th ISBA National Small Firms Conference, Leicester, November.

Blackburn, R. and McClure, R. (1998), *The Use of Information and Communication Technologies (ICTs) in Small Business Service Firms*. Small Business Research Centre, Kingston Business School, London.

Blair, A. (1996), 'Creating an informal investor syndicate: personal experiences of a seasoned informal investor', R. T. Harrison and C. M. Mason (eds.), *Informal Venture Capital: evaluating the impact of business introduction services*, Hemel Hempstead: Prentice Hall, 156–96.

Blanchflower, D. G. (2004), 'Self-Employment: More May Not Be Better', paper presented at the Conference on Self-Employment organised by The Economic Council of Sweden, March.

Blanchflower, D. G. and Oswald, A. (1991), 'SelfEmployment and Mrs. Thatcher's Enterprise Culture', Centre for Economic Performance, LSE Discussion paper No. 30.

Blaschke, J. and Ersoz, A. (1986), 'The Turkish Economy in West Berlin', *International Small Business Journal*, 4(3): 38–47.

Blaschke, J., Boissevain, J., Grotenberg, H. *et al.* (1990), 'European Trends in Ethnic Business', in R. Waldinger, H. Aldrich, and R. Ward (eds.), *Ethnic Entrepreneurs*, London: Sage, 79–105.

Blau, P. (1977), *Inequality and Heterogeneity*, New York: Free Press.

Bleakley, M., Hay, M., Robbie, K. and Wright, M. (1996), 'Entrepreneurial attitudes to venture capital investment realization: evidence from the UK and France', *Entrepreneurship and Regional Development*, 8: 37–55.

Blili, S. and Raymond, L. (1993), 'Information Technology: Threats and Opportunities for Small and Medium-Sized Enterprises', in *International Journal of Information Management*, 13(6): 439–48.

Block, Z. (1982), 'Can corporate venturing succeed?', *Journal of Business Strategy*, 3(2): 21–33.

Block, Z. and MacMillan, I. (1993), *Corporate venturing, creating new businesses within the firm*, Harvard Business School Press, USA.

Blundel, R. (2002), 'Network Evolution and the Growth of Artisanal Firms: a Tale of Two Regional Cheese Makers', *Entrepreneurship and Regional Development*, 14(1): 1–30.

Blundel, R. K. and Smith, D. (2001), 'Business Networking: SMEs and Inter-Firm Collaboration, a Review of the Research Literature with Implications for Policy', Report to Small Business Service PP03/01, Department of Trade and Industry, Small Business Service, Sheffield.

Boatler, R. (1994), 'Manager Worldmindedness and Trade Propensity', *Journal of Global Marketing*, 8(1): 11127.

Boeker, W. (1989), 'Strategic change: the effects of founding and history', *Academy of Management Journal*, 32: 489–515.

Boissevain, J. (1974), *Friends of Friends: Networks, Manipulations and Coalitions*, Oxford: Basil Blackwell.

Bolton Committee (1971), 'Report of the Committee of Enquiry on Small Firms', Cmnd 4811 London: HMSO.

Bonacich, E. and Modell, J. (1980), *The Economic Basis of Ethnic Solidarity: Small business in the Japanese–American Community*, Berkeley, CA: University of California Press.

Bontis, N., Crossan, M. M. and Hulland, J. (2002), 'Managing an organizational learning system by aligning stocks and flows', *Journal of Management Studies*, 39(4): 437–69.

Boocock, G. and Woods, M. (1997), 'The evaluation criteria used by venture capitalists: evidence from a UK venture capital fund', *International Small Business Journal*, 16(1): 36–57.

Bornstein, D. (1998), 'Changing the world on a shoestring', *Atlantic Monthly*, 281(1): 34–9.

Bornstein, D. (2004), *How To Change The World: Social Entrepreneurs and the Power of New Ideas*, Oxford: Oxford University Press.

Borzaga, C. and Defourny, J. (2001), *The Emergence of Social Enterprise*, New York: Routledge.

Boschee, J. (1995), 'Social Entrepreneurship', *Across the Board*, 32(3): 20–5.

Boschee, J. (2001a), *The Social Enterprise Sourcebook*, Minneapolis: Northland Institute.

Boschee, J. (2001b), 'Eight basic principles for nonprofit entrepreneurs', *Nonprofit World*, July–August: 15–18.

Boschee, J., Emerson, J., Sealey, K. and Sealey, W. (2000), *A Reader in Social Enterprise*, Boston: Pearson

Boswell, J. (1973), *The Rise and Decline of Small Firms*, London: Allen and Unwin.

Bosworth, D. and Jacob, S. C. (1989), 'Management Attitudes, Behaviour and Abilities as Barriers to Growth', in Barber, J., Metcalfe, J. S. and Porteous, M. (eds.), *Barriers to Growth in Small Firms*, London: Routledge, 20–38.

Boubakri, H. (1985), 'Mode de gestion et rein-vestissement chez les commerçants Tunisiens à Paris', *Revue Européenne Des Migrations Internationales*, 1(1): 49–66.

Bouchard, V. (2002), 'Corporate entrepreneurship: lessons from the field, blind spots beyond . . .', Working paper 2002/08, EM Lyon.

Bourdieu, P. (1996), 'On the Family as a Realised Category', *Theory, Culture and Society*, 13(3): 19–26.

Bovaird, T., Hems, L. and Tricker, M. (1995), 'Market Failures in the Provision of Finance and Business Services for Small and Medium Size Enterprises', in *Finance for the Growing Enterprise*, edited by Buckland, R. and Davis, E. W. London: Routledge.

Boyd, N. G. and Vozikis, G. S. (1994), 'The influence of self-efficacy on the development of entrepreneurial intentions and actions', *Entrepreneurship Theory and Practice*, 18(4): 63–77.

Boyle, E. (1994), 'The Rise of the Reluctant Entrepreneurs', *International Small Business Journal*, 12(2): 63–9.

Bracker, J. (1982), 'Planning and financial performance among small entrepreneurial firms: an industry study', Unpublished doctoral dissertation, Georgia State University.

Bracker, J. and Pearson, J. (1986), 'Planning and Financial Performance of Small Mature Firms', *Strategic Management Journal*, 7: 503–22.

Bradach, J. (1994), 'Chains within Chains: The Role of Multi-Unity Franchisees', Proceedings of the 8th Conference of the Society of Franchising, Nevada, 13/14 February.

Brand, A. (1998), 'Knowledge Management and Innovation at 3M', *Journal of Knowledge Management*, 2(1): 17–22.

Brav, A. and Gompers, P. (1997), 'Myth or reality? The long-run underperformance of initial public offerings: evidence from venture capital and non-venture capital-backed companies', *Journal of Finance*, 52: 1791–822.

Brazeal, D. V. (1996), 'Managing an entrepreneurial organizational environment', *Journal of Business Research*, 35(1): 55–68.

Brigham, E. and Smith, K. (1967), 'Cost of capital to the small firm', *The Engineering Economist*, 13(3): 1–26.

Brinckerhoff, P. (2000), *Social Entrepreneurship: The Art of Mission-Based Venture Development*, New York: Wiley.

Brockhaus, R. H. (1980), 'Risk taking propensity of entrepreneurs', *Academy of Management Journal*, 23(3): 509–20.

Brockhaus, R. H. (1982), 'The psychology of the entrepreneur', in C. A. Kent, D. L. Sexton and K. L. Vesper (eds.), *Encyclopedia of Entrepreneurship*, 39–71, Englewoods Cliffs, NJ: Prentice-Hall.

Brogger, J. and Gilmore, D. D. (1997), 'The Matrifocal Family in Iberia: Spain and Portugal compaies', *Ethnology*, 36(1): 13–30.

Brooks, A. (1983), 'Black Businesses In Lambeth: Obstacles To Expansion', *New Community*, 11: 42–54.

Brooks, M. R. and Rosson, P. J. (1982), 'A Study of Behaviour of Small and Medium-sized Manufacturing Firms in Three Canadian Provinces', in Czinkota, M. R. and Tesar, G. (eds.), *Export Management: An International Context*, New York: Praeger Publishers, 39–54.

Brooksbank, R., Kirby, D. and Wright, G. (1992), 'Marketing and Company Performance: An Examination of Medium Sized Manufacturing Firms in Britain', *Small Business Economics*, 4: 221–36.

Brown, B. and Butler, J. E. (1995), 'Competitors as Allies: A Study of the Entrepreneurial Networks in the US Wine Industry', *Journal of Small Business Management*, 33(3): 57–66.

Brown, D. H. and Lockett, N. (2001), 'Engaging SMEs in E-Business: The Role of Intermediaries within eClusters', *EM: Electronic Markets*, 11(1): 52–8.

Brown, D. H. and Lockett, N. (2004), 'The Potential of Critical Applications for Engaging SMEs in E-Business', *European Journal of Information Systems*, 13(1): 21–34.

Brown, D. H. and Lockett, N. (2005), 'An SME Perspective of Vertical Application Service Providers', *International Journal of Enterprise Information Systems*, 1(2).

Brown, L. and McDonald, M. H. B. (1994), Competitive Marketing Strategy for Europe, London: Macmillan, 4.

Bruderl, J. and Preisendorfer, P. (1998), 'Network Support and the Success of Newly Founded Businesses', *Small Business Economics*, 10: 213–25.

Brush, C. G. (1992), 'Research of women business owners: past trends, a new perspective, future directions', *Entrepreneurship Theory and Practice*, 16(4): 5–30.

Brush, C., Carter, N., Greene, P., Gatewood, E. and Hart, M. (2001), 'An Investigation of Women-led Firms and Venture Capital Investment', Report prepared for the US Small Business Administration Office of Advocacy and the National Women's Business Council.

Brush, C. G., Carter, N. M., Greene, P. G., Mart, M. M. and Gatewood, P. (2002), 'The role of social capital and gender in linking financial suppliers and entrepreneurial firms: a framework for future research', *Venture Capital: an international journal of entrepreneurial finance*, 4: 305–23.

Bruton, G., Fried, V. and Hisrich, R. D. (1997), 'Venture capital and CEO dismissal', *Entrepreneurship Theory and Practice*, 21(3): 41–54.

Bryson, J. R., Keeble, D. and Wood, P. (1997), 'The Creation and Growth of Small Business Service Firms in Post-Industrial Britain', *Small Business Economics*, 9: 345–60.

Buchanan, D. (1988), 'Getting in, Getting on, Getting out and Getting back', in Bryman, A. (ed.), *Doing Research in Organisations*, London: Routledge.

Buchanan, J. M. and Di Pierro, A. (1980), 'Cognition, choice, and entrepreneurship', *Southern Economic Journal*, 46: 693–701.

Buckland, R. and Davis, E. W. (1995), *Financing for Growing Enterprises*, London: Routledge.

Burawoy, M. (1979), *Manufacturing Consent: Changes in the labour Process under Monopoly Capitalism*, Chicago: University of Chicago Press.

Burns, P. (1989), 'Strategies for Success and Routes to Failure', in Burns, P. and Dewhurst, J. (eds.), *Small Business and Entrepreneurship*, London: Macmillan, 32–67.

Burt, R. S. (1992), *Structural Holes. The Social Structure of Competition*, Harvard University Press.

Busenitz, L. W., Fiet, J. O. and Moesel, D. D. (2004), 'Reconsidering venture capitalists' "value added" proposition: an interorganisational learning perspective', *Journal of Business Venturing*, 19: 787–807.

Busenitz, L. W., Fiet, J. O. and Moesel, D. D. (2005), 'Signalling in venture capitalist-new venture team funding decisions: does it indicate long-term venture outcomes', *Entrepreneurship Theory and Practice*, 29: 1–12.

Busenitz, L. W., Moesel, D., Fiet, J. O. and Barney, J. B. (1997), 'The framing of perceptions of fairness in the relationship between venture capitalists and new venture teams', *Entrepreneurship Theory and Practice*, 21: 5–21.

Butler, J. E. and Hansen, G. S. (1991), 'Network Evolution, Entrepreneurial Success and Regional Development', *Entrepreneurship and Regional Development*, 3: 1–16.

Buttner, E. H. and Moore, D. P. (1997), 'Women's organizational exodus to Entrepreneurship: self-reported motivations and correlates with success', *Journal of Small Business Management*, January: 34–47.

Buttner, E. H. and Rosen, B. (1988), 'Bank Loan Officers' Perceptions of the Characteristics of Men, Women, and Successful Entrepreneurs', *Journal of Business Venturing*, 3: 249–58.

Buttner, E. H. and Rosen, B. (1989), 'Funding new business ventures: are decision makers biased against women entrepreneurs?', *Journal of Business Venturing*, 4(4): 249–61.

Buzzell, R. D. and Wiersema, F. D. (1981), 'Successful Share-building Strategies', *Harvard Business Review*, 53(1): 135–44.

Bygrave, W. D. (1987), 'Syndicated investments by venture capital firms: a networking perspective', *Journal of Business Venturing*, 2: 139–54.

Bygrave, W. D. (1988), 'The structure of investment networks in the venture capital industry', *Journal of Business Venturing*, 3: 137–54.

Bygrave, W. D., Hay, M., Ng, E. and Reynolds, P. (2003), 'A study of informal investing in 29 nations composing the Global Enterprise Monitor', *Venture Capital: an international journal of entrepreneurial finance*, 5: 101–16.

Bygrave, W. D. and Timmons, J. (1992), *Venture Capital at the Crossroads*, Boston: Harvard Business School Press.

Byrne, D. (1998), 'Class and Ethnicity In Complex Cities – The Cases Of Leicester and Bradford', *Environment and Planning A*, 30: 703–20.

Cabinet Office (1995), *The Government Response to the Deregulation Task Force Report*, 1995.

Cabinet Office (1996a), *Sector Challenge, Bidding Guidance*, Cabinet Office, Office of Public Service, London.

Cabinet Office (1996b), *Competitiveness: Helping Business to Win: The Conclusions of Consultation*, Cabinet Office, Office of Public Service, London.

Cabinet Office (1999), *e-commerce@its.best.uk*, Performance and Innovation Unit, Cabinet Office, UK.

Cable, D. M. and Shane, S. (1997), 'A prisoner's dilemma approach to entrepreneur–venture capitalist relationships', *Academy of Management Review*, 22: 142–76.

Cabrera-Suárez, K., Saá-Pérez, P. D. and García-Almeida, D. (2001), 'The Succession Process from a Resource- and Knowledge-Based View of the Family Firm', *Family Business Review*, 14(1): 37–48.

Calantone, J. R., Cavusil, S. T. and Zhao, Y. (2002), 'Learning orientation, firm innovation capability, and firm performance', *Industrial Marketing Management*, 31: 515–24.

Calder, G. H. (1961), 'The Peculiar Problems of a Family Business', *Business Horizons*, 4(3): 93–102.

Callon, M. (1986), 'The sociology of an Actor-Network', in Callon, M., Law, J. and Rip, A. (eds.), *Mapping the Dynamics of Science and Technology*, Basingstoke: MacMillan, 1–16.

Callon, M. (1999), 'Actor-network theory – the market test', in Law, J. and Hassard, J. (eds.), *Actor Network Theory and After*, Oxford: Blackwell, 35–49.

Caloghirou, Y., Kastelli, I. and Tsakanikas, A. (2004), 'Internal capabilities and external knowledge sources: Complements or substitutes for innovative performance?', *Technovation*, 24: 29–39.

Camagni, R. (1991), 'Local "milieu", uncertainty and innovation networks: towards a new dynamic theory of economic space', in R. Camagni (ed.), *Innovation Networks: spatial perspectives*, London: Belhaven Press.

Cambridge Small Business Research Centre (1992), *The State of British Enterprise*, Department of Applied Economics, University of Cambridge, Cambridge: The Belknap Press.

Campbell, K. (2003), *Smarter Ventures: A survivor's guide to venture capital through the new cycle*, London: FT-Prentice Hall.

Campbell, M. and Daly, M. (1992), 'Self-Employment in The 1990s', *Employment Gazette*, June: 269–92.

Cannon, T. (1992), 'Marketing for Small Business', in Baker, M. J. (ed.), *The Marketing Book*, Oxford: Butterworth-Heinemann.

Cannon, T. and Willis, M. (1981), 'The Smaller Firm in Overseas Trade', *European Small Business Journal*, 1(3): 45–55.

CARF (Campaign against Racism and Fascism) (1997), *Commentary, Race and Class*, 39: 85–95.

Carland, J. W., Hoy, F., Boulton, W. R. and Carland, J. A. C. (1984), 'Differentiating Entrepreneurs from Small Business Owners: A Conceptualisation', *Academy of Management Review*, 9(2): 354–9.

Carlsson, B. (1989), 'Flexibility and the Theory of the Firm', *International Journal of Industrial Organisation*, 7: 179–203.

Carmagini, R. (1991), 'Local "milieu", uncertainty and innovation networks: towards a new dynamic theory of economic space', in

R. Camagni (ed.), *Innovation Networks: Spatial Perspective*, London: Belhaven Press, 121–42.

Carree, M., Van Stel, A., Thurik, R. and Wennekkers, S. (2002), 'Economic Development And Business Ownership: An Analysis Using Data Of 23 OECD Countries In The Period 1976–1996', *Small Business Economics*, 19(3): 271–90.

Carrier, C. (1996), 'Intrapreneurship in small businesses: an exploratory study', *Entrepreneurship Theory and Practice*, 21(1): 5–20.

Carroll, G. and Delacroix, J. (1982), 'Organisational mortality in the newspaper industries of Argentina and Ireland: An ecological approach', *Administrative Science Quarterly*, 27: 169–98.

Carson, D. (1985), 'The Evolution of Marketing in Small Firms', *European Journal of Marketing*, 19(5): 7–16.

Carson, D. (1991), 'Research into Small Business Marketing', *European Journal of Marketing*, 9: 75–91.

Carson, D., Cromie, S., McGowan, P. and Hill, J. (1995), *Marketing and Entrepreneurship in SMEs: An Innovative Approach*, Prentice Hall International.

Carsrud, A., Gaglio, C. and Olm, K. (1987), 'Entrepreneurs-mentors, networks and successful new venture development', *American Journal of Small Business*, 12(2): 13–18.

Carsrud, A. L. and Johnson, R. W. (1989), *Entrepreneurship: a social psychological perspective*. Entrepreneurship and Regional Development, 1: 21–31.

Carter, N. M. and Allen, K. R. (1997), 'Size determinants of women-owned businesses: choice or barriers to resources?', *Entrepreneurship and Regional Development*, 9(3): 211–20.

Carter, N. M., Gartner, W. B. and Reynolds, P. D. (1996), 'Exploring start-up event sequences', *Journal of Business Venturing*, 11: 151–66.

Carter, S. (1993), 'Female business ownership: current research and possibilities for the future', in S. Allen and C. Truman (eds.), *Women in business: perspectives on women entrepreneurs*, London: Routledge, 148–60.

Carter, S. (1999), 'The Economic Potential of Portfolio Entrepreneurship: Enterprise and Employment Contributions of Multiple Business Ownership', *Journal of Small Business and Enterprise Development*, 5(4): 297–306.

Carter, S. and Cannon, T. (1988), 'Female entrepreneurs: a study of female business owners; their motivations, experiences and strategies for success', Department of Employment Research paper No. 65, 1–57.

Carter, S. and Cannon, T. (1992), *Women as entrepreneurs*, London: Academic Press.

Carter, S. and Ram, M. (forthcoming), 'Re-assessing Portfolio Entrepreneurship: Towards a Multidisciplinary Approach', *Small Business Economics*.

Carter, S. and Rosa, P. (1998), 'The financing of male- and female-owned businesses', *Entrepreneurship and Regional Development*, 10(3): 225–41.

Carter, S., Anderson, S. and Shaw, E. (2001), 'Women's business ownership: A review of the academic, popular and internal literature', Report to the Small Business Service, DTI.

Casson, M. (1982), *Entrepreneur: An Economic Theory*. London: Edward Elgar.

Casson, M. (1990), *Entrepreneurship*, Cheltenham: Edward Elgar.

Casson, M. (1994), *The Economics of Business Culture*, Oxford: Clarendon Press.

Castells, M. and Hall, P. (1994), *Technopoles of the World*, London: Routledge.

Catford, J. (1998), 'Social entrepreneurs are vital for health promotion – but they need supportive environments too', *Health Promotion International*, 13(2): 95–7.

Cavanagh, R. E. and Clifford, D. K. (1983), 'Lessons from America's mid-sized growth companies', *The McKinsey Quarterly*, Autumn.

Cavusgil, S. T. (1984), 'Differences Among Exporting Firms Based on their degree of Internationalisation', *Journal of Business Research*, 12(2): 195–208.

Cavusgil, S. T. (1980), 'On the Internationalisation Process of Firms', *European Research*, 8 (November): 273–81.

Cavusgil, S. T. and Zou, S. (1994), 'Marketing Strategy-Performance Relationship: An Investigation of the Empirical Link in Export Market Ventures', *Journal of Marketing*, 58 (January).

CBI (2004), *SME Trends*, London: CBI.

Central Intelligence Agency (1996), *World Factbook*, Washington, DC: Central Intelligence Agency.

Central Intelligence Agency (1996), *World Factbook*, CIA: Washington.

CFDT (1998), Confédération Française Du Travail, Délégation PME, Etude de la délégation sur les relations sociales dans les PME (Research of the CGT on social relations in SMEs), January.

Chaffee, E. (1985), 'Three models of strategy', *Academy of Management Review*, 10: 89–98.

Chaganti, R., DeCarolis, D. and Deeds, D. (1995), 'Predictors of capital structure in small ventures', *Entrepreneurship Theory and Practice*, 20(2): 7–18.

Chakrabati, A. K. and Rubenstein, A. H. (1976), 'Interorganizational transfer of technology – a study of adoption of NASA innovations', *IEEE Transactions on Engineering Management*, 23(1): 20–34.

Chamberlain, N. (1977), *Remaking American Values*, New York: Basic Books.

Chandler, A. (1962), *Strategy and Structure*, Cambridge, Ma: MIT Press.

Chandler, A. D. (1990), *Scale and Scope: the Dynamics of Industrial Capitalism*.

Chandler, A. D. Jr (1997), 'The Computer Industry – The First Half-Century', in *Competing in the Age of Digital Convergence*, ed.: D. B. Yoffie, Boston: Harvard Business School Press, 37–122.

Chandler, G. (1996), 'Business similarity as a moderator of the relationship between pre-ownership experience and venture performance', *Entrepreneurship: Theory and Practice*, 20(3): 51–65.

Chandler, G. N., Dahlqvist, J. and Davidsson, P. (2003), 'Opportunity recognition processes: A taxonomic classification and outcome implications', Academy of Management Meeting. Seattle.

Chaston, I. (1995), 'Small Firm Growth Through the Creation of Value-added Networks', Proceedings of the 18th ISBA National Small Firms Policy and Research Conference, Paisley, 45–57.

Chaston, I. (1996), 'Small Business Networking: Evolving an Appropriate UK National Process Model', paper presented at the 19th 18th ISBA National Small Firms Policy and Research Conference, Birmingham, November.

Chaston, I. and Mangles, T. (1997), 'Small Business Structures and Networking: Identification and Marketing Collaboration Opportunities', paper presented at the MEG Special Interest Group in Entrepreneurial Marketing Meeting, Dublin, January.

Chau, P. and Tam, K. (2000), 'Organizational Adoption of Open Systems: a "Technology-Push, Need-pull" Perspective', *Information and Management*, 37(5): 229–39.

Chell, E. and Baines, S. (2000), 'Networking, Entrepeneurship and Microbusiness Behaviour'. *Entrepreneurship and Regional Development*, 12: 195–215.

Chell, E. and Haworth, J. (1992), 'A Typology of Business Owners and their Orientation towards Growth', in Calay, K., Chell, E., Chittenden, F. and Mason, C. (eds.), *Small Enterprise Development:*

Policy and Practice in Action, London: Paul Chapman.

Chell, E., Haworth, J. and Brearley, S. (1991), *The Entrepreneurial Personality: Concepts, Cases and Categories*, London: Routledge.

Chen, C. C., Gene Greene, P. and Crick, A. (1998), 'Does entrepreneurial self-efficacy distinguish entrepreneurs from managers?' *Journal of Business Venturing*, 13(4): 295–316.

Chen, M. and Hambrick, D. (1995), 'Speed, Stealth and Selective Attack: How Small Firms Differ from Large Firms in Competitive Behaviour', *Academy of Management Journal*, 38(2): 118–27.

CHI Research (2003), *Small Serial Innovators: The Small Firm Contribution to Technical Change*, Washington, 5BA.

Chrisman, J. J., Chua, J. H. and Sharma, P. (2003b), 'Current Trends And Future Directions In Family Business Management Studies: Toward A Theory Of The Family Firm', Part of the Coleman Foundation White paper Series. Available at <http://www.usasbe.org/knowledge/whitepapers/index.asp>.

Chrisman, J. J., Chua, J. H. and Steier, L. P. (2003a), 'An Introduction to Theories of Family Business', *Journal of Business Venturing*, 18(4): 441–8.

Chrisman, J. J., Chua, J. H. and Litz, R. A. (2004), 'Comparing the Agency Costs of Family and Non-Family Firms: Conceptual Issues and Exploratory Evidence', *Entrepreneurship: Theory and Practice*, 28(4): 335–54.

Chrisman, J. J., Chua, J. H. and Litz, R. (2003c), 'A Unified Systems Perspective of Family Firm Performance: An Extension and Integration', *Journal of Business Venturing*, 18: 467–72.

Chrisman, J. J., Chua, J. H. and Zahra, S. A. (2003b), 'Creating Wealth in Family Firms through Managing Resources: Comments and Extensions', *Entrepreneurship: Theory and Practice*, 27(4): 359–65.

Christensen, C. and Bower, J. (1996), 'Customer power, strategic investment, and the failure of leading firms', *Strategic Management Journal*, 17: 197–218.

Chua, J. H., Chrisman, J. and Sharma, P. (1999), 'Defining the Family Business by Behaviour', *Entrepreneurship Theory and Practice*, 23(4): 19–39.

Chua, J. H., Chrisman, J. J. and Steier, L. P. (2003), 'Extending the theoretical horizons of family business research', *Entrepreneurship Theory and Practice*, Summer: 331–8.

Churchill, N. C. and Lewis, V. C. (1983), 'The five stages of small business growth', *Harvard Business Review*, 6(3): 30–9.

Cialdini, R. B. (1988), *Influence: Science and Practice*, HarperCollins Publishers.

Ciavarella, M. A., Buchholtz, A. K., Riordan, C. M., Gatewood, R. D. and Stokes, G. S. (2004), 'The Big Five and venture survival: Is there a linkage?' *Journal of Business Venturing*, 19: 465–83.

Clark, K. and Drinkwater, S. (1998), 'Ethnicity and Self-Employment in Britain', *Oxford Bulletin of Economics and Statistics*, 60: 383–407.

Clark, T. (1995), *Managing consultants: consultancy as the management of impressions*, Buckingham: Open University Press.

Clark, T., Pugh, D. S. and Mallory, G. (1997), 'The Process of Internationalisation in the Operating Firm', *International Business Review*, 6(6): 605–23.

Clegg, C. (2001), *E-Commerce Impacts: A Review of 14 sector studies*, Small Business Service, UK.

Cliff, J. (1998), 'Does One Size Fit All? Exploring the Relationship Between Attitudes Towards Growth, Gender and Business Size', *Journal of Business Venturing*, 13(6): 523–42.

Clutterbuck, D. (1991), 'Everyone Needs a Mentor: fostering talent at work', *2E*, Institute of Personnel Management, London.

Coase, R. (1937), 'The nature of the firm', *Economica N.S.*, 4: 386–405.

Cochrane, A. (1993), *Whatever happened to local government*, Buckingham: Open University Press.

Cockburn, C. (1993), *In the way of Women*, London: Methuen.

Cohen, W. M. and Levin, R. C. (1989), 'Empirical Studies of Innovation and Market Structure', in Richard Schmalensee and Robert Willig (eds.), *Handbook of Industrial Organization*, Volume II, Amsterdam: NorthHolland, 1059–107.

Cohen, W. M. and Levinthal, D. A. (1990), 'Absorptive capacity: a new perspective on learning and innovation', *Administrative Science Quarterly*, 35: 128–52.

Cohn, T. and Lindberg, R. (1972), *How management is different in small companies*, New York: Harper & Row.

Cohn, T. and Lindberg, R. A. (1974), *Survival and Growth: Management Strategies for the Small Firm*, New York: Amacom, 14.

Coleman, S. (2000), 'Access to Capital and Terms of Credit: A Comparison of Men- and Women-Owned Small Businesses', *Journal of Small Business Management*, 38(3): 37–52.

Collins, J. C. and Lazier, W. C. (1993), 'Vision', *ERM*, Spring: 61–75.

Collinson, S. (2000), 'Knowledge Networks for Innovation in Small Scottish Software Firms', *Entrepreneurship and Regional Development*, 12: 217–44.

Collis, J. and Jarvis, R. (2000), *How owner-managers use accounts*, Centre for Business Performance, ICAEW.

Comanor, W. S. (1967), 'Market Structure, Product Differentiation and Industrial Research', *Quarterly Journal of Economics*, 81: 639–57.

COMParative ENtrepreneurship Data for International Analysis (COMPENDIA 2002.1)/ EIM (2003), *COMPENDIA 2000.2: a harmonized data set of business ownership rates in 23 OECD countries*, Zoetermeer: EIM.

Conservative Party (1983), 'Small Firm, Big Future', Conservative Party Pamphlet.

Contractor, F. and Lorange, P. (1988), *Cooperative Strategies in International Business*, Lexington, MA: Lexington Books.

Conway, S. (1994), 'Informal Boundary-Spanning Links and Networks in Successful Technological Innovation', unpublished PhD dissertation. Birmingham, England: Aston Business School.

Conway, S. (1997), 'Informal Networks of Relationships in Successful Small Firm Innovation', in D. Jones-Evans and M. Klofsten (eds.), *Technology, Innovation and Enterprise: The European Experience*, MacMillan, 236–73.

Conway, S. (1998), 'Developing a Classification of Network Typologies', paper presented at the 14th EGOS Colloquium – Subtheme 4: Inter-organisational relations and networks, July.

Conway, S. and Steward, F. (1998), 'Mapping Innovation Networks', *International Journal of Innovation Management*, 2(2): 165–96.

Conway, S., Jones, O. and Steward, F. (2001), 'Realising the Potential of the Social Network Perspective in Innovation Studies', in O. Jones, S. Conway, and F. Steward (eds.), *Social Interaction and Organisational Change: Aston Perspectives on Innovation Networks*, London: Imperial College Press, 349–66.

Cookson, G. (1997), 'Family Firms and business networks: textile engineering in Yorkshire', *Business History*, 39(1): 1–20.

Cooper, A. C. (1970), 'The Palo Alto experience', *Industrial Research*, May: 58–84.

Cooper, A. C. (1973), 'Technical entrepreneurship: what do we know?', *R&D Management*, 3(2): 59–64.

Cooper, A. C., Dunkelberg, W. C. and Woo, C. Y. (1986), 'Optimists and pessimists: 2,994 entrepreneurs and their perceived chances for success', in R. Ronstadt, J. A. Hornaday, R. Peterson, and K. H. Vesper (eds.), *Frontiers of Entrepreneurship Research*, 563–77, Babson Park, MA: Center for Entrepreneurial Studies, Babson College.

Cooper, A. C., Willard, G. and Woo, C. (1986), 'Strategies of high-performing new and small firms: A re-examination of the niche concept', *Journal of Business Venturing*, 1: 247–60.

Cooper, R. B. and Zmud, R. W. (1990), 'Information Technology Implementation Research: A Technological Diffusion Approach', in *Management Science*, 36(2): 123–39.

Cooper, R. G. and Kleinschmidt, E. J. (1994), 'Determinants of timeliness in product development', *Journal of Product Innovation Management*, 11 (December): 381–96.

Cooper, S. Y. (1996), 'Small high technology firms: a theoretical and empirical study of location issues', unpublished PhD thesis, Edinburgh, Heriot-Watt University, Department of Business Organisation.

Cooper, S. Y. (1997a), 'Technological and behavioural influences in the location of high technology small firms', 585–604 in *Generating growth: Proceedings of 20th National Small Firms Policy and Research Conference*, Belfast, Leeds, Institute of Small Business Affairs.

Cooper, S. Y. (1997b), 'You take the high road and I'll take the low road: contrasting routes to entrepreneurship in high technology small firms', Paper presented to IntEnt97, the 7th International Entrepreneurship Conference, Monterey, California, 25–27 June.

Cooper, S. Y. (1998), 'Entrepreneurship and the location of high technology small firms; implications for regional development', 245–67, in R. P. Oakey (eds.), *New technology based firms in the 1990s*, London: Paul Chapman.

Cooper, S. Y. (2001a), 'Inter-organisational relationships and firm size', in M. Tayeb (ed.), *International Business Partnerships: Issues and Concerns*, London: Macmillan, 153–76.

Cooper, S. Y. (2001b), 'Commercialisation and regional economic development: universities and their role in the emergence of new technologies', in W. During, R. P. Oakey and S. Kauser (eds.), *New Technology-Based Firms in the New Millennium*, London: Pergamon, 191–205.

Cope, J., Cave, F. and Eccles, S. (2004), Attitudes of venture capitalists towards entrepreneurs with previous business failure, *Venture*

Capital: an international journal of entrepreneurial finance, 6: 147–72.

Copeland, F. (1992), 'Inventing a tape that breathes', *R&D Innovator*, 1(2).

Copp, C. and Ivy, R. (2001), 'Networking Trends of Small Tourism Businesses in Post-Socialist Slovakia', *Journal of Small Business Management*, 39(4): 345–53.

Corbetta, G. and Salvato, C. (2004), 'Self-Serving or Self-Actualizing? Models of Man and Agency Costs in Different Types of Family Firms. A Commentary on "Comparing the Agency Costs of Family and Non-family Firms: Conceptual Issues and Exploratory Evidence," by Chrisman, J. J., Chua, J. H. and Litz, R. A., *Entrepreneurship Theory and Practice*, 28(4): 355–62.

Corner, J. and Harvey, S. (1991), *Enterprise and Heritage*, London: Routledge.

Corney, M. (1997), 'Beauty contest to woo the favour of small businesses', *Times Educational Supplement*, 28 February.

Cosh, A. and Hughes, A. (eds.) (1996), *The Changing State of British Enterprise*, Cambridge: ESRC Centre for Business Research, University of Cambridge.

Cosh, A. and Hughes, A. (eds.) (1997), *Enterprise Britain*, Cambridge: ESRC Centre for Business Research, University of Cambridge.

Cosh, A. and Hughes, A. (eds.) (2000), *British Enterprise in Transition*, Cambridge: CBR.

Cosh, A. and Hughes, A. (eds.) (2003), *Enterprise Challenged: policy and performance in the British SME sector 1999–2002*, University of Cambridge, ESRC Centre of Business Research.

Costa, M. and Duffy, M. (1991), 'Trade Union Strategy in the 1990s', *Economic and Labour Relations Review*, 1(1): 6–29.

Coulson-Thomas, C. (1999), 'Individuals and enterprise: developing intrapreneurs for the new millennium', *Journal: Industrial and Commercial Training*, 31(7): 258–61.

Coveney, P. and Moore, K. (1998), *Business Angels: Securing Start-Up Finance*, Chichester: Wiley.

Coviello, N. and Munro, H. (1995), 'Growing the Entrepreneurial Firm: Networking for International Marketing Development', *European Journal of Marketing*, 29(7): 49–61.

Coviello, N. and Munro, H. (1997), 'Network Relationships and the Internationalisation Process of Small Software Firms', *International Business Review*, 6(4): 361–86.

Covin, J. and Slevin, D. (1991), 'A conceptual model of entrepreneurship as firm behaviour', *Entrepreneurship Theory and Practice*, Fall: 7–25.

Cowling, M., Samuels, J. and Sugden, R. (1991), *Small Firms and Clearing Banks*, Report Prepared for the Association of British Chambers of Commerce.

Cox, A. and Hines, P. (1997), *Advanced Supply Management: the Best Practice Debate*, UK: Earlsgate Press.

Cox, C. and Jennings, R. (1995), 'The foundations of success: the development and characteristics of British entrepreneurs and intrapreneurs', *Leadership and Organisational Development Journal*, 16(7): 4–9.

Coyne, R. D., Sudweeks, F. and Haynes, D. (1996), 'Who Needs the Internet? Computer-Mediated Communication in Design Firms', in *Environment and Planning B*, 23(6): 749–70.

Cragg, P. B. and King, M. K. (1988), 'Organisational Characteristics and Small Firms' Performance Revisited', *Entrepreneurship Theory and Practice*, Winter: 49–64.

Cragg, P. B. and King, M. K. (1993), 'Small Firm Computing: Motivators and Inhibitors', *MIS Quarterly*, 17(1): 47–60.

Cravens, D., Piery, N. and Shipp, S. (1996), 'New Organisational Forms for Competing in Highly Dynamic Environments: the Network Paradigm', *British Journal of Management*, 7: 203–18.

Creigh, S., Roberts, C., Gorman, A. and Sawyer, P. (1986), 'Self-Employment in Britain: Results from the Labour Force Surveys 1981–1984', *Employment Gazette* (June issue): 183–94.

Cressy, R. (1996), *Small Business Failure: Failure to Fund or Failure to Learn?*, Centre for SMEs, University of Warwick, Coventry.

Cressy, R. (2000), *Tax assistance, compliance and the performance of the smaller business*, Federation of Small Businesses, London.

Cressy, R. and Storey, D. J. (1996), *New Firms and Their Bank*, Nat West/Warwick SME Centre, University of Warwick.

Crick, D. (1995), 'An investigation into the targeting of UK export assistance', *European Journal of Marketing*, 29(8): 76–94.

Crick, D. and Chaudhry, S. (1995), 'Export Practices of Asian SMEs: some preliminary findings', *Marketing Intelligence and Planning*, 13(11): 13–21.

Crick, D. and Czinkota, M. R. (1995), 'Export Assistance: Another look at whether we are supporting the best programmes', *International Marketing Review*, 12(3): 61–72.

Cromie, S. (1990), 'The Problems Experienced by Young Firms', *International Small Business Journal*, 9(3): 43–61.

Cromie, S. and Hayes, J. (1988), 'Towards a typology of female entrepreneurs', *Sociological Review*, 36(1): 87–113.

Crosier, K. (1975), 'What Exactly is Marketing?', *Quarterly Review of Marketing*, 1(2).

Cross, J. (1994), 'Franchising Failures: Definitional and Measurement Issues', Proceedings of the 8th Conference of the Society of Franchising, Nevada, 13/14 February.

Cross, J. and Walker, B. (1987), 'Services Marketing and Franchising: A Practical Business Marriage', *Business Horizons*, 30: 10–20.

Cross, J. and Walker, B. (1988), 'Franchise Failures: More Questions than Answers', Proceedings of the 2nd Conference of the Society of Franchising, California, 31 January/1 February.

Cross, M. and Waldinger, R. (1992), 'Migrants, Minorities and the Ethnic Division of Labour', in S. Feinstein, I. Gordon and M. Harloe (eds.), *Divided Cities: New York and London In The Contemporary World*, Cambridge, MA: Blackwell.

Crossick, G., Haupt, H. G. and Merriman, J. (1996), 'The Petite Bourgeoisie in Europe, 1780–1914: enterprise, family and independence', *Economic History Review*, XLIX(3): 619–20.

Cruickshank, D. (2000), *Competition in UK Banking: A Report to the Chancellor of the Exchequer*, HMSO.

Csikszentmihalyi, M. (1992), *Flow – The Psychology of Happiness*, London: Rider.

Cully, M., O'Reilly, A., Millward, N., Forth, J., Woodland, S., Dix, G. and Bryson, A. (1999), *The 1998 Workplace Employee Relations Survey*, London: Routledge.

Culnan, M. J. and Swanson, E. B. (1986), *Research in Management Information Systems, 1980–1984: Points of Work and Reference*, in MIS Quarterly, 10: 289–302.

Curran, J. (1986a), *Bolton fifteen years on: a review and analysis of small business research in Britain 1971–1986*, London: Small Business Research Trust.

Curran, J. (1986b), 'The Survival Of The Petit Bourgeoisie: Production and Reproduction', in J. Curran, J. Stanworth and D. Watkins (eds.), *The Survival of The Small Firm*, Aldershot: Gower, 204–27.

Curran, J. (1988), 'Training and Research Strategies for Small Firms', *Journal of General Management*, 13(3).

Curran, J. (1990), 'Rethinking Economic Structure: Exploring the Role of the Small Firm and Self Employment in the British Economy', *Work, Employment and Society*, May: 125–46.

Curran, J. (1991), 'Employment and Employee Relations', in J. Stanworth and C. Gray (eds.), *Bolton, 20 Years On: The Small Firm in the 1990s*, London: PCP.

Curran, J. (1993), 'TECs and Small Firms: Can TECs reach the small firms other strategies have failed to reach?' paper presented to the All Party Social Science and Policy Group, House of Commons, London, 17 April.

Curran, J. (1997), *The Role of the Small Firm in the UK Economy*, Kingston, Kingston University.

Curran, J. and Burrows, R. (1986), 'The Sociology of Petit Capitalism: A Trend Report', *Sociology*, 20(2): 265–79.

Curran, J. and Blackburn, R. (1990), *Small Firms and Local Economic Networks: A Report to Midland Bank*, Kingston-upon-Thames, Small Business Research Centre, Kingston Business School.

Curran, J. and Blackburn, R. (1991), 'Small firms and networks:methodological strategies: some findings', *International Small Business Journal*, 11(2): 13–25.

Curran, J. and Blackburn, R. (1992), *Small Business Survey*, February, Small Business Research Centre, Kingston University.

Curran, J. and Blackburn, R. (1993), *Ethnic Enterprise and The High Street Bank*, Kingston Business School, Kingston University.

Curran, J. and Blackburn, R. (1994), *Small Business and Local Economy Networks: The Death of the Local Economy?*, London: Paul Chapman.

Curran, J. and Burrows, R. (1988a), 'Ethnicity and Enterprise: A National Profile', paper presented to the 11th Small Firms Policy and Research Conference, Cardiff.

Curran, J. and Burrows, R. (1988b), *Enterprise in Britain: a national profile of small business owners and the self-employed*, London: Small Business Research Trust.

Curran, J. and Burrows, R. (1989), 'National Profiles of the Self-Employed', *Employment Gazette* (July issue): 376–85.

Curran, J. and Stanworth, J. (1979), 'Self Selection and the Small Firm Worker – A Critique and an alternative view', *Sociology*, 13(4): 427–44.

Curran, J. and Stanworth, J. (1979a), 'Self Selection and the small firm worker – a critique and an alternative view', *Sociology*, 13(3): 427–44.

Curran, J. and Stanworth, J. (1979b), 'Work involvement and social relations in the small firm', *Sociological Review*, 27(2): 317–42.

Curran, J. and Stanworth, J. (1981a), 'Size of workplace and attitudes to industrial relations in the printing and electronics industries', *British Journal of Industrial Relations*, 19(1): 14–25.

Curran, J. and Stanworth, J. (1981b), 'A new look at job satisfaction in the small firms', *Human Relations*, 34(5): 343–65.

Curran, J. and Storey, D. (2002), 'Small business policy in the UK: the injeritance of the Small Business Service and implications for its future effectiveness', *Environment and Planning C: Government and Policy*, 20: 163–78.

Curran, J., Blackburn, R. and Kitching, J. (1995), 'Small Business, Networking and Networks: A Literature Review', *Policy Survey and Research Agenda*, Small Business Research Centre, Kingston University.

Curran, J., Blackburn, R., Kitching, J. and North, J. (1996), *Establishing Small Firms' Training Practices, Needs, Difficulties and Use of Industry Training Organisations*, DfEE Research Studies RS17, London: HMSO.

Curran, J., Jarvis, R., Blackburn, R. A. and Black, S. (1993), 'Networks and Small Firms: Constructs, Methodological Strategies and Some Findings', *International Small Business Journal*, 11(2): 13–25.

Curran, J., Kitching, J., Abbot, V. and Mills, V. (1993), 'Employment and employment relations in the small service sector enterprise – a report', ESRC Centre for research on small service sector enterprises, Kingston Business School.

Curran, J., Stanworth, J. and Watkins, D. (1986), *The Survival of the Small Firm*, Vols I and II, Aldershot: Gower.

Currie, W. (2002), 'Application Outsourcing: A New Business Model for Enabling Competitive Electronic Commerce', *International Journal of Services and Technology Management*, 3(2): 139–53.

Currie, W. (2004), *Value Creation from e-Business Models*, Oxford: Elsevier Butterworth-Heinemann.

Currie, W., Desai, B. and Khan, N. (2004), 'Customer evaluation of application services provisioning in five vertical sectors', *Journal of Information Technology*, 19(1): 39–58.

Curtis, D. A. (1983), *Strategic Planning for Smaller Businesses*, Lexington Books, Toronto.

Cyert, R. M. and March, I. G. (1963), *A Behavioural Theory of the Firm*, Englewood Cliffs, NJ: Prentice-Hall.

Czinkota, M. R. and Johnston, W. J. (1982), 'Exporting: Does Sales Volume Make a Difference? – A Reply', *Journal of International Business Studies*, 16(2): 157–61.

Czinkota, M. R. and Ursic, M. L. (1987), 'A Refutation of the Psychic Distance Effect on Export Development', *Developments in Marketing Science*, 10: 157–60.

Daft, R. L. and Lengel, R. H. (1986), 'Organizational Information Requirement, Media Richness and Structural Design', in *Management Science*, 32(5): 554–71.

Dahlqvist, J., Chandler, G. N. and Davidsson, P. (2004), 'Patterns of search and the newness of venture ideas', paper presented at the Babson College/Kauffman Foundation Entrepreneurship Research Conference, Glasgow.

Daily, C. M. and Dollinger, M. J. (1993), 'Alternative Methodologies for Identifying Family – Versus Non-Family Managed Businesses', *Journal of Small Business Management*, April: 79–90.

Dalgic, T. and Leeuw, M. (1994), 'Niche Marketing Revisited: Concept, Applications and Some European Cases', *European Journal of Marketing*, 20(1): 39–55.

Daly, M. (1991a), 'The 1980s: A Decade Of Growth In Enterprise', *Employment Gazette*, March: 109–34.

Daly, M. (1991b), 'VAT Registrations and De-registrations in 1990', *Employment Gazette*, November: 579–88.

Daniel, W. and Milward, N. (1983), *Workplace Industrial Relations in Britain, The DE/PSI/ SSRC Survey*, London: Heinemann.

Das, T. K. and Teng, B.-S. (1997), 'Time and entrepreneurial risk behavior', *Entrepreneurship Theory and Practice*, 22(2): 69–88.

David, B. L. (1993), 'How internal venture groups innovate', *Research Technology Management*, 37(2): 38–45.

Davidson, W. and Dutia, D. (1991), 'Debt, Liquidity, and Profitability Problems in Small Firms', *Entrepreneurship Theory and Practice*, Fall: 53–64.

Davidsson, P. (1989a), *Continued Entrepreneurship and Small Firm Growth*, Stockholm School of Economics, The Economic Research Institute.

Davidsson, P. (1989b), 'Entrepreneurship – And After? A Study of Growth Willingness in Small Firms', in *Journal of Business Venturing*, 4(3): 211–26.

Davidsson, P. (1994), *Husqvarna Forest and Garden (A Marketing Case)*, Mimeo, Jönköping, Jönköping International Business School.

Davidsson, P. (1995), 'Determinants of entrepreneurial intentions'. paper presented at the Rent IX Conference, Piacenza, Italy.

Davidsson, P. (2000), 'Three cases in opportunity assessment: the Sports Bra, the Solar Mower, and A Decent Cup of Coffee', *Mimeo*. Brisbane: Queensland University of Technology.

Davidsson, P. (2003), 'The domain of entrepreneurship research: Some suggestions', in J. Katz and D. Shepherd (eds.), *Advances in Entrepreneurship, Firm Emergence and Growth: Cognitive Approaches to Entrepreneurship Research*, 6: 315–72. Oxford, UK: Elsevier/JAI Press.

Davidsson, P. (2004), *Researching Entrepreneurship*, New York: Springer.

Davidsson, P. and Delmar, F. (1997), 'High Growth Firms: Characteristics, Job Contribution and Method Observations', paper presented at RENT XI conference, Mannheim, Germany, November 27–8.

Davidsson, P. and Honig, B. (2003), 'The role of social and human capital among nascent entrepreneurs', *Journal of Business Venturing*, 18(3): 301–31.

Davidsson, P. and Klofsten, M. (2003), 'The Business Platform: Developing an instrument to gauge and assist the development of young firms', *Journal of Small Business Management*, 41(1): 1–26.

Davies, P. and Stern, D. (1980), 'Adaptation, Survival, and Growth of the Family Business: An Integrated Systems Perspective', *Human Relations*, 34(4): 207–24.

Davies, S. (1995), 'Training policy and practice in Wales and North-Rhine-Westphalia', in P. Cloke (ed.), *The Rise of the Rustbelt*, London: UCL Press.

Davis, F. D. (1989), 'Perceived Usefulness, Ease of Use, and User Acceptance of Information Technology', in *MIS Quarterly*, 13(3): 319–39.

Davis, G. B. (1980), 'The Knowledge and Skill Requirements for the Doctorate in MIS', in 1st Annual International Conference on Information Systems, Proceedings, Philadelphia, December 1980: 174–86.

Davis, P. (1983), 'Realising the Potential of the Family Business', *Organizational Dynamics*, Summer: 47–56.

Davis, P. and Stern, D. (1988), 'Adaptation, Survival and Growth of the Family Business: An Integrated Systems Perspective', *Family Business Review*, I(1), Spring: 69–85.

Day, S. G. (1994), 'Continuous learning about markets', *California Management Review*, 36 (Summer): 9–31.

Day, S. G. and Nedungadi, P. (1994), 'Managerial representations of competitive advantage', *Journal of Marketing*, 58 (April): 31–44.

de Koning, A. (2003), 'Opportunity development: a socio-cognitive perspective', in J. Katz and D. Shepherd (eds.), *Advances in Entrepreneurship, Firm Emergence and Growth. Cognitive Approaches to Entrepreneurship Research*, 6: 265–314. Oxford, UK: Elsevier/JAI Press.

Deacon, B. (1992), *The New Eastern Europe*, London: Sage.

Deakin, N. and Edwards, J. (1993), *The Enterprise Culture and the Inner City*, London: Routledge.

Deakin, S. and Morris, G. (1995), *Labour Law*, London: Butterworth.

Deakins, D. (1996), *Entrepreneurs and Small Firms*, London: McGraw-Hill.

Deakins, D. and Freel, M. (1997), 'Entrepreneurial Learning and the Growth Process in SMEs', paper presented to the 4th ECLO International Conference, Sophia Antipolis, France, May.

Deakins, D. and Hussain, G. (1994), 'Risk Assessment with Asymmetric Information', *International Journal of Bank Marketing*, 12(1): 24–31.

Deakins, D. and Hussain, G. (1994), 'Financial Information, The Banker, and the Small Business: A Comment', *British Accounting Review*, 26(4).

Deakins, D., Graham, L., Sullivan, R. and Whittam, G. (1997), 'New Venture Support: an analysis of mentoring support for new and early stage entrepreneurs', paper presented to the 20th ISBA National Small Firms Policy and Research Conference, Belfast, November.

Deakins, D., Hussain, G. and Ram, M. (1994), *Ethnic Entrepreneurs and Commercial Banks: Untapped Potential*, Birmingham: University of Central England Business School.

Deakins, D., Majmudar, M. and Paddison, A. (1997), 'Developing Success Strategies for Ethnic Minorities in Business: Evidence from Scotland', *New Community*, 23(3): 325–42.

Deakins, D., Mileham, P. and O'Neill, E. (1998), 'The Role and Influence of Non-Executive Directors in Growing Small Firms', paper presented to Babson Entrepreneurship Research Conference, Ghent, Belgium.

Deakins, D., Mileham, P. and O'Neill, E. (1999), *The Role and Influence of Non-Executive Directors in Growing Small Firms*, ACCA research report, ACCA, London.

Deakins, D., Ram., M. and Smallbone, D. (2003), 'Addressing the Business Support needs of Ethnic Minority Firms in the United Kingdom',

Government and Policy, Environment and Planning C, 21: 843–59.

Deakins, D. (1996), *Entrepreneurship and Small Firms*, London: McGraw-Hill.

DeBrabander, B. and Thiers, G. (1984), 'Successful Information System Development in Relation to Situational Factors which Affect Effective Communication between MIS-Users and EDP-Specialists', in *Management Science*, 30(2): 137–55.

Decarolis, M. D. and Deeds, D. L. (1999), 'The impact of stocks and flows of organizational knowledge on firm performance: An empirical investigation of the biotechnology industry', *Strategic Management Journal*, 20: 953–68.

December, J. (1996), 'Units of Analysis for Internet Communication', in *Journal of Communication*, 46(1): 14–38.

Deci, E. L. (1992a), 'On the nature and functions of motivation theories', *Psychological Science*, 3(3): 167–71.

Deci, E. L. (1992b), 'The relation of interest to the motivation of behavior: A self-determination theory perspective', in K. A. Renninger, S. Hidi and A. Krapp (eds.), *The role of interest in learning and development*, 43–70, Hillsdale, New Jersey: Erlbaum.

Dees, J. G. (1994), *Social Enterprise: Private Initiatives for Common Good*, Harvard: Harvard Business School Press.

Dees, J. G. (1996), *The Social Enterprise Spectrum: from Philanthropy to Commerce*, Harvard: Harvard Business School Press.

Dees, J. G. (1998a), *The Meaning of Social Entrepreneurship* at http://faculty.fuqua.duke.edu/centers/case/files/dees-SE.pdf

Dees, J. G. (1998b), 'Enterprising Nonprofits', *Harvard Business Review*, 76(1): 54–67.

Dees, J. G. (2003), 'Social Entrepreneurship Is about Innovation and Impact, Not Income', discussion paper on *Social Edge*, available at: http://skoll.socialedge.org/?293@218.2JjfaI3NaTC.0@.1ad86d9e

Dees, J. G. and Battle Anderson, B. (2002), 'Blurring Sector Boundaries: Serving Social Purposes Through For-Profit Structures', CASE Working paper Series, 2. Duke Fuqua School.

Dees, J. G., Battle Anderson, B., Wei-Skillern, J. (2004), 'Scaling Social Impact', *Stanford Social Innovation Review*, Spring: 24–32.

Dees, J. G. and Elias, J. (1998), 'The Challenges of Combining Social and Commercial Enterprise', an essay on Norman Bowie's University-Business Partnerships: an Assessment, *Business Ethics Quarterly*, 8(1): 1–17.

Dees, J. G., Emerson, J. and Economy, P. (2001), *Enterprising Non-profits: A Toolkit for Social Entrepreneurs*, New York: Wiley Non-Profit Series.

Dees, J. G., Emerson, J. and Economy, P. (2002), *Strategic Tools for Social Entrepreneurs: Enhancing the Performance of Your Enterprising Non-profit*, New York: Wiley Non-Profit Series.

Delmar, F. (1996), *Entrepreneurial Behavior and Business Performance*, Stockholm: Stockholm School of Economics, Economic Research Institute.

Delmar, F. (1997), 'Measuring growth: methodological considerations and empirical results', in R. Donckels and A. Miettinen (eds.), *Entrepreneurship and SME Research: On its Way to the Next Millennium*, 199–216, Aldershot, England: Ashgate.

Delmar, F. and Holmquist, C. (2004), *Women's Entrepreneurship: Issues and Policies*, Paris: OECD.

Delmar, F. and Shane, S. (2003a), 'Does business planning facilitate the development of new ventures?', *Strategic Management Journal*, 24: 1165–85.

Delmar, F. and Shane, S. (2003b), 'Does founder experience matter? The effect of human capital on the sales of newly founded firms', Working paper, Stockholm: Stockholm School of Economics.

Delmar, F. and Shane, S. (2003c), 'Does the order of organizing activities matter for new venture performance?', in P. D. Reynolds *et al.* (ed.), *Frontiers of Entrepreneurship 2003*, Wellesley, MA: Babson College.

DeLone, W. H. (1988), 'Determinants of Success for Computer Usage in Small Business', in *MIS Quarterly*, 12(1): 51–61.

DeLone, W. H. and McLean, E. R. (1992), 'Information Systems Success: The Quest for the Dependent Variable', in *Information Systems Research*, 3: 60–95.

Dempsey, J., Dvorak, R. E., Holen, E., Mark, D. and Meehan, W. F. (1998), 'A Hard and Soft Look at IT Investment', in *McKinsey Quarterly*, 1: 126–37.

Dennis, C. (2000), 'Networking for marketing advantage', *Management Decision*, 38(4): 287–92.

Department for Education and Employment (1988), *Labour Market Quarterly Report*, May.

Department of Employment (1988), *Employment For The 1990s*, Cmnd, 540, London: HMSO.

Department for Employment (1990), *Think big ... buy small: guidelines on purchasing from small firms*, Department of Employment, London.

Department for Trade and Industry (1992), *A prospectus for One-Stop shops for Business*, London: DTI.

Department for Trade and Industry (1995), *Competitiveness: Helping Smaller Firms*, London: DTI.

Department for Trade and Industry (1996a), *A guide to help for Small Firms*, London: DTI.

Department for Trade and Industry (1996b), *The model Trade Association*, London: DTI.

Department for Trade and Industry (1996c), *Personal Business Advisers: Policy guidelines*, London: DTI.

Department for Trade and Industry (1996d), *Small Firms in Britain Report 1996*, London: DTI.

Department of Trade and Industry (1998a), *Our competitive future: Building the knowledge driven economy*, Cm. 4176, London: HMSO.

Department for Trade and Industry (1998b), *Competitiveness White paper: Building the Knowledge Driven Economy*, London: DTI.

Department for Trade and Industry (1998c), *Our Competitive Future*, Cm4176, London, DTI.

Department for Trade and Industry (1998d), *Moving into the Information Age – An International Benchmarking Study*, Information Society Initiative (ISI), London: DTI.

Department of Trade and Industry (1998e), *Small Business Action Update*, URN98/573.

Department for Trade and Industry (2001), *Opportunity for all in a world of change: white paper on enterprise, skills and innovation*, Cm5052, London: DTI and DEE.

Department for Trade and Industry, Social Enterprise Unit (2002), *Social Enterprise: A Strategy for Success*, London: DTI.

Department for Trade and Industry (2003a), *DTI: The Strategy*, London: DTI.

Department for Trade and Industry, Social Enterprise Unit (2003b), *Social Enterprise: a Progress Report on Social Enterprise: A Strategy for Success*, London: DTI.

Department for Trade and Industry (2003c), *Business into the Information Age: International Benchmarking Study 2003*, London: DTI.

Department for Trade and Industry (2004), *Business into the Information Age: International Benchmarking Study 2004*, London: DTI.

Deregulation Task Force (1995), *Report 1994/95*, Cabinet Office, London.

Deregulation Task Force (1996), *Report 1995/96*, Cabinet Office, London.

Deshpande, S. and Golhar, D. (1994), 'HRM practices in large and small manufacturing firms: A comparative study', *Journal of Small Business Management*, 32(1): 49–56.

Dess, G. G. and Robinson, R. B. Jr. (1984), 'Measuring Organizational Performance in the Absence of Objective Measures: The Case of the Privately-Held Firm and Conglomerate Business Unit', in *Strategic Management Journal*, 5(3): 265–74.

Dess, G. G., Duane Ireland, R., Zahra, S. A., Floyd, S. W., Janney, J. J. and Lane, P. J. (2003), 'Emerging Issues in Corporate Entrepreneurship', *Journal of Management*, 29(3): 351–78.

DfES (2003a), *21st Century Skills: Remaking our potential (Individuals, Employers, Nation)*, CM5810, Department for Education and Skills, London.

DfES (2003b), *Skills for life National Needs and Impact Survey of Literacy, Numeracy and IT Skills*, Department for Education and Skills, London.

Dhaliwal, S. (1998), *Silent Contributors – Asian Female Entrepreneurs and Women in Business*, London: Roehampton Institute.

Dichtl, E., Leibold, M., Koglmayr, H. G. and Muller, S. (1984), 'The Export Decision of Small and Medium-sized Firms: A Review', *Management International Review*, 24(2): 47–60.

Dickson, P. R. and Giglierano, J. J. (1986), 'Missing the boat and sinking the boat: a conceptual model of entrepreneurial risk', *Journal of Marketing*, 50 (July): 58–70.

Dimitratos, P., Johnson, J. E., Slow, J. and Young, S. (2003), 'Micromultinationals: New Types of Firms for the Global Competitive Landscape', *European Management Journal*, 21(2): 164–74.

Disney, R., Haskel, J. and Heden, Y. (2003), 'Restructuring and Productivity Growth in UK Manufacturing', *Economic Journal*, 113: 666–94.

Dixon, R. (1991), 'Venture capital and the appraisal of investments', *Omega*, 5: 333–44.

Dodd, S. and Patra, E. (2002), 'National Differences in Entrepreneurial Networking', *Entrepreneurship and Regional Development*, 14: 117–34.

Dodgson, M. (1989), *Technology Strategy and the Firm, Management and Public Policy*, Harlow: Longman.

Doll, J. and Ajzen, I. (1992), 'Accessability and stability of of predictors in theory of planned behavior', *Journal of Personality and Social Psychology*, 63(5): 754–6.

Donckels, R. and Fröhlich, E. (1991), 'Are Family Businesses Really Different? European

Experiences from STRATOS', *Family Business Review*, 7: 149–60.

Donckels, R. and Lambrecht, J. (1997), 'The Network Position of Small Businesses: An Explanatory Model', *Journal of Small Business Management*, April: 13–25.

Donnelley, R. G. (1964), *'The Family Business'*, Harvard Business Review, March–April, 42: 93–105; the small firm, Human Relations, 34(5): 343–65.

Dosi, G. (1988), 'Sources, procedures and microeconomic effects of innovation', *Journal of Economic Literature*, 26: 1120–71.

Dougherty, D. (1992), 'Interpretive barriers to successful product innovation in large firms', *Organization Science*, 3: 179–202.

Downing, J. and Daniels, L. (1992), *The Growth and Dynamics of Women Entrepreneurs in Southern Africa*, US Agency for International Development, Washington, DC, USA, Gemini Technical Report 47, 1992.

Doz, Y. and Hamel, G. (1998), *Alliance Advantage: The Art of Creating Value through Partnering*, Harvard Business School Press, MA.

Drayton, W. (2002), 'The Citizen Sector: Becoming as Entrepreneurial and Competitive as Business', *California Management Review*, 44(3): 120–32.

Drucker, P. (1977), *Management: Tasks, Responsibilities, Practices*, Pan Books, UK.

Drucker, P. (1985), *Innovation and Entrepreneurship*, Pan Books, London.

Druker, J., Stanworth, C. and Conway, J. (1997), 'The Self-Employed Without Employees – An Unexplored Growth Area – Cases From the U.K.', paper presented to the Canadian Industrial Relations Association Conference, St. John's, Newfoundland, June.

Drury, J. C. and Braund, S. (1990), 'The leasing decision: A comparison of theory and practice', *Accounting and Business Research*, Summer.

Duberley, J. and Walley, P. (1995), 'Assessing the adoption of HRM by small and medium sized manufacturing organisations', *The International Journal of Human Resource Management*, 6(4): 891–909.

Dubini, P. and Aldrich, H. (1991), 'Personal and Extended Networks are Central to the Entrepreneurial Process', *Journal of Business Venturing*, 6: 305–13.

Dugdale, D., Hussey, J. and Jarvis, R. (1998), *Financial Reporting by Small and Medium-Sized Companies*, Small Business Research Centre, Kingston University.

Duncan, R. B. and Weiss, A. (1979), 'Organizational learning: Implications for organizational design, Research', in *Organizational Behavior*, 1(4): 75–124.

Duncan, W. J., Ginter, P. M., Rucks, A. C. and Jacobs, T. D. (1988), 'Intrapreneurship and the reinvention of the corporation', *Business Horizons*, 31(3): 16–21.

Dundon, T., Grugulis, I. and Wilkinson, A. (1999), 'Looking out of the Black Hole: Non-union relations in an SME', *Employee Relations*, 21(3): 251–66.

Duysters, G. (1996), *The Dynamics of Technical Innovation – The Evolution and Development of Information Technology*, Cheltenham, UK: Edward Elgar.

Dyer, W. G. (1989), 'Integrating Professional Management into a Family Owned Business', *Family Business Review*, 2(3): 221–35.

Dyer, W. G., Jr. and Handler, W. (1994), 'Entrepreneurship and Family Business: Exploring the Connections', *Family Business Review*, 19(1): 71–83.

Dyer Jr, W. G. and Sánchez, M. (1998), 'Current State of Family Business Theory and Practice as Reflected in Family Business Review 1988–1997', *Family Business Review*, 11(4): 287–96.

Dyson, J. (1997), *Against the Odds: An Autobiography*, London: Texere, Thomson.

Eagly, A. H. and Chaiken, S. (1993), *The Psychology of Attitudes*, Fort Worth: Harcourt Brace Jovanovich, Inc.

Earl, M. J. (1989), *Management Strategies for Information Technology*, New York: Prentice-Hall.

Earle, N. and Keen, P. (2000), *From .com to .profit: Inventing Business Models that Deliver Value and Profit*, San Francisco, CA: Jossey-Bass.

Earnshaw, J., Goodman, J., Harrison, R. and Marchington, M. (1998), 'Industrial tribunals, workplace disciplinary procedures and employment practice', *Employment Relations Research Series 2*, DTI, London.

Easton, G. (1992), 'Industrial Network: A Review', in B. Axelsson and G. Easton (eds.), *Industrial Network: A New View of Reality*, London: Routledge.

Ebers, M. (1997), *The Formation of Inter-Organisational Networks*, Oxford, UK: Oxford University Press.

Economist (2004), 'Philanthropy: Doing Well and Doing Good', 29 July.

Economist (2005), 'The Good Company: A Survey of Corporate Social Responsibility', 22 January.

Edwards, K. L. and Gordon, T. J. (1984), *Characterization of Innovations Introduced on the U.S. Market in 1982*, The Futures Group, prepared for the U.S. Small Business Administration under Contract No. SBA-6050-OA82.

Edwards, P. (1995), *Industrial Relations, Theory and Practice in Britain*, Oxford: Blackwell.

Edwards, P. K. (2003), *Industrial Relations: Theory and Practice*, London: Blackwell.

EFER (1992), *The Conditions for entrepreneurship in the C.S.F.R.*, EFER, Brussels.

EFER (1996), *Europe's 500 Dynamic Entrepreneurs and Job Creators*, EFER, Brussels.

Egge, K. A. (1987), 'Expectations vs. reality among founders of recent start-ups', in N. C. Churchill, J. A. Hornaday, B. A. Kirchhoff, O. J. Krassner and K. H. Vesper (eds.), *Frontiers of Entrepreneurship Research*, 322–36. Wellesley, MA: Babson College.

Ehrlich, S. B., De Noble, A. F., Moore, T. and Weaver, R. R. (1994), 'After the cash arrives: a comparative study of venture capital and private investor involvement in entrepreneurial firms', *Journal of Business Venturing*, 9: 67–82.

Eisenhardt, K. and Schoonhoven, C. (1990), 'Organisational Growth: Linking Founding Team, Strategy, Environment, and Growth among US Semiconductor Ventures, 1978–1988', *Administrative Science Quarterly*, 35: 504–29.

Eisenhardt, K. M. and Forbes, N. (1984), 'Technical entrepreneurship: an international perspective', *The Columbia Journal of World Business*, 19(4), Winter: 31–8.

Ekanem, I. and Smallbone, D. (2004), 'Investment Decision-Making in Small Manufacturing Firms: a Learning Approach', paper presented to the 27th ISBA Annual Small Firms Research and Policy Conference, University of Teesside.

Elango, B., Fried, V. H., Hisrich, R. D. and Polonchek, A. (1995), 'How venture capital firms differ', *Journal of Business Venturing*, 10: 159–79.

Electrolux (2004), *Automower*. Retrieved 12/06/2004 from www.automower.com.

Elliot, A. J. and Harackiewicz, J. M. (1994), 'Goal setting, achievement orientation and intrinsic motivation: A mediational analysis', *Journal of Applied Psychology*, 66(5): 968–80.

Elliot, S. and Melhuish, P. (1995), 'A Methodology for the Evalation of IT for Strategic Implementation', in *Journal of Information Technology*, 10(2): 87–100.

EMBI (1991), *Assisting Ethnic Minority Businesses: Good Practice Guidelines For Local Enterprise Agencies*, London: Home Office.

Emerson, J. (1999a), 'Social return on investment: exploring aspects of value creation',

REDF box set, 2, chapter 8, San Francisco: Roberts Enterprise Development Foundation.

Emerson, J. (1999b), 'The US Non-Profit Capital Market', *REDF box set*, 2, chapter 10, San Francisco: Roberts Enterprise Development Foundation.

Emerson, J. (2003), 'The Blended Value Proposition: Integrating Social and Financial Returns', *California Management Review*, 45(4): 35–51.

Emerson, J. and Twersky, F. (1996), *New Social Entrepreneurs: The Success, Challenge and Lessons of Non-Profit Enterprise Creation*, San Francisco: Roberts Enterprise Development Foundation.

Employment Gazette (1994), 'Ethnic Minorities and The Labour Market', 2: 147–59.

English, W. and Willems, J. (1994), 'Franchise vs. Non-Franchise Restaurant Attrition: Year-Four of a Yellow Pages Longitudinal Analysis', Proceedings of the 8th Conference of the Society of Franchising, Nevada, 13/14 February.

Engwall, L. and Wellenstal, M. (1988), 'Tit for Tat in Small Steps. The Internationalisation of Swedish Banks', *Scandinavian Journal of Management*, 4(3/4): 147–55.

Ensley, M. D. and Pearce, C. (2001), 'Shared cognition in Top Management Teams: Implications for New Venture Performance', *Journal of Organisational Behaviour*, 22(2): 145–60.

ENSR (1997), *The European Observatory for SMEs – Fifth Annual Report*, European Network for SME Research, Zoetermeer: EIM Small Business Research and Consultancy.

ENSR (2004), *Highlights from the 2003 Observatory*, European Commission, Brussels.

Enterprise Dynamics (n/d), *Small Firms: Survival and job creation: The contribution of enterprise agencies*, London: Business in the Community.

Epstein, J. A. and Harackiewicz, J. M. (1992), 'Winning is not enough: The effect of competition and achievement orientation on intrinsic interest', *Personality and Social Psychology Bulletin*, 18(2): 128–38.

Equal Opportunities Commission (2005), *Facts About Women and Men in Great Britain*, Manchester: Equal Opportunities Commission.

Erickson, C. and Jacoby, S. (2003), 'The Effects of Employer Networks on Workplace Innovation and Training', *Industrial and Labor Relations Review*, 56(2): 203–17.

Ernst and Young (1996), *Evaluation of Business Links*, London: DTI.

Ernst, D. and D. O'Connor, (1992), *Competing in the electronics industry – The experience of newly industrialising economies*, OECD, Paris.

Eroglu, S. (1992), 'The Internationalisation Process of Franchise Systems: A Conceptual Model', *International Marketing Review*, 6(5): 19–30.

Erramilli, M. K. and Rao, P. (1990), 'Choice of Foreign Market Entry Modes by Service Firms: The Role of Market Knowledge', *Management International Review*, 30(2): 135–51.

Espenlaub, S., Garrett, I. and Mun, W.-P. (1999), 'Conflicts of interest and the performance of venture capital-backed IPOs: a preliminary study of the UK', in *Venture Capital: an international journal of entrepreneurial finance*, 1: 325–24.

ESRC Centre for Business Research. (1996), A. Cosh and A. Hughes (ed.), *The Changing State of British Enterprise*, University of Cambridge.

Estades, J. and Ramani, S. (1997), 'Technological Competence and the Influence of Networks: A Comparative Analysis of NBFs in the Biotechnology Sectors in France and Britain', Conference paper.

Etemad, H. (2004), 'Internationalization of small and medium-sized enterprises: a grounded theoretical framework and an overview', *Canadian Journal of Administrative Sciences*, 21(1): 1–21.

Ettlie, J. E., Bridges, W. P. and O'Keefe, R. D. (1984), 'Organization Strategy and Structural Differences for Radical vs Incremental Innovation', in *Management Science*, 30: 682–95.

Etzioni, A. (1973), 'The Third Sector and Domestic Missions', *Public Administration Review*, 33: 314–23.

European Commission (2003a), *Green paper: Entrepreneurship in Europe*, European Commission, COM (2003) 27, Brussels.

European Commission (2003b), *The European E-Business Report 2002/03 edition*, European Commission.

European Commission (2004a), *Action Plan: The European agenda for entrepreneurship*, European Commission, COM (2004) 70, Brussels.

European Commission (2004b), http://www.ebusiness-watch.org/ – accessed 10 November 2004. Economics, 1:1, 51–64.

European Foundation for the Improvement of Living and Working Conditions (EFILWC) (2001), *Employment Conditions in micro and small firms*, prepared by the Basque Institute of Research and Studies (Ikea), www.eurofound.eu.int

European Network for SME Research (ENSR) (2004), *Observatory of European SMEs, 2003*, European Commission: Brussels. See (http://europa.eu.int/comm/enterprise/enterprise_policy/analysis/doc/smes_observatory_2003_report7_en.pdf)

European SMEs Observatory (1994), *First Report*, EIM, Zoetermeer.

European SMEs Observatory (1995), *Second Report*, EIM, Zoetermeer.

European SMEs Observatory (1996), *Third Report*, EIM, Zoetermeer.

European Union (2005), 'Commission adopts a new definition of micro, small and medium sized enterprises in Europe', http://europa.eu.int/rapid/pressReleasesAction.do?reference=IP/03/652&format=HTML&aged=0&language=EN&guiLanguage=en

Euske, N. A. and Roberts, K. H. (1987), 'Evolving Perspectives in Organization Theory: Communication Implications', in *Handbook of Organizational Communication*, F. M. Jablin, L. L. Putnam, K. H. Roberts, L. W. Porter (ed.). Newbury Park: Sage, 41–69.

Evans, P. B. and Wurster, T. S. (1997), 'Strategy and the New Economics of Information', in *Harvard Business Review*, Sep–Oct: 70–83.

Eyton, R. (1996), 'Making innovation fly', *Business Quarterly*, 61(1): 59–65.

Fabowale, L. Orser, B. and Riding, A. (1995), 'Gender, Structural Factors, and Credit Terms Between Canadian Small Businesses and Financial Institutions', *Entrepreneurship: Theory and Practice*, Summer: 41–65.

Fagenson, E. A. (1993), 'Personal value systems of men and women entrepreneurs versus managers', *Journal of Business Venturing*, 8: 409–30.

Fairlie, R. W. (2002), 'Drug Dealing and Legitimate Self-employment', *Journal of Labor Economics*, 20(3): 538–67.

Farrell, A. E. (1998), 'Informal Venture Capital Investment in Atlantic Canada: A Representative View of Angels?', A report submitted to Atlantic Canada Opportunities Agency, Halifax, Canada: St Mary's University.

Fass, M. and Scothorne, R. (1990), *The Vital Economy*, Edinburgh: Abbeystrand Publishing.

Fay, M. and Williams, L. (1993a), 'Gender Bias and the Availability of Business Loans', *Journal of Business Venturing*, 8(4): 363–76.

Fay, M. and Williams, L. (1993b), 'Sex of applicant and the availability of business "start-up" finance', *Australian Journal of Management*, 16(1): 65–72.

Fayol, H. (1949), *General and Industrial Management*, London: Pitman.

Federation of Small Business (2000), 'FSB Delivers damning "Red Tape" dossier to government', 23 May, www.fsb.org

Feeney, L., Haines, G. H. and Riding, A. L. (1999), 'Private investors' investment criteria: insights from qualitative data', *Venture Capital: An International Journal of Entrepreneurial Finance*, 1: 121–45.

Feeney, L., Johnstone, H. and Riding, A. L. (1998), 'A profile of informal investors in Canada: a comparison of Canadian and Maritime investors', paper to the CCSBE 15th annual conference, Halifax.

Feher, A. and Towell, E. (1997), 'Business Use of the Internet', in *Internet Research: Electronic Networking Applications and Policy*, 7(3): 195–200.

Feit, S. C. (1996), *TCP/IP – Architecture, Protocols, and Implementation with IPv6 and IP Security*, 2nd Edition, New York: McGraw-Hill.

Feldman, M. S. and March, J. G. (1981), 'Information in Organizations As Signal and Symbol', in *Administrative Science Quarterly*, 26: 171–86.

Feldman, M. P. (1994), 'An Examination of the Geography of Innovation', *Industrial and Corporate Change*, 2: 312–33.

Felstead, A. (1988), 'Technological Change, Industrial Relations and The Small Firm: A Study of Small Printing Firms', Unpublished PhD thesis, University of London.

Felstead, A. (1993), *The Corporate Paradox – Power and Control in the Business Franchise*, London and New York: Routledge.

Fiedler, F. E. (1967), *A Theory of Leadership Effectiveness*, New York: McGraw-Hill.

Fiegenbaum, A. and Karnini, A. (1991), 'Output flexibility – A competitive Advantage for Small Firms', *Strategic Management Journal*, 12: 101–14.

Fiet, J. O. (1995), 'Risk avoidance strategies in venture capital markets', *Journal of Management Studies*, 32: 551–74.

Fiet, J. O. (2002), *The Search for Entrepreneurial Discoveries*, Westport, CT: Quorum Books.

File, K. M., Judd, B. B. and Prince, R. A. (1992), 'Interactive Marketing: The Influence of Participation on Positive Word-of-Mouth and Referrals, *Journal of Services Marketing*, 6(4), Fall, 5–14.

Filion, L. J. (1990), 'Entrepreneurial Performance, Networking, Vision and Relations', *Journal of Small Business and Entrepreneurship*, 7(3): 3–12.

Financial Times (1997), 'Small Companies Lack IT Support', in *Financial Times*, 2 (December): 14.

Finegold, D. and Soskice, D. (1988), 'The Failure of Training in Britain: Analysis of prescription', *Oxford Review of Economic Policy*, 4(3): 21–53.

Fink, D. (1998), 'Guidelines for the Successful Adoption of Information Technology in Small and Medium Enterprises', in *International Journal of Information Management*, 18(4): 243–53.

Fink, K., Griese, J., Roithmayr, F. and Sieber, P. (1997), 'Business on the Internet – Some (R)Evolutionary Perspectives', in *10th International BLED Electronic Commerce Conference: 'Global Business in Practice'*, Volume 2: Research, D. R. Vogel, J. Gricar, J. Novak (ed.), Bled, Slovenia, 9–11 June.

Fiol, C. M. and Lyles, M. A. (1985), 'Organizational learning', *Academy of Management Review*, 10: 803–13.

Fischer, E. (1992), 'Sex Differences and Small Business Performance among Canadian Retailers and Service Providers', *Journal of Small Business and Entrepreneurship*, 9(4): 2–13.

Fisher, M. (1996), Member of Deregulation of Task Force, Quoted in *Financial Times*, 'Campaign to cut red tape "is a sham"', 6 (December).

Fitzgerald, M. A. and Muske, G. (2002), 'Copreneurs: An Exploration and Comparison to Other Family Businesses', *Family Business Review*, 15(1): 1–16.

Fletcher, D. E. (1997), 'Organisational Networking, Strategic Change and the Family Firm', PhD thesis, Nottingham Business School.

Fletcher, D. E. (1998), 'Swimming around in their own ponds: the weakness of strong ties in developing innovative practices, *International Journal of Innovation Management*, forthcoming.

Fletcher, D. E. (2005), 'The promise of social constructionist ideas for entrepreneurship research', under review, Entrepreneurship and Regional Development.

Fletcher, M. (1994), 'How bank managers make lending decisions to small firms' paper presented to the 17th ISBA UK National Small Firms Policy and Research Conference, Proceedings, Sheffield Hallam University.

Florida, R. L. and Kenney, M. (1988), 'Venture capital, high technology and regional development', *Regional Studies*, 22: 33–48.

Fombrun, C. (1982), 'Strategies for Network Research in Organisations', *Academy of Management Review*, 7(2): 280–91.

Foner, N. (1979), 'West Indians in New York and London: A Comparative Analysis', *International Migration Review*, 13: 284–95.

509

Foner, N. (1987), 'The Jamaicans: Race and Ethnicity Among Migrants In New York City', in N. Foner (ed.), *New Immigrants In New York*, New York: Columbia University Press, 195–217.

Food and Drink Weekly (2002), 'Ocean Spray Cranberries Inc close to sale of Nantucket Nectars', Retrieved 06/12/2004 from www.findarticles.com/p/articles/mi_m0EUY/is_13_8/ai_84376816

Ford, D. (ed.) (1990), *Understanding Business Markets: Interaction, Relationships and Networks*, Academic Press.

Ford, D. and Leonidou, L. (1991), 'Research Developments in International Marketing', in S. J. Paliwoda (ed.), *New Perspectives on International Marketing*, London: Routledge.

Foster, M. J. (1993), 'Scenario Planning for the Small Business', *Long Range Planning*, 26(1): 123–9.

Fox, M., Nilikant, V. and Hamilton, R. T. (1996), 'Managing Succession in Family-Owned Businesses', *International Small Business Journal*, 15(1)(57): 15–25.

Franco, A. and Winqvist, K. (2002), 'The Entrepreneurial Gap Between Women and Men; *Statistics in Focus*, Population and Social Conditions Theme 3, 11/2002. Brussels: Eurostat.

Frank, H., Plaschka, G. and Roessl, D. (1989), 'Planning behaviour of successful and non-successful founders of new ventures', *Entrepreneurship and Regional Development*, 1: 191–206.

Fraser, N. (1992), 'Rethinking the Public Sphere: A Contribution to the Critique of Actually Existing Democracy', in C. Calhoun (ed.), Habermas and the Public Sphere, 109–42. Cambridge: MIT Press.

Frazier, E. F. (1957), *Black Bourgeoisie*, New York: The Free Press.

Fredrickson, J. and Mitchell, T. (1984), 'Strategic Decisions Processes: Comprehensiveness and performance in an industry with an unstable environment', *Academy of Management Journal*, 27(2): 399–423.

Freear, J., Sohl, J. E. and Wetzel, W. E. Jr (1994a), 'Angels and non-angels: are there differences?', *Journal of Business Venturing*, 9: 109–23.

Freear, J., Sohl, J. E. and Wetzel, W. E. Jr (1994b), 'The private investor market for venture capital', *The Financier*, 1(2): 7–15.

Freear, J., Sohl, J. E. and Wetzel, W. E. Jr (1995a), 'Angels: personal investors in the venture capital market', *Entrepreneurship and Regional Development*, 7: 85–94.

Freear, J., Sohl, J. E. and Wetzel, W. E. Jr (1995b), 'Who Bankrolls Software Entrepreneurs', in W. D. Bygrave, B. J. Bird, S. Birley, N. C. Churchill, M. Hay, R. H. Keeley and W. E. Wetzel Jr (eds.), *Frontiers of Entrepreneurship Research* (1995), Center for Entrepreneurial Studies, Babson College, 394–406.

Freear, J. and Wetzel, W. E. (1990), 'Who bankrolls high-tech entrepreneurs?', *Journal of Business Venturing*, 5: 77–89.

Freel, M. (2000), 'External Linkages and Product Innovation in Small Manufacturing Firms', *Entrepreneurship and Regional Development*, 12: 245–66.

Freeman, C. (1991), 'Networks of Innovators: A Synthesis of Research Issues', *Research Policy*, 20(5): 499–514.

Freeman, C. and Soete, L. (1997), *The Economics of Industrial Innovation*, London: Pinter.

Fried, V. H. and Hisrich, R. D. (1994), 'Toward a model of venture capital investment decision making', *Financial Management*, 23(93): 28–37.

Fried, V. H., Bruton, G. D. and Hisrich, R. D. (1998), 'Strategy and the board of directors in venture capital-backed firms', *Journal of Business Venturing*, 13: 493–503.

Fried, V. H., Hisrich, R. D. and Polonchek, A. (1993), 'Research note: venture capitalists' investment criteria: a replication', *Journal of Small Business Finance*, 3(1): 37–42.

Friedman, D. (1988), *The misunderstood miracle: Industrial development and political change in Japan*, Ithaca: Cornell University Press.

Friedman, A. (1977), *Industry and Labour*, London: Macmillan.

Fry, A. (1987), 'The Post-It note: an intrapreneurial success', *SAM Advanced Management Journal*, 52(3): 4–9.

Fry, F. L. and Stoner, C. R. (1995), *Strategic Planning for the New and Small Business*, Chicago: Upstart, 3–19.

Frydman, R. and Rapaczynski (1994), *Privatisation in Eastern Europe: Is the state withering away?*, Central European University Press, Budapest.

Fryer, P. (1984), *The History of Black People in Britain*, London: Pluto Press.

Fukyama, F. (1995), *Trust: The Social Virtues and the Creation of Prosperity*. London: Penguin.

Fuller, P. B. (1994), 'Assessing Marketing in Small and Medium-sized Enterprises', *European Journal of Marketing*, 28(12): 34–49.

Fuller, T. and Southern, A. (1999), 'Small Firms and Information and Communication Technologies: Policy Issues and some Words of Caution', *Environment and Planning: Government and Policy*, 17: 287–302.

Fulop, L. (1991), 'Middle managers: victims or vanguards of the entrepreneurial movement?', *Journal of Management Studies*, 28(1): 25–44.

Furnham, A. and Steele, H. (1993), 'Measuring locus of control: A critique of general, children's, health- and work-related locus of control questionnaires', *British Journal of Psychology*, 84: 443–79.

Furtado, A. (1997), 'The French System of Innovation in the Oil industry: some Lessons about the Role of Public Policies and Sectoral Patterns of Technological Change in Innovation Networking', *Research Policy*, 25(8): 1243–59.

Galbraith, C. S. (1985), 'High technology location and development – the case of Orange County', *California Management Review*, 28(1): 98–109.

Galbraith, J. K. (1967), *The New Industrial State*, London: Penguin.

Galbraith, R. J. (1973), *Designing complex organizations*, Reading, Mass: Addison-Wesley.

Garnier, G. (1982), 'Comparative Export Behaviour of Small Canadian Firms in the Printing and Electrical Industries', in M. R. Czinkota and G. Tesar (eds.), *Export Management: An International Context*, New York: Praeger Publishers, 113–31.

Garnsey, E. (1998), 'The genesis of the high technology milieu: a study in complexity', *International Journal of Urban and Regional Research*, 22: 361–77.

Garnsey, E. and Wright, S. M. (1990), 'Technical innovation and organizational opportunity', *International Journal of Technology Management*, 5(3): 267–91.

Garris, J. M. and Burch, E. E. (1983), 'Small Businesses and Computer Panic', in *Journal of Small Business Management*, 21(3): 19–24.

Garrison, T. (1996), *International Business Culture*, Huntingdom: ELM Publications.

Gartner, W. B. (1988), 'Who is the entrepreneur? Is the wrong question', *American Journal of Small Business*, 12(4): 11–32.

Gartner, W. B. (1990), 'What are we talking about when we talk about entrepreneurship', *Journal of Business Venturing*, 5(1): 15–28.

Gartner, W. B. and Carter, N. (2003), 'Entrepreneurial behavior and firm organising processes', in Z. J. Acs and D. B. Audretsch (eds.), *Handbook of Entrepreneurship Research*, Dordrecht, NL: Kluwer.

Garvin, D. A. (1993), *Building a learning organization*, Harvard Business Review, 71 (July–August): 78–91.

Gaston, R. J. (1989), *Finding venture capital for your firm: a complete guide*, New York: John Wiley and Sons.

Gaston, R. J. (1990), 'Financing entrepreneurs: the anatomy of a hidden market', in R. D. Bingham, E. W. Hill and S. B. White (eds.), *Financing Economic Development*, Newbury Park: Sage, 266–84.

Gavron, R., Cowling, M., Holtham, G. and Westall, A. (1998), *The Entrepreneurial Society*, IPPR, London.

Gee, R. E. (1994), 'Finding and commercializing new businesses', *Research Technology Management*, 37(1): 49–56.

Geisler, E. (1992), 'Managing IT in Small Business: Some Practical Lessons and Guidelines', in *Journal of General Management*, 18(1): 74–81.

Gergen, K. K. (1999), *An Invitation to Social Construction*, London: Sage.

Gersick, K. E., Davis, J. A. and McCollom Hampton, Lansberg, I. (1997), *Generation to Generation: Lifecycles of Family Business*, Boston, Mass: Harvard Business School Press.

Gibb, A. A. (1983), *Enterprise Agencies: Exploring their future potential*, Durham: Durham University Business School.

Gibb, A. A. (1983), 'The Small Business Challenge to Management Education', *Journal of European Industrial Training*, 7(5): 6–8.

Gibb, A. A. (1988), 'The Enterprise Culture: threat or opportunity?', *Management Decision*, 26(4): 5–12.

Gibb, A. A. (1990), 'Entrepreneurship and intrapreneurship – exploring the differences', in R. Donckels and A. Miettinen (eds.), *New findings and perspectives in Entrepreneurship*, Aldershot: Avebury.

Gibb, A. A. (1993), 'Key factors in the design of policy support for SME development process: An overview', *Entrepreneurship and Regional Development*, 5: 1–24.

Gibb, A. A. (1996), 'Entrepreneurship and Small Business Management: Can We Afford to Neglect them in the Twenty First Century Business School?', *British Journal of Management*, 7(4): 309–22.

Gibb, A. A. (1997), 'Small firms training and industrial competitiveness: Building on the small firm as a learning organisation', *International Small Business Journal*, 15(3): 13–29.

Gibb, A. and Davies, L. (1990), 'In Pursuit of Frameworks for the Development of Growth

Models of the Small Business', *International Small Business Journal*, 9(1): 15–31.

Gibb, A. and Davies, L. (1991), 'Methodological Problems in the Development and Testing of a Growth model of Business Enterprise Development', in *Recent Research in Entrepreneurship*, Aldershot: Avebury, 286–323.

Gibb, A. and Dyson, J. (1982), 'Stimulating the Growth of the Owner-Managed Firms', UK National Small Business Policy and Research Conference, Glasgow.

Gibb, A. and Dyson, J. (1984), 'Stimulating the growth of owner managed firms, 249–58', in J. Lewis, J. Stanworth and A. Gibb (eds.), *Success and failure in Small Business*, Aldershot: Gower.

Gibb, A. A. and Haas, Z. (1995), 'Strategic issues in the development of Local Enterprise Agency support for small business in Central and Eastern Europe and the CIS', paper presented to the 25th EFMD European Small Business Seminar, Industrial Training Authority, Cyprus, 20–22 September.

Gibb, D. and Handler, W. (1994), 'Entrepreneurship and Family Business: Exploring the Connections', *Entrepreneurship Theory and Practice*, Autumn: 71–83.

Gibb, W., Dyer, W. G., Jr and Handler, W. (1994), 'Entrepreneurship and Family Business: Exploring the Connection', *Entrepreneurship Theory and Practice*, 19(1): 71–84.

Gibb, A. and Scott, M. (1985), 'Strategic Awareness, Personal Commitment and the Process of Planning in Small Business', *Journal of Management Studies*, 22(6): 597–632.

Gibson, D. (1991), *Technology Companies and Global Markets: Programs, Policies and Strategies to Accelerate Innovation and Entrepreneurship*, Rowan and Littlefield.

Giddens, A. (1984), *The Constitution of Society: Outline of the Theory of Structuration*, Cambridge: Polity Press.

Giddens, A. (1998), *The Third Way*, Cambridge: Polity Press.

Giddens, A. (2000), *The Third Way and Its Critics*, Cambridge: Polity Press.

Gifford, S. (1997), 'Limited attention and the role of the venture capitalist', *Journal of Business Venturing*, 12: 459–82.

Gilder, G. (1971), *The Spirit of Enterprise*, New York: Simon and Schuster.

Gillan, C., Graham, S., Levitt, M., McArthur, J., Murray, S., Turner, V., Villars, R. and McCarty Whalen, M. (1999), 'The ASPs' Impact on the IT Industry: An IDC-Wide Opinion', *International Data Corporation*.

Gilley, K. M., McGee, J. E. and Rasheed, A. A. (2004), 'Perceived environmental dynamism and managerial risk aversion as antecedents of manufacturing outsourcing: The moderating effects of firm maturity', *Journal of Small Business Management*, 42(2): 117–33.

Gillman, M., Edwards, P., Ram, M. and Arrowsmith, J. (2002), 'Pay Determination in small firms in the UK: the case of the response to the National Minimum Wage', *Industrial Relations Journal*, 33(1): 52–68.

Gilroy, P. (1987), *There Ain't No Black In The Union Jack: The Cultural Politics Of Race and Nation*, London: Macmillan.

Ginsberg, A. and Hay, M. (1994), 'Confronting the challenges of corporate entrepreneurship: guidelines for venture managers', *European Management Journal*, 12(4): 382–90.

Glazer, R. (1991), 'Marketing in an information-intensive environment: strategic implications of knowledge as an asset', *Journal of Marketing*, 55: 1–19.

Global Entrepreneurship Monitor (2003), *GEM 2002 Executive Report*, Babson College: Babson Park.

Global Entrepreneurship Monitor (2004), *GEM 2003 Executive Report*, Babson College: Babson Park.

Godfrey, M. and Richards, P. (eds.) (1997), *Employment policies and programmes in Central and Eastern Europe*, ILO, Geneva.

Godfrey, P. (1990), 'Management – Theories and Practice', in The New Manager's Handbook, M. Armstrong (ed.), Kogan Page: 37–49.

Goffee, R. and Scase, R. (eds.) (1985a), *Entrepreneurship in Europe*, London: Croom Helm.

Goffee, R. and Scase, R. (1985b), *Women in charge: the experience of female entrepreneurs*, London: Allen and Unwin.

Goffee, R. and Scase, R. (1995), *Corporate Realities: The dynamics of large and small organisations*, London: Routledge.

Goh, S. and Richards, G. (1997), 'Benchmarking the learning capability of organizations', *European Management Journal*, 15(5): 575–83.

Goldberg, L. R. (1993), 'The structure of phenotypic personality traits', *American Psychologist*, 48(1): 26–34.

Goman, C. K. (1994), *Managing in a Global Economy: Keys to Success in a Changing World*, California: Crisp Publications.

Gompers, P. A. (1994), 'The rise and fall of venture capital', *Business and Economic History*, 23(2): 1–26.

512

Gompers, P. and Lerner, J. (2001a), 'The venture capital revolution', *Journal of Economic Perspectives*, 15(2): 145–68.

Gompers, P. and Lerner, J. (2001b), 'The Money of Invention', Boston: Harvard Business School Press.

Gordon, C. (1996), *The Business Culture in France*, Oxford: Butterworth-Heinemann.

Gorman, G., Hanlon, D. and King, W. (1997), 'Some research perspectives on entrepreneurship education, enterprise education and education for small business management: a ten-year literature review', *International Small Business Journal*, 15(3): 56–77.

Gorman, M. and Sahlman, W. A. (1989), 'What do venture capitalists do?', *Journal of Business Venturing*, 4: 231–48.

Goshal, S. and Bartlett, C. A. (1995), 'Changing the role of top management: beyond structure to processes', *Harvard Business Review*, 73(1): 86–76.

Goss, D. (1988), 'Social Harmony and the Small Firm: a reappraisal', *Sociological Review*, 36(1): 114–32.

Goss, D. (1991), *Small Business and Society*, Routledge, London.

Gouldner, A. (1964), *Patterns of Industrial Bureaucracy*, RKP, London.

Govindarajan, V. and Lang, J. B. (2002), *3M Corporation – a case study*, Dartmouth College, NH.

Grabher, G. (ed.) (1993), *The Embedded Firm On the SocioEconomics of Industrial Networks*, London: Routledge.

Graham (2004), *Graham Review of the Small Firms Loan Guarantee*, HM Treasury.

Graham, T. (2004), *Task Force studies new ideas to reduce regulatory and administrative burden*, Better Regulation Task Force, Cabinet Office, London, Press Release, 6 December.

Grandori, A. and Soda, G. (1995), 'Interfirm Networks: Antecedents, Mechanisms and Forms', *Organisational Studies*, 16(2): 183–214.

Granger, B., Stanworth, J. and Stanworth, C. (1995), 'Self-Employment Career Dynamics: The Case Of 'Unemployment Push', *Work, Employment and Society*, 9(3): 499–516.

Granovetter, M. S. (1973), 'The Strength of Weak Ties', *American Journal of Sociology*, 78(6): 1361–81.

Granovetter, M. S. (1982), 'The Strength of Weak Ties: A Network Theory Revisited', in P. V. Marsden and V. Lin (eds.), *Social Structure and Network Analysis*, London: Sage, 105–30.

Granovetter, M. S. (1985), 'Economic and Social Structure; The Problem of Embeddedness', *American Journal of Sociology*, 91(3): 481–510.

Granovetter, M. S. (1992), 'Networks and Organisations: Problems of Explanation in Economic Sociology', in N. Nohria and R. G. Eccles (eds.), *Networks and Organisations: Structure, Form and Action*, Boston, Massachusetts: Harvard Business School Press.

Grant, R. M. (1996), 'Toward a knowledge-based theory of the firm', *Strategic Management Journal*, 17: 109–22.

Grant, W. and Sargent, J. (1987), *Business and Politics in Britain*, Basingstoke: MacMillan Education Ltd.

Grant Thornton International and Business Strategies Ltd (1998), *European Business Survey*, 31.

Green, H. and Cruttenden, M. (1990), *Enterprise support agencies in Leeds: An analysis of current patterns – A report for Leeds TEC*, Leeds: CUDEM, Leeds Polytechnic.

Green, H. and Johnson, S. (1992), 'Localisation and quasi-markets and enterprise support: Implications for TECs', paper presented to the 15th National Small Firms Policy and Research Conference, Southampton, November.

Greene, F. and Kirby, D. (1998), 'Overcoming asymmetries in the relationship between accountants and their small business clients', paper presented to the 21st National Small Firms Policy and Research Conference, Durham, 18–20 November.

Greene, F. J. (2002), 'An Investigation into Enterprise Support For Younger People, 1975–2000', *International Small Business Journal*, 20(3): 315–36.

Greene, F. J., Mole, K. F. and Storey, D. J. (2004), 'Does More Mean Worse? Three Decades of Enterprise Policy in the Tees Valley', *Urban Studies*, 41(7): 1207–28.

Greene, P., Brush, C., Hart, M. and Saparito, P. (1999), 'An Exploration of the Venture Capital Industry: Is Gender an Issue?', in P. D. Reynolds, W. Bygrave, S. Manigart, C. Mason, G. D. Meyer, H. Sapienza and K. G. Shaver (eds.), *Frontiers of Entrepreneurship Research*, Wellesley, MA: Babson College.

Greene, P., Brush, C., Hart, M. and Saparito, P. (2001), 'Patterns of Venture Capital Funding: Is Gender a Factor?', *Venture Capital: An International Journal of Entrepreneurial Finance*, 3(1): 63–83.

Greenstein, S. and Khanna, T. (1997), 'What Does Industry Convergence Mean?', in: *Competing in the Age of Digital Convergence*, D. B. Yoffie (ed.), Boston: Harvard Business School Press, 201–26.

Greenwood, R. (2003), 'Toward a Theory of Agency and Altruism in Family Firms', *Journal of Business Venturing*, 18(4): 491–4.

Greiner, L. E. (1972), 'Evolution and revolution as organisations grow', *Harvard Business Review*, July–August: 37–46.

Grell, O. P. and Woolf, S. (ed.) (1996), 'Domestic Strategies: work and the family in France and Italy 1600–1800', *Historical Journal*, 39(1): 257–63.

Greve, A. and Salaff, J. (2003), 'Social Networks and Entrepreneurship', *Entrepreneurship Theory and Practice*, 28(4): 1–22.

Griliches, Z. (1979), 'Issues in Assessing the Contribution of R&D to Productivity Growth', *Bell Journal of Economics*, 10 (Spring): 92–116.

Griliches, Z. (1990), 'Patent Statistics as Economic Indicators: A Survey', *Journal of Economic Literature*, 28(4): 1661–707.

Gubrium, J. F. and Holstein, J. A. (1990), *What is Family?* Mayfield Publishing.

Guclu, A., Dees, J. and Battle Anderson, B. (2002), 'The process of social entrepreneurship: creating opportunities worthy of serious pursuit', *CASE Working paper Series*, 3. Duke Fuqua School.

Gummesson, E. (1987), 'The New Marketing – Developing Long Term Interactive Relationships', *Long Range Planning*, 20(4): 10–20.

Gustafsson, V. (2004), 'Entrepreneurial Decision-Making', Doctoral dissertation, Jönköping: Jönköping International Business School.

HM Government (1994), *Competitiveness: Helping Businesses to Win*, Cm2563, HMSO, London.

HM Government (1995), *Competitiveness: Forging Ahead*, Cm2867, HMSO, London.

HM Government (1996), *Competitiveness: Creating the Enterprise Centre of Europe*, Cm3300, HMSO, London.

Haahti, A. (1987), 'A Word on Theories of Entrepreneurship and Theories of Small Business Interface. A Few Comments', Helsinki School of Economics, *Working papers F-170*. Finland.

Habbershon, T. G., Williams, M. and Kaye, K. (1999), 'A Resource-Based Framework For Assessing The Strategic Advantages Of Family Firms', *Family Business Review*, 12(1): 1–15.

Haberfellner, R. (2003), 'Austria: still a highly regulated economy', in R. Kloosterman and J. Rath (eds.), *Immigrant Entrepreneurship: Venturing Abroad in the Age of Golbalisation*, Oxford: Berg.

Habermas, J. (1989), *The Structural Transformation of the Public Sphere*, Cambridge: MIT Press.

Habermeier, K. (1990), 'Product Use and Product Improvement', *Research Policy*, 19(3): 271–83.

Haggett, P. (1983), *Geography, A Modern Synthesis*, New York: HarperCollins.

Hagmann, C. and McCahon, C. (1993), 'Strategic Information Systems and Competitiveness', *Information and Management*, 25(2): 183–92.

Haines, G. H., Jr, Madill, J. J. and Riding, A. L. (2003), 'Informal investment in Canada: financing small business growth', *Journal of Small Business and Entrepreneurship*, 16(3/4): 13–40.

Haines, G. H., Orser, B. J. and Riding, A. L. (1999), 'Myths and Realities: An Empirical Study of Banks and the Gender of Small Business Clients', *Canadian Journal of Administrative Sciences*, 16(4): 291–307.

Hakansson, H. and Snehota, I. (1995), *Developing Relationships in Business Networks*, London: Routledge.

Hakim, C. (1988a), 'Women at Work: Recent Research on Women's Employment', *Work, Employment and Society*, 2(1): 103–13.

Hakim, C. (1988b), 'Self-Employment in Britain: Recent Trends and Current Issues', *Work, Employment and Society*, 2(4): 421–50.

Hakim, C. (1989a), 'Identifying Fast Growth Small Firms', *Employment Gazette* (January issue): 29–41.

Hakim, C. (1989b), 'New Recruits to Self-Employment in the 1980s', *Employment Gazette* (June issue): 286–97.

Hall, E. (1959), *The Silent Language*, New York: Doubleday.

Hall, G. (1989), 'Lack of finance as a Constraint on the Expansion of Innovative Small Firms', in J. Barber, J. Metcalfe and M. Porteous (eds.), *Barriers to Growth in Small Firms*, London: Routledge.

Hall, G. (1995), *Surviving and Prospering in the Small Firm Sector*, London: Routledge.

Hall, J. and Hofer, C. W. (1993), 'Venture capitalists' decision criteria in new venture evaluation', *Journal of Business Venturing*, 8: 25–42.

Hall, P., Breheny, M., McQuaid, R. and Hart, D. (1987), *Western Sunrise: The Genesis and Growth of Britain's Major High Tech Corridor*, London: Allen and Unwin.

Hall, S., Held, D. and McGrew, T. (1992), *Modernity and its Futures*, Cambridge: Polity Press.

Hamel, G. (2000), *Leading the Revolution*, Boston: Harvard Business School Press.

Hamill, J. (1997), 'The Internet and International Marketing', in *International Marketing Review*, 14(5): 300–23.

Hamill, J. and Gregory, K. (1997), 'Internet Marketing in the Internationalisation of UK SMEs', in *Journal of Marketing Management*, 13(1–3): 9–28.

Hamilton, D. (1990), 'An "ecological" basis for the analysis of gender differences in the predisposition to self-employment', paper presented to the Research in Entrepreneurship (RENT) Conference, Cologne.

Hamilton, D., Rosa, P. and Carter, S. (1992), 'The impact of gender on the management of small business: some fundamental problems', in R. Wetford (ed.), *Small business and small business development – a practical approach*, Bradford: European Research Press, 33–40.

Hamilton, E. (2002), 'One Lifetime Is Not Enough: Stories Of Intergenerational Influence And Succession In Family Business', in Proceedings of the 25th Institute for Small Business Affairs National Small Firms Policy and Research Conference, Brighton, 13–15 (November): 333–52.

Hamilton, E. (2004), 'Whose Story Is It Anyway? Narrative Accounts Of The Role Of Women In Founding And Establishing Family Businesses', Lancaster University Management School Working paper, Lancaster, LUMSWP2004/041.

Hammer, M. and Champy, J. (1993), *Reengineering the Corporation – A Manifesto for Business Revolution*. New York: HarperCollins.

Hammer, M. and Mangurian, G. (1987), 'The Changing Value of Communication Technology', *Sloan Management Review*, 28(2): 65–71.

Hampden-Turner, C. and Trompenaars, F. (1994), *The Seven Cultures of Capitalism*, New York: Doubleday.

Handy, C. (1976), *Understanding Organisations*, Middlesex: Penguin, 176–211.

Handy, C. (1997), 'New language of organising', *Executive Excellence*, May: 13–14.

Hannah, L. (1976), *The rise of the corporate economy*, Second edition, London: Methuen.

Hansen, J. V. and Hill, N. C. (1989), 'Control and Audit of Electronic Data Interchange', in *MIS Quarterly*, 13(4): 402–13.

Hansford, A., Hasseldine, T. and Haworth, C. (2003), 'Factors affecting the costs of UK VAT compliance for small and medium-size enterprises', *Environment and Planning C: Government and Policy*, 21: 479–92.

Harackiewicz, J. M. and Elliot, A. J. (1993), 'Achievement goals and intrinsic motivation', *Journal of Personality and Social Psychology*, 65(5): 904–15.

Harding, R. and Cowling, M. (2004), *Social Entrepreneurship Monitor: United Kingdom 2004*, London: Global Entrepreneurship Monitor.

Hareven, T. (1975), 'Family Time and Industrial Time: Family and Work 1912–22: The Role of Family and Ethnicity in the Adjustment to Urban Life', *Labor History*, 16: 249–65.

Harhoff, D. and Licht, G. (1996), *Innovationsaktivitaeten kleiner und mittlerer Unternehmen*, Baden-Baden: Nomos Verlagsgesellschaft.

Harland, C. M. (1995), 'Networks and Globalisation: A Review of Research', Warwick University Business School Research paper, ESRC Grant No: GRK 53178.

Harland, C. M. (1996), 'Supply Chain Management: Relationships, Chains and Networks', *British Journal of Management*, 7: 63–80.

Harris, B., Holt C. P., Hatsopoulos, G. N., DeSimone, L. D. and O'Brien, W. F. (1995), 'How can big companies keep the entrepreneurial spirit alive?', *Harvard Business Review*, 73(6): 183–90.

Harris, D. (1993), 'Where those Business Angels Fear to Tread', *The Times*, 13 March.

Harrison, B. (1994), *Lean and Mean*, New York: Basic Books.

Harrison, R. (2002), *Learning and Development*, London: CIPD.

Harrison, R., Cooper, S. and Mason, C. (2004), 'Entrepreneurial activity and the dynamics of cluster development: the case of Ottawa', *Urban Studies*, 41(5/6): 1045–70.

Harrison, R. T. and Mason, C. M. (1987), 'The regional impact of the small firms loan guarantee scheme', in K. O'Neil, R. Bhambri, T. Faulkner and T. Cannon (eds.), *Small business development: Some current issues*, Aldershot: Avebury, 121–44.

Harrison, R. T. and Mason, C. M. (1992), 'The roles of investors in entrepreneurial companies: a comparison of informal investors and venture capitalists', in N. C. Churchill, S. Birley, W. D. Bygrave, D. F. Muzyka, C. Wahlbin and W. E. Wetzel Jr (eds.), *Frontiers of Entrepreneurship Research 1992*, Babson Park, MA: Babson College, 388–404.

Harrison, R. T. and Mason, C. M. (1995), 'The Role of Informal Venture Capital in Financing the Growing Firm', in *Finance for Growing Enterprises*, edited by Buckland, R. and Davis, E. W., London: Routledge.

Harrison, R. T. and Mason, C. M. (2000), 'Venture capital market complementarities: the links between business angels and venture capital funds in the UK', *Venture Capital: An International Journal of Entrepreneurial Finance*, 2: 223–42.

Harrison, R. T. and Mason, C. M. (2004), 'A critical incident analysis technique approach to entrepreneurial research: developing a methodology to analyse the value-added contribution of informal investors', paper to the Babson-Kauffman Entrepreneurship Research Conference, University of Strathclyde, 3–5 June.

Harrison, R. T. and Mason, C. M. (eds.) (1995), *Informal Venture Capital: evaluating the impact of business introduction services*, Hemel Hempstead: Prentice Hall.

Harrison, R. T., Mason, C. M. and Girling, P. (2004), 'Financial bootstrapping and venture development in the software industry', *Entrepreneurship and Regional Development*, 16: 307–33.

Hart, M. and Blackburn, R. (2004), 'Employment Regulation in the European Context', in S. Marlow, D. Patton and M. Ram, *Managing Labour in Small Firms*, London: Routledge.

Hartwick, J. and Barki, H. (1994), 'Explaining the Role of User Participation in Information Systems Use', in *Management Science*, 40(4): 440–65.

Harvey-Jones, J. (1994), in Leach, P., *The Stoy Hayward Guide to the Family Business*, London: Kogan Page.

Hasek, G. (1998), 'Stretch before exercising genius', *Industry Week*, 17 August.

Haughton, G. (1993), 'The local provision of small and medium enterprise advice services', *Regional Studies*, 27(8): 835–42.

Hawkins, P. (1994), 'The Changing View of Learning', in *Towards the Learning Company: Concepts and Practices*, J. Burgoyne, M. Pedlar and T. Boydell (eds.), McGraw-Hill Europe, 9–27.

Hawkins, R. and Prencipe, A. (2000), *Business to Business E-Commerce in the UK: A Synthesis of Sector Reports*, Department of Trade and Industry, UK.

Hay, M., Verdin, P. and Williamson, P. (1993), 'Successful New Ventures: Lessons for entrepreneurs and innovators', *Long Range Planning*, 26(5): 31–44.

Hayek, F. (1979), *Law, Legislation and Liberty*, London: RKP.

Haynes, G. W. and Haynes, D. C. (1999), 'The Debt Structure of Small Businesses Owned by Women in 1987 and 1993', *Journal of Small Business Management*, 37(2): 1–19.

Hayton, K. (1991), 'The coming of age of local economic development?' *Local Government Policy Making*, 18: 53–6.

Heath, C. and Tversky, A. (1991), 'Preference and belief: Ambiguity and competence in choice under uncertainty', *Journal of Risk and Uncertainty*, 4: 5–28.

Heck, Z. and Kay, R. (2004), 'A Commentary on Entrepreneurship in Family vs. Non-Family Firms: A Resource-Based Analysis of the Effect of Organizational Culture', by Shaker A. Zahra, James C. Hayton and Carlo Salvato, *Entrepreneurship Theory and Practice*, 28(4): 383–9.

Hedberg, B. (1981), 'How organizations learn and unlearn', in Nystrom, P. C. and Starbuck, W. H. (eds.), *Handbook of Organizational Design*, Oxford, Oxford University Press, 3–27.

Heelas, P. and Morris, P. (1992), *The Values of the Enterprise Culture*, London: Routledge.

Heikkilä, J., Saarinen, T., Sääksjärvi, M. (1991), 'Success of Software Packages in Small Businesses: An Exploratory Study', in *European Journal of Information Systems*, 1(3): 159–69.

Heintz, T. J. (1981), 'On Acquiring Computer Services for a Small Business', in *Journal of Small Business Management*, 19(3): 1–7.

Hellman, P. (1996), 'The Internationalisation of Finnish Financial Service Companies', *International Business Review*, 3(2): 191–207.

Hellman, T. and Puri, M. (2000), 'The interaction between product market and financing strategy: the role of venture capital', *Review of Financial Studies*, 13: 959–84.

Henderson, R. and Clark, K. (1990), 'Architectural innovation: The reconfiguration of existing product technologies and the failure of established firms', *Administrative Science Quarterly*, 35(1): 9–30.

Hendry, C. and Brown, J. (2001), 'Local skills and knowledge as critical contributions to growth of industry clusters in biotechnology', in W. During, R. Oakey and S. Kauser (eds.), *New Technology-Based Firms in the New Millennium*, Oxford: Pergammon, 127–40.

Hendry, C., Jones, A., Arthur, M. and Pettigrew, A. (1991), 'Human Resource Development in Small to Medium Sized Enterprises', Research paper No. 88, Sheffield: Employment Department.

Henriquez, C., Verheul, I. and van der Geest, Bischoff, C. (2002), 'Determinants of Entrepreneurship in France', in Audretsch, D. B., Thurik, R., Verheul, I. and Wennekers, S. (eds.), *Entrepreneurship: Determinants and Policy in a European-US Comparison*, Dordrecht: Kluwer.

Henry, J. and Walker, D. (1991), *Managing Innovation*, London: Sage.

Henton, D., Melville, J. and Walesh, K. (1997), 'The age of the civic entrepreneur: restoring civil society and building economic community', *National Civic Review*, 86(2): 149–56.

Herron, L. and Robinson, R. B. J. (1993), A structural model of the effects of entrepreneurial characteristics on venture performance, *Journal of Business Venturing*, 8: 281–94.

Heuberger, G. (ed.) and Gutwein, D. (1997), 'The Rothschilds: essays on the history of a European Family (review)', *Journal of Economic History*, 57(1): 214–16.

Holland, P. G. and Boulton, W. B. (1984), 'Balancing the "Family" and the "Business" in Family Business', *Business Horizons*, March–April: 16–21.

HFEP (1996), *Annual Report State of Small and Medium Sized Businesses in Hungary*, Budapest.

Hicks, D., Breitzman, T., Olivastro D. and Hamilton, K. (2001), 'The changing composition of innovative activity in the U.S. – a portrait based on patent analysis', *Research Policy*, 30(4): 681–703.

Higashide, H. and Birley, S. (2002), 'The consequences of conflict between the venture capitalist and the entrepreneurial team in the United Kingdom from the perspective of the venture capitalist', *Journal of Business Venturing*, 17: 59–81.

Higson, C. (1993), *Business Finance*, 2nd ed., London: Butterworth.

Hill, C. J. and Neeley, S. E. (1991), 'Differences in consumer decision processes for professional vs. generic services', *Journal of Services Management*, 2(1): 17–23.

Hills, G. E. and Hultman, C. M. (2005), 'Marketing, entrepreneurship and SMEs: knowledge and education revisited', paper presented at the 10th Annual Research Symposium of the Academy of Marketing Special Interest Group on Entrepreneurial and SME Marketing, Southampton University, 6–7 January.

Hinden, R. M. (1996), 'IP Next Generation Overview', in *Communications of the ACM*, 39(6): 61–71.

Hipple, J. Hardy, D., Wilson, S. A. and Michalski, J. (2001), 'Can corporate innovation champions survive?' *Chemical innovation*, 31(11): 14–22.

Hirschman, A. O. (1970), *Exit, Voice, and Loyalty*, Cambridge, MA: Harvard University Press.

Hisrich, R. and Brush, C. G. (1986), *The woman entrepreneur: starting, financing and managing a successful new business*, Lexington, Mass.: Lexington Books.

Hisrich, R. D. and Peters, M. P. (1992), *Entrepreneurship, starting, developing, and managing a new enterprise*, Illinois: Irwin.

Hite, J. (2005), 'Evolutionary Processes and Paths of Relationally Embedded Network Ties in Emerging Entrepreneurial Firms', *Entrepreneurship Theory and Practice*, 30(1): 113–44.

Hite, J. and Hesterly, W. (2001), 'The Evolution of Firm Networks: From Emergence to Early Growth of the Firm', *Strategic Management Journal*, 22(3): 275–86.

Hitt, L. and Brynjolfsson, E. (1996), 'Productivity, Profit and Consumer Welfare: Three Different Measures of Information Technology's Value', *MIS Quarterly*, 20(2): 121–42.

Hitt, M. A., Ireland, R. D. and Hoskisson, R. E. (1999), *Strategic Management: Competitiveness and Globalisation*, Cincinnati, OH: Southwestern Publishing.

HM Government (1994), 'Competitiveness: Helping Business to Win', Cmnd 2563, HMSO, London.

HM Government (1995), 'Competitiveness: Forging Ahead', A report to Parliament, HMSO, London.

HM Treasury (2002), 'Cross cutting review of services to small businesses', HM Treasury, London.

HM Treasury/SBS (2003), *Bridging the Finance Gap: A Consultation on improving access to growth capital for small businesses*.

Hmieleski, K. M. and Ensley, M. D. (2004a), 'An Investigation of Improvisation as a Strategy for Exploiting Dynamic Opportunities', paper presented at the 2004 BKERC Conference, Glasgow.

Hmieleski, K. M. and Ensley, M. D. (2004b), 'An Investigation of the Linkage Between Entrepreneur Intelligence and New Venture Performance', paper presented at the 2004 BKERC Conference, Glasgow.

HMSO (1985), *Lifting the burden*, London.

HMSO (1994), *Competitiveness: Helping Business to Win*, London.

HMSO (1995), *Competitiveness: Forging Ahead*, London.

HMSO (1996), *Competitiveness: Creating the Enterprise Centre of Europe*, London.

Hoang, H. and Antoncic, B. (2003), 'Network-Based Research in Entrepreneurship: A Critical

Review', *Journal of Business Venturing*, 18: 165–87.

HoC (1996a), Trade and Industry Committee Fifth Report, Business Links, 3 Vols., HC302, HMSO, London.

HoC (1996b), Trade and Industry Committee, Third Special Report, Government Observations on the Fifth Report from the Trade and Industry Committee Session (1995–96), Business Links, HC712, HMSO, London.

Hofer, C. (1975), 'Toward a contingency theory of business strategy', *Academy of Management Journal*, 18: 784–810.

Hofstede, G. (1991), *Cultures and Organisations: Software of the Mind*, London: McGraw Hill.

Hofstede, G. (1994), 'Defining Culture and its Four Dimensions', *European Forum for Management Development*: Focus: Cross-cultural Management, Forum 94/1: 4.

Hofstede, G. (1996), *Cultures and Organisations*, London: HarperCollins.

Hogan, R. T. (1991), 'Personality and personality measurement', in M. D. Dunnette and L. M. Hough (eds.), *Handbook of Industrial and Organizational Psychology* 2 ed., 2, 873–919. Palo Alto, California: Consulting Psychologists Press, Inc.

Hogan, R. T., Hogan, J. and Roberts, B. W. (1996), 'Personality measurement and employment decisions: Questions and answers', *American Psychologist*, 51(5): 469–77.

Hogarth, R. (1987), *Judgment and Choice* (2 ed.), Chichester: John Wiley and Sons.

Hogia (2004), *The Hogia Group*. Retrieved 6 December from www.hogia.com.

Hogsved, B.-I. (1996), *Klyv företagen! Hogias tillväxtmodell (Split the companies! Hogia's growth model)*, Falun: Ekerlids Förlag.

Holland, P. G. and Boulton, W. B. (1984), 'Balancing the "Family" and the "Business" in Family Business', *Business Horizons*, March–April: 16–21.

Hollander, B. (1984), 'Toward a Model for Family-Owned Business', paper presented at meeting of the Academy of Management, Boston.

Hollander, B. and Elman, N. S. (1988), 'Family-Owned Businesses: An Emerging Field of Inquiry', *Family Business Review*, 1(2): 145–64.

Holliday, R. (1995), *Nice Work?: Investigating Small Firms*, London: Routledge.

Holliday, R. and Letherby, G. (1993), 'Happy Families or Poor Relations – An Exploration of Familial Analogies in the Small Firm', *International Small Business Journal*, 11(2): 54–63.

Holme, C. (1992), *Self Development and the Small Organisation*, Training and Development UK, August: 16–19.

Holmquist, C. and Sundin, E. (1989), 'The growth of women's entrepreneurship – push or pull factors?', paper presented to the EIASM Conference on Small Business, University of Durham Business School.

Honeycutt, E. D. Jr., Flaherty, T. B., Benassi, K. (1998), 'Marketing Industrial Products on the Internet', in *Industrial Marketing Management*, 27: 63–72.

Honig, B. and Karlsson, T. (2001), 'Business planning and the nascent entrepreneur: an empirical study of normative behaviour', *Journal of Management*, 30(1): 29–48.

Hoogstra, G. J. and Van Dijk, J. (2004), 'Explaining Small Firm Growth: Does Location Matter?', *Small Business Economics*, 22(3–4): 179–92.

Hornaday, J. A. (1982), 'Research about living entrepreneurs', in C. A. Kent, D. L. Sexton, and K. L. Vesper (eds.), *Encyclopedia of Entrepreneurship*, 281–90, Englewood Cliffs, NJ: Prentice-Hall.

Hornaday, R. (1992), 'Thinking about entrepreneurship: a fuzzy set approach', *Journal of Small Business Management*, 30(4): 12–23.

Hoselitz, B. (1951), *The Early History of Entrepreneurial Theory, Explorations in Entrepreneurial Theory*, 3: 193–220.

HOST (1994), *ITO Non-Members Survey – Summary Report*, Sheffield: Employment Department.

Housden, J. (1984), *Franchising and Other Business Relationships in Hotel and Catering Services*, London: Heinemann.

Howells, J., James, A. and Malik, K. (2003), 'The sourcing of technological knowledge: Distributed innovation processes and dynamic change', *R&D Management*, 33(4): 395–409.

Hoy, F. and Stanworth, J. (2003), *Franchising: An International Perspective* (eds.), London and New York: Routledge.

Hoy, F. and Verser, T. G. (1994), 'Emerging Business, Emerging Field: Entrepreneurship and The Family Firm', *Entrepreneurship Theory and Practice*, Autumn: 9–23.

Huff, A. and Reger, R. (1987), 'A review of strategic process research', *Journal of Management*, 13(2): 211–36.

Huff, J. O., Huff, A. S. and Thomas, H. (1992), 'Strategic renewal and the interaction of cumulative stress and inertia', *Strategic Management Journal*, 13: 55–75.

Hughes, A. (1992), 'The Problems of Finance for Smaller Businesses', Working paper No. 15, University of Cambridge: Small Business Research Centre.

Hussey, R. (ed.) (1995), *A Dictionary of Accounting*, Oxford University Press.

Hutton, W. (1996), *The State We're In*, London: Vintage.

Hyland, T. (1994), *Competence, Education and NVQs – Dissenting Perspectives*, London: Cassell.

Hyland, T. and Matlay, H. (1997), 'Small Businesses, Training Needs and VET Provision', *Journal of Education and Work*, 10(2): 129–39.

Hynes, B. (1996), 'Entrepreneurship education and training – introducing entrepreneurship into non-business disciplines', *Journal of European Industrial Training*, 20(8): 10–17.

Hyvarinen, L. (1990), 'Innovativeness and its indicators in Small and Medium-sized Industrial Enterprises', *International Small Business Journal*, 9(1): 65–79.

Iacovou, C., Benbassat, I. and Dexter, A. (1995), 'EDI and Small Organisations: Adoption and Impact of Technology', *MIS Quarterly*, 19(4): 465–85.

Ibarra, H. (1993), 'Personal Networks and Minorities in Management: A Conceptual Framework', *Academy of Management Review*, 18(1): 56–87.

Ibeh, K. I. N. (1998), 'Analysing the Critical Influences on Export Entrepreneurship in a Developing Country Environment', Unpublished PhD thesis, Department of Marketing, University of Strathclyde, Glasgow.

Ibeh, K. I. N. (2001), 'On the resource-based, integrative view of small firm internationalisation', in Taggart, J. Berry, M. M. J. and McDermott, M. (eds.), *The Multinational in the New Era*, Palgrave, Academy of International Business Series, 8: 72–87.

Ibeh, K. I. N. (2005), 'Toward Greater Firm-level International Entrepreneurship within the UK Agribusiness Sector: Resource Levers and Strategic Options', *Management International Review*, 45(3): 59–81.

Ibeh, K. I. N., Johnson, J., Dimitratos, P. and Slow, J. (2004), 'Micromultinationals: some preliminary evidence on an emergent star of the international entrepreneurship field', *Journal of International Entrepreneurship*, 2(4): 289–303.

Ibeh, K. I. N., Young, S. and Lin, H. C. (2004), 'Information Technology and the electronics firms from Taiwan Province of China in the United Kingdom: emerging trends and implications', *Transnational Corporations Journal*, 13(3): 21–52.

Igbaria, M., Zinatelli, N. and Cavaye, L. M. (1998), 'Analysis of Information Technology Success in Small Firms in New Zealand', in *International Journal of Information Management*, 18(2): 103–19.

Igbaria, M., Zinatelli, N., Cragg, P. and Cavaye, A. L. M. (1997), 'Personal Computing Acceptance Factors in Small Firms: A Structural Equation Model', in *MIS Quarterly*, 21(3): 279–305.

IKEI and ENSR Partners (1997), Training Processes in SMEs: Practices, Problems and Requirements, project funded by the Leonardo Programme, Donostia-San Sebastián.

Ingham, G. K. (1970), *Size of Industrial Organisation and Worker Behaviour*, London: CUP.

Institute of Directors (1993), *Late Payment of Debt – A Position paper*, IOD, London.

Institute of Directors (1996), *Business Link IoD Research paper*, IOD, London.

Institute of Directors (1996), *Your Business matters: Report from the Regional Conferences*, IOD, London, on behalf of IOD, CBI, BCC, TNC, FSB and FPB.

Institute of Export (1995), *Survey of international services provided to exporters*, Institute of Export, London.

Ives, B. and Learmonth, G. (1984), 'The Information System as a Competitive Weapon', in *Communications of the ACM*, 27(12): 1193–201.

Ives, B. and Olson, M. H. (1984), 'User Involvement and MIS Success: A Review of Research', in *Management Science*, 30(5): 586–603.

Izard, C. E. (1984), 'Emotion-cognition relationships and human development', in C. E. Izard, J. Kagan, and R. B. Zajonc (eds.), *Emotions, Cognition, and Behavior*, 17–37, Cambridge: Cambridge University Press.

Jack, S. and Anderson, A. (2002), 'The Effects of Embeddedness on the Entrepreneurial Process', *Journal of Business Venturing*, 17: 467–87.

Jackson, G. I. (1981), 'Export from the importer's viewpoint', *European Journal of Marketing*, 15: 3–15.

Jaffe, Adam B. (1989), 'Real Effects of Academic Research', *American Economic Review*, 79(5): 957–70.

Jansen, P. G. W. and van Wees, L. L. G. M. (1994), 'Conditions for internal entrepreneurship', *Journal of Management Development*, 13(9): 34–51.

Jarillo, J. (1988), 'On Strategic Networks', *Strategic Management Journal*, 9(1): 31–41.

Jarillo, J. (1989), 'Entrepreneurship and Growth: The Strategic Use of External Resources', *Journal of Business Venturing*, 4(2): 133–47.

Jarvis, R. (1996), *Users and Uses of Unlisted Companies' Financial Statements: A Literature Review*, The Institute of Chartered Accountants in England and Wales.

Jarvis, R., Kitching, J., Curran, J. and Lightfoot, G. (1996), *The Financial Management of Small Firms: An Alternative Perspective*, Research Report No. 49, The Association of Chartered Certified Accountants, London.

Jarvis, R., Lipman, H., Macallan, H. and Berry, A. (1994), *Small Business Finance: The Benefits and Constraints of Leasing*, Occasional paper No. 28, Kingston University.

Jeffries, I. (1996), *A guide to the economies in transition*, London: Routledge.

Jenkins, A. (1998), *Trends in business support*, Durham: Small Business Foresight.

Jenkins, C., Jackson, M., Burden, P. and Wallis, J. (1998), 'Searching the World Wide Web: An Evaluation of Available Tools and Methodologies', in *Information and Software Technology*, 39(14/15): 985–94.

Jenkins, R. (1984), 'Ethnic Minorities In Business: A Research Agenda', in Ward, R. and Jenkins, R. (eds.), *Ethnic Communities in Business*, Cambridge: Cambridge University Press, 231–8.

Jenkins, S. P. (1994), 'Winners and Losers: A Portrait of the UK Income Distribution During the 1980s', University College of Swansea Department of Economics Discussion paper No. 94–07.

Jensen, M. (2002), 'Angel investors: opportunity amid chaos', *Venture Capital: an international journal of entrepreneurial finance*, 4: 295–304.

Jensen, M. C. and Meckling, W. H. (1976), 'Theory of the firm: managerial behavior, agency costs, and ownership structure', *Journal of Financial Economics*, 3: 305–60.

Johannisson, B. (1986a), 'New Venture Creation: A Network Approach', in *Frontiers of Entrepreneurship Research*, Wellesley, Mass: Babson College, 236–40.

Johannisson, B. (1986b), 'Network Strategies, Management Technology for Entrepreneurship and Change', *International Small Business Journal*, (5)1.

Johannisson, B. (1987a), 'Anarchists and Organisers: Entrepreneurs in a Network Perspective', *International Studies of Management and Organisations*, XVII(1): 49–63.

Johannisson, B. (1987b), 'Toward a Theory of Local Entrepreneurship', in Wyckham R., Meredith, L. and Bushe, G. (eds.), *The Spirit of Entrepreneurship*, Proceedings 32nd International Congress of Small Business, Vancouver.

Johannisson, B. (1987c), 'Beyond Process and Structure: Social Exchange Networks', *International Studies of Management and Organisation*, XVII(i): 3–23.

Johannison, B. (1988), 'Business Formation: A Network Approach', *Scandinavian Journal of Management*, 4: 83–99.

Johannisson, B. (2000), 'Networking and Entrepreneurial Growth', in D. Sexton and H. Landstrom, (eds.), *The Blackwell Handbook of Entrepreneurship*, Oxford: Blackwell.

Johannisson, B. and Peterson, R. (1984), 'The Personal Networks of Entrepreneurs', paper presented at the Third Canadian Conference of the International Council for Small Business, Toronto, 23–25 May.

Johanson, J. and Mattsson, L. G. (1988), 'Internationslisation in Industrial Systems – A Network Approach', in Hood, N. and Vahlne, J. E. (eds.), *Strategies in Global Competition*, Kent: Croom Helm.

Johanson, J. and Vahlne, J. (1977), 'The Internationalisation Process of the Firm – A Model of Knowledge Development and Increasing Foreign Market Commitments', *Journal of International Business Studies*, 8(1): 23–32.

Johanson, J. and Vahlne, J. E. (1978), 'A Model for the Decision Making Affecting the Pattern and Pace of Internationalisation of the Firm', in Ghertman, M. and Leontiades, J. (eds.), *European Research in International Business*, New York: Croom Helm, 283–305.

Johanson, J. and Vahlne, J. E. (1984), 'The Mechanism of Internationalisation', *International Marketing Review*, 7(4): 11–23.

Johanson, J. and Vahlne, J. E. (1990), 'The Mechanism of Internationalisation', *International Marketing Review*, 7(4): 11–24.

Johanson, J. and Vahlne, J. E. (1992), 'Management of Foreign Market Entry', *Scandinavian International Business Review*, 1(3): 9–27.

Johanson, J. and Wiedersheim-Paul, F. (1975), 'The Internationalisation of the Firm – Four Swedish Cases', *The Journal of Management Studies*, 12: 305–22.

Johnson, B. R. (1990), 'Toward a multidimensional model of entrepreneurship: The case of achievement motivation and the entrepreneur', *Entrepreneurship Theory and Practice*, 14(3), 39–54.

Johnson, G. and Scholes, K. (2004), *Exploring Corporate Strategy: Text and Cases*, London: Prentice-Hall International.

Johnson, S. (1990), 'Small firms policy – an agenda for the 1990s', paper presented to the 13th National Small Firms Policy and Research Conference, Harrogate.

Johnson, S. (1993), 'TEC's and enterprise support: Developing a strategic role', paper presented to the Skills and Enterprise Network Conference, University of Nottingham, 29 March.

Johnson, S. (2000), 'Literature Review on Social Entrepreneurship', Canadian Centre for Social Entrepreneurship Discussion paper, available at: http://www.bus.ualberta.ca/ccse/WhatIs/

Johnson, S. and Gubbins, A. (1991), 'Training in Small and Medium Sized Enterprises: Lessons from North Yorkshire', paper Presented at the 14th National Small Firms Policy and Research Conference, Blackpool, 20–22 November.

Johnson, S. and Storey, D. (1993), 'Male and female entrepreneurs and their businesses', in S. Allen and C. Truman (eds.), *Women in business: perspectives on women entrepreneurs*, London: Routledge, 70–85.

Johnstone, H. (2001), 'Equity gaps in depleted communities: an entrepreneurial response', in W. During, R. Oakey and S. Kauser (eds.), *New Technology-Based Firms in the New Millennium*, Oxford: Pergamon, 84–94.

Johnston, H. R. and Vitale, M. R. (1988), 'Creating Competitive Advantage with Inter-organisational Information Systems', in *MIS Quarterly*, June: 153–65.

Jones, A. and Moskoff, W. (1991), *Ko-ops: the rebirth of entrepreneurship in the Soviet Union*, Bloomington and Indianapolis: Indiana University Press.

Jones, G. (1991), *Starting Up*, 2nd ed., Natwest Business Handbooks, London: Pitman Publishing.

Jones, M. (1995), 'Business Link: One stop (or Enterprise Monster) shop?', paper presented to the ESRC seminar programme on the North in the 1990s, University of Durham, 4–5 July.

Jones, M. (1996), 'Business Link: A critical commentary', *Local Economy*, 11(1): 71–8.

Jones, M. V. (1999), 'The Internationalization of Small High Technology Firms', *Journal of International Marketing*, 7(4): 15–41.

Jones, O. (2005), 'Manufacturing regeneration through corporate entrepreneurship: Middle managers and organizational innovation', *International Journal of Operations and Production Management*, 25: 491–511.

Jones, O. and Conway, S. (2004), 'The International Reach of Entrepreneurial Social Networks: The Case of James Dyson in the UK', in H. Etemad (ed.), *International Entrepreneurship in Small and Medium-sized Enterprises: Orientation, Environment and Strategy*, Volume 3, McGill International Entrepreneurship Series: Edward Elgar, 87–106.

Jones, O., Conway, S. and Steward, F. (2001), 'Introduction: Social Interaction and Organisational Change', in O. Jones, S. Conway and F. Steward (eds.), *Social Interaction and Organisational Change: Aston Perspectives on Innovation Networks*, London: Imperial College Press, 1–40.

Jones, O., Cardoso, C. and Beckinsale, M. (1997), 'Mature SMEs and Technological Innovation: Entrepreneurial Networks in the UK and Portugal', *International Journal of Innovation Management*, 1(3): 201–27.

Jones, T. (1981), 'Small Business Development and The Asian Community In Britain', *New Community*, 9: 467–77.

Jones, T. (1989), 'Ethnic Minority Business and The Post-Fordist Entrepreneurial Renaissance', paper presented to the conference on Industrial Restructuring and Social Change In Western Europe, University Of Durham, 26–28 September.

Jones, T. (1993), *Britain's Ethnic Minorities*, London: Policy Studies Institute.

Jones, T., Barrett, G. and McEvoy, D. (2000), 'Market Potential as a Decisive Influence on the Performance of Ethnic Minority Business', in Rath J., *Immigrant Businesses*, Basingstoke: Macmillan Press Ltd.

Jones, T. and McEvoy, D. (1986), 'Ethnic Enterprise: The Popular Image', in J. Curran, J. Stanworth and D. Watkins (eds.), *The Survival of The Small Firm*, Aldershot: Gower, 197–219.

Jones, T., Cater, J., De Silva, P. and McEvoy, D. (1989), 'Ethnic Business and Community Needs', Report To The Commission For Racial Equality, Liverpool: Liverpool Polytechnic.

Jones, T., McEvoy, D. and Barrett, G. (1992), *Small Business Initiative: Ethnic Minority Business Component*, Swindon: ESRC.

Jones, T., McEvoy, D. and Barrett, G. (1993), 'Labour Intensive Practices in the Ethnic Minority Firm', in J. Atkinson and D. Storey (eds.), *Employment, The Small Firm and the Labour Market*, London: Routledge.

Jones, T., McEvoy, D. and Barrett, G. (1994a), 'Labour Intensive Practices In The Ethnic Minority Firm', in J. Atkinson and D. Storey (eds.), *Employment, The Small Firm and The Labour Market*, London: Routledge, 172–205.

Jones, T., McEvoy, D. and Barrett, G. (1994b), 'Raising Capital For The Ethnic Minority Small Firm', in A. Hughes and D. Storey (eds.), *Finance and The Small Firm*, London: Routledge, 145–81.

Jones, T. and Ram, M. (2003), 'South Asian Businesses in Retreat? The Case of the United Kingdom', *Journal of Ethnic and Migration Studies*, 29(3): 485–500.

Jones-Evans, D. (1995), 'A typology of technology-based entrepreneurs – a model based on previous occupational background', *International Journal of Entrepreneurial Behaviour and Research*, 1(1): 26–47.

Jones-Evans, D. (1996a), 'Technical entrepreneurship, strategy and experience', *International Small Business Journal*, 14(3): 15–39.

Jones-Evans, D. (1996b), 'Experience and entrepreneurship: technology-based owner-managers in the UK', *New Technology, Work and Employment*, 11(1): 39–54.

Jones-Evans, D. and Klofsten, M. (1997), *Technology, Innovation and Enterprise: The European Experience*, London: MacMillan.

Jones-Evans, D. and Steward, F. (1995), 'Technology, Entrepreneurship and the Small Firm', in D. Bennett and F. Steward (ed.), *Technological Innovation and Global Challenges: Proceedings of the First IAMOT European Conference on Management of Technology*, 272–9.

Jovanovic, B. (1982), 'Selection and Evolution of Industry', *Econometrica*, 50(2): 649–70.

Jovanovic, B. (2001), 'New Technology and the Small Firm', *Small Business Economics*, 16(1): 53–5.

Joyce, P., Woods, A. and Black, S. (1995), 'Networks and Partnerships: Managing Change and Competition', *Small Business and Enterprise Development*, 2: 11–8.

Joynt, P. and Warner, M. (1996), *Managing Across Cultures*, London: International Thomson Business Press.

Julien, P., Andriambeloson, E. and Ramangalahy, C. (2004), 'Networks, Weak Signals and Technological Innovations Among SMEs in the Land-Based Transportation Equipment Sector', *Entrepreneurship and Regional Development*, 16(4): 251–70.

Julien, P. A. (1995), 'New Technologies and Technological Information in Small Businesses', *Journal of Business Venturing*, 10(6): 459–75.

Kagan, A., Lau, K. and Nusgart, K. R. (1990), 'Information System Usage within Small Business Firms', in *Entrepreneurship: Theory and Practice*, 14(3): 25–37.

Kahneman, D. and Tversky, A. (1979), 'Prospect theory: An analysis of decision under risk', *Econometrica*, 47(2): 263–91.

Kaish, S. and Gilad, B. (1991), 'Characteristics of opportunities search of entrepreneurs versus executives: Sources, interests, general alertness', *Journal of Business Venturing*, 6(1): 45–61.

Kalakota, R. and Robinson, M. (2000), *e-Business 2.0: Roadmap for Success*, Upper Saddle River, NJ: Addison Wesley.

Kalakota, R. and Whinston, A. (1996), *Frontiers of Electronic Commerce*, Reading, MA: Addison Wesley.

Kaleka, A. and Katsikeas, C. S. (1995), 'Exporting Problems: The Relevance of Export Development', *Journal of Marketing Management*, 11: 499–515.

Kalleberg, A. and Leicht, K. (1991), 'Gender and Organisational Performance: Determinants of Small Business Survival and Success', *Academy of Management Journal*, 34(1): 136–61.

Kanfer, R. (1991), 'Motivation theory and industrial and organizational psychology', in Dunnette, D. D. (ed.), *Handbook of Industrial and Organizational Psychology*, Palo Alto, CA: Consulting Psychologists Press, 75–170.

Kanter, R. M. (1979), 'How the top is different', in R. M. Kanter and B. A. Stein (eds.), *Life in organizations: Workplaces as people experience them*, New York: Basic Books.

Kanter, R. (1984), *The Change Masters: Innovation and Entrepreneurship in the American Corporation*, New York: Simon and Schuster.

Kanter, R. (1988), *The Change Masters*, London: Allen and Unwin.

Kanter, R. (1999), 'From Spare Change to Real Change. The Social Sector as Beta Site for Business Innovation', *Harvard Business Review*, May–June: 122–32.

Kanter, R. M. (1989a), 'Work and Family in the United States: A Critical Review and Agenda for Research and Policy', *Family Business Review*, 2(1), Spring: 77–114.

Kanter, R. M. (1989b), *When Giants Learn to Dance – mastering the challenges of strategy, management and careers in the 1990s*, Lndon: Unwin.

Kanter, R. M. and Eccles, R. G. (1992), 'Making Network Research Relevant to Practice', in Nohria, N. and Eccles, R. G. *Networks and Organisations*, Boston, MA: Harvard University Press.

Kanter, R. M. (1989), 'Becoming PALS: Pooling, Allying and Networking Across Companies', *Academy of Management Executive*, III(3): 183–93.

Kaplinsky, R. (1990), *The Economies of Small*, London: Intermediate Technology Publications.

Kappelman, L. A. (1995), 'Measuring User Involvement – A Diffusion of Innovation Perspective', in *Data Base for Advances in Information Systems*, 26(2–3): 65–86.

Kasarda, J. D. (1989), 'Urban Industrial Transition and the Underclass', *Annals of the American Academy of Political and Social Science*, 501: 26–47.

Katsikeas, C. S. (1994), 'Perceived Export Problems and Export Involvement: The Case of Greek Exporting Manufacturers', *Journal of Global Marketing*, 7(4): 29–57.

Katz, J. A. (1992), 'A psychosocial cognitive model of employment status choice', *Entrepreneurship Theory and Practice*, 17(1), 29–37.

Katz, J. A. and Williams, P. M. (1997), 'Gender, self-employment and weak-tie networking through formal organizations', *Entrepreneurship and Regional Development*, 9(3): 183–98.

Katz, L. and Krueger, A. (1992), 'The Effect of the Minimum Wage on the Fast Food Industry', National Bureau of Economic Research Working paper No. 3997, Cambridge, Mass.

Katz, R. and Allen, T. J. (1982), 'Investigating the Not Invented Here (NIH) syndrome: A look at 50 R&D project groups', *R&D Management*, 12(1): 7–19.

Katz, R. L. (1970), *Cases and Concepts in Corporate Strategy*, Englewood Cliffs, NJ: Prentice-Hall.

Kazanjian, R. K. (1988), 'Relation of Dominant Problems to Stages of Growth in Technology-Based New Ventures', *Academy of Management Journal*, 31(2): 257–79.

Kazuka, M. (1980), 'Why So Few Black Businessmen?', Report on the Findings Of The Hackney Ethnic Minority Business Project, London.

Keasey, K. and Watson, R. (1992), 'Investment and Financing Decisions and the Performance of Small Firms', A study commissioned by the National Westminster Bank, September.

Keasey, K. and Watson, R. (1993), *Small Firm Management: Ownership, Finance and Performance*, Blackwell.

Keat, R. and Abercrombie, N. (eds.) (1991), *Enterprise Culture*, London: Routledge.

Keeble, D. (1987), 'Entrepreneurship, high-technology industry and regional development in the United Kingdom: the case of the Cambridge Phenomenon', paper presented to the seminar on 'Technology and Territory: Innovation Diffusion in the Regional Experience of Europe and the

USA', Instituto Universitario Orientale, University of Naples, February 20–21.

Keeble, D. (1993), 'Small Firm Creation, Innovation and Growth and the Urban-Rural Shift', in J. Curran and D. Storey (eds.), *Small Firms in Urban and Rural Locations*, London: Routledge, 54–78.

Keeble, D. and Wilkinson, F. (eds.) (2000), *High-Technology Clusters, Networking and Collective Learning in Europe*, Aldershot: Ashgate.

Keeble, D. Bryson, J. and Wood, P. (1992), 'The Rise and Role of Small Business Service Firms in the United Kingdom', *International Small Business Journal*, 11(1): 11–22.

Keeble, D., Tyler, P., Broom, G. and Lewis, J. (1992), *Business Success in the Countryside: the Performance of Rural Enterprise*, London: HMSO.

Keen, L. and Scase, R. (1998), *Local Government Management: The Rhetoric and Reality of Change*, Milton Keynes: Open University Press.

Keep, E. and Mayhew, K. (1997), 'Vocational Education and Training and Economic Performance', paper presented to the ESRC Seminar Presentation, Cranfield University.

Kelley, M. and Brooks, H. (1991), 'External Learning Opportunities and the Diffusion of Process Innovations to Small Firms: The Case of Programmable Automation', *Technological Forecasting and Social Change*, 39: 103–25.

Kelly, G. A. (1955), *The Psychology of Personal Constructs*, 1 and 2, Norton.

Kelly, P. and Hay, M. (1996), 'Serial investors and early stage finance', *Journal of Entrepreneurial and Small Business Finance*, 5: 159–74.

Kelly, P. and Hay, M. (2000), ' "Deal-makers": reputation attracts quality', *Venture Capital: an international journal of entrepreneurial finance*, 2: 183–202.

Kelly, P. and Hay, M. (2003), 'Business angel contracts: the influence of context', *Venture Capital: an international journal of entrepreneurial finance*, 5: 287–312.

Kendall, J., Tung, L., Chua, K., Ng, C. and Tan, S. (2001), 'Receptivity of Singapore's SMEs to Electronic Commerce Adoption', *Journal of Strategic Information Systems*, 10(3): 223–42.

Kent, C., Sexton, D. and Vesper, K. (1982), *Encyclopaedia of Entrepreneurship*, New Jersey: Prentice-Hall.

Kepner, E. (1983), 'The Family and the Firm: A Co-Evolutionary Perspective', *Organisational Dynamics*, 12(1): 57–70.

Kern, T., Kreijer, J. and Willcocks, L. (2002), 'Exploring ASP as sourcing strategy: Theoretical

Perspectives, Propositions for Practice', *Journal of Strategic Information Systems*, 1(2): 153–77.

Kessler, E. H., Bierly, P. E. and Gopalakrishnan, S. (2000), 'Internal vs. external learning in new product development: Effects on speed, costs and competitive advantage', *R&D Management*, 30(3): 213–23.

Kesteloot, C. and Mistiaen, P. (1997), 'From Ethnic Minority Niche to Assimilation: Turkish Restaurants in Brussels', *Area*, 29(4): 325–34.

Kets de Vries, M. (1977), 'The Entrepreneurial Personality: a Person at the Crossroads', *Journal of Management Studies*, 14: 34–57.

Kets de Vries, M. (1985), 'The dark side of the entrepreneur', *Harvard Business Review*, 63(6): 160–7.

Keynes, J. M. (1926), *The end of laissez-faire*, London: L. and V. Woolf.

Kiesler, S. and Sproull, L. (1982), 'Managerial response to changing environments: Perspectives on problem sensing from social cognition', *Administrative Science Quarterly*, 27: 548–70.

Kilby, P. (1971), 'Hunting the Heffalump', in Kilby, P. (ed.), *Entrepreneurship and Economic Development*, New York: The Free Press.

Kim, H. D. (1993), 'The link between individual and organizational learning', *Sloan Management Review*, Fall, 37–50.

Kim, I. (1981), *New Urban Immigrants: The Korean Community in New York*, Princeton, NJ: Princeton University Press.

Kim, M.-S. and Hunter, J. E. (1993), 'Attidude-behavior relations: A meta-analysis of attitutinal relevance and topic', *Journal of Communication*, 43(1), 101–42.

Kimhi, A. (1997), 'Intergenerational succession in small family businesses: borrowing constraints and optimal timing of succession', *Small Business Economics*, August, 9(4): 309–18.

Kinsella, R. and Mulvenna, D. (1993), 'Fast Growth Businesses: Their Role in the Post-Culliton Industrial Strategy', *Administration*, 41(1), 3–15.

Kinsella, R., Clarke, W., Coyne, D., Mulvenna, D. and Storey, D. J. (1993), *Fast Growth Firms and Selectivity*, Dublin: Irish Management Institute.

Kirby, D. A. (2003), *Entrepreneurship*. Maidenhead: McGraw-Hill.

Kirchhoff, B. (1991), 'Entrepreneurship's Contribution to Economics', *Entrepreneurship, Theory and Practice*, 16(2): 93–112.

Kirzner, I. M. (1973), *Competition and Entrepreneurship*. Chicago, IL: University of Chicago Press.

Kirzner, I. M. (1979), *Perception, Opportunity and Profit Studies in the Theory of Entrepreneurship*, Chicago: University of Chicago Press.

Kisfalvi, V. (2002), 'The entrepreneur's character, life issues, and strategy making. A field study', *Journal of Business Venturing*, 174: 489–518.

Klein, E. H. and Newman, H. W. (1980), 'How to integrate environmental forces into strategic planning', *Management Review*, 69 (July): 40–8.

Klepper, S. (2002), 'Firm survival and the evolution of oligopoly', *RAND Journal of Economics*, 33(1): 37–61.

Klofsten, M. (1994), 'Technology-based firms: critical aspects of their early development', *Journal of Enterprising Culture*, 2(1): 535–57.

Kloosterman, R. and Rath, J. (2003), 'Introduction', in R. Koosterman and J. Rath (eds.), *Immigrant Entrepreneurship: Venturing Abroad in the Age of Globalisation*, Oxford: Berg.

Kloosterman, R., van Der Leun, J. and Rath, J. (1998), 'Across the Border: Economic Opportunities, Social Capital and Informal Business Activities Of Immigrants', *Journal of Ethnic and Migration Studies* 24(2): 249–68.

Knight, F. H. (1921), *Risk, Uncertainty and Profit*, Boston: Houghton Mifflin Company.

Knight, G. A. and Cavusgil, S. T. (1996), 'The born global firm: a challenge to traditional internationalization theory', *Advances in International Marketing*, 8: 11–26.

Knight, J., Bell, J. and McNaughton, R. (2003), 'Satisfaction with paying for government export assistance', in C. N. Wheeler, H. Tuselmann and I. Greaves (eds.), *International Business*, London: Palgrave, 223–42.

Knight, R. M. (1987), 'Corporate innovation and entrepreneurship: a Canadian study', *Journal of Product Innovation Management*, 4: 284–97.

Kogut, B. and Zander, U. (1992), 'Knowledge of the firm, combinative capabilities, and the replication of technology', *Organization Science*, 3(3): 383–97.

Kolvereid, L. (1992), 'Growth aspirations among Norwegian entrepreneurs', *Journal of Business Venturing*, 7: 209–22.

Kolvereid, L. (1996a), 'Organizational employment versus self-employment: Reasons for career choice intentions', *Entrepreneurship Theory and Practice*, 20(3): 23–31.

Kolvereid, L. (1996b), 'Prediction of employment status choice intentions', *Entrepreneurship Theory and Practice*, 21(1): 47–57.

Kolvereid, L. and Bullvag, E. (1996), 'Growth intentions and actual growth: the impact of entrepreneurial choice', *Journal of Enterprising Culture*, 4(1): 1–17.

Kotler, P. (1997), *Marketing Management*, 9th edition, Englewood Cliffs, NJ: Prentice-Hall.

Kowtha, N. and Choon, T. (2001), 'Determinants of website development: a study of electronic commerce in Singapore', *Information and Management*, 39: 227–42.

Krackhardt, D. and Hanson, J. (1993), 'Informal Networks: The Companies Behind the Chart', *Harvard Business Review*, July–August: 104–11.

Krantz, S. (1999), 'Small Business', in *Sunday Business Essex*, 11 April.

Kreiner, K. and Schultz, M. (1993), 'Informal Collaboration in R&D: The Formation of Networks Across Organizations', *Organization Studies*, 14(2): 189–209.

Krueger, A. (1991), 'Ownership, Agency and Wages: An Examination of Franchising in the Fast Food Industry', *Quarterly Journal of Economics*, 56 (Issue 1): 75–101.

Krueger, N. F. (1993), 'The impact of prior entrepreneurial exposure on perceptions of new venture feasibility and desirability', *Entrepreneurship Theory and Practice*, 18(1): 5–21.

Krueger, N. F. (1998), 'Encouraging the identification of environmental opportunities', *Journal of Organizational Change Management*, 11(2): 174–83.

Krueger, N. F. and Brazeal, D. V. (1994), 'Entrepreneurial potential and potential entrepreneur', *Entrepreneurship Theory and Practice*, 18(3): 91–104.

Krueger, N. F. and Carsrud, A. L. (1993), 'Entrepreneurial intentions: Applying the theory of planned behavior', *Entrepreneurship and Regional Development*, 5(4): 315–30.

Krueger, N. F. and Dickson, P. R. (1993), 'Percieved self-efficacy and perceptions of opportunity and threats', *Psychological Reports*, 72: 1235–40.

Krueger, N. J. and Dickson, P. R. (1994), 'How believing in ourselves increases risk taking: Perceived self-efficacy and opportunity recognition', *Decision Sciences*, 25(3): 385–400.

Krugman, P. (1991), *Geography and Trade*, Cambridge: MIT Press.

Kuratko, D. F. (1993), 'Intrapreneurship: Developing innovation in the corporation. Advances in Global High Technology Management', *High Technology Venturing*, 3: 3–14.

Kuratko, D. F. and Hodgetts, R. M. (2001), *Entrepreneurship: A Contemporary Approach*. Orlando, Fl: Harcourt College Publishers.

Labour Force Survey (2005), *Quarterly Survey*, London: HMSO.

Labour Market Trends (2005), http://www.statistics.gov.uk/statbase/Product.asp?vlnk=550&More=N

Landström, H. (1992), 'The relationship between private investors and small firms: an agency theory approach', *Entrepreneurship and Regional Development*, 4: 199–223.

Landström, H. (1998), 'Informal investors as entrepreneurs', *Technovation*, 18: 321–33.

Landström, H. (ed.) (2006), *Handbook of Research on Venture Capital*, Cheltenham: Edward Elgar.

Lange, J. E., Bygrave, W., Nishimoto, S., Roedel, J. and Stock, W. (2001), 'Smart money? The impact of having top venture capitalists and underwriters backing a venture', *Venture Capital: an international journal of entrepreneurial finance*, 3: 309–26.

Langlois, A. and Razin, E. (1995), 'Self-Employment Among French-Canadians: The Role Of The Regional Milieu', *Ethnic and Racial Studies*, 18(3): 581–604.

Larson, A. (1992), 'Network dyads in Entrepreneurial Settings: A Study of the Governance of Exchange Relationships', *Administrative Science Quarterley*, 37: 76–104.

Larson, A. and Starr, J. (1993), 'A Network Model of Organization Formation', *Entrepreneurship Theory and Practice*, 17(2): 5–15.

Latour, B. (1993), *We have never been modern*, Boston, MA: Harvard University Press.

Lawrence, P. A. and Lee, R. A. (1989), *Insight into Management*, Oxford: Oxford University Press, 73–91.

Leach, P. (1994), *The Stoy Hayward Guide to the Family Business*, London: Kogan Page.

Leadbeater, C. (1997), *The Rise of the Social Entrepreneur*, London: Demos.

Leadbeater, C. and Goss, S. (1998), *Civic Entrepreneurs*, London: Demos.

Lechner, C. and Dowling, M. (2003), 'Firm Networks: External Relationships as Sources for the Growth and Competitiveness of Entrepreneurial Firms', *Entrepreneurship and Regional Development*, 15(1): 1–26.

Lee, W.-Y. and Brasch, J. J. (1978), 'The Adoption of Export as an Innovation', *Journal of International Business Studies*, 9(1): 85–93.

Lefebvre, L., Harvey, J. and Lefebre, E. (1991), 'Technological Experience and Technology Adoption Decisions in Small Manufacturing Firms', *R&D Management*, 21(3): 241–9.

Legge, K. (1995), *Human Resource Management, Rhetorics and Realities*, Houndmills: Macmillan.

Leiblein, M. J., Reuer, J. J. and Dalsace, F. (2002), 'Do make or buy decisions matter? The influence of organizational governance on technological performance', *Strategic Management Journal*, 23: 817–33.

Lengyel, Z. and Gulliford, J. (1997), *The Informal Venture Capital Experience*, London: Local Investment Networking Company.

Leonard-Barton, D. (1984), 'Interpersonal Communication Patterns Among Swedish and Boston-area Entrepreneurs', *Research Policy*, 13(2): 101–14.

Leonard-Barton, D. (1995), *Wellsprings of knowledge: Building and sustaining the sources of innovation*, Boston, MA: Harvard Business School Press.

Leonidou, L. C. (1995), 'Empirical Research on Export Barriers: Review, Assessment and Synthesis', *Journal of International Marketing*, 3(1): 29–43.

Lepley, B. (2000), 'Régulations sociales, relations professionnelles et petites enterprises – Etudes des facteurs constitutifs de la norme sociale dans le PE/TPE du secteur tertiaire', (Social Regulations, Professional Relations and small firms; constitutive factors of the social norm in SMEs and very small firms of the third sector), *Groupement d'Intérêt Public sur les Mutations Industrielles*, May.

Levin, I. (1993), 'Family as Mapped Realities', *Journal of Family Issues*, 14 (Part 1): 82–91.

Levitt, B. and March, J. C. (1988), 'Organizational learning', *Annual Review of Sociology*, 14: 319–40.

Levy, M. and Powell, P. (2000), 'Information Systems Strategy for SMEs: an Organisational Perspective', *Journal of Strategic Information Systems*, 9(1): 63–84.

Levy, M. and Powell, P. (2003), 'Exploring SME Internet Adoption: Towards a Contingent Model', *EM – Electronic Markets*, 13(2).

Levy, M., Powell, P. and Yetton, P. (2001), 'SMEs: Aligning IS and the Strategic Context', *Journal of Information Technology*, 16(1): 133–44.

Liao, Y. (1992), 'The Geography of the Chinese Catering Trade in Greater Manchester', *Manchester Geographer*, 14: 54–82.

Light, I. (1972), *Ethnic Enterprise In America: Business and Welfare Among Chinese, Japanese and Blacks*, Berkeley, CA: University Of California Press.

Light, I. (1984), 'Immigrant and Ethnic Enterprise In North America', *Ethnic and Racial Studies*, 7: 195–216.

Light, I. (1995), *Race, Ethnicity, and Entrepreneurship in Urban America*, New York: Aldine De Gruyter.

Light, I. and Bonacich, E. (1988), *Immigrant Entrepreneurs*, Berkeley, CA: University Of California Press.

Light, I. and Rosenstein, C. (1995), *Race, Ethnicity and Entrepreneurship in Urban America*, New York: Aidine de Gruyter.

Light, I., Sabagh, G., Bozorgmehr, M. and Der-Martirosian, C. (1993), 'Internal ethnicity in the ethnic economy', *Ethnic and Racial Studies*, 16(4): 581–97.

Lindahl, C. and Skagegård, L.-Å. (1998), *Stay In Place: Från Idé till Företag (Stay In Place: From Idea to Firm)*, Uppsala: ALMI/Konsultförlaget.

Lindholm Dahlstrand, Å. (1999), 'Technology-based SMEs in the Göteborg Region: their origin and interaction with universities and large firms', *Regional Studies*, 33: 379–89.

Lindqvist, M. (1988), 'Internationalisation of Small Technology-based Firms: Three Illustrative Case Studies on Swedish Firms', Stockholm School of Economics Research paper 88/15.

Link, A. N. and Barry Bozeman (1991), 'Innovative Behavior in Small-Sized Firms', *Small Business Economics*, 3(3): 179–84.

Link, A. N. and Rees, J. (1990), 'Firm Size, University Based Research, and the Returns to R&D', *Small Business Economics*, 2(1): 25–32.

Litz, R. A. (1995), 'The Family Business: Toward Definitional Clarity', *Family Business Review*, 8(2), Summer: 71–81.

Liu, H. (1995), 'Market Orientation and Firm Size: an Empirical Examination in UK firms', *European Journal of Marketing*, 29(1): 57–71.

Locke, E. A. (1991), 'The motivation sequence, the motivation hub and the motivation core', *Organizational Behavior and Human Decision Processes*, 50: 288–99.

Lockett, A. and Wright, M. (1999), 'The syndication of private equity: evidence from the UK', *Venture Capital: an international journal of entrepreneurial finance*, 1: 303–24.

Lockett, A. and Wright, M. (2002), 'Editorial: venture capital in Asia and the Pacific Rim', *Venture Capital: an international journal of entrepreneurial finance*, 4: 195.

Lockett, A., Murray, G. and Wright, M. (2002), 'Do UK venture capitalists still have a bias against investment in new technology firms?' *Research Policy*, 31: 1009–30.

Lockett, N. and Brown, D. H. (2006), 'Aggregation and the Role of Trusted Third Parties in SME E-Business Engagement: A Regional Policy

Issue', *International Small Business Journal*, 24(1).

Lombardini, S. (1996), 'Family, Kin and the quest for Community: a study of three social networks in early modern Italy', *History of the Family*, 1(3): 227–58.

Lorenzoni, G. and Ornati, O. A. (1988), 'Constellations of Firms and New Ventures', *Journal of Business Venturing*, 3: 41–57.

Loveman, G. and Segenberger, W. (1991), 'The Re-emergence of Small-Scale Production: An International Comparison', *Small Business Economics*, 1(3): 1–37.

Low, M. B. and MacMillan, I. C. (1988), 'Entrepreneurship: past research and future challenges', *Journal of Management*, 14(2): 139–61.

Luffman, G., Sanderson, S., Lea, E. and Kenny, B. (1991), *Business Policy: An Analytical Introduction*, Oxford: Blackwell, 3–17.

Lukas, A. B., Hult, G. T. M. and Ferrell, O. C. (1996), 'A theoretical perspective of the antecedents and consequences of organizational learning in marketing channels', *Journal of Business Research*, 36: 233–44.

Lumme, A., Mason, C. and Suomi, M. (1998), *Informal Venture Capital: Investors, Investments and Policy Issues in Finland*, Dordrecht, Netherlands: Kluwer Academic Publishers.

Luostarinen, R. (1980), *The Internationalisation of the Firm*, Helsinki School of Economics.

Luostarinen, R. (1994), *Internationalisation of Finnish Firms and their Response to Global Challenges*, 3rd ed., Helsinki: UNU/WIDER.

Lybaert, N. (1998), 'The Information Use in a SME: its Importance and Some Elements of Influence', *Small Business Economics*, 10(2): 171–91.

Ma Mung, E. (1994), 'L'entreprenariat ethnique en France', *Sociologie du Travail*, 2: 195–209.

Ma Mung, E. and Guillon, M. (1986), 'Les Commerçants Etrangers Dans L'agglomeration Parisienne', *Revue Européenne Des Migrations Internationales*, 2(3): 105–34.

Ma Mung, E. and Lacroix, T. (2003), 'France: the narrow path', in R. Kloosterman and J. Rath (eds.), *Immigrant Entrepreneurship: Venturing Abroad in theAge of Globalisation*, Oxford: Berg.

Ma Mung, E. and Simon, G. (1990), *Commerçants Maghrebins Et Asiatiques En France: Agglomération Parisienne Et Villes De L'est*, Paris: Masson.

Macaulay, S. (1963), 'Non-contractual relations in business: a preliminary study', *American Sociological Review*, 45: 55–69.

MacKinnon, D., Capman, K. and Cumbers, A. (2004), 'Networking, Trust and Embeddedness Amongst SMEs in the Aberdeen Oil Complex', *Entrepreneurship and Regional Development*, 16(2): 87–106.

Macmillan Committee (1931), *Report of the Committee on Finance and Industry*, Cmnd 3897, London: HMSO.

MacMillan, I. C., Kulow, D. M. and Khoylian, R. (1988), 'Venture capitalists' involvement in their investments: extent and performance', *Journal of Business Venturing*, 4: 27–47.

MacMillan, I. C., Siegel, R. and SubbaNarasimha, P. N. (1985), 'Criteria used by venture capitalists to evaluate new venture proposals', *Journal of Business Venturing*, 1(1): 119–28.

MacMillan, I. C., Siegel, R. and SubbaNarasimha, P. N. (1995), 'Criteria used by venture capitalists to evaluate new venture proposals', in J. A. Hornaday, E. B. Shils, J. A. Timmons and K. H. Vesper (eds.), *Frontiers of Entrepreneurship Research 1985*, Wellesley, MA: Babson College, 126–41.

Macrae, D. (1991), 'Characteristics of High and Low Growth Small and Medium Sized Businesses', paper presented at 21st European Small Business Seminar, Barcelona, Spain.

Macrae, N. (1976), 'The Coming Entrepreneurial Revolution', *The Economist*, Christmas edition, London.

Madill, J. J., Haines, G. H. Jr and Riding, A. L. (2005), 'The role of angels in technology SMEs: a link to venture capital', *Venture Capital: an international journal of entrepreneurial finance*, 7: 107–29.

Madsen, T. K. and Servais, P. (1997), 'The Internationalisation of Born Globals: an Evolutionary Process?', *International Business Review*, 6(6): 561–83.

Mahot, P. (1997), 'Funding for Women Entrepreneurs: A Real – Though Disputed – Problem', Proceedings of the OECD Conference on Women Entrepreneurs in Small and Medium Enterprises: A Major Force in Innovation and Job Creation, Paris, April, 217–26.

Malecki, E. J. (1981), 'Product cycles, innovation cycles, and regional economic change', *Technological Forecasting and Social Change*, 19: 291–306.

Malecki, E. J. (1991), *Technology and Economic Development*, Harlow: Longman Scientific and Technical.

Manigart, S. and Sapienza, H. (2000), 'Venture capital and growth', in D. L. Sexton and H. Landström (eds.), *The Blackwell Handbook of Entrepreneurship*, Oxford: Blackwell Publishers, 240–58.

Manigart, S. and Struyf, C. (1997), 'Financing high technology start-ups in Belgium: an exploratory study', *Small Business Economics*, 9: 125–35.

Manigart, S., de Waele, K., Wright, M., Robbie, K., Desbrières, P., Sapienza, H. J. and Beekham, A. (2002), 'Determinants of required return in venture capital investments: a five-country study', *Journal of Business Venturing*, 17: 291–312.

Manimala, M. (1999), *Entrepreneurial Policies and Strategies: The Innovator's Choice*, New Delhi: Sage.

Mansfield, E. (1984), 'Comment on Using Linked Patent and R&D Data to Measure Interindustry Technology Flows', in Z. Griliches (ed.), *R&D, Patents, and Productivity*, Chicago, IL: University of Chicago Press, 462464.

Marable, M. and Mullings, L. (1994), 'The Divided Mind of Black America: Race, Ideology and Politics in the Post-Civil Rights Era', *Race and Class*, 36(1): 61–72.

Marcucci, P. N. (2001), 'Jobs, gender and small enterprises in Africa and Asia: Lessons drawn from Bangladesh, the Philippines, Tunisia and Zimbabwe', SEED Working paper 2001/18, WEDGE series, 2001.

Markusen, A. (1985), *Profit Cycles, Oligopoly, and Regional Development*, Cambridge MA: MIT Press.

Marlow, S. (1992), 'Take-Up of Business Growth Training Schemes by Ethnic Minority-Owned Small Firms', *International Small Business Journal*, 10: 34–46.

Marlow, S. (1997), 'Self-employed women – new opportunities, old challenges?', *Entrepreneurship and Regional Development*, 9(3): 199–210.

Marlow, S. (1998), 'So much opportunity, so little take up – training in small firms', *Journal of Small Business and Enterprise Development*, 5(1): 38–49.

Marlow, S. (2002), 'Regulating Labour Management in small firms', *Human Resource Management*, 12(3): 25–43.

Marlow, S. and Gray, C. (2005), 'Information and consultation in small and medium sized firms', in J. Storey (ed.), *Adding Value Through Information and Consultation*, London: Palgrave Macmillan.

Marlow, S. and Patton, D. (1993), 'Managing the employment relationship in the small firm: possibilities for HRM', *International Small Business Journal*, 11(4): 57–64.

Marlow, S., Patton, D. and Ram, M. (2004), *Managing Labour in Small Firms*, London: Routledge.

Marshak, K. J. (1993), 'Copreneurial couples: a literature review on boundaries and transitions among copreneurs', *Family Business Review*, 6(4): 355–69.

Marshall, J. N., Alderman, N., Wong, C. and Thwaites, W. (1993), 'The impact of government-assisted management training and development on small and medium-sized enterprises in Britain', *Environment and Planning C: Government and Policy*, 11: 331–48.

Martello, W. E. (1994), 'Developing Creative Business Insights: Serendipity and its Potential', *Entrepreneurship and Regional Development*, 6(2): 239–58.

Martin, C. J. (1989), 'Information Management in the Smaller Business: The Role of the Top Manager', in *International Journal of Information Management*, 9(3): 187–97.

Martin, S. and Oztel, H. (1996), 'The business of partnership: Collaborative-competitive partnerships in the development of Business Links', *Local Economy*, 11(2): 131–42.

Mason, C. and Rogers, A. (1996), 'Understanding the Business Angel's Investment Decision', Venture Finance Working paper No. 14, Southampton: University of Southampton and University of Ulster.

Mason, C. and Rogers, A. (1997), 'The business angel's investment decision: an exploratory analysis', in D. Deakins, P. Jennings and C. Mason (eds.), *Entrepreneurship in the 1990s*, London: Paul Chapman Publishing, 29–46.

Mason, C. and Stark, M. (2004), 'What do investors look for in a business plan? A comparison of the investment criteria of bankers, venture capitalists and venture capitalists', *International Small Business Journal*, 22: 227–48.

Mason, C., Cooper, S. and Harrison, R. (2002), 'Venture capital and high technology clusters: the case of Ottawa', in R. Oakey, W. During and S. Kauser (eds.), *New Technology-Based Firms in the New Millennium*, Volume II, Oxford: Pergammon, 261–78.

Mason, C. (2006), 'Informal sources of venture finance', in S. Parker (ed.), *The International Handbook of Entrepreneurship*. Volume 2: The Life Cycle of Entrepreneurial Ventures (Kluwer) forthcoming.

Mason, C. M. and Harrison, R. T. (1991), 'The small firm equity gap since Bolton', in

J. Stanworth and C. Gray (eds.), *Bolton 20 years on: The small firm in the 1990s*, London: Paul Chapman Publishing, 112–50.

Mason, C. M. and Harrison, R. T. (1992), 'Promoting Informal Venture Capital: Some operational considerations for business introduction services', Venture Finance Research Project, paper No. 5, University of Southampton.

Mason, C. M. and Harrison, R. T. (1993), 'Strategies for expanding the informal venture capital market', *International Small Business Journal*, 11(4): 23–38.

Mason, C. M. and Harrison, R. T. (1994), 'The informal venture capital market in the UK', in A. Hughes and D. J. Storey (eds.), *Financing Small Firms*, London: Routledge, 64–111.

Mason, C. M. and Harrison, R. T. (1995), 'Informal Venture Capital and the Financing of Small and Medium Sized Enterprises', *Small Enterprise Research*, 3(1): 33–56.

Mason, C. M. and Harrison, R. T. (1996a), 'Why business angels say no: a case study of opportunities rejected by an informal investor syndicate', *International Small Business Journal*, 14(2): 35–51.

Mason, C. M. and Harrison, R. T. (1996b), 'Informal venture capital: a study of the investment process and post-investment experience', *Entrepreneurship and Regional Development*, 8: 105–26.

Mason, C. M. and Harrison, R. T. (1999), 'Financing entrepreneurship: venture capital and regional development', in R. L. Martin (ed.), *Money and the Space Economy*, Wiley, 157–83.

Mason, C. M. and Harrison, R. T. (2000), 'The size of the informal venture capital market in the United Kingdom', *Small Business Economics*, 15: 137–48.

Mason, C. M. and Harrison, R. T. (2002a), 'Barriers to investment in the informal venture capital sector', *Entrepreneurship and Regional Development*, 14: 271–87.

Mason, C. M. and Harrison, R. T. (2002b), 'Is it worth it? The rates of return from informal venture capital investments', *Journal of Business Venturing*, 17: 211–36.

Massey, D. (1996), 'Masculinity, dualisms and high technology', in N. Duncan (ed.), *Bodyspace – Destabilizing geographies of gender and sexuality*, London: Routledge, 109–26.

Masters, R. and Meier, R. (1988), 'Sex differences and risk-taking propensity of entrepreneurs', *Journal of Small Business Management*, 26(1): 31–5.

Mathias, P. (1969), *The First Industrial Revolution: An Economic History of Britain 1700–1914*, London: Methuen.

Matthews, C. H. and Moser, S. B. (1995), 'Family Background and gender: implications for interest in small firm ownership', *Entrepreneurship and Regional Development*, 7: 365–77.

May, J. and O'Halloran, E. F. (2003), *Cutting Edge Practices in American Angel Investing*, Charlottesville, VA: The Darden School, Batten Institute, University of Virginia.

May, J. and Simmons, C. (2001), *Every Business Needs An Angel: getting the money you need to make your business grow*, New York: Crown Business.

May, T. C. and McHugh, J. (1991), 'Government and small business in the UK: The experience of the 1980s', paper presented at the Annual Conference of the Political Studies Association of the United Kingdom.

Mayoux, L. (1995), 'From Vicious to Virtuous Circles? Gender and Micro-Enterprise Development', Occasional paper No. 3, UN Fourth World Conference on Women, United Nations Research Institute for Social Development, Geneva, May 1995.

Mazzi, P. (2001), 'Small Business eBusiness: Bringing SMEs Online', The IDC European eCommerce Forum 2001, International Data Corporation.

McClelland, D. C. (1961), *The Achieving Society*, Princeton, New Jersey: Van Nostrand.

McClelland, D. C. and Winter, D. G. (1969), *Motivating Economic Achievement*, New York: Free Press.

McCloy, U. A., Campbell, J. P. and Cudeck, R. (1994), 'A confirmatory test of a model of performance. Determinants', *Journal of Applied Psychology*, 79: 493–503.

McCollom, M. E. (1988), 'Integration in the Family Firm: When the Family System Replaces Controls and Culture', *Family Business Review*, 1(4): 399–417.

McCollom, M. E. (1992), 'Organizational Stories in a Family Owned Business', *Family Business Review*, V(1), Spring, 3–23.

McConaugby, D. L., Matthews, C. H. and Fialko, A. S. (2001), 'Founding Family Controlled Firms: Performance, Risk and Value', *Journal of Small Business Management*, 39(1): 31–49.

McDonald, M. H. (1980), *Handbook of Marketing Planning*, Bradford: MCB Publications, 2.

McDonald, M. H. (1984), *Marketing Plans: How to prepare them and use them*, London: Heineman, 1–8.

McDougall, P. and Robinson, R. (1990), 'New Venture Strategies: An empirical identification of eight "archetypes" of competitive strategies for entry', *Strategic Management Journal*, 11: 447–67.

McEvoy, D. and Cook, I. G. (1993), 'Transpacific Migration: Asians in North America', paper delivered at 2nd British Pacific Rim Seminar, School of Social Science, Liverpool John Moores University, September.

McGee, J. (1989), 'Barriers to Growth: the Effects of Market Structure', in *Barriers to Growth in Small Firms*, op. cit., 173–95.

McGill, M. and Slocum, J. W. (1993), 'Unlearning the organization', *Organizational Dynamics*, 67–79.

McGrath, R. G. (2002), 'Entrepreneurship, small firms and wealth creation: a framework using real options reasoning', in A. Pettigrew, H. Thomas and R. Whittington (eds.), *Handbook of Strategy and Management*, London: Sage, 299–325.

McGrath, R. G. (undated), L'Art d'Entreprendre. Comment la parcimonie peut mener au profit, Les Echos, retrieved 6 December 2004 from www.lesechos.fr/formations/entreprendre/articles/article_2_9.htm#Top.

McGrath, R. G. and MacMillan, I. (2000), *The Entrepreneurial Mindset: Strategies for Continuously Creating Opportunity in an Age of Uncertainty*, Boston, Mass: Harvard Business School Press.

McGrath, R. G., MacMillan, I. C. and Scheinberg, S. (1992), 'Elitits, risk-takers and rugged individualists? An exploratory analysis of cultural differences between entrepreneurs and non-entrepreneurs', *Journal of Business Venturing*, 7: 115–35.

McGuinness, N. W. and Little, B. (1981), 'The Influence of Product Characteristics on the Export Performance of New Industrial Products', *Journal of Marketing*, 45 (Spring): 110–22.

McKay, S. (2001), 'Between flexibility and regulation: rights, protection and equality at work', *British Journal of Industrial Relations*, 39(36): 285–303.

McKechnie, S. Ennew, C. and Read, L. (1998), 'The Nature of the Banking Relationship: A Comparison of the Experiences of Male and Female Small Business Owners', *International Small Business Journal*, 16(3): 39–55.

McKenna, E. (2000), *Business Psychology and Organisational Behaviour: A Student's Handbook*, Hove, East Sussex: Psychology Press.

McKinney, G. and McKinney, M. (1989), 'Forget the corporate umbrella: Entrepreneurs shine in the rain', *Sloan Management Review*, 30(4): 77–82.

Meager, N. (1991), 'Self-Employment in the United Kingdom', IMS Report No. 205 Institute of Manpower Studies.

Meager, N. (1992), 'Does Unemployment Lead to Self-Employment?', *Small Business Economics*, 4: 87–103.

Meager, N., Court, G. and Moralee, J. (1996), 'Self-Employment and the Distribution of Income', in J. Hills (ed.), New Inequalities, Cambridge: Cambridge University Press.

Megginson, W. and Weiss, K. (1991), 'Venture capitalist certification in Initial Public Offerings', *Journal of Finance*, 46: 879–903.

Mehrtens, J., Cragg, P. and Mills, A. (2001), 'A Model of Internet Adoption by SMEs', *Journal of Information and Management*, 39(3): 165–76.

Mellers, B. A., Schwartz, A. and Cooke, A. D. (1998), 'Judgment and decision making', *Annual Review of Psychology*, 49: 447–77.

Metcalf, H., Modood, T. and Virdee, S. (1996), *Asian Self-Employment: The Interaction Of Culture and Economics in England*, London: Policy Studies Institute.

Michaelas, N., Chittenden, F. and Poutziouris, P. (1996), *Determinants of Capital Structure in Small Privately Held Firms*, The Institute of Small Business Affairs Research Series, Monograph 2.

Middlemas, K. (1983), *Industry, Unions and Government: twenty-one years of NEDC*, London: Macmillan.

Miesenbock, K. J. (1988), 'Small Business and Exporting: A Literature Review', *International Small Business Journal*, 6(2): 42–61.

Miles, R. and Snow, C. (1986), 'Organisations: New Concepts for New Forms', *California Management Review*, 28(2): 62–73.

Miller, D. (1987a), 'Material Culture and Mass Consumption', Oxford: Basil Blackwell.

Miller, D. (1987b), 'Strategy making and structure: Analysis and implications for performance', *Academy of Management Journal*, 30(1): 7–32.

Miller, D. (1993), 'The architecture of simplicity', *Academy of Management Review*, 18(1): 116–38.

Miller, D. and Droge, C. (1986), 'Psychological and traditional determinants of structure', *Administrative Science Quarterly*, 31: 539–60.

Miller, D. and Friesen, H. P. (1980), 'Momentum and revolution in organizational adaptation', *Academy of Management Journal*, 23(4): 591–614.

Miller, D. and Toulouse, J.-M. (1986), 'Chief executive personality and corporate strategy and structure in small firms', *Management Science*, 32(11): 1389–409.

Milward, N. and Stevens, M. (1986), *British Workplace Industrial Relations, 1980–1984*. Aldershot: Gower.

Milward, N., Stevens, M., Smart, D. and Hawes, W. R. (1992), *Workplace Industrial Relations in Transition*, Aldershot: Gower.

Min, P. Y. (1991), 'Cultural and economic boundaries of Korean ethnicity: A comparative analysis,' *Ethnic and Racial Studies* 14: 225–41.

Min, P. Y. and Bozogmehr, M. (2003), 'Immigrant Entrepreneurship and Business Patterns: A Comparison of Korean and Iranians in Los Angeles,' *International Migration Review*, 34(3): 707–38.

Miner, J. B., Crane, D. P. and Vandenberg, R. J. (1994), 'Congruence and fit in professional role motivation theory', *Organization Science*, 5(1): 86–97.

Miner, J. B., Smith, N. R. and Bracker, J. S. (1989), 'Role of entrepreneurial task motivation in the growth of technologically innovative firms', *Journal of Applied Psychology*, 74(4): 554–60.

Miner, J. B., Smith, N. R. and Bracker, J. S. (1992), 'Predicting firm survival from a knowledge of entrepreneur task motivation', *Entrepreneurship and Regional Development*, 4: 145–53.

Minitti, M., Arenius, P. and Langowitz, N. (2005), *Global Entrepreneurship Monitor 2004 Report on Women and Entrepreneurship*, Babson Park, MA: Babson College.

Mintzberg, H. (1979), *The Structuring of Organisations*, Englewood Cliffs, NJ: Prentice-Hall.

Mintzberg, H. (1994), 'Rethinking Strategic Planning, Part I: Pitfalls and Fallacies', *Long Range Planning*, 27(3): 12–21.

Mintzberg, H. and Quinn, J. (1991), *The Strategy Process, Concepts, Contexts, Cases*, 2nd Edition, Prentice-Hall International.

Mintzberg, H. and Waters, J. (1982), 'Tracking Strategy in an Entrepreneurial Firm', *Administrative Science Quarterly*, 25: 465–99.

Mirchandani, K. (1999), 'Feminist insight on Gendered Work: New Directions in Research on Women and Entrepreneurship', *Gender, Work and Organization*, 6(4): 224–35.

Mitchell, F., Reid, G. and Terry, N. (1995), 'Post Investment Demand for Accounting Information by Venture Capitalists', *Accounting and Business Research*, 25.

Mitchell, J. C. (1969), 'The Concept and Use of Social Networks', in J. C. Mitchell (ed.), *Social Networks in Urban Situations*, Manchester: University of Manchester Press.

Mitchell, J. C. (1973), 'Networks, Norms and Institutions', in J. Boissevain and J. C. Mitchell (eds.), *Network Analysis: Studies in Human Interaction*, London: Mouton and Company.

Mitchell, R. K. and Seawrigth, K. W. (1995), 'The implication of multiple cultures and entrepreneurial expertise for international public policy', in W. D. Bygrave, B. J. Bird, S. Birley, N. C. Churchill, M. G. Hay, R. H. Keeley and W. E. J. Wetzel (eds.), *Frontiers of Entrepreneurship Research*, 143–71, Babson Park, MA: Center for Entrepreneurial Studies, Babson College.

Mitter, S. (1986), 'Industrial Restructuring and Manufacturing Homework', *Capital and Class*, 27: 37–80.

Mittlestaedt, R. and Peterson, M. (1980), 'Franchising and the Financing of Small Business', a paper in the Studies of Small Business Finance series prepared by The Inter-agency Task Force on Small Business Finance.

Modigliani, F. and Miller, M. H. (1958), 'The Cost of Capital, Corporation Investment and the Theory of Investment', *American Economic Review*, 48: 261–97.

Moini, A. H. (1997), 'Barriers Inhibiting Export Performance of Small and Medium-sized Manufacturing Firms', *Journal of Global Marketing*, 10(4): 67–93.

Mole, K. (2002a), 'Business advisers' impact on SMEs: an agency theory approach', *International Small Business Journal*, 20(2): 139–62.

Mole, K. (2002b), 'Street-level technocracy in UK small business support: Business Links, personal business advisers and the Small Business Service', *Environment and Planning C: Government and Policy*, 20: 179–94.

Monck, C. S. P., Quintas, P., Porter, R. B., Storey, D. J. and Wynarczyk, P. (1988), *Science Parks and the Growth of High Technology Firms*, London: Croom Helm.

Moorman, C. (1995), 'Organizational market information process: Cultural antecedents and new product outcomes', *Journal of Marketing Research*, 32: 318–35.

Moorman, C. and Miner, A. S. (1997), 'The impact of organizational memory on new product performance and creativity', *Journal of Marketing Research*, 34: 91–106.

Moran, P. (1999), 'Growth Strategies and Owner-Manager Personality: What is the Relationship?', paper presented to the 22nd ISBA National Small Firms Policy and Research Conference, Leeds, November.

Morck, R. and Yeung, B. (2003), 'Agency Problems in Large Family Business Groups', *Entrepreneurship: Theory and Practice*, 27(4): 367–82.

Morgan, R. E. and Katsikeas, C. S. (1997), 'Export Stimuli: Export Intention Compared with Export Activity', *International Business Review*, 6(5): 477–99.

Morrissey, C. A. (2000), 'Managing innovation through corporate venturing – new management models boost large firms in emerging markets', *The Graziadio Business Report*, Spring.

Moule, C. (1998), 'The Regulation of Work in Small Firms', *Work, Employment and Society*, 12(4): 635–54.

Mower and *A Decent Cup of Coffee*, Mimeo, Brisbane: Queensland University of Technology.

Mowery, C. D., Oxley, J. E. and Silverman, B. (1998), 'Technological overlap and interfirm cooperation: Implications for the resource-based view of the firm', *Research Policy*, 27: 507–23.

Moyes, A. and Westhead, P. (1990), 'Environment for new Firm Formation in Great Britain', *Regional Studies*, 24: 123–36.

Muller, M. (1996), 'Good Luck or Good Management? Multigenerational Family Control in two Swiss Enterprises since the 19th century', *Entreprises et Histoire*, 12: 19–48.

Mullins, D. (1979), 'Asian Retailing in Croydon', *New Community*, 7: 403–5.

Mullins, J. (1996), 'Early growth decisions of entrepreneurs: the influence of competency and prior performance under changing market conditions', *Journal of Business Venturing*, 11(2): 89–105.

Mullins, J. W. and Forlani, D. (2005), 'Missing the boat or sinking the boat: a study of new venture decison making', *Journal of Business Venturing*, 20: 47–69.

Muncie, J. and Sapsford, R. (1997), 'Issues in the Study of "The Family" Family', in J. Muncie, M. Wetherell, M. Langan, Dallos and A. Cochrane (eds.), *Understanding the Family*, London: Sage.

Munir, K. (2003), 'Competitive Dynamics in Face of Technological Discontinuity: A Framework for Action', *Journal of High Technology Management Research*, 14(1): 93–109.

Murphy, G. B., Trailer, J. W. and Hill, R. C. (1996), 'Measuring Performance in Entrepreneurship', *Journal of Business Research*, 36: 15–23.

Murray, C. (1990), *The Emerging British Underclass*, London: Institute of Economic Affairs.

Murray, G. (1995), 'Third-Party Equity – The Role of The UK Venture-Capital Industry', in *Finance for Growing Firms*, R. Buckland and E. Davis (eds.), London: Routledge.

Murray, G. and Lott, J. (1995), 'Have UK venture capital firms a bias against investment in new technology-based firms?', *Research Policy*, 24: 283–99.

Murray, J. A. and O'Gorman, C. (1994), 'Growth Strategies for Smaller Business', *Journal of Strategic Change*, 3: 175–83.

Muzyka, D., Birley, S. and Leleux, B. (1996), 'Trade-offs in the investment decisions of European venture capitalists', *Journal of Business Venturing*, 11: 273–87.

Myers, S. C. (1984), 'The Capital Structure Puzzle', *Journal of Finance*, 34(3): 575–92.

Mytelka, L. K. and Farinelli, F. (2000), 'Local clusters, innovation systems and sustained competitiveness', UNU/INTECH Discussion papers #2005, Maastricht, Netherlands.

Namiki, N. (1988), 'Export Strategy for Small Business', *Journal of Small Business Management*, 26(2): 32–7.

Namiki, N. (1994), 'A Taxonomic Analysis of Export Marketing Strategy: An Exploratory Study of US Exporters of Electronic Products', *Journal of Global Marketing*, 8(1): 27–50.

Nantucket Nectars (2004), '2004 Nantucket Nectar's Recap', retrieved 12 June 2004 from www.juiceguys.com.

National Statistical Institute (2000), *Conditions for the development of Micro-enterprises in Bulgaria*, Sofia.

National Westminster Bank/British Franchise Association Franchise Survey (The), NatWest Bank/BFA, 1987–2005 (annual surveys).

National Women's Business Council (2004), *Key Facts About Women Business Owners and Their Enterprises*. Washington DC: National Women's Business Council.

Nelson, D. (1975), *Managers and Workers: Origins of the New Factory System in the United States, 1880–1920*, Madison: University of Wisconsin Press.

Nelson, R. R. and Winter, S. G. (1982), *An evolutionary theory of economic change*. Cambridge MA: Harvard University Press.

Nevis, C. E., Dibella, A. J. and Gould, M. J. (1995), 'Understanding organizations as learning systems', *Sloan Management Review*, Winter, 73–85.

New Economics Foundation (2004), *Social Return on Investment: Valuing What Matters*. London: New Economics Foundation.

Newby, H. (1977), *The Deferential Worker: A Study of Farm Workers in East Anglia*, Harmondsworth: Penguin.

Newell, S., Swan, J. and Galliers, R. (2000), 'A Knowledge-focused Perspective on the Diffusion and Adoption of Complex Information Technologies: the BPR example', *Information Systems Journal*, 10: 239–59.

Nicholls, A. and Opal, C. (2005), *Fair Trade: Market-Driven Ethical Consumption*, London: Sage Publications.

Nicholls-Nixon, C., Cooper, A. and Woo, C. (2000), 'Strategic experimentation: Understanding change and performance in new ventures', *Journal of Business Venturing*, 15: 493–521.

Nicolaou, N. and Birley, S. (2003), 'Academic Networks in a Trichotomous Categorisation of University Spinouts', *Journal of Business Venturing*, 18: 333–59.

NOIE (2005), http://www2.dcita.gov.au/ie/ebusiness/developing/itol – accessed 10 February 2005.

Noon, M. and Blyton, P. (1997), *The Realities of Work*, London: Macmillan.

North, D. and Smallbone, D. (1996), 'Small Business Development in Remote Rural Areas: the Example of Mature Manufacturing Firms in Northern England', *Journal of Rural Studies*, 12(2): 151–67.

North, J., Blackburn, R. and Curran, J. (1997), 'Reaching small businesses? Delivering advice and support to small businesses through Trade Bodies', in M. Ram, D. Deakins and D. Smallbone (eds.), *Small firms: Enterprising Futures*, London: Paul Chapman Publishing, 121–35.

Norton, E. (1990), 'Similarities and Differences in Small and Large Corporation Beliefs About Capital Structure Policy', *Small Business Economics*.

Norton, E. (1991a), 'Capital Structure and Public Firms', *Journal of Business Venturing*.

Norton, E. (1991b), 'Capital Structure and Small Growth Firms', *Journal of Small Business Finance*, 1(2).

Norton, E. and Tenenbaum, B. H. (1992), 'Factors affecting the structure of US venture capital deals', *Journal of Small Business Management*, 30(3): 20–9.

Nowikowski, S. (1984), 'Snakes and Ladders', in Ward and R. Jenkins (eds.), *Ethnic Communities in Business*, Cambridge: Cambridge University Press, 149–65.

Nystrom, C. P. and Starbuck, H. W. (1984), 'To avoid crisis, unlearn', *Organizational Dynamics*, 12(4): 53–65.

Nystrom, C. P., Hedberg, B. and Starbuck, H. W. (1976), 'Interacting processes as organization process', in H. K. Ralph, R. P. Louis and P. D. Slevin (eds.), *The management of organization design*, New York: Elsevier North-Holland, 1: 203–30.

O'Farrell, P. N. and Hitchens, D. M. (1988), 'Alternative Theories of Small Firm Growth: A Critical Review', *Environment and Planning. A.*, 20: 1365–83.

O'Grady, S. and Lane, H. W. (1996), 'The Psychic Distance Paradox', *Journal of International Business Studies*, 2nd Quarter, 309–33.

O'Shea, M. (1995), *Venture Capital in OECD Countries*, Paris: OECD, Directorate for Financial, Fiscal and Enterprise Affairs.

Oakey, R. P. (1984), *High Technology Small Firms*, London: Frances Pinter.

Oakey, R. P. (1985), 'British university science parks and high technology small firms: a comment on the potential for sustained industrial growth', *International Small Business Journal*, 4(1): 58–67.

Oakey, R. P. (1995), *High-Technology New Firms: Variable Barriers to Growth*, London: Paul Chapman.

Oakey, R. P. and Cooper, S. Y. (1989), 'High technology industry, agglomeration and the potential for peripherally sited small firms', *Regional Studies*, 23(4): 347–60.

Oakey, R. P. and Cooper, S. Y. (1991), 'The relationship between product technology and innovation performance in high technology small firms', *Technovation*, 11(2): 79–92.

Oakey, R. P., Cooper, S. Y. and Biggar, J. (1993), 'Product marketing and sales in high-technology small firms', 201–22, in P. Swann (ed.), *New Technologies and the Firm*, London: Routledge.

Oakey, R. P., Faulkner, W., Cooper, S. Y. and Walsh, V. (1990), *New Firms in the Biotechnology Industry*, London: Pinter Publishers.

Oakey, R. P., Rothwell, R. and Cooper, S. Y. (1988), *The Management of Innovation in High Technology Small Firms*, London: Pinter Publishers.

OECD (1986), 'Self-Employment in OECD Countries', *OECD Employment Outlook*, Paris: September.

OECD (1997a), *Globalisation and Small and Medium Enterprises (SMEs)*, 1, Paris: OECD.

OECD (1997), *Information Technology Outlook 1997*, Paris: OECD.

OECD (1998), *Use of Information and Communication Technologies at Work*, Paris: OECD.

OECD (2000), *Employment Outlook 2000*, Paris: OECD.

Office for National Statistics (2003), *Business Monitor PA1003 Size Analysis of United Kingdom Businesses*, London: HMSO.

Office for National Statistics (2005a), *UK Workforce Jobs, Seasonally Adjusted, 1959–2004*.

Office for National Statistics (2005b), RP02 Retail Prices Index (RPI) all items, April.

Oldfield, C. (1999), 'Red Tape is Strangling Enterprise', *Sunday Times*, 31 October: 7.

Oman, C. (1984), *New Forms of International Investment in Developing Countries*, Paris: OECD.

Orr, A. (1995), 'Customers for Life', *Target Marketing*, 18(3), March.

Orser, B. J. and Foster, M. K. (1994), 'Lending Practices and Canadian Women in Micro-based Businesses', *Women in Management Review*, 9(5): 11–9.

Ortega, F. (1997), *La Pequena y mediana empresa en el ordenamiento juridico-laboral (SMEs in the labour legal ordinance)*, Ministry of Labour and Social Issues, Survey on Labour Situation.

Osbourne, D. and Gaebler, T. (1992), *Reinventing Government*. Reading, Mass.: Addison-Wesley.

Oviatt, B. M. and McDougall, P. P. (1994a), 'Global start-ups: Entrepreneurs on a worldwide stage', *Academy of Management Executive*, 25(2): 30–43.

Oviatt, B. M. and McDougall, P. P. (1994b), 'Toward a theory of international new ventures', *Journal of International Business Studies*, 25(1): 45–64.

Owualah, S. (1987), 'Providing the Necessary Economic Infrastructure for Small Business: Whose Responsibility?', *International Small Business Journal*, 6(1): 10–30.

Ozanne, U. and Hunt, S. (1971), *The Economic Effects of Franchising*, US Select Committee on Small Business, Washington, DC.

Padmanabhan, K. (1986), 'Are the Franchised Businesses Less Risky than the Non-Franchised Businesses?', Proceedings of the 1st Conference of the Society of Franchising, Nebraska, January 28–30.

Pajackowska, C. and Young, L. (1992), 'Race, representation and psychoanalysis', in J. Donald and A. Rattansi (eds.) *Race, Culture, Difference*, London: Sage.

Pakes, A. and Griliches, Z. (1980), 'Patents and R&D at the Firm Level: A First Report', *Economics Letters*, 5: 377–81.

Parker, D. (1994), 'Encounters Across The Counter: Young Chinese People In Britain', *New Community*, 20: 621–34.

Parker, K. T. and Vickerstaff, S. (1996), 'TECs, LECs and small firms: Differences in provision and performance', *Environment and Planning C: Government and Policy*, 14: 251–67.

Parker, S. (2004), *The Economics of Self-employment and Entrepreneurship*, Cambridge: Cambridge University Press.

Parker, S. (ed.) (2006), *The International Handbook of Entrepreneurship*, Volume 2: The Life Cycle of Entrepreneurial Ventures, Dordrecht: Kluwer.

Parker, S. C. (1997), 'The Distribution of Self-Employment Income in the United Kingdom, 1976–1991', *Economic Journal*, 107(441): 455–66.

Parker, S., Brown, R., Child, J. and Smith, M. (1972), *The Sociology of Industry*, London: George Allen and Unwin.

Patel, S. (1988), 'Insurance and Ethnic Community Business', *New Community*, 15: 79–89.

Pavitt, K., Robson, M. and Townsend, J. (1987), 'The size distribution of innovating firms in the UK: 1945–83', *Journal of Industrial Economics*, 35(3): 297–316.

Pavord, W. C. and Bogart, R. G. (1975), 'The Dynamics of the Decision to Export', *Akron Business and Economic Review*, 6(Spring): 6–11.

Peach, C. (1996), 'A Question Of Collar', *Times Higher*, 23 August.

Peacock, P. (1986), 'The influence of risk-taking as a cognitive judgmental behavior of small business success', in R. Ronstadt, J. A. Hornaday, R. Peterson and K. H. Vesper (eds.), *Frontiers of Entrepreneurship Research*, 110–8, Babson Park, MA: Center for Entrepreneurial Studies, Babson College.

Pearson, G. J. (1989), 'Promoting entrepreneurship in large companies', *Long Range Planning*, 22(3): 87–97.

Peel, M. J. and Bridge, J. (1998), 'How Planning and Capital Budgeting Improve SME Performance', *Long Range Planning*, 31(6).

Peng, M. W. (2001), 'The resource-based view and international business', *Journal of Management*, 27: 803–29.

Penrose, E. (1959), *The Theory of the Growth of the Firm*, London: John Wiley.

Perez, M. and Sanchez, A. (2002), 'Lean Production and Technology Networks in the Spanish Automotive Supplier Industry', *Management International Review*, 42(3): 261–72.

Perren, L. (undated), 'Comparing Entrepreneurship and Leadership: A textual analysis'. Working paper. London: Council for Excellence in Management and Leadership.

Perren, L. and Grant, P. (2001), 'Management and Leadership in UK SMEs: Witness Testimonies from the World of Entrepreneurs and SME Managers', London: Council for Excellence in Leadership and Management.

Perry, C., MacArthur, R., Meredith, G. and Cunnington, B. (1986), 'Need for achievement and locus of control of Australian small business owner-managers and super-entrepreneurs', *International Small Business Journal*, 4(4): 55–64.

Peters, T. and Waterman, R. (1982), *In Search of Excellence*, London: Harper and Row.

Pharoah, C., Scott, D. and Fisher, A. (2004), *Social Enterprise in the Balance; Challenges for the Voluntary Sector*, West Malling: CAF.

Philips, B. and Kirchhoff, B. (1989), 'Formation, Growth and Survival: Small Firm Dynamics in the US economy', *Small Business Economics*, 1(1): 65–74.

Phizacklea, A. (1990), *Unpacking The Fashion Industry*, London: Routledge.

Phizacklea, A. and Ram, M. (1996), 'Open For Business? – Ethnic Entrepreneurship In Comparative Perspective', *Work, Employment and Society*, 10(2): 319–39.

Pilat, D. (2004), *The Major Growth Regions in Comparison: Some Findings from recent OECD Work on Growth Productivity and Productivity*, OECD Breakfast Series in partnership with NABE, 18 February.

Pinchot, G. (1986), *Intrapreneuring*, New York: Harper and Row.

Pinchot, G. (1987), 'Innovation through intrapreneuring', *Research Management*, 30(2).

Pinchot, G. and Pinchot, E. S. (1978), 'Intra corporate entrepreneurship', research note.

Piore, M. and Sabel, C. (1984), *The Second Industrial Divide*, New York: Basic Books.

PIU (2000), *Reaching Out: The role of Central Government at Regional and Local Level*, Performance and Innovation Unit, Strategy Unit, Cabinet Office, London.

Pizarro, I., Real, J. C. and Sousa (2002), 'Corporate Entrepreneurship, a knowledge-based view', paper presented at the European Academy of Management Conference, Stockholm, 9–11 May.

Politis, D. and Landström, H. (2002), 'Informal investors as entrepreneurs – the development of an entrepreneurial career', *Venture Capital: an international journal of entrepreneurial finance*, 4: 77–101.

Poon, S. and Swatmann, P. (1999), 'An Exploratory Study of Small Business Internet Commerce Issues', *Journal of Information and Management*, 35(1): 9–18.

Porter, M. E. (1980), *Competitive Strategy – Techniques for Analysing Industries and Competitors*, New York: Free Press.

Porter, M. E. (1985), *Competitive Advantage: Creating and Sustaining Superior Performance*, New York: Free Press.

Porter, M. (1990), *The Competitive Advantage of Nations*, London: Macmillan.

Porter, M. E. (1998), 'Clusters and the New Economics of Competition', *Harvard Business Review*, 96(6): 77–91.

Porter, M. E. and Millar, V. E. (1985), 'How Information Gives You Competitive Advantage', in *Harvard Business Review*, 63(4): 149–60.

Portes, A. and Bach, R. L. (1985), *Latin Journey: Cuban and Mexican Immigrants In The United States*, Berkeley: University of California Press.

Poutziouris, P. and Chittenden, F. (1996), 'Family Businesses or Business Families?' UK Institute for Small Business Affairs Monograph in association with National Westminster Bank, Leeds.

Poutziouris, P. (2005), 'Performance of family firms, *Financial Times*, 28th January.

Poutziouris, P., Chittenden, F. and Michaelas, N. (1999), 'Modelling the impact of taxation on the small business economy: the NatWest/MBS tax index for the self-employed, sole-traders and partnerships', *Environment and Planning C: Government and Policy*, 17: 577–92.

Poutziouris, P., Chittenden, F. and Michaelas, N. (2001), 'Modelling the impact of taxation (direct and compliance costs) on the UK small business economy', in C. Evans, J. Hasseldine and J. Pope (eds.), *Tax Compliance costs*: Festschrift for Cedric Sandford, Prospect Media, Sydney.

Poutziouris, P., Chittenden, F., Watts, T. and Soufari, K. (2003), 'A comparative analysis of the impact of taxation on the SME Economy in the case of UK and US – New York State in the year 2000', *Environment and Planning C: Government and Policy*, 21: 493–508.

Powell, W. W. (1990), 'Neither Market nor Hierarchy: New Forms of Organisation', in L. L. Commings and Brustaw (eds.), *Research in Organizational Behaviour*, 295–336.

Powell, W., Koput, K. and Smith-Doerr, L. (1996), 'Interorganizational collaboration and the locus of innovation: Networks of learning in biotechnology', *Administrative Science Quarterly*, 41: 116–45.

Prahalad, C. and Hamel, G. (1990), 'The core competence of the corporation', *Harvard Business Review*, 68(3): 79–91.

Prais, S. J. (1976), *The Evolution of Giant Firms in Britain*, Cambridge: Cambridge University Press.

Pratt, M. G. (2000), 'The good, the bad, and the ambivalent: Managing identification among Amway distributors', *Administrative Science Quarterly*, 45(3): 456–93.

Premaratne, S. (2001), 'Networks, Resources and Small Business Growth: The Experience in Sri Lanka', *Journal of Small Business Management*, 39(4): 363–71.

Preston, S. L. (2004), *Angel Investment Groups, Networks and Funds: A Guidebook to Developing the Right Angel Organisation For Your Community*, Kansas City.

Priest, S. J. (1999), 'Business Link services to small and medium-sized enterprises: targeting, innovation and charging', *Environment and Planning C: Government and Policy*, 17: 177–94.

Provan, K. and Milwood, H. (1995), 'A Preliminary Theory of Interorganisational Network Effectiveness', *Administrative Science Quarterly*, 40: 1–33.

Pryke, R. (1981), *The nationalised industries*, Martin Robertson, Oxford.

Pryor, A. K. and Shays, E. M. (1993), 'Growing the business with intrapreneurs', *Business Quarterly*, 43–50.

Pugliese, E. (1993), 'Restructuring of the Labour Market and The Role of Third World Migrations In Europe', *Environment and Planning D: Society and Space*, 11: 513–22.

Putnam, R. (2001), *Bowling Alone*, New York: Simon and Schuster.

Putnam, R. (ed.) (2004), *Democracies in Flux: The Evolution of Social Capital in Contemporary Society*, New York: Oxford University Press.

Pyke, E. (1992), *Industrial Development Through Small Firm Cooperation*, Geneva: International Labour Office.

Pyke, F. and Sengenberger, W. (eds.) (1992), *Industrial districts and local economic regeneration*, ILO, Geneva.

Quayle, M. (2002), 'E-Commerce: the challenge for UK SMEs in the twenty-first century', *Journal of Operations and Production Management*, 22(10): 11–48.

Quinn, R. and Cameron, K. (1983), 'Organisational life cycles and shifting criteria of effectiveness', *Management Science*, 29: 33–51.

Rainnie, A. (1989), *Industrial Relations in Small Firms, Small Isn't Beautiful*, London: Routledge.

Rainnie, A. (1991), 'Small firms: Between the enterprise culture and New Times', in R. Burrows (eds.), *Deciphering the enterprise culture*, London: Routledge.

Rainnie, A. and Scott, M. (1986), 'Industrial Relations in the Small Firm', *International Small Business Journal*, 4(4): 42–60.

Ram, M. (1991), 'The Dynamics of Workplace Relations in Small Firms', *International Small Business Journal*, 12(3): 42–53.

Ram, M. (1992), 'Coping With Racism: Asian Employers In The Inner City', *Work Employment and Society*, 6: 601–18.

Ram, M. (1994a), 'Unravelling Social Networks in Ethnic Minority Firms', *International Small Business Journal*, 12(3): 42–53.

Ram, M. (1994b), *Managing to Survive – Working Lives in Small Firms*, Oxford: Blackwell.

Ram, M. (1997), 'Supporting ethnic minority enterprise: Views from the providers', in M. Ram, D. Deakins and D. Smallbone (eds.), *Small firms: Enterprising Futures*, London: Paul Chapman Publishing, 148–60.

Ram, M. (1998), 'Enterprise Support and Ethnic Minority Firms', *Journal of Ethnic and Migration Studies*, 21(1): 143–58.

Ram, M. and Deakins, D. (1995), *African-Caribbean Entrepreneurship in Britain*, University of Central England, Birmingham.

Ram, M. and Deakins, D. (1996), 'African-Caribbean Entrepreneurship In Britain', *New Community*, 22(1): 67–84.

Ram, M. and Edwards, P. (2003), 'Praising Caesar not burying him', *Work, Employment and Society*, 17(4): 719–30.

Ram, M. and Holliday, R. (1993a), 'Keeping it in the Family: Family Culture in Small firms', Chapter 10 in F. Chittenden, M. Robertson and D. Watkins, *Small Firms: Recession and Recovery*, London: Paul Chapman.

Ram, M. and Holliday, R. (1993b), 'Relative Merits: Family Culture and Kinship in Small Firms', *Sociology*, 2(4): 629–48.

Ram, M. and Jones, T. (1998), *Ethnic Minorities in Business*, Milton Keynes: Open University Press.

Ram, M. and Smallbone, D. (2001), *Ethnic Minority Enterprise: Policy in Practice*, DTI Small Business Service Research Report.

Ram, M. and Smallbone, D. (2002), 'Ethnic Minority Business Support in the Era of the Small Business Service', *Environment and Planning 'C': Government and Policy*, 20: 235–49.

Ram, M., Abbas, T., Sanghera, B., Barlow, G. and Jones, T. (2001), '"Apprentice Entrepreneurs"? Ethnic Minority Workers in the Independent Restaurant Sector', *Work, Employment and Society*, 15(2): 353–72.

Ram, M., Edwards, P. and Jones, T. (2002), *The Employment of Illegal Immigrants in SMEs*, DTI Central Unit Research Report.

Ram, M., Edwards, P., Gilman, M. and Arrowsmith, J. (2001), 'The Dynamics of Informality: Employment Relations in Small Firms and the Effects of Regulatory Change', *Work, Employment and Society*, 15(4): 845–61.

Ram, M., Sanghera, B., Abbas, T. and Jones, T. (2000), 'Ethnic minority business in comparative perspective: the case of the independent restaurant sector', *Journal of Ethnic and Migration Studies*, 26(3): 405–510.

Ram, M., Smallbone, D., Deakins, D. and Jones, T. (2003), 'Banking on "break-out": Finance and the Development of Ethnic Minority Businesses', *Journal of Ethnic and Migration Studies*, 29(4): 663–81.

Ramsden, M. and Bennett, R. J. (2005), 'The benefit of external supports to SMEs: "Hard" versus "soft" outcomes and satisfaction levels', *Journal of Small Business and Enterprise Development*.

Rapoport, R. and Rapoport, R. (1976), *Dual-Career Families Re-Examined: New Integrations of Work and Family*, New York: Harper and Row.

Rath, J. (ed.) (1998), *Immigrant Businesses on The Urban Fringe. A Case for Interdisciplinary Analysis*, Basingstoke: Macmillan.

Rath, J. (2000), *Immigrant Businesses: The Economic, Political and Social Environment*, Houndmills: Macmillan Press.

Rath, J. and Kloosterman, R. (2003), 'The Netherlands: a Dutch treat', in R. Kloosterman and J. Rath (eds.), *Immigrant Entrepreneurship: Venturing Abroad in the Age of Globalisation*, Oxford: Berg.

Ray, D. M. (1986), 'Perceptions of risk and new enterprise formation in Singapore: an exploratory study', in R. Ronstadt, J. A. Hornaday, R. Peterson and K. H. Vesper (eds.), *Frontiers of Entrepreneurship Research*, 119–45. Wellesley, MA: Babson College.

Ray, D. M. (1994), 'The role of risk-taking in Singapore', *Journal of Business Venturing*, 9: 157–77.

Raymond, L. (1987), 'The Presence of End-User Computing in Small Business: An Exploratory Investigation of Its Distinguishing Organisational and Information Systems Context', in *INFOR – Information Systems and Operational Research*, 25(3): 198–213.

Raymond, L. (1989), 'Management Information Systems: Problems and Opportunities', in *International Small Business Journal*, 7(4): 44–53.

Raymond, L. (1990), 'Organizational Context and IS Success: A Contingency Approach', in *Journal of Management Information Systems*, 6(4): 5–20.

Raymond, L. and Magenat-Thalmann, N. (1982), 'Information Systems in Small Business: Are They Used in Managerial Decisions?', in *American Journal of Small Business*, 6(4): 20–6.

Razin, E. (1993), 'Immigrant Entrepreneurs in Israel, Canada and California', in I. Light and P. Bhachu (eds.), *Immigration and Entrepreneurship*, New Brunswick, NJ: Transaction.

Read, L. (1994), 'The financing of women-owned businesses: a review and research agenda', Venture Finance Working paper No. 8, University of Southampton, Department of Geography.

Read, L. (1998), *The Financing of Small Business: A Comparative Study of Male and Female Business Owners*, London: Routledge.

Read, S., Wiltbank, R. and Sarasvathy, S. D. (2003), 'What do entrepreneurs really learn from experience? The difference between expert and novice entrepreneurs', in P. D. Reynolds *et al.* (ed.), *Frontiers of Entrepreneurship Research 2003*. Wellesley, MA: Babson College.

Rees, H. and Shah, A. (1986), 'An empirical analysis of self-employment in the UK', *Journal of Applied Econometrics*, 1: 95–108.

Rees, T. (1992), *Women and The Labour Market*, London: Routledge.

Reeves, F. and Ward, R. (1984), 'West Indian Business in Britain', in R. Ward and R. Jenkins (eds.) Ethnic Communities In Business, Cambridge: Cambridge University Press, 125–46.

Rehn, A. and Taalas, S. (2004), 'Znakomstva I Svyazi (Acquaintances and Connections) – Blat, the Soviet Union, and Mundane Entrepreneurship', *Entrepreneurship and Regional Development*, 16(3): 235–50.

Reid, G. and Jacobsen, L. (1988), *The Small Entrepreneurial Firm*, David Hume Institute, Aberdeen: University Press.

Reid, S. (1982), 'The Impact of Size on Export Behaviour in Small Firms', in M. R. Czinkota and G. Tesar (eds.), *Export Management: An International Context*, New York: Praeger Publishers, 18–38.

Reid, S. D. (1981), 'The Decision-maker and Export Entry and Expansion', *Journal of International Business Studies*, 12(2): 101–12.

Reid, S. D. (1983a), 'Export Research in a Crisis', in Czinkota, M. R. (ed.), *Export Promotion, the Public and Private Sector Interaction*, New York: Praeger, 129–53.

Reid, S. D. (1983b), 'Firm Internationalisation: Transaction Cost and Strategic Choice', *International Marketing Review*, 1(2): 45–55.

Reid, S. D. (1985), 'Exporting: Does Sales Volume Make a Difference? – Comment', *Journal of International Business Studies*, Summer, 153–5.

Renard, M.-C. (2002), 'Fair trade quality, market and conventions', *Journal of Rural Studies*, 19: 87–96.

Renzulli, L., Aldrich, H. and Moody, J. (2000), 'Family Matters: Gender, Family, and Entrepreneurial Outcomes', *Social Forces*, 79(2): 523–46.

Revans, R. W. (1982), *The Origin and Growth of Action Learning*, Hunt: Chatwell-Bratt.

Rex, J. (1982), 'West Indian and Asian Youth', in E. Cashmore and B. Troyna (eds.), *Black Youth in Crisis*, London: Routledge and Kegan Paul, 53–71.

Reynolds, P. D., Bygrave, W. D. and Autio, E. (2003), *GEM 2003 Global Report*. Kansas, MO: Kauffman Foundation.

Reynolds, P. D., Storey and Westhead, P. (1994), 'Cross National Comparisons of the Variation in New Firm Formation Rates', *Regional Studies*, 28: 443–56.

Richardson, P., Howarth, R. and Finnegan, G. (2004), SEED Working paper 2004/47. 'Jobs, gender and small enterprises in Africa and Asia: Lessons drawn from Bangladesh, the Philippines, Tunisia and Zimbabwe', ILO Geneva, WEDGE Series, 2001.

Riddle, D. F. (1986), *Services and Growth: the role of the special service sector in world development*, Praeger: New York.

Riding, A. L. and Swift, C. S. (1990), 'Women business owners and terms of credit: some empirical findings of the Canadian experience', *Journal of Business Venturing*, 5(5): 327–40.

Riding, A. L., Dal Cin, P., Duxbury, L., Haines, G. and Safrata, R. (1993), *Informal Investors in Canada: The Identification of Salient Characteristics*, Ottawa: Carleton University.

Riding, A. L., Duxbury, L. and Haines, G., Jr (1995), *Financing enterprise development: decision-making by Canadian angels*, mimeo, Ottawa: School of Business, Carleton University.

Ring, P. and Van de Van, A. (1994), 'Developmental Processes of Cooperative Interorganizational Relationships', *Academy of Management Review*, 19(1): 90–118.

Riordan, D. A. and Riordan, M. P. (1993), 'Field Theory: An Alternative to Systems Theories in Understanding the Small Family Business', *Journal of Small Business Management*, April: 66–78.

Roberts, E. B. (1991a), *Entrepreneurs in High Technology*, Oxford: Oxford University Press.

Roberts, E. B. (1991b), 'High stakes for high-tech entrepreneurs: understanding venture capital decision-making', *Sloan Management Review*, 32: 9–20.

Robinson, R. and Pearce, J. (1984), 'Research Thrusts in Small Firm Strategic Planning', *Academy of Management Review*, 9(1): 128–37.

Robinson, V. and Flintoff, I. (1982), 'Asian Retailing In Coventry', *New Community*, 10: 251–58.

Robson, M. (1996a), 'Housing Wealth, Business Creation and Dissolution in the UK Regions', *Small Business Economics*, 8: 39–48.

Robson, M. (1996b), 'Macroeconomic Factors in the Birth and Death of UK Firms: Evidence from Quarterly VAT Registrations', *Manchester School of Economic and Social Studies*, 64(2): 170–88.

Robson, M. T. (1998), 'Self-Employment in the UK Regions', *Applied Economics*, 30: 313–22.

Robson Rhodes (1984), *A Study of Business Financed Under the Small Firms Loan Guarantee Scheme*, Department of Trade and Industry, London, HMSO.

Roet, B. (2001), *Positive Action for Health and Wellbeing: The practical guide to taking control of your life and health*, London: Class Publishing.

Rogers, E. (1962; 1995; 2003), *Diffusion of Innovations* – 1st, 4th and 5th Ed, New York: Free Press.

Rogers, E. and Kincaid, D. (1981), *Communication Networks*, New York: Free Press.

Rogoff, E. G., Kay, R. and Heck, Z. (2003), 'Evolving Research in Entrepreneurship and Family Business: Recognizing Family as the Oxygen that Feeds the Fire of Entrepreneurship', *Journal of Business Venturing*, 18(5): 559–66.

Romanelli, E. (1989), 'Environments and strategies of organisation start-up: Effects on early survival', *Administrative Science Quarterly*, 34: 369–87.

Romme, G. and Dillen, R. (1997), 'Mapping the landscape of organizational learning', *European Management Journal*, 15(1): 68–78.

Rosa, P. (1993), 'Gender and Small Business Co-ownership: Implications for Enterprise Training', paper presented at INTENT, Stirling University.

Rosa, P. and Hamilton, D. (1994), 'Gender and Ownership in UK small firms', *Entrepreneurship Theory and Practice*, 18(3): 11–25.

Rosa, P., Carter, S. and Hamilton, D. (1996), 'Gender as a determinant of small business performance: insights from a British study', *Small Business Economics*, 8: 463–78.

Rosa, P., Hamilton, D., Carter, S. and Burns, H. (1994), 'The impact of gender on small business management: preliminary findings of a British study', *International Small Business Journal*, 12(3): 25–33.

Rose, E. (2003), *Employment Relations*, London: Prentice Hall.

Rosenkopf, L. and Nerkar, A. (2001), 'Beyond local search: Boundary-spanning, exploration, and impact in the optical disk industry', *Strategic Management Journal*, 22: 287–306.

Rosenstein, J., Bruno, A. V., Bygrave, W. D. and Taylor, N. T. (1993), 'The CEO, venture capitalists and the board', *Journal of Business Venturing*, 8: 99–113.

Ross, G. C. (1977), 'The Determination of Financial Structure: The Incentive Signalling Approach', *Bell Journal of Economics and Management Science*, Spring.

Rothwell, R. (1986), 'The Role of the Small Firm in Technical Innovation', in J. Curran (ed.), *The Survival of the Small Firm*, Aldershot: Gower.

Rothwell, R. (1989), 'Small Firms, Innovation and Industrial Change', *Small Business Economics*, 1(1): 51–64.

Rothwell, R. (1991), 'External Networking and Innovation in Small and Medium-Sized Manufacturing Firms in Europe', *Technovation*, 11(2): 93–111.

Rothwell, R. and Gardiner, P. (1985), 'Invention, Innovation, Re-Innovation and the Role of the User: A Case Study of British Hovercraft Development', *Technovation*, 3: 167–86.

Rotter, J. B. (1966), 'Generalized expectancies for internal versus external control of reinforcement', *Psychological Monograph*, 80: 1–28.

Royer, S. (2004), 'Editorial: Small business in a global environment', *International Journal of Globalisation Small Business*, 1(1): 1–6.

Rubenson, G. C. and Gupta, A. K. (1990), 'The Founder's Disease: A Critical Re-examination', in *Frontiers of Entrepreneurship Research*, Wellesley, MA: Babson Center for Entrepreneurship Research.

Rubin, P. (1978), 'The Theory of the Firm and the Structure of the Franchise Contract', *Journal of Law and Economics*, 23: 223–33.

Ruda, W. (1999), 'Innovative High Growth Start-Ups in Germany: the Neuer Markt as a Possibility for IPOs', paper presented at the Thirteenth Research into Entrepreneurship Conference, London, November.

Ruhnka, J. C., Feldman, H. D. and Dean, T. J. (1992), 'The "living dead" phenomenon in venture capital investments', *Journal of Business Venturing*, 7: 137–55.

Rumelt, R. (1991), 'How much does industry matter?', *Strategic Management Journal*, 12: 167–85.

Saari, E. (1996), 'Work with flexibility? Exception to the Contracts of Employment Act and the Contract to Improve Employment Preconditions for Young Adults', Studies in Labour Policy, 139, Ministry of Labour, Helsinki.

Sadler-Smith, E., Spicer, D. P. and Chaston, I. (2001), 'Learning orientations and growth in smaller firms', *Long Range Planning*, 34: 139–58.

Sadowski, B., Maitland, C. and van Dongen, J. (2002), 'Strategic use of the Internet by small to medium-sized companies: an exploratory study', *Information Economics and Policy*, 14(1): 192–203.

Sætre, A. S. (2003), 'Entrepreneurial perspectives on informal venture capital', *Venture Capital: an international journal of entrepreneurial finance*, 5: 71–94.

Sahlman, W. A. (1988), 'Aspects of financial contracting in venture capital', *Journal of Applied Corporate Finance*, 1: 23–36.

Sahlman, W. A. (1990), 'The structure and governance of venture-capital organisations', *Journal of Financial Economics*, 27: 473–521.

Sahlman, W. A. and Stevenson, H. H. (1985), 'Capital market myopia', in J. A. Hornaday, E. B. Shils, J. A. Timmons and K. H. Vesper (eds.), *Frontiers of Entrepreneurship Research 1985*, Wellesley, MA: Babson College, 80–104.

Salaff, J. and Hu, S. M. (1996), 'Working Daughters of Hong Kong: filial piety or power in the family', *Asian Thought and Society*, Sept–Dec., XXI(61): 187–89.

Salamon, L. (1994), 'The Rise of the Nonprofit Sector', *Foreign Affairs*, 73(4): 109–22.

Salamon, L. and Anheier, H. (1999), *The Emerging Sector Revisited*, Baltimore: John Hopkins University.

Salamon, L., Sokolowski, M. and List, R. (2003), *Global Civil Society: An Overview*, Baltimore: Kumarian Press.

Samuelsson, M. (2001), 'Modelling the nascent venture opportunity exploitation process across time', in W. D. Bygrave, E. Autio, C. G. Brush,

P. Davidsson, P. G. Green, P. D. Reynolds and H. J. Sapienza (eds.), *Frontiers of Entrepreneurship Research 2001*, Wellesley, MA, 66–79.

Samuelsson, M. (2004), 'Creating New Ventures: A Longitudinal Investigation of the Nascent Venturing Process', Doctoral dissertation, Jönköping: Jönköping International Business School.

Sandberg, W. and Hofer, C. (1987), 'Improving new venture performance: The role of strategy, industry structure, and the entrepreneur', *Journal of Business Venturing*, 2: 5–28.

Sanders, J. and Nee, V. (1996), 'Immigrant Self-employment: The Family as Social Capital and the Value of Human Capital', *American Sociological Review*, 61(2): 231–49.

Sandford, C. (ed.) (1989), *Administrative and compliance costs of taxation*, Trowbridge: Fiscal Publications.

Sandford, C. (ed.) (1995), *Tax compliance costs: measurement and policy*, Trowbridge: Fiscal Publications.

Sapienza, H. J. and Gupta, A. K. (1994), 'The impact of agency risks and task uncertainty on venture capitalist-CEO interaction', *Academy of Management Journal*, 37: 1618–32.

Sapienza, H. J. and Korsgaard, M. A. (1996), 'Procedural justice in entrepreneur-investor relations', *Academy of Management Journal*, 39: 544–74.

Sapienza, H. J. and Timmons, J. A. (1989), 'The roles of venture capitalists in new ventures: what determines their importance?' Academy of Management Best papers Proceedings, 74–8.

Sapienza, H. J., Manigart, S. and Vermeir, W. (1996), 'Venture capitalist governance and value added in four countries', *Journal of Business Venturing*, 11: 439–69.

Sarasvathy, S. (1999), *Decision making in the absence of markets: An empirically grounded model of entrepreneurial expertise*, School of Business, University of Washington.

Sarasvathy, S. (2001), 'Causation and effectuation: towards a theoretical shift from economic inevitability to entrepreneurial contingency', *Academy of Management Review*, 26(2): 243–88.

Sarasvathy, S., Dew, N., Velamuri, R. and Venkataraman, S. (2003), 'Three views of entrepreneurial opportunity', in A. Z. J. and D. B. Audretsch (eds.), *Handbook of Entrepreneurship Research*, Dordrecht, NL: Kluwer.

Sassen, S. (1991), *The Global City: New York, London, Tokyo*, Princeton University Press.

Sassen, S. (1997), *Globalization and its Discontents: Collected Essays*, New York: New Press.

Sathe, V. (1989), 'Fostering entrepreneurship in the large, diversified firm', *Organizational Dynamics*, 18(1): 20–32.

Saxenian, A. (1985), 'Silicon Valley and Route 128: Regional Prototypes or Historic Exceptions?', in M. Castels (ed.), *High Technology, Space and Society*, Beverly Hills: Sage.

Saxenian, A. (1996), *Regional Advantage: Culture and Competition in Silicon Valley and Route 128*, Cambridge, Massachusetts: Harvard University Press.

Saxenian, A. L. (1990), 'Regional Networks and the Resurgence of Silicon Valley', *Californian Management Review*, 33(1): 89–112.

Say, J.-B. (2001), *A Treatise on Political Economy*, Quddus, M. and Rashid, S. (eds.), London: Transaction Publishing.

SBA (1996), *The state of small business 1996*, Washington DC: Small Business Administration.

SBC (2004a), *Small Business Council: Annual Report 2004*, Small Business Council, London.

SBC (2004b), *Evaluation of government employment regulations and their impact on small business*, Small Business Council, London.

SBRC (1992), *The State of British Enterprise: Growth, Innovation and Competitive Advantage in Small and Medium-Sized Firms*, University of Cambridge, Small Business Research Centre.

SBS (2002), *Small business and government*, Small Business Services, London.

SBS (2004), *A Government Action Plan for Small Business: making the UK the best place in the world to start-up and grow a business: The Evidence Case*, Small Business Services, Department of Trade and Industry, London.

Scarman, Lord (1981), *The Brixton Disorders 10–12 April 1981*, Cmnd 8427, London: HMSO.

Scarpetta, S., Hemmings, P., Tressel, T. and Woo, J. (2002), 'The Role of Policy and Institutions for Productivity and Firm Dynamics: Evidence from Micro and Industry Data', OECD working paper 329, OECD: Paris.

Scase, R. (2003), 'Employment Relations in Small Firms', in P. Edwards (ed.), *Industrial Relations, Theory and Practice in Britain*, Oxford: Blackwell.

Scase, R. (2004), 'Managerial Strategies in Small Firms', in S. Marlow, D. Patton and M. Ram (eds.), *Management Labour in Small Firms*, London: Routledge.

Scheré, J. (1982), 'Tolerance of ambiguity as a discriminating variable between entrepreneurs and managers', Academy of Management Best papers Proceedings, Academy of Management, 404–8.

Scherer, F. M. (1980), *Industrial Market Structure and Economic Performance*, Chicago: Rand McNally.

Scherer, F. M. (1983a), 'Concentration, R&D, and Productivity Change', *Southern Economic Journal*, 50: 221–5.

Scherer, F. M. (1983b), 'The Propensity to Patent,' *International Journal of Industrial Organization*, 1: 107–28.

Scherer, F. M. (1988), 'Testimony before the Subcommittee on Monopolies and Commercial Law', Committee on the Judiciary, U.S. House of Representatives, February 24.

Scherer, F. M. (1991), 'Changing Perspectives on the Firm Size Problem,' in Z. J. Acs and D. B. Audretsch (eds.), *Innovation and Technological Change: An International Comparison*, Ann Arbor: University of Michigan Press, 24–38.

Scherer, R. F., Brodzinski, J. D. and Wiebe, F. A. (1991), 'Examining the relationship between personality and entrepreneurial career preference', *Entrepreneurship and Regional Development*, 3: 195–206.

Scholhammer, H. and Kuriloff, A. (1979), *Entrepreneurship and Small Business Management*, New York: John Wiley.

Schreier, J. (1973), *The female entrepreneur: a pilot study*, Milwaukee, Wis.: Center for Venture Management.

Schulze, W. S., Lubatkin, M. H. and Dino, R. N. (2003), 'Toward a Theory of Agency and Altruism in Family Firms', *Journal of Business Venturing*, 18(4): 473–90.

Schumacher, E. F. (1974), *Small is Beautiful*, London: Abacus.

Schumpeter, J. A. (1934), *History of Economic Analysis*, New York: Oxford University Press.

Schumpeter, J. A. (1942), *Capitalism, Socialism and Democracy*, New York, NY: Harper and Row.

Schumpeter, J. A. (1980), *Theory of Economic Development*. London: Transaction Publishing.

Schutgens, V. and Wever, E. (2000), 'Determinants of New Firm Success', papers in Regional Science, 79: 135–59.

Schwab, B. and Schwab, H. (1997), 'Better risk management: a key to improved performance', *Journal of General Management*, 22(4): 65–75.

Schwartz, E. B. (1976), 'Entrepreneurship: a new female frontier', *Journal of Contemporary Business*, Winter: 47–76.

Schwenk, C. and Shrader, C. (1993), 'Effects of Formal Strategic Planning on Financial performance in Small firms: A Meta-Analysis', *Entrepreneurship Theory and Practice*, Spring: 53–64.

Schwer, R. K. and Yucelt, U. (1984), 'A Study of risk-taking propensities among small business entrepreneurs and managers: An empirical evaluation', *American Journal of Small Business*, 8(3): 31–40.

Scott, J. (1991), *Social Network Analysis: A Handbook*, London: Sage.

Scott, M. and Rosa, P. (1997), 'New Businesses from Old: the Role of Portfolio Entrepreneurs in the Start-up and Growth of Small Firms', in M. Ram, D. Deakins and D. Smallbone (eds.), *Small Firms: Enterprising Futures*, London: Paul Chapman, 33–46.

Scott, M., Roberts, I., Holroyd, G. and Sawbridge, D. (1989), 'Management and Industrial Relations in Small Firms', Research paper no 70, Department of Employment, London.

Scott, T. (1998), *Two men and a bottle. Inc.* 15 May.

Sear, L. and Agar, J. (1996), *A survey of Business Link Personal Advisers: Are they meeting expectations?* Durham: Durham University Business School.

Sear, L. and Green, H. (1996), 'Small business development and enterprise support', in G. Haughton and C. Williams (eds.), *Corporate City? Partnership, participation and partition in urban development in Leeds*, Aldershot: Avebury.

Sear, L. and Agar, J. (1996), 'Business Links and personal business advisers: selling services irrespective of client's needs?', in Proceedings of 19th ISBA Conference, Birmingham.

Segal Quince and Partners (1985), *The Cambridge Phenomenon*, Cambridge: Segal Quince and Partners.

Sen, C. and Lee, H. (1994), 'The Impact of Information Technology on the Franchise Decision', Proceedings of the 8th Conference of the Society of Franchising, Nevada, 13/14 February.

Senge, M. P. (1990), 'The leader's new work: Building learning organizations', *Sloan Management Review*, Fall: 7–23.

Seringhaus, F. H. R. and Rosson, P. J. (1991), 'Export Promotion and Public Organisations: The State of the Art', in R. F. Seringhaus and P. J. Rosson (eds.), *Export Development and Promotion: The Role of Public Organisations*, Boston, MA: Kluwer Academic Publishers, 3–18.

Sexton, D. L. (1987), 'Advancing Small Business Research: Utilizing Research from Other Areas', *American Journal of Small Business*, 11(3): 25–30.

Sexton, D. L. and Bowman-Upton, N. (1985), 'The entrepreneur: A capable executive and more', *Journal of Business Venturing*, 1: 129–40.

Sexton, D. L. and Bowman-Upton, N. (1990) 'Female and Male Entrepreneurs: Psychological Characteristics and Their Role in Gender Discrimination', *Journal of Business Venturing*, 5(1): 29–36.

Sexton, D. L. and Landström, H. (eds.) (2000) *The Blackwell Handbook of Entrepreneurship*, Oxford: Blackwell Publishers.

Shakeshaft, C. and Nowell, I. (1984), 'Research on themes, concepts and models of organisational behaviour: the influence of gender', *Issues in Education*, 2(3): 186–203.

Shane, S. (2000), 'Prior knowledge and the discovery of entrepreneurial opportunities', *Organizational Science*, 11(4): 448–69.

Shane, S. (2003), 'A General Theory of Entrepreneurship: the Individual-Opportunity Nexus', Cheltenham, UK, and Northampton, Mass: Edward Elgar Publishing Ltd.

Shane, S. and Eckhardt, J. (2003), 'The individual-opportunity nexus', in Z. J. Acs and D. B. Audretsch (eds.), *Handbook of Entrepreneurship Research*, 161–94, Dordrecht, NL: Kluwer.

Shane, S. and Venkataraman, S. (2000), 'The promise of entrepreneurship as a field of research', Academy of Management Review, 25(1): 217–26.

Shane, S. and Venkataraman, S. (2001), 'Entrepreneurship as a field of research: a response to Zahra and Dess, Singh, and Erikson', *Academy of Management Review*, 26(1): 13–16.

Shanklin, W. L. and Ryans, J. K. (1988), 'Organising for high-tech marketing', 487–98, in M. L. Tushman and W. L. Moore (eds.), *Readings in the Management of Innovation*, 2nd Edition, New York: HarperCollins.

Sharma, D. (1993), 'Introduction: Industrial Networks in Marketing', S. T. Cavusgil and D. Sharma (eds.), *Advances in International Marketing*, 5: 1–9, Greenwich: JAI Press.

Sharma, P. (1999), 'Towards a reconciliation of the definitional issues in the field of corporate entrepreneurship', *Entrepreneurship, Theory and Practice*, 23(3): 11–18

Shaver, K. G. and Scott, L. R. (1991), 'Person, process, choice: The psychology of new venture creation', *Entrepreneurship Theory and Practice*, 16(2): 23–45.

Shaw, E. (1997), 'The Real Networks of Small Firms', in D. Deakins, P. Jennings and C. Mason (eds.), *Small Firms: Entrepreneurship in the 1990s*, London: Paul Chapman Publishing.

Shaw, E. (1998), 'Social Networks: Their Impact on the Innovative Behaviour of Small Service Firms', *International Journal of Innovation Management*, 2(2): 201–22.

Shaw, E. and Conway, S. (2000), 'Networking and the Small Firm', in *Enterprise and Small Business: Principles, Practice and Policy*, S. Carter and D. Jones-Evans (eds.), UK: Pearson Education.

Shepherd, D. A. (1999), 'Venture capitalists' introspection: a comparison on "in use" and "espoused" decision policies', *Journal of Small Business Management*, 37(2): 76–87.

Shepherd, D. A. and Zacharakis, A. (1999), 'Conjoint analysis: a new methodological approach for researching venture capitalists decision policies', *Venture Capital: An International Journal of Entrepreneurial Finance*, 1: 197–217.

Shepherd, D. A. and Zacharakis, A. (2001), 'The venture capitalist-entrepreneur relationship: control, trust and confidence in co-operative behaviour', V*enture Capital: an international journal of entrepreneurial finance*, 3: 129–49.

Shepherd, D. A. and Zacharakis, A. (2002), 'Venture capitalists' expertise: a call for research into decision aids and cognitive feedback', *Journal of Business Venturing*, 17: 1–20.

Shutt, J. and Whittington, R. (1987), 'Fragmentation Strategies and the Rise of Small Units: Cases from the North West', *Regional Studies*, 21: 13–23.

Silva, J. (2004), 'Venture capitalists' decision-making in small equity markets: a case study using participant observation', *Venture Capital: an international journal of entrepreneurial finance*, 6: 125–45.

Simmel, G. (1955), *Conflict and the Web of Group-Affiliations*, translated by K. Wolff and R. Bendix, New York: Free Press.

Singh, R. P. (2001), 'A comment on developing the field of entrepreneurship through the study of opportunity recognition and exploitation', *Academy of Management Review*, 26(1): 10–12.

Sinkula, M. J. (1994), 'Market information processing and organizational learning', *Journal of Marketing*, 58: 35–45.

Sinkula, M. J., Baker, W. E. and Noordewier, T. (1997), 'A framework for market-based organizational learning: Linking values, knowledge, and behavior', *Journal of the Academy of Marketing Science*, 25(4): 305–18.

Sjöberg, L. (1993), *Life-styles and Risk Perception* (14), Stockholm, Sweden: Center for Risk Research, Stockholm School of Economics.

Skinner, B. F. (1971), *Beyond Freedom and Dignity*, New York: Alfred A Knopf.

Slater, F. S. and Narver, J. C. (1995), 'Market orientation and the learning organization', *Journal of Marketing*, 59 (July): 63–74.

Slater, S. (1995), 'Learning to change', *Business Horizons*, Nov–Dec: 13–20.

Smailes, R. and Cooper, S. (2004), 'Academic enterprise and sustainable wealth-creation', in K. Tang, A. J. Vohora and R. Freeman (eds.), *Taking Research to Market: How to Build and Invest in Successful University Spinouts*, London: Euromoney Books, 21–30.

Small Business Foresight (1996), *Small Business Foresight Digest*, Edition 1.1, Durham: University of Durham.

Small Business Research Trust (2003), *NatWest Quarterly Survey of Small Business Customers*.

Small Business Service (SBS) (2003a), *A Strategic Framework for Women's Enterprise*, London: DTI Small Business.

Small Business Service (SBS) (2003b), www.sbs.gov.uk/content/statistics/stats 2001.xls.

Small Business Service (SBS) (2004), *SME Statistics*, http://www.sbs.gov.uk/smes.

Small Business Service (SBS) (2005), www.sbs.gov.uk/sbsgov/action/layer?topicId=7000011759.

Small Business Service (Various years), *SME Statistics*, http://www.sbs.gov.uk/smes.

Smallbone, D. (1990), 'Success and Failure in New Businesses', *International Small Business Journal*, 8(2): 34–47.

Smallbone, D. (1997), 'Selective targeting in SME policy: criteria and implementation issues', 126–140, in D. Deakins, P. Jennings and C. Mason (eds.), *Small Firms: entrepreneurship in the Nineties*, London: Paul Chapman.

Smallbone, D. and North, D. (1996), 'Survival, Growth and Age of SMEs: Some Implications for Regional Development', in M. Davison (ed.), *Small Firm Formation and Regional Economic Development*, 36–64.

Smallbone, D. and Wyer, P. (1994), 'SMEs and Exporting: Developing an Analytical Framework', paper presented to Small Business and Enterprise Development Conference, Manchester, 28–29 March 1994.

Smallbone, D. and Wyer, P. (1997), 'Export Activities in SMEs: A Strategic Framework', Centre for Enterprise and Economic Development Research, Middlesex University Working paper Series, CEEDR Publication No. 6, October 1997.

Smallbone, D., Baldock, R. and Burgess, S. (2002), 'Targeted Support for High Growth Start-Ups: Some Policy Issues', *Environment and Planning C, Government and Policy*, 20(2): 195–209.

Smallbone, D. J., Leigh, R. and North, D. (1995), 'The Characteristics and Strategies of High Growth Firms', *International Journal of Entrepreneurial Behaviour and Research*, 1(3): 44–62.

Smallbone, D., North, D. and Kalantaridis, C. (1999a), 'Adapting to Peripherality: a Study of Small Manufacturing Firms in Northern England,' *Entrepreneurship and Regional Development*, 11(2): 109–28.

Smallbone, D., North, D. and Leigh, R. (1992), 'Managing Change for Growth and Survival: the Study of Mature Manufacturing Firms in London in the 1980s', Working paper No. 3, Planning Research Centre, Middlesex Polytechnic.

Smallbone, D., North, D. and Leigh, R. (1993), 'The Growth and Survival of Mature Manufacturing SMEs in the 1980s: an Urban-Rural Comparison', in J. Curran and D. Storey (eds.), *Small Firms in Urban and Rural Locations*, London: Routledge, 8: 79–131.

Smallbone, D., Piasecki, B., Damyanov, A., Labriandis, L. and Venesaar, U. (1998), 'Internationalisation, Inter-firm Linkages and SME Development in Central and Western Europe'. Final report to EU Phare (ACE) Committee, Centre for Enterprise and Economic Development Research, Middlesex University, London.

Smallbone, D., Piasecki, B., Venesaar, U., Todorov, K. and Labrianidis, L. (1999b), 'Internationalisation and SME Development in Transition Economies: an International Comparison', *Journal for Small Business and Enterprise Development*, 5(4): 363–75.

Smart, C. and Vertinsky, I. (1984), 'Strategy and the environment: A study of corporate responses to crisis', *Strategic Management Journal*, 5: 199–213.

Smart, G. H. (1999), 'Management assessment methods in venture capital: an empirical analysis of human capital evaluation', *Venture Capital: an international journal of entrepreneurial finance*, 1: 59–82.

Smith, M. and Kumar, R. (2004), 'A Theory of Application Service Provider (ASP) Use from a Client Perspective', *Information and Management*, 41(8): 977–1002.

Smith, N. R. (1967), *The Entrepreneur and His Firm: The Relationship between Type of Man and Type of Company*, East Lansing, MI: Michigan State University.

Smith-Hunter, A., Kapp, J. and Yonkers, V. (2003), 'A Psychological Model of Entrepreneurial Behaviour', *Journal of the Academy of Business and Economics*, April.

Snyder, M. and Cantor, N. (1998), 'Understanding personality and social behavior: a functionalist strategy', in D. T. Gilbert, S. T. Fiske and G. Lindzey (eds.), *The Handbook of Social Psychology*, 4 ed., 1: 635–79, Boston, MA: The McGraw-Hill Companies, Inc.

Sohl, J. E. (1999), 'The early stage equity market in the United States', *Venture Capital: An International Journal of Entrepreneurial Finance*, 1: 101–20.

Sohl, J. E. (2003), 'The private equity market in the USA: lessons from volatility', *Venture Capital: an international journal of entrepreneurial finance*, 5: 29–46.

Sohl, J. E., Van Osnbrugge, M. and Robinson, R. J. (2000), 'Models of angel investing: portals to the early stage market', paper to the Babson-Kauffman Entrepreneurship Research Conference, Babson College, 8–10 June.

Solemn, O. and Stiener, M. (1989), 'Factors for Success in Small Manufacturing Firms – and with Special Emphasis on Growing Firms', paper presented at Conference on Small and Medium Sized Enterprises and the Challenges of 1992, Mikkeli, Finland.

Solomon, G. T. and Fenald, L. W. (1988), 'Value profiles of male and female entrepreneurs', *International Small Business Journal*, 6(3): 24–33.

Sørheim, R. and Landström, H. (2001), 'Informal investors – a categorisation with policy implications', *Entrepreneurship and Regional Development*, 13: 351–70.

Southern, A. and Tilley, F. (2000), 'Small Firms and Information and Communication Technologies: (ICTs): Toward a Typology of ICT Usage', *New Technology Work and Employment*, 15(2).

Spence, J. T. (1985), 'Achievement American style – The rewards and costs of individualism', *American Psychologist*, 40(12): 1285–95.

Spengler, J. and Ford, T. (2002), 'From the Environmentally Challenged City to the Ecological City', available at: http://www.earthscape.org/p3/ger01/ger02.pdf

Spinosa, C., Flores, F. and Dreyfus, H. (1997), *Disclosing New Worlds*, Cambridge, Mass: MIT Press.

Srinavasan, S. (1992), 'The class position of the Asian petite bourgeoisie', *New Community*, 19(1): 61–74.

Srinavasan, S. (1995), *The South Asian Petite Bourgeoisie in Britain*, Aldershot: Avebury.

Stacey, R. D. (1990), 'Dynamic Strategic Management', in *The New Manager's Handbook*, Armstrong, M. (ed.), London: Kogan Page, 299–333.

Stacey, R. D. (1996), *Strategic Management and Organisational Dynamics*, London: Pitman, 21–49; 62–4.

Stafford, W. (1995), 'Ferdinand Tonnies on gender, women and the family', *History of Political Thought*, Autumn, XVI(3): 391–415.

Stanworth, C. and Stanworth, J. (1995), 'The Self-Employed without Employees – Autonomous or Atypical?', *Industrial Relations Journal*, 26(3): 221–9.

Stanworth, J. (1977), *A Study of Franchising in Britain: A Research Report*, University of Westminster.

Stanworth, J. (1984), *A Study of Power Relationships and their Consequences in Franchise Organisations*, University of Westminster.

Stanworth, J. and Curran, J. (1976), 'Growth and the Small Firm – an Alternative View', *Journal of Management Studies*, 13: 95–110.

Stanworth, J. and Gray, C. (eds.) (1991), *Bolton 20 Years On: The Small Firm in the 1990s*, London: Paul Chapman Publishing.

Stanworth, J. and Purdy, D. (1993), The Blenheim Group plc/University of Westminster Franchise Survey, International Franchise Research Centre, Special Studies Series paper No. 1.

Stanworth, J. and Purdy, D. (2003), *SME Facts and Figures*, Report to the All-Party Parliamentary Small Business Group, University of Westminster.

Starbuck, W. H. (1992), 'Learning by knowledge-intensive firms', *Journal of Management Studies*, 713–40.

Staring, R. (2000), 'International migration, undocumented immigration and immigrant entrepreneurship', in J. Rath (ed.), *Immigrant Businesses: The Economic, Political and Social Environment*, London: Macmillan.

Starr, J. A. and Fondas, N. (1992), 'A model of entrepreneurial socialization and organization formation', *Entrepreneurship Theory and Practice*, 17(1): 67–76.

Stata, R. (1989), 'Organizational learning – The key to management innovation', *Sloan Management Review*, Spring: 63–74.

Steensma, H. K. and Fairbank, J. F. (1999), 'Internalizing external technology: A model of governance mode choice and an empirical assessment', *The Journal of High Technology Management Research*, 10(1): 1–35.

Steering Group (1996), *Statistical Surveys: easing the burden on business*, Report of a Steering group, Chair E. Osmotherly, Cabinet Office, London.

Steier, L. (2003), 'Variants of Agency Contracts in Family-Financed Ventures as a Continuum of Familial Altruistic and Market Rationalities', *Journal of Business Venturing*, 18(5): 597–618.

Steier, L. and Greenwood, R. (1995), 'Venture capitalist relationships in the deal structuring and post-investment stages of new firm creation', *Journal of Management Studies*, 32: 337–57.

Steinmetz, L. L. (1969), 'Critical Stages of Small Business Growth', *Business Horizons*, 12(1): 29–34.

Sternberg, R. J. (2004), 'Successful intelligence as a basic for entrepreneurship', *Journal of Business Venturing*, 19: 189–201.

Sternberg, R. J. and Lubart, T. I. (1996), 'Investing in creativity', *American Psychologist*, 51(7): 677–88.

Stevens, T. (1998), 'Idea Dollars: funds set aside for in-company entrepreneurial activity can pay big dividends in new product development', *Industry Week*, 16 February.

Stevenson, H. and Gumpert, D. (1985), 'The Heart of Entrepreneurship', *Harvard Business Review*, 63(2): 85–94.

Stevenson, L. (1983), 'An investigation into the entrepreneurial experience of women', paper presented to the ASAC Conference, Vancouver, University of British Columbia.

Stimpson, D. V., Robinson, P. B., Waranusuntikule, S. and Zheng, R. (1990), 'Attitudinal characteristics of entrepreneurs and non-entrepreneurs in United States, Korea, Thailand, and the People's Republic of China', *Entrepreneurship and Regional Development*, 2: 49–55.

Stogdill, R. M. (1948), 'Personal Factors Associated with Leadership: A Survey of the Literature', *Journal of Psychology*, 25: 35–71.

Stohr, W. (ed.) (1990), *Global Challenge and Local Response*, Mansell, London.

Stokes, D. R. (1997), 'A Lesson in Entrepreneurial Marketing from the Public Sector', *Marketing Education Review*, 7(3): Fall.

Stokes, D. R. (1998), *Small Business Management*, 3rd edition, London: Letts Educational.

Stokes, D. R., Fitchew, S. and Blackburn, R. (1997), *Marketing in Small Firms: a Conceptual Approach*, Report to the Royal Mail, Small Business Research Centre, Kingston University.

Stone, M. and Brush, C. (1996), 'Planning in ambiguous contexts: The dilemma of meeting needs for commitment and demands for legitimacy', *Strategic Management Journal*, 17: 633–52.

Stopford, J. M. and Baden-Fuller, C. (1994), 'Creating corporate entrepreneurship', *Strategic Management Journal*, 15(7): 521–36.

Storey, D. (1982), *Entrepreneurship and the New Firm*, London: Croom Helm.

Storey, D. J. (1985), 'Manufacturing Employment Change in Northern England 1965–78: The Role of Small Business', in *Small Firms in Regional Economic Development*, D. J. Storey (ed.), Cambridge: Cambridge University Press.

Storey, D. J. (1992), 'Should we abandon support to start-up businesses?' Working paper No. 7, Warwick, Warwick Business School Small and Medium Enterprise Centre.

Storey, D. J. (1993), 'Should We Abandon Support to Start-up Businesses', in F. Chittenden and M. Robertson (eds.), *Small Firms: Recession and Recovery*, London: Paul Chapman Publishing, 1–26.

Storey, D. (1994), *Understanding The Small Business Sector*, London: Routledge.

Storey, D. J. and Johnson, S. (1986), 'Job Generation in Britain: A Review of Recent Studies', *International Small Business Journal*, 4(4): 29–46.

Storey, D. J. and Johnson, S. (1987), *Job Generation and Labour Market Change*, London: Macmillan.

Storey, D. J. and Strange, A. (1992), 'Entrepreneurship in Cleveland, 1979–1989: a study of the effects of the enterprise culture', Employment Department, Research Series No. 3.

Storey, D. and Westhead, P. (1994), 'Management Training and Small Firm Performance: A Critical Review', Working paper No. 18, Warwick University: SME Centre.

Storey, D. J. and Westhead, P. (1996), 'Management training and small firm performance: Why is the link so weak?', *International Small Business Journal*, 14(4): 13–24.

Storey, D., Keasey, K., Watson, R. and Wynarczyk, P. (1987), *The Performance of Small Firms: Profits, Jobs and Failures*, London: Croom Helm.

Storey, J. (ed.) (1995), *Human Resource Management: A Critical Text*, London: Routledge.

Storey, J. (ed.) (1989), *New Perspectives on Human Resource Management*, London: Routledge.

Stratos Group (1990), *Strategic Orientations of Small European Businesses*, Aldershot, UK: Gower Publishing.

Styles, C. and Ambler, C. (1997), *The First Step to Export Success*, PAN'AGRA Research Programme, London Business School.

Styles, C. and Ambler, T. (1994), 'Successful Export Practice: The U.K. Experience', *International Marketing Review*, 11(6).

Sullivan Mort, G., Weerawardena, J. and Carnegie, K. (2003), 'Social entrepreneurship: Towards conceptualisation', *International Journal of Nonprofit and Voluntary Sector Marketing*, 8(1): 76–88.

Sullivan, D. and Bauerschmidt, A. (1990), 'Incremental Internationalisation: A Test of Johanson and Vahlne's Thesis', *Management International Review*, 30(1): 19–30.

Sunley, P., Klagge, B., Berndt and Martin, R. (2005), 'Venture capital programmes in the UK and Germany: in what sense a regional problem?' Regional Studies, 39: 255–73.

Susarla, A., Barua, A. and Whinston, A. (2003), 'Understanding the Service Component of Application Service Provision: An Empirical Analysis of Satisfaction with ASP services', *MIS Quarterly*, 27(1): 91–123.

Swan, J. and Newell, S. (1995), 'The Role of Professional Associations in Technology Diffusion', *Organization Studies*, 16(5): 847–74.

Swann, P. and Prevezer, M. (1996), 'A comparison of the dynamics of industrial clustering in computing and biotechnology', *Research Policy*, 25: 1139–57.

Swanson, E. B. and Ramiller, N. C. (1993), 'Information Systems Research Thematics: Submissions to a New Journal, 1987–1992', in *Information Systems Research*, 4(4): 299–330.

Swartz, L. N. (1995), *Worldwide Franchising Statistics: A Study of Worldwide Franchise Association*, Arthur Anderson (in co-operation with the World Franchising Council).

Sweeney, G. P. (1987), *Innovation, Entrepreneurs and Regional Development*, London: Francis Pinter.

Sydow, J. and Windeler, A. (1998), 'Organising and Evaluating Interfirm Networks: A Structurationist Perspective on Network Processes and Effectiveness', *Organisation Science*, 9(3): 263–84.

Sykes, H. B. and Block, Z. (1989), 'Corporate venturing obstacles: Sources and solutions', *Journal of Business Venturing*, 4: 59–167.

Tann, J. and Laforet, S. (1998), 'Assuring consultant quality for SMEs: The role of Business Links', *Small Business and Enterprise Development*, 5(1): 7–18.

Tannenbaum, R. and Schmidt, W. H. (1973), 'How to Choose a Leadership Pattern', *Harvard Business Review*, May–June, 62–80.

Taylor, A. (1993), 'DTI will talk only to large lobby groups, Heseltine says', *Financial Times*, 18 June.

Taylor, F. W. (1947), *Scientific Management*, London: Harper and Row.

Taylor, S. (2004), 'The Hunting of the Snark: A critical analysis of HRM discourses in relation to managing labour in smaller organisations', in S. Marlow, D. Patton and M. Ram (eds.), *Managing Labour in Small Firms*, London: Routledge.

Taylor, S. E. (1998), 'The social being in social psychology', in D. T. Gilbet, S. T. Fiske and G. Lindsey (eds.), *The Handbook of Social Psychology*, 1: 58–95. Boston, MA: The McGraw-Hill Companies, Inc.

Tesar, G. and Tarleton, J. S. (1982), 'Comparison of Wisconsin and Virginia Small- and Medium-sized Exporters: Aggressive and Passive Exporters', in M. R. Czinkota and G. Tesar (eds.), *Export Management: An International Context*, New York: Praeger Publishers, 85–112.

Thompson, G. (1993), 'Network Coordination', in R. Maidment and G. Thompson (eds.), *Managing the United Kingdom*, London: Sage.

Thompson, J. (2002), 'The world of the social entrepreneur', *International Journal of Public Sector Management*, 15(5): 412–31.

Thompson, J., Alvy, G. and Lees, A. (2000), 'Social entrepreneurship – a new look at the people and the potential', *Management Decision*, 38(5): 328–38.

Thorelli, H. (1986), 'Networks: Between Markets and Hierarchies', *Strategic Management Journal*, 7: 37–51.

Thornberry, N. (2001), 'Corporate Entrepreneurship: Antidote or Oxymoron?', *European Management Journal*, 19: 526–33.

Thornberry, N. (2003), 'Corporate entrepreneurship: teaching managers to be entrepreneurs', *Journal of Management Development*, 22(4): 329–44.

Tichy, N. M. (1981), 'Networks in Organizations', in P. C. Nystrom and W. H. Starbuck (eds.), *Handbook of Organisational Design*, Volume 2: Remodelling Organisations and their Environments, Oxford: Oxford University Press.

Tichy, N. M. and Cohen, E. (1998), 'The Leadership engine: How Winning Companies Build Leaders at Every Level', Dallas Tx: Pritchett and Associates, Inc.

Tichy, N. M., Tushman, N. L. and Forbrun, C. (1979), 'Social Network Analysis for Organisations', *Academy of Management Review*, 4(4): 507–19.

Tidd, J. and Trewhella, M. J. (1997), 'Organizational and technological antecedents for knowledge acquisition and learning', *R&D Management*, 27(4): 359–75.

Tiebout, C. M. (1957), 'Location theory, empirical evidence and economic evolution', papers and Proceedings of the Regional Science Association, 3: 74–86.

Timmers, P. (2000), Electronic Commerce: Strategies and Models for Business to Business Trading, Chichester, UK: John Wiley and Sons.

Timmons, J. A. (1990), *New Venture Creation: Entrepreneurship in the 1990s*, 4th ed., Boston: Irwin.

Timmons, J. A. (1994), *New Venture Creation: Entrepreneurship for the 21st Century*, 4th ed., Illinois: Irwin.

Timmons, J. A. (1999), *New Venture Creation: Entrepreneurship for the 21st Century*, 5th ed. Boston: Irwin/McGraw-Hill.

Trutko, J., Trutko, J. and Kostecka, A. (1993), *Franchising's Growing Role in the US Economy, 1975–2000*, US Small Business Administration.

Tsur, Y., Sternberg, M. and Hochman, E. (1990), 'Dynamic modeling of innovation process adoption with risk aversion and learning', *Oxford Economic paper*, 42: 336–55.

Turban, E., Lee, J., King, D. and Chung, H. (2004), *Electronic Commerce: A Managerial Perspective*, 3rd ed., Upper Saddle River, NJ: Prentice-Hall.

Turnbull, P. W. (1987), 'A Challenge to the Stages Theory of the Internationalisation Process', in P. J. Rosson and S. D. Reid (eds.), *Managing Export Entry and Expansion*, New York: Praeger, 21–40.

Tushman, M. L. and O'Reilly, C. A. (1996), 'Ambidextrous organizations: Managing evolutionary and revolutionary change', *California Management Review*, 38(4): 8–30.

Tyebjee, T. and Bruno, A. (1984), 'A model of venture capitalist investment activity', *Management Science*, 30: 1051–66.

UK Franchise Directory (1993), 9th Edition, Franchise Development Services Limited.

UNDP (1998), Human Development Report 1998, New York. United Nations Development programme, September.

UNICE (1999), *Fostering Entrepreneurship in Europe – The UNICE Benchmarking Report*.

US Department of Commerce (c. 1997, undated), *India: Marketing U.S. Products and Services*, Country Commercial Guide.

Ucbasaran, D., Lockett, A., Wright, M. and Westhead, P. (2003), 'Entrepreneurial Founder Teams: Factors Associated with Member Entry and Exit', *Entrepreneurship Theory and Practice*, 28(2).

US Department of Commerce (2005), www.censusgov/mrts/www/ecommhtml – accessed 20 February 2005.

Valliere, D. and Peterson, R. (2004), 'Inflating the bubble: examining dot-com investor behaviour', *Venture Capital: an international journal of entrepreneurial finance*, 6: 1–22.

Valliere, D. and Peterson, R. (2005), 'Venture capitalist behaviours: frameworks for future research', *Venture Capital: an international journal of entrepreneurial finance*, 7: 167–83.

Van der Veen, M. and Wakkee, I. A. M. (2004), 'Understanding the Entrepreneurial Process', in D. S. Watkins (ed.), *Annual Review of Progress in Entrepreneurship Research*, 2, Brussels: European Foundation for Management Development, 114–52.

van der Wees, C. and Romijn, H. (1987), *Entrepreneurship and small enterprise development for women in developing countries*, Geneva: ILO Management Development Branch.

Van Osnabrugge, M. and Robinson, R. J. (2000), *Angel investing: matching start-up funds with start-up companies*, San Francisco: Jossey-Bass.

Vandermerwe, S. and Birley, S. (1997), 'The corporate entrepreneur: leading organizational transformation', *Long Range Planning*, 30(3).

Venkatraman, N. and Ramanujam, V. (1987), 'Measurement of Business Economic Performance: An Examination of Method Convergence', in *Journal of Management*, 13(1): 109–22.

Venkataraman, S. (1997), 'The distinctive domain of entrepreneurship research. An editor's perspective', in J. Katz and R. Brockhaus (eds.), *Advances in Entrepreneurship, Firm Emergence, and Growth*, 3: 119–38. Greenwich, CT: JAI Press.

Verheul, I. and Thurik, R. (2000), 'Start-up capital: Differences Between Male and Female Entrepreneurs. Does Gender Matter?', EIM Research Report 9910/E, Rotterdam: Erasmus University.

Vesper, K. H. (1990), *New Venture Strategies*, Englewood-Cliffs, NJ: Prentice-Hall.

Vesper, K. H. (1991), 'New venture ideas: do not overlook the experience factor', in W. A. Sahlman and H. H. Stevenson (eds.), *The Entrepreneurial*

Venture, 73–80, Boston: Harvard Business School.

Veugelers, R. (1997), 'Internal R&D expenditure and external technology sourcing', *Research Policy*, 26: 303–15.

Veugelers, R. and Cassiman, B. (1999), 'Make and buy in innovation strategies: Evidence from Belgian manufacturing firms', *Research Policy*, 28: 63–80.

Von Bergen, C. W. and Soper, B. (2002), 'Entrepreneurial Leadership Styles: What works and What Doesn't', *The Entrepreneurial Executive*, 7: 63–78.

Walczuch, R., Van Braven, G. and Lundgren, H. (2000), 'Internet Adoption Barriers for Small Firms in the Netherlands', *European Management Journal*, 18(5): 565–71.

Waldinger, R. (1995), 'The "other side" of embeddedness: A case-study of the interplay of economy and ethnicity', *Ethnic and Racial Studies*, 18: 555–80.

Waldinger, R., Aldrich, H. and Ward, R. (eds.) (1990), *Ethnic Entrepreneurs*, London: Sage.

Waldinger, R., McEvoy, D. and Aldrich, H. (1990), 'Spatial Dimensions of Opportunity Structures, in R. Waldinger, H. Aldrich and R. Ward (eds.), *Ethnic Entrepreneurs*, London: Sage, 106–30.

Waldinger, R. and Perlmann, J. (1998), 'Second Generations: Past, Present, Future', *Journal of Ethnic and Migration Studies*, 24(1): 5–24.

Walker, C. O. and Ruekert, W. R. (1987), 'Marketing's role in the implementation of business strategies: A critical review and conceptual framework', *Journal of Marketing*, 51 (July): 15–33.

Walsh, J. and Dewar, R. (1987), 'Formalisation and the organisational life cycle', *Journal of Management Studies*, 24: 215–31.

Ward, J. L. (1987), *Keeping the Family Business Healthy: How to Plan for Continuing Growth, Profitability and Family Leadership*, San Francisco: Jossey-Bass Publishers.

Ward, L. (2004), 'Student debt hits £12,000, says study', The Guardian Unlimited, http://www.guardian.co.uk/uk_news/story

Ward, R. (1991), 'Economic Development and Ethnic Business', in J. Curran and R. A. Blackburn (eds.), *Paths Of Enterprise: The Future Of The Small Business*, London: Routledge, 51–67.

Ward, R. and Jenkins, R. (eds.) (1984), *Ethnic Communities in Business*, Cambridge: Cambridge University Press.

Warren, L. and Hutchison, W. (2000), 'Success factors for high technology SMEs: a Case Study from Australia', *Journal of Small Business Management*, 38(3): 86–91.

Watkins, D. S. (1973), 'Technical entrepreneurship; a Cis-Atlantic view', *R&D Management*, 3(2).

Watkins, J. and Watkins, D. (1984), 'The female entrepreneur: background and determinants of business choice – some British data', *International Small Business Journal*, 2(4): 21–31.

Watkins, J. and Watkins, D. (1986), 'The female entrepreneur: her background and determinants of business choice – some British data', in J. Curran, J. Stanworth and D. Watkins (eds.), *The Survival of the Small Firm*, Aldershot: Gower, 220–32.

Watson, J. and Robinson, S. (2003), 'Adjusting for Risk in Comparing the Performance of Male and Female Controlled SMEs', *Journal of Business Venturing*, 18(6): 773–88.

Weber, A. (1929), *Theory of the Location of Industries*, Chicago: University of Chicago Press.

Webopedia (2005), www.webopedia.com – accesssed 10 February 2005.

Webster, F. E. Jr (1992), 'The Changing Role of Marketing in the Organisation', *Journal of Marketing*, 56 (October): 1–17.

Weidenbaum, M. (1996), 'The Chinese Family Business Enterprise', *California Management Review*, 38(4).

Weill, P. and Vitale, M. (2001), *Place to Space: Migrating to eBusiness Models*, Harvard Business School Press.

Weiner, B. (1985), 'An attributional theory of achievement motivation and emotion', *Psychological Review*, 92(4): 548–73.

Weiner, B. (1992), *Human motivation: metaphors, theories, and research*, Newbury Park, California: Sage Publications, Inc.

Weinrauch, J. D., Mann, K., Robinson, P. A. and Pharr, J. (1991), 'Dealing with Limited Financial Resources: a Marketing Challenge for Small Business', *Journal of Small Business Management*, 29(4): 44–54.

Welch, L. S. and Luostarinen, R. (1988), 'Internationalisation: Evolution of a Concept', *Journal of General Management*, 14(2): 34–55.

Welsh, J. A. and White, J. F. (1984), 'A Small business is not a Little Big Business', in *Growing Concerns: Building and Managing the Smaller Business*, D. E. Gumpert (ed.), New York: Wiley, 149–67.

Wennekers, S. and Thurik, R. (1999), 'Linking Entrepreneurship and Economic Growth', *Small Business Economics*, 13: 27–55.

Werbner, P. (1980), 'From Rags To Riches: Manchester Pakistanis In The Garment Trade', *New Community*, 9: 84–95.

Werbner, P. (1984), 'Business on Trust: Pakistani entrepreneurship in the Manchester garment trade', in R. Ward and R. Jenkins (eds.), *Ethnic Communities In Business*, Cambridge: Cambridge University Press, 166–88.

Werbner, P. (1990), 'Renewing An Industrial Past: British Pakistani Entrepreneurship In Manchester', *Migration*, 8: 17–41.

West, A. (1988), *A Business Plan*, London: Pitman Publishing.

Westerberg, M. (1998), *Managing in Turbulence: An Empirical Study of Small Fimrs Operating in a Turbulent Environment*, Luleå, Sweden: Luleå Technological University.

Westhead, P. (1997), 'Ambitions, "external" environment and strategic factor differences between family and non-family companies', *Entrepreneurship and Regional Development*, Apr–Jun, 19(2): 127–57.

Westhead, P. and Birley, S. (1993), *Employment Growth in New Independent Owner-Managed Firms in Great Britain*, University of Warwick, UK.

Westhead, P. and Cowling, M. (1997), 'Performance Contrasts Between Family and Non-Family Unquoted Companies in the UK', *International Journal of Entrepreneurial Behaviour and Research*, 3(1): 30–52.

Westhead, P., Cowling, M., Storey, D. and Howorth, C. (2002), 'The Scale and Nature of Family Businesses', in D. E. Fletcher (2002) (ed.), *Understanding the Small Family Business*, London: Routledge.

Wetzel, W. E. (1981), 'Informal risk capital in New England', in K. H. Vesper (ed.), *Frontiers of Entrepreneurship Research 1981*, Wellesley, MA: Babson College, 217–45.

Whatmore, S. (1991), *Farming Women: Gender, Work and Family Enterprise*, London: Macmillan.

Wheelock, J. (1990), *Husbands at Home: the domestic economy in a post-industrial society*, London: Routledge.

Wheelock, J. (1991), 'The Flexibility of Small Business Family Work Strategies', in K. Caley, E. Chell, F. Chittenden and C. Mason (eds.), *Small Enterprise Development: Policy and Practice in Action*, London: Paul Chapman Publishing.

Wheelock, J. and Baines, S. (1998), 'Dependency or Self Reliance? The Contradictory Case of Work in UK Small Business Families', *Journal of Family and Economic Issues*, 19(1): 53–74.

Wheelock, J. and Oughton, E. (1996), 'The Household as a Focus for Research', *Journal of Economic Issues*, 30(1): 143–59.

Wickham, P. (1998), *Strategic Entrepreneurship*, London: Pitman.

Wickens, P. (1999), *Energise Your Enterprise*. Hampshire, Basingstoke: MacMillan Press Ltd.

Wiedersheim-Paul, F., Olson, H. C. and Welch, L. S. (1978), 'Pre-Export Activity: The First in Internationalisation', *Journal of International Business Studies*, 9(1): 47–58.

Wiklund, J. (1998), *Small Firm Growth and Performance*, Jönköping, Sweden: Jönköping International Business School.

Wiklund, J. and Shepherd, D. (2005), 'Entrepreneurial orientation and small business performance: a configuration approach', *Journal of Business Venturing*, 20: 71–91.

Wiklund, J., Davidsson, P. and Delmar, F. (2003), 'What do they think and feel about growth? An expectancy-value approach to small business managers' attitudes toward growth', *Entrepreneurship Theory and Practice* (Spring): 247–70.

Wilkinson, J. (1997), 'A new paradigm for economic analysis? Recent convergences in French social science and an exploration of the convention theory approach with a consideration of its application to the analysis of the agro-food sector', *Economy and Society*, 26(3): 305–39.

Williamson, O. (1975), *Markets and Hierarchies: Analysis and Antitrust Implications*, New York: The Free Press.

Williamson, O. (1985), *The Economic Institutions of Capitalism*, New York: Free Press.

Williamson, O. (1991), 'Corporate Economic Organization: The Analysis of discrete Structural Alternatives', *Administrative Science Quarterly*, 36: 269–96.

Williamson, O. (1996), 'Economic Organisation: The Case for Candor', *Academy of Management Review*, 21(1): 48–57.

Wilpert, C. (2003), 'Germany: from workers to entrepreneurs', in Kloosterman, R. and Rath, J. (eds.), *Immigrant Entrepreneurship: Venturing Abroad in the Age of Globalisation*, Oxford: Berg.

Wilson Committee (1979), *The Financing of Small Firms: Interim Report of the Committee to Review the Functioning of the Financial Institutions*, Cmnd 7503, London: HMSO.

Wilson, R. (2004), *Business Finance 2004*, Institute of Directors, London.

Winborg, J. and Landström, H. (2001), 'Financial bootstrapping in small businesses: examining small business managers' resource acquisition behaviours', *Journal of Business Venturing*, 16: 235–54.

Winckles, K. (1986), *The Practice of Successful Business Management*, London: Kogan Page, 61.

Windrum, P. and de Berranger, P. (2003), 'The Adoption of E-Business Technology by SMEs', in O. Jones and F. Tilley (eds.), *Competitive Advantage in SMEs*, Cheltenham, UK: John Wiley and Sons.

Withey, J. J. (1980), 'Differences between Exporters and Non-exporters: Some Hypotheses concerning Small Manufacturing Business', *American Journal of Small Business*, 4(3): 29–37.

Woo, C., Cooper, A., Dunkelberg, W., Daellenbach, U. and Dennis, W. (1989), 'Determinants of Growth for Small and Large Entrepreneurial Start Ups', paper presented at Babson Entrepreneurship Conference, Babson, USA.

Wood, R. and Bandura, A. (1989), 'Social cognitive theory of organizational management', *Academy of Management Review*, 14(3): 361–84.

Woods, A., Blackburn, R. and Curran, J. (1993), *A Longitudinal Study of Small Enterprises in the Service Sector*, Brunel University: Small Business Research Centre and Department of Management Studies.

Woodward, M. D. (1997), *Black Entrepreneurs In America: Stories Of Struggle and Success*, New Brunswick, NJ: Rutgers University Press.

Workplace Employment Relations Survey (1998), www.dti.gov.uk/er/emar/1998wers.htm

Wright, M., Lockett, A. and Pruthi, S. (2002), 'Internationalisation of Western venture capitalists into emerging markets: risk assessment and information in India', *Small Business Economics*, 19: 13–29.

Wright, M., Sapienza, H. J. and Busenitz, L. W. (eds.) (2003), *Venture Capital*, Cheltenham: Edward Elgar (three volumes).

Wyer, P. and Smallbone, D. (1999), 'Export Activity in SMEs: a Framework for Strategic Analysis', *Journal of the Academy of Business Administration*, 4(2): 9–24.

Wyer, P. (1990), 'The Effects of Varying Forms and Degrees of Government Intervention Upon the Effective Competitiveness of UK Small Businesses', unpublished PhD thesis, University of Aston, Birmingham.

Wyer, P. (1997), 'Small Business Interaction with the External Operating Environment – the Role of Strategic Management and Planning within the Small Business', paper presented to Small Business and Enterprise Development Conference, Sheffield, 30–31 March 1998.

Wyer, P. and Boocock, G. (1996), 'The Internationalisation of Small and Medium Sized Enterprises: An Organisational Learning Perspective', paper presented to the 7th ENDEC World Conference on Entrepreneurship, Singapore, 5–7 December 1996.

Wyer, P. and Mason, J. (1998a), 'Recognising the Complexity of the Small Business Management Task within Malaysia: Toward an Understanding of "Best Management Practice" ', paper presented to the Second Global Change Conference – The Impact of Change in the 21st Century, Manchester, 6 April 1998.

Wyer, P. and Mason, J. (1998b), 'An Organisational Learning Perspective to Enhancing Understanding of People Management in Small Businesses', *International Journal of Entrepreneurial Behaviour and Research*, 4(2): 112–28.

Wyer, P., Mason, P. and Theodorakopoulos, N. (2000), 'An Examination of the Concept of the Learning Organisation within the Context of Small Business Development', *International Journal of Entrepreneurial Behaviour and Research*, 6(4).

Wynarczyk, P., Watson, R., Storey, D., Short, H. and Keasey, K. (1993), *Managerial Labour Markets in Small Firms*, London: Routledge.

Yap, C. S. and Thong, J. Y. L. (1997), Programme Evaluation of a Government Information Technology Programme for Small Businesses, in *Journal of Information Technology*, 12(2): 107–20.

Yap, C. S., Soh, C. P. and Raman, K. S. (1992), 'Information Systems Success Factors in Small Business', in *Omega – International Journal of Management Science*, 20(5/6): 597–609.

Yellow Pages (1993a), *The Business Database*, London: British Telecommunications Plc.

Yoffie, D. B. (1997), 'Competing in the Age of Digital Convergence', in *California Management Review*, 38(4): 31–53.

Yoo, S. J., Jones-Evans, D. and Tan, W. L. (2004), Organizational Learning within Innovative Smes – The Effect if Attitude, Culture and Prior Experience on Knowledge Development in Entrepreneurial Firms, paper presented at the 18th RENT Conference, Copenhagen, November 24–26.

Young, S. (1987), 'Business Strategy and the Internationalisation of Business: Recent Approaches', *Managerial and Decision Economics*, 8: 31–40.

Young, S. (1990), 'Internationalisation: Introduction and Overview', *International Marketing Review*, 7(4).

Young, S., Hamill, J., Wheeler, C. and Davis, J. R. (1989), *International Market Entry and Development*, Hertfordshire: Harvester Wheatsheaf.

Yukl, G. (2002), *Leadership in Organizations*. Upper Saddle River, NJ: Prentice Hall.

Zacharakis, A. L. and Meyer, G. D. (1995), 'The venture capitalist decision: understanding process versus outcome', in W. D. Bygrave, B. J. Bird, S. Birley, N. C. Churchill, M. Hay, R. H. Keeley and W. E. Wetzel Jr (eds.), *Frontiers of Entrepreneurship Research 1995*, Center for Entrepreneurial Studies, Babson College, 465–78.

Zacharakis, A. L. and Meyer, G. D. (1998), 'A lack of insight: do venture capitalists really understand their own decision processes?', *Journal of Business Venturing*, 13: 57–76.

Zafarullah, M., Ali, M. and Young, S. (1998), 'The Internationalisation of the Small Firm in Developing Countries – Exploratory Research from Pakistan', *Journal of Global Marketing*, 11(3): 21–38.

Zahra, S. A. (1999), 'The Changing Rules of Global Competitiveness and Leadership in the 21st Century', *Academy of Management Executive*, 13: 36–42.

Zahra, S. A. (2004), 'A Theory of International New Ventures: a decade of research', *Journal of International Business Studies*, 35(12): 1–9.

Zahra, S. A., Hayton, H. and Salvato, C. (2004), 'Entrepreneurship in Family vs. Non-Family Firms: A Resource-Based Analysis of the Effect of Organizational Culture', *Entrepreneurship Theory and Practice*, 28(4): 363–81.

Zahra, S. A., Sapienza, H. J. and Davidsson, P. (forthcoming), 'Entrepreneurship and the creation of dynamic capabilities', *Journal of Management*.

Zajac, E. and Olsen, C. (1993), 'From Transaction Cost to Transaction Value Analysis: Implications for the Study of Interorganizational Strategies', *Journal of Management Studies*, 30: 131–45.

Zewde and Associates (2002), 'Jobs, Gender and Small Enterprises in Africa: Women Entrepreneurs in Ethiopia', A Preliminary Report, Geneva: ILO, IFP/SEED-WEDGE, October.

Zider, B. (1998), 'How venture capital works', *Harvard Business Review*, Nov–Dec, 131–9.

Zimmer, C. and Aldrich, H. (1987), 'Resource Mobilization Through Ethnic Networks', *Sociology Perspectives*, 30(4): 422–45.

Zmud, R. W. (1984), 'An Examination of Push-pull Theory Applied to Process Innovation in Knowledge Work', *Management Science*, 30(6): 727–38.

Zmud, R. W. and Apple, L. E. (1992), 'Measuring Technology Incorporation/Infusion', in *Journal of Product Innovation Management*, 9(2): 148–55.

Index